T

BIRD

The ultimate illustrated guide to
the birds of Britain and Europe

BIRD

The ultimate illustrated guide to the birds of Britain and Europe

PETER HAYMAN & ROB HUME   MITCHELL BEAZLEY

To Henry Birch, the Thorogoods, and my parents for their generous encouragement from the beginning RH

Bird: The Ultimate Illustrated Guide to the Birds of Britain and Europe
Peter Hayman and Rob Hume

First published as *The Complete Guide to the Birdlife of Britain & Europe* in 2001 by Mitchell Beazley

This revised edition published in 2007 by Mitchell Beazley,
an imprint of Octopus Publishing Group Ltd
2–4 Heron Quays, London, E14 4JP
An Hachette Livre UK Company
www.octopusbooks.co.uk

ISBN 978 1 84533 338 6

A CIP catalogue copy of this book is available from the British Library.

Commissioning Editor Jon Asbury
Art Director Tim Foster
Executive Art Editor Yasia Williams-Leedham
Senior Editor Suzanne Arnold
Editor Theresa Bebbington
Designer Ash Weston
Proofreader Howard Watson
Indexer Helen Snaith
Production Controller Peter Hunt

Photos:
Page 1 Coal Tit; **2–3** Whooper Swan; **4** Black-headed Bunting; **6** Kingfisher

Set in DIN and Agency

Colour reproduction by Fine Arts, China
Printed and bound by C&C, China

Contents

Introduction

This book is as much about the fascination of birds as how to tell them apart. If it conveys our own enthusiasm for discovering birds, and our enjoyment of their behaviour, then it will, we hope, inspire a similar excitement in our readers.

We cover all the birds that breed in Europe, as well as all the regular visitors. We have avoided taking on the whole of the Western Palearctic – a zone that includes north Africa and the Middle East – yet we wanted to include some of the many rarities that visit Europe, some of which are more easily seen than some European breeders. We would have liked to include even more: we were sometimes tempted to write "compare with..." only to remember that the other bird was not in the book. In the event, we have omitted the really rare species, allowing us to do full justice to the non-European breeders that we have included.

An increasingly obvious challenge, but a richly rewarding one, was to meet the needs of readers new to the joys of watching and identifying birds while at the same time ensuring that the new information we had was communicated to the experienced bird-watcher. Even the most experienced enthusiast, however, enjoys a new book with new illustrations to pore over, and the size and scope of the book, and its wealth of illustrations will, we trust, appeal to anyone wishing to learn more. In this enlarged and revised edition, we have been able to include photographs to supplement the illustrations: they help to convey the character of the birds, and show, too, how a bird's appearance can be affected quite dramatically by local conditions, especially light and shade.

We found, and indeed have long known, that there is much to learn about even the most familiar species. Much of the new information comes from a detailed study of specimens, mostly from the unrivalled collection of the Natural History Museum at Tring, Hertfordshire. Such study can never replace a good knowledge of the living bird, and we do not suggest that it should, but it adds an altogether different dimension. In fact, problems encountered in the field and explored in the museum often set us off on another line of enquiry in the field.

For most of us, for example, a Garden Warbler is just that (if we can identify it at all). If it sings, we assume it is a male. Measurements, however, reveal differences between the sexes that can be seen if you get a good enough view and try hard enough. Species after species showed the same distinctions, which were frequently defined by variations in the length of the bird's body: a measurement rarely taken, even by the specialists who catch birds for ringing and measure their wings, tails, claws, bills, and weight, and even record their state of moult. In the spirit of presenting new information where we have it, we have included as much of this material as possible in the available space. It may seem a little esoteric to the beginner, but gives the expert something extra to find within these pages, and explains the subtle and sometimes not so subtle differences within many species.

Whether you are an expert or a beginner, we hope you enjoy this book. More importantly, we hope it encourages you to get out and watch the birds themselves, and share our enthusiasm for some of the most attractive, intriguing, and inspiring of creatures.

Peter Hayman and Rob Hume

How to use this book

The illustrations provide an instant visual impression of each bird for quick identification. The text provides vital facts to check this visual judgement and gives a wealth of extra information on behaviour and habitat. Both the illustrations and text go much deeper, exploring subtle distinctions of age, sex, and populations in enough detail to intrigue and inform the most advanced bird-watcher.

DIMENSIONS AND STATUS
The length, wingspan, and weight of each species are given. The status is colour-coded: green for secure (no conservation concern); yellow for vulnerable (experiencing large or continuing decline in numbers or threats to habitat through, for instance, climate change, sea-level rise, or intensification of agriculture; or having a very small range within Europe); red for endangered (with a small population more immediately under threat) or rare (whose main range is outside Europe).

SCALE IMAGE
A silhouette shows each species' size in comparison with either a Pigeon (standing) or a Woodpigeon (in flight).

MAIN TEXT
This includes information on habitat, food and feeding techniques, displays and calls, breeding details, and migration as relevant. The breeding details have been omitted for some species that do not nest in Europe.

HABITAT AND RANGE
There are brief details of the seasonal presence of the bird within Europe (When Seen) and its habitat and range (Where Seen). It is highly unlikely that you will see a bird outside its usual range or at the wrong time of year. A piechart and map give an at-a-glance summary. The symbols indicate the status of the species in Britain and its preferred habitat. A key can be found below and on the back flap of the book cover.

INTRODUCTION
This provides a general impression of the bird, often invaluable in identification. It may be the way the bird stands, flicks its wings, or bobs its head, the general pattern of its head or back, or some other part of its "character" that catches your eye. It is rather like picking out a good friend in a crowd of people: you may not be able to explain why, but you can do it, instantly.

SCIENTIFIC NAME
Scientific names convey a lot of information. The species name has two words. The first word indicates the genus. All species in the same genus are closely related: something that is not always apparent from their English names. The Blackcap and Garden Warbler, for example, are near relatives, and this is made plain by their scientific names: they are both in the genus *Sylvia*. The second word is the specific name. Together with the genus, this gives every species its own "label", so the Blackcap is *Sylvia atricapilla*, while the Garden Warbler is *Sylvia borin*.

COLOUR-CODING
Each species is colour-coded, so you can see at a glance to which group of birds it belongs. If you know which group you want, use the colour to turn quickly to the right pages.

PHOTOGRAPH
A photograph shows each species in its natural habitat, often displaying typical behaviour. A brief caption explains what is happening or draws attention to salient points.

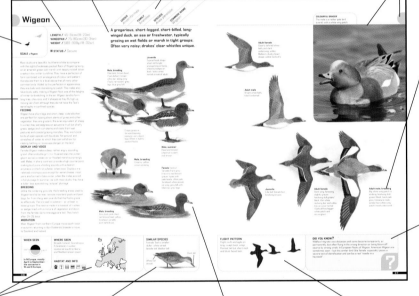

CAPTIONS
The captions to the illustrations pick out points to check to identify a bird. They also reveal much more, such as differences in plumage or structure between the sexes or individuals at different times of year, or in different parts of Europe.

EXTRA INFORMATION
Species illustrated across two pages have a box giving additional interesting or unexpected details.

SIMILAR SPECIES
Where relevant, attention is drawn to a bird that is easily confused with the species, pointing out ways of telling them apart.

ILLUSTRATIONS
The accurate, yet evocative illustrations show as much information about each species as possible, with several different views of the bird in a variety of postures. They show all the common plumage variations, as well as some rarer forms, and include many details derived from careful research and measurement.

FLIGHT PATTERN
Interesting flight patterns are illustrated, with a brief explanation of how to recognize the bird by the shapes it makes and its style of movement.

■ KEY TO SYMBOLS

- Not recorded in Britain
- Rare vagrant in Britain
- Resident in Britain
- Rare, but annual, visitor to Britain
- Summer visitor to Britain
- Winter visitor to Britain
- Passage migrant to Britain

- Town and built-up areas
- Freshwater marsh
- Coast and sea
- Farmland
- Low scrub
- High scrub
- Lakes and reservoirs

- Mountains, moorlands, and crags
- Rivers and streams
- Cliffs and islands
- Broadleaved woods
- Pine woods
- Mixed woods

The parts of a bird

Throughout this book we have tried to avoid technical terms as far as possible, but some of the more precise details cannot be effectively described in any other way. So it is worth taking the time to study the basic anatomy of a typical bird, and to become familiar with the names of all the main feather groups and facial markings. You will find a number of these terms shown on the diagrams below, which will also provide a useful reference when reading the main species descriptions.

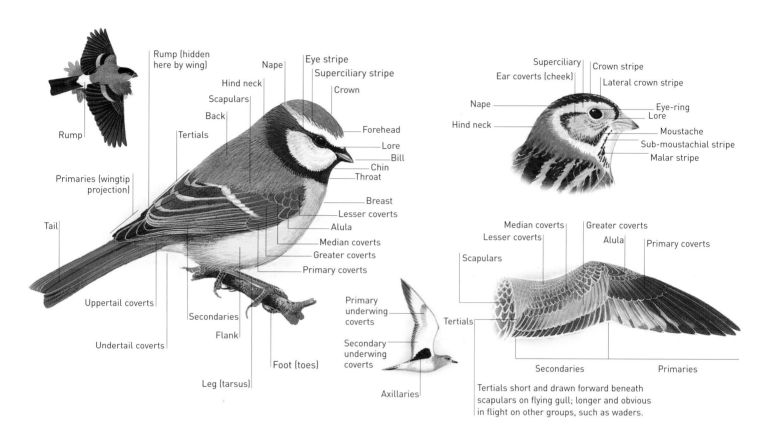

Tertials short and drawn forward beneath scapulars on flying gull; longer and obvious in flight on other groups, such as waders.

The patterns and colours of a bird's plumage are important clues to its identity, but they can be surprisingly easy to forget. This is partly because most people are not familiar with bird anatomy, so they cannot define the actual positions of colour patches or markings. Learning the parts of a bird, and especially the wing feathers, enables you to name the details you see through your binoculars. Even if you do this only mentally, it makes the details much easier to check later.

Memory can play tricks, though, so one of the best ways to ensure you can identify a bird is to write a description in a notebook as you watch it. Better still, make a drawing, even the roughest sketch, with the various parts labelled. It may sound laborious, but making a fully annotated drawing requires that you look at all the parts of a bird, or at least as much as you can see while you are watching it. It is not easy, but practice makes perfect – and writing down such things as leg colour, bill colour, eye colour, and all the feather patterns reinforces your observation and helps you to memorize what you see. Once you have seen, described, and identified something in this way, you are much more likely to remember the bird in future.

The shapes and proportions of the various feather tracts vary greatly between the bird families. On a perched finch or bunting, for example, all the wing feathers – the lesser, median, and greater coverts, the tertials, secondaries, and primaries, and even the primary coverts and alula – are often clearly visible. On a swimming duck, however, the bird's scapulars often droop down to overlie its flanks, covering its wing feathers so that none of them can be seen except for the tertials, which are often prominent, and the tips of the primaries. It is only when the duck stretches, rises up, and flaps its wings, or actually takes flight, that you get to see its various wing feathers.

The measured drawings in this book allow detailed comparison of the exact proportions of the most prominent feathers, such as the main wing and tail feathers. This can be very helpful when you are trying to identify a bird with confusing plumage. A perched falcon such as a Kestrel, for example, will typically show long, slim wingtips because it has long primaries, but a Sparrowhawk in the same situation will show almost no exposed primary tips. Such distinctions may provide the only sure way of identifying birds such as larks, which are often indistinguishable at a glance.

How this book was created

The illustrations for this book are the culmination of several years' research based on the experience of a lifetime studying birds. They not only capture the essential character of each species, but are highly accurate and detailed.

Each illustration in these pages has been created after many years spent watching birds out in the field. In addition, museum specimens have been painstakingly studied – in particular, those preserved in spirit, rather than skins or stuffed birds, which are fixed rigidly in position. Countless photographs have also been examined and scores of books and identification papers read. The combination of expertise in the museum, field experience, and field notes and sketches has produced vivid, accurate illustrations with a wealth of useful detail.

Many of the details concern lengths and proportions. Most books give a simple measure of bill tip to tail tip for each species. More specialized works add the length of the folded wing, from the bend to the tip, and sometimes the lengths of the tail and bill. These are useful in some circumstances, but they are of limited value in judging the shape of a living bird.

Body length, for example, is never given, yet it is fundamental to a bird's proportions. It determines the extent to which the tip of the tail extends beyond the tips of the folded wings when perched. Measuring the wings and tail may not give this information, but a measure of body length does. When folded, the wings are more or less fixed in position relative to the body. A long body makes the tail project farther beyond the wingtips, while a short body reduces the projection or eliminates it altogether. This can be a valuable means of identifying species with nondescript plumage.

The research for the book has also revealed that body size frequently varies from male to female within a species. Consequently, many of the illustrations show the wing-to-tail proportions of males and females, allowing the sexes to be distinguished even when their plumage is identical. This reveals why, for example, some gulls have long wingtips reaching well beyond their tails, but others do not. The difference is not a random variation between individuals, but sexual dimorphism, and often adds to the complexity of identification.

The detailed measurements used as a basis for the illustrations have also revealed some surprising differences in other proportions, such as the length and breadth of the open wing. In some species, a different ratio of wing length to breadth can make a flying male look quite different from a female. People who have studied a species for years often find they are able to tell the males and females apart at a glance, yet they do not know why. As a result they may even doubt their own judgement. The subtle differences in proportion explain how they do it. The ability of the human eye and brain to judge such subtleties is remarkable.

In most cases, these distinctions are not necessary for the simple identification of a species, but they take us a step further toward understanding the birds we are watching. In other cases, such details can be critical to identification: there are some extremely difficult species among European birds that challenge even the experts, and the more information we have, the better. You only have to look at some of the streaky brown larks, pipits, and plain brown warblers to appreciate this. It is also amazing how much you can discern in the field once you know the difference is there.

TAXONOMIC TANGLES

Taxonomy is the study of classification, of relationships in the natural world. It sounds dull, but it is not: it creates a great deal of heated debate.

The classification of a species may change as our knowledge increases and our interpretation of the data alters. Such changes are often based upon the views of very few influential people. The research for this book has raised a number of queries over thorny issues, in some cases revealing facts that suggest that a new classification is desirable. These are noted on the appropriate pages. For examples, see the "Mediterranean" shearwaters, the White-backed Woodpecker, the Rock and Water Pipit complex, Booted and Olivaceous Warblers, and redpolls and crossbills. Such changes may already have been made by the time you read these words, but they will not alter the nature of the birds themselves.

The measurements
Each scale drawing of a standing or flying bird requires approximately 70 measurements of the wings, tail, wing bones, individual feathers, bill, legs, and feet. Male, female, and juvenile may be different. Whole birds are the most useful, but skins are used if necessary. The measurements enable a grid to be built up showing the main proportions of the bird.

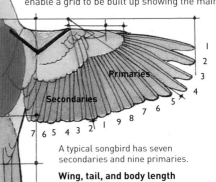

Primaries

Secondaries

A typical songbird has seven secondaries and nine primaries.

The illustrations
The measurements and scale drawing form the basis for five or more drawings on tracing paper showing the bird's shape and character. When this is right the final drawing is rubbed down onto the paper to be worked up into the finished illustration.

Wing, tail, and body length
Birds of equal wing and tail length may be different shapes because their body length varies: usually males have a longer body than females, more rarely the reverse is the case. The difference affects, for example, the amount of tail projection when perched or in flight.

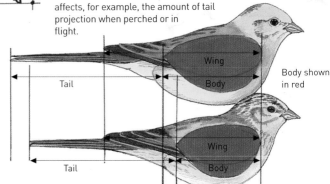

Wing

Tail

Body

Body shown in red

Wing

Tail

Body

How to identify birds

There is no quick way to learn your birds – but that means you have years of enjoyment ahead of you. Much of the appeal of bird-watching is discovering species that are new to you, and when you are starting out, they are all new.

Identifying birds takes practice. It isn't reasonable to dabble once or twice a year while on holiday and expect to become really proficient. But so what? It doesn't matter how good you are, you can still enjoy watching the birds around you. Even so, knowing more about them and being able to tell one from another adds to the enjoyment; it certainly doesn't reduce it.

As well as practice, identifying birds requires careful observation. First of all, when you see an unfamiliar bird, try to get an idea of its size. This may not always be easy: if it flies overhead against a plain sky, you have nothing to go on. But there is usually some sort of reference – foliage, grass, other birds – that allows you to make a judgement. Compare it to something familiar: "about the size of a pigeon", "smaller than a sparrow", and so on. For more advanced cases, such as the rarer warblers, your judgement of size may have to be more subtle than this!

Check the shape. Is the bird basically long and slim, or round and dumpy? Is it squat or elegant, tall or short? Is it heavy or light in its actions? A Grey Partridge, for example, might be about the size of a pigeon, but it is short-legged, short-billed, and round-bodied, with a small head and short tail. A Jackdaw, on the other hand, although also about the size of a pigeon, has a longer tail, longer wings, and a longer bill, creating a quite different general effect. When you start looking at birds like this you will soon learn the overall appearance of major groups, such as the wildfowl, birds of prey, gamebirds, waders, gulls, pigeons, owls, thrushes, and finches, and begin to fit what you see into some sort of order to give you a clue where to start. This is one of the main steps to identifying birds: getting a clue, rather than being altogether lost.

GETTING DOWN TO DETAIL

Once you have an idea of size and general shape, try to make a note (mental, or in a notebook) of any details that strike you about the bird's form. If you have decided it is a wader, you might be looking at things such as bill length and shape, and leg length.

Colours and patterns are next. If your wader flies away, does it have a wingbar? Or a white rump? Did it have black or pale legs? Do your best to make a note of as much as you can, because once it has gone, you will not be able to check again. If the bird really has flown, and you are none the wiser but you want to find out what it was, scribble down all you saw right away. It is extremely important to put down what you actually saw, before you look at a book. Once you start flicking through pages, reading bits of text, and looking

at pictures, then what you saw, what you think you saw, what you have just read, and what you would like it to have been, become so mixed up that any kind of objective identification is no longer possible. We have seen this process many times. We haven't quite seen black called white, but we have been in a hide with people watching a Greenshank (which has a bill that curves slightly upward) and, on checking a field guide, pronounce "Ah, it had a curved bill: it must have been a Curlew" (which has a bill that curves markedly down). Confusion sets in, memory plays tricks, the real bird is forgotten...

CALLS AND SONG

The voices of birds are amazingly useful to bird-watchers for locating birds as much as identifying them. Most birds are first noticed because they make some sort of sound, especially in woodland. You will soon be picking up birds by their calls even though you don't know what they are.

Some bird sounds are only useful for location, but other calls and songs are valuable to identification: indeed, some can be vital. If you see a Marsh Tit or Willow Tit, for example, you may be unable to decide which it is, but if it calls with a clear *pit-chew!* the answer is easy: Marsh Tit. The song of a Chiffchaff quickly answers a similar identification problem in spring: no Willow Warbler – which looks almost the same – ever produces the sequence of simple, deliberate notes that gives the Chiffchaff its name. Rarer birds may also betray their identity with a call. A "Greenish or Arctic" Warbler can be a challenge, but should it call *zik*, Greenish is instantly ruled out of the argument.

Calls, then, are important, and you will soon learn many of them, especially if you can watch a bird while it is calling and really make a lasting mental link between the sound and the bird. But how do you describe these sounds? In this book, we have tried to do exactly this for the most important calls and songs of vocal species. If you listen closely, you find that birds generally don't have sharp, hard consonants in their calls: something that is written as "*zip*" or "*tik*" is little more than an emphatic "*i*" sound when heard well. But writing down a series of vowels is useless in trying to convey a bird call, and a more imaginative use of letters and combinations such as "*z*", "*t*", "*zzz*", or "*tikitiki-tik*" can give the right impressions of buzzy, sharp, slurred, or rattled notes.

Despite this, the transcriptions in the book are really *aides-mémoire* at best. Usually you have little idea what the bird really sounds like until you hear it: then *zit-zit-chew* becomes clear! If you like, remember it as *zit-zit-chew* from then on, but the chances are you will hear it as *zap-zap-sue* and if so, think of it like that. Or maybe "what's up, you?" might suit the purpose. But do try to get the best impression you can of inflexion and character: descriptions such as "plaintive", "sweet", "rasping", "nasal", "emphatic", and "explosive" are common in bird books, and they are all attempts to give information that really does help separate one bird from another. It is, anyway, all part of the fun.

The living bird

The illustrations in this book show birds in all their plumage variations and in a wide variety of poses. Yet a living bird can look quite unlike any picture. Its behaviour, the state of its feathers, and even the weather conditions can give it a unique appearance for the few minutes that you have it in view, and you need to allow for this.

The basic shape of a bird is defined by its skeleton, its bill, and its feathers. These help give a bird of a particular species, sex, age, and season an overall appearance that is usually remarkably stable. A juvenile Robin looks like any other juvenile Robin; a first winter Common Gull looks like hundreds of thousands, indeed millions, of other first winter Common Gulls. Yet other factors can change them, and you must remember these when looking at birds in the wild – or "in the field" as biologists say.

The stability of basic structure can be seen on the wing of a small warbler. The lengths of the outer feathers, the primaries, may not be precisely identical in every individual, but they nevertheless conform to a distinctive pattern, just like the fingers of your hand. On a Willow Warbler, this pattern is recognizably different from that of the very similar Chiffchaff. It is a function of the fact that the Willow Warbler is a long-distance migrant that winters in Africa, so it needs a longer, stronger wing for such epic flights; the Chiffchaff is a short-distance migrant, so it can make do with a shorter, rounder wing.

Close examination of the wing structure also reveals a tapered outer edge (emargination), and a more sharply stepped or notched inner web on some, but not all, of the feathers. The combination of the relative lengths of the feathers and their emarginations and notches is unique to each species. On millions of individuals, this structural difference proves to be the same: a constant element that, if necessary, can be used to separate one species from another.

PATTERN AND COLOUR

Similarly, the pattern on some feathers can often be used to identify a bird with equal certainty. This is more useful to most of us than detailed structure, if only because it can be seen at a distance. You can see, for example, that a Mistle Thrush has white outer tail feathers, while a Song Thrush does not; a Brambling has a white rump, while a Chaffinch's rump is green. More subtly, there are a few broad dark bars on a Green Sandpiper's tail, while a Wood Sandpiper has several narrower ones. An adult Knot in winter has plain feathers on its back, while each back feather of a juvenile is delicately fringed with dark and light lines. Such consistency of pattern, repeated millions of times within a species, allows us to tell species apart and often to separate the different sexes and ages.

The actual colours of feathers are also remarkably consistent. Tens of thousands of Black-headed Gulls show precisely the same shade of pale grey on their backs, and it is exceptional to see one that is paler or darker than its fellows. So, if you see a darker grey back within a flock of Black-headed Gulls, it is worth a second look because it may belong to a different species. In the same way, the precise shade of green on the back of a Blue Tit, or of pink on the breast of a Bullfinch, is repeated again and again.

WEAR AND TEAR

If birds are characterized by such striking consistency of structure, pattern, and colour, how is it that a living bird can look so unlike "the bird in the book"?

Superimposed upon these consistent patterns are the effects of wear and tear. Feathers, after all, have a rough time over the course of many months, since they are subject to knocks, abrasion, and bleaching by the sun or, in seabirds, by salt. Dark areas in feathers are coloured by pigments that contain melanin, which adds strength to a feather. White areas, on the other hand, have no melanin; they are therefore weaker, so they wear more quickly. If you find an old feather from a bird such as a Curlew, with pale spots along its edge, you may see that the pale parts are actually worn right away, giving a saw-tooth edge. The white spots on the wingtip of a gull can wear off, leaving a solid patch of dull black (gull feathers can often be picked up on a beach, and are worth a close look). Patterns can and do change with time as the feathers are physically altered.

The other factor that modifies a bird's appearance over time is the effects of moult: the regular replacement of old feathers by new ones. This also proceeds with a marked regularity, and in most species there is a precise "programme" of feather replacement. During moult a wingtip, for example, may have a very old, battered outermost feather, a gap where the adjacent feather is completely missing, and alongside that a pristine new feather, still only half grown. The wingtip pattern (and indeed shape) will therefore be a little unlike that shown in the book. Moult also affects a bird's colour. A Robin in fresh plumage looks immaculate, but after a hard breeding season it is pale and dowdy, bleached and tattered; when it moults in late summer it renews its plumage, and after a short time when it is inconspicuous, it reappears as fresh and bright as ever.

CHANGING POSTURE

The Robin also illustrates another factor that affects a bird's appearance. On a hot day it is positively skinny: taut and tight-feathered, standing upright on long, fully exposed legs. On a cold day in winter, as every Christmas card shows, it will be as round as a tennis ball, its legs all but hidden within loose, fluffed-out belly feathers that retain a layer of warm air as insulation against the frost. A Crested Lark can look equally round and dumpy on a cold morning, but in the semi-desert of southern Spain at midday it might appear as thin as a stick.

The posture of a bird is also influenced by what it is doing. A resting Grey Heron usually looks dumpy, its head withdrawn into rounded shoulders. When searching out a fish, though, it can look extraordinarily long and thin, tall, and forward-leaning, its head and neck stretched to their full extent: the very essence of concentration. Another familiar example is the Mallard, so round, squat, and pot-bellied as it sleeps beside a park pond, but slender and alert when feeding in a salt marsh where it faces the dangers of predators or wildfowlers hidden in the creeks.

Birds also use posture to deliberately change their appearance. A displaying male Chaffinch spreads its wing feathers in such a way that the broad white wingbars show to greatest advantage. Yet the same Chaffinch, feeding quietly beneath a shady tree, cleverly covers its white feathers by tucking them under darker ones, so it is much harder to see – and therefore less vulnerable to attack.

TRICKS OF THE LIGHT

Light has a huge influence on the way we see things. Everyone knows this, but we sometimes forget. A white bird silhouetted against a bright, white sky can look dark grey; similarly, a dark bird, moving against a shaded background but lit by a strong, low sun, can look misleadingly pale. A female Hen Harrier against a pale green field looks dark, but it may look surprisingly pale against a dark brown heather moor in bright sunshine.

A warbler in the dappled light of sun-washed leaves in spring may look green and yellow, yet the same bird in a bare bush of grey and brown twigs on a dull day looks grey. Gulls standing on white snow in dull weather look beautifully clear in their various shades of grey and white, but low sun turns the snow blue and the gulls orange. Conversely, strong sun at noon makes the gulls dazzling white and the subtle variations of their pale greys are invisible. Strong light can shine through feathers and change their appearance. Viewed against the sun, a slightly spread outer tail feather may seem to have a white edge that does not really exist.

Reflected light can be particularly misleading because it is often coloured. A bright blue bird once seen flying over a hotel swimming pool proved to be a House Sparrow, illuminated from below by blue light. That is an extreme example, but the influence of light reflected off snow is familiar enough: it produces a marvellous effect, projecting a ghostly or sometimes remarkably solid whiteness onto the underside of a bird flying above. A Common Gull over snow, for example, has a wonderful whiteness with most strikingly contrasted inky black wingtips.

A bird in a tree against the sky is always likely to create identification problems. Even the brightest colours and strongest contrasts can be elusive in such circumstances. In late evening, birds can look surprisingly orange: we usually compensate for this without thinking about it, because the birds surroundings are washed with orange light too, but published photographs taken in evening light may be misleading.

Tricks of the light also affect our impressions of size and sometimes shape. A distant pale bird may look bigger than it really is, while a dark bird may appear smaller. The infinite variety of such effects can be confusing, but it also adds to the appeal of living, moving birds. Just bear in mind that, while all birds are essentially constant in their structure, pattern, and colour, the appearance of an individual bird can – and does – vary greatly, almost from moment to moment.

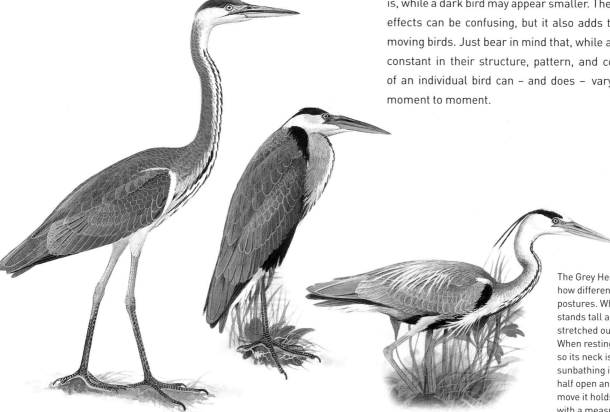

The Grey Heron is a fine example of how different a bird can look in varying postures. While searching for fish it stands tall and thin, with its neck stretched out to its fullest extent. When resting it withdraws its head so its neck is invisible, and when sunbathing it stands with its wings half open and turned back. On the move it holds its body horizontal, with a measured, purposeful stride.

The families of birds

With a very few exceptions, the sequence of birds in this book follows the widely accepted "scientific" order of birds, and their position in the order indicates the closeness of their relationships. The species are arranged in colour-coded groups, most of which consist of species from several families. This introduction to the various groups follows the sequence used in the book, and the different families within the groups are described in the text.

Demoiselle Crane

The scientific classification of birds into families was originally achieved by comparing their appearance, anatomy, and behaviour. In general, the classification reflects their true relationships, but the status of some species is still debated, as are the links between some families. Species that seem very different may actually be close relatives, while others that look similar are not closely related at all, but examples of "convergent evolution" by which species that live in similar ways have evolved to resemble each other. Swifts, swallows, and martins, for example, all feed on flying insects and have evolved much the same look and habits, but the swifts are not closely related to the others. Zoologists are now able to establish these relationships by studying the DNA of contentious species and families, and ultimately this will clarify the relationships of the different families of birds beyond all doubt.

WILDFOWL

This single family includes all the swans, geese, and ducks, and displays a wide variety of adaptations. Swans are large, short-legged, long-necked birds that feed in water or on land. Geese are stockier than swans, but larger than most ducks, with longer legs that make them more mobile on land. They feed in large flocks and fly in wonderful V-formations, lines, and chevrons. They form two basic groups, the "grey geese" (grey-brown and white with variously coloured legs and bills) and the "black geese" (grey or dark brown with a lot of black, and black legs and bills). The shelducks are more or less intermediate between geese and true ducks.

Dabbling or surface-feeding ducks feed by filtering water through fine "combs" in their bills to extract food; they also feed underwater by "up-ending", but rarely diving, and graze or pick up grain on land. They have short legs, but walk moderately well, and long wings, which despite their heavy bodies allow fast and powerful flight. Diving ducks feed underwater, diving from the surface. Some species live at sea, others mostly on freshwater or both. The sea ducks include maritime species such as eiders and scoters. Finally, the sawbills are fish-catching species whose bills have toothed edges for gripping slippery prey.

GROUSE, PHEASANTS, AND PARTRIDGES

The game birds are a small but diverse group of seed-eating species with short, curved bills, longish legs with sharp "spurs", and a low, fast, whirring flight. They include the various types of grouse that are mainly upland or northern birds adapted to harsh climates, and the partridges, pheasants, and quails. Partridges are squat, short-tailed birds, but pheasants are larger, with long or very long tails. Quails are tiny and secretive, living in dense crops.

DIVERS AND GREBES

The divers and grebes are two small families of aquatic birds, rarely seen on land except when on the nest. Perfectly adapted for life on water, they are remarkably capable swimmers both on and beneath the surface. Yet their legs are set so far back on their bodies – for efficiency while swimming – that they are virtually useless on land, forcing the birds to slide on their bellies. Their long, slim, pointed bills are ideal for seizing slippery fish.

SHEARWATERS, CORMORANTS, AND GANNETS

The shearwaters and petrels are weak-legged ocean birds that live at sea, but come to land to nest in burrows. Unable to walk well, many visit the shore under cover of darkness to avoid predators, making a loud, unearthly cacophony of calls as they do so. They are superb fliers and travel vast distances at sea. Storm Petrels are small, delicate-looking relatives of the petrels that live in a similar way, spending most of their lives at sea. The gannets and cormorants appear very different, but share several structural features, including having all four toes joined by webbing. Their wings also reveal a remarkably similar basic structure when spread wide. Gannets are huge birds that fly superbly well and feed by plunge-diving; cormorants are adapted for swimming underwater and are less efficient in the air.

Fulmar

Red-crested Pochard

HERONS AND PELICANS

The herons, bitterns, and egrets are long-billed, long-necked, long-legged birds of the waterside. They are all slender-bodied birds that move easily through vegetation. Some inhabit open shores, while others live a secretive life in heavily overgrown marshes, but they all require access to water for catching fish (with the exception of the Cattle Egret, which feeds largely on insects in drier places and even forages on refuse tips). Several species nest colonially in trees, building large and obvious nests. Cranes are large birds resembling herons, but they are heavy-bodied and have smaller bills. Cranes require large areas of undisturbed land both in winter and in summer, and such shy, large birds find life increasingly difficult in the busy, heavily-populated Europe of today. The large, long-legged, long-billed storks look stately on the ground and magnificent in the air, travelling great distances by gliding. They are long-distance migrants, wintering in Africa. The spoonbills and ibises are closely allied to the storks, and also to the extraordinary flamingos, which, like the spoonbills, are highly adapted for feeding in shallow water. Pelicans are actually related to the gannets and cormorants, and have the same type of feet with all four toes webbed. In their way, pelicans are among the world's finest flying birds, able to exploit rising air currents to perfection, but they are better known for their capacious throat pouches, which they use to scoop fish from the water.

Red Kite

BIRDS OF PREY

Well known for their hooked bills and often their sharp, curved claws, the birds of prey catch live food or forage for dead animals (carrion) or refuse. Many are superb in the air, but spend long periods inactive on perches. The vultures, kites, harriers, hawks, buzzards, and eagles all belong to the same family, the Accipitridae. Vultures are carrion-eaters that exploit air currents to stay aloft as they search the ground for food; however repellent their eating habits, they are sensational in the sky. The kites are elegant fliers that both kill live prey and eat dead meat and rubbish of all kinds. Harriers are long-winged birds with sharp claws and a long reach, adapted for snatching prey while hunting at low level over grassy or reed-covered areas and open moors.

Bird-eating hawks such as the Sparrowhawk also have a long reach, with long needle-sharp claws; they are short-winged, long-tailed, fast, agile hunters of woods and gardens. The buzzards both soar and hover; they catch live food and eat a lot of carrion, and even plod about in fields in search of earthworms and beetles. The biggest members of this family – the eagles – vary from medium-sized to very large. Most of them are powerful hunters and expert fliers that kill much of their food, but they often survive winters by scavenging meat from dead animals. The falcons belong to a different family. Long-winged and long-tailed, they range from hunters of insects and small birds to powerful predators of larger birds and mammals.

Moorhen

CRAKES AND RAILS

The crakes and rails are waterside birds with long toes, sometimes lobed, that allow them to walk over waterlogged ground and floating weed. Some are common and obvious, often on open water, while others are rare and secretive, living in dense vegetation. All are rather round-looking birds from the side, but their bodies are extremely slim for slipping through the dense vertical stems of reed beds. The bustards combine some of the features of the game birds with those of waders; they are rare and restricted, having declined as a result of hunting, disturbance, and loss of habitat.

WADERS

This is a very large, mixed, complex group of families. In North America, they are usually termed "shorebirds", but neither term fully describes all the species. Many live far from any shore and rarely wade; some breed in dry areas but spend the winter on shorelines. The strangest waders are the Stone-curlews, with just one European species: a big-eyed, partly nocturnal ground bird of dry, open terrain. The pratincoles are quite different, with a somewhat swallow-like form, although much larger; they share with swallows and some terns an aerial, insectivorous lifestyle. The stilts and Avocets are true wading birds that exploit shallow water. Stilts wade deeply and snatch insects from the surface with needle-like bills, while Avocets sweep their upturned bills sideways through shallow watery mud to catch tiny shrimps and other small animals. Oystercatchers eat shellfish when they can,

Avocet

Pin-tailed Sandgrouse

smashing or prising them open with their strong red bills, but when food is short they are forced into fields to look for worms. They are noisy, eye-catching birds, and often highly gregarious. The plovers include the widespread but declining Lapwing that breeds and spends the winter on arable land and marshes, the "ringed" plovers that nest on beaches, and the Dotterel that breeds on mountain grasslands and the northern tundra. The sandpipers include some very numerous and gregarious species such as the Knot, which flies in huge, spectacular, highly coordinated flocks. Many species breed far to the north and winter far to the south (the Sanderling, for example, migrates from the Arctic almost to the Antarctic). The Dunlin is one of the most widespread and familiar of the sandpipers, and a "standard" by which others are judged and identified. The "shanks" are larger and have longer legs than typical sandpipers; the *Tringa* sandpipers – which include the Green Sandpiper and Wood Sandpiper – are medium-small, and the "stints" are tiny and small-billed. Some species mix together freely. The sandpiper family also includes specialized waders like the very long-billed, short-legged, large-eyed Snipe, which needs soft, oozy, wet ground, and the cryptically coloured Woodcock, a woodland wader that emerges at dusk to feed in wet places with thick layers of soft leaf-mould. Finally, the phalaropes are remarkable for their sexual role reversal, the female being more brightly coloured than the male and taking the dominant role in courtship. Unlike most waders, they feed while swimming and spend the winter at sea, often far from land.

Razorbill

GULLS, TERNS, AND AUKS

This group includes the skuas: long-winged, elegant fliers that are both predatory and piratical, stealing much of their food from other species. The more abundant and widespread gulls range from small and neat to large and aggressive, with several "generalist" and opportunist species, such as the Black-headed Gull, and some specialized ones, including Audouin's Gull. The similar terns include pale-plumaged "sea terns" that plunge-dive for prey, and "marsh terns" that dip the surface for food while flying and have a good deal of black on their plumage in summer. The auks are a small group of seabirds that spend most of their life well out at sea and come to land only to nest, like the shearwaters. Unlike the shearwaters, however, they spend their time swimming rather than flying, being heavy-bodied and short-winged. They are capable of riding out most storms so long as they are not driven close against a shore, when they may be found washed up in an exhausted "wreck". They are also susceptible to oil pollution. They are highly gregarious when breeding, gathering in spectacular nesting colonies on sea cliffs and islands.

SANDGROUSE, PIGEONS, AND CUCKOOS

The sandgrouse are seed-eating ground birds that live in arid terrain. They resemble game birds, which explains their name, but they are actually close relatives of the pigeons and doves. These are common and successful birds of woods, farmland, and suburbs: small-billed, round-headed, and rather long-tailed, with soft, dense plumage. They have familiar cooing songs, but no obvious flight calls; to some extent their sharp, loud "wing claps" in display and clattering wing noise in alarm replace calls. The cuckoos are superficially hawk-like birds, well known for placing their eggs in the nests of other birds, who then rear the cuckoo chicks as their own. The Cuckoo is celebrated for its unmistakable two-note song, but few people would recognize it on sight.

OWLS

These round-headed, mostly nocturnal predators have large, forward-facing eyes and large ears to help them locate prey at night, and most have soft plumage that is silent in flight. There are two families: the barn and bay owls, which in Europe consists of just the Barn Owl, and the typical owls. Larger species eat mammals and birds, smaller ones mostly insects. Some species are nomadic, opportunist breeders that rear large families when food is abundant, but few or no chicks at all in poorer years.

SWIFTS, WOODPECKERS, AND ALLIES

The swifts are almost exclusively aerial birds: unable to perch or walk, they spend years aloft, catching flying insects, and come to land only to nest. They are long-range migrants, spending very little time in Europe. The nightjars are similar, but larger. They hunt at night for moths and flying beetles, and are known for their strange, mechanical, churring songs. Of more than 90 species of kingfishers found worldwide, only one breeds in Europe, but it is widespread and surprisingly common. Brilliantly coloured, it is closely related to three other families with glorious plumage: the bee-eaters, which really do eat bees, the larger but otherwise similar rollers, and the unmistakable, high-crested Hoopoe, which is the only species in the hoopoe family. This collection of small, unrelated families also includes the woodpeckers: stout-billed, sharp-clawed, stiff-tailed birds that excavate tree holes for nesting. Some woodpeckers extract prey from tree bark and rotten wood, but the various "green" woodpeckers and the Wryneck eat ants. They have loud calls and some also "drum" on resonant, dead timber in spring.

Green Woodpecker

Pied Wagtail

LARKS, SWALLOWS, AND PIPITS

The larks are short-billed birds that perform extended song flights in the breeding season. They have long hind claws for walking through short vegetation, and anonymous streaky brown plumages that make some species difficult to tell apart. Swallows and martins are long-winged, fork-tailed, swift-like birds that catch insects in flight with their wide-open mouths. They have tiny feet, but unlike the swifts they are well able to perch. They are often seen gathering on overhead wires before undertaking their long-range migrations. The pipits and wagtails are ground-feeding birds with long legs, long hind claws, and short bills. Wagtails have striking plumage patterns or colours, while most pipits are duller, streaky, and brown. They have an undulating flight and launch themselves into song flights from trees or from the ground.

WRENS AND ALLIES

This selection of birds consists of the few European representatives of four families: the waxwings, dippers, wrens, and accentors. The Waxwing is a plump tree-dwelling bird usually seen feeding on berries in small flocks. The Dipper is very different: a songbird that, uniquely for its kind, specializes in feeding underwater in fast-flowing streams. The Wren is a tiny, noisy insect-eater, common and widespread throughout much of the Northern Hemisphere. The accentors, which include the familiar Dunnock, are small, rather secretive birds, some of which breed at very high altitudes.

THRUSHES AND CHATS

A single, large, varied family, this includes such familiar species as the Robin, rarer ones such as the Rufous Bush-robin, and the striking wheatears of more open habitats. These smaller species are collectively known as chats. Thrushes are mostly rather larger, with stout bills and legs, and feed on fruit and berries or specialize in catching earthworms or snails. Many of this family are exceptionally fine songsters. Some, such as the Blackbird and Robin, have become familiar garden birds. Gardens can provide a reasonable replacement for a woodland glade or edge, although the food supply is usually poorer.

Redwing

WARBLERS AND FLYCATCHERS

The small, slim, but varied warblers include some widespread, common, and easily identified birds, as well as a few rare and local ones, rare visitors, and many that are very hard to identify. They fall into several distinct generic groups. The secretive *Locustella* warblers have prolonged reeling or trilling songs, round tails, curved wings, and long undertail coverts. *Acrocephalus* warblers are streaked or plain birds with distinctive song patterns that live in reeds or marsh vegetation. *Hippolais* warblers are small or medium-large, stocky, large-billed, strong-legged, and square-tailed. *Phylloscopus* leaf warblers are small, sleek, mostly greenish, and rather weak-looking birds of leafy trees and bushes, with distinctive songs. *Sylvia* warblers are heavier in their movements, generally more colourful and well-marked, but with scratchy songs; they are often found in scrub or low bushes. "Crests", such as the Goldcrest, are minute warblers with striped crowns and needle-sharp calls that test our high-frequency hearing. The flycatchers are a family of rather upright, short-legged, specialist insect-eaters, which typically catch prey in short flights from a perch.

TITS, TREECREEPERS, AND NUTHATCHES

Stout, small, fast-moving, with strong feet and short, thick bills, the tits are acrobatic birds that are well equipped for foraging in the trees; they are also familiar visitors to bird feeders in gardens. The treecreepers and nuthatches are mostly specialized for picking food from tree bark: the treecreepers use their tails for support as they creep over bark, while nuthatches use their strong feet. The Wallcreeper is an exception – it lives on cliffs and crags in mountain regions.

Blue Tit

SHRIKES, STARLINGS, AND CROWS

The shrikes are medium-small birds with hooked bills and strong, sharp claws, capable of catching small birds and large insects, which they often impale on thorns. The starlings are sharp-billed, stocky birds with strong legs and a fast walk. They fly straight and fast, and form large, coordinated flocks. Gregarious and often associated with people, they are found in woodland, farmland, and suburbs. The rather larger crows are stout-billed birds with nostrils covered by dense bristly feathers. Most are good fliers, the choughs especially so. They are typically black, but magpies and jays are boldly patterned.

SPARROWS, FINCHES, AND BUNTINGS

Small birds with short, stout, or sharply triangular bills and short legs, the sparrows are drab brown at a glance, but actually strongly patterned, some with marked differences between the sexes. The finches are very varied, ranging from crossbilled pine cone specialists to stout-billed seed crackers. Some breed semi-colonially, sharing sources of abundant food, while others are territorial and defend scarcer, more dispersed food supplies. Finally, the buntings have slightly differently shaped bills, mostly longer tails, and live in a variety of open places from moors and fields to marshland.

Brambling

Bird habitats of Europe

The illustrations in this book show birds in all their plumage variations and in a wide variety of poses. Yet a living bird can look quite unlike any picture. Its behaviour, the state of its feathers, and even the weather conditions can give it a unique appearance for the few minutes that you have it in view, and you need to allow for this.

The largest numbers of oceanic birds are to be seen from western headlands and on cliffs and islands, mostly in the north-west. The western shores of Britain and Ireland, especially, support huge colonies of breeding Gannets, Manx Shearwaters, Storm Petrels, Guillemots, Puffins, Kittiwakes, and Fulmars. These seabird colonies are among Europe's most exciting bird-watching sites.

The Mediterranean has its own shearwaters, gulls, and terns, but it is often associated with waders, especially where the coast is backed with lagoons or salt pans. Some of these have big flocks of Greater Flamingos and rare ducks. Migrant waders can be numerous on the lagoons, but as the sea is non-tidal its beaches are rather disappointing.

ESTUARIES AND BAYS

The North Sea and Irish Sea coasts, by contrast, have large tidal ranges that create big, muddy estuaries and bays. These shallows teem with waders and wildfowl feeding on mud, sand, and marshes that are enriched twice a day by the incoming tide. In winter, they attract great flocks of migrants escaping the harsh climates of the far north and east, and some also come from the north-west, from Greenland and beyond. Wigeon, Pintails, Teal, and Brent Geese feed on the marshes and mud flats, along with great gatherings of Knots, Oystercatchers, Dunlins, and Bar-tailed Godwits. The smaller, more sheltered estuaries may harbour Black-tailed Godwits and Avocets, while Redshanks, Grey and Ringed Plovers, Curlews, and Turnstones are widespread. Estuaries also provide opportunities to watch Black-necked and Slavonian Grebes, Red-throated Divers, and other marine birds that drift in with the tide.

WETLANDS AND LAKES

Freshwater wetlands often have extensive reed beds that may support Bitterns, Bearded Tits, and Marsh Harriers. Lagoons in the north may have Avocets, while farther south you can expect Kentish Plovers, Black-winged Stilts, and Little Egrets. In winter, marshy places near the coast may attract groups of Snow Buntings, Lapland Buntings, and Shore Larks, as well as larger numbers of Twites, Greenfinches, and Chaffinches feeding on seeds washed up on the strand line and caught up in the marsh vegetation.

Lakes and reservoirs vary greatly in their bird life. Lowland waters are usually richer than the cold, acid pools of the uplands.

They may attract ducks such as Mallards, Shovelers, Gadwalls, Tufted Ducks, and Pochards, as well as Goosanders, Goldeneyes, and others locally in winter. Larger reservoirs are often used as secure roosts by gulls almost all year round. On far northern pools, you may find Red-throated and Black-throated Divers, Whooper Swans, and Slavonian Grebes. Ospreys fish in all kinds of water in summer and can be widespread on migration in spring and autumn. Reedy freshwater margins are good for Reed and Sedge Warblers; in eastern Europe you may see Penduline Tits and Purple Herons. In the Low Countries and Scandinavia, the reeds may be enlivened in summer by the stunning song of the Bluethroat.

Flocks of Arctic Terns sometimes fly over land in spring, stopping off at reservoirs for an hour or two, and Black Terns may appear in spring and autumn. The autumn gales are likely to bring rare seabirds inland: waifs and strays such as Grey Phalaropes, Leach's Petrels, and Little Auks. If the water level of a reservoir falls in late summer, it could be excellent for migrant waders in autumn.

Low-lying marshland and seasonally flooded pastures have special birds too, but such habitats are becoming more difficult to find. Ruffs and Black-tailed Godwits, Snipe, Redshanks, Lapwings, Yellow Wagtails, and Reed Buntings breed in such places, while Wigeon, Bewick's Swans, White-fronted Geese, and Golden Plovers arrive in winter.

FIELDS AND PASTURES

Farmland used to be rich in birds, but the intensification of farming has caused massive declines throughout Europe. Corn Buntings, Tree Sparrows, Skylarks, Grey Partridges, Turtle Doves, and many others are becoming rare, and breeding Lapwings and Curlews have vanished from vast areas. Hay meadows used to be found everywhere and were full of Corncrakes: both are now practically extinct in many regions, although for the time being Corncrakes survive in surprising numbers in eastern Europe.

Changing patterns of farming have a huge influence on birds. Quails may be abundant in less-intensively farmed cereal fields in southern Europe, but disappear when the fields are planted with oilseed rape. Black Kites are everywhere along the coast of Spain, but intensive olive cultivation gives them little chance to thrive inland. Rice fields can be marvellous for Whiskered and Gull-billed Terns, Black-winged Stilts, and other species, but plans to intensify rice cultivation threaten to drive them out for good.

Grassy pastures used to support an abundance of wagtails, Swallows, Starlings, and Jackdaws, but many are now almost deserted. It is not always clear why, although pesticides may be to blame. Many small, seed-eating birds of arable land also seem to be suffering from a lack of food in winter, primarily because the adoption of autumn-sown cereals eliminates the winter stubbles with their spilt grain and seed-bearing weeds. Nevertheless, some farmland can still be excellent for birds. Old-fashioned fields in the south and east have White Storks, Red-backed and Woodchat

Shrikes, and even, in places, Great and Little Bustards. Winter farmland in the Low Countries can be stunningly rich in geese of several species, wild swans, and wintering birds of prey, including Common and Rough-legged Buzzards, Merlins, Sparrowhawks, and the occasional Goshawk and White-tailed Eagle.

FORESTS, WOODLANDS, AND GARDENS

Forests and woodlands vary greatly in their bird populations. There are some special woodland types, often shaped by human influence: the Spanish cork oak forests, for example, are splendid places, with Hoopoes, Orphean Warblers, Imperial Eagles, and a host of common species such as Serins and Greenfinches. Holm oak forests produce great crops of acorns that are harvested by Common Cranes and vast numbers of Woodpigeons all winter.

Magnificent conifer woodlands grow high on the shoulders of the Alps, the Pyrenees, and other mountain ranges throughout Europe. These remote, wild woods may support Capercaillies, Crossbills, elusive Hazel Hens, and Tengmalm's Owls. Other exciting owls live in the great conifer forests of the north.

Beech woods cast deep shade and have little growing beneath them, yet this is much to the liking of Wood Warblers and Nuthatches. Their crops of beech mast also attract some of Europe's largest bird flocks: the great concentrations of Bramblings that, in parts of central Europe, occasionally number in their millions. Old oak woods with tangles of holly, cherry, elder, hawthorn, and many other shrubs can boast a range of birds including Blackcaps, Garden Warblers, Lesser Whitethroats, Marsh Tits, Great Spotted Woodpeckers, Woodpigeons, Stock Doves, Jackdaws, Song Thrushes, Blackbirds, and Dunnocks. Nightingales make the air throb with their songs in many Mediterranean areas; in south-east England they largely rely on woods and thickets managed by people, especially coppices that produce dense growths of stems almost from ground level. Nightingales are showing disturbing signs of decline in Britain, but Woodlarks, which like felled plantations rather than woods, are doing well and spreading.

Robins, Chaffinches, Blue Tits, and Great Tits are often abundant in woods. In rural and suburban areas, they also spill out into gardens, finding them good substitutes in the main. But tits, especially, require endless supplies of caterpillars to feed their chicks, and sometimes cannot breed very successfully in gardens because they are too poor in insect life. Sparrowhawks are the typical avian predators of most woods, and they too have learned to exploit gardens, often raiding bird tables in winter.

HEATHLANDS, MOORS, AND MOUNTAINS

Mediterranean heaths – variously called *garrigue* or *maquis* – support a whole suite of warblers. Some are common almost everywhere, such as the Sardinian Warbler, while others are locally frequent like the Subalpine Warbler. A few are rather scarce like the Dartford Warbler, and some are decidedly rare and very local, such as the Spectacled and Marmora's Warblers. Woodlarks and Tawny Pipits sing overhead, Ortolan and Cirl Buntings sing repetitively from bush tops, while high above soar Short-toed Eagles, Booted Eagles, Black and Red Kites, and Griffon Vultures.

Dartford Warblers are also found on southern heaths in England, where they are doing well and spreading. British heaths may also have Linnets, Stonechats, Yellowhammers, and Hobbies, and Nightjars often appear at dusk in summer.

In winter, there are few birds up on the moors of the north and west, but in summer Meadow Pipits, Whinchats, and Wheatears join the resident Red Grouse, while Curlews and Golden Plovers breed among the heather. On lower ground farther north, the rich pickings of summer attract a variety of waders, including Whimbrels, Dunlins, Oystercatchers, and Ringed Plovers.

The habitat of the far north is more or less replicated on higher hills farther south, and both share such birds as Ptarmigan, Dotterels, Ring Ouzels, and Shore Larks. Mountain peaks in southern and central Europe, however, boast birds that do not extend to the north, such as the incomparably beautiful Wallcreeper and the stunning Lammergeier.

SPECIALISTS AND GENERALISTS

Some species have adapted along such specialist lines that they are tied strictly to a particular habitat, or a particular situation. Others are "generalists" and occupy a variety of landscapes. The "specialists" include the Dipper, which spends its life by a clean, tumbling river, the Treecreeper, whose day is entirely devoted to probing tree bark with its slim, curved bill, and the Bittern, found throughout the year in wet reed beds. Only unusual circumstances, such as a hard frost that exiles the Dipper to the coast, drive such birds from their usual habitats.

Many other birds are not so exacting, but still have special requirements. They include birds such as the Grey Heron: this feeds by hunting fish in shallow water, but it can do so in a river, beside a lake, in a salt-marsh creek, or from seaweedy rocks on the shore. Similarly, the Wood Warbler can occupy beech woods, oak woods, or even larch plantations, so long as they have a dense canopy high up and open space beneath, with a ground layer of dead leaves.

The generalists include such birds as the Black-headed Gull, which breeds near water – on a coastal marsh, an inland lake, or even a peaty pool high on a moor – but might feed anywhere from a beach to a ploughed field, a garden, a town park lake, or even a mountain top.

Most birds are not quite so adaptable, but they still enjoy a little variety. Often the "edge" of a habitat, or where two or three habitat types meet, is a very good place to see birds since it offers a range of feeding opportunities and brings several kinds of birds together. It is worth getting into the habit of recognizing such places: looking carefully along hedgerows, walking quietly up to bridges to glance quickly each way along streams, treading softly as you enter woodland clearings, or checking the edges of a ploughed field for feeding finches or buntings. You will also soon realize that water is usually a magnet to birds, and since there is always some sort of dry habitat alongside, this doubles the chances of seeing something interesting.

What you need to watch birds

All you need to watch birds is a pair of eyes, but anyone really interested in watching birds will want a closer view. The best way to achieve that is to obtain a good pair of binoculars.

Binoculars are near-essential equipment for every bird-watcher. A telescope may come later, or not at all. Looking through binoculars does not allow you to see farther than you can without them, but it enlarges what you can see so that the detail becomes clear.

The size of the enlarged image depends on the magnification, and this is shown in the figures that are used to describe the binoculars. These might be 8x30, 10x50, or perhaps 10x42. The first of the two figures is the magnification: the number of times an object is increased in size. A figure of 8x simply means that a bird you see with the naked eye will be increased in apparent size by eight times. Eight to ten is the range to consider. Don't be tempted by offers of binoculars that allow you to "see craters on the Moon", with magnifications of 12, 15, or 20. The bigger the magnification, the duller the image, the narrower the field of view, and the more problems you have keeping them still. A large magnification magnifies "handshake" too, and the image dances about in front of your eyes unless you are able to steady the binoculars against a solid support. The higher the magnification, the worse the effect.

So forget high magnification. What you really need is a bright image: plenty of light. This means one (or both) of two things. The first is large "object lenses": the bigger lenses at the far end of the binoculars. Their diameter in millimetres is the second of those two figures: 8x30 means your binoculars magnify eight times and have 30mm diameter object lenses. The bigger the lenses, the more light they let in, but after 50mm they get too big, too heavy, and too difficult to handle. The other option is to go for the best possible quality, with special coatings and special glass that increase light transmission. This means that a really top-class pair of 10x40s can be as bright or brighter than modest 10x50s. Quality costs money, though, and the best binoculars can be very expensive.

You also need a good field of view, meaning that you see a reasonably wide picture and not just a tiny part of the landscape. Typically, the larger the magnification, the narrower the field of view. This makes it hard to locate a bird that you have spotted with your naked eye, and may mean you miss other birds just out of view. Miniature binoculars also tend to suffer in this way. Close focus is useful, too: sometimes it is wonderful to focus on a bird perched nearby so that you can see every detail. Binoculars of lower magnification tend to be better in this respect.

So binocular choice is a compromise between good magnification (higher than six), a stable image (magnification no more than ten), plenty of light (bigger object lenses), light weight and ease of use (smaller object lenses), a wide field of view (lower magnification),

close focus (lower magnification), good quality (high cost), and something you can afford (low cost). Not easy! Also, you need something you feel comfortable with. You could pay a small fortune for "the best that money can buy" and find that they don't fit comfortably in your hands, or the eyecups don't feel comfortable around your eyes. You must try them out first.

You must also learn how to focus properly. Most important, you have to set the right-hand eyepiece to balance any difference between your eyes, or the best binoculars available will produce only blurred images. Aim the binoculars at something with sharp detail like a wire fence, shut your right eye, and focus using the centre focus wheel. Then shut your left eye and adjust the individual eyepiece on the right until the image is sharp. Open both eyes, and you should have a perfect stereoscopic image. Memorize the setting and check it regularly.

A telescope adds greater magnification: perhaps 30x or even higher, up to 60x. It will have a smaller field of view and be much less easy to handle: you might take several seconds to locate a bird. It will also need a rigid support like a tripod. So a telescope is not for ordinary, everyday bird-watching, and certainly not in a wood or other confined space, and you might do without one altogether. Yet if you regularly watch birds on an estuary or reservoir, you may need the extra power. The considerations listed for binoculars apply here too: you must compromise between power, light-gathering performance (big lens, heavy glass), weight, quality, and cost. Telescopes do not come cheap. You will also need a big, solid (and therefore heavy) tripod to mount it on.

Both binoculars and telescopes should last a lifetime if you look after them. Don't drop them, don't scratch the lenses, don't smear your fingers over the glass, and don't scrub them with coarse cloths. They should be treated as delicate instruments.

You may be tempted into bird photography or even recording birdsong. These are really specialist activities, although you can achieve quite a lot in the garden with modest equipment. Out in the field the birds are much more wary and further away, so the problems tend to escalate, expensively. You may need to build a hide, and you will certainly be spending a lot of time waiting for that elusive critical moment. If you have the money, time, and dedication, good luck – but be warned!

Once you have your optics sorted, you need a good field guide: perhaps the pocket version of this one. And a notebook. You don't have to draw or describe everything you see, but it is great fun and teaches you a lot about birds. It makes you look more carefully at each bird and helps fix the details in your head. It is hopeless trying to remember everything, then looking through a book and trying to decide whether the bird really had red legs or brown legs – or were they green? A notebook also allows you to describe the bird as you see it, instead of getting your descriptions second-hand. Once you start doing that, you are well on the way to becoming not just a bird-watcher, but an ornithologist.

USEFUL CONTACTS IN BRITAIN AND IRELAND

Britain and Ireland are well served with a network of amateur bird and wildlife clubs. The bird club network in particular is remarkably good, with many expert people involved. A typical bird club will have regular indoor meetings and monthly outings to see birds. You can meet other bird-watchers at all levels of experience and ability; in particular, you can pick the brains of the experts and learn from them. The club will probably produce a bulletin or newsletter that gives invaluable details of local birds, and an annual report that brings together the year's records and relates them to the experience gained over past decades. These are enormously helpful in telling you what to expect and where. You can see where other people are going bird-watching and find out the best places to see many species – where to see winter wildfowl or migrant waders, for example. The reports help you to put your own experiences into context: have you seen a rare or unexpected species, or something quite common?

In Scotland, the Scottish Ornithologists' Club is the national body, playing in part the role of regional and county bird clubs in England. The Welsh Ornithological Society has a similar role in Wales. Local members' groups of the Royal Society for the Protection of Birds (RSPB) also perfom some of the functions of bird clubs, but are essentially a means to promote and support the society locally. The RSPB is probably the largest bird conservation body in the world; it has more than a million members, and owns or manages more than 200 nature reserves. It organizes research into the needs of birds and threats to their survival, and plays an important role in promoting legislation favouring wildlife, as well as policies such as the agricultural schemes that help farmers conserve wildlife on their land.

The RSPB is the UK partner of BirdLife International, a global federation of similar organizations that has its base in England. The RSPB's increasing international work is largely focused through BirdLife International projects, including the training of conservation staff from all over the world, while BirdLife International also has partners worldwide working to improve prospects for birds and people.

The British Trust for Ornithology (BTO) is another national organization, which mobilizes amateur (but often expert) bird-watchers in projects and monitoring schemes such as the Breeding Bird Survey. It also oversees activities such as bird ringing in the UK. Much of its work provides crucial data that enables government agencies and the RSPB to promote conservation policies: it provides many of the facts and figures that back up their arguments.

Specializing in wetlands and their birds, particularly ducks, geese, and swans worldwide, the Wildfowl & Wetlands Trust is an organization with worldwide responsibilities and involvement in conservation issues. Its British centres include its famous headquarters at Slimbridge, which attracts many wild ducks, geese, and swans in winter. There are the county wildlife trusts, which have a broader interest in wildlife of all kinds and perhaps do more conservation work than the organizations that concentrate on birds: they often own or manage several nature reserves. Each county in England has its own trust with its own headquarters, but they are supervised by the umbrella body, The Wildlife Trusts.

All of these and more deserve the support of bird-watchers who gain so much from their hobby and naturally wish to help to ensure that birds have a place in the future in our increasingly hostile world.

There are also several magazines and journals for bird-watchers: monthlies include the long-established *British Birds*, the younger *Birding World*, and even more recent *Birding Scotland*, all available on subscription only, while the bookstalls and newsagents offer *Bird Watching* and *Birdwatch*. BBC Wildlife has some bird content, too. The RSPB magazine, *Birds*, which is concerned with bird conservation issues as well as RSPB nature reserves and other bird material, is a members-only publication, not available from shops or independent of RSPB membership. Details of nature reserves, bird clubs, RSPB members' groups, wildlife trusts, and other relevant bodies are published annually in *The Birdwatcher's Yearbook*, which may be available in your local library or can be ordered through any good bookshop.

USEFUL ADDRESSES

Royal Society for the Protection of Birds (RSPB), The Lodge, Sandy, Bedfordshire SG19 2DL. Tel: 01767 680551 www.rspb.org.uk

British Trust for Ornithology (BTO), The Nunnery, Thetford, Norfolk IP24 2PU. Tel: 01842 750050 info@bto.org www.bto.org

Birdwatch Ireland, 1 Springmount, Newtown, Mount Kennedy, Co. Wicklow, Ireland. Tel: 00 353 (0) 1 281 9878 info@birdwatchireland.ie www.birdwatchireland.ie

Scottish Ornithologists' Club, Waterston House, Aberlady, East Lothian, EH32 0PY. Tel: 01875 871330 mail@the-soc.org.uk www.the-soc.org.uk

Welsh Ornithological Society, 196 Chester Road, Hartford, Northwich CW8 1LG. PKenyon196@aol.com www.welshornithologicalsociety.org.uk

Society of Wildlife Artists, 17 Carlton House Terrace, London SW1Y 5BD. Tel: 020 7930 6844 www.swla.co.uk

Wildfowl & Wetlands Trust, Slimbridge, Gloucestershire GL2 7BT. Tel: 01453 891900 enquiries@wwt.org.uk www.wwt.org.uk

Wildlife Sound Recording Society, enquiries@wildlife-sound.org www.wildlife-sound.org

The Wildlife Trusts, The Kiln, Waterside, Mather Road, Newark NG24 1WT. Tel: 0870 036 7711 enquiry@wildlifetrusts.org www.wildlifetrusts.org

British Birds, Unit 3, The Applestore, Workhouse Lane, Icklesham, East Sussex TN36 4BJ. Tel: 01424 815132 subscriptions@britishbirds.co.uk www.britishbirds.co.uk

Birding Scotland, c/o Stuart Rivers, Flat 8, 10 Waverley Park, Edinburgh, Lothian, EH8 8EU. Tel: 0131 6612 661 slrivers@bee-eater.fsnet.co.uk www.birdingscotland.org.uk

Birding World, Stonerunner, Coast Road, Cley next the Sea, Norfolk NR25 7RZ. Tel: 01263 740 913 sales@birdingworld.co.uk www.birdingworld.co.uk

Birdwatch, Solo Publishing Ltd, The Chocolate Factory, 5 Clarendon Road, London N22 6XJ. Tel: 020 8881 0550 editorial@birdwatch.co.uk www.birdwatch.co.uk

Bird Watching, Bretton Court, Peterborough PE3 8DZ. Tel: 01733 465972

Mute Swan

LENGTH / 1.45–1.6m (4³/₄–5¹/₄ft)
WINGSPAN / 2–2.4m (6¹/₂–7³/₄ft)
WEIGHT / 10–12kg (22–26lb)

SCALE v Pigeon

■ **STATUS /** Secure

A huge, white, long-necked, short-legged water bird. Elegant on water, it is heavy and waddling on land. Flight powerful and direct with loud humming or throbbing sound from wings.

Few birds are so visible at such great range and that may be part of the reason swans are so large and white. No need for a song: visibility acts as a territorial statement in itself. Mutes are the largest swans, but also the most approachable, in many areas effectively semi-domesticated.

FEEDING
Mute Swans graze freely on short grass or cereals, but they mostly feed in shallow water, up-ending to reach down for the shoots and roots of aquatic plants with their long necks.

DISPLAY AND VOICE
Far from mute, a Mute Swan uses a range of hisses, snorts, and strangled trumpetings. Displays include elegant posturing with entwined necks and an aggressive territorial display, with arched wings and an S-shaped neck, that often leads to violent battles with intruders.

BREEDING
Swan nests are huge piles of reeds and stems at the water's edge. The usual clutch is of 5–8 eggs.

MIGRATION
Most long-distance flights are connected with migrations to safe places to moult in the late summer.

Adult female
Orange-red bill; black basal knob larger on male.

Long neck obvious; wing noise much louder than anything from Whooper or Bewick's Swan; occasionally spend time on the sea.

Immature
Grey bill at first; later dull orange with black base.

Wings arched during display and territorial disputes.

Pointed tail, often raised above water; neck often slightly curved; head and bill usually angled down.

THE EVERYDAY SWAN
The big basal knob and down-tilted bill create a unique effect.

WHEN SEEN

All year.

WHERE SEEN
Britain, Ireland, S Scandinavia, France, and Germany; locally in E Europe, including N Greece.

HABITAT AND INFO

SIMILAR SPECIES
Whooper Swan has tendency to hold neck more erect; wedge-shaped head and bill; short, square tail.

Square tail

Yellow on bill

ORDER
Anseriformes

FAMILY
Anatidae

SPECIES
Cygnus columbianus

COMMON NAME
Bewick's Swan

Bewick's Swan

A smaller swan than the Mute or Whooper, often more goose-like and chunky, but its neck can look equally long and slim. It has a compact shape with square tail.

LENGTH / 115–130cm (45–51in)
WINGSPAN / 1.8–2.1m (6–6³/₄ft)
WEIGHT / 5–6.5kg (11–14lb)

■ **STATUS /** Vulnerable

SCALE v Pigeon

Frequent noisy displays with wing flapping and forward-thrusting head; musical calls frequent.

Powerful flight, but no heavy, rhythmic wing noise.

A breeding bird of the High Arctic tundra that winters in Europe, Bewick's Swan is a most romantic, inspiring species, even though it is easy to see at close range at a handful of nature reserves where flocks are fed and overlooked by public hides. At other places, it is always an exciting bird to find, wild and wary of people.

FEEDING
Bewick's usually feed on land, grazing or eating potatoes, waste carrots, spilt grain, or other crops. Their feet often become caked with mud when they feed on wet, ploughed fields.

DISPLAY AND VOICE
Like larger Whooper Swans, Bewick's have elaborate greeting and triumph ceremonies and whole groups (often in family parties) may be watched bobbing their outstretched heads, spreading their wings, and calling loudly. Their calls are less ringing than a Whooper's: a softer bugling honk. Flocks have a musical babble, audible at long range.

MIGRATION
Bewick's reach western Europe in October or November, leaving in February or March.

Adult
Bill has rounded yellow patch each side; very variable central black stripe, often broken.

Juvenile
Pink, black, and whitish bill.

Juvenile
Dull grey-fawn.

Adult
White overall.

More agile and flatter-backed than Mute Swan on land.

Short-tailed, thick-necked on water.

GENTLE EXPRESSION
This is the most goose-like in shape of the swans.

WHEN SEEN

November to March; not found in Europe in summer.

WHERE SEEN
Baltic, Low Countries; locally in Britain and Ireland, N France.

HABITAT AND INFO

SIMILAR SPECIES
Whooper Swan has longer neck; larger, more wedge-shaped, less concave head/bill profile; triangular yellow patch.

Flatter bill with more yellow

Whooper Swan

LENGTH / 1.45–1.6m (4³/₄–5¹/₄ft)
WINGSPAN / 2–2.4m (6¹/₂–7³/₄ft)
WEIGHT / 9–11kg (20–24lb)

■ **STATUS /** Secure

SCALE v Pigeon

A huge swan with a long, wedge-shaped head and bill extensively marked with yellow. It has a rather straight, slim neck, and a short, square tail.

Compared with Mute Swans, Whoopers are much wilder, far less approachable, and not very familiar to most people. Their range is much more restricted, but in many traditional wintering sites they mix with Mutes and Bewick's Swans.

FEEDING
Whoopers feed in water like Mutes, but they spend more time on dry land grazing on grasses and eating grain and roots, including potatoes.

DISPLAY AND VOICE
Whoopers use a variety of calls based on a trumpeting, slightly yodelling *whoop-whoop*. They do not arch their wings in display, but have noisy greeting and dominance displays with wings half-open and head and neck thrust forward.

BREEDING
They nest beside northern lakes and in remote marshes, laying 3–5 eggs in a mound of vegetation.

MIGRATION
Icelandic Whooper Swans move south in winter to Britain and Ireland. Scandinavian birds move mostly to the Low Countries and the southern Baltic area.

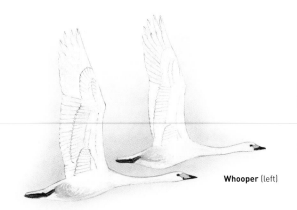

Whooper has longer neck and longer "arm" than Bewick's.

Bewick's

Whooper (left)

Bewick's (near left)
Rounded yellow patch, pink streak at base of bill where black thicker.

Juvenile
Bill dull white, pink, and black, progressively brighter; pattern echoes adult's.

Adult Whooper (top left)
Yellow forms long wedge beyond nostril; underside has longer yellow patch than Bewick's (top right).

Adult
May look thick-necked on water; square tail.

Adult
Extended neck very long and slim; often bolt upright or kinked at base.

Juvenile
Dull grey-brown overall.

Horizontal bill with diamond-shaped yellow; black "grin".

TRUMPETING ON THE WING
Call frequently in flight, but wings make no rhythmic throbbing sound.

WHEN SEEN

Sept — March

In W Europe, mostly September to March. A few remain all year.

WHERE SEEN
Breeds Iceland, N and E Scandinavia; winters Baltic, North Sea, locally Britain and Ireland.

HABITAT AND INFO

SIMILAR SPECIES
Mute Swan has head and bill tilted down; knob on bill base; rounder back; and longer, pointed, often uptilted tail.

Knob on bill base

Pointed tail

Canada Goose

Egyptian Goose

Canada is a large, heavy, long-necked goose, boldly patterned. Egyptian is stocky, rufous, or greyish, with bold white forewing.

CANADA GOOSE
LENGTH / 90–110cm (35½–43in)
WINGSPAN / 1.5–1.8m (5–6ft)
WEIGHT / 4.3–5kg (9½–11lb)

■ STATUS / Secure

EGYPTIAN GOOSE
66–71cm (26–28in)
110–130cm (43–51in)
1.5–2.3kg (3¼–5lb)

■ Vulnerable

SCALE v Pigeon

Both of these geese were introduced into Britain as ornamental birds. The Canada Goose has now spread to adjacent parts of Europe and is abundant in many places, especially around gravel pits, reservoirs, and park lakes. The Egyptian Goose, however, remains scarce.

FEEDING
Both feed on grassland near water, or in the shallows, taking shoots, roots, grasses, and seeds.

VOICE
Canada Geese have the deepest, throatiest honk of any goose: a penetrating *ah-honk*. Egyptian Geese have a shorter, wheezing, chuffing bark or cackle.

BREEDING
Canadas nest mostly on small, sandy islands, laying 5–6 eggs on a thick pad of downy feathers. The eggs hatch after 28 to 30 days.

MIGRATION
Although they are mostly resident, Canadas have developed some regular movements to safe areas in which to moult. Rarely, genuine vagrants from North America reach western Europe in autumn.

Egyptian (above)
White underwing;
compare Ruddy Shelduck.

Canada
Unique black neck "stocking" with white chinstrap; white breast.

Typically raised tail reveals white stern.

Generally brown appearance.

Grey Egyptian

Rufous Egyptian

Juvenile

Egyptian
Brown eye-patch; short pink bill; rufous and grey forms, both with long, red-pink legs.

Long red-pink legs.

GARRULOUS GOOSE
Egyptian Geese are social birds, giving loud, guttural calls in unison.

WHEN SEEN

All year

WHERE SEEN
Canada Goose in Britain and Ireland, Low Countries, S Scandinavia; Egyptian mostly in E England.

HABITAT AND INFO

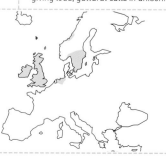

Pink-footed Goose

LENGTH / 60-75cm (23½-29½in)
WINGSPAN / 1.4-1.7m (4½-5½ft)
WEIGHT / 2.5-2.7kg (5½-6lb)

SCALE v Pigeon

■ **STATUS /** Secure

A grey and buff-brown goose with a round, dark head, short neck, stubby bill, and extensive mid-grey on the upperwing. Distinctive calls help identify flocks. Pale chest and very dark head are visible at long range.

Perhaps the most attractive of the grey geese, this is a neatly turned-out, subtly beautiful bird. Its large flocks are the essence of "wild geese" – hard to approach but familiar in many regions where migrating flocks are symbols of the passing seasons.

FEEDING
These geese are attracted to salt marshes, wet grazing meadows, stubbles, and ploughed fields, where they eat a variety of grasses, cereals, carrots, potatoes, waste sugar beet roots, and leaves.

VOICE
While the flock chorus is generally quite deep and nasal, based on cackling *unk-unk* sounds, frequent high-pitched, quick *wink-wink* notes make Pink-footed Geese easy to identify by call.

BREEDING
This goose breeds in eastern Greenland, small parts of Iceland, and in Svalbard, nesting on the ground in quite barren regions.

MIGRATION
Svalbard geese move to the Low Countries bordering the North Sea in winter. Iceland and Greenland populations winter in Britain.

Adult
Grey of forewing can be very pale in some lights; grey of upperwing more obvious than on White-fronted, which is darker than Greylag's.

Juvenile
Round head; delicate bill; short, waisted neck.

Adult
White tailband much broader than White-fronted Goose's; juvenile slightly narrower than adult.

A dark adult resembles a Bean Goose but has pink legs and billband.

Adult
Grey upperparts with fine white bars, bluish and pale in strong light; head and bill look dark; pink billband in good view; chest pale fawn.

Adult's legs pale pink to deep cerise-pink.

Juvenile
Browner than adult; scaly; no white flank line; dull legs; dark bill, unlike White-fronted.

SMOOTH LINES
A sinuous but short-necked elegance is characteristic.

WHEN SEEN

Sept — April

September to April in wintering areas.

WHERE SEEN
Breeds in Iceland; winters Denmark to Belgium, locally E England, and S and central Scotland.

HABITAT AND INFO

SIMILAR SPECIES
Bean Goose is longer-necked and has longer bill with orange band, orange legs, and darker forewing.

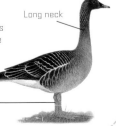

Long neck

Orange legs

Bean Goose

A large, long-necked, long-legged, elegant goose. Individuals in mixed flocks can be picked out by size, shape, dark brown head and neck, and bold upperpart bars.

LENGTH / 66–88cm (26–34½in)
WINGSPAN / 1.4–1.8m (4½–6ft)
WEIGHT / 2.6–3.2kg (6–7lb)

■ STATUS / Secure

SCALE v Pigeon

These large, dark, handsome geese gather for the winter in traditional areas – in Britain they use just two or three specific sites – but one or two often turn up in flocks of other species and are always a challenge for the keen goose-watcher. There are several forms: currently regarded as races, these may actually represent separate species.

FEEDING
Bean Geese feed in flocks, often mixed with Pink-footed and White-fronted Geese. They eat grass, sedges, grain, and root crops.

VOICE
The call is a noisy, cackling, bass note: *kayakak* or *kay-ak*.

BREEDING
Their nests are simple depressions on the ground, in tundra, peat bogs, and open river deltas.

MIGRATION
Breeding birds from north Scandinavia and Siberia move west and south in the autumn. Very few reach England and Scotland, but large numbers stay in the Low Countries, parts of central Europe, and Spain.

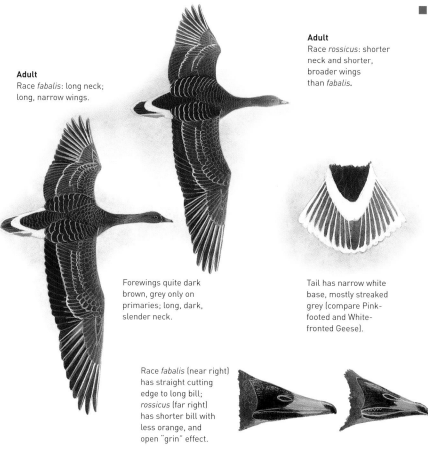

Adult
Race *fabalis*: long neck; long, narrow wings.

Adult
Race *rossicus*: shorter neck and shorter, broader wings than *fabalis*.

Forewings quite dark brown, grey only on primaries; long, dark, slender neck.

Tail has narrow white base, mostly streaked grey (compare Pink-footed and White-fronted Geese).

Race *fabalis* (near right) has straight cutting edge to long bill; *rossicus* (far right) has shorter bill with less orange, and open "grin" effect.

Both races have very dark head, dark neck, dull chest (unlike Pink-footed), orange billband, orange legs.

Adult
Race *fabalis*: white flank stripe often striking.

Dark back with neat, parallel white bars.

Adult
Race *rossicus*: dumpier, shorter rear, shorter neck than *fabalis*.

LARGE AND DARK
The Bean Goose is a large, long-winged, bulky bird.

WHEN SEEN

Sept — April

Mostly September or October to April or early May.

WHERE SEEN
Breeds in the far north, from N Scandinavia eastward; migrates to Denmark, Germany, Netherlands, Belgium, France, Spain; rare in Britain, N Italy, Balkans.

HABITAT AND INFO

SIMILAR SPECIES
Pink-footed Goose is greyer above; rounder head; pink legs; narrow tailband.

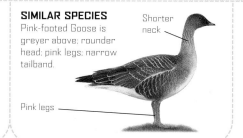

Shorter neck

Pink legs

White-fronted Goose

LENGTH / 65–78cm (25½–30½in)
WINGSPAN / 1.3–1.7m (4¼–5½ft)
WEIGHT / 1.9–2.5kg (4¼–5½lb)

■ STATUS / Secure

SCALE v Pigeon

A pale-brown goose. Adults have white forehead blaze and black belly bars; juveniles plainer. It has only moderately pale grey patch on upperwing.

Of the grey geese, this is the most colourful and often the most lively and nervous. Flocks winter in well-defined, traditional localities, although in Britain several sites have been abandoned in recent decades. Meanwhile, numbers have increased in the Low Countries.

FEEDING
Fields and grazing marshes supply a diet of grass, cereals, potatoes, and grain. The Greenland race also feeds in boggy moorland areas, plucking the leaves and roots of sedges.

DISPLAY AND VOICE
Lively dominance and threat displays are a feature of winter flocks. The high, laughing calls have a catch in the middle, giving a yodelling quality: *lyo-lyok*, or *kow-yow*, like a pack of dogs at a distance.

BREEDING
White-fronts nest on the ground in the northern tundra.

MIGRATION
Greenland breeders move to Scotland and Ireland in winter. Most Siberian birds go to the Netherlands, but some winter in northern France, England, and south-east Europe.

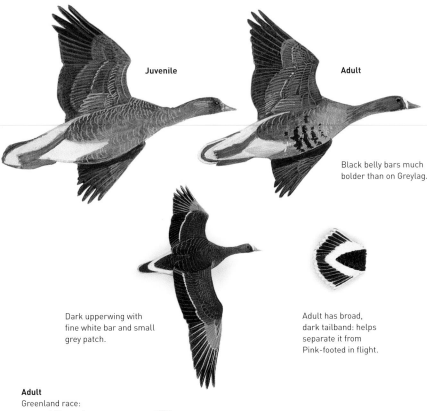

Juvenile

Adult

Black belly bars much bolder than on Greylag.

Dark upperwing with fine white bar and small grey patch.

Adult has broad, dark tailband: helps separate it from Pink-footed in flight.

Adult
Greenland race: orange bill; may be solidly black below.

White forehead usually obvious even in side view.

Adult
Russian race: mostly pink bill; typically paler overall, less boldly marked below than Greenland race.

Vivid orange legs (both races).

Juvenile
Scaly pattern; no white on forehead or black on belly, but pale bill unlike Pink-footed; wings darker than Greylag Goose's.

TYPICAL "GREY GOOSE"
The mid-grey upperwing is darker than a Greylag's.

WHEN SEEN

Oct — March

October to March.

WHERE SEEN
Greenland race in S Scotland, Hebrides, Ireland; Russian race in the Low Countries, France, very locally S and E England, and SE Europe.

HABITAT AND INFO

SIMILAR SPECIES
Pink-footed Goose has rounder, darker head and shorter, blacker bill; pink legs; purer grey on forewing.

Dark head and bill

Pink legs

Lesser White-fronted Goose

A small, neat, round-headed, short-billed goose with long wingtips, a yellow eye-ring, and high-pitched calls. Usually found in ones and twos among flocks of White-fronted Geese.

LENGTH / 53–66cm (21–26in)
WINGSPAN / 110–140cm (43–55in)
WEIGHT / 1.5–2kg (3¼–4½lb)

■ **STATUS** / Endangered

SCALE v Pigeon

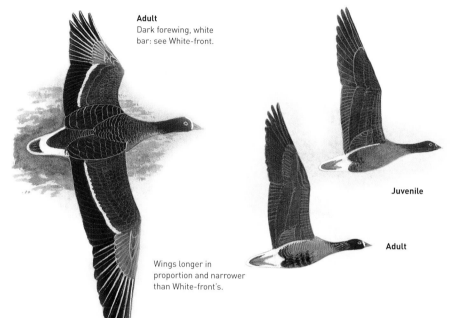

Adult
Dark forewing, white bar: see White-front.

Juvenile

Adult

Wings longer in proportion and narrower than White-front's.

Sadly diminished in Scandinavia, the Lesser White-front is most often seen in western Europe as a result of reintroduction schemes. It is a neat, delicate goose, but when in company with White-fronts – as it usually is – it can be extremely difficult to pick out. In Britain, it is most regularly seen at Slimbridge in Gloucestershire.

FEEDING
Although they feed on grass and other vegetation like White-fronts, smaller individuals at least have a faster pecking rate and move forward at a quicker pace.

VOICE
The call is noticeably higher-pitched and more ringing than a White-front's, like *dyee-yeek* or *dyee-yik*.

BREEDING
Very few breed in open birch and willow woodland in north Scandinavian mountains, and on more open tundra farther east.

MIGRATION
Most move south or south-east, but a few wild birds get caught up in flocks of White-fronted Geese moving west in the autumn.

Adult
Upperparts plainer than White-front's; underparts less barred.

Short neck.

Wingtips project beyond tail (equal in White-front); feeding action quicker.

Orange legs.

Juvenile
Rear flanks often dark.

Juvenile
Yellow eye-ring thin but clear; white may be more extensive.

Adult
White extends back in V onto crown; bright yellow eye-ring.

Head neat, round, or flat-topped, or with high, vertical forehead; bill triangular, bright shocking pink.

SHOCKING PINK BEAK
The small bill and neat head shape are distinctive.

WHEN SEEN

Nov — March

In western Europe, November to March.

WHERE SEEN
Breeds N Scandinavia; in winter very rare in Netherlands, rare and decreasing in Britain and SE Europe.

HABITAT AND INFO

SIMILAR SPECIES
White-fronted Goose has longer, deeper bill; flatter head; no yellow eye-ring.

Bigger bill

Shorter wingtip

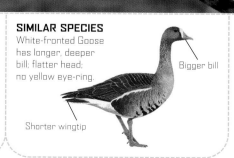

Greylag Goose

SCALE v Pigeon

LENGTH / 75–90cm (29½–35½in)
WINGSPAN / 1.5–1.7m (5–5½ft)
WEIGHT / 2.9–3.7kg (6½–8lb)

■ **STATUS /** Secure

A big goose, marked by pale grey forewings above and below, big orange bill, and pinkish legs, but with little or no white on the face or black on the belly.

Familiar as a semi-tame, introduced species in some areas, the Greylag is genuinely wild in most of its range. It is a rather heavy-bodied goose, less elegant and romantic than most.

FEEDING
Flocks feed on meadows and arable land in winter, eating grass, grain, root crops, and cereals.

DISPLAY AND VOICE
Its posturing with outstretched head and neck is familiar from the similar actions of farmyard geese, which are descended from Greylags. The calls are similar, based on a loud, hard, rattling repetition of nasal *krang-ang-ang* notes.

BREEDING
Pairs nest on the ground in heather (in the north) or among rushes and other waterside vegetation. Up to six eggs take 27–28 days to hatch. The goslings fly at 50–60 days.

MIGRATION
Wild Greylags from Iceland move to Britain and Ireland in winter. Those from Scandinavia and eastern Europe move south and west.

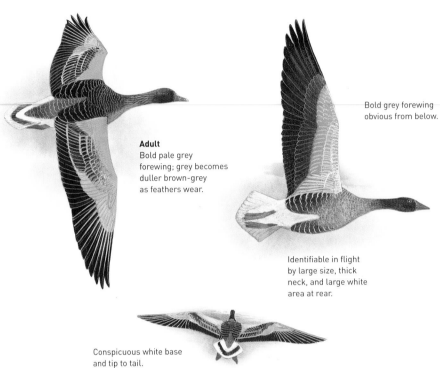

Adult
Bold pale grey forewing; grey becomes duller brown-grey as feathers wear.

Bold grey forewing obvious from below.

Identifiable in flight by large size, thick neck, and large white area at rear.

Conspicuous white base and tip to tail.

Adult
Some show quite obvious dark spots below.

Eastern race has pink bill.

Western race has orange bill.

Adult
Strong light creates very dark/light contrast on body.

Legs dull pale pink to pinkish-orange.

ANCESTOR OF FARMYARD GOOSE
Its heavy build is characteristic of the Greylag Goose.

WHEN SEEN

All year in Britain, migrants September to April; summer N and E Europe; winter Spain, Greece.

WHERE SEEN
Breeds Iceland, locally N and E Europe, Britain (most introduced, but native in N Scotland); large numbers winter locally S Europe and Low Countries.

HABITAT AND INFO

SIMILAR SPECIES
Juvenile White-fronted Goose has orange legs; irregular scaling on back; much darker-winged in flight.

Smaller bill

Orange legs

COMMON NAME
Barnacle Goose

SPECIES
Branta leucopsis

FAMILY
Anatidae

ORDER
Anseriformes

Barnacle Goose

A handsome grey, black, and white goose, often pale bluish at long range with a bold black chest and pale face. Flocks fly in shapeless groups with loud, yapping barks.

LENGTH / 58–70cm (23–27½in)
WINGSPAN / 130–140cm (51–55in)
WEIGHT / 1.5–2kg (3¼–4½lb)

■ STATUS / Vulnerable

SCALE v Pigeon

Long wings give easy, relaxed flight.

Grey on wings lost by spring, so looks quite dark.

Adult
Immaculate; some more solidly black on upper back (below left).

Face varies from dead white to yellow-buff.

White belly, sharp contrast with black breast, and bold white face unique.

While many wildfowl are very attractive birds, few geese are so immaculately turned out as the Barnacle Goose. It is a highly social species that uses traditional migration routes and wintering areas, where it may be seen in large flocks, although these are often restricted to nature reserves until after the shooting season, when they move onto nearby farmland.

FEEDING
Dense flocks graze fields and salt marshes for grass, clover, and seeds.

VOICE
Individually, the call is a sharp yapping or barking note, but flocks produce a noisy and more rhythmic chorus like the barking of dogs.

BREEDING
Barnacles breed far to the north on open tundra and cliffs.

MIGRATION
Breeding birds from Greenland fly to western Scotland in autumn and some move on to Ireland. Those from Svalbard move to the Solway Firth, mostly on the Scottish side. From farther east, many thousands fly to the Netherlands each winter.

Juvenile
Markings on back more diffuse than on adult's.

CONFUSION OF WINGS
Flocks fly in irregular packs rather than V-shapes.

WHEN SEEN

Sept — April

In W Europe, September to April; some feral outside usual range all year.

WHERE SEEN
W and SW Scotland, Ireland, E England, Netherlands, and Belgium, and some feral breeders in Baltic.

HABITAT AND INFO

SIMILAR SPECIES
Canada Goose is larger; longer-necked; brown; chest white; white chinstrap.

Brown body

White chest

Brent Goose

LENGTH / 56-61cm (22-24in)
WINGSPAN / 110-120cm (43-47in)
WEIGHT / 1.3-1.6kg (2¾-3½lb)

■ STATUS / Vulnerable

SCALE v Pigeon

Brent is a small, chunky, dark goose, with black breast, all-dark head, and small neck patches.

On a muddy estuary in winter the deep, rolling calls of Brent Geese make pleasant background music. Although scarcely longer than Mallards, Brents look bigger and heavier, and a big flock makes a fine sight. In recent decades they have increased and have also taken much more to feeding on farmland adjacent to the estuaries.

FEEDING
Flocks tend to feed in dense, irregular packs, so they "puddle" the ground beneath their feet when it is wet and damage crops. They eat eelgrass and algae on the mud flats, and grasses, cereals, linseed, and other crops.

VOICE
Flocks make a grunting chorus of nasal *krronk-krronk* calls.

BREEDING
Brents breed in the extreme north, on open tundra.

MIGRATION
Flocks move faster than Barnacles, flying in shapeless packs rather than lines. Greenland breeders (pale-bellied) winter in Ireland and NE England. Siberian ones head to southern Britain, the Low Countries, and France.

Adult
Upperwing all dark; uppertail coverts all white, covering tail.

Juvenile
Pale bars across inner wing reveal age.

Adult
Dark-bellied.

Adult (left)
Light-bellied.

Adult (left)
Dark-bellied.

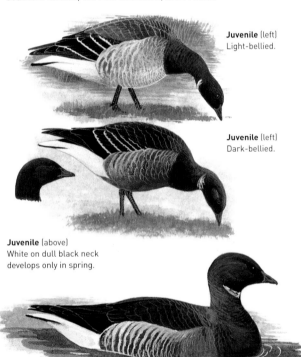

Juvenile (left)
Light-bellied.

Juvenile (left)
Dark-bellied.

Juvenile (above)
White on dull black neck develops only in spring.

Adult "Black Brant"
N American race, vagrant in Europe; white neck patch complete across throat; white flank above black belly.

WHEN SEEN

Sept — May

September to May.

WHERE SEEN
Pale-bellied in Ireland, Northumberland; dark-bellied in S Wales, S and E England, NW France, and S North Sea; migrates through Baltic.

HABITAT AND INFO

ORDER
Anseriformes

FAMILY
Anatidae

SPECIES
Branta ruficollis

COMMON NAME
Red-breasted Goose

Red-breasted Goose

Red-breasted is a strikingly marked goose, yet it is easy to miss when individuals are grazing among flocks of Brent or Barnacle Geese.

LENGTH / 53–56cm (21–22in)
WINGSPAN / 110–120cm (43–47in)
WEIGHT / 1.2–1.6kg (2½–3½lb)

■ **STATUS /** Endangered

SCALE v Pigeon

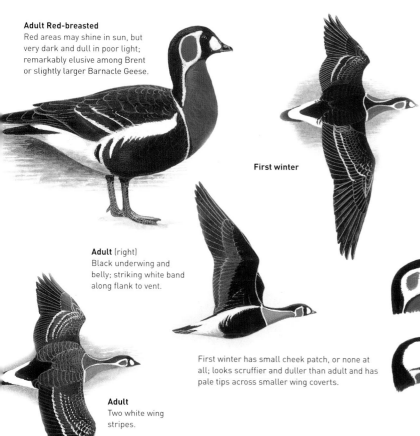

Adult Red-breasted
Red areas may shine in sun, but very dark and dull in poor light; remarkably elusive among Brent or slightly larger Barnacle Geese.

First winter

Adult (right)
Black underwing and belly; striking white band along flank to vent.

First winter has small cheek patch, or none at all; looks scruffier and duller than adult and has pale tips across smaller wing coverts.

Adult
Two white wing stripes.

Extraordinary in its appearance, yet surprisingly easy to overlook when a single bird is feeding with Brent or Barnacle Geese, the Red-breasted Goose is a prized find in western Europe. Its status as a wild bird is, however, blurred by the presence of small numbers of escapees from captivity, for it is highly rated as an ornamental goose.

FEEDING
Grazes on grass and other short vegetation or on eelgrass on estuary mud.

VOICE
A sharp, high, staccato *pik-wik!* becoming a loud, jumbled chatter from flying flocks.

BREEDING
Its nesting areas are in the extreme north on the tundra, often in the company of Peregrines or Rough-legged Buzzards, which provide a measure of protection against Arctic foxes and other predators.

MIGRATION
Most Red-breasted Geese move south to the Danube area of eastern Europe each winter, but as if by mistake a few associate with Brent Geese, and turn up among flocks of Brents in western Europe.

STRIKING COLOURS
This is a striking goose, but if one joins a flock of Brent or Barnacle Geese, it can be hard to spot.

Light-bellied

Dark-bellied

WHEN SEEN

Oct

April

October to April

WHERE SEEN
E Europe bordering the Black Sea; rare in flocks of other geese in Baltic, Netherlands, S Britain.

HABITAT AND INFO

DID YOU KNOW?
Early in the 20th century, Brent Geese were reduced to such low numbers that strict protection was introduced. They suffered from a lack of food when eelgrass was drastically reduced on north-west European estuaries by disease. Numbers are now much higher, but fluctuate widely, especially with years of varying breeding success in the Arctic. On average, 120,000 winter in Britain.

Shelduck

LENGTH / 58–71cm (23–28in)
WINGSPAN / 110–130cm (43–51in)
WEIGHT / 0.85–1.4kg (1¾–3lb)

■ STATUS / Secure

SCALE v Pigeon

A boldly pied, large, somewhat goose-like duck, often terrestrial. Juvenile unexpectedly different.

A link between ducks and geese, the Shelduck has some of the terrestrial character of grazing geese, including an easy walk on relatively long legs. It is among the more arresting birds to be seen on an estuary or marsh, easily identified at very long range. This might leave it vulnerable to predation, but perhaps aids territorial defence in spring and summer.

FEEDING
It takes tiny snails from estuarine mud with a side-to-side sweep of its bill, which filters food from soft mud and water. Various other crustaceans and insects are also eaten.

DISPLAY AND VOICE
Displays involve much head-bobbing and gentle aerial chasing. Calls include a squeaky whistle and a deep, rhythmic, cackling *ga-ga-ga-ga-ga* from the female.

BREEDING
Pairs nest under brambles, in rabbit holes, and in many artifical situations, lining them with down. The 8–10 eggs hatch after 29–31 days.

MIGRATION
Most western European Shelducks go to the Waddenzee in late summer to moult. Some UK birds go to the south side of the Severn estuary.

Sparkling white in flight – black patterns stand out well; heavy, direct action.

Female

Male

Male has broader breast band and black belly patch.

Very bow-winged on short flights.

Female
Whitish face marks; duller bill.

Juvenile
White face.

Male
Bold red knob on bill.

Juvenile
Drab white body with dark brown bands and cap; pale pink legs.

DUCK OF DUNES AND MARSH
Rough coastal grassland is a typical nesting habitat.

WHEN SEEN

All year.

WHERE SEEN
Breeds on Scandinavian coast, UK, and Ireland (sparse inland); in winter on Biscay coasts, Mediterranean.

HABITAT AND INFO

SIMILAR SPECIES
Male Shoveler has shorter legs and less goose-like stance; longer, black bill; darker underside.

Dark belly

Black bill

COMMON NAME
Ruddy Shelduck

SPECIES
Tadorna ferruginea

FAMILY
Anatidae

ORDER
Anseriformes

Ruddy Shelduck

Large and goose-like, very like Shelduck, but its rusty body colour is instantly obvious.

LENGTH / 61–67cm (24–26½in)
WINGSPAN / 110–140cm (43–55in)
WEIGHT / 0.75–1.2kg (1¾–2½lb)

■ STATUS / Vulnerable

SCALE v Pigeon

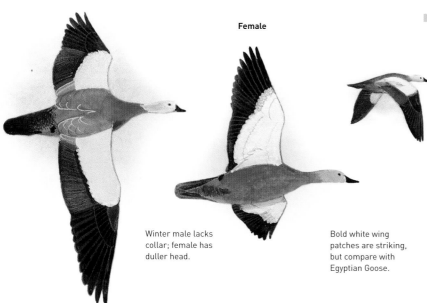

Male, winter

Female

Winter male lacks collar; female has duller head.

Bold white wing patches are striking, but compare with Egyptian Goose.

A clear view of the Ruddy Shelduck reveals a handsome bird with rich, rusty-orange plumage and sharp black features. It is a surprise in flight, with eye-catching black-and-white wings dominating the rusty body. Sadly, its ability to escape from ornamental collections makes its status in western Europe difficult to ascertain.

FEEDING

Its diet and feeding habits are much like those of the Shelduck, but Ruddy Shelducks also feed on wet grassland and swamps around lakes and estuaries.

VOICE

Various calls include a goose-like *gag-ag* or *pok-pok-pok* and a rolling, growling *porr porr porrr* in flight.

BREEDING

The nest is in a natural or artificial hole in a bank, building or tree, lined with down and a little grass. The 8–9 eggs are laid and incubated by the female for 28–29 days. The chicks are cared for by both parents, first flying when about eight weeks old. They breed at two years old.

MIGRATION

There is some limited dispersal in late summer and autumn and stragglers occasionally fly north and west. When the European population was larger, a century or more ago, such movements occasionally amounted to sizeable invasions of western Europe.

Female
Paler face than male's.

Juvenile
Greyer head than adult's.

Male, summer
Black collar.

Rich orange-buff to coppery body; black bill and legs. Beware confusing it with escaped near-relatives with different head patterns.

RUSTY ORANGE
The black bill and pale head are always obvious.

WHERE SEEN
Only about 200 pairs breed in E Europe (Romania, Bulgaria, Greece) after serious decline; rare vagrant elsewhere but frequent escapee.

HABITAT AND INFO

SIMILAR SPECIES
Shelduck is much whiter on body; chestnut only on breast band; black head.

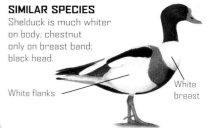

White flanks

White breast

Wigeon

LENGTH / 45–51cm (17½–20in)
WINGSPAN / 75–86cm (29½–34in)
WEIGHT / 500–900g (18–32oz)

■ **STATUS /** Secure

SCALE v Pigeon

A gregarious, short-legged, short-billed, long-winged duck, on sea- or freshwater, typically grazing on wet fields or marsh in tight groups. Often very noisy. Drakes' clear whistles unique.

Most ducks are beautiful, but there is little to compare with the sight of a densely packed flock of Wigeon grazing on an emerald-green salt marsh with deeply incised, silver creeks in low winter sunshine. They have a perfection of form combined with an elegance of colour and pattern that elevate them to a level above that of many other common birds. Added to this perfection in appearance, they are lively and interesting to watch. The males also have lovely calls, making a Wigeon flock one of the delights of winter bird-watching. In the air, Wigeon tend to form long lines, chevrons, and V-shapes as they fly high up, moving very fast, although they do not have the Teal's aerial agility in confined spaces.

FEEDING

Wigeon have short legs and short, deep, wide bills that are perfect for nipping short stems of grass and other vegetation: they are grazers, the avian equivalent of sheep. In winter they eat eelgrass on estuarine mud, but chiefly grass, sedge, and rush stems and roots from wet pastures and coastal grazing marshes. They are typical birds of open spaces with big skies, flat ground, and stretches of water to which they can withdraw for resting, bathing, or avoiding danger on the land.

DISPLAY AND VOICE

Female Wigeon make a deep, rather angry-sounding growl, often a double *grr-rrrr*. It penetrates the winter gloom across a reservoir or flooded marsh surprisingly well. Males, in sharp contrast, provide a high counterpoint, making loud, pure whistling sounds with a distinct emphasis on the first syllable: *whee-oooo*. Displays are relatively inconspicuous except for aerial chases. Most pairs are formed in late winter when the males are still in full plumage. In summer, as with most ducks, they have a duller, less eye-catching "eclipse" plumage.

BREEDING

Unlike the wintering grounds, the breeding areas used by Wigeon tend to be near remote moorland pools and peat bogs, far from the green swards that the flocks graze so effectively. Pairs breed in isolation – or, at best, in loose groups. The nest is made in a tussock of rushes or sedge, lined with a mixture of vegetation and down from the female. Up to nine eggs are laid. They hatch after 24–25 days.

MIGRATION

Most Wigeon from northern Europe move south-west in autumn, returning in April. Icelandic breeders move to Scotland and Ireland.

Juvenile
Typical head shape; short bill; bright orange-brown flanks; chestnut edges on back; lacks white tertial streak of adult.

Male, breeding
Pale body; brown head (Teal's darker); broad white bar along wing (Teal's narrower); grey legs; blue-grey bill.

Crops grass in forward-leaning posture; very short legs; often in tightly packed flocks.

Male, summer
Head and breast chestnut to dark red-brown.

Male, breeding
Creamy-yellow crown striking.

Female (below)
Variable from grey-brown to red-brown; greyer types with pale heads, often pale forehead; white streak on wing; grey bill with black tip; grey legs.

Male, breeding
Grey body; pink chest; red-brown head; yellow forehead; variable dark behind eye.

WHEN SEEN

Sept —— April

In N Europe, mostly April to September; the converse in W and S Europe.

WHERE SEEN

Breeds Iceland, Scandinavia, N Scotland; in winter scattered south to Iberia and Mediterranean coast.

HABITAT AND INFO

SIMILAR SPECIES

Female Teal is smaller; duller; white streak beside tail; blacker bill.

White tail streak   Dark bill

COLOURFUL GRAZER
The male is a rather pale bird
overall, with a white wing patch.

Adult female
Clearly defined
white belly and dark
underwing, unlike
Mallard's; chunky head
shape, unlike Gadwall's.

Adult male
Bright white belly;
black undertail.

Juvenile
Like dull female but
hindwing brown.

Adult female
Dark wing; forewing
slightly greyer; hindwing
dull green/ black; thin
white midwing bar and
white line on outer
tertial (Gadwall has
bigger white patch
and no wingbar).

Adult male, breeding
Big white wing patch is
striking; hindwing dull
green/black; back pale
grey; immature male
similar but white wing
patch mostly obscured.

FLIGHT PATTERN

Flight swift and agile on
long, swept-back wings.
Pointed tail, but short neck
and blunt-faced look.

DID YOU KNOW?

Wildfowl migrate vast distances and some can become
temporarily, or permanently, lost after flying in the wrong direction
or being blown off course by strong winds. In European flocks of
Wigeon, American Wigeon are sometimes seen. This bird
(especially the female) bears a close resemblance to
its European relative, and trying to spot an American
Wigeon in a flock of European Wigeon poses a
severe test of identification, much like finding
a needle in a haystack.

?

Mallard

LENGTH / 51–62cm (20–24½in)
WINGSPAN / 81–95cm (32–37in)
WEIGHT / 0.75–1.5kg (1¾–3¼lb)

■ **STATUS /** Secure

SCALE v Pigeon

The common wild duck, one of the largest ducks with a loud quack, sometimes shows features and varied patterns of semi-domestic ducks, but always has a blue wing patch. Drakes retain curly central tail feathers.

There are Mallards on most town and village ponds, although many are of various colour forms that are not found in the wild. Dark brown ones with white bibs, khaki birds with dull brown heads, and white ones with yellow bills all betray the influence of centuries of domestication. Yet truly wild Mallards remain among the most beautiful of all ducks. The drakes have extraordinary, glossy green heads that are shot with blue, lovely purple-blue patches on each wing, and the typical curly black tail feathers that often remain even in domestic forms. Wild Mallards are often unapproachable and nervous – with good reason, because so many are shot. The species is almost too familiar in its duck-pond persona but should not be overlooked as a handsome, wild bird in its own right.

FEEDING
Many Mallards feed at night, when they are safer on dry land. They glean grain from harvested fields, search out acorns from among fallen leaves at woodland edges, and dabble in shallow water for seeds that have fallen onto lakes and rivers and been washed up on the shore. They often up-end, and sometimes dive, to reach shoots, roots, aquatic insects, and shellfish.

DISPLAY AND VOICE
Most courtship takes place in late autumn and through the winter, when the drakes are in immaculate plumage. They get together around a female, bobbing their heads and calling with low whistling sounds. They force their attentions on the females, often chasing them in the air and forcing them to the ground. Only the ducks (females) quack, making the familiar loud, descending series of vulgar *quaarrk quarrk quark quack* notes.

BREEDING
Drakes take no part in rearing the ducklings, moving away to moult into dark, dull "eclipse" plumage while the ducks hide themselves away on nests in dense vegetation, often under brambles or in tussocks of sedge. Some nest in artificial sites, especially near town park lakes. The usual clutch is 9–13 eggs. They hatch after 27–28 days and the ducklings are led to the nearest water (often crossing busy roads), where they remain for 50–60 days before their first flight.

MIGRATION
Mallards from northern and eastern Europe move south and west in autumn, so Scandinavia and areas east of the Baltic have Mallards only as summer visitors. Much of western Europe has residents, migrants, and winter visitors, too.

Adult female
Bill has different orange pattern from Gadwall's; legs vivid orange like Shoveler's (Gadwall's yellower).

Male in summer resembles female, but darker, more rufous, dark crown, and stripe through eye separated by pale band; retains yellow bill.

Adult male, autumn to spring
Grey with dusky dark-brown band along body; chocolate breast; white neckring; glossy head; legs brilliant orange; bill green-yellow.

Up-ends in shallow water; female shows whitish tail and shorter wingtips than Shoveler's; male reveals white-edged curly tail.

Male, autumn to spring

Female

WHERE SEEN
Almost throughout Europe except in the most barren and mountainous regions.

HABITAT AND INFO

SIMILAR SPECIES
Female Gadwall has neater, squarer head; white belly; legs yellower; orange side of bill in neat patch; white wing patch.

Orange bill panels

White wing patch

ECLIPSE PLUMAGE
The striped head and dark breast show
this is a male in summer plumage.

Male

Striking white
underwing.

Female
Dark belly, unlike
Wigeon's or Gadwall's.

**Male, autumn
to spring**

Broad purple-blue
panel, edged black, and
white front and back.

Female

Male
White tail and double
white bar on hindwing.

FLIGHT PATTERN
Heavy in flight, head well
forward, tail short, wings
beat below body level.
Several males chase
each female in spring.

DID YOU KNOW?
Two species of ducks are the basis of almost all domestic ducks
worldwide: the South American Muscovy Duck and the Mallard. Various
"farmyard duck" varieties sometimes fly free and join wild flocks,
especially dark ones with white breasts and white ones with bright
yellow bills.

Gadwall

LENGTH / 46–56cm (18–22in)
WINGSPAN / 84–95cm (33–37in)
WEIGHT / 650–900g (23–32oz)

SCALE v Pigeon

■ **STATUS /** Vulnerable

A large duck, more delicate than the Mallard, with a squarer head, flatter, slimmer bill, no green, no blue, but a square, white patch on the wing. Beautiful in close-up, but rather plain and drab at longer ranges.

This is a large duck, but noticeably smaller, neater, and more finely built than the Mallard. It is a delicately patterned, rather handsome bird, but at long range it tends to look quite dull compared with some more vividly patterned waterfowl. In some ways it is a connoisseur's bird: one to pick out, not too easily, from a flock of Mallards and to appreciate for its subtlety. It is nothing like as widespread as the Mallard: its range is wide, but peculiarly patchy. In some areas, Gadwall populations have been increased by past introduction schemes. It is not usually found on saltwater but may feed in brackish areas at the edges of salt marsh and coastal grazing marsh.

FEEDING
Gadwalls frequently swim close to Coots, waiting until a Coot dives and brings up a beakful of weed, then moving in. They don't appear to steal food from the Coots, but they snatch up scraps that would otherwise float away. They are dabblers, like Mallards: they filter food from the water with filaments in their bills, dibbling or dabbling by rapidly opening and closing the bill while holding it almost along the water surface. They up-end, too, to reach food below the surface. They eat a variety of aquatic plants, seeds, and insects.

DISPLAY AND VOICE
Gadwall displays are quite subdued and include aerial chases with nasal calls from the drakes and a variety of postures on water. They make short croaks and whistles, including a nasal *ehk ehk*. Females have a more refined version of a Mallard's quack, the call being quieter, more even, and slightly higher in pitch.

BREEDING
The female finds a nesting site on the ground at the edge of a pool, usually well hidden in tall grass, sedge, or rushes. She makes the nest using grass stems and leaves, and lines it with down from her breast. She lays up to 12 eggs and incubates them for 24–26 days. She also takes sole charge of caring for the ducklings, which fly when they are about seven weeks old.

MIGRATION
Gadwalls breeding in eastern Europe head west and south in autumn. Those in the west disperse more randomly, often simply gathering in large groups on broad expanses of freshwater such as lakes, reservoirs, and large complexes of flooded gravel pits.

Male
Becomes paler-headed with wear; legs more yellow-orange than Mallard's.

Juvenile
Bright, orange-buff with bold dark streaks and V-shapes; buff belly unlike adult's.

Tertials sometimes reflect light, creating pale patch above black.

Black bill.

Female
Like Mallard, but neat bill with orange sides; white wing patch; may be pale with bold, large black mottles on flanks.

Male
Black stern; pale brown scapulars; otherwise exquisitely barred grey; some have grey tertials.

Up-ends to reveal black vent in male; white vent in female; orange legs.

WHEN SEEN

Mostly summer in E Europe: April to August. All year but most widespread in winter in W Europe.

WHERE SEEN
Breeds in parts of Spain, France, UK, S Scandinavia, NE Europe; in winter scattered locally but more widely south to Mediterranean.

HABITAT AND INFO

SIMILAR SPECIES
Female Mallard is bigger and darker – whole underside dark; purple-blue wing patch.

Blue wing patch

Dark belly

Male
In flight shows black
stern with white edge to
tail; striking white
underwing and belly.

Female
White underwing (often
visible head-on) but
square white belly
unlike Mallard's or
Shoveler's; juvenile
similar but has
buff belly.

Male
Grey; bold black
stern; wing colours
hard to see except
striking white patch.

Female
Brighter and browner
than male; bold white
wing patch is bigger
than Wigeon's.

Sharp wings and tail
give delicate, spiky
look, with a more
cruciform profile than
beefier Mallard's.

Some (perhaps first
winter) males show very
little red on wing.

Juvenile
White on wing reduced
to thin sliver; more like
Wigeon, but slimmer
and longer-necked.

DID YOU KNOW?

Gadwalls in many areas, including eastern Britain, derive from
introduced stock released for shooting. More recently, introductions
of birds have generally been closely controlled and in most cases
are illegal. Introduced wildfowl in some parts of the world, such
as Mallards in New Zealand, pose serious conservation
challenges because they interbreed with native species.

Shoveler

SCALE v Pigeon

LENGTH / 48–52cm (19–20½in)
WINGSPAN / 70–84cm (27½–33in)
WEIGHT / 400–1,000g (14–35oz)

■ **STATUS /** Secure

A large duck with a long, heavy bill, usually held low on the water as it swims with shoulders almost awash. In flight, the grotesque bill is obvious. Much quieter than the larger Mallard, but wings are noisy on takeoff.

There are times when a female Shoveler at moderate range is not immediately obvious, looking rather like a female Mallard. At close range, however, it seems almost inconceivable that such a huge bill could be overlooked: it makes the Shoveler look uniquely front-heavy. A drake in full plumage is unmistakable even at a distance, with its richly coloured and boldly contrasted pattern. Compared with the Mallard, which seems to be almost everywhere, the Shoveler is more sporadically distributed: over much of its range it is a scarce breeding bird. In winter, in places where other wildfowl gather in hundreds or thousands, there may be fewer than 20 Shovelers to be seen except in the most favoured spots. They prefer rich, lowland lakes with plenty of shoreline vegetation, but they can also be found on salt marshes and sometimes on quite open reservoirs and flooded pits in autumn and winter.

FEEDING
The Shoveler uses its long, broad bill to filter food from the water. Plankton, floating seeds, insects, crustaceans, and molluscs are caught in fine filaments called *lamellae* along each side of the bill as the bird squeezes water out with its tongue. As they feed, Shovelers swim slowly forward, their shoulders almost awash. Sometimes they gather in dense groups, which may spin like a huge wheel. Shovelers also up-end to feed, showing off their particularly long wingtips crossed over a short tail.

DISPLAY AND VOICE
Pairs and small parties fly over breeding areas in spring, often performing rapid twists and turns as several males pursue a single female. Males make a short, double note and the females call with a short, low quack. At other times Shovelers are fairly quiet birds, but their wings make a loud "whoofing" noise, especially on takeoff.

BREEDING
The Shoveler nests near water, in a hollow in thick vegetation, lined with leaves, grass stems, and the duck's own down. Up to 12 eggs are incubated solely by the female for 22–23 days. The ducklings fly at 40–45 days old.

MIGRATION
Eastern European birds move south and west in autumn, replacing many western European breeders that move south to the Mediterranean from late summer to early spring.

Head blacker than Mallard's; bill black; eye yellow.

Breeding male
Large white patch on rear flank between black stern and chestnut body; vivid orange legs.

Juvenile female (left)
More regular dark spots along flanks than on adult female (below).

Female (right)
Head plainer than Mallard's; bill longer, broad-tipped, orange near base.

Male (left, breeding)
In summer, heavily blotched rusty-brown with grey head, dark forehead, and crescent of white curving up in front of eye.

Female
Note low shape, long wingtips, obvious when up-ending, no white on greenish wing panel.

WHEN SEEN

In E Europe mostly March to September; in W Europe all year, but breeders move south in winter.

WHERE SEEN
Britain and Ireland; locally North Sea coasts, W France, E Europe; in winter south to Mediterranean coasts, Italy, and Spain.

HABITAT AND INFO

SIMILAR SPECIES
Female Mallard's bill is less broad at tip, less orange; upperwing brown.

Whiter tail

Smaller bill

ALMOST IMMACULATE
This male is moulting into breeding
plumage. Not yet fully white-breasted.

Adult female
Like Mallard but
blue-grey forewing,
green hindwing without
white bars; similar dark
body; white underwing.

Adult male
Striking combination
of blue forewing above,
green-black head,
broad white band
around chest, and
deep rufous body.

DID YOU KNOW?
Shapes and proportions can be surprisingly difficult to judge when wild
birds are seen, especially in unexpected circumstances. The long,
broad, heavy-tipped bill of a Shoveler looks highly distinctive on the
page – and can be so in reality – but on occasion a swimming female
Shoveler may be remarkably hard to separate from a
female Mallard.

Pintail

LENGTH / Male 61–76cm (24–30in);
female 51–57cm (20–22½in)
WINGSPAN / 80–95cm (31½–37in)
WEIGHT / 550–1,200g (19–42oz)

SCALE v Pigeon

■ **STATUS /** Secure

An elegant surface-feeding duck with a slender bill, slim, often-raised neck, narrow wings, and pointed tail. Males in winter are strikingly patterned while females are pale and rather plain-faced.

No duck has a greater elegance of form and pattern than the Pintail, although its subtle plumage lacks the vivid colours of some other species. Females have a typical female Mallard's streaky-brown pattern, but are more neatly marked with more uniform, paler heads and necks. They are a test for the keen duck-watcher because, along with eclipse males in late summer and early autumn, they can be hard to pick out from among scores or hundreds of Mallards. In winter, however, the startling white breasts of adult drakes are obvious at great range, making them hard to miss on the marsh or mud flat. Pintails are unusually local in occurrence: some traditional sites attract hundreds or thousands of them, but in most areas a handful, at best, might be found on a few occasions each winter. They are rather wild and elusive, rarely allowing a close approach in the wide open spaces that they prefer.

FEEDING
On estuaries, Pintails take tiny snails from mud. On lakes and freshwater floods, they are able to reach food in deeper water than other dabbling ducks by up-ending and using their particularly long necks. They take seeds, berries, shoots, roots, and a variety of aquatic insects and crustaceans. Many also move onto fields to eat spilled grain and root crops such as potatoes and sugar beet.

DISPLAY AND VOICE
The white breast and long, white neck stripes of males are shown off to advantage in their head-bobbing and stretching postures. During these displays the males call with a nasal *wheee*. Normally, Pintails are quite quiet: females have a low quack and a Wigeon-like growl and males make a quiet whistle.

BREEDING
Few breed in western Europe: in Britain only a handful at most. The nest is typical of dabbling ducks, made in a waterside hollow among tall grasses or sedge, lined with leaves, stems, and some down from the duck. Up to nine eggs are incubated by the female for 22–24 days and the ducklings fly at 40–45 days old. Males take no part in rearing the family.

MIGRATION
Pintails from Iceland, Scandinavia, and north-east Europe move south and west in autumn. They reach the western coasts of France, much of Spain and Portugal, and most of Britain and Ireland, but most concentrate on a handful of favoured estuaries and flooded grasslands inland.

Female
Note grey bill, grey legs, and pale, plain head; shape is best clue at distance.

Black shoulder.

Male
Unique shape and pattern, with long, white neck stripe.

Resting male shows white breast; both sexes have dark legs (Shoveler has orange legs); female shows pale tail sides.

Male
Bill striped grey and black; eye-catching white breast.

Tail tip curls up in breeze.

WHEN SEEN

Sept — April

In W Europe mostly September to April.

WHERE SEEN
Breeds Scandinavia, NE Europe, Iceland; in winter W and S locally to Ireland and Mediterranean.

HABITAT AND INFO

SIMILAR SPECIES
Female Wigeon has steeper forehead; often more rufous overall; square white belly; lacks long white hindwing stripe.

Pale bill

Rufous flanks

PICTURE OF ELEGANCE
This is a long-bodied duck
with an elegant head shape.

Male
Preparing to land.

Male
Long tail point; yellow-
buff vent against black
undertail; white trailing
edge to wing and
orange-buff wingbar;
bright white breast.

Narrow white trailing
edge to inner wing
catches the eye.

Buff wingbar browner
on juvenile.

Female
Less extreme than
male, but still slim
with long neck
and pointed tail.

FLIGHT PATTERN
Graceful profile makes
Pintails easy to pick out
in flight, which is swift
and direct.

DID YOU KNOW?
Like other ducks, the males (or drakes) have a dull summer plumage,
called "eclipse", much like the female. In autumn, males moult into
distinctive breeding colours and can be seen in assorted intermediate
plumages, not illustrated in most books: pale grey-brown with dark
spots and patches of finely barred grey feathers gradually
increasing on the body.

Teal

SCALE v Pigeon

LENGTH / 34–38cm (13½–15in)
WINGSPAN / 58–64cm (23–25in)
WEIGHT / 250–400g (9–14oz)

■ **STATUS /** Secure

Common, widespread duck in marshes and around the edges of pools and floods. Small and dark, often revealed by the drakes' sharp, whistling calls. Male has dark head and long, white stripe along side. Female has bright-green wing patch.

The smallest and most agile of surface-feeding ducks, the Teal could almost be taken for a wader at times, especially if a small group flies up from a muddy pond, twisting and turning before getting under way at top speed. Teal are lovely ducks, but a close view is needed to appreciate their dark, varied colours fully. Even then, a little bright sunlight is best for all the highlights to show well. It is worth trying to get close but, unless they are watched from a hide, Teal tend to be suspicious, easily alarmed, and difficult to approach.

FEEDING
Teal can be found on both salt- and freshwater, but they are most common on shallow lakes and winter floods. They eat all kinds of seeds, roots, and shoots, along with some aquatic insects. In the late summer and autumn they can gather in hundreds, especially at reservoirs where the level has fallen to expose areas of mud well stocked with freshly ripened seeds of waterside plants. Often they stay half-hidden in the vegetation and their numbers might not be apparent unless something disturbs them and they fly off or swim out onto open water. Flocks often feed on marshes and around estuaries at night. In summer they feed in the sphagnum and deep, peaty creeks of upland bogs and moors.

DISPLAY AND VOICE
Pairs chase each other over breeding pools and marshes. The male has a wonderful ringing call, far-carrying in still winter air, of a bell-like or piping, cricket-like *krik* or *kreek*. Females make a high quack and a lower growling sound.

BREEDING
Most Teal breed in the north, around moorland pools or lakes within areas of forest. They nest on the ground in thick vegetation near water, lining the nest with down from the female's breast. She lays 8–11 eggs and incubates them alone for 21–23 days. The ducklings soon leave the nest but cannot fly until they are 25–30 days old. Males take no part in rearing the family.

MIGRATION
Large numbers of Teal from western Asia and northern Europe move south and west in autumn to spend the winter scattered locally over much of Europe. Others join them from Iceland and a handful of North American Green-winged Teal arrive in western Europe each autumn. Some go as far as north Africa and part of the breeding population of western Europe moves south.

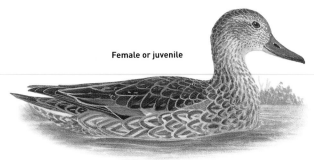

Female or juvenile

Female, juvenile, and eclipse male all have dull plumage relieved by green wing patch, pale streak by tail; head often dark-capped, pale-cheeked.

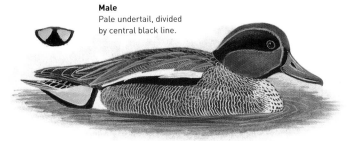

Male
Pale undertail, divided by central black line.

Male, breeding
Dark head, brown with broad, dark-green stripe and dark bill; rich cream triangle under tail; white stripe along body; short, dark legs.

Female
Pale stripe along tail side; bright green wing patch; dark legs; wing may have violet sheen when seen from rear.

WHEN SEEN

All year; mostly August to April in non-breeding areas. In N and E Europe, only in summer.

WHERE SEEN
Breeds Iceland, locally Britain and Ireland, France, N and E throughout Scandinavia into Asia; in winter, also in SE Europe, Italy, S France, and Iberia.

HABITAT AND INFO

SIMILAR SPECIES
Female Garganey has more dark blotches on body; bolder pale lines and dark cheek band on face; double white line on hindwing in flight.

Bold line over eye

Dull wing patch

EUROPE'S SMALLEST DUCK
The male is a dark, small-headed,
slim-billed duck.

Male, breeding
Dark, with pale line
along midwing;
green-and-black
hindwing patch.

Female
Wing like male's; duller
brown body with no
white lines; juvenile
has narrower wingbar
than adult female's.

Female or juvenile
Whitish underwing;
grey forewing (not
dark as on Garganey).

FLIGHT PATTERN
Small, quick, and agile in flight,
more like wader than duck; flocks
often tight and coordinated.

DID YOU KNOW?
North America's Common Teal looks similar, but the male has little or
no pale buff around the green head patch and no white bar along the
body. However, it has a vertical white line each side of the chest. For
centuries it was treated as a race, or sub-species, of the Teal, but it
has recently been separated, or split, by taxonomists as a
separate species, the Green-winged Teal.

Garganey

LENGTH / 37–41cm (14½–16in)
WINGSPAN / 60–63cm (24–26in)
WEIGHT / 250–500g (9–18oz)

■ **STATUS /** Vulnerable

SCALE v Pigeon

A small, fast-flying, elegant duck, with dark legs and bill and typically a rather striped head pattern.

In a way, this species reverses the usual duck pattern, as it is a summer visitor to Europe. It is not much bigger than a Teal and is found in similar places with shallow water, often temporary floods, and plenty of vegetation.

FEEDING
It eats small beetles, snails, and other aquatic creatures, along with a variety of plant material.

VOICE
Males in spring have a strange, dry, rattling note, a short crackling *crrrk*. Females quack quietly.

BREEDING
Nests are near water, often in grass tussocks, and lined with down. The 8–11 eggs hatch after 21–23 days. The male ignores the ducklings, which fly when 35–40 days old.

MIGRATION
The winter months are spent in tropical Africa. In the Middle East and south-east Europe, large migrant flocks reappear in spring. In western Europe it is much scarcer and very local, most places seeing only a pair or two in spring and up to a dozen or so on their return in autumn.

Plain rump; no white V like Teal's.

Outer wing grey.

Darker beneath forewing than Teal's.

Juvenile (above)
Brown wing patch, lacks black of Teal's; two equal wingbars.

Flight shapes as Teal's, but bill longer.

Female
Dull wing; greyish wing patch; two prominent white bars of equal width, unlike Teal's.

Midwing bar on male is broader than hindwing bar.

Distinctive grey on primaries as if light reflects from outer wing.

Male, spring
Forewing bluish; gets duller grey before July moult.

Juvenile male
Dark crown; pale stripe over eye and on upper cheek; pale spot by bill; white chin.

Male, spring
Striking head stripe; drooped, spiky scapulars.

Female
Large spots, thin pale edges, more solid than Teal's.

SPRING DANDY
A spring male is a strongly patterned but subtly coloured duck, with distinctively pale wings.

WHEN SEEN

Sept — March

Early March to late September.

WHERE SEEN
E Europe, E Scandinavia, Baltic area; locally and irregularly scattered farther west to England.

HABITAT AND INFO

SIMILAR SPECIES
Female Teal is more uniform and drab; upperwing with broader central stripe; brighter green on hindwing.

Duller face pattern

Bright green wing patch

Marbled Duck

A rare duck of southern Europe, looking pale and poorly marked at any distance except for a dark eye smudge and, in flight, a white underwing.

LENGTH / 39–42cm (15½–16½in)
WINGSPAN / 63–70cm (25–27½in)
WEIGHT / 400–500g (14–18oz)

■ **STATUS** / Endangered

SCALE v Pigeon

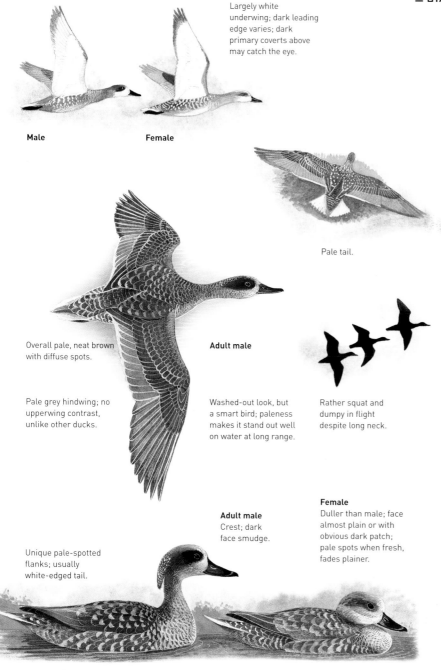

Largely white underwing; dark leading edge varies; dark primary coverts above may catch the eye.

Male

Female

Pale tail.

Overall pale, neat brown with diffuse spots.

Adult male

Pale grey hindwing; no upperwing contrast, unlike other ducks.

Washed-out look, but a smart bird; paleness makes it stand out well on water at long range.

Rather squat and dumpy in flight despite long neck.

Adult male
Crest; dark face smudge.

Female
Duller than male; face almost plain or with obvious dark patch; pale spots when fresh, fades plainer.

Unique pale-spotted flanks; usually white-edged tail.

This rare and threatened bird has disappeared from many of its former breeding sites across southern Europe, although in some places in south-west Spain, its numbers have recently shown signs of increasing. It prefers shallow lakes with plenty of waterside vegetation, flooded salt pans, and, in winter, the margins of undisturbed estuaries.

FEEDING
Unless disturbed, it usually keeps well within areas of vegetation where it feeds on shoots and stems, dabbling in the shallows, up-ending, and occasionally diving.

VOICE
This is a quiet bird. Males call in spring with a squeaky *eeeeep*. Ducks have a similar call and a weaker, high *pleep pleep*.

BREEDING
It nests on the ground under bushes or in dense, low thickets. Up to 14 eggs are incubated for 25–27 days. Other details are little known.

MIGRATION
Spanish breeding birds move out of their nesting areas in late summer, mainly to nearby coasts.

SUBTLE COLOURS
Fierce Mediterranean light tends to wash out the darker patterning at a distance.

WHEN SEEN

All year.

WHERE SEEN
Very local near southern and eastern coasts of Spain.

HABITAT AND INFO

SIMILAR SPECIES
Female Teal is darker; head usually less contrasted; pale central wing stripe.

Plainer head

Green wing patch

Pochard

SCALE v Pigeon

LENGTH / 42-49cm (16½-19in)
WINGSPAN / 72-82cm (28½-32in)
WEIGHT / 700-1,000g (25-35oz)

■ STATUS / Secure

A gregarious, freshwater diving duck. It often sleeps by day in tight flocks with Tufted Ducks on lakes and reservoirs. Dark front and back, pale middle helps to identify males. Females are much dowdier.

Typically, Pochards spend much of the day asleep, drifting in flocks, often mixed with Tufted Ducks. They are common and widespread, except in summer, when they are local and scarce breeders in much of Europe.

FEEDING
Pochards dive underwater to find seeds, shoots, and roots, taking only a small amount of animal food. They tend to be most active at night.

DISPLAY AND VOICE
Displays are subdued, including various head-stretching postures with wheezy, rising, double *aawoo* notes from the male and quiet whistles from the female. Otherwise the most usual call is a low, gruff, short growl.

BREEDING
Pochards nest near water in reeds, laying 8–10 eggs on a thick pad of waterweed and down. The eggs hatch after 25 days.

MIGRATION
Large numbers reach western Europe from eastern Europe and Asia. In the UK, there is a marked autumn migration in most areas with large flocks in October and November.

Larger, broader than Tufted; rufous head, grey sides distinguish from Scaup.

Male
Broad midwing panel paler than forewing, but no white.

Female

Female

Male, non-breeding

Immature male
Plumage of immatures and females variable and confusing.

Male

Red eye; blue band on bill.

Pale billband.

Male, breeding
Handsome winter drake, pale with black breast and stern.

Female, winter

SLEEPY CUSTOMER
An active male has a sharp, dynamic look, but they spend much of the day asleep.

WHEN SEEN

All year, but increased numbers in W Europe October–March.

WHERE SEEN
Widespread from UK, Ireland, and Iceland to east through central and NE Europe; locally S Scandinavia; in winter also Iberia, S France, Italy, Balkans.

HABITAT AND INFO

SIMILAR SPECIES
Male Scaup has round black head; whiter flanks; broad, pale grey bill.

Black head

White sides

ORDER
Anseriformes

FAMILY
Anatidae

SPECIES
Netta rufina

COMMON NAME
Red-crested
Pochard

Red-crested Pochard

A bulky duck that feeds by dabbling as well as diving. The extraordinary male is easy to identify, but female can be confused with maritime Common Scoter.

LENGTH / 53–57cm (21–22½in)
WINGSPAN / 85–90cm (33½–35½in)
WEIGHT / 0.9–1.4kg (2–3lb)

■ **STATUS /** Vulnerable

SCALE v Pigeon

One of the more flamboyant European ducks, this rare and local species combines characteristics of both diving and surface-feeding ducks. In places, escapees can be seen outside the usual range and some of these birds regularly nest successfully.

FEEDING

Although capable of diving well, Red-crested Pochards often feed at the surface, dabbling and even up-ending like Mallards as they search for seeds, shoots, and leaves of water plants.

DISPLAY AND VOICE

Males pursue females in flight over nesting areas in spring, like most dabbling ducks, showing their big white wingbars. The males often raise their bushy, orange crown feathers and call with a nasal, sneezing *keuvik*. The usual call is a short *gik*.

BREEDING

Nests are hidden in dense vegetation beside reedy lakes and swamps and overgrown saltpans. The 8–10 eggs hatch after 26–28 days.

MIGRATION

In Spain, most are resident. Some from NE Europe move south in autumn, mostly to Greece and Turkey. In most places, they occur irregularly. In UK, most are semi-resident feral birds, with very few wild ones in autumn.

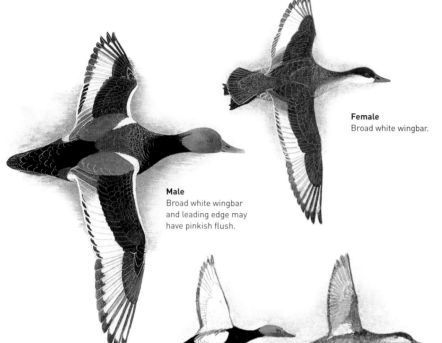

Female
Broad white wingbar.

Male
Broad white wingbar and leading edge may have pinkish flush.

Male

Female

Male, summer
Retains red bill.

Juvenile
No pink on bill.

Male, breeding
Fuzzy ginger crown; red bill; black breast; ragged white sides.

Female (right)
Brown cap and dull white cheeks; dark bill.

BOLD FEATURES
Males are extravagantly coloured and look big and bulky among Pochards.

SIMILAR SPECIES
Female Common Scoter has darker body; blacker cap; all-dark wings.

Triangular grey bill

Dark brown body

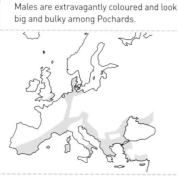

Ferruginous Duck

LENGTH / 38–42cm (15–16½in)
WINGSPAN / 60–67cm (23½–26½in)
WEIGHT / 500–600g (18–21oz)

SCALE v Pigeon

■ **STATUS** / Endangered

A dark, richly coloured duck with white beneath the tail and broad white wingbars revealed in flight or when flapping wings. Head peaked, its forehead slopes into bill profile.

The Ferruginous Duck has suffered a rapid decline in recent years: it evidently has specialized needs which it finds more difficult to meet as the shallow, rich lakes that it favours are drained, disturbed, or polluted. At first glance it seems a plain bird, but a close view reveals a finely built, elegant duck with great depth of colour.

FEEDING
It dives underwater for seeds and plant matter, and a much smaller proportion of animal food.

DISPLAY AND VOICE
Small groups display unobtrusively on the water. Males have short *chuk* notes. Females give a loud, frequent, grating *err err err* in flight.

BREEDING
They breed in the marshy fringes of lowland lakes with plenty of aquatic plants, hiding their nests in the reeds. Fish ponds are used in the east. The 8–10 eggs hatch in 25–27 days.

MIGRATION
Those from far eastern Europe move south through the Middle East into Africa in autumn. A few move west or remain in the Balkans in winter.

Very broad white panel under wing; sharp white belly patch on male; female has blurred belly; juvenile dusky belly until September.

Female
Inner wingbar narrower than male's; outer part duller.

Male
Broad white bar on blackish wing extends to wingtip.

Male

Female

Small white stern shows in flight.

White leading edge to wing.

No greyer scaling on back; no contrast between breast and flanks (these would indicate a hybrid).

Adult male
Bluish bill with tiny black nail; white eye; dark neckring hard to see.

Pale band on bill of female, behind black tip.

Female
Duller than male; darker eye; bill may have duskier area at tip.

Adult male
Deep mahogany over breast and flanks; no hint of barring; white stern edged black.

SMALL SEXUAL DIFFERENCES
This female shows the duller, browner eye that makes it less obvious than a bright, white-eyed male.

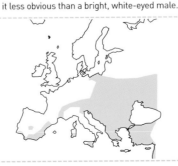

WHEN SEEN

Sept — April

Mostly September to April in W Europe; all year in Greece.

WHERE SEEN
Very local; in UK, now only rare vagrant; in winter, locally Spain, France, Italy, Balkans; more regular on reedy lakes in Greece.

HABITAT AND INFO

SIMILAR SPECIES
Female Tufted Duck has small head tuft; yellow eyes; less or no white under tail.

Dull undertail

Darker, duller body

COMMON NAME
White-headed Duck
SPECIES
Oxyura leucocephala
FAMILY
Anatidae
ORDER
Anseriformes

White-headed Duck

A stiff-tailed, dumpy bodied, large-headed diving duck with a distinctive swollen bill base. In Europe, only the Ruddy Duck resembles it, but hybrids between the two may cause identification problems – and the possible extinction of the White-headed Duck.

LENGTH / 43–48cm (17–19in)
WINGSPAN / 60–70cm (23½–27½in)
WEIGHT / 600–900g (21–32oz)

■ **STATUS /** Endangered

SCALE v Pigeon

Rare and declining for several decades, the White-headed Duck has made a welcome comeback in Spain, but its future is far from secure. Possibly genuine vagrants have turned up in England, but it is difficult to prove their origin.

FEEDING
It finds its food underwater in frequent dives: insect larvae, other aquatic invertebrates, and some seeds.

DISPLAY AND VOICE
The male raises its peculiar stiff tail as it bobs its head up and down, showing off its head pattern and swollen bill to the female. It is generally a silent species.

BREEDING
These ducks prefer shallow lakes with open water but a broad fringe of vegetation. Their nests are large structures hidden in dense reeds. Up to 10 eggs are incubated by the female for about 25 days.

MIGRATION
Most are more or less resident, with local movements to open lakes and salt pans in winter. In Turkey, large numbers concentrate outside the breeding season on a few lakes.

Male
Very broad-bodied end-on.

Male

Male
Heavy-bodied and short-winged in flight; dark except for belly and paler underwing.

Juvenile
Short bar across pale face; bill shape unlike Ruddy Duck's; dark undertail.

First-summer male
Not all have black heads.

Female (left)
Bold black and white face marks; bill grey in winter, bluer in spring; dark undertail.

Male
Pale, gingery, very finely barred; lacks broad black nape of Ruddy Duck; bill swollen.

Male, eclipse
Variable dark head mottles.

BULKY HEAD AND BILL
The white forehead and pale body help to rule out the Ruddy Duck.

WHEN SEEN

All year.

WHERE SEEN
S Spain, Turkey.

HABITAT AND INFO

SIMILAR SPECIES
Ruddy Duck has slender bill; male has more black on crown; female less contrasted on face.

More black on crown

Richer red body

Ruddy Duck

SCALE v Pigeon

LENGTH / 35–43cm (14–17in)
WINGSPAN / 53–62cm (21–24½in)
WEIGHT / 350–800g (12½–28oz)

■ STATUS / Vulnerable

Ruddy Duck is round-backed, big-headed, and stiff-tailed; it bobs like a cork. In winter, it is often in flocks. Other "escapees" are stocky and small-billed Mandarin (male is exotically multicoloured) and Wood Duck (the male is less flamboyant).

The Ruddy Duck established itself in Europe after a few escaped in Britain in the 1950s. It is harmless in most places, but in Spain it interbreeds with the endangered White-headed Duck, prompting real concern for the rarer bird. The dazzling Mandarin and the similar North American Wood Duck now breed in the wild.

FEEDING
Ruddies dive for food, eating small insects, crustaceans, and seeds.

DISPLAY AND VOICE
Male Ruddies raise their tails, draw back their heads, and rattle their bills against fluffed-out breast feathers, forcing out a flow of bubbles. They also make low, deep, grunting noises.

BREEDING
Ruddy Duck nests are platforms of stems, sometimes domed, in reeds, often beside small pools. Up to 10 eggs hatch after 25–26 days. Ducklings fly at 50–55 days old.

MIGRATION
Most Ruddies move short distances to gather on large lakes and reservoirs for the winter. Some move further to Spain and central Europe.

Ruddy Duck
Wings plain, dark; flight low, fast, almost whirring.

Mandarin (above) has dark underwing; **Wood Duck** (above right) is paler.

Female Wood Duck
Broad white spectacle; dull below; yellow eye-ring.

Male Wood Duck
Occasionally escapes from waterfowl collections

Female Mandarin
Thin white spectacle; frosted white below.

Mandarin Duck (right and left) Occurs in local feral groups.

Male Mandarin
Chestnut and green crest; bright orange sails.

Female Ruddy Duck
Darker face crossed by dark bar; bill dark; tail often flat on water.

Male Ruddy Duck, spring
Bold white face; black cap and neck; body rich rufous.

Male Ruddy Duck, winter
Cold white face; dark brown body.

ALMOST UNMISTAKABLE
Males are flamboyant, active little ducks with great character.

WHEN SEEN

All year.

WHERE SEEN
S Britain, rare Ireland; locally in small numbers in NW Europe and south to Spain.

HABITAT AND INFO

SIMILAR SPECIES
Female Smew has bright white lower face; white on wings; greyer body.

Slimmer bill

Greyer body

ORDER
Anseriformes

FAMILY
Anatidae

SPECIES
Aythya marila

COMMON NAME
Scaup

Scaup

A large, thickset but elegant diving duck, seen in flocks on the sea, small numbers on freshwater. It combines features of Pochard and Tufted Duck.

LENGTH / 42–51cm (16½–20in)
WINGSPAN / 67–73cm (26½–28½in)
WEIGHT / 0.8–1.3kg (1¾–2¾lb)

■ STATUS / Vulnerable

SCALE v Pigeon

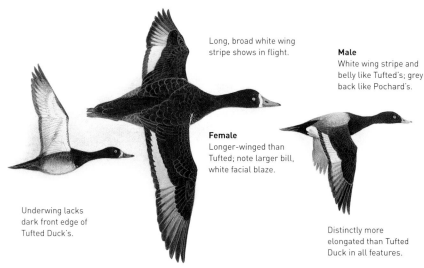

Long, broad white wing stripe shows in flight.

Male
White wing stripe and belly like Tufted's; grey back like Pochard's.

Female
Longer-winged than Tufted; note larger bill, white facial blaze.

Underwing lacks dark front edge of Tufted Duck's.

Distinctly more elongated than Tufted Duck in all features.

Scaup may turn up in many different situations: in lively, buoyant flocks on choppy seas, on large rafts drifting sleepily on smooth, sheltered estuaries, or as isolated individuals among dense flocks of Tufted Ducks and Pochards on inland lakes. However, most spend winter on traditional coastal feeding sites.

FEEDING
Scaup dive for molluscs and invertebrates, but also eat waste grain and other food discharged into the sea.

DISPLAY AND VOICE
Males can be seen courting females in winter, gathering in groups around them and calling with deep whistles. The usual call is a low, short growling note.

BREEDING
In northern Europe, Scaup breed near the coast and beside remote upland lakes with sparse vegetation. They lay 8–11 eggs in a ground nest.

MIGRATION
Breeding birds from Iceland, northern Scandinavia, and Siberia move south-west, with large numbers in the Baltic region and parts of northern and eastern Britain.

Female, breeding
Broader beam than Tufted's, noticeable in mixed group; long-necked in alarm.

Juvenile
(right)
Dull, small facial spot; pale ear crescent; dusky bill tip.

Female, breeding
Broad blaze; pale ear crescent.

Female, non-breeding
Grey bars wear off; round, dark head with white face; broader, paler than Tufted's.

Male, non-breeding
Large body; large high-crowned head sweeps into long, heavy bill; sides pure white, black at both ends.

CLOSE SCRUTINY REQUIRED
A good view is needed to be sure of the distinctive bill tip pattern.

WHEN SEEN

Sept — April

In W Europe, mostly September–April; in north, only in summer.

WHERE SEEN
Breeds Iceland, N and central highland Scandinavia; in winter, Britain and Ireland, Baltic and North Sea coasts; scarce south to Mediterranean.

HABITAT AND INFO

SIMILAR SPECIES
Male Tufted Duck has black back; head tuft; narrower bill with bigger black tip.

Tuft on nape

Black back

Tufted Duck

LENGTH / 40–47cm (15½–18½in)
WINGSPAN / 67–73cm (26½–28½in)
WEIGHT / 450–1,000g (16–35oz)

■ **STATUS /** Secure

SCALE v Pigeon

Stocky, round-headed and buoyant, a common freshwater duck, often in flocks with Pochards and Coots; it dives frequently.

This is one of the most familiar ducks in Europe, for while entirely wild and highly migratory, many Tufteds have taken advantage of park lakes and other areas of water in and around cities. They may even come to be fed bread with the local Mallards and Coots. Yet they are equally likely to be seen on sheltered estuaries and coastal bays, or on remote pools and marshes. Tufteds are frequently found with Pochards and these mixed flocks may attract a variety of rarer birds inland, such as Scaup, vagrant Ring-necked Ducks, and Ferruginous Ducks. There are natural variations in appearance according to age, sex, and season in all these species, but the possibility of escapees from waterfowl collections and even hybrids with intermediate features make these mixed flocks quite fascinating to determined wildfowl-watchers.

FEEDING
Tufteds dive, bouncing back to the surface like corks. They are much more active by day than Pochards and eat different food, so the mixed flocks do not compete too much. Tufteds eat more animals, taking a variety of molluscs, crustaceans, and insects as well as some plant matter.

DISPLAY AND VOICE
Males swim quite quietly around females, bobbing their heads and calling with pleasant, low whistling sounds. The most usual call at other times is the female's deep growl, most often heard from a bird as it takes flight.

BREEDING
Tufteds use a variety of sites, usually in lowland areas, from broad rivers and town lakes to reservoirs and flooded gravel pits. Nests are lined with vegetation and down from the duck's own breast. The female incubates 8–11 eggs for about 25 days. The young are typically lively, engaging, inquisitive ducklings that begin to fly at about seven weeks old.

MIGRATION
Their movements are complicated, but most Tufted Ducks winter in big flocks on larger waters, or move to sheltered coasts such as the IJsselmeer where they gather in huge numbers. In Iceland, northern Europe, and eastward from Germany and Scandinavia, they are summer visitors, flying south and west to escape the hard winters. These birds move into central Europe and as far as Spain, Italy, and Greece, and many supplement the mostly resident breeding population of Britain and Ireland.

Female
Greyer variant.

Female, winter
All dark, but some have small dull or bright white patch under tail; pale mark by bill.

Female, breeding
Very dark overall; slight crest; often pale face but dark cheeks.

Male, winter
Pure white side panel is striking.

Female, winter
Tufted Ducks stand elegantly, clear of the ground, but do not walk much.

Male, summer
Brownish above, flanks smudged warm brown; immature male is the same.

Male
Note broad, black bill tip.

WHEN SEEN

All year; April to October in NE Europe, September to April in SW and S Europe.

WHERE SEEN
Breeds Iceland, Britain, and Ireland, locally France and Sweden eastward; in winter, also farther south-west and south to Mediterranean.

HABITAT AND INFO

SIMILAR SPECIES
Female Scaup has bigger, rounder head; broad bill with tiny black tip; often pale ear patch.

Broader body

Broader bill

PATTERING TAKEOFF
Diving ducks rise less easily from the water than surface-feeders, needing a short run.

Female Tufted
May show white blaze, less extensive than Scaup's (below); note head shape and slimmer, upcurved bill with more black at tip.

Scaup

Scaup female
(near right)
Broader crown; wider bill with small black tip; often pale ear patch.

Tufted female
Narrower bill with more black.

Flight fast; wings rather straight; rapid beats.

Female
Dark brown; belly may be darker.

Female
Long white wing stripe, like flattened M.

Male, winter
Striking black-and-white, drooped crest; bright yellow eye.

DID YOU KNOW?
Many wildfowl are found around the Northern Hemisphere, common both in Europe and North America, such as the Scaup, Pintail, and Shoveler. Tufted Ducks, however, are replaced by a similar but distinctive species in North America: the Ring-necked Duck, which is sometimes identified in western Europe. Its grey flanks with a peak of white beside the chest are characteristic of the bird.

Red-breasted Merganser

LENGTH / 51–62cm (20–24½in)
WINGSPAN / 70–85cm (27½–33½in)
WEIGHT / 0.85–1.3kg (1¾–2¾lb)

■ STATUS / Secure

SCALE v Pigeon

A large sawbilled duck that is long, elegant, slim-necked, and sharp-billed. Males boldly pied, females rather blurred and dingy. Both swim low in the water, diving often.

The fine lines typical of sawbills combine with the Red-breasted Merganser's rich colour and pattern to create a supremely elegant bird. Unlike many diving ducks, it is also lively and active: a fascinating bird to watch.

FEEDING
Like all sawbills, it is a fish-eater, diving energetically and staying submerged for long periods as it drives itself along underwater with its feet.

DISPLAY AND VOICE
Displays involve dramatic posturing by the males: their tails down, backs arched, heads thrown back, and bills jerked upward and open. They use a low, purring call during courtship. Females make a low, harsh *krr* call as they fly.

BREEDING
The nests are on the ground in tall grass or among rocks or roots, close to the shore. Up to 11 eggs are incubated by the female for 31–32 days. The chicks fly after nine weeks.

MIGRATION
Breeding birds from northern Europe move south in winter to North Sea and Atlantic coasts.

In flight, looks long, with humped back, slightly drooped head, wings set well back, more angled than Goosander's.

Male

Female

Underwing tip darker than Goosander's; dark chest.

Female
Slimmer wings than similar Goosander's; drabber, browner.

Long, broad, grey rear body.

Male
Pied with black lines across inner wing; white collar.

Female (below)
Grey-brown; head pale gingery; chin and throat pale, blurred; crest spiky.

Male

Goosander
Sharp chin patch.

Bill slimmer than Goosander's; slight upturn, sometimes with smiling effect.

FREQUENTLY FOUND ASHORE
On dry ground, the Merganser has a long, slim appearance.

WHEN SEEN

Summer in N Europe; all year in Britain; winter in S and SW Europe.

WHERE SEEN
Breeds Scandinavia, Iceland, N Britain, and Ireland; winters south to Mediterranean, locally central Europe.

HABITAT AND INFO

SIMILAR SPECIES
Female Goosander has paler, greyer body; sharply defined dark head, and white chin patch.

Sharper neck pattern

Purer grey back

ORDER
Anseriformes

FAMILY
Anatidae

SPECIES
Mergus merganser

COMMON NAME
Goosander

Goosander

Large, elongated, heavy sawbilled duck with a big head. The males are very striking; females are clean-cut grey, white, and red-brown.

LENGTH / 58–66cm (23–26in)
WINGSPAN / 82–98cm (32–39in)
WEIGHT / 1–1.6kg (2¼–3½lb)

■ STATUS / Secure

SCALE v Pigeon

Female
Crisp grey; square white wing patch.

Long grey rear body.

Male
Long white neck; unmarked white inner wing.

Long neck; sharp white throat and chin patch.

Straight-winged in flight; adult and juvenile female alike under wing; young male like adult male.

Spindle-shaped body.

Male

A big, fish-eating, sawbilled duck, the Goosander is one of the most impressive of Europe's wildfowl. It can be seen on the sea, but is more of a freshwater bird than the Red-breasted Merganser, both when breeding and in winter. Both are persecuted because of their fish-eating habits, although there is no proof that they affect the numbers of fish in the rivers they occupy.

FEEDING
They dive underwater from the surface to catch a variety of fish, including small trout and salmon parr.

DISPLAY AND VOICE
Males posture in much the same way as Red-breasted Mergansers, with quiet croaks. Otherwise this is a very quiet species.

BREEDING
Goosanders nest in holes in riverside trees, and less often in banks or among tree roots. Up to 11 eggs hatch after 30–34 days. The chicks soon drop from the nest hole and make their way to water. They fly after 10 weeks.

MIGRATION
Northern breeding birds migrate to central and western Europe to spend the winter.

Male, breeding
Rich salmon-pink fades in late winter.

Female
Dark shaggy crest; white chin; dark foreneck.

Hooked, deep plum-red bill.

CLOSE FAMILY TIES
A lively family of ducklings maintains close contact with the adult female.

WHEN SEEN

Summer in N Europe; September to April in C Europe and S Britain; all year in N and W Britain.

WHERE SEEN
Breeds Scandinavia, Iceland, Britain; winters south to France.

HABITAT AND INFO

SIMILAR SPECIES
Female Red-breasted Merganser is duller, browner, with ginger head and neck blending into pale throat.

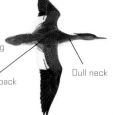

Browner back

Dull neck

Smew

SCALE v Pigeon

LENGTH / 38–44cm (15–17½in)
WINGSPAN / 55–69cm (21½–27in)
WEIGHT / 500–800g (18–28oz)

■ STATUS / Vulnerable

A beautiful duck, small-headed except when crest erected in display. It is lively, often flying, but dives out of sight for long periods. Usually adult males are in minority.

The smallest of the sawbills, the stockily built Smew is one of the liveliest ducks, especially where it is common and found in flocks of scores or hundreds together. These are scenes of constant activity, with Smews always diving, chasing, or flying swiftly back and forth in small parties. Even when wintering in ones and twos with large numbers of commoner ducks, Smews often move about restlessly and are sometimes very elusive.

FEEDING
Smews dive for fish but take a variety of other aquatic creatures such as insect larvae and crustaceans.

DISPLAY AND VOICE
Males often display in winter, sometimes alongside displaying Goldeneyes, drawing back their heads and bobbing up and down. They are generally silent birds.

BREEDING
Nests are in tree holes near lakes in forested northern regions.

MIGRATION
In autumn, Smews move south-west to the Baltic and North Sea regions, especially the Low Countries.

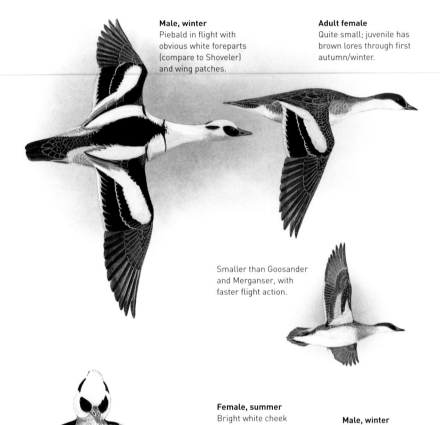

Male, winter
Piebald in flight with obvious white foreparts (compare to Shoveler) and wing patches.

Adult female
Quite small; juvenile has brown lores through first autumn/winter.

Smaller than Goosander and Merganser, with faster flight action.

Female, summer
Bright white cheek patch; face becomes blacker in winter.

Male, winter
Stunning; often yellowish-white with striking black patterns and grey flanks (appears white mostly at front).

NON-STOP ENERGY
Smews are very active, lively ducks, especially when in large flocks.

WHEN SEEN

Nov
April

In W Europe, mostly November to April.

WHERE SEEN
Breeds N Scandinavia and east into Russia; in winter, sparsely in Britain, France, central Europe; most common in IJsselmeer and S Baltic area.

HABITAT AND INFO

SIMILAR SPECIES
Male Goldeneye has black head with white face spot; more black on back; spotless white sides.

White face spot

Spotless white sides

Goldeneye

A round-backed, round-headed duck with a stubby bill, typically with dark grey females and immatures far outnumbering adult males.

LENGTH / 42–50cm (16½–20in)
WINGSPAN / 65–80cm (26–32in)
WEIGHT / 600–1,200g (21–42oz)

■ **STATUS /** Secure

SCALE v Pigeon

Although not a sawbill, the Goldeneye is similar in many ways to the scarcer Smew. Indeed, the two occasionally hybridize. Goldeneyes tend to keep apart from other ducks such as Tufted Ducks in winter, forming separate feeding and roosting groups. It may seem that only a few are present, as they dive so constantly, but if disturbed they gather together and may fly off in surprising numbers. They are usually nervous and quite difficult to approach.

FEEDING
They gather molluscs, crustaceans, and insect larvae from the bottom in lengthy dives.

DISPLAY AND VOICE
Males display to females in late winter, raising their heads and suddenly arching them back over their rumps. The courtship call is a nasal, slightly grating or creaking *ay-eeek*. Females make quick croaks.

BREEDING
Nests are in holes in trees or nest boxes. Up to 11 ducklings take to the water as soon as they hatch.

MIGRATION
Breeding populations move south and west in winter.

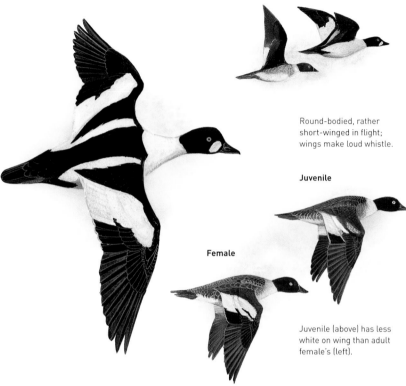

Round-bodied, rather short-winged in flight; wings make loud whistle.

Juvenile

Female

Juvenile (above) has less white on wing than adult female's (left).

Note high crown, steep forehead, low, round nape, and triangular bill.

Female

Female
White collar on adult female; white wing patch often hidden on water; immature looks dark and dull.

Male
Green-glossed head and large white spot; juvenile males develop white patch in winter.

Long tail, cocked at rest but inconspicuous when feeding.

INFLEXIBLE BEHAVIOUR
Ducks mate on water after long, ritualized courtship displays.

WHEN SEEN

Oct — April

In south, mostly October to April; summer visitor in N and E Europe.

WHERE SEEN
Breeds Scandinavia, Scotland; winters Britain, North Sea and Baltic coasts, locally in central Europe.

HABITAT AND INFO

SIMILAR SPECIES
Female Tufted Duck is browner overall; dark neck; longer, less triangular bill.

Longer bill

More uniform brown body

Common Scoter

LENGTH / 45–54cm (17½–21in)
WINGSPAN / 79–90cm (31–35½in)
WEIGHT / 1.2–1.4kg (2½–3lb)

■ **STATUS /** Secure

SCALE v Pigeon

A heavy-bodied but elegant sea duck, with a large head, very slim neck, and pointed tail. Often seen in long flocks well offshore.

A true sea duck, the highly sociable Common Scoter lives in dense flocks in sandy bays and firths, often associating with Eiders, smaller numbers of Velvet Scoters, and Long-tailed Ducks. Often they are far offshore and not easy to see well.

FEEDING
Common Scoters dive deep for their food, taking a variety of shellfish, worms, and other aquatic life.

DISPLAY AND VOICE
Displays are quite subdued, but the males' soft whistling or piping calls can be heard on calm days. Females have a deeper growl.

BREEDING
They nest on the ground, on islands, or on the shores of moorland lakes. The 6–8 eggs hatch after 30–31 days' incubation by the female.

MIGRATION
Movements are complex: breeding birds move south in winter, and large moulting flocks appear in traditional areas offshore in July and August. In spring and late summer, small parties often appear briefly on inland lakes and reservoirs.

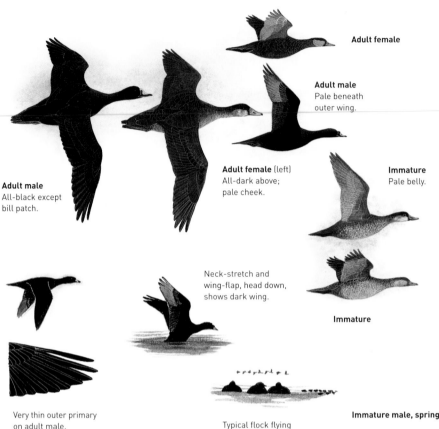

Adult female

Adult male
Pale beneath outer wing.

Adult male
All-black except bill patch.

Adult female (left)
All-dark above; pale cheek.

Immature
Pale belly.

Neck-stretch and wing-flap, head down, shows dark wing.

Immature

Very thin outer primary on adult male.

Typical flock flying low over sea.

Immature male, spring

Thin tail often cocked.

Adult female (above)
Pale greyish face; double patch at first (top).

Adult male

Adult male
All-black except for yellow bill patch; sometimes thin line extends over basal knob.

SEA-GOING DUCKS
The pale flight feathers make a surprisingly useful identification feature in flight.

WHEN SEEN

All year; in south, mostly July to April.

WHERE SEEN
Breeds in Iceland, N Scandinavia, rarely N Scotland and Ireland; winter south to Portugal; scarce E Spain; numerous Baltic and North Sea.

HABITAT AND INFO

SIMILAR SPECIES
Male Velvet Scoter has bigger, flatter head shape; white near eye; white wing patch.

Flatter forehead

White wing patch

ORDER
Anseriformes

FAMILY
Anatidae

SPECIES
Melanitta fusca

COMMON NAME
Velvet Scoter

Velvet Scoter

A big, eider-like sea duck, usually seen with more numerous Common Scoters, and most readily identified by white wing patches.

LENGTH / 51–58cm (20–23in)
WINGSPAN / 90–99cm (35–39in)
WEIGHT / 1.1–2kg (2½–4½lb)

■ **STATUS /** Vulnerable

SCALE v Pigeon

Always scarcer than Common Scoters, Velvet Scoters are best found by visually searching through flocks of more numerous species. At long range they are hard to spot, but if they fly the problem is resolved. It is worth getting a close view, for they are big, handsome, and impressive ducks.

FEEDING
Like other scoters and eiders, Velvet Scoters dive for their food: mostly mussels, shrimps, crabs, and other small marine creatures, which they crush with their stout bills.

VOICE
Males make a whistling call and females a gruff croak or growl, but these are rarely heard in winter.

BREEDING
Nests are often far from water, near northern lakes and coasts. Up to nine eggs hatch within 28 days.

MIGRATION
The breeding season is late, but males move in summer to moulting areas while the females incubate their eggs and rear their young. These then move south from September, returning in April and May.

Adult male

Adult male

All have broad white hindwing patch; most have red legs.

Adult female

Adult female

Immature male
White belly; black legs.

Wing-flap, head up, reveals white: a clinching feature at long range.

Juvenile
Dark face at first; dark wedge bill.

Adult female
Two pale spots on face below blacker cap become brighter white with wear.

Adult male
White under eye; yellow bill panel.

CLOSE-UP FEATURES
The white eye-patch is a close-range feature; the wing patch is often hidden.

WHEN SEEN

All year; in north, April to October; in North Sea, July onward, mostly November to March.

WHERE SEEN
Breeds Norway, Baltic coasts; winters in S Baltic, North Sea including E Scotland and NE England; some south to Spain, a few to S France.

HABITAT AND INFO

SIMILAR SPECIES
Female Common Scoter has paler lower face; dark legs; all-dark wings.

Large pale cheek

All-dark wing

Surf Scoter

SCALE v Pigeon

LENGTH / 45–56cm (17½–22in)
WINGSPAN / 85–95cm (33½–37in)
WEIGHT / 650–1,100g (23–39oz)

■ STATUS / Rare

ORDER Anseriformes
FAMILY Anatidae
SPECIES Melanitta perspicillata
COMMON NAME Surf Scoter

A large, eider-like scoter with a wedge-shaped bill, like the Velvet Scoter, but with all-dark wings. Adult drakes have obvious head and bill patterns.

Although little more than a rare vagrant from North America, the Surf Scoter is nevertheless discovered in mixed scoter flocks somewhere in the North Sea each year. The males are relatively easy to identify, as their white nape patches stand out well even when they are very far offshore, but the females require a closer view that is rarely forthcoming.

FEEDING
Like the other scoters with which it associates, the Surf Scoter dives to find molluscs, crabs, starfish, and similar prey, mostly in sandy bays or over offshore mussel scarps. As its name implies, it is quite at home in the rough and tumble of a sandy bay with enormous breakers rolling onshore.

MIGRATION
A few individuals appear to be regularly associating with Common Scoters, and move around with them in northern Europe. One or two "new" birds probably reach western European coasts each autumn. Very rarely one appears inland.

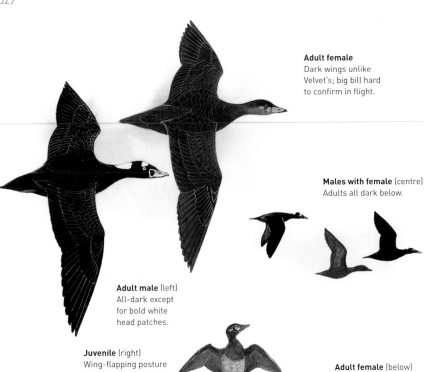

Adult female
Dark wings unlike Velvet's; big bill hard to confirm in flight.

Males with female (centre)
Adults all dark below.

Adult male (left)
All-dark except for bold white head patches.

Juvenile (right)
Wing-flapping posture reveals young bird's pale belly.

Adult female (below)
Two face spots; compare to Velvet.

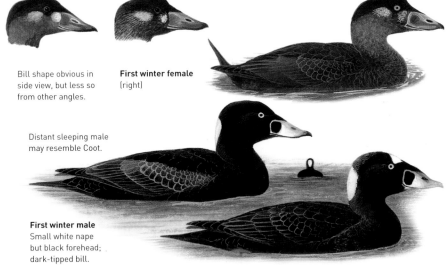

Bill shape obvious in side view, but less so from other angles.

First winter female (right)

Distant sleeping male may resemble Coot.

First winter male
Small white nape but black forehead; dark-tipped bill.

Adult male
Glossy black with bold white forehead and nape patches; bright bill; red legs.

BOLDLY MARKED RARITY
All scoters are powerful, heavy-bodied birds in flight, with deep wing beats.

WHEN SEEN

Oct — March

October to March.

WHERE SEEN
Very rare except in a few places in NE Britain, where one or two are seen each year.

HABITAT AND INFO

SIMILAR SPECIES
Female Velvet Scoter has white wing patch; slimmer bill and less bulky head.

Slimmer bill

White wing patch

Steller's Eider
King Eider

Steller's is small and unlike other eiders. King is a distinctive and obvious eider, but females are easily overlooked.

STELLER'S EIDER
LENGTH / 42–48cm (16½–19in)
WINGSPAN / 68–77cm (27–30in)
WEIGHT / 500–900g (18–32oz)

■ STATUS / Rare

KING EIDER
55–63cm (22–25in)
87–100cm (34–39in)
1.6–2kg (3½–4½lb)

■ Secure

SCALE v Pigeon

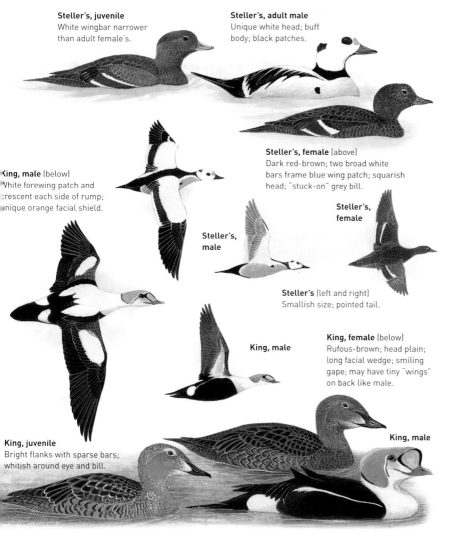

Steller's, juvenile
White wingbar narrower than adult female's.

Steller's, adult male
Unique white head; buff body; black patches.

King, male (below)
White forewing patch and crescent each side of rump; unique orange facial shield.

Steller's, female (above)
Dark red-brown; two broad white bars frame blue wing patch; squarish head; "stuck-on" grey bill.

Steller's, female

Steller's, male

Steller's (left and right)
Smallish size; pointed tail.

King, female (below)
Rufous-brown; head plain; long facial wedge; smiling gape; may have tiny "wings" on back like male.

King, male

King, juvenile
Bright flanks with sparse bars; whitish around eye and bill.

King, male

Steller's Eider is an extremely rare vagrant in Europe away from the extreme north of Scandinavia; it breeds farther east in Siberia. The King Eider breeds in Siberia and Greenland, and appears rarely but more regularly in north-west Europe, typically with large flocks of Eiders. In both species, the adult male is distinctive, but other plumages are much more difficult to pick out, especially out at sea.

FEEDING
Both are diving ducks that feed on shellfish and other marine creatures in sheltered, shallow seas.

MIGRATION
Steller's Eiders are regular visitors to the extreme north of Europe and move into the Baltic at times. King Eiders may sometimes be seen with Eiders in summer, but they are chiefly winter visitors. Some individuals return to the same places regularly for several years.

FLAMBOYANT EIDER
The male King Eider has uniquely striking head and bill features.

WHEN SEEN

Oct / April

Steller's all year; King mostly October to April or May.

WHERE SEEN
Steller's mostly extreme N Norway, rare in Baltic; King mostly NW Scandinavia, Iceland, Scotland, on sandy coasts and estuaries.

HABITAT AND INFO

SIMILAR SPECIES
Female Eider has bigger head with long wedge of feathers near bill; less obvious double wingbars; lacks smiling gape line.

Longer facial wedge

Smooth back

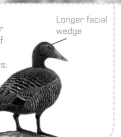

Eider

LENGTH / 50–71cm (19½–28in)
WINGSPAN / 80–108cm (31½–43in)
WEIGHT / 1.2–2.8kg (2½–6lb)

■ STATUS / Secure

SCALE v Pigeon

A large, powerful, fast-flying diving duck of coastal waters. Females are dark and closely barred all over. Males are strikingly contrasted, beautifully clean and neat. Their wedge-shaped face is distinctive.

Like the scoters, Eiders are often found in flocks well offshore, yet they are much more likely to be seen pottering about in harbours, at the mouths of estuaries, or around the myriad rocky islets, headlands, and weedy bays that characterize many north European coastlines. They are sociable, unhurried, unflappable. Their plumage variations are complicated and there are several racial varieties, so they are always interesting to look at, but it is the colours and calls of the drakes and confiding behaviour of the ducks that make them such enjoyable birds to watch.

FEEDING
Eiders find their food underwater, diving from the surface with a forward roll and half-opened wings. They eat mussels and other molluscs, crabs (which they bring to the surface to dismember), starfish, and other invertebrates. Sometimes they up-end in shallow water, or simply dip their heads into the shallows or among drifts of seaweed between the rocks.

DISPLAY AND VOICE
Males have a typical head-throwing display, pulling their heads well back with their bills pointing upward. During this display whole groups of males make highly distinctive loud, deep, crooning calls sounding like *ah-aaooh!* Females have a low, guttural *kok-ok-ok*.

BREEDING
Individual pairs or small, loose groups nest close to the shore in rocky places, or on rocky islands. The nests are in hollows, under driftwood or sometimes exposed, lined with the prized down from the female's body. Just 4–6 eggs are incubated by the female for 25–28 days. The ducklings do not fly until about 10 weeks old. Incubating females sit tight when approached. They rely on their excellent camouflage, but often do not move even when it is obvious that they have been discovered. The ducklings gather together in large groups, or crèches, to seek safety in numbers from predators, but they are still vulnerable, especially to large gulls.

MIGRATION
Northern breeders move south along Scandinavian coasts, including the Baltic, reaching northern France. In Britain, breeding birds gather in large flocks, making local movements, but relatively few continental birds arrive in winter. Non-breeding groups are regularly seen in isolated but traditional spots around the coasts of southern Britain.

Male, breeding

Female
Looks dark when worn.

Juvenile
Dark with diffuse bars; pale over eye.

Female

Male, eclipse
Young or moulting males have complex plumage variations.

Male
Breast yellowish or white when worn, strong pink when fresh.

Often swims low, head sunk in but short tail cocked; dives with slightly open wings; sometimes in very large, elongated flocks; may stand out on rocks or sandbars.

Male, first summer

Female
Plumage quite pale and bright when fresh; sharp bars.

Male (right)
Green nape patches; unique bill structure; white rear flank patch.

WHEN SEEN

All year; in N Baltic, in summer; in S Baltic and southern North Sea, September to May.

WHERE SEEN
Breeds Iceland, all coasts of Scandinavia, Scotland, and NE England; non-breeders S Britain; winter south to Biscay coasts.

HABITAT AND INFO

SIMILAR SPECIES
Female Common Scoter is more uniform except pale face; dark in flight with paler underwing.

Whitish face

Plain dark body

PIED SEA DUCK
The white upperside and black underside
create a distinctive effect on a male Eider.

Female
Dark bars over
upperparts; typically
(but not always) finely
barred white on wing.

Male
Eye-catching in flight
with complicated
chequered patterns.

Flight direct, strong; low
over water; head held
low; often forms lines.

Female
Small pale areas
under the wings, but
may look all dark.

Common Scoter has
shorter, rounder head;
thinner neck; paler
flight feathers.

FLIGHT PATTERN

Strong, regular wing
beats give fast
progression low
over the sea, despite
heavy build.

DID YOU KNOW?

Ducks have thick, waterproof body plumage, with a thick layer of down
feathers to add insulation. This down – fine, loose feathering with little
structure – is used to line the nest, most famously by the Eider. Eiders
are farmed in Iceland for the down, gathered harmlessly from their
colonies, and down was farmed in England at least as far
back as the 14th century.

Long-tailed Duck

LENGTH / Male 58–60cm (23–23½in); female 37–41cm (14½–16in)
WINGSPAN / 73–79cm (28½–31in)
WEIGHT / 520–950g (18–34oz)

SCALE v Pigeon

■ **STATUS /** Secure

A chunky, short-billed, buoyant sea duck; dark-winged, blunt-tailed except in adult male, with a confusing variety of patterns. Typically has round head with pale eye-patch, dark cheeks. It dives constantly. Social, often with scoters, but stray individuals turn up inland and in estuaries.

This is one of several sea ducks that live in flocks, often far offshore and frequently associated with scoters and Eiders. The flocks are very active, often flying fast over the sea, and can resemble auks as they whirr along, flashing black and white and rolling between the wavetops. In a few areas they move close inshore, especially at the mouths of estuaries, where they are brought in by the tides, but on more exposed coasts they tend to be harder to see at close range. This is a pity, because they are among the most attractive of the sea ducks, full of vigour and lively interaction. All sea ducks have their charms, but the stub-billed, round-headed profile and wispy central tail feathers of the drakes add extra character and individuality to the Long-tailed Duck.

FEEDING

They feed mainly on small molluscs and crustaceans such as crabs, taken from the sea floor in deep dives. In summer they also eat insects and their larvae, and these form the main diet of the ducklings.

DISPLAY AND VOICE

Drakes bob their heads and raise their long tails to impress the ducks. They create a loud, attractive chorus of soft, cooing *ow-owdl-ow* or *owdl-ee* calls. In courtship chases, sometimes far out at sea, several drakes pursue single females in fast flights with abrupt, splashing descents to the water before flying up again in a constant whirl of activity.

BREEDING

Small numbers breed in Scandinavia, with many more in Iceland and Arctic Russia. They nest near small pools on the tundra, or in mountain areas farther south. In Iceland they nest around lakes with an abundance of insect life in summer. Often several pairs cluster on small islands out of reach of foxes and other predatory mammals. The nest is a hollow, lined with down, sometimes well-hidden but often quite exposed. The 5–7 eggs are incubated by only the female and take 24–29 days to hatch. The ducklings soon move to the nearest water, where several broods may group together. They fly at about 40 days old, by which time the female may have moved away to moult.

MIGRATION

After breeding, Long-tailed Ducks move out to sea and then south, often through the Baltic. Many pass north through the Baltic and the Gulf of Finland in late May, often arriving on the tundra well before the lakes are free from ice.

Male's tail is longer and more flexible than Pintail's.

Male, summer

Male, summer (left) Some have white faces; billband may be grey, usually pink.

Male, winter At distance a confusing jumble of white and dark brown; white areas striking in good light; grey face patch fades browner.

Males look spectacled from front.

Male, summer   **Male, winter**

Male, spring Pink on bill.

Dives with open wings, like bigger Eider and smaller Little Auk.

Juvenile, first winter Dark cheeks; pale collar; eye-ring.

Female, breeding Head pattern varies with wear (near left).

Steep forehead; round nape; thick, triangular bill always distinctive.

White sides or rear flank patch obvious.

Female, winter

WHEN SEEN

Oct — May

In W Europe, mostly October to May.

WHERE SEEN

Breeds Iceland, N and central Scandinavia; winter Britain and Ireland, S Baltic, S North Sea coasts.

HABITAT AND INFO

SIMILAR SPECIES

Male Eider is bigger; pale breast; dark belly; longer wedge-shaped bill.

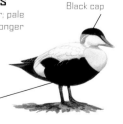

Black cap

Black belly

Male, winter

Male, summer

Pot-bellied, squat
appearance, but
flight fast, low,
rocking sideways.

Female

Female,
winter

Dark tail and white
sides to rump
recall Guillemot.

All-dark wing;
white flank/vent,
unlike scoter's.

Female, winter
Unique head pattern.

Male, winter
White on head and
foreparts shows at
great range.

DID YOU KNOW?

In North America, this lively, sociable bird is known as the Old Squaw.
Populations around the Northern Hemisphere are all of the same race
and look alike, unlike the situation with scoters. Velvet and Common
Scoters in Europe have nearly identical counterparts in North America
– until recently treated as races, these are now thought to
be separate species, albeit difficult to separate in the wild.

Pheasant

ORDER Galliformes   **FAMILY** Phasianidae   **SPECIES** *Phasianus colchicus*   **COMMON NAME** Pheasant

LENGTH / Male 75–90cm (30–35½in); female 52–64cm (20½–25in)
WINGSPAN / 70–90cm (27½–35½in)
WEIGHT / 0.9–1.4kg (2–3lb)

SCALE v Pigeon

■ **STATUS /** Secure

This is a striking, long-tailed, heavy-bodied game bird. It is often tame where released for shooting, but more wary and wild where it has become naturalized.

Two thousand years ago Pheasants from Asia were introduced to Greece. They were widely introduced to most of north-west Europe only 200 years ago, but in Britain they have been present since about the 11th century. Bred and released in huge numbers for shooting, they have become widespread and familiar. Many released birds are ridiculously tame, and some enter parks and large gardens where they may survive as ornamental birds. A few, however, live much wilder lives in woodland, on the bushy edges of heathland, and, in winter, in and around freshwater marshes with reed beds, assorted scrub, and mixed woodland. Because of the history of introductions from various parts of Asia, coupled with the effects of breeding and releasing a wide variety of forms, wild Pheasants can be seen in a number of colour variations – but they all have the same basic shape that makes them easy to identify.

FEEDING
A Pheasant uses its strong legs and feet to scratch and scrape for earthworms, grubs, and berries in soft earth and thick leaf litter. Its muscular neck gives it a powerful, chicken-like lunge and pecking action. Coupled with its stout, slightly hooked beak, this makes the Pheasant a capable predator, able to kill and eat small creatures from beetles to lizards, and sometimes even small snakes. Much of its food, however, consists of grain, seeds, and berries.

DISPLAY AND VOICE
A male trying to impress a female uses his colourful plumage and long tail to best effect. He corners the hen, striding around and in front of her, demanding attention as he leans toward her, twisting his tail over and drooping one wing. His territorial call is a loud crow, *korrk-kok*, followed by a burst of rapid wing beats. Alarm calls are repeated *kok-kok* notes, often becoming a series of calls with a squeaky, hiccuping quality, *kok-kok-i-kok, i-kok, i-kok*. Females are quieter but make a variety of purring and *kia kia* sounds.

BREEDING
Females nesting wild rear one brood each year with no help from the male. The nest is on the ground among dead leaves, dense brambles, or other thick plants, with little or no lining. Up to 15 plain olive eggs hatch after 23–28 days. The chicks can fly when still small, just 12 days old, but are not fully grown or properly independent for up to 12 weeks.

MIGRATION
Pheasants are sedentary.

Male
Variant with no white neckring.

Male
Males variable: most have white neckring; variants look blacker, creamy-bodied, or even brown-headed.

Male
Scarce variety, almost completely glossy green-black.

Juvenile
Smaller, shorter-tailed than female at first, can fly well before fully grown.

Female
Longer-legged, longer-tailed, more triangular and chicken-like than partridges or grouse.

Male
Typical plumage: richly varied with coppery flanks, redder back, and dark brown, creamy or green rump.

Roosts in trees, but otherwise a ground bird.

WHEN SEEN

All year.

WHERE SEEN
N and central Europe except N Scandinavia.

HABITAT AND INFO

SIMILAR SPECIES
Grey Partridge has squarer tail with rufous sides; narrower wings.

Squarish tail

Narrower wings

70

FLAUNTING IT
Male Pheasants are extravagantly coloured and shaped – and act as if they know it.

Female   Male   Male

FLIGHT PATTERN
Flies low and straight with bursts of fast wing beats between flat glides. When disturbed at close range bursts up with startling call and clatter of wings.

DID YOU KNOW?
It is said that the weight of Pheasants in the British countryside in autumn is equal to that of all other birds put together. About 20 million are released for shooting; 12 million are shot, the rest succumb to disease, starvation, predation, and accident, especially on roads. It is a pity that few are properly appreciated for their spectacular appearance.

?

Capercaillie

LENGTH / 60–86cm (24–33³⁄₄in)
WINGSPAN / 87–125cm (34–49in)
WEIGHT / 1.5–4.4kg (3¹⁄₄–9³⁄₄lb)

SCALE v Pigeon

■ **STATUS /** Vulnerable

A giant woodland grouse, it is rare and elusive, usually seen only at long range flying away from an open area, or at close range flushed from a tree top or dense heather, clattering away in a flurry of powerful wing beats.

An encounter with a belligerent, rogue male Capercaillie in spring is a memorable experience. It might end in tears, with a hefty, vicious peck from that big, hooked bill. A few highly charged individuals famously attack anything, and they are not to be taken lightly. In the main, however, Capercaillies are shy and secretive: so elusive, in fact, that to see one at all is an achievement. Usually the best that can be expected is a distant view of one in flight, retreating from a forest clearing into the depths of the woods, or a brief, close view as one clatters up from the deep heather to disappear almost instantly behind a big pine. In most parts of their fragmented range, such as the Pyrenees, Capercaillies are so scarce that it is extremely difficult to find one. In northern Scotland, they have declined and are restricted to a few extensive tracts of ancient Caledonian pine – some of the most wonderful and attractive forests in the world. They are threatened by the effects of overgrazing by sheep and deer (which reduces the shrub and herb layer and prevents the forest from regenerating), and deer fencing: Capercaillies often fly into these high fences, with fatal results. Predators and cold, wet spring weather also take their toll on one of Europe's most fascinating, unusual birds.

FEEDING
Capercaillies eat mainly shoots, seeds, berries, and buds, in particular of bilberry and cowberry, supplemented by pine needles in winter. In summer, they feed mainly on the ground; in winter, they are more often in the tree tops.

DISPLAY AND VOICE
A male Capercaillie displays with drooped wings, raised and fanned tail, and head erect, and with his beard of spiky throat feathers puffed out and his bill open, producing a peculiar mixture of crackles and rattling sounds running into loud, hollow "popping" notes like a series of pulled corks. Where they are still numerous, the males display at forest leks, while the females look on from the sidelines to choose the best, fittest males with which to mate. Females make a Pheasant-like *kok-kok*.

BREEDING
Nests are on the ground, at the foot of trees. Up to eight eggs are laid. They hatch after 24–26 days. The young flutter when still small at 14 days. They become independent after 10–12 weeks. Only the females take an interest in rearing the chicks.

MIGRATION
Resident, moving only locally in bad weather.

Male
Big, turkey-like, with waxy dark tail feathers barred white; white shoulder spot; green gloss on chest; displays with fanned tail to female, shown to same scale.

Roosts low in tree with clear escape route.

Female
Grey above with tail and breast band contrastingly rusty; white legs.

Juvenile female
Darker above than adult; darker legs.

Male
Brown wings; pale bill; tail feathers large, square-tipped, waxy, with white spots; moulted tail feathers often found in woods.

Female is bigger than female Black Grouse, with rounder, redder tail, brighter chest and bolder black flank bars.

WHEN SEEN

All year.

WHERE SEEN
Pine forests; locally in Scandinavia, E Europe, N Scotland, Alps, Pyrenees.

HABITAT AND INFO

SIMILAR SPECIES
Female Black Grouse is duller, less rusty; pale wingbar; squarer or notched tail.

Smaller tail

Yellowish breast

TURKEY-LIKE GROUSE
An enormous, displaying male
Capercaillie has a unique character.

Female
Bright orange-chestnut
breast band; much
white underneath.

Male
Grey-brown contrast
often lost at longer
range or in poor
light; can look almost
black overall.

Shown to
larger scale
than male
for clarity
of detail.

Male
Flying away, gliding
on stiff, drooped,
fingered wings; head
outstretched; tail long
and rounded.

Male has bold white
underwing patch; round
tail held closed in flight.

Juvenile female
Richly coloured,
beautifully patterned
with inky-black, much
white barring on fresh
feathers; broad, round
tail rufous barred
black, contrasts
with grey rump.

DID YOU KNOW?
Male Capercaillies may become so obsessed with displaying their
strength and sexual prowess to anything that moves that they
may attack humans and their vehicles: an aggressive caper cock
is certainly not to be underestimated. Yet Capercaillies are also
extremely vulnerable. A simple deer fence at the edge of
a forest can wipe out a small, local population through
fatal collisions.

?

Ptarmigan

LENGTH / 34–36cm (13½–14in)
WINGSPAN / 54–60cm (21–23½in)
WEIGHT / 400–600g (14–21oz)

■ STATUS / Vulnerable

SCALE v Pigeon

In much of Europe, this is a mountain bird. In the far north, it lives on lower, exposed ground. White wings separate it from the similar Willow Grouse in the north. In winter, the male's black face patch is distinctive.

Throughout the year the Ptarmigan thrives in some of the most inhospitable terrain on the earth: the cold, near-barren tundra of the far north. Where tundra conditions prevail on high mountains, it occurs further south at increasing altitudes in the Highlands of Scotland, the Alps, and the Pyrenees. In these regions, it lives on the highest ground on gravelly, boulder-strewn ridges and plateaux with short shrubby vegetation, but in Iceland it lives practically at sea level.

FEEDING
In summer, small insects are its main food, especially for chicks, but otherwise it relies on a dry, tough diet of shoots, buds, berries, and seeds.

DISPLAY AND VOICE
Males fly up steeply then glide down, calling with deep, throaty croaks: *err-ook-kakakaka, kwa, kwa, kwa*. Other calls are hard, cackling notes with an accelerating rhythm.

BREEDING
The hen incubates up to nine eggs in a shallow scrape between boulders for 21–26 days. The chicks fly when just two weeks old.

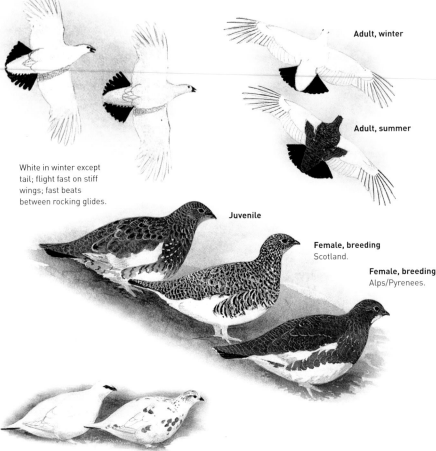

Adult, winter

Adult, summer

White in winter except tail; flight fast on stiff wings; fast beats between rocking glides.

Juvenile

Female, breeding
Scotland.

Female, breeding
Alps/Pyrenees.

Male, winter (above)

Female, early spring (above)

Adult male
White feathers appear in autumn and may remain in spring to give heavily spotted look.

Female, late summer

SEASONAL COLOURS
Ptarmigan plumage changes to match the environment.

ORDER
Galliformes

FAMILY
Tetraonidae

SPECIES
Tetrao tetrix

COMMON NAME
Black Grouse

Black Grouse

A beautiful large grouse of the moorland edge, the male is unmistakable. The female is like other grouse or Pheasant, but with notched tail and pale wingbars.

LENGTH / 40–55cm (15½–21½in)
WINGSPAN / 65–80cm (26–31in)
WEIGHT / 0.75–1.4kg (1¾–3lb)

■ **STATUS /** Endangered

SCALE v Pigeon

Juvenile female

Fine white wingbar.

Female tail notched (can look square); lacks dark corners of Red Grouse's.

Northern, greyer Scandinavian and Russian females can have male-type wingbars, central white spot, or none at all; some females have lyre tails.

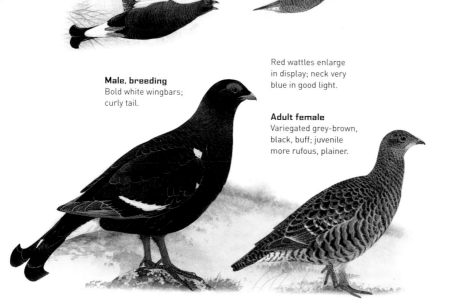

Bold white underwing.

Long wings white below.

Male, breeding
Bold white wingbars; curly tail.

Red wattles enlarge in display; neck very blue in good light.

Adult female
Variegated grey-brown, black, buff; juvenile more rufous, plainer.

Whitish undertail.

Sadly this spectacular bird is one of the most threatened in Europe. It is declining fast, and already long gone from many parts of its former range. It requires a mixture of grassland, heather moorland, or rough heath, and damp, rushy hillsides, plus open woodland (for which young plantations are only a poor substitute). Such diversity of habitat is becoming scarce, especially under the pressure of modern farming.

FEEDING
The Black Grouse's diet reflects its habitat, and it successively takes buds, shoots, leaves, berries, and fruit from heather, bilberry, and other shrubs and trees. Insects, including caterpillars, are extremely important for young chicks in summer.

DISPLAY AND VOICE
Males display competitively at traditional lek sites, sparring with fanned tails, fluffed-out body plumage, and swollen wattles. The watching females select the fittest mates. Calls include explosive sneezes and a far-carrying, musical cooing.

BREEDING
Females incubate 6–10 eggs for 23–27 days in a scrape. The chicks flutter at just 10–14 days old.

RITUAL COMBAT
Male Black Grouse pose and challenge, with little real damage being done.

WHEN SEEN

All year.

WHERE SEEN
Rare UK, Alps; more in Scandinavia; rare Germany; and E Europe.

HABITAT AND INFO

SIMILAR SPECIES
Male Capercaillie is less glossy blue-black; broad, white-flecked tail; much bigger.

Round tail

White flank stripe

Willow Grouse

SCALE v Pigeon

LENGTH / 37–42cm (14½–16½in)
WINGSPAN / 55–66cm (21½–26in)
WEIGHT / 650–750g (23–26oz)

■ STATUS / Vulnerable

A thickset, short-legged, round-headed game bird of northern forest and tundra, it has white wings (and white body in winter) similar to Ptarmigan.

Male, summer   Adult, winter

This is the same species as the Red Grouse of Britain and Ireland, but in its mainland continental form. It has a more striking appearance in spring, when the males are partly white, and in winter when they become white all over like the Ptarmigan. It is more typical of forest clearings and willow scrub than the Red Grouse and is generally found in high, mountainous regions.

FEEDING
Like the Ptarmigan, the Willow Grouse has a diet restricted to mainly leathery leaves and shoots, and hard, dry seeds. It eats berries in late summer and insects when they are available: these are most important to the development of the chicks.

DISPLAY AND VOICE
In spring, males stretch upward, their red wattles swollen, and call loudly with a series of accelerating croaks. Startling, nasal calls, frog-like but very loud, include a rapid *ke-uk kekekekekekuh-uh-uhk*.

BREEDING
Hens incubate 6–9 eggs in a scrape on the ground for 19–25 days.

MIGRATION
Resident.

Female, spring

Male, winter
Note heavy bill; neither sex has black face of male Ptarmigan.

Male, late summer
More rufous than Ptarmigan; much less barred.

Male, spring
Reddish head contrasts with white body, unlike Ptarmigan's.

Female, late summer
Slightly larger, thicker-billed than Ptarmigan; face and throat more buff, less grey.

SHARP CONTRASTS
The crisply divided red and white areas make this a distinctive game bird.

WHEN SEEN

All year.

WHERE SEEN
Norway, N Sweden, Finland, Estonia, and eastward into Russia.

HABITAT AND INFO

SIMILAR SPECIES
Ptarmigan is slimmer; smaller bill; less rufous; in winter male has black face.

Thin bill

Greyer body

Red Grouse

The "Willow Grouse" of Britain and Ireland is found on heather moorland. It never has white wings or body plumage – but is darker, redder, and more barred than any partridge.

LENGTH / 37–42cm (14½–16½in)
WINGSPAN / 55–66cm (21½–26in)
WEIGHT / 650–750g (23–26oz)

■ **STATUS /** Vulnerable

SCALE v Pigeon

Glides between bursts of wing beats.

Underwing shows variable amount of white that may change with moult, but usually looks a dark bird.

Flight fast, direct, on stiff, arched wings, with long glides.

Male
In display flight.

Male
Black tail, dark outer wing, unlike partridges' or female Black Grouse's.

Male, spring
Large red wattle; some have white on belly, white spots on wing.

Irish birds greyer on back.

Female
Paler, yellower than male; less olive than female Black Grouse.

Unique to Britain and Ireland, the Red Grouse is now treated as a race of the Willow Grouse. It lives mainly on extensive heather moorland, and it is common only where this unnatural habitat is maintained and managed for shooting. A few Red Grouse live in more natural heathery clearings in open, upland woods, and on higher, exposed ground extending up to the kind of mountain terrain inhabited by Ptarmigan.

FEEDING
It eats a variety of leaves, shoots, and berries such as bilberry, crowberry, and cowberry fruits. In winter, it plucks haws from trees at the edge of the moor. The chicks need moth caterpillars and other nutritious invertebrates in summer.

DISPLAY AND VOICE
In spring, displaying males defy each other with loud, crowing challenges from prominent perches. The evocative calls are sudden, loud outbursts of deep, grating, rapid notes: *kr-rrrr r r kuk-kuk-ku huk, go-bak go-bak go-bak, bak, bak*.

BREEDING
Females lay 6–9 eggs in a scrape and incubate them for 19–25 days.

POWERFUL FLIER
Grouse fly fast and low, but for relatively short distances before they tire.

WHEN SEEN

All year.

WHERE SEEN
Scotland, N England; scarce SW England, Wales; Ireland.

HABITAT AND INFO

SIMILAR SPECIES
Grey Partridge is smaller, paler; less boldly mottled; paler wings and tail sides.

Paler wings

Barred flanks

Rock Partridge

SCALE v Pigeon

LENGTH / 32–35cm (12½–14in)
WINGSPAN / 46–53cm (18–21in)
WEIGHT / 500–750g (18–26½oz)

■ **STATUS /** Vulnerable

A boldly marked partridge of high or barren rocky areas, it is found mostly in south-east Europe. Close examination is necessary for certain identification.

This scarce, or even rare, and elusive bird lives on rocky or craggy slopes, often high up on mountains, sometimes where there is a scattering of bushes but often in really open, apparently barren locations. It prefers south-facing slopes. Hard to see on the ground, it usually reveals itself when accidentally flushed at close range. Even then it is not easy to distinguish from its relatives, but the range and habitat are useful clues.

FEEDING
Like the Chukar, the Rock Partridge finds its food on the ground, taking insects when it can but mostly subsisting on seeds and shoots.

VOICE
The usual call is a four-syllable phrase, repeated at intervals: *chair tsirit-chee*. Other notes are sharp, clear calls: *vit vit* or *pit-chee pit-chee*.

BREEDING
The nest is a simple scrape with a skimpy lining of leaves and stems. The 8–14 eggs are incubated for about 25 days. The chicks are fully grown at about eight weeks.

Tail feathers all-rufous, unlike Chukar's.

Black against base of upper mandible distinctive if present.

Head pattern varies; some have black under bill and gape.

Brown bloom on back wears off to give greyer colour.

Pure white throat, unlike Chukar's.

Birds in Swiss Alps have narrow flank bars.

SHOW OFF
Like its related partridges, this is a handsome bird with crisply defined patterns.

WHEN SEEN

All year.

WHERE SEEN
Alps and Balkans, including most of Greece; highlands of Italy including Sicily.

HABITAT AND INFO

SIMILAR SPECIES
Red-legged Partridge is smaller, darker, with streaked necklace.

Speckled neckband

ORDER	Galliformes
FAMILY	Phasianidae
SPECIES	Alectoris chukar
COMMON NAME	Chukar
COMMON NAME	Galliformes
FAMILY	Phasianidae
SPECIES	Alectoris barbara
COMMON NAME	Barbary Partridge

Barbary Partridge

Chukar is a large, pale partridge of the warm south-east, scarce in Europe except where introduced. Barbary is similar, but it has distinctive head and neck.

	CHUKAR	BARBARY PARTRIDGE
LENGTH /	32–34cm (12½–13½in)	32–34cm (12½–13½in)
WINGSPAN /	47–52cm (18½–20½in)	46–49cm (18–19in)
WEIGHT /	500–600g (17½–21oz)	500g (17½oz)
◾ STATUS /	Secure	◾ Vulnerable

SCALE v Pigeon

In the extreme south-east of Europe and the Middle East, the Chukar is familiar and frequent on warm, open ground and dry farmland, as well as rough, barren slopes to a high altitude in the mountains. It has been widely introduced (belatedly made illegal in the UK) so it occurs – either in pure form or as a hybrid with the Red-legged Partridge – in many areas where it is not native. The Barbary Partridge is a bird of rocky hillsides, found in Gibraltar and Sardinia.

FEEDING
Chukars forage like chickens on open ground, sometimes scratching with their feet. In summer, insects supplement their vegetarian diet of seeds, shoots, and berries.

VOICE
A series of short, loud, abrupt notes sound like a rhythmic *chuk chuk chuk chuk-ke-cher chuk-ke-cher*.

BREEDING
Up to 12 eggs are laid in a scrape on the ground and incubated by the hen for about 25 days. As with other game birds, the young can fly moderately well when still only half or three-quarters grown.

Red-legged x Chukar hybrid
Border of bib spotted beneath.

Chukar

Chukar
Face cream; border of bib neat, black.

All-rufous tail.

Chukar
Base of tail feathers grey, unlike Rock Partridge's and Red-legged Partridge's.

Barbary Partridge
Gibraltar, Sardinia.

Barbary Partridge
Gibraltar, Sardinia.

Grey face; spotted brown gorget; pale stripe beside nape.

BOLD BIB
The black-edged white bib is characteristic of this group of species.

WHEN SEEN

All year.

WHERE SEEN
Chukar: extreme E Europe; widely introduced (but often hybridized) elsewhere. Barbary: Gibraltar and Sardinia.

HABITAT AND INFO

SIMILAR SPECIES
Rock Partridge very similar, but with subtle differences in face pattern and purer white throat.

Whiter throat

Red-legged Partridge

SCALE v Pigeon

LENGTH / 32–34cm (12½–13½in)
WINGSPAN / 45–50cm (17½–19½in)
WEIGHT / 400–550g (14–19oz)

■ STATUS / Vulnerable

Of the plain-backed, white-faced partridges, this is the neatest and most attractive, but it is threatened by interbreeding with released Chukars. Compared with Grey Partridge, it is larger, heavier, and boldly patterned on the face.

Perhaps the most beautiful of the partridges, the Red-legged faces an uncertain future since in some places it hybridizes with the irresponsibly introduced Chukars. It is the western representative of the *Alectoris* group.

FEEDING
Red-legs share the chicken-like ground-feeding behaviour of other partridges. They find leaves, shoots, roots, and seeds of cereals and grasses, as well as tree seeds such as beech mast.

DISPLAY AND VOICE
Males often call loudly and rhythmically from high perches, including stacks of straw bales and roofs. The song has a "chuffing" effect, like *kok-chak-kok-chak-kok-chak-chak*. Other calls are short, rather hollow *chuk*, *chuk-ar*, or *tschreg* notes.

BREEDING
A scrape in the ground, lined with leaves, serves as the nest. The 10–16 eggs hatch after 23–24 days' incubation by the female. The male may incubate a second clutch nearby. The young fly after 10 days, but are not full-grown for several weeks.

Few Red-legged now remain in E England – most are hybrids with Chukars.

Red-legged

Compared with Grey, note plain back; broader flank bars; red legs and bill; white face.

Grey

Larger, often more upright, faster-running, paler than Grey.

Red-legged   Grey

All-rufous tail.

Red bill; white face bordered by black; spotted neck and chest.

Long white stripes over eyes almost meet on hindneck.

BEAUTIFUL PARTRIDGE
Of several similar species, this is perhaps the most prettily patterned.

WHEN SEEN

All year.

WHERE SEEN
France, N Italy, Spain, Portugal, Balearics, Corsica; also introduced in Britain, mostly England and S and E Scotland.

HABITAT AND INFO

SIMILAR SPECIES
Chukar has bigger pale face patch with neat black border; bolder flank streaks.

Sharp black border

COMMON NAME
Grey Partridge

SPECIES
Perdix perdix

FAMILY
Phasianidae

ORDER
Galliformes

Grey Partridge

The native partridge of northern Europe and Britain, this small, shy, dumpy bird is a subtle beauty compared with the more colourful Red-legged Partridge and bolder Chukar.

LENGTH / 29–31cm (11½–12in)
WINGSPAN / 45–48cm (17½–19in)
WEIGHT / 350–450g (12½–16oz)

■ **STATUS /** Vulnerable

SCALE v Pigeon

The Grey, or "English", Partridge is the only one native to Britain and Ireland. It was once a distinctive feature of arable farmland and hay meadows, especially when calling in spring or in winter coveys, but like many farmland birds it has declined dramatically over most of western Europe in recent decades. Like other partridges, it is sociable, often seen in groups of 10–20 or so.

FEEDING
Chicks require insect larvae in summer. Otherwise its diet consists largely of seeds, berries, green leaves, and shoots. It is the loss of insects and weed seeds from intensively cultivated farmland that has caused its decline.

DISPLAY AND VOICE
Males have a frequent song, especially in the evening: a loud, creaky, very pleasant *kee-err-ik*. As the bird takes flight it gives sharp, quick *ker-ik*, *krrip-krrip* and *kit-it* alarm notes.

BREEDING
The 10–20 or more eggs are laid in a shallow nest in dense vegetation, and hatch after 23–25 days. Chicks flutter when 10 days old, but are not fully grown for about 14 weeks.

Grey

Red-legged

Red-legged

Grey flies on bowed wings; Red-legged flies with wings almost flat, slightly raised, before final landing flutter.

Sides of tail rufous.

Male

Female

Cream underwing coverts; pale vent; dark breast patch is distinctive.

Dark horseshoe on lower breast most marked on male.

Male

Female

Simple deep brown flank bars; streaked upperparts; pale legs.

Some birds have very rufous back feathers.

FARMLAND VOICE
The spring song of a Grey Partridge is a familiar, but declining, element of the countryside.

WHEN SEEN

All year.

WHERE SEEN
Sparse and very local in Ireland; more widespread in Britain; widely from N Spain, France, S Norway eastward.

HABITAT AND INFO

SIMILAR SPECIES
Female Pheasant is larger; more spotted; pointed tail lacking rufous sides.

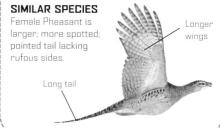

Longer wings

Long tail

Hazel Grouse

LENGTH / 35–37cm (14–14½in)
WINGSPAN / 48–54cm (19–21in)
WEIGHT / 350–490g (12½–17¼oz)

SCALE v Pigeon

■ STATUS / Vulnerable

A Woodpigeon-sized game bird of dark forests with dense undergrowth. It flies off early when approached and is hard to see.

Principally a bird of mixed forest, found deep in shady, often damp, luxuriant places, the Hazel Grouse is usually seen when disturbed as it flies a short distance to settle in a tree. It is a wary bird, difficult to approach for a better view. In summer, it spends most of its time on the ground, where it is quite agile, but in winter it lives mostly up in the trees.

FEEDING
Hazel Grouse eat buds and shoots, leaves, berries, and seeds according to availability, plus ants, beetles, and caterpillars in summer.

DISPLAY AND VOICE
Males advertise their territories with whirring wings and calls, a sharp whistling song of 5–9 notes and a pipit-like *srit-srit*.

BREEDING
Pairs are monogamous. Nests are well-hidden beneath bushes or tree stumps. Up to 11 eggs hatch after 25 days. The chicks can fly at 15–20 days, but are not fully grown until about five weeks old.

MIGRATION
Resident apart from short-distance movements in search of food in autumn and winter.

Male flies with arched wings; grey tail/rump with black band.

Scandinavian birds tend to be grey (below); those living to south and west are more rufous (below right).

Male
Long tail with black band; many white spots; scapular spots aligned in curved braces; pale shafts and outer webs on primaries.

Loses some of rufous colour with wear; much minor individual variation in detail of pattern.

Female

Spiky nape.

Male
Face pattern distinctive if seen.

FOREST RECLUSE
Hazel Grouse are hard to see in their dense forest habitats.

WHEN SEEN

All year.

WHERE SEEN
Locally Norway; most of Sweden, Finland, Baltic states, Russia; local in Germany, Alps, Balkans, E Europe.

HABITAT AND INFO

SIMILAR SPECIES
Female Black Grouse is more yellow-brown, less black, white, and rufous; shorter tail.

Barred brown tail

Browner body

Andalusian Hemipode

A tiny, secretive ground-living bird of dry heathy ground with dwarf palm and similar scrub. It is exceedingly rare and elusive in Europe, although common in Africa (where it is known as the Small Button Quail).

LENGTH / 15–16cm (6–6¼in)
WINGSPAN / 25–30cm (9⅞–11⅞in)
WEIGHT / 60–70g (2–2½oz)

■ STATUS / Extinct in Europe?

SCALE v Pigeon

Although this is a common and quite widespread bird in Africa south of the Sahara, in Europe it is all but extinct (indeed, it may be so) after a drastic decline during the past 150 years. In southern Spain, it used to be common in coastal scrub, especially with dwarf palmetto; it was also found rarely in Sicily. It is still to be seen in Morocco, although the population is dwindling. It is very hard to observe in the wild, and therefore little known.

FEEDING
It takes seeds and insects from the ground.

DISPLAY AND VOICE
Females dominate courtship, calling to males with a resonant, slowly repeated call, like wind through a pipe: *hoo, hoo, hoo*.

BREEDING
The pattern of "successive polyandry" is extremely unusual in European birds. The females probably mate with several males in succession. They lay a clutch of eggs for each male to incubate and the males care for the young. Incubation takes 12–14 days.

MIGRATION
Probably sedentary in Europe and north Africa.

If flushed, reveals broad, diffuse pale area on upperwing, with darker flight feathers.

Slightly smaller, shorter wings than Quail's; equally difficult to flush; runs fast in horizontal pose.

Adult male
Paler, more gingery, than female; bolder black spotting onto flanks.

Adult female
Darker, especially on back, than male.

May still be present in Spain and Sicily; lack of habitat knowledge may have prevented sightings; waste areas and land near human habitation are possible sites.

ENIGMATIC RARITY
In Africa, this species is widespread, but in Europe, it is extraordinarily elusive.

WHEN SEEN

All year.

WHERE SEEN
Uncertain: perhaps a handful of pairs remain in extreme SW Spain, but possibly extinct in Europe.

HABITAT AND INFO

SIMILAR SPECIES
Quail is more striped on body; dark lines on face and throat; dark eyes.

Streaked back

Striped face

Quail

SCALE v Pigeon

LENGTH / 16–18cm (6¼–7in)
WINGSPAN / 32–35cm (12½–14in)
WEIGHT / 70–135g (2½–4¾oz)

■ **STATUS /** Vulnerable

A small, plump game bird, it is rarely seen but frequently heard in breeding areas in summer. A liquid triple note is repeatedly given from dense cereal crops or hay meadows.

A mysterious voice in the cereal fields, the Quail is easy to hear, but hard to see. In many areas it fluctuates, declining locally in years when cereals are replaced by other crops such as rape. It may cope well with clover, however, and still breeds in its natural habitat of extensive grasslands and steppe.

FEEDING
Quail pick seeds from the ground. Insects are important in summer, especially for the chicks.

DISPLAY AND VOICE
The male circles the female with his throat feathers puffed out. His far-carrying territorial song is a liquid but abrupt *whit, whit-it*, repeated for long spells throughout the summer. A nasal, doll-like *ma-ma* can sometimes be heard at close range.

BREEDING
The clutch is usually 8–13 eggs, but may be as many as 18, laid in thick cover. They hatch in 17–20 days.

MIGRATION
Quails once gathered in their thousands on the Mediterranean coast. Now they migrate in smaller numbers, although they can still be abundant, especially in the east.

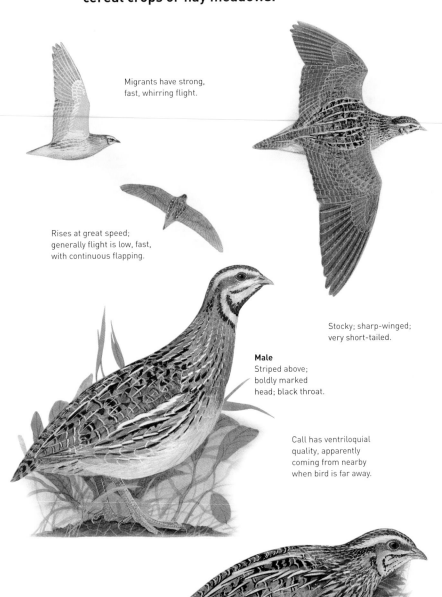

Migrants have strong, fast, whirring flight.

Rises at great speed; generally flight is low, fast, with continuous flapping.

Stocky; sharp-winged; very short-tailed.

Male
Striped above; boldly marked head; black throat.

Call has ventriloquial quality, apparently coming from nearby when bird is far away.

Female
Bright with weaker version of male's face pattern.

A DISEMBODIED VOICE
The Quail is almost always heard, but not seen, calling from deep within a dense crop.

WHEN SEEN
Oct — March

March to October.

WHERE SEEN
Widespread north to North Sea and Baltic; fluctuating numbers, especially in north of range in Britain, Ireland, Scandinavia, W Russia.

HABITAT AND INFO

SIMILAR SPECIES
Juvenile Grey Partridge has wider, squarer wings; darker tail sides; plainer face.

Barred flanks

Orange face

Great Northern Diver

A goose-sized diver with a massive, dagger bill, it has a very broad body with bulging shoulders, often obvious when viewed end-on.

LENGTH / 70–80cm (27½–31½in)
WINGSPAN / 1.3–1.5m (4¼–5ft)
WEIGHT / 3–4kg (6½–9lb)

■ **STATUS /** Secure

SCALE v Pigeon

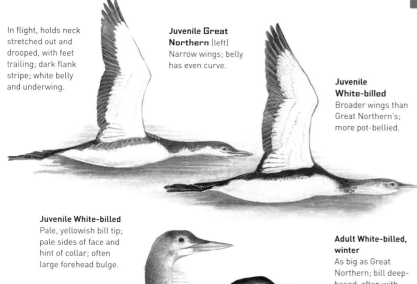

In flight, holds neck stretched out and drooped, with feet trailing; dark flank stripe; white belly and underwing.

Juvenile Great Northern (left) Narrow wings; belly has even curve.

Juvenile White-billed Broader wings than Great Northern's; more pot-bellied.

Juvenile White-billed Pale, yellowish bill tip; pale sides of face and hint of collar; often large forehead bulge.

Adult White-billed, winter As big as Great Northern; bill deep-based, often with straight upper and upcurved lower edge, dark only at base of bill ridge; paler eye-ring and cheeks.

Adult Great Northern, breeding Evenly chequered back, unlike Black-throated Diver's.

Black head and bill; striped necklace and broken collar; White-billed's similar but with pale bill.

Adult Great Northern, non-breeding Compare juvenile Cormorant.

Bluish or ivory bill with black ridge.

Black patch on side of neck; dark nape; often a forehead bulge.

Juvenile Great Northern Square pale feather fringes on back; nape blacker than back; rear flank dark.

The Great Northern and White-billed are the biggest divers. Both have chequerboard plumage and black heads in summer, but their winter colours are dull. In winter, Great Northerns range from wide, sandy bays and sheltered estuaries to the wilder coasts of north-west Scotland, and may appear on large, inland lakes. The White-billed is more elusive and rarely nests outside the Arctic.

FEEDING
These divers capture fish and crabs in long, deep dives, often bringing larger prey back to the surface to deal with.

VOICE
All divers are silent in winter, but the Great Northern's loud, evocative wails and bubbling, laughing calls may occasionally be heard before it leaves in spring.

BREEDING
Both species lay two large, dark eggs at the edge of a lake.

MIGRATION
Autumn movements take Great Northerns south into the North Sea and along west European coasts. The White-billed is much rarer.

UNDERWATER HUNTER
Moulting into breeding plumage creates an intermediate pattern.

WHEN SEEN

Sept · April

A few immatures all year in non-breeding areas; most September to April.

WHERE SEEN
Breeds on large lakes in Iceland; winters on coasts from Scandinavia to France.

HABITAT AND INFO

SIMILAR SPECIES
Immature Cormorant has bill angled up, blunt, hook-tipped; flatter head; longer tail.

Hooked bill

Perches upright out of water

Black-throated Diver

LENGTH / 60–70cm (23½–27½in)
WINGSPAN / 110–130cm (43–51in)
WEIGHT / 2–3kg (4½–6½lb)

■ **STATUS /** Vulnerable

SCALE v Pigeon

A supremely elegant diver, immaculately patterned in summer, without the bulk and angularity of the Great Northern.

Of all the divers, a Black-throat in full breeding plumage is arguably the most beautiful. It lacks the impact of the huge Great Northern, but makes up for it with the most delicate of plumage patterns, almost too perfect to be true. Yet most people see it, if at all, in winter or immature plumage, which is much duller but still highlights the perfect form of this superb bird.

FEEDING
It takes fish, frogs, and a few aquatic invertebrates, hunting underwater in long dives.

VOICE
Silent in winter, the Black-throated Diver has wonderful howling or wailing calls in summer and a deep, short *kwok* in flight.

BREEDING
It lays two dark eggs at the water's edge on an islet, or on an artificial raft in some Scottish lochs.

MIGRATION
Breeding birds move to the sea in late summer and are thinly scattered southward in winter, mostly in broad, sandy bays. They are rare inland but sometimes stay for weeks on larger reservoirs or lakes.

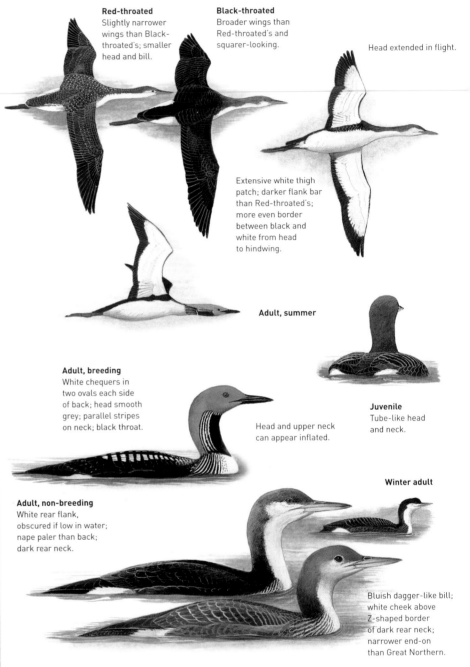

Red-throated
Slightly narrower wings than Black-throated's; smaller head and bill.

Black-throated
Broader wings than Red-throated's and squarer-looking.

Head extended in flight.

Extensive white thigh patch; darker flank bar than Red-throated's; more even border between black and white from head to hindwing.

Adult, summer

Adult, breeding
White chequers in two ovals each side of back; head smooth grey; parallel stripes on neck; black throat.

Head and upper neck can appear inflated.

Juvenile
Tube-like head and neck.

Adult, non-breeding
White rear flank, obscured if low in water; nape paler than back; dark rear neck.

Winter adult

Bluish dagger-like bill; white cheek above Z-shaped border of dark rear neck; narrower end-on than Great Northern.

Juvenile
White rear flank patch; fine pale scaling on back.

OP-ART PERFECTION
No bird has a more immaculate and intricate plumage pattern.

WHEN SEEN

Nov
April

In the south, mostly November to March or April.

WHERE SEEN
Breeds on large lakes in Norway, Sweden, Scotland; winters in estuaries and sandy bays south to Biscay coasts.

HABITAT AND INFO

SIMILAR SPECIES
Great Northern Diver has black head in summer; in winter, head blacker than back; dark collar.

Black head

Evenly spotted back

Red-throated Diver

A snake-necked diver with a tip-tilted bill held upward, it has dark, plain plumage in summer. It is pale in winter, with a white face.

LENGTH / 55–69cm (21½–27in)
WINGSPAN / 110–120cm (43–47in)
WEIGHT / 1.2–1.6kg (2½–3½lb)

■ **STATUS /** Vulnerable

SCALE v Pigeon

The smallest diver, about the size of a Mallard, the Red-throated Diver is best distinguished by its slender bill, which it holds tilted slightly upward. It sits low in the water, rolling forward to dive and often reappearing far away. It comes to land only to breed, but it flies frequently, especially in summer, making regular trips from the small lakes on which it nests to hunt for food at sea.

FEEDING
It catches small fish during lengthy dives, but feeds its small young on insects and crustaceans.

DISPLAY AND VOICE
Although silent in winter, it makes loud, quacking flight notes in summer and produces weird, far-carrying, syncopated wailing and rattling sounds during its strange, ritualized courtship displays.

BREEDING
Nests are simple scrapes on lake shores in northern Europe. Pairs rear one or two young each summer.

MIGRATION
In autumn, Red-throats move south around the coasts as far as the Mediterranean, but are rare inland.

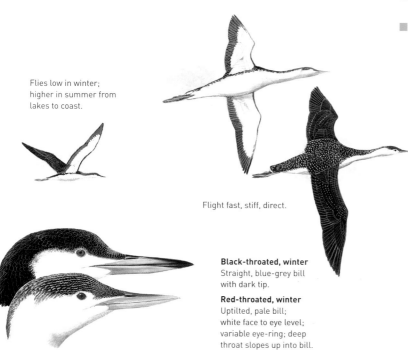

Flies low in winter; higher in summer from lakes to coast.

Flight fast, stiff, direct.

Black-throated, winter
Straight, blue-grey bill with dark tip.

Red-throated, winter
Uptilted, pale bill; white face to eye level; variable eye-ring; deep throat slopes up into bill.

Breeding adult, summer
Grey head and dark red throat; finely striped hindneck; broader stripes on sides of breast.

White encircles eye.

Dark brown upperparts in summer; rounder back than other divers.

Non-breeding adult, winter (left)
Speckled white.

Tail projection on female shorter than male's.

Only diver with white spots on secondary and covert feathers.

Juvenile
Throat pale; neck sometimes darker.

COMFORT AFLOAT
Divers often rise up in the water to flap their wings.

WHEN SEEN

All year; on breeding lakes April to August, otherwise at sea.

WHERE SEEN
Breeds on small lakes from Scotland and S Sweden northward; in winter widespread on coasts.

HABITAT AND INFO

SIMILAR SPECIES
Black-throated Diver has bill held horizontal, not upswept; dark around eye; darker back.

White back spots

Black throat

Great Crested Grebe

LENGTH / 46–51cm (18–20in)
WINGSPAN / 85–90cm (33½–35½in)
WEIGHT / 0.8–1kg (1¾–2¼lb)

■ STATUS / Secure

SCALE v Pigeon

This round-bodied, stump-tailed, long-necked swimming bird is rarely on land and dives frequently. It holds its thin neck upright or withdrawn into its shoulders.

Unmistakable facial adornments make the Great Crested Grebe a distinctive bird in spring and summer. The colourful ruffs are absent in winter, when it looks very white-faced and white-breasted, with a slender neck and dagger bill.

FEEDING
These grebes eat small fish and other aquatic creatures, caught during lengthy underwater dives.

DISPLAY AND VOICE
During courtship, pairs rise breast-to-breast and face each other with their crests and ruffs spread wide, wagging their heads in a ritual display and offering rags of waterweed to each other. The voice is a loud quacking and growling.

BREEDING
They nest at the water's edge, laying up to six eggs on floating heaps of dank weed. The chicks quickly leave the nest and make loud, whistling calls during the summer.

MIGRATION
After nesting many move to the coast, or gather on reservoirs that are free from ice. Those from northern and eastern Europe move to the North Sea or Mediterranean coasts.

Adult, non-breeding
Black eye stripe; white line below cap, unlike Red-necked Grebe.

Flies rarely, low, fast, direct, with wings whirring, legs and neck drooped.

Big white patches on inner wing.

White face, thin cap (Red-necked has deeper cap, no white over eye).

Juvenile
Striped face and neck; otherwise plain pale brown.

Winter flocks gather on large lakes; ones and twos on sea.

Neck may be held upright or withdrawn.

Dagger-like, pink-and-black bill; triangular, forward-tilted head.

Adult, breeding
Black crest and chestnut ruff from late winter.

Breast gleaming white all year.

Size deceptive: may look large on water at distance.

Body largely dull olive-brown.

Adult, non-breeding

DANK NEST
A grebe's nest is always more or less wet, but is semi-floating, anchored to a stem.

WHEN SEEN

All year in south and west; April to October in north and east.

WHERE SEEN
Freshwater lakes, large rivers, coasts; locally in all Europe except N Scandinavia.

HABITAT AND INFO

SIMILAR SPECIES
Red-necked Grebe in winter is bigger-headed, thicker-necked; bill yellow at base; dark cap to below eye.

Stocky neck

Less white on wing

Red-necked Grebe

A chunky grebe, with a large, round head and a thick bill. Its body lies low in water and often looks short, exaggerating size of head and thickness of neck. It may dive deep, with a leap from the surface like a Shag.

LENGTH / 40–50cm (15½–19½in)
WINGSPAN / 77–85cm (30–34in)
WEIGHT / 700–900g (25–32oz)

■ **STATUS /** Secure

SCALE v Pigeon

While not so large as the Great Crested Grebe, the Red-necked Grebe is stocky, thick-necked and big-headed, with a heavy bill, and it can look deceptively big out on the water. Like other grebes it dives easily and often, flies with some difficulty, and almost never comes onto dry land.

FEEDING
Red-necked Grebes eat more insects and crustaceans than fish.

DISPLAY
Their black-and-white faces, contrasted bills, and deep red necks are important in displays that involve much bill-to-bill dancing on water.

BREEDING
They nest among reeds or rushes, laying 4–5 eggs on a sodden mass of weed. The young fly after 10 weeks and do not breed until they are two years old.

MIGRATION
After breeding on inland lakes, mostly in eastern Europe, many move to the coast or larger lakes in winter to avoid ice. Only then are they frequent around the North Sea and Adriatic coasts.

White inner wing patches smaller than on Great Crested Grebe.

Adult (below) Bill black, small yellow base; eye blackish; face white to dusky grey.

Trailing legs and feet in flight.

Immature Eye yellow (red on Great Crested).

Juvenile Dark head stripes.

Breeding adult, summer Neck and breast deep rusty-red.

Non-breeding adult, winter Head round; black surrounds eye, no white stripe above, unlike Great Crested Grebe.

Double bump on rear crown in summer.

Foreneck grey in winter (bright white on Great Crested); often a flash of white on upper flank.

Lacks snaky elegance of Great Crested Grebe; at long range in winter more like Slavonian Grebe.

CHUNKY GREBE
This is a large, round-headed, rather large-billed grebe.

WHEN SEEN

Aug — May

Mostly August to May in west; from March or April onward on breeding territories.

WHERE SEEN
Breeds on lakes from Denmark eastward; in winter on S Scandinavian and North Sea coasts; E Britain, where scarce inland.

HABITAT AND INFO

SIMILAR SPECIES
Slavonian Grebe in summer has dark face; pale yellowish wedge behind eye.

Small bill

Yellow wedge

Slavonian Grebe

LENGTH / 31–38cm (12–15in)
WINGSPAN / 59–65cm (23–25½in)
WEIGHT / 375–450g (13–16oz)

■ **STATUS /** Secure

SCALE v Pigeon

A well-proportioned, round-headed grebe, with a lower forehead profile and straighter bill than Black-necked's. It is colourful in breeding plumage; very black-and-white in winter.

The middle-sized grebe of northern waters, the Slavonian is a glorious bird in summer when it prefers cold, shallow lakes with shoreline vegetation. It is more familiar, however, in its neat, clean-cut black-and-white winter plumage, when it is usually seen on the coast.

FEEDING
Dives underwater to find aquatic insects and their larvae, and various species of small fish.

BREEDING
Nests among reeds and rushes in shallow water. The nest is a typical grebe heap of dank weed, nearly always floating but anchored to a stem, holding 4–5 eggs. The young fly after 45 days and return to breed when two years old.

MIGRATION
After nesting, all Slavonian Grebes move south and west to the coast, becoming widespread but scarce around Scandinavia, Britain, and the North Sea. Some arrive in autumn in full breeding colours and look equally colourful again before moving north in spring.

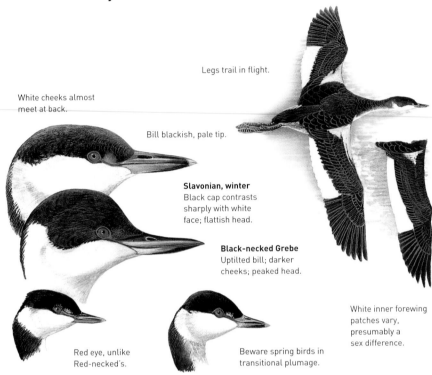

Legs trail in flight.

White cheeks almost meet at back.

Bill blackish, pale tip.

Slavonian, winter
Black cap contrasts sharply with white face; flattish head.

Black-necked Grebe
Uptilted bill; darker cheeks; peaked head.

White inner forewing patches vary, presumably a sex difference.

Red eye, unlike Red-necked's.

Beware spring birds in transitional plumage.

Usually pale spot in front of eye.

Back tapers to tail, less blunt than Black-necked's.

Non-breeding, winter
Black-and-white.

Black head; wedge-shaped golden tufts.

Breeding adult, summer
Flanks and neck all rusty-red.

BUOYANT SWIMMER
Smaller, round-bodied grebes are lively, buoyant birds on the water.

WHEN SEEN

Aug — May

August to May on coasts.

WHERE SEEN
Remote breeding lakes in Iceland, N Scotland, Scandinavia; on coasts in winter, especially estuaries.

HABITAT AND INFO

SIMILAR SPECIES
Black-necked Grebe in winter has thinner, upswept, dark-tipped bill; dusky cheek; broader, dark hindneck.

Darker neck

Uptilted bill

Black-necked Grebe

A round, tailless grebe with a steep forehead and peaked crown; its bill is uptilted. It dives constantly and swims very buoyantly even on rough seas.

LENGTH / 28–34cm (11–13½in)
WINGSPAN / 56–60cm (22–24in)
WEIGHT / 250–350g (9–12½oz)

■ **STATUS /** Secure

SCALE v Pigeon

No forewing white patch.

Black cap to below eye in winter, but pattern varies; sunlight increases contrast.

Pale hook on ear coverts typical.

Extensive white only on trailing edge of wing.

Slavonian (right)
Flatter head; narrower cap; whiter foreneck; pale bill tip.

Non-breeding adult, winter

Uptilted bill tip.

Dusky sides of neck may meet under throat.

Slavonian (below far left)
Black-necked (below left)
Winter birds are confusing: bill and head shape are best clues.

Juvenile, autumn
Drab; often trace of buff on ear coverts.

Breeding adult, summer
Black head with drooped fan of coppery-gold or yellow; coppery-red on flanks.

Although colourful in summer, the Black-necked Grebe becomes a dusky grey, black, and white in winter, less spick-and-span than the slightly larger Slavonian. It is distinguished by its peaked head and thin, slightly uptilted bill. It prefers freshwater lakes with plenty of bankside vegetation in summer. In winter many move to estuaries and other sheltered coasts.

FEEDING
It feeds on insects and tiny fish caught during frequent dives.

DISPLAY AND VOICE
Courtship displays involve head-wagging with golden ear-tufts fanned, synchronized dives, and rapid dashes across the water accompanied by shrill, trilling calls.

BREEDING
The 3–4 eggs are laid in a typical grebe nest of damp weed anchored to vegetation. The young are independent after just three weeks.

MIGRATION
After breeding, those from eastern Europe, Denmark, and the Low Countries move west and south, mostly to the sea. Scattered sites in southern Europe are occupied all year.

HALF AND HALF
In spring and autumn, grebes can be seen like this, in transition between breeding and winter colours.

WHEN SEEN

All year; on southern and western coasts August to May.

WHERE SEEN
Breeds on reedy lakes, mainly E Europe; scarce and scattered west to UK; winters on lakes and estuaries.

HABITAT AND INFO

SIMILAR SPECIES
Slavonian Grebe in winter is very similar, but has a sharper black-and-white look, with a neat cap and a straight bill.

Sharp facial division

Straight bill with pale tip

Little Grebe

LENGTH / 25–29cm (9¾–11½in)
WINGSPAN / 40–45cm (15½–17½in)
WEIGHT / 100–120g (3½–4¼oz)

■ STATUS / Secure

SCALE v Pigeon

A squat water bird with a peaked, rounded head and a short, fairly thick bill with a pale spot at base. Its body is very rounded. It is often heard calling in spring: a sudden, loud, whinnying sound.

This smallest and dumpiest of grebes lives on small freshwater pools and even quite narrow rivers, although many move to larger lakes or the coast in winter. Its short bill, round head, tailless appearance, and constant diving habit make it impossible to confuse with other water birds. It is not often seen in flight, which is hurried, low, and weak.

FEEDING
Little Grebes eat molluscs and insects and their larvae, caught underwater. They also catch small fish.

DISPLAY AND VOICE
Posturing is less extravagant than in larger grebes, but involves head-shaking and swimming together side by side, with frequent loud calls. Little Grebes are often heard more than seen, giving sudden loud, whinnying trills in summer.

BREEDING
The nest is a floating heap of weed, and the parent bird covers the clutch of 4–6 eggs with weed if it leaves them unattended. The chicks can fly after 45 days.

Shy and easily disturbed.

Non-breeding adult

Legs trail in flight.

Breeding, summer
Blackish with rufous cheeks; pale bill spot.

No white on upperwing.

Non-breeding, winter
Head buff with darker cap; pale spot near bill still there, but less contrasted.

Fluffs out rear flanks: whitish in winter, rufous in summer.

Frequently dives; hides in weeds.

Breeding, summer
No sign of ear tufts; flanks reveal bright orange-buff when feathers fluffed out.

Non-breeding, winter
Brown and buff; face contrasts less with cap than on Black-necked's.

Rufous cheeks may look sharply-defined or blend into black in strong light and shade.

HITCHING A RIDE
Like other grebes, it sometimes carries small chicks on its back.

WHEN SEEN

All year.

WHERE SEEN
UK, central and S Europe.

HABITAT AND INFO

SIMILAR SPECIES
Black-necked Grebe in winter is more black and white; brighter white chin and cheeks; blacker back.

White hook on cheek

Silvery flanks

Fulmar

Gull-like but really a petrel, the Fulmar is heavy-bodied, with a large white head but grey tail, unlike a gull. It glides and soars on stiff, almost straight wings.

LENGTH / 45–50cm (17½–19½in)
WINGSPAN / 100–112cm (39–44in)
WEIGHT / 700–900g (25–32oz)

■ STATUS / Secure

SCALE v Pigeon

Fulmars have increased hugely in the 20th century, thanks to the vast amount of dead fish and offal thrown overboard by bigger trawler fleets. Nesting colonies have spread to quite low cliffs and, in the north, even grass banks and ruined buildings. Fulmars are otherwise entirely seabirds.

FEEDING
Fulmars eat fish, crustaceans, and all kinds of floating waste and offal from ships. They always feed at sea.

DISPLAY AND VOICE
Pairs and immature birds visit potential nesting cliffs and soar to and fro along them. The pairs are noisy at the nest, making a hoarse, throaty, rapid cackling. They are quiet at sea.

BREEDING
Fulmar pairs breed from seven years old, choosing a broad ledge or an earth scrape on a sea cliff. Some colonies are well inland where there are few cliffs. Each pair incubates a single egg for 52–53 days, and the chick flies when seven weeks old.

MIGRATION
Most Fulmars disperse widely in the Atlantic after breeding, but a few remain inshore all year. Immatures remain at sea all year.

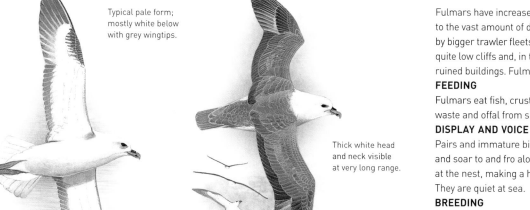

Typical pale form; mostly white below with grey wingtips.

Thick white head and neck visible at very long range.

Flies low and heavily in calm weather; glides masterfully in wind, rising high and banking over in gales.

Dark forms blue-grey to dull brownish; (compare Sooty Shearwater).

Pale inner primaries make obvious patch; no black on wingtips; often uneven, blotchy effect on upperwing.

Tube-nosed bill obvious at close range.

Unique appearance when squatting on cliff ledge; unable to stand, and merely shuffles; loud cackling distinctive.

CACKLING DUET
The hoarse, rattling calls of a Fulmar pair echo around the cliffs.

WHEN SEEN

All year; fewest inshore in late autumn.

WHERE SEEN
Breeds Iceland, Britain, Ireland, N France, locally to N Norway; widespread in North Sea and N Atlantic.

HABITAT AND INFO

SIMILAR SPECIES
Herring Gull holds wings more angled and arched; whiter tail; black on wingtips.

White tail

Black on wingtip

Cory's Shearwater

LENGTH / 45–55cm (17½–21½in)
WINGSPAN / 100–125cm (39–49in)
WEIGHT / 700–800g (25–28oz)

■ STATUS / Vulnerable

SCALE v Woodpigeon

Bigger and longer-winged than a Fulmar, Cory's Shearwater uses lazy flaps of bowed wings in light winds, but high, towering flight in gales. Its head lacks strong contrast, unlike Great Shearwater's, but its pale bill can be seen at long range.

Large, brown, lazy-looking shearwaters of the Mediterranean and mid-Atlantic, Cory's Shearwaters usually fly in small groups but occasionally in large flocks. They may be seen drifting by headlands in southern Spain or Majorca in small, unhurried parties all day long.

FEEDING
They catch fish, squid, and other marine creatures, mostly at night, and scavenge from trawlers.

VOICE
Sobbing, rasping *kaa-ough* notes are repeated several times at the breeding colony at night, creating an unearthly cacophony. It is silent at sea.

BREEDING
Breed in colonies on rocky islands, using rock cavities or burrows, which they visit only at night. The single egg hatches after 53 days. The young bird wanders at sea for some years before returning to breed.

MIGRATION
After breeding, many move west and north, appearing close to the coasts of Ireland, more rarely the UK, in July, August, and September.

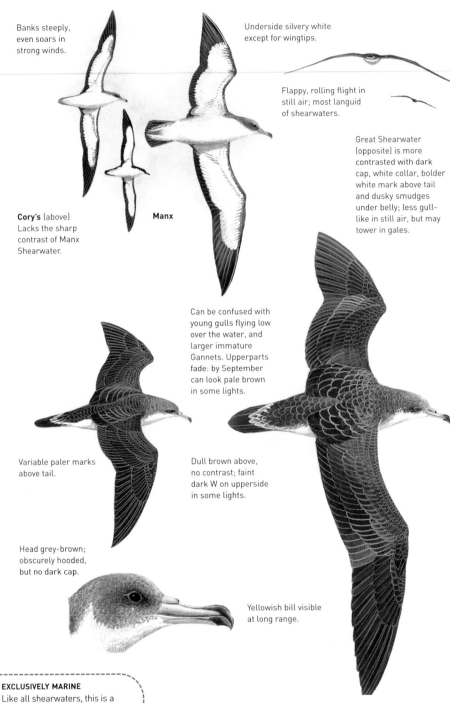

Banks steeply, even soars in strong winds.

Underside silvery white except for wingtips.

Flappy, rolling flight in still air; most languid of shearwaters.

Great Shearwater (opposite) is more contrasted with dark cap, white collar, bolder white mark above tail and dusky smudges under belly; less gull-like in still air, but may tower in gales.

Cory's (above) Lacks the sharp contrast of Manx Shearwater.

Manx

Can be confused with young gulls flying low over the water, and larger immature Gannets. Upperparts fade: by September can look pale brown in some lights.

Variable paler marks above tail.

Dull brown above, no contrast; faint dark W on upperside in some lights.

Head grey-brown; obscurely hooded, but no dark cap.

Yellowish bill visible at long range.

EXCLUSIVELY MARINE
Like all shearwaters, this is a seabird through and through.

WHEN SEEN

Oct — March

March to October.

WHERE SEEN
Breeds on rocky islands throughout Mediterranean, Portugal, Canaries; winters far offshore in open Atlantic; rare SW Britain and Ireland.

HABITAT AND INFO

SIMILAR SPECIES
Great Shearwater has dark cap and sharp white collar; dark marks on underside.

Black bill

Dark cap

94

Great Shearwater
Sooty Shearwater

COMMON NAME	Great Shearwater
SPECIES	Puffinus gravis
FAMILY	Procellariidae
ORDER	Procellariiformes

ORDER	Procellariiformes
FAMILY	Procellariidae
SPECIES	Puffinus griseus
COMMON NAME	Sooty Shearwater

Great Shearwater is large and elegant, with very long wings. Its dark cap and white collar are distinctive.

Sooty Shearwater is dark all over except for its underwing. It is very angular and heavy-bodied.

GREAT
LENGTH / 43–51cm (17–20in)
WINGSPAN / 105–122cm (41–48in)
WEIGHT / 720–950g (25–43oz)

■ **STATUS /** Secure

SOOTY
40–51cm (15½–20in)
95–110cm (37–43in)
700–970g (25–34oz)

Secure

SCALE v Woodpigeon

These two large, long-winged, oceanic shearwaters from the Southern Hemisphere visit European waters in the autumn. They fly over the ocean in the fiercest gales, riding up-currents and exploiting the winds to carry them over vast distances. They are quite gregarious, but small numbers of both species often mix loosely with bigger flocks of Manx Shearwaters. Of the two, the Great Shearwater is much the rarer in western Europe. Sooty Shearwaters are regular visitors to the North Sea, moving in from the north and often seen close to north-east British coasts as they return northward.

FEEDING
They eat small fish and squid, caught in shallow dives.

BREEDING
Great Shearwaters breed in burrows on the South Atlantic island of Tristan da Cunha, while Sooty Shearwaters breed in the Falklands.

MIGRATION
Both species migrate in a loop around the North Atlantic from their southern breeding grounds.

Great Shearwater (above)
White underside with dark belly and wingpit smudges (white on Cory's).

Sooty Shearwater (below)
Very narrow, angled or straight wings, pot belly; can be confused with dark skuas gliding in strong wind with angled wings.

Narrow white rump crescent.

Great Shearwater
Rises in long, high arcs in strong winds; uses quicker, stiffer wing beats than Cory's in a light breeze.

Great Shearwater
Dark brown, sharply defined cap (diffused on Cory's) and black bill (pale on Cory's).

Dark Balearic Shearwater is smaller, more Manx-like, with blunter, straighter wings.

Sooty Shearwater
All dark except for paler underwing panel; Sooty tilts over onto wingtip in long glides.

OCEAN TOURIST
The Great Shearwater performs huge migrations around the Atlantic.

WHEN SEEN

Sept
July
July to September.

WHERE SEEN
Offshore, open ocean; Sooty frequent UK; Great rare British Isles.

HABITAT AND INFO

Levantine Shearwater

SCALE v Woodpigeon

LENGTH / 30–36cm (11¾–14in)
WINGSPAN / 76–89cm (30–35in)
WEIGHT / 350–420g (12½–15oz)

■ STATUS / Vulnerable

A relatively short-headed, short-tailed, Manx-type shearwater, looking fairly compact, with slim wings but a chunky body, and with a rather fast, low, scurrying flight. Its feet project beyond tail – an identifiable feature separating it from the Manx Shearwater.

Traditionally all European, "Manx" shearwaters have been treated as one species. Now it is clear that the Mediterranean birds deserve specific status, and must be split further into the Levantine Shearwater in the east and the Balearic Shearwater in the west. The Levantine is closest to the Manx in its clean, brown-and-white appearance. It is the species often glimpsed speeding through the straits at Istanbul, or seen floating in rafts off Greek beaches or from ferries passing between the Greek islands.

FEEDING
It catches fish in shallow plunges from the surface.

VOICE
This bird is a nocturnal visitor to its nest, where it is noisy. It is silent at sea.

BREEDING
It nests in a deep burrow, laying a single egg that hatches after 48–52 days.

MIGRATION
It probably remains in the Mediterranean and Black Sea all year.

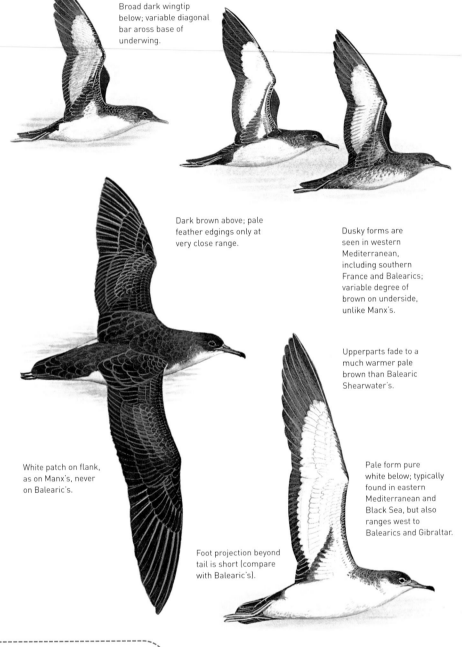

Broad dark wingtip below; variable diagonal bar aross base of underwing.

Dark brown above; pale feather edgings only at very close range.

Dusky forms are seen in western Mediterranean, including southern France and Balearics; variable degree of brown on underside, unlike Manx's.

Upperparts fade to a much warmer pale brown than Balearic Shearwater's.

White patch on flank, as on Manx's, never on Balearic's.

Pale form pure white below; typically found in eastern Mediterranean and Black Sea, but also ranges west to Balearics and Gibraltar.

Foot projection beyond tail is short (compare with Balearic's).

White vent on pale birds.

SQUAT SHEARWATER
This bird looks a little less elegant and elongated than a Manx Shearwater.

WHEN SEEN

All year.

WHERE SEEN
Breeds very locally in S France, Sardinia, Italy, Balkans, Greek Islands, Crete; widespread in E Mediterranean and Black Sea.

HABITAT AND INFO

SIMILAR SPECIES
Manx Shearwater is blacker above, purer white below, including underwing; feet shorter than tail tip.

Short legs

Greater contrast

Balearic Shearwater

A rather long, slim, dusky shearwater, with a long neck and longer toes than the very similar Levantine and Manx Shearwaters.

LENGTH / 34–38cm (13½–15in)
WINGSPAN / 85–90cm (33½–35½in)
WEIGHT / 490–570g (17–20oz)

■ **STATUS /** Endangered

SCALE v Woodpigeon

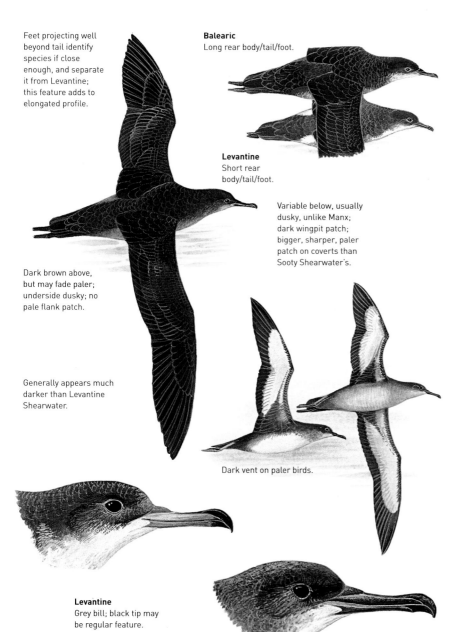

Feet projecting well beyond tail identify species if close enough, and separate it from Levantine; this feature adds to elongated profile.

Balearic
Long rear body/tail/foot.

Levantine
Short rear body/tail/foot.

Variable below, usually dusky, unlike Manx; dark wingpit patch; bigger, sharper, paler patch on coverts than Sooty Shearwater's.

Dark brown above, but may fade paler; underside dusky; no pale flank patch.

Generally appears much darker than Levantine Shearwater.

Dark vent on paler birds.

Levantine
Grey bill; black tip may be regular feature.

Balearic
Longer, all-dark bill.

Closely resembling the Manx and Levantine Shearwaters, this is a rare bird of the western Mediterranean, with only a few thousand pairs known. It moves out into the Atlantic and North Sea after breeding, so despite its rarity it may be seen by seabird-watchers in north-west Europe.

FEEDING
It catches fish and squid by plunging from the air and surface. Large flocks gather over shoals and follow fishing boats.

VOICE
Like the Manx and Levantine Shearwaters, it makes noisy visits to its nesting colonies at night, but at sea it is quiet.

BREEDING
One egg is incubated for 52 days. The chick does not fly for a further 72 days.

MIGRATION
Breeding is very early and most leave the Mediterranean from May onward, moulting off western France in late summer and autumn.

DUSKY BROWN SHEARWATER
The smudgy, brownish appearance is characteristic.

WHEN SEEN

All year; off Britain and France mostly June to October.

WHERE SEEN
Breeds Balearics.

HABITAT AND INFO

SIMILAR SPECIES
Sooty Shearwater has bigger, heavier body; much blacker overall with narrower white underwing patch.

Much blacker

Longer wings

Manx Shearwater

LENGTH / 35cm (14in)
WINGSPAN / 76–82cm (30–32in)
WEIGHT / 350–450g (12½–16oz)

■ **STATUS /** Secure

SCALE v Pigeon

A stiff-winged, low-flying seabird, flashing white beneath during frequent tilts onto wingtip. It holds its wings straight and rather stiff in glides between bursts of fast and shallow wing beats. It comes to land only at night at colonies, or when blown inland by gales.

This is the common North Atlantic shearwater: a small, fast-moving, black-and-white bird of the open ocean. Long, straggling lines fly low over the waves, their wingtips almost shearing the water, while resting flocks sit on the sea in elongated rafts.

FEEDING
Manx Shearwaters dive from the surface or just above to snatch small fish, sometimes in excited groups.

VOICE
Noisy at the colony, they create a unique, maniacal chorus as they return to their nesting burrows at night. At sea they are silent.

BREEDING
Nests in colonies on offshore islands and remote mainland cliffs, in burrows dug in turf, or among rocks on high, barren hills. The single chick does not return to breed until 5–8 years old.

MIGRATION
After breeding they move to the mid-Atlantic, far offshore. Many pass by headlands in summer and autumn, especially in onshore winds, all around the UK but most commonly in the north and west, and around Ireland.

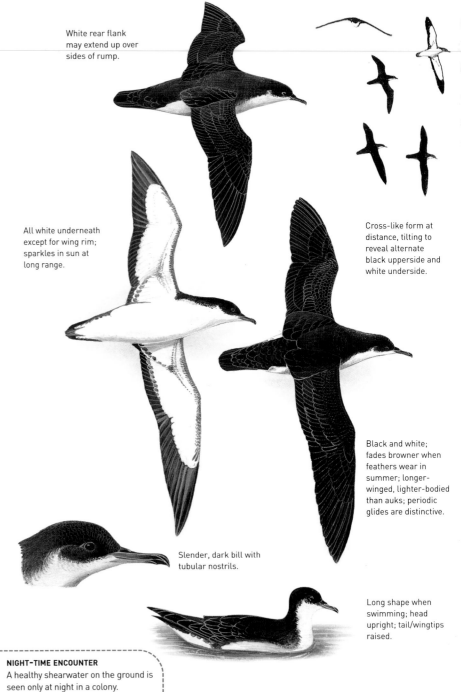

White rear flank may extend up over sides of rump.

All white underneath except for wing rim; sparkles in sun at long range.

Cross-like form at distance, tilting to reveal alternate black upperside and white underside.

Black and white; fades browner when feathers wear in summer; longer-winged, lighter-bodied than auks; periodic glides are distinctive.

Slender, dark bill with tubular nostrils.

Long shape when swimming; head upright; tail/wingtips raised.

NIGHT-TIME ENCOUNTER
A healthy shearwater on the ground is seen only at night in a colony.

WHEN SEEN

Oct
April

April to October.

WHERE SEEN
Islands from S Iceland to N France; frequent in offshore waters, but oceanic in winter.

HABITAT AND INFO

SIMILAR SPECIES
Fulmar is bigger, heavier silhouette, especially head and broad-based tail; paler back in good light.

Broad pale tail

White head

Leach's Petrel
Storm Petrel

ORDER	FAMILY	SPECIES	COMMON NAME
Procellariiformes	Hydrobatidae	Oceanodroma leucorhoa	Leach's Petrel
Procellariiformes	Hydrobatidae	Hydrobates pelagicus	Storm Petrel

	LEACH'S	STORM
LENGTH /	19–22cm (7½–8¾in)	14–18cm (5½–7in)
WINGSPAN /	43–48cm (17–19in)	36–39cm (14–15½in)
WEIGHT /	40–50g (1½–1¾oz)	20–30g (¾–1oz)
■ STATUS /	Vulnerable	Vulnerable

SCALE v Woodpigeon

Leach's Petrel is angular, the size of a Black Tern and has an erratic, bounding, twisting flight with frequent glides.

Storm Petrel is more like a Swallow, swooping and fluttering low over the sea on swept-back wings.

These two tiny, dark seabirds look ill-suited to life at sea. They are delicately built, barely bigger than sparrows, and are the most appealing creatures. Yet they are oceanic for most of the year, coming to land only to nest – and then only in darkness.

FEEDING
They fly low over the waves, seeking tiny crustaceans, fish, jellyfish, and squid: pattering, hovering, and dipping to the surface to snatch food without alighting and never diving.

VOICE
They are silent at sea, but have soft, purring calls at the nest.

BREEDING
Storm Petrels breed on many western islands, but Leach's Petrels are found on only a handful of remote islets between northern Scotland and Iceland. Both birds nest in crevices in walls or broken rocks. The single egg does not hatch for more than 40 days. Juveniles will not breed for 4–5 years, spending their time over the mid-Atlantic.

MIGRATION
Both move out to sea in autumn; Leach's is more prone to be blown into coasts or even inland.

Storm Petrel
Distinct white bar under wing (not on Leach's); sooty with broad white rump.

Leach's Petrel, female (below) Broad, paler band across inner wing (not on Storm's).

Angular, pointed wings.

May skip across water with feet.

Leach's Petrel, male
Tail notched or forked; white rump divided by dark line or hint of dark notch; long-tailed birds presumed male.

Storm Petrel (right)
Rounder wingtips than Leach's, tapered to a shorter point when swept back to form less angular, broader-based shape.

Storm Petrel

Tail rounded.

Leach's Petrel

Rump wraps around slightly in side view.

Often trails feet, skips on surface.

NOCTURNAL RETURN
Storm Petrels come to their nesting crevices only in darkness.

WHEN SEEN

Oct — April

April to October.

WHERE SEEN
Breeds on a few islands in NW Europe; at sea; offshore in autumn storms.

HABITAT AND INFO

Gannet

ORDER Pelecaniformes   **FAMILY** Sulidae   **SPECIES** Morus bassana   **COMMON NAME** Gannet

LENGTH / 90–100cm (35½–39in)
WINGSPAN / 1.7–1.8m (5½–6ft)
WEIGHT / 2.8–3.2kg (6–7lb)

■ **STATUS /** Vulnerable

SCALE v Pigeon

A powerful seabird with long, narrow wings held out straight and pointed head protruding on thick neck. Adults are gleaming white; immatures are dark or piebald. It has a distinctive dive from height into the sea.

The Gannet is the most dramatic and impressive North Atlantic seabird simply because of its size and power. It has a charismatic presence that smaller birds lack. A Gannet at sea looks dynamic and elegant. A closer view at the colony reveals a fascinating bird, with its dagger-like bill, forward-facing eyes, fluttering gular (throat) pouch, its strange, striped, completely webbed feet, and peculiarly stereotyped communication postures. In normal flight in still air, a Gannet moves steadily over the open sea, its wings held out straight and beating with a regular, shallow action, flexing at the tip. Given a good wind, however, the Gannet shows itself a master of its element, soaring on up-currents over the waves, frequently banking onto one wingtip and travelling for miles with scarcely a wing beat.

FEEDING
Gannets eat fish: usually fast muscular fish such as mackerel and herring, which are difficult to catch and subdue. To do so they fly over the sea, using their sharp eyes to spot the fish, then dive headlong from the air – either from a great height with a loud splash, or from low level, spearing into the water at an angle – to reach deep down to the shoals of potential prey.

DISPLAY AND VOICE
Loud, rhythmic, repetitive calls create an almost mechanical chorus at the colony. The displays are ritualized communications between paired birds and with other pairs nearby. Males advertise nest sites with a headshaking action, but attack approaching females with a bite to the nape. Reunited pairs greet each other standing breast-to-breast, shaking their heads and fencing with their bills; each will preen the head and neck of the other. When one of the pair is about to fly off, leaving the other to protect the nest, it points its head skyward to make its intention clear.

BREEDING
A breeding colony in full swing is a vibrant, noisy scene, full of action. The nests are built of seaweed, discarded netting, and twine on broad ledges, usually on islands but increasingly on mainland cliffs. A single chick fledges after 90 days. It will not breed for 5–6 years, although it may survive to 15–20 years of age.

MIGRATION
A fledged Gannet flies south to the ocean off the west African coast for its first year of life. Mature birds spend the winter in the North Sea and North Atlantic.

Adult
Against a dark sea, adult looks sparkling white and jet black; plunges headlong from a height with a great splash, but may dive from low level at shallow angle.

Black wingtips.

Yellow-buff head fades in winter.

Pointed tail.

Looks slender-bodied at long range, but is really quite deep-chested and solidly built; a powerful flier.

WHEN SEEN

All year; at colonies March to October.

WHERE SEEN
Breeds in isolated colonies from N France, UK to Iceland; widespread off coasts.

HABITAT AND INFO

SIMILAR SPECIES
Juvenile Great Black-backed Gull has paler rump above rounded tail; wings more bowed; bill blunter.

Square tail   White rump

Juvenile
Dusky grey with fine white speckling.

Older juvenile
Whiter on body; wings become chequered.

HEAVY TAKEOFF
Gannets rise from the water in a series of clumsy hops.

Juvenile

Beware similarity with immature gulls, especially Great Black-backed, which can approach sub-adult Gannet pattern, but have blunter head and tail.

Eyes face forward, set in broad, round head.

Adult, breeding
All-white except for rich buff head and black wingtips.

Juvenile

Black facial skin.

Striped toes of adult visible at close range.

The juvenile grows quickly at the nest, eventually refusing food when it is already too fat and heavy to fly; it flops into the sea and swims away, starving until it is light enough to take off again.

All four toes joined by web (like Cormorants' but unlike gulls').

Near adult
Yellow head, wings spotted black.

FLIGHT PATTERN
Flight direct, with slow, steady rhythm in calm air; in wind, frequent glides; in gales, rises high over waves on wingtip in fast, powerful action.

DID YOU KNOW?
Gannets dive for fish from a height of up to 25m (80ft) and may reach 100km (60 miles) per hour when they plunge into the water. An extensive network of air sacs between the muscles and skin around the base of the bill cushions this impact. The dive typically creates a narrow, upright splash of white water that is visible from a long distance; but a more angled dive may have a much smoother entry.

?

Cormorant

SCALE v Pigeon

LENGTH / 80–100cm (31½–39in)
WINGSPAN / 1.3–1.6m (4¼–5¼ft)
WEIGHT / 2–2.5kg (4½–5½lb)

■ **STATUS /** Secure

Cormorant is goose-sized but more slender, with longer tail and slim, hook-tipped bill. It is often found in small, loose flocks or at nesting colonies on cliffs or in tall trees. It flies well, often in lines or V-formation at moderate height, or in ones and twos at much greater heights on long fishing trips.

Cormorants eat fish and, although there is no evidence that they cause lasting damage to fish stocks, they have been vilified by anglers. Hundreds are shot under licence, even though there is no apparent benefit to the fisheries as a result. Yet to others, Cormorants are a welcome sight, especially in Britain where such large, dramatic birds are uncommon. Some colonies have developed inland, in the tops of trees beside lakes, reservoirs, and gravel pits. These are spectacular places, especially when groups of birds return from fishing trips, flying in at a height and spiralling or twisting down in aerobatic dives. On the water, Cormorants are goose-sized but much flatter, with lower backs and slender bills. A close view of the bill reveals a sturdy hooked tip, ideal for handling slippery, muscular fish. After feeding, Cormorants often stand on the shore, on buoys or in tree tops with their wings half outspread. Birds adopting this attitude have always been assumed to be drying their wings, but it may have more to do with the digestion of a good meal.

FEEDING
They take fish of many kinds, from both fresh- and saltwater. In lakes and rivers, they prefer eels, but they may catch almost anything that is available and of suitable size.

DISPLAY AND VOICE
At the nest, they are noisy and display with fanned tails and half-open wings raised up from the body. The white face patches, long white nape plumes, and white thigh patches are all shown off to advantage by the display. Their calls are deep, croaking notes, while young in the nest make a higher, chattering chorus.

BREEDING
Cormorants nest in colonies that may be from a few to hundreds of nests strong. The nest is a great heap of sticks or, at the coast, of seaweed, piled up in the fork of a tree or on a broad cliff ledge. The area around each nest soon becomes liberally splashed with white droppings, and trees may eventually die from the effects. The clutch of 3–4 eggs hatches within 30–31 days. It is a further 50 days before the young first fly.

MIGRATION
Some Cormorants that breed on the Continent reach the UK, and UK breeders (and especially immatures) move south to Spain. Even those living inland make long and irregular movements.

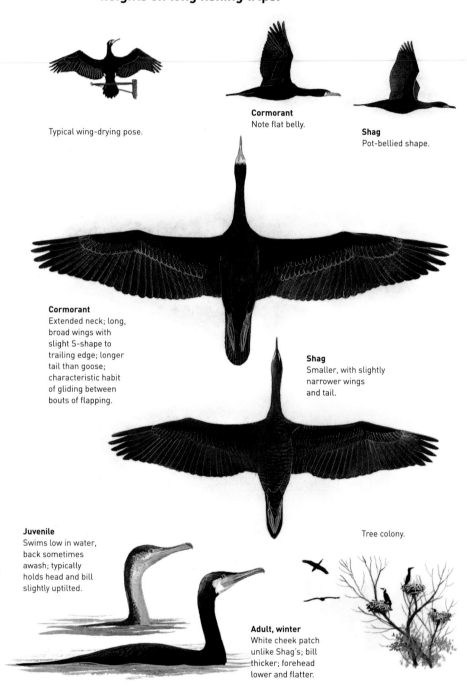

Typical wing-drying pose.

Cormorant
Note flat belly.

Shag
Pot-bellied shape.

Cormorant
Extended neck; long, broad wings with slight S-shape to trailing edge; longer tail than goose; characteristic habit of gliding between bouts of flapping.

Shag
Smaller, with slightly narrower wings and tail.

Juvenile
Swims low in water, back sometimes awash; typically holds head and bill slightly uptilted.

Tree colony.

Adult, winter
White cheek patch unlike Shag's; bill thicker; forehead lower and flatter.

WHEN SEEN

All year.

WHERE SEEN
Breeds locally by coasts of UK and Ireland, and a few places inland; also breeds by coasts of NW Europe, rivers of E Europe; more widespread in winter on large lakes, estuaries, and sheltered coastal waters.

HABITAT AND INFO

SIMILAR SPECIES
Juvenile Shag has thinner bill; rounder head with steep forehead; snaky neck; darker beneath.

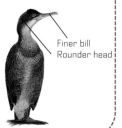

Finer bill
Rounder head

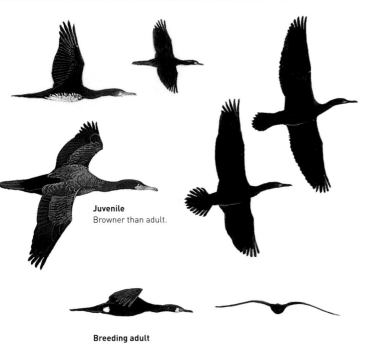

Juvenile
Browner than adult.

Breeding adult
White thigh patch never
seen on Shag.

TYPICAL POSE
Cormorants often hold their wings
open, but the reason why is uncertain.

Breeding adult
White thigh patch
develops in late winter.

Winter adult

Juvenile
Dark type.

Shag

Juvenile

Adult
Race *sinensis:* some
British birds have as
much white; face
patterns variable.

Sub-adult

Short, thick, dark legs;
all toes joined by webs
like Gannet's.

FLIGHT PATTERN
Flight shape is goose-like,
but slender-bodied
and longer-tailed. The
Cormorant often glides.

DID YOU KNOW?
All four toes are joined by a thick, leathery web, a feature that is
shared by the gannets, boobies, shags, and pelicans, which are all part
of the same worldwide order – the Pelecaniformes, The shape and
structure of the wings, although at first looking rather different, also
reveal a close relationship between these fish-eating birds.

Shag

SCALE v Pigeon

LENGTH / 65–80cm (25½–31½in)
WINGSPAN / 90–105cm (35½–41in)
WEIGHT / 1.7–2.3kg (3¾–5lb)

■ **STATUS /** Secure

Shag is slightly smaller, rounder-headed than Cormorant, with a slimmer bill, steeper forehead, and more snaky neck. It generally flies low over water in small, irregular groups. Large flocks may gather in good fishing areas. It is often seen on rocks and cliffs, but not in trees inland.

Shags are more strictly marine than Cormorants. They are scarce inland, and even at the coast they rarely fly over headlands. Small groups are seen flying low over the sea, looking much quicker in their actions than heavier Cormorants. They may concentrate in bigger flocks to feed in shallow bays and tide races, and they are equally at home in the roughest seas just off fearsome rocks.

FEEDING
Fish form their staple food: mostly quite small fish, especially sandeels taken at a considerable depth.

DISPLAY AND VOICE
Shags indulge in various head-wagging and aggressive displays at the nest, producing raucous calls and harsh, rattling notes, both in alarm or to threaten intruders.

BREEDING
They nest on well-sheltered cliff ledges, often just inside caves. Some are low down but they may be 100m (330ft) above the waves. Up to eight eggs are laid and hatch in 28–31 days. Usually two chicks fledge, after 53 days.

MIGRATION
There is dispersal along coasts after the breeding season. Far northern birds and immatures go farthest south.

Mediterranean
Adult has short crest in spring.

Breeding adult, spring
Upstanding crest unlike any Cormorant.

Flies low over sea with rapid wing beats.

Juvenile (right)
Wing panel distinctive: whiter on Mediterranean race.

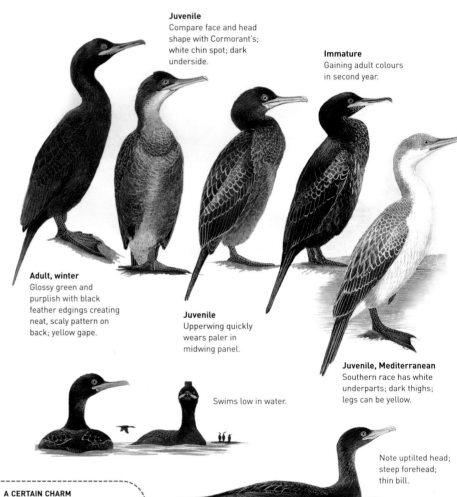

Juvenile
Compare face and head shape with Cormorant's; white chin spot; dark underside.

Immature
Gaining adult colours in second year.

Adult, winter
Glossy green and purplish with black feather edgings creating neat, scaly pattern on back; yellow gape.

Juvenile
Upperwing quickly wears paler in midwing panel.

Juvenile, Mediterranean
Southern race has white underparts; dark thighs; legs can be yellow.

Swims low in water.

Note uptilted head; steep forehead; thin bill.

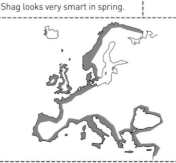

A CERTAIN CHARM
Unconventionally beautiful, the Shag looks very smart in spring.

WHEN SEEN

All year.

WHERE SEEN
Appears on the coasts of NW and W Europe, and around the Mediterranean.

HABITAT AND INFO

SIMILAR SPECIES
Juvenile Cormorant is whiter below; thicker bill runs into flatter forehead; slower, heavier roll when diving.

Flatter head

Whiter belly

Pygmy Cormorant

A small, handsome, but stub-billed freshwater cormorant, with bronze or chestnut brown on the head and long, fine, whitish plumes on the head and breast in spring.

LENGTH / 45–55cm (17½–21in)
WINGSPAN / 75–90cm (29½–35in)
WEIGHT / 570–870g (20–31oz)

■ STATUS / Vulnerable

SCALE v Pigeon

This small, chunky cormorant is a freshwater species, restricted to reed-fringed lakes and rivers in south-east Europe. It is often found in mixed colonies with egrets and herons, but is rare and declining, and may even be threatened.

FEEDING
It eats mainly fish, which it catches by diving in shallow water. It is usually solitary when fishing.

DISPLAY AND VOICE
Posturing in spring reveals fine, spiky, hair-like crest feathers. Breeding birds give deep, guttural calls at the nest.

BREEDING
It nests in reeds and waterside bushes, often over water, with 4–6 eggs hatching in 27–30 days. The young do not fly until 70 days old.

MIGRATION
Breeders from the Balkans move toward coastal lagoons and marshes in winter. Black Sea birds make longer southward migrations.

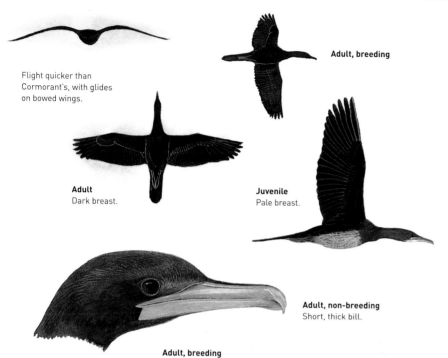

Flight quicker than Cormorant's, with glides on bowed wings.

Adult, breeding

Adult
Dark breast.

Juvenile
Pale breast.

Adult, non-breeding
Short, thick bill.

Adult, breeding
Gains bronze or brown head and fine white plumes.

Rounded head, steep forehead.

Adult, non-breeding
Duller brown head loses white plumes; some have white on chin.

Long tail and heavy body.

STIFFLY OUTSTRETCHED
The Pygmy Cormorant has a wide, straight-winged drying posture.

WHEN SEEN

All year.

WHERE SEEN
On reed-fringed rivers and lagoons in SE Europe; rare on coast.

HABITAT AND INFO

SIMILAR SPECIES
Cormorant is bigger; shorter tail; longer, thick bill and flatter head shape; heavier flight.

Long wings

Short tail

Bittern

LENGTH / 70–80cm (27½–31½in)
WINGSPAN / 120–140cm (47–55in)
WEIGHT / 0.9–1.1kg (2–2½lb)

SCALE v Woodpigeon

■ STATUS / Vulnerable

A richly marked, golden-buff, heron-like bird, with a thick neck, big green feet, broad wings, and a dagger bill.

Restricted as it is to dense reed beds, the Bittern is a rarely seen, mysterious bird of the marshes. If it appears close to the water's edge, it is still difficult to spot because its camouflage is remarkably effective against golden reed stems. In flight, it is an odd, unlikely-looking bird: vaguely owl-like with bowed wings, trailing feet, and a long, thickly feathered, half-withdrawn neck.

FEEDING
It stands still or strides slowly forward looking for fish, which it catches with a typically heron-like strike, grabbing its prey in its bill.

VOICE
Males produce a deep, booming *whoomp*, as if blowing across the wide neck of a large bottle. The calls carry for miles and can be analyzed to identify individual males.

BREEDING
The nest is a large heap of reeds. The 5–6 eggs hatch in 25–26 days.

MIGRATION
In winter, many fly west to avoid frost on the European mainland, some to regular wintering sites in quite small marshes.

Black crown.

Arched wings show it is a heron, but looks more compact; otherwise resembles a huge owl in flight.

Pale forewing shows as broad band in flight.

Thick feathers conceal kinked neck in flight.

Upperparts have complex blotches and bars, usually looking pale at a distance.

Eyes face forward; blackish moustache.

Striped foreneck.

Neck much thicker than that of immature Purple Heron.

Flies high over breeding areas in spring.

Long toes provide support when body tilts forward, and help grasp reed stems above water level.

Leans forward when fishing; may shake body from side to side.

HIDING IN THE REEDS
A Bittern in the open is a rare sight.

WHEN SEEN

All year, but more widely in winter.

WHERE SEEN
Reed beds; rarely other waterside places; very local, all Europe.

HABITAT AND INFO

SIMILAR SPECIES
Juvenile Purple Heron has more slender, much thinner neck; longer legs; much less streaked.

Plainer back

Long, slender neck

COMMON NAME
Squacco Heron

SPECIES
Ardeola ralloides

FAMILY
Ardeidae

ORDER
Ciconiiformes

Squacco Heron

A squat, well-camouflaged heron, it is often hard to spot. In summer, it is quite pink. In winter, it is much duller in colour.

LENGTH / 44–47cm (17½–18½in)
WINGSPAN / 71–86cm (28–34in)
WEIGHT / 230–350g (8–12½oz)

■ STATUS / Vulnerable

SCALE v Woodpigeon

Breeding adult
Black-edged head plumes.

Bill blue and black in spring.

White wings contrast with dark back, unlike all-white egrets; sudden shock of white as bird takes flight.

Shows little white when standing, but reveals eye-catching white wings in flight.

Juvenile
Darkest, most streaked plumage.

First winter

Non-breeding adult
No head plumes; bill yellow and black.

Typically stands leaning forward, head and neck withdrawn into shoulders in tapered oval shape; lunge for fish reveals startlingly long neck.

Immature
Broad, soft neck streaks.

MINIATURE HERON
The oval body and spray of dark plumes at the nape are distinctive.

A beautiful little heron, pinkish-buff or sandy at rest, the Squacco reveals startlingly white wings when it flies. It is usually seen in waterside vegetation or on floating weed, either on or beside rivers and still lakes.

FEEDING

It catches small aquatic creatures in its bill after long, patient waiting and watching. It is much less active in its feeding than the egrets, preferring to wait for prey to come within range.

DISPLAY AND VOICE

Usually silent except for an occasional harsh *karr* at dusk, or during a pairing display, which involves leaning forward with outstretched neck, passing sticks from bill to bill, and temporary blushing of face and bill colours.

BREEDING

It nests in a thicket of willows or dense reeds, in a loose colony or with other herons and egrets. The 4–6 eggs hatch after 22–24 days.

MIGRATION

In autumn, Squacco Herons move south to Africa, returning in late March and April.

WHEN SEEN

Sept — March

March to September.

WHERE SEEN
Reedy marshes, swamps, richly vegetated rivers; scattered in S Europe; very rare in the UK.

HABITAT AND INFO

SIMILAR SPECIES
Female Little Bittern is smaller with darker cap and back; dark wingtips in flight.

Dark cap

Dark back

Little Bittern

LENGTH / 33–38cm (13–15in)
WINGSPAN / 49–58cm (19–23in)
WEIGHT / 140–150g (5–5¼oz)

■ STATUS / Vulnerable

SCALE v Woodpigeon

A small, shy, round-winged swamp bird with a short tail and a dagger bill.

This tiny, colourful heron is very secretive and hard to see, which is a pity for such a handsome species. It is often glimpsed as a Moorhen-sized bird with big, pale wing patches, flying low and flat over a reed bed or riverside marsh before dropping out of sight into the reeds.

FEEDING
It is most active around dusk, moving to good feeding sites at the water's edge, where it catches small fish, frogs, newts, and large insects.

VOICE
During courtship the male produces a monotonous song: a hollow *kok* repeated every two seconds mostly at dusk.

BREEDING
The nest is a pile of reed stems built in willows or reeds over shallow water. The 5–6 eggs hatch after an incubation of 17–19 days.

MIGRATION
Little Bitterns leave Europe between August and October, spending the winter south of the Sahara. They return from Africa in March and April.

Female

Male

In flight, both sexes look front-heavy.

Clambers to top of reeds and flutters up to take flight.

Both sexes show big pale patches on the inner wing, contrasted with black: an easy identification mark.

Juvenile
More streaked than female; wing coverts mottled; cap paler brown.

Female
More striped than male; cap dark; wing coverts buff; back lined with buff and white.

Male, breeding
Bright, clean-looking, warm buff and green-black; greyer on cheeks; softly striped on neck.

IMMACULATE HUNTER
Smaller bitterns like the male Little Bittern are beautifully neat.

WHEN SEEN

Oct — March

Late March to October.

WHERE SEEN
Reed beds, reed-fringed rivers; locally through S Europe and north to the Baltic states; vagrants to UK seen mostly in spring.

HABITAT AND INFO

SIMILAR SPECIES
Juvenile Night Heron is heavier; thicker bill; more uniform upperwing.

Pale spots

Bulky body

Night Heron

A thickset, sociable heron of well-wooded watersides. Active at twilight and at night, it often flies in small groups that rise and scatter if disturbed at the roost.

LENGTH / 58–65cm (23–25½in)
WINGSPAN / 90–100cm (35–39in)
WEIGHT / 600–800g (21–28oz)

■ STATUS / Secure

SCALE v Woodpigeon

A handsome, medium-sized heron, most active at dusk and dawn, the Night Heron is widespread in five continents but has a restricted distribution in Europe, where suitable wet habitats are few and far between. It spends the day in a willow thicket or waterside tree and moves at dusk to find good feeding beside a lake or river.

FEEDING
Usually active after dark, it catches fish, frogs, insects, small mammals, and small birds.

DISPLAY AND VOICE
Males display by stretching erect, swaying from one foot to the other, then gradually subsiding into the usual hunched pose. The usual call is a crow-like *quok*.

BREEDING
Night Heron nests are fragile but become increasingly robust after several years' use. Small colonies nest in reeds, bushes, or tall trees, often with other species. The 3–5 eggs hatch after 21–22 days.

MIGRATION
Night Herons migrate to Africa in October and return in March and April.

Juvenile
Brown, spotted with white.

Adult, breeding
Looks pale except for a black saddle; the wings are uniform, unlike Grey Heron's.

Adult, breeding
(below left)
Spring adults have two long, white plumes from the nape.

Adult   Juvenile
Short-necked, bow-winged in flight.

Typical hunched pose.

Legs pink-red in spring.

Juvenile
Brown with white, drop-shaped spots above.

Immature, first year
Loses pale spots.

Immature, second year
More or less mottled above; streaked on breast.

SPOTTED JUVENILE
Despite the extensive dull brown, immatures can look pale.

WHEN SEEN

Oct   March

Late March to October.

WHERE SEEN
Rivers, lakes, fishponds, and adjacent thickets; locally through Europe north to Netherlands; rare in UK – vagrants to UK seen mostly in spring

HABITAT AND INFO

SIMILAR SPECIES
Grey Heron is much bigger; longer-legged; longer-necked; much heavier flight on long, bowed wings.

Pale grey back

Long legs

Great White Egret

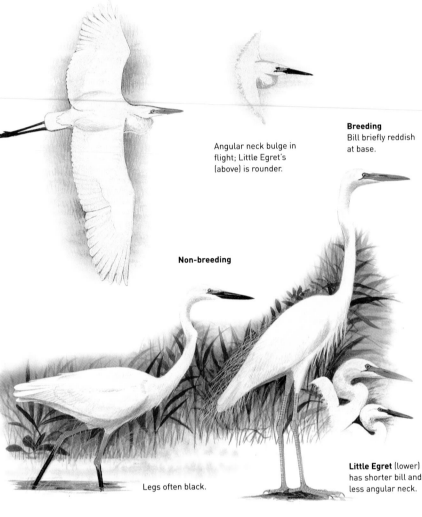

LENGTH / 85–102cm (33½–40in)
WINGSPAN / 1.4–1.7m (4½–5½ft)
WEIGHT / 1–1.5kg (2¼–3¼lb)

SCALE v Pigeon

■ **STATUS /** Secure

A very large white heron, at least Grey Heron-sized, but more like a giant Little Egret in appearance and actions.

Also known as the Great White Heron, this large, dramatic bird has the white plumage of a Little Egret but the size and dagger bill of a Grey Heron. It is a particularly angular bird, with a long, slim, kinked neck, which makes a deep bulge when its head is withdrawn in flight.

FEEDING
It searches for fish to snatch up in its bill, using the patient, waterside wait-and-see or more active hunting methods typical of herons.

DISPLAY AND VOICE
The courtship and territorial displays involve ritual postures that show off the elongated plumes to best effect in beautiful and dramatic performances. Calls are short, low, harsh monosyllables.

BREEDING
Nests are usually in trees, made of sticks and lined with finer stems. The clutch varies from 2–5 eggs, which hatch after 25 days.

MIGRATION
Most move south in winter, but some wander erratically into western Europe.

Angular neck bulge in flight; Little Egret's (above) is rounder.

Breeding
Bill briefly reddish at base.

Non-breeding

Little Egret (lower) has shorter bill and less angular neck.

Legs often black.

Great White Heron

Little Egret

Yellow on bill outside breeding season; Little Egret has blue-black bill all year.

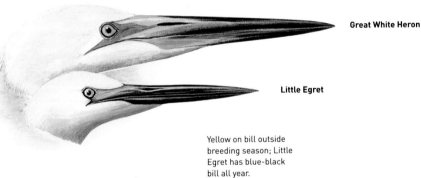

DRAMATIC DISPLAY
Courtship involves striking poses and a wide spray of plumes.

WHEN SEEN

All year, but mostly March to October.

WHERE SEEN
Very localized in SE Europe; increasingly in the Netherlands, S France, and as a vagrant to Britain.

HABITAT AND INFO

SIMILAR SPECIES
Little Egret is smaller, with finer dark bill; black legs with yellow feet.

Contrasting yellow feet

Shorter neck

Little Egret

A small, startlingly-white heron-like bird of both fresh- and saltwater margins. It nests in colonies in trees, often with other herons.

LENGTH / 55–65cm (21½–25½in)
WINGSPAN / 88–106cm (35–42in)
WEIGHT / 400–600g (14–21oz)

■ **STATUS /** Secure

SCALE v Pigeon

Little Egrets are fun-to-watch, superb, lively, elegant white herons. They are spreading in north-west Europe, but are most familiar in the warmer south.

FEEDING
Little Egrets wade in shallow water, sometimes belly-deep, often running to and fro to stir fish and other prey into tell-tale action and grasping them with their long, sharp beaks. They have a habit of perching on floating weed, flapping their half-open wings for balance.

DISPLAY AND VOICE
In display, Little Egrets make full use of their nuptial plumes: long, wispy, white back feathers and two slender head plumes. The voice is a nasal croak, not at all fitting for such a beautiful bird.

BREEDING
They nest in tree colonies, often with other herons and egrets. Each pair incubates 3–5 eggs in a stick nest for 25 days.

MIGRATION
In winter, most move south to the Mediterranean area or into north Africa, but some stay as far north as southern Britain.

Flight is heron-like with bowed wings, withdrawn neck, and trailing legs, but quite quick wing beats.

Non-breeding

Breeding
Spreads plumes of head, back, and breast in courtship display; bill grey-black, never yellow.

Non-breeding

Feeds in shallows, from rocks, or from floating vegetation; often dashes jerkily sideways with raised head and open wings.

Yellow feet distinctive, but beware muddy feet looking dark.

Yellow feet rule out other European egrets and herons.

AERIAL BALLET
In any situation, the Little Egret looks delicately elegant.

WHEN SEEN

All year, but mostly March to October.

WHERE SEEN
Southern and central Europe; increasingly in S Britain, with a few breeding since 1996.

HABITAT AND INFO

SIMILAR SPECIES
Great White Egret is bigger; longer-necked; often yellow on bill; paler legs.

Variable leg colour with dark feet

Longer neck and bill

Cattle Egret

LENGTH / 48–53cm (19–21in)
WINGSPAN / 82–95cm (32–37in)
WEIGHT / 300–400g (10½–14oz)

■ STATUS / Secure

SCALE v Woodpigeon

Small, gregarious egret, far less tied to watersides than the Little Egret, but usually nesting and roosting in trees near water.

In parts of Iberia, and also far more commonly in Africa and the Middle East, Cattle Egrets are a familiar sight along watersides, in fields with livestock or recently-tilled earth, on roadside verges, and even in town parks and rubbish tips. Adaptable, successful birds, they bring a touch of elegance to some of the world's poorest regions.

FEEDING
They often feed around the feet of cattle and horses (or take ticks from their backs), or follow the plough to snatch worms and grubs. They also eat frogs, lizards, insects, and offal.

DISPLAY AND VOICE
Most displays are at the nest, exploiting the birds' elegant, elongated plumes. Calls include hoarse, short notes and a rapid quack.

BREEDING
They nest in trees, in sizeable colonies, often with other egrets, ibises, and herons. The 4–5 eggs hatch after 22–26 days.

MIGRATION
Many move south in winter into Africa. A rare vagrant in north-west Europe, including Britain.

Flies fast, with head withdrawn and legs trailing; usually in flocks.

Adult, breeding
Bill becomes red in spring; face flushes red and green.

Adult, non-breeding

Immature
Dark bill turns yellow.

Non-breeding (below)
Yellow bill; dark legs (Little Egret has dark bill; yellow feet).

Breeding (left)
Buff plumes and cap; yellow to red bill; yellow or reddish legs; the only white egret with buff patches.

IMMACULATE WHITE
In non-breeding plumage, this is a startlingly white egret.

WHEN SEEN

All year.

WHERE SEEN
Wetlands and adjacent fields and trees, refuse tips; very local in Europe, mostly SW Spain; a few elsewhere in Iberia and extreme S France.

HABITAT AND INFO

SIMILAR SPECIES
Little Egret has dark bill; dark legs with yellow feet; finer, more tapered facial profile.

Yellow feet

Fine dark bill

Spoonbill

A big, heron-like bird of shallow water and reedy marshes, with a unique flattened bill tip. It is much sturdier and thicker-legged than the white egrets.

LENGTH / 80–90cm (31–35in)
WINGSPAN / 120–140cm (47–55in)
WEIGHT / 1–1.5kg (2¼–3¾lb)

■ **STATUS /** Endangered

SCALE v Woodpigeon

Flies with neck outstretched, unlike herons and egrets, more like swan.

Immature
Black wingtips.

Although white like an egret, the Spoonbill is a quite different bird, identifiable at great range. Its thick legs, solid build, and almost human walk (and its habit of feeding in small, tight groups) create a much more stable and sedate impression, although it can become quite agitated and move fast when chasing prey.

FEEDING
It typically walks slowly forward through shallow water, its bill half open and immersed, detecting prey by touch. It eats small fish, tadpoles, and other aquatic creatures.

DISPLAY AND VOICE
Pairs preen each other at the nest, stretch up their heads and bills to display the coloured skin beneath their throats, and spread their peculiar, spiky pineapple crests. They are usually silent birds.

BREEDING
They nest in colonies in reeds and tall trees, often with herons. The bulky stick nests hold 3–4 eggs, which hatch in 24–25 days.

MIGRATION
Moves south into Africa in the autumn. It is scarce in Britain.

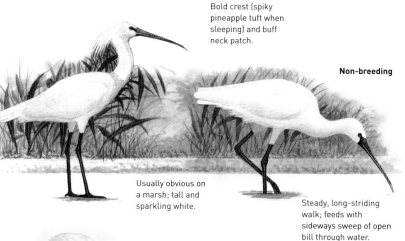

Breeding (left)
Bold crest (spiky pineapple tuft when sleeping) and buff neck patch.

Non-breeding

Usually obvious on a marsh; tall and sparkling white.

Steady, long-striding walk; feeds with sideways sweep of open bill through water.

Adult has variable yellow bill tip and throat patch.

Juvenile (far right)
Pink bill of young bird gradually darkens to black; yellow tip develops later.

DOWDY IMMATURE
Before striking adulthood, there is a dull-billed, nondescript stage.

WHEN SEEN

March to October.

WHERE SEEN
Freshwater lakes and reed beds, brackish lagoons; extremely local in Netherlands, Spain, E Europe.

HABITAT AND INFO

SIMILAR SPECIES
Great White Egret is more elegant; much longer-necked; thinner, dagger bill; head withdrawn in flight.

Dagger bill

Slender legs

Purple Heron

LENGTH / 78–90cm (30½–35½in)
WINGSPAN / 1.1–1.5m (3½–5ft)
WEIGHT / 1–1.5kg (2¼–3¾lb)

■ STATUS / Vulnerable

SCALE v Woodpigeon

A large, elegant, snaky-headed heron with a long, slim bill. In flight, it reveals rather narrow wings and the curved neck makes a deep, narrow bulge. The long legs and toes trail noticeably far beyond the tail.

This is a slender, snaky-necked southern heron of reed beds and dense marshes. It is often hard to see well, preferring to hide in reeds more like a Bittern than a Grey Heron. However, from time to time it appears on the edge of the marsh beside open water, perches in a low tree, or flies overhead on its way to a new feeding place. Whatever it is doing, it is an elegant bird: more finely-drawn than a Grey Heron, slightly longer and more slender in the bill, head, neck, and legs, and narrower in the wing. Compared to the Grey Heron, it is much more restricted to extensive wetlands with clean water invading tall marshland vegetation: it cannot make do with wet ditches, reservoir edges, or sea coasts like the more adaptable Grey. Nor does it use nesting platforms or nest in tall trees, and it is far less tolerant of human disturbance.

FEEDING

The Purple Heron usually feeds alone, mostly in the cover of waterside vegetation and typically in the early morning and evening. It stands silently, then swiftly darts out its long neck to snatch small fish or large aquatic insects. More rarely, it takes small snakes, birds, and voles. Fish prey includes bream, carp, perch, roach, sticklebacks, rudd, and eels.

DISPLAY AND VOICE

Rather quiet compared with the Grey Heron, the Purple Heron has a rough, rasping note, especially as it flies up when disturbed. It produces various raucous calls at the nest, and the male makes rhythmic rattles with his bill. Displays include a rather exaggerated stretch display compared with the Grey Heron's version, pointing its head and neck vertically upward for a moment before making a sudden deep bowing movement with back plumes raised; the male clatters his bill.

BREEDING

Most nests are built of dead reed stems among reeds, some of twigs in low bushes. The birds make new nests each year, often in small colonies. The 4–5 eggs are laid in May or June and incubated for 26 days by both parents. The chicks fly after about seven weeks. They are ready to breed themselves at one year old.

MIGRATION

European Purple Herons move south to Africa, south of the Sahara, in September and October, returning in March. A few reach Britain each spring, but do not breed. Juveniles tend to be more nomadic in late summer and reach areas well outside the usual breeding range.

Juvenile
No black crown; much browner than Grey Heron.

Immature
Second-year bird looks dark; plumage variable as adult colours gradually assumed.

Adult female
Tendency to have more buff, less clear grey, on wing coverts than male; raised head and neck extremely long and slim; very long bill.

Looks much darker than Grey Heron, more steely-grey, with sandy-buff plumes and chestnut flanks and thighs.

Juvenile
Rufous when first fledged, gradually becomes duller, browner or tawny; can look very pale.

Legs vivid orange-yellow with black front in spring.

Remarkably long toes.

WHEN SEEN

Oct   March

March to October.

WHERE SEEN

S and central European swamps and marshes; north to the Low Countries; rare visitor to UK.

HABITAT AND INFO

SIMILAR SPECIES

Grey Heron has no brown or rufous; broader wing base; less protruding feet; rounder neck shape in flight.

Smaller feet

Plain grey back

Adult
Dark rufous under forewing.

Juvenile
Paler sandy colour under forewing.

SNAKE-NECKED HERON
A Purple Heron has a long, slender neck merging into a long dagger bill.

Juvenile
Almost uniform pale rufous neck; pale buff "landing lights" on leading edge of wing.

Adult male
Forewing clear zinc-grey; often more buff on female; white "landing lights"; coiled neck striped black and chestnut.

FLIGHT PATTERN
Flight silhouettes reveal long wings with often prominent secondary bulge and narrow base; very deep neck; long legs. Sometimes flies in small flocks on passage, over land and at sea in the Mediterranean.

DID YOU KNOW?
While Purple Herons in Europe are largely known as birds of reed beds, in the tropics they frequently feed in mangrove swamps, where they may watch for fish from prominent perches on the mangrove tops. Sometimes, when a fish is seen in the middle of a lagoon, the heron will launch itself from the mangrove thicket and dive in to catch its prey in its bill.

Grey Heron

SCALE v Pigeon

LENGTH / 90–98cm (35½–39in)
WINGSPAN / 1.75–1.95m (5½–6½ft)
WEIGHT / 1–2.3kg (2–5lb)

■ **STATUS /** Secure

A large, upstanding bird, ghostly grey in most lights, contrasted dark grey, silver, and white in strong sun. It flies with neck coiled back, legs trailed, wings bowed: one of the slowest wing actions of any common bird in active flight.

A familiar, upstanding, grey bird of the waterside, the Grey Heron often stands motionless in shallow water with its neck withdrawn, or stretched upright if it is fishing. It also spends a lot of time in nearby fields or trees, surprising people who expect to see it only at the water's edge. There are regular standing grounds where Grey Herons are frequent, sometimes far from water. Here the birds gather in rather loosely scattered small groups, like grey, hunched old men standing quiet and aloof. Compared with the more specialized Purple Heron and Bittern, the Grey Heron is much more able to thrive in suburban habitats where town park lakes, riverside parks, and even garden ponds are available. It steals in at dawn to take goldfish, and even stands boldly beside ornamental pools and streams if it is not persecuted or disturbed.

FEEDING
The Grey Heron's usual hunting method is to stand still or move slowly forward through the shallows, watching for prey. It grabs fish, tadpoles, large beetles, and even voles in a sudden forward lunge, grasping prey in its bill rather than stabbing it.

DISPLAY AND VOICE
Its typical note is a loud strident call in flight, like *fraarnk*. It has many other calls and makes loud mechanical rattling sounds with its bill at the nest. Displays include an upward stretch, with its body at an angle and its head and neck curved upward in a bow, less straight than in the equivalent pose of the Purple Heron. Most postures form a rigid, stereotyped pattern of actions and reactions. The pair frequently preen each other at the nest, especially early in the breeding season.

BREEDING
The nests are in the tops of trees (or bushes if there are no tall trees available). They are made of thick sticks and stems and are reused in subsequent years, so they become huge platforms. Others are remarkably small and flat. The colonies may be tiny or more than 100 strong. The 4–5 eggs are laid early in the year, from March onward, and hatch after 25–26 days. The young remain in the nest for 50 days, making a lot of noise as they get older, sometimes drawing attention to otherwise surprisingly unobtrusive small colonies or individual nests.

MIGRATION
Grey Herons that breed in eastern Europe move south and west in winter. Most others move only to the coast in severe weather.

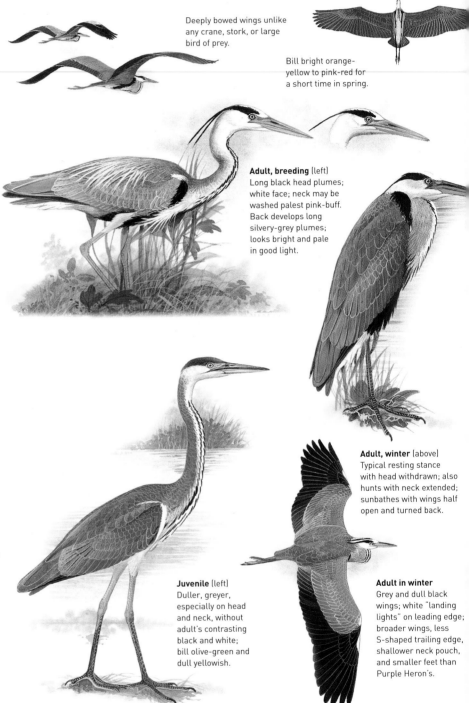

Deeply bowed wings unlike any crane, stork, or large bird of prey.

Bill bright orange-yellow to pink-red for a short time in spring.

Adult, breeding (left)
Long black head plumes; white face; neck may be washed palest pink-buff. Back develops long silvery-grey plumes; looks bright and pale in good light.

Adult, winter (above)
Typical resting stance with head withdrawn; also hunts with neck extended; sunbathes with wings half open and turned back.

Juvenile (left)
Duller, greyer, especially on head and neck, without adult's contrasting black and white; bill olive-green and dull yellowish.

Adult in winter
Grey and dull black wings; white "landing lights" on leading edge; broader wings, less S-shaped trailing edge, shallower neck pouch, and smaller feet than Purple Heron's.

WHEN SEEN

Sept — March

September to March

WHERE SEEN
Widespread in W. and central Europe, but absent from large areas of the north and Mediterranean region.

HABITAT AND INFO

NOT A FUSSY EATER
Anything edible by the waterside
is at risk from a heron.

FLIGHT PATTERN
Direct flight steady, almost
ponderous, with regular beats of
broad, bowed wings; head drawn
in, legs stretched behind.
Capable of sudden twists and
dives to feeding area and
sometimes acrobatic over
breeding colonies.

DID YOU KNOW?
The Grey Heron's food is generally slimy and its feathers often
become soiled. It uses a special soft, absorbent down from its own
feathers – powder down – to soak up this mess, then combs it from its
plumage using a specially toothed, or pectinated, claw. It often finishes
preening by standing with its wings opened "inside out"
in the sunshine.

Crane

SCALE v Woodpigeon

LENGTH / 115–130cm (45–51in)
WINGSPAN / 2.3m (7½ft)
WEIGHT / 4.5–6kg (10–13lb)

■ **STATUS /** Vulnerable

The Crane is a large, erect, grey bird with white head stripes, dark wingtips, and bushy secondaries over its tail when standing. It walks with a long, elegant stride.

Cranes are superb, giant birds, best known for their spectacular courtship dances involving lovely, rhythmic posturing. In the far north, their noisy, migrating flocks are symbols of the changing seasons.

FEEDING
Although Cranes eat insects, voles, frogs, and some young birds, they feed mainly on roots, leaves, seeds, and fruits picked from the ground.

DISPLAY AND VOICE
In courtship, each bird performs a deep bow followed by an elegant upward stretch and a leap into the air with raised wings. The calls include a duetting *krruee-krruee* and trumpeting notes in flight.

BREEDING
Crane nests are mounds of vegetation on the ground, in open areas of bog or marshland. Cranes are very shy at the nest and require large areas of undisturbed wilderness. The two eggs hatch after a 30-day incubation.

MIGRATION
A very few may spend the winter in Britain and elsewhere. Most fly south to Iberia and Africa.

Red on rear of crown difficult to see unless at close range.

Juvenile Crane (above)
Dull grey-brown, with unmarked browner head.

Crane, non-breeding (above)
Blue-grey with black forehead and throat; white neck stripe.

Crane, breeding
Drooping black secondaries create bushy tail; variable dark spots on coverts; long, slender black legs.

Crane
Flies with head and neck outstretched, unlike heron's: flocks fly in long lines and V-formations with loud, clanging calls.

ELEGANT MOVERS
Being such big birds, Cranes almost seem to move in slow motion.

DID YOU KNOW?
All the world's cranes dance, using a bowing action followed by a graceful, rhythmic, upward sweep of the head, continued in one elegant movement into a two-footed leap with open wings. Performed by single birds, pairs, or groups at any season, its function is unclear, but it is infectious: even a human imitating the action can start a flock dancing.

WHEN SEEN

All year; March to September in north.

WHERE SEEN
Breeds on bogs and marshes from Scandinavia and N Germany eastward; winters in Spain, France.

HABITAT AND INFO

Demoiselle Crane

The Demoiselle Crane is smaller, slimmer, more elegant than Crane, with a long, white neck stripe. Black on its foreneck extends lower down as wispy plumes, and greyer secondaries create a longer, paler, bushy tail.

LENGTH / 90–100cm (35½–39in)
WINGSPAN / 2m (6½ft)
WEIGHT / 4–5kg (9–11lb)

■ STATUS / Vulnerable

SCALE v Woodpigeon

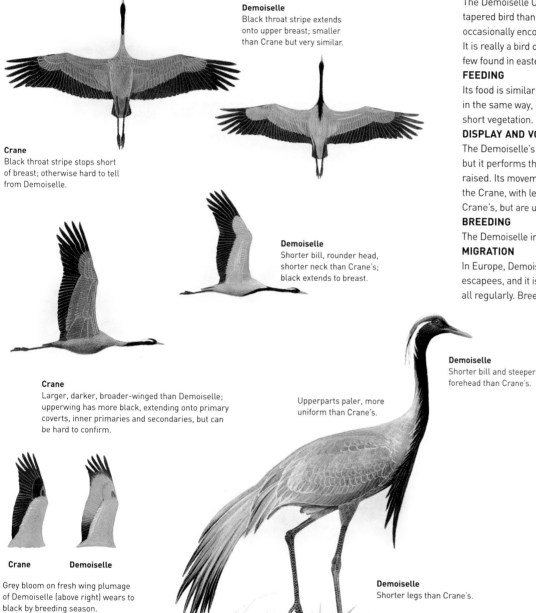

Demoiselle
Black throat stripe extends onto upper breast; smaller than Crane but very similar.

Crane
Black throat stripe stops short of breast; otherwise hard to tell from Demoiselle.

Demoiselle
Shorter bill, rounder head, shorter neck than Crane's; black extends to breast.

Crane
Larger, darker, broader-winged than Demoiselle; upperwing has more black, extending onto primary coverts, inner primaries and secondaries, but can be hard to confirm.

Upperparts paler, more uniform than Crane's.

Demoiselle
Shorter bill and steeper forehead than Crane's.

Crane   **Demoiselle**

Grey bloom on fresh wing plumage of Demoiselle (above right) wears to black by breeding season.

Demoiselle
Shorter legs than Crane's.

The Demoiselle Crane is a slightly smaller, more tapered bird than the Crane, much rarer in Europe (but occasionally encountered as an escapee from captivity). It is really a bird of the central Asian steppe, with a very few found in eastern Turkey and Cyprus.

FEEDING
Its food is similar to that of the Crane and taken in the same way, in the bill, from damp ground or short vegetation.

DISPLAY AND VOICE
The Demoiselle's displays include typical Crane dances, but it performs these with its bushy tail flat rather than raised. Its movements are more balletic than those of the Crane, with less leaping. Its calls are rather like the Crane's, but are usually higher-pitched.

BREEDING
The Demoiselle incubates two eggs for 27–29 days.

MIGRATION
In Europe, Demoiselle Cranes are usually vagrants or escapees, and it is only in Cyprus that they can be seen at all regularly. Breeding birds migrate to Africa each winter.

WHEN SEEN

Oct
April

April to October.

WHERE SEEN
Extensive lakes and marshes around Black Sea.

HABITAT AND INFO

White Stork

SCALE v Pigeon

LENGTH / 100–115cm (39–45in)
WINGSPAN / 1.8–2.2m (6–7¼ft)
WEIGHT / 2.5–4.5kg (5½–10lb)

■ **STATUS /** Vulnerable

A huge, stately, long-legged black-and-white bird with a deliberate, long-striding walk. In flight, wing beats are deep and slow. It soars on flat wings with neck outstretched.

A popular bird in European villages, the White Stork builds huge stick nests on roof tops, church towers, special man-made poles, and less often in trees. It has declined in many regions, possibly because of problems in Africa as well as wetland drainage and pesticide use in Europe.

FEEDING
It feeds on farmland and around lakes, eating beetles, grasshoppers, frogs, and voles. Land drainage and intensive cultivation drives storks away from traditional feeding sites.

DISPLAY AND VOICE
Courtship displays at the nest include noisy bill-rattling with heads bent back, and rhythmic, ritualized bowing with spread wings. Otherwise, storks are silent.

BREEDING
The 3–5 eggs hatch in 30 days. Young birds migrate with adults but do not breed until 3–7 years old.

MIGRATION
In August, White Storks form huge flocks and cross the Mediterranean at its narrowest points, bound for the east African plains, where they feed on insects disturbed by grazing herds. They return in March.

Wings broad, deeply-fingered.

White with black flight feathers from below.

Fresh flight feathers edged whitish; all-black when worn.

Soars to great heights, often in tight flocks.

Birds in flocks circle independently, crossing and recrossing as they rise; pelicans usually more coordinated, whole flock circling as one.

Adult
Bill red, dagger-like.

Juvenile
Blackish bill.

Walks with long, slow, elegant strides.

Red legs often chalky-white with droppings.

EYE-CATCHING NESTERS
White storks nest in obvious places in and around towns.

WHEN SEEN

Sept — March

March to September.

WHERE SEEN
Open farmland, wet pastures, marshes; Iberia and eastward from the Low Countries; rarely UK.

HABITAT AND INFO

SIMILAR SPECIES
White Pelican does not have trailing legs; neck and bill much thicker; flocks more synchronized.

Thick bill and neck

Short legs

Black Stork

A dramatic bird, much bigger than a Grey Heron and more sedate and upstanding. It soars on flat, fingered wings; direct flight has deep, heavy beats. Its black neck and chest distinguish it from the White Stork.

LENGTH / 95–100cm (37–39in)
WINGSPAN / 1.6–1.8m (5¼–6ft)
WEIGHT / 2.5–3kg (5½–6½lb)

■ STATUS / Vulnerable

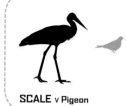

SCALE v Pigeon

At long range beware confusion with circling, immature Cormorant.

Head and neck extended in flight; looks giant but slimmer, more elegant than White Stork.

From below, white only on underbody and wingpits; black tail may be obscured by spread coverts.

Typical stork flight ends in long, descending glide on outstretched wings that flex to reduce lift; legs lowered in final descent.

More a bird of forests and wooded gorges than the White Stork, the Black Stork is almost as large but more slender, with a longer bill. It is by no means so closely linked with human settlements and is rather shy and elusive. In flight, it is as grand and expert as the White Stork, but rarely forms large flocks. In spring, it may be seen spiralling upward to gain height before crossing mountain ranges such as the Pyrenees on its way north.

FEEDING
It eats mainly fish, hunting in shallow water and wet pastures.

DISPLAY AND VOICE
Like the White Stork, the Black Stork rarely calls. Its displays are mostly confined to bill-clattering and posturing at the nest.

BREEDING
Its nest is large yet well hidden, in a tree or on a cliff ledge. It does not nest on buildings like the White Stork. It lays 3–5 eggs. The young fly when 35 days old.

MIGRATION
After breeding, all but a few Iberian pairs migrate to southern Africa. Some of the few breeding birds in central Spain remain all year.

Red skin around eye.

Juvenile
Duller, browner or washed olive; less glossy than adult.

Green bill.

Adult
Whole upperside glossy greenish-black.

Long, red, slightly upcurved bill; red legs.

Green legs.

BIG AND ANGULAR
Black Storks are huge birds, with long, gangly legs and necks.

WHERE SEEN
Forests, cliffs, open areas; Spain, Belgium, central and N Europe; rarely UK.

HABITAT AND INFO

SIMILAR SPECIES
White Stork has more white on back, underwing, and tail; thicker white neck.

White head

White chest

Dalmatian Pelican

LENGTH / 1.6–1.8m (5¼–6ft)
WINGSPAN / 2.9m (9½ft)
WEIGHT / 11kg (24lb)

■ STATUS / Endangered

SCALE v Woodpigeon

A huge, dramatic, and now rare bird, often seen with the commoner White Pelican. It is identified by its long, heavy bill combined with a short tail and enormous broad wings in flight, and by distinctive dull plumage on the water.

This magnificent bird is virtually restricted to Europe, where it is dangerously threatened by persecution, disturbance, and drainage of its wetland habitats. It breeds around the Black Sea and very locally in the Balkans.

FEEDING
Dalmatians feed sociably like other pelicans, often gathering to drive shoals of fish into the shallows where they can scoop them up in their grotesque, fleshy bill pouches. Only rich, shallow, warm waters with thriving fish populations can support large numbers of these pelicans.

DISPLAY AND VOICE
The males display in groups. The voice is a quiet croak.

BREEDING
The nests are huge heaps of vegetation, built in reed beds and on semi-floating islands. There are usually 2–3 (rarely 5–6) eggs, incubated for 30–32 days. The chicks fly at 85 days.

MIGRATION
Most remain in south-east Europe and Turkey in winter. A few non-breeding sub-adults may be found with breeding White Pelicans and on lakes in summer.

Juvenile (left)
Grey with darker outer flight feathers, whiter rump; paler than White.

Adult, fresh non-breeding (left)
Plain-looking.

Grey bloom on rear wing.

Adult
Grey bloom worn off wing.

Underside dull and plain at all ages, with no black; paler panel along midwing; short dark legs may be evident.

Breeding
Curly grey-white crest; bill grey-brown with rich pale orange to deep red-orange pouch; pale eye hard to see (dark and obvious on White Pelican); blunt forehead feathering.

Non-breeding
Bill grey with yellow-pink to yellow-grey pouch.

Legs grey at all times (pink on White Pelican).

GIANT WINGS
This bird has one of the largest wingspans in the world.

WHEN SEEN

All year.

WHERE SEEN
Black and Caspian Seas, Balkans, Turkey.

HABITAT AND INFO

SIMILAR SPECIES
White Pelican has brighter, often pinker body; more sharply defined black-and-white wing pattern.

Black flight feathers

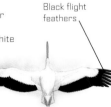

White Pelican

A giant, strikingly black-and-white bird with long wings, long bill, and short tail. Flocks coordinate their movements on the water and in flight.

LENGTH / 1.4–1.7m (4½–5½ft)
WINGSPAN / 2.4–3m (7¾–9¾ft)
WEIGHT / 10–11kg (22–24lb)

■ **STATUS /** Vulnerable

SCALE v Woodpigeon

White Pelicans are massive and solid on water, swimming like battleships, and huge and upstanding on land. Yet it is in flight that they reveal their true majesty, soaring to great heights, circling in synchrony (much more coordinated than storks) or forming long lines and chevrons.

FEEDING
Their staple diet is fish, taken in warm, rich, shallow lakes and deltas. Large flocks sometimes form horseshoes that gradually drive fish toward the shore and entrap them. In many areas, pelicans fly long distances each day to and from feeding areas.

DISPLAY AND VOICE
Males display to females in groups, croaking quietly.

BREEDING
They build their nests within reed beds and on more open islands, often in large colonies. The two eggs hatch after 29–30 days, and the chicks fly at 65–70 days.

MIGRATION
Large flocks move south in autumn, soaring on thermals to save energy, like storks and large birds of prey. They pass through the Middle East, where many remain all winter, with others moving on to Africa.

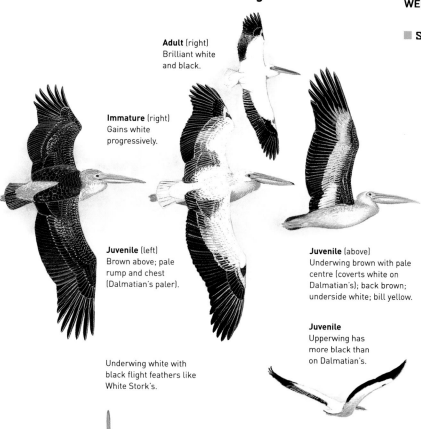

Adult (right)
Brilliant white and black.

Immature (right)
Gains white progressively.

Juvenile (left)
Brown above; pale rump and chest (Dalmatian's paler).

Underwing white with black flight feathers like White Stork's.

Juvenile (above)
Underwing brown with pale centre (coverts white on Dalmatian's); back brown; underside white; bill yellow.

Juvenile
Upperwing has more black than on Dalmatian's.

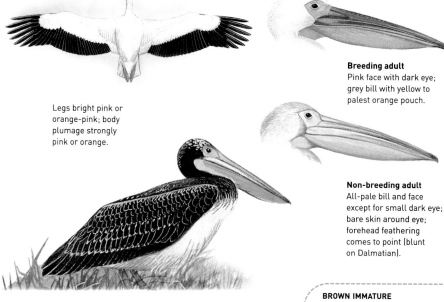

Legs bright pink or orange-pink; body plumage strongly pink or orange.

Breeding adult
Pink face with dark eye; grey bill with yellow to palest orange pouch.

Non-breeding adult
All-pale bill and face except for small dark eye; bare skin around eye; forehead feathering comes to point (blunt on Dalmatian).

BROWN IMMATURE
Young pelicans are harder to tell apart than their parents.

WHEN SEEN

All year.

WHERE SEEN
Balkans, Turkey, Black Sea.

HABITAT AND INFO

SIMILAR SPECIES
White Stork has long, thin neck, trailing legs; soaring flocks tend to be less coordinated in movements.

Long legs

Long thin neck

Greater Flamingo

LENGTH / 1.2–1.4m (4–4½ft)
WINGSPAN / 1.4–1.7m (4½–5½ft)
WEIGHT / 3–4kg (6½–8¾lb)

STATUS / Vulnerable

SCALE v Pigeon

A tall, long-necked, long-legged bird with down-curved bill, it is unique in Europe except for escaped individuals of other species.

Flamingos are familiar from their many stylized representations, as well as captive flocks in ornamental collections and wildlife parks. Wild flamingos are superb, but in Europe they are almost confined to the far south. They are worth going a long way to see, being among the most spectacular wildlife sights in Europe.

FEEDING
A flamingo feeds on tiny invertebrates and algae, sweeping its head sideways through the water to trap them in a complex mesh of fine structures within its specialized bill.

DISPLAY AND VOICE
Displays include remarkable coordinated marching and head-waving by tightly packed flocks. Most calls are loud, clanging, goose-like notes, especially a double, grunting *gagg-agg* or *gegg-egg*.

BREEDING
Large colonies move between several traditional sites around the Mediterranean, settling wherever conditions are best. Sometimes they do not breed at all, but occasional bumper years produce thousands of young.

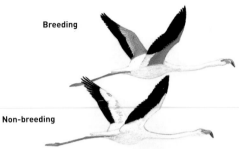

Breeding

Non-breeding

Adults
Reveal glorious crimson-and-black wings in flight.

Immature
Lacks red in wings.

Bright pink-and-black bill.

Flies with amazing extension of neck and legs.

Adult, breeding
Pale pink or whitish with a hint of crimson visible at rest.

Immature
Dull, browner, with darker bill, grey legs.

Feeds by sweeping bill through shallow water; may also wade much more deeply or swim, swan-like, on lakes; dense flocks look pale pink; smaller flocks like scattered pink/white spots.

Adult
Bright pink legs; escaped Chilean race has grey legs with pink joints.

Non-breeding
Duller; less pink.

Juvenile

EXTRAORDINARY SHAPE
This is a remarkable European bird, with exceptional adaptations.

WHEN SEEN

All year.

WHERE SEEN
Saline lakes, lagoons, and salt pans in France, S and E Spain, Balearics, Corsica, Sardinia, Sicily, Balkans.

HABITAT AND INFO

COMMON NAME
Glossy Ibis

SPECIES
Plegadis falcinellus

FAMILY
Threskiornithidae

ORDER
Ciconiiformes

Glossy Ibis

An elegant, slim-bodied, long-winged, blackish marsh bird with long legs and a curved bill. It is often in small groups.

LENGTH / 55-65cm (22-26in)
WINGSPAN / 88-105cm (35-41in)
WEIGHT / 550-750g (19-26oz)

■ **STATUS /** Vulnerable

SCALE v Pigeon

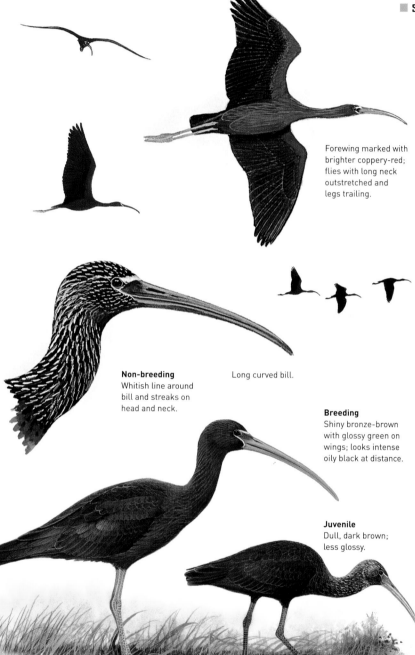

Forewing marked with brighter coppery-red; flies with long neck outstretched and legs trailing.

Non-breeding
Whitish line around bill and streaks on head and neck.

Long curved bill.

Breeding
Shiny bronze-brown with glossy green on wings; looks intense oily black at distance.

Juvenile
Dull, dark brown; less glossy.

A bird of lakesides, deltas, and rivers flanked with quagmires and swamps of wet vegetation, the Glossy Ibis is chiefly found in south-east Europe. Its habitat is often destroyed or fragmented, so its numbers and distribution fluctuate considerably. The birds often fly between feeding and roosting areas at dawn and dusk, frequently in mixed flocks with egrets.

FEEDING
The Glossy Ibis uses its long, curved bill to probe into shallow water, wet mud, and ooze to detect and seize worms and other invertebrates.

VOICE
The usual call is a throaty, crow-like, grunting *kraa kra kra*.

BREEDING
Ibises breed in colonies, with each pair building a nest of thin twigs and sticks among reeds, bushes, or taller trees. They often nest and feed alongside various herons and egrets.

MIGRATION
Some European breeders remain in the Mediterranean area all winter, wandering widely, but most migrate south to central Africa. A few reach western Europe, at almost any time of year.

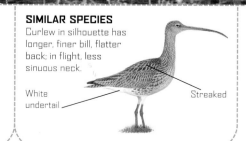

WARM WATER WADER
The slender Glossy Ibis prefers shallow pools in warm countries.

WHEN SEEN

Oct
March

March to October.

WHERE SEEN
Marshes and lakes; mainly SE Europe, occasionally UK.

HABITAT AND INFO

SIMILAR SPECIES
Curlew in silhouette has longer, finer bill, flatter back; in flight, less sinuous neck.

White undertail

Streaked

Griffon Vulture

LENGTH / 95–105cm (37–41in)
WINGSPAN / up to 2.7m (8¾ft)
WEIGHT / 7–10kg (15–22lb)

■ **STATUS /** Vulnerable

SCALE v Woodpigeon

An immense, impressive bird, it is capable of fast glides and dives around the colony (often three to five in tight formation). It typically soars in wide, rising circles or takes long, direct glides toward its feeding site or roost.

One of Europe's great birds, in terms of both size and sheer presence, the Griffon is glorious in the air. Early on cold days, Griffons use updraughts where the wind meets steep slopes. On hot days, they appear later, riding the rising masses of warm air (thermals) over cliffs and hillsides. Both techniques show their skill at manoeuvring to gain height for long-distance gliding with little expenditure of energy.

FEEDING
Griffons eat dead animals. Rarely, in Spain, where the population is too big for the amount of carrion available, they attack live lambs. In places, they are fed offal and carcasses.

DISPLAY AND VOICE
Other than angry hissing sounds, Griffons are silent. They display chiefly in the air. Close formation flying in groups clearly has an important social function.

BREEDING
The stick nests are on cliff ledges, usually in small colonies. A single egg hatches after 52 days. The chick flies when it is about 16 weeks old.

MIGRATION
Most are resident.

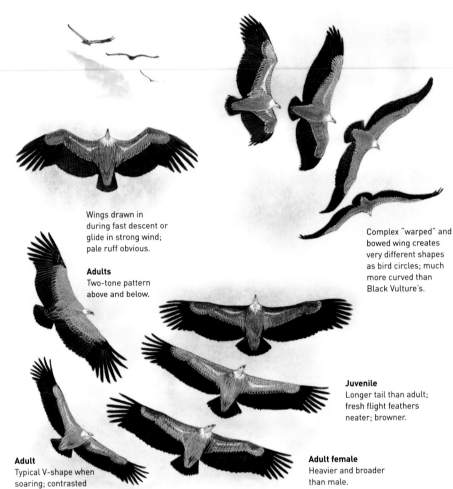

Wings drawn in during fast descent or glide in strong wind; pale ruff obvious.

Adults
Two-tone pattern above and below.

Complex "warped" and bowed wing creates very different shapes as bird circles; much more curved than Black Vulture's.

Juvenile
Longer tail than adult; fresh flight feathers neater; browner.

Adult
Typical V-shape when soaring; contrasted pattern below.

Adult female
Heavier and broader than male.

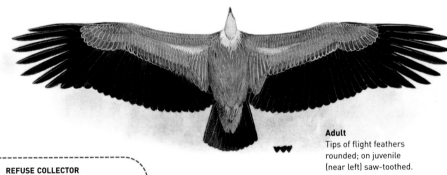

Adult
Tips of flight feathers rounded; on juvenile (near left) saw-toothed.

REFUSE COLLECTOR
The pale upperside is usually strikingly obvious in flight.

WHEN SEEN

All year.

WHERE SEEN
Spain, Portugal, S France, Sardinia; sparsely in Balkans.

HABITAT AND INFO

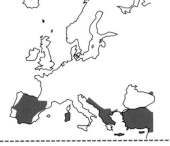

SIMILAR SPECIES
Golden Eagle in flight has longer head and tail; narrower wings with less two-tone contrast.

Protruding head

Longer tail

Black Vulture

The biggest, heaviest, squarest-looking of all the great birds of prey – a "flying door".

LENGTH / 100–110cm (39–43in)
WINGSPAN / up to 2.8m (9ft)
WEIGHT / 7–11.5kg (15–25lb)

■ STATUS / Vulnerable

SCALE v Woodpigeon

Griffon gliding.
Griffon soaring.
Black soaring.

Only tips of wings curve up.

Griffon soaring.

Soars on flat wings; pale feet.

Bill and facial colour vary, perhaps with age, from blue to pink or white.

Stands with body more horizontal than Griffon's.

Griffon
Much paler, tawny body.

Less elegant and shapely than a Griffon, the Black Vulture is bigger and its spread wings are more "plank-like": it is a mightily impressive bird in the air. It is less a bird of cliffs, although it does search for food over mountain ranges, but it is more typical of undulating, wooded areas. Central Spain, with rolling landscapes dotted by cork oaks and open woodland, suits it perfectly.

FEEDING
Like Griffons, Black Vultures eat dead animals. They dominate Griffons at carcasses and are able to rip into thicker hides with their huge bills.

DISPLAY AND VOICE
Display flights include impressive tumbling by pairs with feet interlocked, and high circling over the nest site. Black Vultures are practically silent birds.

BREEDING
Pairs breed when they are 5–6 years old. They make a bulky nest of sticks in a tree, and only exceptionally on a cliff. Both sexes incubate a single egg for 50–55 days. The chick flies when it is around 15 weeks old.

MIGRATION
Resident.

Griffon soars on raised wings and glides on bent wings, while Black Vulture keeps its wings flat.

Always looks very dark: contrasts in wing subtle at best.

BIG BRUISER
Unlike the Griffon, this is a tree-nesting species.

WHEN SEEN

All year.

WHERE SEEN
Central Spain; rare Majorca; very rare in SE Europe.

HABITAT AND INFO

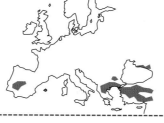

SIMILAR SPECIES
Griffon Vulture has paler forewing; paler underwing; wings raised in V-shape.

Wings raised in a V-shape

Pale forewing

Lammergeier

LENGTH / 100–115cm (39–45in)
WINGSPAN / up to 2.4m (7¾ft)
WEIGHT / 5–7kg (11–15lb)

■ **STATUS** / Endangered

SCALE v Woodpigeon

A spectacular, long-tailed vulture with a slow, sailing flight and occasional very deep, languid wing beats. It looks smaller beside a Griffon Vulture in the air.

Also known as the Bearded Vulture, the Lammergeier is a magnificent bird. Seen with Griffons it looks less bulky, sometimes obviously smaller, but its huge wingspan, long tail, white head, and orange breast give it a superior air. It looks the part as one of Europe's rarest, biggest, and most legendary birds.

FEEDING
Although capable of killing prey, Lammergeiers typically feed on large carcasses, including the marrow bones that they drop from a height to break them against rocks.

DISPLAY AND VOICE
In winter, pairs chase each other near the nest site, sometimes linking talons and falling toward the ground. They may then make oddly thin, squeaky calls. They often patrol the cliff face in long, slow glides.

BREEDING
Nests are on cliff ledges, especially in caves. The 1–2 eggs are laid in midwinter and incubated by both parents for 55–60 days. Usually only one chick flies after 110 days.

MIGRATION
Resident.

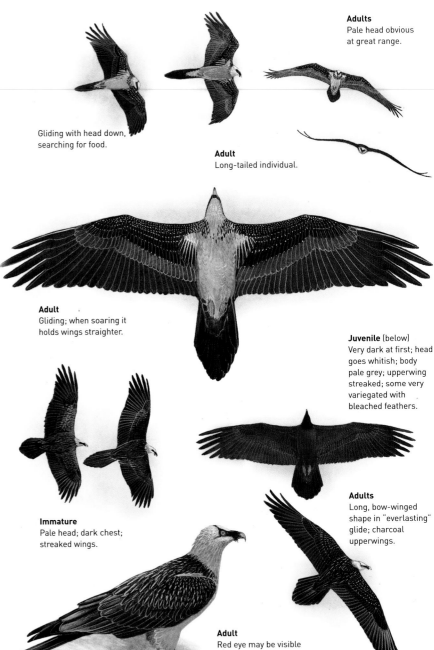

Adults
Pale head obvious at great range.

Gliding with head down, searching for food.

Adult
Long-tailed individual.

Adult
Gliding; when soaring it holds wings straighter.

Juvenile (below)
Very dark at first; head goes whitish; body pale grey; upperwing streaked; some very variegated with bleached feathers.

Immature
Pale head; dark chest; streaked wings.

Adults
Long, bow-winged shape in "everlasting" glide; charcoal upperwings.

Adult
Red eye may be visible at reasonable range; "beards" easier to see; some much whiter-headed.

SAILPLANE
A perfect flying machine, it soars endlessly without effort.

WHEN SEEN

All year.

WHERE SEEN
Pyrenees, Corsica (very rare), Alps (reintroduced), Greece, Crete

HABITAT AND INFO

SIMILAR SPECIES
Juvenile Egyptian Vulture in flight is much smaller; thinner head and bill; shorter tail more triangular.

Sharper head

Egyptian Vulture

A small yet impressive vulture, it soars on flat wings with few wing beats, over cliffs or near rubbish tips.

LENGTH / 60–70cm (24–28in)
WINGSPAN / 1.5–1.7m (5–5½ft)
WEIGHT / 1.6–2.1kg (3½–4¾lb)

■ STATUS / Secure

SCALE v Woodpigeon

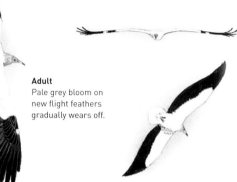

Adult
Pale grey bloom on new flight feathers gradually wears off.

Adult
Pattern like larger White Stork's, White Pelican's, or smaller Booted Eagle's, but note white, wedge-shaped tail; thin yellow head.

Sub-adult
Two years old.

Immatures
Dark brown; juvenile in Europe up to September, but most older immatures remain in Africa.

Immature
Adults far outnumber dark immatures in Europe.

Adult
Unique thin bill; yellow face; may look pristine white or very dirty.

Its unspeakable habits mean that the Egyptian Vulture is not everyone's favourite bird of prey. Yet it is a most impressive sight as it sails through the air, especially when seen against a bright blue sky when its plumage may look almost translucent.

FEEDING
Although most famous for using stones to break Ostrich eggs in Africa, Egyptian Vultures often feed at refuse tips and relish the most awful rubbish and excrement. They also feed in proper vulture fashion, at carcasses, as well as taking insects, eggs, and sometimes even nestling birds.

DISPLAY AND VOICE
On arrival at a nesting area in spring, pairs perform energetic diving display flights with high-speed, acrobatic manoeuvres. They are, however, usually silent.

BREEDING
Nests are typically on cliffs, less often in trees. Pairs breed at 4–5 years old. Two eggs are usual, and they hatch after 42 days. The chicks fly when about 10–11 weeks old.

MIGRATION
Adults fly south in August, juveniles later, to Africa, where juveniles remain for a few years.

SHARP-FACED SCAVENGER
This bird is immaculate in the air, but it looks unkempt on the ground.

WHEN SEEN

March
Sept

March to September.

WHERE SEEN
Iberia, S France, S Italy, SE Europe; migrants over Gibraltar, Istanbul.

HABITAT AND INFO

SIMILAR SPECIES
White Stork in flight has long head and neck, trailing legs; broader wings.

Long neck

Long legs

Red Kite

LENGTH / 60–65cm (23½–25½in)
WINGSPAN / 1.4–1.7m (4½–5½ft)
WEIGHT / 0.75–1.3kg (1¾–2¾lb)

■ STATUS / Secure

SCALE v Woodpigeon

The most elegant of large raptors, with long, angled wings, a forked tail, and fluent flight.

While predominantly a scavenger, the Red Kite has a brightness of colour, strength of pattern, elegance of form, and mastery of flight that make it a star in the bird world. In Britain, it is a symbol of conservation: a truly rare bird, once on the edge of extermination, that is now on the verge of a remarkable comeback. Elsewhere in Europe, it is now not so rare as was recently thought: in Spain, especially, it has staged a fine recovery.

FEEDING
Kites search for food from the air, dropping down to pick up worms and scraps, but also catching birds as large as crows and Black-headed Gulls in short, swift chases.

DISPLAY AND VOICE
Display flights over territories are frequent in spring. Kites make loud, wavering squeals, less powerful or emphatic than a buzzard's.

BREEDING
Large nests of sticks, leaves, earth, scraps of paper, and cloth are built in trees. The 2–4 eggs hatch after 31–32 days' incubation.

MIGRATION
Many north European birds move south and west in autumn.

Black Kite

Red Kite

Juvenile

Black Kite

Adult
Narrow wings; white patch on underwing; dark upperwing.

Adult
Tail more forked than a juvenile's.

Juvenile
Tail less forked.

Juvenile

Juvenile

Juvenile (left)
Secondaries and greater coverts have white tips; adult (below) lacks these.

Adult
Grey-white head with neat fine streaks; bright yellow eye.

STANDING OUT
The Red Kite's colour and pattern are striking for a bird of prey.

WHEN SEEN

All year; March or April to October only in central and E Europe.

WHERE SEEN
Locally UK; common Iberia, SE France, Balearics; scarcer N and E Europe, N Balkans.

HABITAT AND INFO

SIMILAR SPECIES
Common Buzzard holds wings up in V; round tail; stiffer wing beats.

Broader wings

Rounder tail tip

Black Kite

Slightly chunkier, less rangy than Red Kite, but also exceptionally agile in flight. Note its generally duller underwing and shorter tail.

LENGTH / 55–60cm (22–24in)
WINGSPAN / 1.3–1.5m (4¼–5ft)
WEIGHT / 650–1,100g (23–39oz)

■ STATUS / Vulnerable

SCALE v Woodpigeon

Compare angled and bowed wings, tail twisting, hint of wing patch, and especially broad pale band across inner wing with Marsh Harrier's.

Juvenile (above)
Broad, pale buff feather edges wear off to leave whitish spots by September.

Juvenile
May show strong whitish wing patch

Black Kites are common in parts of Europe, but they are less able to cope in areas of intensive farming or modern urban development. In coastal areas of southern Spain and parts of the Pyrenees, they are still numerous, but as the traditional landscapes are threatened, so too are the kites.

FEEDING
They eat all kinds of offal, scraps, and refuse, along with insects, small mammals, and fish; Black Kites are often found close to water. They are remarkably agile in the air.

DISPLAY AND VOICE
Courtship consists largely of flights over the nest site. Calls are mostly gull-like, vibrant, or whining notes like *kueee-ee-ee-eee*.

BREEDING
Nests are made in tree tops, well-hidden in foliage although quite large, and made of sticks and debris. The 2–4 eggs hatch in 31–32 days.

MIGRATION
Black Kites head south in autumn, crossing the Mediterranean in thousands at Gibraltar in August and September, with fewer passing through Sicily, Malta, and over the Bosphorus at Istanbul. Most return in April.

Adult
Wings angled; tail notched when closed.

Adult
Muddy brown with little pattern below.

Red Kite

Adult (above)
By contrast, Red Kite has paler head; whiter wing patch; brighter tail and underbody.

Juvenile
Rusty with marked pale feather edges.

SQUAT SHAPE
Shorter legs give kites a different stance from a buzzard's.

WHEN SEEN

March/April to October.

WHERE SEEN
S and central Europe, to Finland; rare Scandinavia, UK, Low Countries.

HABITAT AND INFO

SIMILAR SPECIES
Female Marsh Harrier is more uniformly dark without pale upperwing band; sharply defined pale head.

Square tail

Plain upperwing

Marsh Harrier

SCALE v Woodpigeon

LENGTH / 48–55cm (19–21½in)
WINGSPAN / 110–120cm (43–47in)
WEIGHT / 400–800g (14–28oz)

■ STATUS / Secure

The largest, heaviest harrier with the shortest tail. The male is distinctive. The female is usually obvious but needs care at long range or high up, when she may resemble a Black Kite, buzzard, or even Booted Eagle.

This bird of prey is usually instantly recognizable as a harrier, despite being rather larger and bulkier than other harriers. It tends to fly low, flapping gently between wavering glides on slightly raised wings. Yet it is also capable of high soaring flights, and can be taken for a buzzard or a Black Kite if its plumage details cannot be seen against a bright sky. Marsh Harriers are often associated with marshes, but they travel widely when hunting over adjacent farmland and sometimes turn up in very dry areas while on migration.

FEEDING
The Marsh Harrier eats a variety of small waterside birds and animals such as voles, moles, and young rabbits, as well as birds of drier places near the nesting marsh. It hunts with a low, floating flight, switching instantly to a fast dive as it targets a frog, Coot, or duckling, often with a sideways twist or turning back onto its course.

DISPLAY AND VOICE
The display flights follow a typical harrier pattern, with the male swooping and climbing high over the nesting territory. He brings food to the female, and gives it to her in a thrilling mid-air pass from foot to foot as she rolls beneath him. This continues when the male hunts for food to feed the growing chicks and calls the hen from the nest to receive it. Calls are a loud, nasal, Lapwing-like *way-oo* from the male, a harsher chattering rattle, and various mewing notes or whistles. Often a male pairs with two or three females. It seems to be a matter of chance whether he mates with a particular female in successive years.

BREEDING
The female builds a bulky nest of reeds and twigs in reeds, on the ground, or over shallow water. She lays 4–5 (sometimes up to 8) eggs, which are often quickly stained by the damp. They hatch after 31–38 days' incubation solely by the female. The chicks fly when about 35–40 days old. The youngest often die when food is short and many clutches fail completely, succumbing to flooding or predators. The young are fed by their parents for another 2–3 weeks after they leave the nest.

MIGRATION
Marsh Harriers breeding in northern and eastern Europe move to the Mediterranean area in winter, or even along the Nile Valley into central and eastern Africa. Those from western Europe may go to west Africa, but some remain in eastern England and the Low Countries.

Adult male
Trailing edge and forewing all pale.

Sub-adult male (above)
Breeds in this plumage with dark trailing edge to wing.

Adult female
Some are more marked on breast; longer than male.

Adult male
Head may be very pale or streaked; tail pale grey or faintly barred on sides; solid rufous underbody.

Adult female
Cream crown and throat; cream wing patches can be much bigger; juvenile plumage varies greatly, can be difficult to age; usually pale edges to wing coverts visible close up.

Juvenile
Typical pale crown and throat; paler on face.

WHEN SEEN

Oct — April

Mostly April to October; a few in winter in W Europe.

WHERE SEEN
E Britain; locally most of Europe except extreme north and mountain ranges.

HABITAT AND INFO

SIMILAR SPECIES
Black Kite has pale diagonal on upperwing; sharp-cornered tail; wings held bowed or angled.

Notched tail

Pale underwing patch

CONTRASTING UNDERSIDE
The adult male is pale with black wingtips but a browner body.

Male
When soaring, shows longer, less broad tail than buzzard's.

Juveniles have narrower wings than adults', males narrower than females'.

Juvenile male

Juvenile female

Adult female
Some have clear cream forewing patch.

Juvenile male
Dark chocolate; paler edges to wing coverts.

Sub-adult male

Floats low over reeds and open, damp ground.

Gliding, hunting, sailing profile with raised wings, unlike Black Kite's.

Adult male

FLIGHT PATTERN
Flight shapes recall Black Kite and other harriers, but this is the bulkiest, broadest-winged harrier.

DID YOU KNOW?
Persecution, and the drainage of marshlands, brought Marsh Harriers close to extinction in the UK several times. In 1971, there was only one breeding pair in England. By the early 21st century, protection, plus an expansion of suitable habitat, brought a terrific recovery to more than 300 breeding pairs across the UK. The species still faces problems in parts of Europe.

Hen Harrier

LENGTH / 43–50cm (17–19½in)
WINGSPAN / 100–120cm (39–47in)
WEIGHT / 300–700g (10½–25oz)

■ **STATUS /** Vulnerable

SCALE v Woodpigeon

A large, long-winged, white-rumped bird of prey that flies low and apparently slowly on raised wings. The sexes are entirely different in colour, but they need careful observation to distinguish them from other harriers.

For centuries the males and females of the three smaller harriers were thought to be different species because, while the adult males are grey, the females and immatures are brown with white rumps and barred or "ringed" tails. These harriers can be difficult to distinguish; all prefer hunting over open ground, heaths, marshes, and extensive areas of cultivation. They use a low, often slightly wavering flight with relaxed wing beats between glides on slightly raised wings. It looks slow, but they cover a lot of ground quickly. Of the three, Hen Harriers are by far the most likely to be found on higher ground, typically with heathery slopes and rushy valleys in summer.

FEEDING
Hen Harriers eat rodents and small birds, or the chicks of ground-nesting birds. They catch them on the ground, often with a sudden, twisting pounce. Harriers have long, bare legs, ideal for snatching prey from tall vegetation. They often carry their prey to a small hummock, rock, or fence post to pluck and eat it at leisure.

DISPLAY AND VOICE
In spring, males perform an exciting sky dance. They fly over the territory in a deeply undulating flight, bouncing at the bottom of each dive and rolling or tumbling as if out of control at the top of each climb. They call with a hard, even, quick *chuk-uk-uk-uk*, while females make a less even, higher, whickering *chek-ek-ek-ek-ek-ek*.

BREEDING
Males may pair with 2–3 females and supply them all with food while they incubate eggs and brood young. The grass-lined stick nests are built on the ground, often in heather or rushes on a slope with a wide view. Each female lays 3–6 eggs, incubating them until they hatch after 29–31 days. The last eggs may hatch some days after the first, and these later, smaller chicks die if food is short. Surviving chicks fly when 32–42 days old. Intruders at the nest are often attacked by females and some bold males: they may strike people on the head with their feet.

MIGRATION
Northern and eastern breeders move south and west. In western Europe, they may move shorter distances, perhaps to low ground or coastal marshes. In much of southern and south-eastern Europe, Hen Harriers are seen only as winter visitors.

Adult male
Grey chest; white underwing with dark trailing edge; secondaries sometimes faintly barred.

Juvenile male
Narrower wings than adult's.

Adult male (right)
Pale grey; sub-adults look dingy, marked browner, less pearly-grey; dark band on tips of secondaries, not across base as on Montagu's Harrier.

Adult female
Facial disc gives slightly owl-like effect; older females greyer when fresh, wear browner; some have paler shoulder area.

Long legs and toes.

WHEN SEEN

In UK and Ireland all year, S and E winter only; NW, W, central Europe, mostly winter; Scandinavia and E Europe, summer.

WHERE SEEN
N Scandinavia, N Europe, and locally E Europe, UK, and Ireland; locally Denmark to France and Spain; locally in SE Europe in winter.

HABITAT AND INFO

SIMILAR SPECIES
Montagu's Harrier has slimmer, longer wingtip; bolder white and dark bands under eye.

Streaked flanks

Dark wingbar

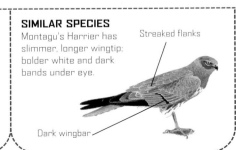

IMMACULATE MALE
Black, white, and palest grey create a superbly contrasted effect.

Male pale and gull-like against dark moorland or ploughed field.

Adult male
Faint dark hindwing bar becomes darker with wear.

Adult female
Longer than male.

Adult female
Some have lighter barring on flight feathers.

Juvenile female
Some have lighter primary barring.

Compare four-fingered, long primaries with narrow-winged Pallid and Montagu's Harriers'.

Juvenile male (above)
Rich, dark brown, paler forewing panel; has white rump and banded tail like adult female's; male has narrower wings than female's.

Juvenile female
Typical raised-wing profile.

DID YOU KNOW?
Not only were the Hen Harrier and Montagu's Harrier not separated, but the male and female Hen Harriers were frequently thought to be separate species by early ornithologists, such is the difference in their appearance. Harriers have long legs and toes, adapted to catch small prey from deep down in long vegetation, such as grasses, heather, and reeds.

Montagu's Harrier

LENGTH / 43–50cm (17–19½in)
WINGSPAN / 100–120cm (39–47in)
WEIGHT / 225–450g (8–16oz)

SCALE v Woodpigeon

■ **STATUS /** Secure

A graceful, slender-winged harrier with typical strong sexual differences. Adult males are easiest to identify.

Perhaps the most elegant of the harriers, Montagu's is a bird of warm, open landscapes with rolling cereal fields and grassy steppe. Changing agricultural practices have made life more difficult for nesting harriers in many parts of Europe. Very few Montagu's Harriers now breed in semi-natural grassland habitats.

FEEDING

They eat lizards, mice, voles, small birds, and nestlings, which are caught on or near the ground in a sudden pounce from a low, wavering flight.

DISPLAY AND VOICE

Males perform an undulating sky dance over the nesting territory. They call with a very high, staccato *kyek-kyek-kyek*. Otherwise this is a rather silent bird.

BREEDING

Twig nests are built on the ground in grass, crops, or reeds. The 4–5 eggs hatch after 27–30 days. The male delivers food to the female and young in a dramatic mid-air food pass.

MIGRATION

All Montagu's Harriers move to Africa in winter, most leaving by September and returning in April.

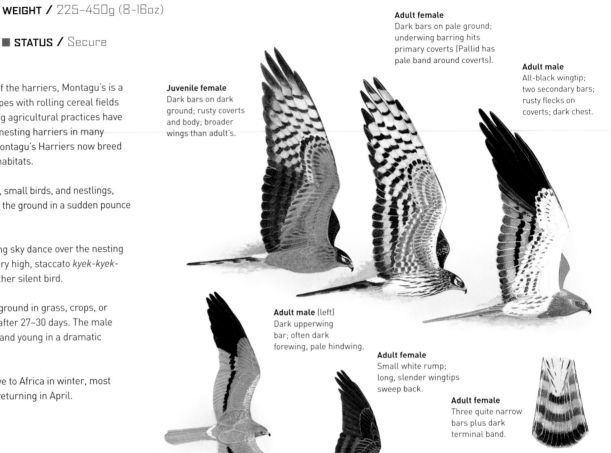

Adult female
Dark bars on pale ground; underwing barring hits primary coverts (Pallid has pale band around coverts).

Juvenile female
Dark bars on dark ground; rusty coverts and body; broader wings than adult's.

Adult male
All-black wingtip; two secondary bars; rusty flecks on coverts; dark chest.

Adult male (left)
Dark upperwing bar; often dark forewing, pale hindwing.

Adult female
Small white rump; long, slender wingtips sweep back.

Adult female
Three quite narrow bars plus dark terminal band.

Juvenile
Two narrow bars; narrow pale tip.

Adult male
Black crossbar on wing; rufous streaks.

Compare diffuse paler area on wing coverts with juvenile Pallid Harrier's.

Juvenile female
Wingtips fall short of tail (equal on male).

FLOATING EASILY
Montagu's is the lightest, most agile of the harriers.

WHEN SEEN

Sept
April

Mid-April to late September.

WHERE SEEN
Iberia, E Europe; very local from Italy north to Denmark, E England.

HABITAT AND INFO

SIMILAR SPECIES
Hen Harrier has blunter, broader wingtip; plainer face pattern with owl-like ruff.

White rump

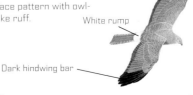

Dark hindwing bar

Pallid Harrier

A striking harrier. The male is small and elegant, but the female is larger than Montagu's Harrier.

LENGTH / 40–48cm (15½–19in)
WINGSPAN / 97–118cm (38–46in)
WEIGHT / 300–500g (10½–18oz)

■ **STATUS /** Rare

SCALE v Woodpigeon

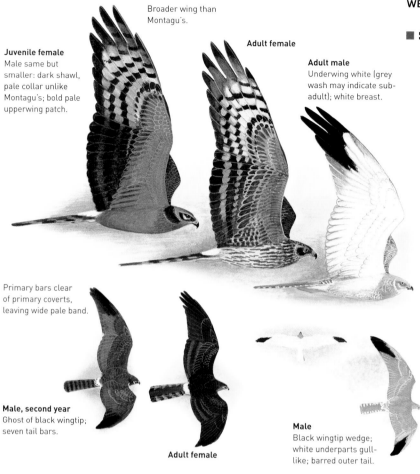

Juvenile female
Male same but smaller: dark shawl, pale collar unlike Montagu's; bold pale upperwing patch.

Broader wing than Montagu's.

Adult female

Adult male
Underwing white (grey wash may indicate sub-adult); white breast.

Primary bars clear of primary coverts, leaving wide pale band.

Male, second year
Ghost of black wingtip; seven tail bars.

Adult female

Male
Black wingtip wedge; white underparts gull-like; barred outer tail.

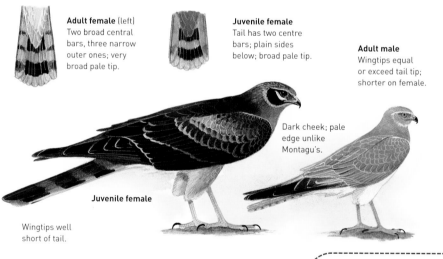

Adult female (left)
Two broad central bars, three narrow outer ones; very broad pale tip.

Juvenile female
Tail has two centre bars; plain sides below; broad pale tip.

Adult male
Wingtips equal or exceed tail tip; shorter on female.

Juvenile female

Wingtips well short of tail.

Dark cheek; pale edge unlike Montagu's.

A very rare and much-prized bird in most of Europe, the Pallid Harrier is small and slight, and lives in dry, open steppes and extensive cereal fields.

FEEDING
It eats mainly lemmings, wood mice, voles, and a few small birds. It pounces upon prey from a low hunting flight like other harriers, but it often moves more quickly than other harriers when hunting. Its numbers vary locally with fluctuations in small rodent populations.

DISPLAY AND VOICE
The bouncing display flight is accompanied by a sharp, high *kek-kek-kek-kek* chatter. Otherwise this species is very quiet.

MIGRATION
In autumn, Pallid Harriers move to India and Africa, where they hunt over the open savannah, often close to large herds of grazing animals. In spring, they return, taking a more westerly route, but in both seasons most of them pass through the Middle East. Small numbers travel through Turkey. In most years, a few are seen much farther west in Europe.

WINGTIP WEDGE
The black wedge is characteristic of a male Pallid Harrier.

WHEN SEEN

Oct / April
Aug / May
Most April–May and August–October; very few in winter.

WHERE SEEN
Rare in SE Europe; very rare vagrant elsewhere.

HABITAT AND INFO

SIMILAR SPECIES
Montagu's Harrier has narrower central bands under tail; less prominent cheek patch.

Weaker cheek patch

Sparrowhawk

LENGTH / 28–38cm (11–15in)
WINGSPAN / 60–80cm (23½–31½in)
WEIGHT / 150–320g (5¼–11oz)

■ STATUS / Secure

SCALE v Woodpigeon

A quick, snappy, broad-winged, long-tailed hawk, it is usually seen hunting low down but sometimes soaring to great heights.

This is the main predator of small woodland birds such as tits and finches, although it is also quick to take advantage of concentrations of prey on fields, in gardens, and even on salt marshes or other open places. It suffered particularly badly in the pesticide era of the 1960s, being completely wiped out in many places where it had been common. Changes in the pesticides used on farmland have allowed it to regain most of its lost ground, but ironically it has declined again in many places because of a reduction in numbers of prey, also thought to be caused by changes in farming methods.

FEEDING
Males take small prey, especially tits and sparrows, while females, being much bigger and more powerful, are able to take more thrush-sized prey and even birds as large as a Woodpigeon. It is thought that this difference in prey allows a pair to occupy a smaller territory, since they do not compete with each other for food. A Sparrowhawk hunts by flying low and taking prey by surprise: for example, it may dart from one side of a hedge to the other to fall upon an unsuspecting flock of finches. It also hunts by sitting and watching, then chasing prey that flies within range. It may be very determined, chasing birds over long distances, sometimes to quite a height, or even following birds into dense hedges or bushes and continuing the chase on foot through the branches. Some Sparrowhawks may lie in wait inside hedges to ambush foraging tit flocks. Others specialize in raiding garden feeders, snatching Blue Tits from peanut baskets, often hitting windows or fences during the chase.

DISPLAY AND VOICE
In spring, they may be seen flying over the nesting woods with a rather harrier-like action, patrolling their territories. Both sexes also perform remarkable bouncing flights: undulations so fast and steep that, at the bottom of each dive, the bird appears to bounce off some unseen surface. They also perform headlong dives with completely closed wings, plunging at full speed into the woodland canopy. Calls are mostly high, chattering *kyi-kyi-kyi-kyi* sounds.

BREEDING
Sparrowhawks nest in trees, often close to the main stem on a flat branch, building a flattish platform of twigs. Up to seven eggs hatch after 33–35 days. The chicks fly when 24–30 days old.

MIGRATION
Many northern breeders move south in winter. In Britain and Ireland, most are resident.

Soaring.

Gliding.

Typical flight.

Female
Gliding.

Male
Broad wings angle back to sharp tip.

Male
Narrow square tail; short head.

Male, displaying
Both sexes display with strange, slow, deep beats of their extended wings.

Carries prey in laboured, tail-down flight.

Adult male
Blue-grey and rufous like Merlin, but short-winged, long-legged shape.

Juvenile male
Chestnut-buff feather edges above; short wings, unlike Kestrel's.

Adult female
Upperparts darker grey than male's, but wear browner; white below with dark bars; compare with Goshawk.

Long upper leg extends to give great reach; long toes and sharp claws to grasp prey.

WHEN SEEN

All year.

WHERE SEEN
All of Europe except Iceland; summer only in extreme north.

HABITAT AND INFO

SIMILAR SPECIES
Kestrel has striking two-tone wings; less distinct flap-glide action.

Barred back

Rufous colouring

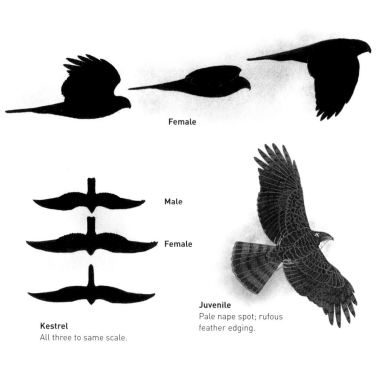

Female

Male

Female

Kestrel
All three to same scale.

Juvenile
Pale nape spot; rufous feather edging.

FOREST NEST
Nests are usually close to the trunk of a tall tree.

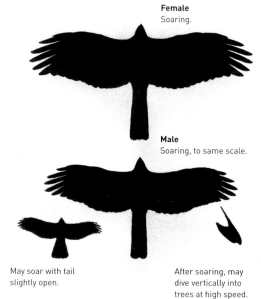

Adult male

Adult female

Juvenile male
Some are whiter; variable amounts of barring on wings on both sexes.

Juvenile female

Female
Soaring.

Male
Soaring, to same scale.

May soar with tail slightly open.

After soaring, may dive vertically into trees at high speed.

FLIGHT PATTERN
Typical flight is a fast flap-flap-flap with wings drawn in, then a flat glide.

DID YOU KNOW?
Sparrowhawks were almost wiped out from England in the 1960s by the effects of pesticides. This gave an opportunity to compare the numbers of prey species, such as blue and great tits, studied in some areas before the pesticide period, when Sparrowhawks were common. The numbers of prey species were compared during the period when Sparrowhawks were absent, and again later, when they returned. Numbers of prey birds showed no change overall.

?

Goshawk

LENGTH / 48–61cm (19–24in)
WINGSPAN / 95–125cm (37–49in)
WEIGHT / 500–1,350g (18–48oz)

■ **STATUS /** Secure

SCALE v **Woodpigeon**

A large, powerful, spectacular woodland predator with rather long, broad wings and a long tail.

Essentially a larger version of the Sparrowhawk that takes much bigger prey, the Goshawk is far less familiar than its smaller relative. Even where a pair or two are resident, they may be surprisingly difficult to see for such big birds, except during their spring display flights. Optimistic bird-watchers often misidentify female Sparrowhawks as Goshawks, but on seeing a genuine Goshawk for the first time they wonder at their mistake. A female Goshawk is so big and dramatic that it cannot be taken for the smaller bird: it is more like a buzzard or even an oversized female Peregrine. The smaller male can be more of a problem, unless seen with other birds for a good size comparison.

FEEDING

Male Goshawks take quite small prey, such as thrushes, as well as pigeons, doves, Magpies, and other medium-sized birds. Females take many pigeons, but also bigger species including crows, Pheasants, grouse, various waders, even smaller hawks and owls. Both also catch many squirrels, some rabbits, and even hares. Hunting flights may include steep, fast stoops like a Peregrine, or relatively short, fast, acrobatic chases over open ground or between large trees. Most hunts are low over the ground. They use regular plucking posts in forests, which become surrounded by feathers, uneaten scraps, and white droppings.

DISPLAY AND VOICE

Males soar with spread tails. Both sexes fly over the nest with white undertail coverts fluffed out and prominent. They also perform vertical plunges into the nesting wood. Near the nest their calls include a powerful, Green Woodpecker-like *kyee-kyee-kyee* and a weaker or more melancholy *peee-yeh* from the female.

BREEDING

Nests used for several years can become huge, flat platforms of sticks, regularly decorated with green sprays during the season. They are usually in big pines or tall oaks, often close to the main bole of the tree. Some Goshawks breed in immature plumage, but most begin when 2–3 years old; pairs remain together for life. The 2–5 eggs are laid mostly in April. They hatch after 35–38 days. The chicks fledge when 35–42 days old. Some females, especially, may be aggressive to people near the nest.

MIGRATION

Young birds move south and west in autumn, but most adults are resident unless forced to move by deep snow or prolonged hard frost.

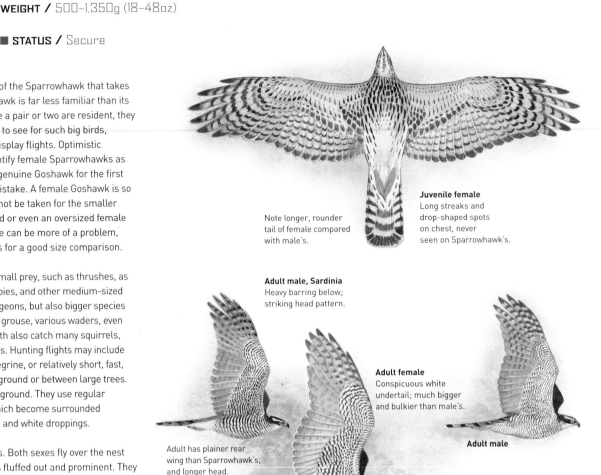

Juvenile female
Long streaks and drop-shaped spots on chest, never seen on Sparrowhawk's.

Note longer, rounder tail of female compared with male's.

Adult male, Sardinia
Heavy barring below; striking head pattern.

Adult female
Conspicuous white undertail; much bigger and bulkier than male's.

Adult has plainer rear wing than Sparrowhawk's, and longer head.

Adult male

Juvenile female
Compact, dark form found over most of Europe.

Juvenile female
Large, pale northern form.

WHEN SEEN

All year.

WHERE SEEN
Most of Europe, but very local in most areas.

HABITAT AND INFO

SIMILAR SPECIES
Sparrowhawk has shorter, squarer head; squarer wings; longer tail.

Long, slender legs

FIERCE PREDATOR
A Goshawk's eyes and beak give it
a ferocious appearance.

Male

Female
Note long head.

Male Sparrowhawk
To same scale; short
head; sharp-cornered
tail; quick wing flaps.

Female Sparrowhawk
To same scale.

Woodpigeon
To same scale.

Can look falcon-like
when gliding away.

Worn adult may
look very brown.

Adult can be grey
or blue above.

Adult female, Italy
Heavy barring;
some immature
(browner) plumage
in wing coverts.

Gliding, wings flat
at full stretch.

Juvenile female

Male

Female
Much bigger, heavier,
squarer, more robust
than Sparrowhawk.

Younger adults not
so dark-headed as
older birds.

Male   Woodpigeon

FLIGHT PATTERN
Glides and soars on flattish,
droop-tipped wings. Flap-
flap-glide flight flatter
than Sparrowhawk's, less
undulating; wing beats
slower, lack "snap".

DID YOU KNOW?
Goshawks vary considerably in appearance from area to area, being
especially large and pale in the north. In the UK, in recent decades,
several forms have been released illegally and the population is
somewhat mixed. The Goshawk, unlike the Sparrowhawk,
is also found in North America, in a more strikingly
patterned, red-eyed form.

?

Rough-legged Buzzard

LENGTH / 50–60cm (19½–23½in)
WINGSPAN / 1.2–1.5m (4–5ft)
WEIGHT / 600–1,300g (21–46oz)

■ **STATUS /** Secure

SCALE v Woodpigeon

A big, elegant, long-winged buzzard with a flexible, relaxed flight, frequently hovering, usually with a striking plumage pattern. However, variability in pattern makes structure and flight action a better identification guide than plumage.

This species replaces the Common Buzzard in the far north. As would be expected for a bird that lives in a colder climate, it is slightly larger so it has less surface area relative to its body size, and therefore loses less heat. In most respects, it is very similar to the Common Buzzard, but it is a little more elegant in flight, with a more elastic, flexible action. It is more accomplished at hovering than the Common Buzzard, but it may also spend long periods perched motionless in a tree, on a post, or even on flat ground. The "rough legs", or tightly-feathered tarsi, are not at all easy to see.

FEEDING

In summer, Rough-legged Buzzards feed on small rodents, principally field voles, bank voles, and lemmings. They also kill young hares and even stoats, as well as a few small birds, young ducks, and waders. In winter, they still prey mainly on voles, but supplement them with dead meat such as rabbits killed on roads. If voles are scarce, as they are every few years, they eat more birds.

DISPLAY AND VOICE

Pairing probably takes place in winter, as most birds arrive at breeding sites already paired. Displays include soaring and diving flights over the nest, but these are performed in silence, without the Common Buzzard's piercing calls. The alarm calls are longer and higher-pitched than the Common Buzzard's, and not usually heard away from the nest.

BREEDING

Much depends on the rodent population: in Scandinavia, rodent numbers fluctuate on a four-year cycle, and in years with few rodents, Rough-legged Buzzards either do not breed or wander far and wide until they find a better food supply and settle to breed there. The nest is built on a cliff or, in wooded areas, in a tree. In open tundra, it may simply be on a hummock on the ground. The 3–4 (sometimes as many as 7) eggs are incubated for 31 days, mostly by the female. The young fly after 34–43 days, but remain dependent on the adults for a few weeks.

MIGRATION

All breeding birds and their young leave Norway and Sweden in the autumn, but their wanderings southward depend largely on the availability of food. Many reach Denmark, Germany, and the Low Countries, but they are much more irregular in Britain. Some travel as far as the Balkans and the Black Sea.

Juvenile female

All ages/sexes show broad pale area on upper primaries.

Juvenile

Juvenile
Pale eye.

Adult (below left) has dark eye; juvenile (right) has pale eye.

Delicate head; fine bill.

Adult female
Female's wingtips very long, equal tail tip.

Juvenile male
Male's wingtips are shorter than tail.

WHEN SEEN

Oct — April

In breeding areas April to October; in S and W Europe mostly October to April.

WHERE SEEN

Breeds N and central Scandinavia and eastward; in winter, regular from Belgium and Netherlands east to Black Sea; erratic and usually rare E Britain.

HABITAT AND INFO

SIMILAR SPECIES

Common Buzzard usually has less contrast on top of tail; paler belly; less striking wing pattern.

Paler belly

Plainer tail

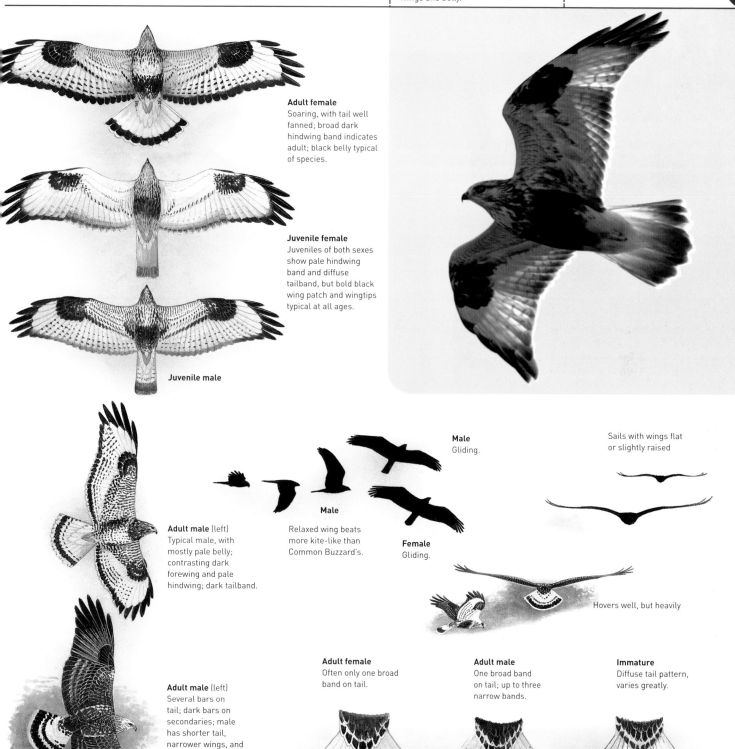

Adult female
Soaring, with tail well fanned; broad dark hindwing band indicates adult; black belly typical of species.

Juvenile female
Juveniles of both sexes show pale hindwing band and diffuse tailband, but bold black wing patch and wingtips typical at all ages.

Juvenile male

Adult male (left)
Typical male, with mostly pale belly; contrasting dark forewing and pale hindwing; dark tailband.

Male
Gliding.

Sails with wings flat or slightly raised

Male
Relaxed wing beats more kite-like than Common Buzzard's.

Female
Gliding.

Hovers well, but heavily

Adult male (left)
Several bars on tail; dark bars on secondaries; male has shorter tail, narrower wings, and much more elongated profile than female's.

Adult female
Often only one broad band on tail.

Adult male
One broad band on tail; up to three narrow bands.

Immature
Diffuse tail pattern, varies greatly.

FLIGHT PATTERN
Sails with wings flat or slightly raised.

DID YOU KNOW?
Rough-legged Buzzards feed mostly on small mammals such as lemmings and voles, and their numbers, breeding success, and winter migrations depend largely on the cyclical fluctuations in the numbers of their prey. In normal years, many visit the Low Countries in winter, but very few cross the North Sea. In good years (in reality stressful for the birds), 100 or even 200 may appear in the UK.

?

Common Buzzard

LENGTH / 51–57cm (20–22½in)
WINGSPAN / 110–130cm (43–51in)
WEIGHT / 550–1,200g (19–42oz)

■ STATUS / Secure

SCALE v Woodpigeon

A generally common, widespread, stocky, medium-large bird of prey, often seen perched on poles, wires, or fences, or soaring with wings held up in a V-shape. Most individuals bear an unremarkable pattern.

In much of western Britain, this is the most common and obvious bird of prey, even more numerous than the Kestrel and certainly much easier to see than the secretive Sparrowhawk. It is also common in a variety of habitats over large areas of Europe. It is well able to survive in farmland regions: indeed, a mixture of cultivated fields, permanent pasture, hedges, and woodland makes perfect Buzzard habitat. Ideally, it needs undulating or hilly ground, which helps to generate the varied winds and rising air currents that allow it to take full advantage of its skill in the air. It soars on thermals or up-currents for long periods, but it also spends hours perched on telegraph poles, trees, and fence posts, or even standing on the ground. Yet, despite its fondness for such mixed, farmed landscapes, it is equally a bird of remote moors, bogs, and cliffs, although normally not far from at least some scattered trees or open woodland.

FEEDING

Buzzards enjoy a varied diet. They prey mainly on small mammals such as voles, mice, small rabbits, and moles, but also eat a lot of earthworms, big beetles, and grasshoppers. They vary their prey according to location, often taking frogs, toads, slow-worms, lizards, or even fish. In many places, dead rabbits and other animals killed on roads make up a large part of their food, especially in winter. Buzzards watch for prey from the air, either soaring in wide arcs or hovering (especially in the wind over steep hillsides). They also use the "wait and see" technique, simply sitting on high perches and watching for movement.

DISPLAY

Buzzards perform exciting displays with extravagant switch-backs, steep climbs, and plunges with half-closed wings. A pair soar and dive together, and sometimes one dives at the other, which rolls over and reaches out with its feet.

BREEDING

The nest, a bulky structure of sticks, wool, and various scraps, is built in a woodland tree or at the base of a tree sprouting from a cliff face. Incubated by both parents, 2–4 eggs hatch after 33–38 days. Chicks fly after 50–55 days and are fed by their parents for a further 6–7 weeks.

MIGRATION

Birds from Scandinavia and the far north-east of Europe move south-west in autumn; thousands pass through southern Sweden. Elsewhere they are mostly resident, but many cross over Gibraltar. Asian birds migrate south over the Bosphorus in September and October.

Juvenile female

Typically dark with paler tail, barred inner wing, and obvious pale patch toward tip.

Soars on raised wings in wide, wavering, slow circles.

Glides on lower, arched wings.

Tail feathers: juvenile (left) has narrow dark bars; adult (right) has broad bar near tip.

Juvenile female
Male's wings longer: almost reach tail tip.

Juvenile

Adult

Loud, ringing, challenging or mewing *pee-ow* call.

WHEN SEEN

All year; in N and NE Europe, April to October.

WHERE SEEN
Most of Europe except Iceland and N Scandinavia; absent from most of Ireland and much of E England.

HABITAT AND INFO

SIMILAR SPECIES
Golden Eagle has bigger, longer head and tail; longer wings with more obvious bulging trailing edge; no obvious dark wrist patch.

Paler upperwing band

Longer head and tail

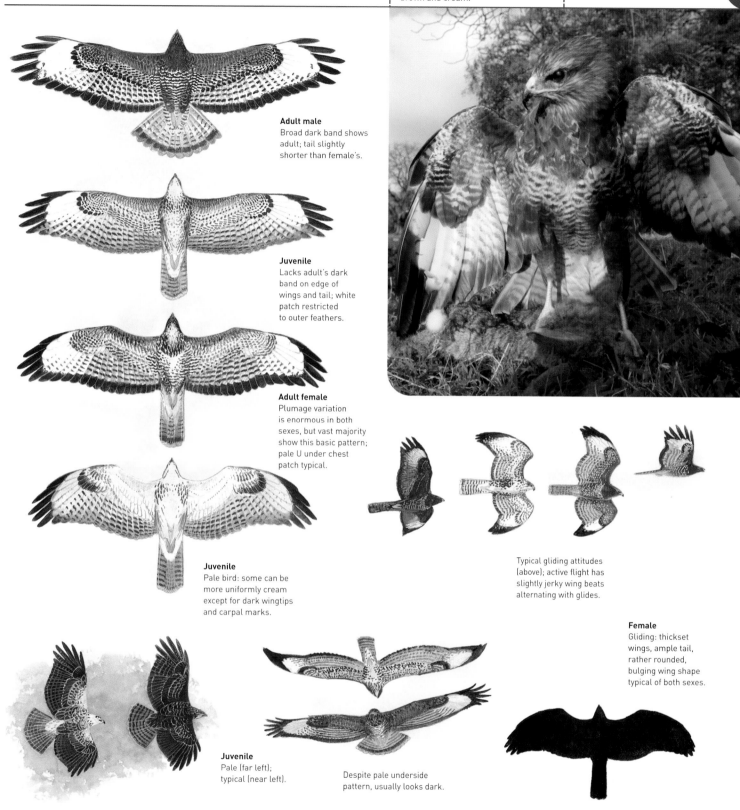

Adult male
Broad dark band shows adult; tail slightly shorter than female's.

Juvenile
Lacks adult's dark band on edge of wings and tail; white patch restricted to outer feathers.

Adult female
Plumage variation is enormous in both sexes, but vast majority show this basic pattern; pale U under chest patch typical.

Juvenile
Pale bird: some can be more uniformly cream except for dark wingtips and carpal marks.

Typical gliding attitudes (above); active flight has slightly jerky wing beats alternating with glides.

Female
Gliding: thickset wings, ample tail, rather rounded, bulging wing shape typical of both sexes.

Juvenile
Pale (far left); typical (near left).

Despite pale underside pattern, usually looks dark.

FLIGHT PATTERN
Typical profiles (far right) and head-on soaring shape with wings in V (near right); quite broad, longish wings with bulging rear edge; shortish, round tail.

DID YOU KNOW?
In Scotland, the Common Buzzard is sometimes known as the "tourist's eagle", because so many visitors, over optimistic when they first see a Buzzard on a roadside telegraph pole, assume it is an eagle. A real eagle is highly unlikely to be seen in such a situation: indeed, it might take many hours of scanning high, distant skylines for a soaring "dot" before a Golden Eagle is seen.

Long-legged Buzzard

SCALE v Woodpigeon

LENGTH / 50–65cm (19½–25½in)
WINGSPAN / 1.3–1.5m (4¼–5ft)
WEIGHT / 1–1.3kg (2¼–2¾lb)

STATUS / Vulnerable

A large, agile buzzard with long, rather narrow wings, a pale tail, and a vigorous wing action recalling a small eagle. Its character is constant despite having variable plumage.

This is a true buzzard of warm, dry areas, often found on almost semi-desert steppes, but, in the Balkans, it occurs in more wooded areas in hilly country. It is easily mistaken for a Common Buzzard.

FEEDING
It eats small mammals such as voles, rats, and ground squirrels, plus some small birds, lizards, frogs, even snakes. It watches from perches such as telegraph poles, or soars in high circles over open ground. It hovers more often than the Common Buzzard, typically hanging head-to-wind over dry, hot fields or open scrub.

DISPLAY AND VOICE
Displays include an undulating flight with steep climbs and fast plunges. It is quieter than a Common Buzzard, its higher-pitched calls seldom heard.

BREEDING
It nests on cliff ledges, and incubates 3–4 eggs for 28 days. The young fly after five weeks.

MIGRATION
Breeders from north of the Caspian Sea move south in autumn into Africa. Some migrate south from Greece, but others remain all winter.

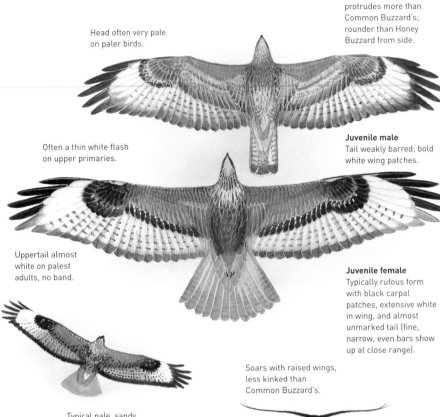

Head often very pale on paler birds.

Small, narrow head protrudes more than Common Buzzard's; rounder than Honey Buzzard from side.

Juvenile male
Tail weakly barred; bold white wing patches.

Often a thin white flash on upper primaries.

Uppertail almost white on palest adults, no band.

Juvenile female
Typically rufous form with black carpal patches, extensive white in wing, and almost unmarked tail (fine, narrow, even bars show up at close range).

Typical pale, sandy to cinnamon tail.

Soars with raised wings, less kinked than Common Buzzard's.

Sails with inner wing raised, wingtips level.

Adult male
Pale type.

Juvenile female
Rufous type.

Adult female
Dark rufous form.

Adult female
Dark form.

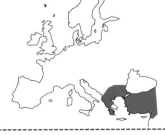

TYPICAL BUZZARD
The shape and stance are much like other buzzards.

WHEN SEEN

All year.

WHERE SEEN
E and NE Greece; very rare vagrant NW Europe.

HABITAT AND INFO

SIMILAR SPECIES
Common Buzzard is shorter-winged; more bars on darker tail; less gingery or tawny.

More barred tail

Steppe Buzzard

A possible race of the Common Buzzard, but consistent physical structure from Finland and Poland through Russia to Caspian suggests a separate species. Supposed area of hybridization in central Europe needs more research.

LENGTH / 50–60cm (19½–23½in)
WINGSPAN / 1.1–1.2m (3½–4ft)
WEIGHT / 600–1,100g (21–39oz)

■ STATUS / Secure

SCALE v Woodpigeon

Adult female
Grey-brown; belly barred (streaked on juvenile).

Juvenile female
Foxy-red form: note all-orange tail.

Juvenile
Grey-brown form.

Adult
Very dark form.

Soars (top) with flatter wings than Common Buzzard's; sails/glides (lower) on flat wings; direct flight has more rapid beats; looks more dainty, with petite head

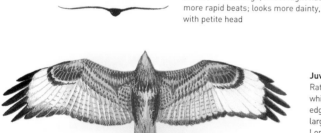

Juvenile female
Rather rusty, with much white in wing; weak trailing edge band; pale tail; compare larger, longer-winged Long-legged Buzzard.

Much colour variation in both sexes, at all ages, with dark, grey, brown, and rufous forms.

Adult male
Distinctive foxy-red form, with rufous upperside to tail, rufous underwing coverts and body.

Adult female
Grey-brown type; tail paler, often with whitish patch at base.

Smaller than Common Buzzard: large adult female same size as small young male Common; proportionately shorter bodied, more lightly built, with longer, more slender wing but more S-shaped trailing edge; greater difference between sexes than in Common Buzzard.

Usually treated as a race of the Common Buzzard, this is really a distinct form best separated as a species in its own right. More research into its status and distribution is required, especially in central Europe. It is a common migrant in eastern Europe and the Middle East, crossing the Bosphorus in large flocks between mid-September and mid-October.

FEEDING
Its food and foraging behaviour are much like those of the Common Buzzard, with small mammals forming the bulk of its diet.

DISPLAY AND VOICE
Displays include soaring and more active flights, with pairs often diving at each other and sometimes grasping each other's feet. Its calls are like a Common Buzzard's, but are rarely heard outside the breeding area.

BREEDING
The stick nest is made in a tree. The 2–4 eggs are incubated for 33–35 days, and the chicks fly after about seven weeks.

MIGRATION
In autumn, they fly south, mostly over narrow sea crossings. It is rare in NW Europe in late autumn.

LONG-RANGE MIGRANT
Steppe Buzzards migrate in sizeable flocks.

WHEN SEEN

Oct — April

April to October.

WHERE SEEN
Breeds NE Europe through to Russia and into Asia; very few in winter in SE Europe.

HABITAT AND INFO

SIMILAR SPECIES
Common Buzzard is less rufous or strikingly patterned on underwing; more barred on tail.

Weaker wing pattern

Duller tail

Honey Buzzard

LENGTH / 52–60cm (20½–23½in)
WINGSPAN / 1.4–1.5m (4½–5ft)
WEIGHT / 600–1,100g (21–39oz)

SCALE v Woodpigeon

■ **STATUS** / Secure

A big, long-winged, supple, bird of prey, with pale eyes, a small head, and a rather long tail with three dark bands. Its pattern is highly variable, but often strongly barred underneath. Identification is by its distinctive shape and actions.

Despite its name this is not a true *Buteo* buzzard. It resembles one superficially, but close views reveal several distinctions; its behaviour and ecology are also quite different. It is particularly variable in its plumage pattern, which makes its distinctive flight shape and the set of its wings all the more vital for identification. Usually seen in flight, Honey Buzzards are secretive when feeding and breeding, and they keep within the confines of extensive woodland. They are most easily seen when they concentrate at short sea crossings while on migration, or when displaying over their territories in late spring.

FEEDING

A Honey Buzzard spends long periods perched within woodland, watching for wasps and bees. When it sees one it follows it back to its nest, which it then digs out with its feet. Stiff, short feathers on its face probably help protect it from stings. It eats wasp and bee grubs, adults, and honeycomb, as well as ant grubs and various other insects. In early spring, it may need to supplement this insectivorous diet with frogs, worms, small birds, and other prey.

DISPLAY AND VOICE

For a short period in spring, Honey Buzzards display over the woodlands where they nest. The male flies upward, raises its wings over its back and claps them together two or three times. It then rises again and repeats the performance, then rises still higher in a sequence of steep climbs and wing claps. The usual call is a slightly whining, clear *peee-u*.

BREEDING

Both sexes build the nest, characteristically of leafy twigs, high in a tree – often a spruce, oak, or beech. Usually two eggs are incubated for 30–35 days. The chicks fly when 33–45 days old.

MIGRATION

Honey Buzzards spend the winter in Africa south of the Sahara. Like most birds of prey, they find flying over open sea difficult; they prefer to soar on warm, rising air, which occurs only over land. Their migration routes therefore concentrate over short sea crossings. These include the Bosphorus at Istanbul, where large flocks move through in early September and return in April and May, and Gibraltar, where even larger numbers pass through. Other good sites include Falsterbo in southern Sweden. Sadly, many Honey Buzzards migrating over Sicily and Malta are illegally shot by hunters.

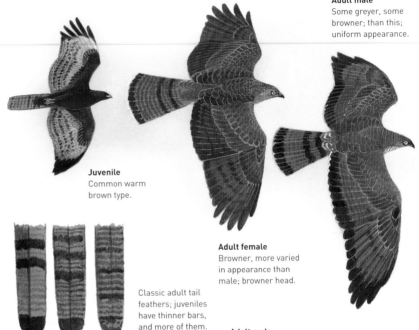

Adult male
Some greyer, some browner; than this; uniform appearance.

Juvenile
Common warm brown type.

Classic adult tail feathers; juveniles have thinner bars, and more of them.

Male Female Juvenile

Adult female
Browner, more varied in appearance than male; browner head.

Adult male
Yellow eye, unlike true buzzards; bristly facial feathers; dark bill base.

Adult female
Brown head (grey on male).

Juvenile
Much white on head; dark eye; yellow base to bill.

Walks about on ground when feeding, digging out wasps' nests with quite straight claws.

WHEN SEEN

Sept — April

April to September.

WHERE SEEN
Extremely rare breeder in UK; local from Spain through France and N Italy north to Baltic; frequent S Scandinavia, Finland, and east into Russia; migrants Gibraltar, Sicily, Malta, Greece, Bosphorus.

HABITAT AND INFO

SIMILAR SPECIES
Common Buzzard has wings held up in V; shorter, squarer head; broader tail with even barring.

Broader head

Plainer tail

Rather dark individual with obvious black wrist (carpal) patches, bold black trailing edge, and long dark bars curving across base of flight feathers.

Head rather round but small, quite slim, protruding on slim neck, sometimes with Cuckoo-like effect in side view.

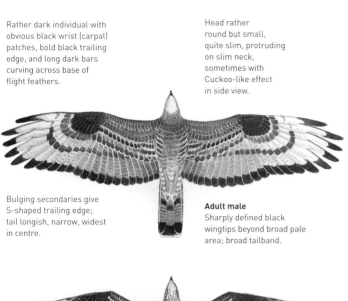

Bulging secondaries give S-shaped trailing edge; tail longish, narrow, widest in centre.

Adult male
Sharply defined black wingtips beyond broad pale area; broad tailband.

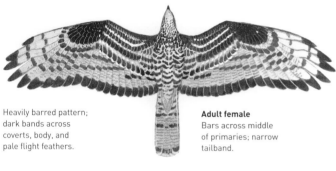

Heavily barred pattern; dark bands across coverts, body, and pale flight feathers.

Adult female
Bars across middle of primaries; narrow tailband.

Buzzard (lower bird)
Broad, squat head and neck; shorter, broader wings pushed forward and raised; shorter, broader tail.

Tail pattern sometimes obscure from below, more obvious above, with two basal dark bands and one at tip; juveniles more barred on primaries, more like Common Buzzard.

Juvenile male
Pale juvenile (some almost white-headed): thin, even barring across flight feathers; streaks on body; male narrower-winged, smaller than female.

Migrant juveniles seen only on autumn passage; remain in Africa for 2–3 years before returning to Europe.

May soar with wings slightly raised; sometimes flies with feet lowered; kinks wings up when turning.

Cuckoo-like head, thinner than Common Buzzard's.

Relaxed, quite "floppy" wing action, unlike that of Common Buzzard; migrants use distinctive easy, continuous, elastic flaps.

Juvenile female
Broad-winged and larger than male, looking shorter-tailed.

Typcal glide and soar; with slightly drooped, smoothly-bowed wings, unlike stiffer-winged Common Buzzard.

FLIGHT PATTERN
Distinctive narrow head and flat, or drooped, wings.

DID YOU KNOW?
The status of the Honey Buzzard in Britain is shrouded in secrecy. While it is common in parts of Europe, in Britain it has always been rare, and its whereabouts closely guarded. Some published sources have suggested that as few as 10–20 pairs breed, but recent claims suggest that there may have been several times that number present for decades.

Booted Eagle

SCALE v Woodpigeon

LENGTH / 45–50cm (17½–19½in)
WINGSPAN / 110–130cm (43–51in)
WEIGHT / 700–1,000g (25–35oz)

■ STATUS / Vulnerable

A small eagle with a broad, rounded head, gliding on flat or drooped wings, with a rounded look and longish tail.

Unusually well-marked pale individual.

This is the smallest of the eagles, a summer visitor to southern parts of Europe, where it is just one of a whole suite of birds of prey. It is more or less buzzard-like, but some features recall a kite or even a harrier at times. It has two forms: pale and dark. Seen against a vivid blue sky in bright sun, the pale type is an extremely handsome bird. It is often harried by other birds of prey, Ravens, and crows. It seems to get the worst of it in many aerial battles, although it is usually capable of defending itself well enough by rolling over and presenting its talons. It is found in much the same places as buzzards and kites, especially where open woodland, particularly oak, and aromatic Mediterranean scrub clothe rolling hills and lower mountain slopes. In many areas, Booted Eagles have declined in recent decades, largely because of poisoning, shooting, general disturbance, and habitat loss. In particular, the destruction of native, broadleaved woodland for farming or coniferous plantations usually drives out the eagles.

FEEDING

Booted Eagles soar over woods and bushy hillsides, often at a great height, searching for almost anything they can get hold of: lizards, snakes, frogs, small mammals such as voles and young rabbits, small birds, and even large insects. They hang in the wind looking down intently, then stoop dramatically to strike their prey with a killing blow. They also chase birds in fast, low pursuits.

DISPLAY AND VOICE

Spring and summer display flights are exciting to see: high-soaring and steep, fast undulations, with headlong plunges at great speed. The call is a distinctive loud, piping *chi-dee*, often repeated. During display flights more mellow, plover-like *heeup* calls carry far and wide over the hills.

BREEDING

The nest is a bulky affair of sticks and roots, built by both sexes in a tree. A dry, warm slope with open oak woods is preferred. Two eggs make up the usual clutch. They hatch after an incubation of 36–38 days, mostly by the female. The young fly when about 50–60 days old, but as a rule only a single chick survives to fledge.

MIGRATION

Booted Eagles spend the winter in Africa just south of the Sahara. Small numbers cross the Bosphorus in autumn, but many more move south through Gibraltar in mid-September. They return in late March and April. Young, non-breeding birds may disperse more widely to the north, but very few reach areas far outside the breeding range.

Adult
Pale form; forehead often white.

Juvenile
Pale form.

Dives during display or when hunting.

Feathered legs, unlike Common Buzzard's.

Dark form.

Intermediate form.

Pale phase more constant; darker birds variable.

WHEN SEEN

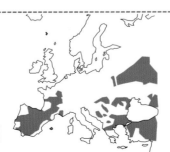

March
Sept

March to September.

WHERE SEEN

Spain and Portugal, S and central France, Balkans.

HABITAT AND INFO

SIMILAR SPECIES

Common Buzzard glides with wings raised, has a plainer back without pale upperwing band or rump patch.

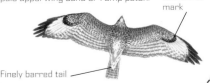

Dark wrist mark

Finely barred tail

Male

Slightly paler inner primaries; translucent tips to flight feathers and tail.

Tail plain, or with slight dark tip or very faint bars.

Dark form; paler behind bend of wing; paler tail with hint of dark tip.

Translucent trailing edge; white "spotlights" on shoulders.

Female
Slightly longer tail than male's.

Head-on glide with slightly bowed, droop-tipped wings.

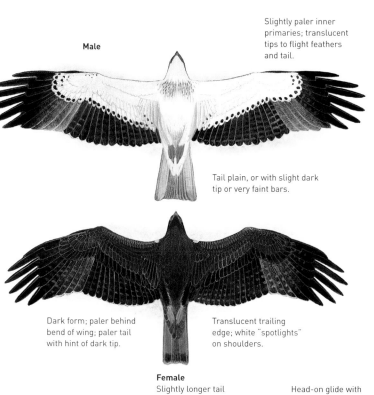

Pale form (about 80 per cent of west European adults); much smaller than Egyptian Vulture and White Stork, which share similar pattern.

White "spotlights" best seen head-on; Honey Buzzard may show similar marks, but not such striking white spots.

Adult (left)
Medium-dark, rufous phase, with heavier bars; commonest in E Europe.

Adult
Medium-dark.

Rufous individual with dark midwing line, like small Bonelli's; round head, white "spotlights" helpful; upperparts give best clues.

Adult
Dark form; pale V above tail; pale band across wing.

Juvenile
Pale form; upperwing bands very striking on some birds.

DID YOU KNOW?
Many birds of prey avoid long sea crossings over the Mediterranean by using the narrowest possible routes, such as at Gibraltar and the Bosphorus. At such sites large flocks occur, especially in autumn, but, even where it is relatively common, the Booted Eagle characteristically travels singly or in twos and threes, and keeps away from other migrating species.

Bonelli's Eagle

LENGTH / 70–74cm (27½–29in)
WINGSPAN / 1.4–1.7m (4½–5½ft)
WEIGHT / 1.5–2.5kg (3¼–5½lb)

SCALE v Woodpigeon

■ **STATUS /** Endangered

A big, dramatic, impressive eagle, hunting almost like a huge hawk, but spending long periods perched.

Generally rare and hard to see, this is an exciting bird of prey. It combines the size and power of an eagle with the speed, agility, and impact of a Goshawk. In the unlikely event of a really close view, its whole bearing and facial expression create a wonderfully memorable impression. Sadly, in most areas, it is rare and declining owing to continuing persecution, disturbance in once-remote areas, and loss of habitat. Bonelli's Eagles prefer the fringes of mountainous regions, where rocky cliffs and gorges mix with steep, wooded slopes and extensive *maquis:* the bushy scrub so characteristic of the Mediterranean area but now so often replaced by farmland or dense commercial forestry. A pair will often fly at particular times of the day when they can usually be seen over their breeding cliffs, but otherwise they are secretive and easily overlooked.

FEEDING
Often hunting in pairs, Bonelli's Eagles patrol the slopes in search of likely quarry, flying low over the ground. Typical prey includes rabbits and medium-sized birds such as Jackdaws and partridges. This staple diet is varied by all kinds of birds, from ducks to larks, and other mammals such as hares and rats. It is a dramatic hunter, combining manoeuvrability with the strength and stamina to pursue a chase to its conclusion. Most prey, however, is taken by surprise and quickly caught and killed.

DISPLAY AND VOICE
Owing to the very early breeding season, display flights may take place well before the turn of the year and continue until February or March, when the eggs are laid. They have a typical eagle/buzzard pattern, with soaring developing into steeply undulating displays and plunges. Unlike the Booted Eagle, however, voice does not play any significant part.

BREEDING
Pairs form at about 3–4 years of age and last for life. The nest is a pile of sticks on a ledge or inside a cavity on a sheer cliff face. Two eggs are normal; they hatch after 37–40 days. In two out of three cases, only one chick survives to fledge.

MIGRATION
The adults are resident and rarely move far from their breeding territories, but young birds must disperse and sometimes wander a short distance outside the usual breeding range. Very few Bonelli's Eagles cross the Mediterranean into north Africa.

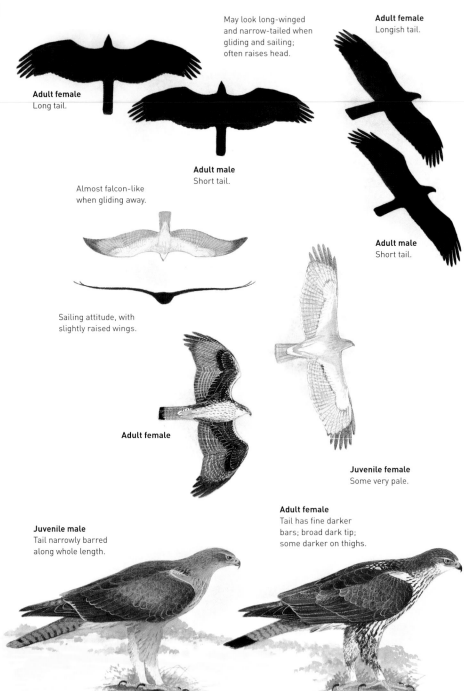

Adult female
Long tail.

May look long-winged and narrow-tailed when gliding and sailing; often raises head.

Adult female
Longish tail.

Adult male
Short tail.

Almost falcon-like when gliding away.

Adult male
Short tail.

Sailing attitude, with slightly raised wings.

Adult female

Juvenile female
Some very pale.

Adult female
Tail has fine darker bars; broad dark tip; some darker on thighs.

Juvenile male
Tail narrowly barred along whole length.

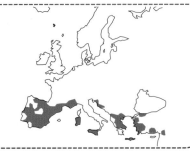

WHEN SEEN

All year.

WHERE SEEN
Spain, extreme S France, Sardinia, Sicily; rarely Greece.

HABITAT AND INFO

SIMILAR SPECIES
Booted Eagle has stronger upperside contrast with pale wing bands and white rump.

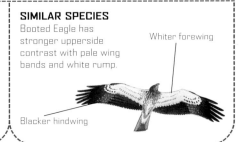

Whiter forewing

Blacker hindwing

POWERFUL HUNTER
This bird combines the power of an
eagle with the agility of a Goshawk.

Juvenile male
Pale wing covert
edges; barred tail.

Adult female
White on back; pale
tail with black band.

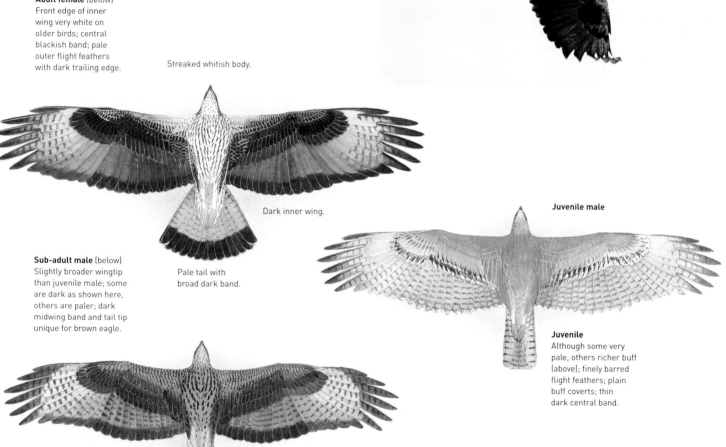

Adult female (below)
Front edge of inner
wing very white on
older birds; central
blackish band; pale
outer flight feathers
with dark trailing edge.

Streaked whitish body.

Dark inner wing.

Juvenile male

Sub-adult male (below)
Slightly broader wingtip
than juvenile male; some
are dark as shown here,
others are paler; dark
midwing band and tail tip
unique for brown eagle.

Pale tail with
broad dark band.

Juvenile
Although some very
pale, others richer buff
(above); finely barred
flight feathers; plain
buff coverts; thin
dark central band.

DID YOU KNOW?
Rabbits and Red-legged Partridges are common prey; birds are mostly
taken on the ground or as they try to take off. In southern Europe,
birds predominate from August to April, with rabbits increasing
sixfold as prey at other times. However, this powerful eagle takes
anything that is available and concentrates on whatever is
most frequent, from lizards to herons, and even other
birds of prey.

Osprey

LENGTH / 55–65cm (21½–25½in)
WINGSPAN / 1.4–1.7m (4½–5½ft)
WEIGHT / 1.2–2kg (2½–4½lb)

■ STATUS / Secure

SCALE v Woodpigeon

A big, spectacular bird of prey, with long, angled wings, that feeds on fish caught after a headlong plunge from the air.

Although found worldwide, the Osprey is a rarity in Britain. Persecution and collecting had led to its extinction in Scotland by 1910, but in the 1950s it returned, entirely of its own accord. Since then a long story of protection combined with public viewing at selected nests has made the Osprey a symbol of conservation success in the Highlands, and it has thrived sufficiently well in recent years to reach a total of more than 100 breeding pairs. In spring and autumn, they can be seen almost anywhere in Britain as they journey between their northern breeding areas and Africa.

FEEDING

What catches the public imagination about the Osprey is its spectacular fishing method. It patrols above the water at a great height until it spots a fish, then hovers like a giant Kestrel. Having judged the position of its next meal, it plunges headlong, folding back its wings for speed. Just before striking the water it swings back, thrusting out its feet at full stretch ready to grasp the fish in its long, curved, needle-sharp claws. It can swing its outer toe sideways like an owl to get a secure grip on twisting, muscular, slippery fish, and the soles of its feet are equipped with sharp-edged, roughened scales. As it rises, shaking the water from its feathers, the Osprey often manoeuvres the fish into a more streamlined, head-first position so it is easier to carry back to the nest or to a perch, where it will eat it. Most of its victims are medium-sized fish such as pike, trout, flatfish, and mullet.

DISPLAY AND VOICE

The early spring displays over the nest involve steeply undulating flights together with loud, high-pitched, shrill whistling calls, *pyew-pyew-pyew*. Ospreys also make a lot of fuss over refurbishing their nest, breaking off dead twigs and green sprays from pine trees or lifting larger branches from the ground.

BREEDING

Nests are used year after year, by a succession of different Ospreys, so they soon build up into huge, rounded piles of thick sticks. They are usually on tall pines, often on a broken branch or in a strong fork. Some Ospreys used to nest on ruined buildings in Scotland, and elsewhere today they still use a variety of artificial sites. The 2–3 eggs hatch after 37 days. The young fly when about 44–59 days old. They return to breed on their own account when three years old.

MIGRATION

North European Ospreys, including those from Scotland, spend the winter in west Africa.

Glides and flaps with kinked wings; wing beats deliberate; long or short glides.

Hovering: compare with Short-toed Eagle.

Adult
Wingtips well past tail.

Juvenile
Pale patch on lower shoulder obvious on some, but not all.

Juvenile (left) has buff feather edges; adult (right) uniform dark brown above.

Juvenile
Wingtips equal tail.

WHEN SEEN

Oct　March

March to October.

WHERE SEEN
A migrant through much of England and S Scotland; breeds in N Europe from Scotland through Scandinavia and N Germany; locally in Iberia and Mediterranean islands.

HABITAT AND INFO

SIMILAR SPECIES
Great Black-backed Gull's wings taper to neater point; whiter rump area; no central dark band or wrist patch under wing.

Longer, plainer head

Dark tailband

SPLASHDOWN
Ospreys are easily identified once they plunge into water for fish.

Juvenile
Diving for fish; feet brought forward at last moment; shakes off water after dive.

Black wingtips, carpal patch, and trailing edge (narrow on some juveniles); barred flight feathers look dull against white coverts at a distance.

Juvenile

Hovering: broad-winged, winnowing action.

White crown, broad black band across head obvious at long range.

Very white individual with small dark carpal patch at bend of wing.

Carries fish head-first.

Adult
Gliding with typical angled wing; breast band varies; striking white body.

DID YOU KNOW?

Cases have been reported of Osprey skeletons attached to large fish, as if drowned when being too optimistic in their hunting. One such case seemed well documented and the skeleton, fixed to a large carp, was photographed. This was the undoing of the story, however, as the pictures proved a fraud. No Osprey would keep its hold while being drowned.

?

Short-toed Eagle

LENGTH / 62–67cm (24½–26½cm)
WINGSPAN / 1.6–1.8m (5¼–6ft)
WEIGHT / 1.5–2.5kg (3¼–5½lb)

■ STATUS / Vulnerable

SCALE v Woodpigeon

A big, pale, large-headed snake-eagle with bare legs and bright yellow eyes. Its pale underwings have no dark wrist patches or tips.

In much of southern Europe, this is one of the most conspicuous raptors: a large eagle that spends much of its time in the air. It is a magnificent sight, its pale underside often catching the sunlight as it turns against a bright blue sky. In a close view – which is more likely than with other big eagles – the barring on the underside shows crisp and clear, while the large, round, cold, yellow eyes give a piercing, intelligent expression. This is a snake-eagle: a European representative of a group that is more widespread and varied in Africa. They are all distinguished by similarly large, rounded, owl-like heads, yellow eyes, and strong, bare-shanked legs.

FEEDING
Hunting flights are long, high-level patrols over open ground and warm, bushy hillsides, punctuated by regular periods of hovering. The eagle stares intently at the ground, head-to-wind. With tail fanned and angled downward, and wings fanned or beating with an almost wobbling action, depending on the wind, it pinpoints a snake or lizard, or sometimes in dull or wet weather perhaps a small mammal. Then it drops onto its prey. Sometimes it dives from a great height, plunging at high speed with its feet down, breast pushed forward, and head pulled back in a dramatic stoop. At other times it hunts by watching from a perch, often a tall electricity pylon. Its usual food includes grass snakes, European whip snakes, Montpellier snakes, and less often adders, which it typically grips behind the head and carries off to a perch to eat.

DISPLAY AND VOICE
Like other eagles and buzzards, it displays in flight, performing deep undulations above the breeding territory. Pairs may often be seen flying together, their tails closed, heads thrust forward, and wings stretched out flat and straight in a marked cross-shape. The various calls recall the squealing sounds of gulls.

BREEDING
In spring, the eagles always return to the same place, so pairs form life-long bonds. Together, they build a nest of sticks in a tall tree such as an oak. Just one egg is incubated, mostly by the female, for 45–47 days. The chick flies at 10 weeks old. They breed when 3–4 years old.

MIGRATION
In autumn, all European Short-toed Eagles migrate to mid-Africa, with concentrated movements over Gibraltar and the Bosphorus in August and September. The adults return in March and April.

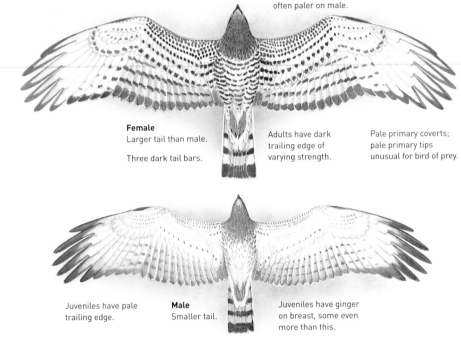

Adult
Head/chest can be dark and hooded; often paler on male.

Female
Larger tail than male.

Three dark tail bars.

Adults have dark trailing edge of varying strength.

Pale primary coverts; pale primary tips unusual for bird of prey.

Juveniles have pale trailing edge.

Male
Smaller tail.

Juveniles have ginger on breast, some even more than this.

Hovers expertly, but looks heavy; wing beats deep, or it may just wobble outer wing.

White underside often has dull or silvery effect at long range; crisp barring shows in close view.

Juvenile

Large, owl-like, loose-feathered head; magnificent yellow eye.

Pale, unfeathered legs.

Adult

WHEN SEEN

Sept — March

March or April to September.

WHERE SEEN
Spain, S France, Italy, and the Balkans; only a rare vagrant outside breeding range.

HABITAT AND INFO

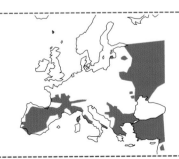

SIMILAR SPECIES
Osprey has more angled wings; obvious dark wrist patch; darker upperside.

Black wrist patch

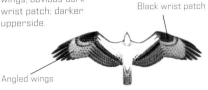

Angled wings

SNAKE EAGLE
The big, round head, yellow eyes, and
bare legs characterize this big eagle.

Adult
Upperside can look
patchy with fading
and moult.

Juvenile
Looks neat, without
irregular patchy effect.

Soaring, wings raised.

Gliding, wings
flat/drooped.

Pale juvenile
Gliding away.

Looks slim- or broad-
winged, depending on
angle and attitude;
displays with wings
straight and flat,
head outstretched.

Adult
Gliding on angled wings.

Variable extent and
weight of barring at
all ages; older females
have dark hood, some
with white chin.

DID YOU KNOW?

This bird's reliance on eating snakes, up to 1m (3ft) long, is shown by
many studies. At a nest in France, 67 of 70 items brought to a nest
were snakes (two were lizards, one a finch). Venomous snakes are
usually less frequent in the diet than in the local snake population and
the eagle is not immune to venom.

White-tailed Eagle

SCALE v Woodpigeon

LENGTH / 77–92cm (30½–36in)
WINGSPAN / 2–2.4m (6½–7¾ft)
WEIGHT / 3.1–7kg (7–15lb)

■ **STATUS** / Vulnerable

One of Europe's giants, it is a broad, flat-winged bird of prey with a massive yellow bill, bare legs, a protruding head, and a short tail.

Drainage of lakes and marshes, disturbance of previously untouched wildernesses, pollution, and persecution have dealt a succession of severe blows to the White-tailed Eagle. Like many other large European birds of prey, it has dwindled in both numbers and range, and in some countries, its populations have been reduced to the tiniest remnants. Nevertheless, protection measures have encouraged a small recovery in parts of northern Europe. The Norwegian population is thriving and a concerted effort to reintroduce it to Scotland is, so far, succeeding. So the future of this magnificent bird is, for a time, secure, if only in a small part of its past range. Unlike Golden Eagles, which are typically shy and aloof, White-tailed Eagles may settle close to coastal or lakeside villages, especially where small harbours offer the chance of free handouts of fish and offal.

FEEDING

It eats mainly fish, finding most of them dead, washed up onto shores or floating on the surface. It also captures live fish in its feet as it swoops onto lakes or sheltered coastal bays, and may even catch large fish in shallow water by hunting on foot. It kills medium-sized or large birds with a short, surprise stoop, but also takes wildfowl and Coots by forcing them to dive repeatedly until, exhausted, they are no longer able to escape.

DISPLAY AND VOICE

Pairs remain in their territories all year, but increase their displays in spring. They soar together, sometimes with shallow undulations, and one will dive at the other. Sometimes the lower bird will roll over and the two interlock their feet. Occasionally the two then spin down toward the ground, one upside down beneath the other. They call much more often than Golden Eagles, with various dog-like yapping sounds or screeches, higher-pitched from the male, often in an accelerating sequence of 15–20 calls.

BREEDING

The nests are built of thick sticks, on ledges or in particularly large, old, sturdy trees. When close to villages or towns, they are always in inaccessible places: in Norway, often on small, rocky offshore islands. Up to three eggs hatch after 34–42 days. Often only one, sometimes two, very rarely three young fledge after about 10 weeks. They breed at five years old.

MIGRATION

Adults are resident, but immatures wander quite widely.

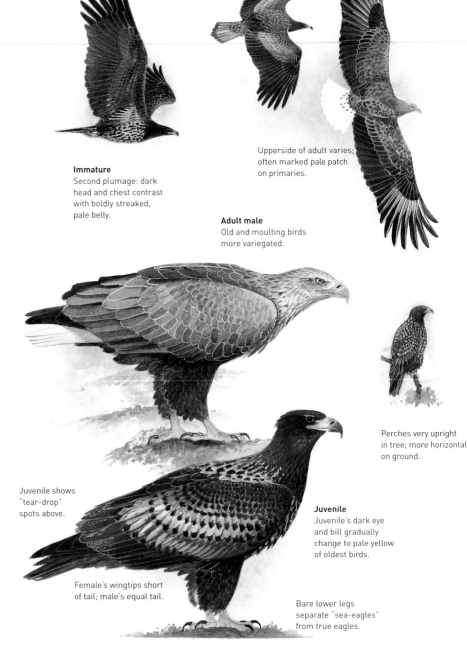

Immature
Second plumage: dark head and chest contrast with boldly streaked, pale belly.

Upperside of adult varies; often marked pale patch on primaries.

Adult male
Old and moulting birds more variegated.

Perches very upright in tree; more horizontal on ground.

Juvenile shows "tear-drop" spots above.

Juvenile
Juvenile's dark eye and bill gradually change to pale yellow of oldest birds.

Female's wingtips short of tail; male's equal tail.

Bare lower legs separate "sea-eagles" from true eagles.

WHERE SEEN
Breeds NW Iceland, Norway, Baltic coasts, very locally Scotland, NE Europe, Balkans; very rare in winter in N France, Low Countries, and some central European lakes and marshes.

HABITAT AND INFO

SIMILAR SPECIES
Osprey is much smaller, much whiter beneath and more contrasted, and has a small, dark bill.

Whiter head

Slender wingtips

Adult female
Wedge-shaped
tail; pale head.

Adult male
Tail squarer; head
even paler.

Sailing/gliding,
wings arched.

Soaring, wings raised,
well forward.

Gliding away: wingtips
look pointed at this angle,
as on big vultures.

Head protrudes well
forward; may appear to
droop, unlike neater
Golden Eagle.

Flapping flight –
"all wings".

Huge, square, fingered wings give
door-like impression, unlike
Golden Eagle; constant heavy
flapping on long flights.

Juvenile's pale inner
wing patch often
conspicuous.

Juvenile male
Rear of wing curves
forward into body on
male; straighter on
female (below).

Upper side of juvenile's
tail has whitish feathers
edged and tipped
dark; feathers become
whiter with each
succeeding moult.

Juveniles have pointed flight
feathers, giving saw-tooth
trailing edge.

Juvenile female
Longer body gives
impression of longer
tail than male.

Adults look magnificent
against blue sky
in sunshine.

FLIGHT PATTERN
Heavy with flat or arched
wings. Soars expertly.

DID YOU KNOW?
It is hard to decide whether food eaten by White-tailed Eagles is
caught alive, scavenged after it has died, or (in either case) stolen
from other predators. They catch fish, adult and young seabirds and
herons, and rarely birds as large as swans, and steal from Ospreys,
kites, buzzards, Peregrines, gulls, and even Snowy Owls.

Spotted Eagle

ORDER / Falconiformes
FAMILY / Accipitridae
SPECIES / Aquila clanga
COMMON NAME / Spotted Eagle

LENGTH / 62–74cm (24½–29in)
WINGSPAN / 1.5–1.8m (5–6ft)
WEIGHT / 2.4–4.8kg (5½–11lb)

■ STATUS / Endangered

SCALE v Woodpigeon

A medium-sized but heavy, square-looking, short-tailed eagle, usually very dark, with a pale crescent that is more or less obvious toward the wingtip.

A very rare bird in Europe, this is smaller than the widespread Golden Eagle but in some ways recalls the large and less closely related White-tailed Eagle. It is usually associated with water, but needs extensive woodlands in summer.

FEEDING
Typically a rodent-eater, catching field voles and water voles, the Spotted Eagle may turn to birds in years when voles are scarce. It snatches young herons, gulls, Rooks, and doves from nests, but is not agile enough to catch many adult birds such as Coots or ducks on the water.

DISPLAY AND VOICE
Screeching dip-dip-dip-dip calls are often heard over breeding sites.

MIGRATION
The breeding grounds are occupied in March and April, and vacated in September and October. A few Spotted Eagles winter in southern Europe, but most spend the winter (and their first three years of immaturity) in east Africa.

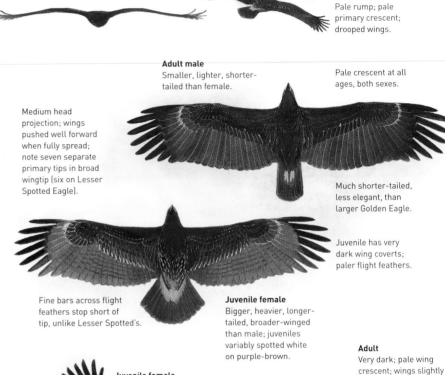

Sub-adult
Pale rump; pale primary crescent; drooped wings.

Adult male
Smaller, lighter, shorter-tailed than female.

Pale crescent at all ages, both sexes.

Medium head projection; wings pushed well forward when fully spread; note seven separate primary tips in broad wingtip (six on Lesser Spotted Eagle).

Much shorter-tailed, less elegant, than larger Golden Eagle.

Juvenile has very dark wing coverts; paler flight feathers.

Fine bars across flight feathers stop short of tip, unlike Lesser Spotted's.

Juvenile female
Bigger, heavier, longer-tailed, broader-winged than male; juveniles variably spotted white on purple-brown.

Adult
Very dark; pale wing crescent; wings slightly drooped, not raised as in Golden Eagle's.

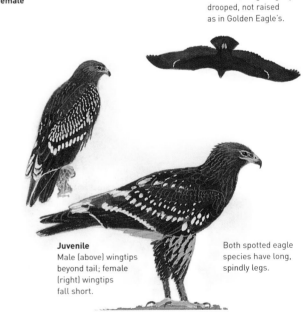

Juvenile female

Adult female

Juvenile
Male (above) wingtips beyond tail; female (right) wingtips fall short.

Both spotted eagle species have long, spindly legs.

LONG-LEGGED EAGLE
Spotted Eagles have rather long thighs and bare, slender lower legs.

WHEN SEEN
All year.

WHERE SEEN
Breeds east of Baltic; in winter, very rare in France, Italy, Greece; only a very rare vagrant elsewhere.

HABITAT AND INFO

SIMILAR SPECIES
Lesser Spotted Eagle has more distinct pale forewing/dark hindwing; narrower wing.

Paler forewing

Slimmer shape

Lesser Spotted Eagle

A medium-sized brown eagle, generally paler than the Spotted Eagle but best identified with experience and care by its shape and often paler wing coverts.

LENGTH / 57–64cm (22–25in)
WINGSPAN / 1.4–1.7m (4³⁄₄–5¹⁄₂ft)
WEIGHT / 1.3–2kg (2³⁄₄–4¹⁄₂lb)

■ **STATUS /** Vulnerable

SCALE v Woodpigeon

Adults mid-brown; slight pale crescent on wing; coverts paler than flight feathers (reverse on Spotted).

Adult male
Wing, head, and bill length as female; tail shorter.

Juvenile female
Bars on flight feathers extend to tip; thin whitish line along midwing; many have ginger body/covert feathers with paler central streak.

Lighter, more agile than Spotted; smaller, shorter-tailed than Golden and Imperial; head projects well forward; tail has slight wedge shape; six separated primary tips.

Male Lesser Spotted
Adult brown with pale rump, pale coverts and head.

Spotted, Adult female

Lesser Spotted, Adult female

Juvenile

Male Spotted

Juvenile female
Paler than juvenile Spotted; white midwing bar rather than rows of spots.

Slightly drooped wing flatter in soar or glide than Spotted's.

A few hundred pairs of Lesser Spotted Eagles breed in Europe, making this a much more regular European bird than its slightly larger relative. It is a bird of forested areas with large clearings, marshes, and damp plains.

FEEDING
Small mammals, especially voles, as well as frogs and small birds make up a diet that is more typical of buzzards than eagles. It hunts either by soaring, watching from a perch such as a post or a tree top, or by wandering about on the ground on foot, jumping or running after prey on its relatively long, slim legs.

DISPLAY AND VOICE
A high, musical, rhythmic *dip-dip-dip* is often heard.

BREEDING
Nests are big platforms of sticks and leaves in trees. Usually two eggs hatch after being incubated for 38–41 days by the female only. The chicks fly after another eight weeks.

MIGRATION
In September and early October, thousands pass over the Bosphorus on their way to Africa. Many fewer return in April.

NEAT RAPTOR
Lesser Spotteds are smart, tidy-looking, sharp-faced eagles.

WHEN SEEN

April to October.

WHERE SEEN
Breeds N Germany eastward, locally south to Greece; migrates south-east in autumn; a very few head north-west in error and reach Scandinavia.

HABITAT AND INFO

SIMILAR SPECIES
Golden Eagle has longer, broader wings; longer tail; no pale crescent at base of primaries; often darker tailband.

Pale upperwing band

Dark tailband

Golden Eagle

LENGTH / 76-89cm (30-35in)
WINGSPAN / 1.9-2.2m (6¼-7¼ft)
WEIGHT / 3-6.7kg (7-15lb)

■ **STATUS /** Vulnerable

SCALE v Woodpigeon

A majestic, elegant, and powerful raptor, it soars on broad wings and mounts spectacular high-speed display flights in winter and spring. It is one of Europe's most impressive birds.

Combining great size and power with real grace and poise, the Golden Eagle is one of Europe's most inspirational species. Its expression manages to combine ferocity and purpose with intelligence and a truly regal bearing. Such attributes have not, however, saved it from centuries of persecution, and in common with many other raptors, it has also suffered from habitat degradation, disturbance, and pollution. Yet, like the Osprey and Peregrine, it retains a remarkably wide distribution worldwide, and flourishes in parts of Spain and Scotland. It particularly likes mountainous regions, exploiting both harsh, barren moors and more varied terrain with rocky peaks, extensive crags, and thickly-forested mountainsides.

FEEDING

A Golden Eagle finds much of its food already dead: carrion, in the form of sheep and deer that have died of exposure or starvation during the harsh upland winter and early spring. At other times it captures medium-sized mammals and birds, including mountain hares, brown hares, rabbits, grouse, Ptarmigan, waders, and gulls. It is an opportunist, taking a wide range of prey. It kills young deer, foxes, and badgers at times, as well as voles, mice, lizards, and even tortoises.

DISPLAY AND VOICE

In winter and spring, a Golden Eagle performs dramatic display flights: diving, climbing, and then half-closing its wings and looking from side to side before tilting over and diving down again. It soars high, then drops in a steep or near-vertical plunge, wingtips held tight over its tail but the front of each wing pushed out from the body to give a broad tear-drop shape. In such dives, it probably outpaces almost any other bird. It is not often heard, but has a variety of sharp yelping calls, one a sharp *kip* recalling an Oystercatcher's call.

BREEDING

The nests are rebuilt in late winter and decorated with green sprays in spring, so over many years they become vast piles of sticks, sprays, and bits of earth, sited on inaccessible cliff ledges or in big trees, especially old Scots pines. There may be three, four, or several more alternative nests, of which one or two are particularly favoured, depending partly on the snow cover in spring. Two eggs are usual, incubated by the female for 43–45 days. Typically one chick will kill the other before fledging after 65–70 days.

MIGRATION

Most are resident, with random dispersal by young birds. In north-eastern Europe and Asia, there are winter movements to the south and west.

Glides between beats in direct flight on flatter wings.

Marked bulge to inner wing in rear view.

Dramatic switchback displays and steep dives at extremely high speed.

Adult male

Adult female

Big bill; flat head; strong feet; thighs heavily feathered.

Juvenile
Fresh plumage rich dark brown; crown and nape pale; white patches on thighs.

Adult
New feathers black-brown, paler at base; old feathers bleach paler, golden, buff or greyish; tail often pale grey at base with thin dark bars.

WHEN SEEN

All year.

WHERE SEEN
Breeds Scotland, Scandinavia, Spain, Alps, Italy, Balkans, some Mediterranean islands, and NE Europe.

HABITAT AND INFO

SIMILAR SPECIES
Spotted Eagle has shorter, broader wings; shorter head; is more uniformly dark.

Broad round wingtips

Short tail

MAJESTIC PRESENCE
A massive eagle, with an undoubted
regal bearing and expression.

Juvenile
Striking wing and tail
patches aid instant
recognition; white
reduces with age.

Adult
Paler with wear,
especially across
upperwing coverts.

Adult female
Predominantly dark;
underwing faintly
barred; weak,
dark tailband.

Adult male
As female but smaller,
with slimmer wings
and longer tail.

Juvenile
Can look blackish
except for bold white
wing patches and
white tail base; broad
black tailband.

Soars with wings at full
stretch, pushed well
forward, fingers widely
spread, tail either
fanned or closed.

Much bigger, longer-
winged, plainer than
Common Buzzard,
typically silent and
seen at long range;
Common Buzzard
often close, perches
on posts, calls a lot.

Soaring.

Gliding fast.

FLIGHT PATTERN
Soars with wings in
quite deep V; pale
forewing evident.

DID YOU KNOW?
Adult Golden Eagles are essentially plain brown but exhibit a wide
range of patterns, largely due to the fading of feathers with age and
exposure. A new, dark, purple-brown feather can fade to a pale straw
colour within a single sunny summer. The areas of feathers usually
hidden beneath adjacent ones remain dark, while the
exposed parts bleach quickly.

?

Imperial Eagle

SCALE v Woodpigeon

LENGTH / 74–84cm (29–33in)
WINGSPAN / 1.7–2.1m (5½–6¾ft)
WEIGHT / 2.4–4kg (5½–9lb)

■ STATUS / Endangered

A large, dark, flat-winged eagle, most like Golden but with distinctive immature plumage patterns. Has two forms.

The two separate races of Imperial Eagles may well be two distinct species: if they are not yet, they must be well on the way to becoming so. In Spain, a few scores of pairs of the form *adalberti* breed on forested plains and near coastal marshes. Farther east, the *heliaca* group occupies a variety of terrain from steppe grassland to wooded hillsides and large deltas. Whether considered together or separately, these must be the most threatened eagles in Europe, suffering from persecution, pollution, disturbance, and habitat loss. Imperial Eagles look much like Golden Eagles and are equally imposing when perched, but they do not have quite the same poise and shapeliness in flight.

FEEDING
Their main prey includes medium-sized mammals, such as sousliks and young hares, rabbits, and marmots, as well as a wide variety of birds, especially young waterfowl, herons, Magpies, and crows. More rarely, they kill lizards and snakes. Birds are usually taken by surprise and caught as they try to fly off. Frequently, one eagle will startle the prey while its mate takes up the ideal position to capture it when it is flushed. They kill mammals in short, fast stoops from soaring flight or from a perch, the weight of the bird and the power in its legs and feet delivering a killing blow.

DISPLAY AND VOICE
Pairs perform display flights from almost the beginning of the year, circling for hours over their breeding territory. They grasp talons together and fall toward the ground, or call loudly as they circle in the clear air. Much more vocal than Golden Eagles, they call with a goose-like or Raven-like bark: a gruff *krrr-krrr-krrr*.

BREEDING
The nest is a big, flat-topped affair made of thick sticks, built by both sexes in the top of a broad tree. Both birds incubate 2–3 eggs for 43 days. Like other eagles, they begin to incubate when the first egg is laid, so the later eggs hatch several days after the first. Despite this – which means that the later young are much smaller and weaker than the first – two, sometimes even three, chicks often survive to fledge after 65–77 days.

MIGRATION
Spanish Imperial Eagles are resident. In eastern Europe, most of the young birds move south in autumn to spend the winter in Africa and the Middle East. A small proportion of the adults migrate to the edge of the breeding range, but many remain on their territories throughout the year.

Spanish adults
Sail along (above) on bent, uplifted wings; glide (right) on bowed wings; soar (left) on flexible, upturned wings.

Sub-adult female (above)
Black spots appear on ginger underwing and body; already has pale vent.

Square shape unlike that of other eagles.

Pale inner primary patch; pale trailing edge and tail tip on juveniles.

Juvenile male
Streaked body unique to young Imperial; pale outer wing; dark hindwing with buff tip when fresh.

Golden Eagle, juvenile male
Spanish bird: larger, broader wings than Imperial's (even more pronounced in female).

Spanish adult
Eastern birds do not have extensive white forewing (variable braces only).

Eastern juvenile
Spots/lines above seen on no other eagle; Spanish juvenile solid rufous.

Unique breast/belly streaks on eastern juveniles and adult females.

Wings equal tail on female; longer on male.

WHEN SEEN

All year.

WHERE SEEN
Central and SW Spain; locally Bulgaria, Romania, Greece.

HABITAT AND INFO

SIMILAR SPECIES
Golden Eagle holds wings in V; less contrasted tail; lacks white on forewing; more shapely wings.

Browner tail base

Paler upperwing band

BANDED IMMATURE
Adults look plain, but immature birds
are brightly patterned.

Juvenile female

Female

Male (left)
Short tail distinctive.

Eastern adult
Pale head; white
braces; grey tail
fades browner.

Juvenile female

Tail feathers: from
juvenile (left), to full
adult at nine years
old (right).

Immature male
Pale inner primaries;
white uppertail coverts
appear as juvenile
gets older.

Square-winged, crow-like shape,
head well forward; pale feet and
vent; two-tone tail.

Spanish adult female
Spanish birds blacker;
eastern adults
much browner;
profiles identical.

Adult male
Tail shorter than
female's; not
always so square.

DID YOU KNOW?
Although one of the rarest birds of prey of Europe, the Imperial Eagle
is still illegally shot, trapped, and poisoned. Recent research reveals a
higher population than previously thought, with 600–900 pairs in
European Russia. Nevertheless, elsewhere it is declining: it is now
absent from Greece, and there are just 20–25 pairs in
Bulgaria and 10–50 pairs in Turkey.

Red-footed Falcon

ORDER Falconiformes
FAMILY Falconidae
SPECIES *Falco vespertinus*
COMMON NAME Red-footed Falcon

LENGTH / 28–31cm (11–12in)
WINGSPAN / 65–76cm (25½–30in)
WEIGHT / 130–195g (4½–7oz)

■ STATUS / Secure

SCALE v Woodpigeon

A gentle-looking, small-billed, lightweight falcon, it is usually seen perched or flying in pursuit of insects, combining some characteristics of the Kestrel and the Hobby. Male and female plumages are very different, but are equally distinctive.

Not all falcons are dramatic, fast-flying, solitary bird-eaters: the Red-footed is not, but it is nevertheless a true falcon and it can fly with speed and precision when required. Rather than travelling alone it flies in small flocks; it even breeds in large colonies. In other ways it most closely resembles the Lesser Kestrel, the Hobby, and Eleonora's Falcon.

FEEDING

This small falcon likes open areas such as grassy steppes, woodland clearings, and the edges of marshes, over which it flies in pursuit of insect prey. It watches from a tree, post, wire, or other suitable perch, rather like a shrike, until it spots a suitable victim and gives chase. It may also hunt from the air, more like a Hobby (indeed, frequently in association with Hobbies). It hunts mainly in the morning and evening. It catches grasshoppers, beetles, caterpillars, ants, and spiders on the ground, and neatly plucks dragonflies, bees, wasps, mayflies, and craneflies from the air with its feet and transfers them to its bill to be eaten in flight.

DISPLAY AND VOICE

Pairs soar together in spring and the male will dive at the female. The male also flies fast over the territory and dives toward the female on the nest, calling loudly. Calls are typical falcon *kew-kew-kew-kew* notes, fast and rhythmic, but weaker than the calls of a Kestrel or Hobby.

BREEDING

Typically Red-footed Falcons take over the nests of Rooks. Several pairs will occupy a colony, from a few to a couple of dozen. Today, 50 pairs are considered a large colony, but in the past, as many as 500 pairs bred in colonies in eastern Europe. The 3–4 (rarely as many as 6) eggs are incubated by both sexes for 28 days. The chicks fledge after a month.

MIGRATION

All Red-footed Falcons migrate in autumn to spend the winter in Angola, Namibia, Zimbabwe, and Botswana. They leave in September and October and return, using a more westerly route, from March onward. In spring and summer, there are sporadic occurrences well to the west of the breeding range, mainly involving immatures, but rarely adult males. These influxes usually occur in May and June, and the birds may range as far west as Britain. In some years, they involve so many birds that they amount to small irruptions.

First-summer male
Commoner in western Europe than adults.

First-summer male
Rufous collar, brown on wings, rufous beneath tail; all vary in strength.

Juvenile
Very white around face and each side of neck, with thin central stripe; tail barred, unlike Hobby's.

Adult female (right)
Orange crown and nape fade to white; unique grey back and orange breast; barred grey tail.

First-summer female
Head gradually fades paler.

First-summer female
New, broadly-barred grey feathers and old, browner, narrowly-barred ones on back, wings, and tail.

Adult male
Red bill base, eye-ring, and legs; rusty vent.

WHEN SEEN

Oct — April

April to October.

WHERE SEEN

Breeds Hungary, Romania, Bulgaria, and farther east; rarely and irregularly elsewhere; sporadic visitor, sometimes rare but widespread, west to Britain, Balearics, Sweden.

HABITAT AND INFO

SIMILAR SPECIES

Juvenile Hobby has sharper wings; darker cap; darker above with plainer tail.

Darker head pattern

Plainer tail

SMOKY-GREY BEAUTY
Adult males have a lovely soft, grey
plumage and bright red on the bill.

Adult female
Unique all-orange
underparts and
red legs.

First-summer male
Strongly chequered
underwing.

First-year male
Moulting to adult in
autumn: new dark
flight feathers among
old barred ones.

Adult male
All-dark head
and breast; rufous
beneath tail.

Eating insect in flight.

Hovering.

Glides on slightly
drooped wings.

First-summer male
Variable barring on
underwing, rufous on
chest; legs orange,
pinkish, or pale red.

Juvenile
Whitish throat and
vent; may have pale
forehead; dark trailing
edge to wing.

Juvenile
White throat and white
spot each side of nape;
buff feather edges on
upperparts.

Adult female
Distinctive rufous cap;
barred grey tail.

Adult male
Pale on wing shines
silvery in good light;
dark hood, back, tail.

DID YOU KNOW?
Unusually for a bird of prey, most of the population of Red-footed
Falcons migrates south into eastern Africa in autumn. However the
majority move north much farther west in spring. As a vagrant in
north-west Europe it is much more common in May and June than
at other times, with small numbers of non-breeding birds
regularly overshooting their regular range.

Hobby

LENGTH / 28–35cm (11–14in)
WINGSPAN / 70–84cm (27½–33in)
WEIGHT / 130–340g (4½–12oz)

■ **STATUS /** Secure

SCALE v Woodpigeon

An elegant, long-winged, and short-tailed falcon, with a bold head pattern and dark body. It is able to accelerate to a great pace from its relaxed patrolling flight.

Like the Red-footed Falcon, this is largely an insect-eater, but it is faster, slightly more powerful, and also takes a lot of birds in some seasons. Few birds match Hobbies for sheer grace and brilliance of flight: it is a joy to watch them in summer as they cover wide areas using a minimum of energy. Somehow they contrive to fly long distances with scarcely a wing beat, employing a few flaps every so often to accelerate smoothly, gain height, and snatch an insect from the air with lethal accuracy before moving on as before: fast, smooth, effortless. Close views reveal that they are also beautifully patterned, always well turned out, and extremely handsome.

FEEDING
Half the Hobby's diet consists of large flying insects such as dragonflies, wasps, bees, cockchafers, big beetles, and butterflies. It eats flying ants with relish, as well as much bigger termites in winter in Africa. It also catches small birds of many kinds, mostly in the air: Swallows, larks, martins, sparrows, and finches. Many are caught at dusk as they go to roost, and mixed Swallow, martin, and wagtail roosts in reed beds often attract Hobbies in the autumn. The falcon takes birds to a perch to dismember and eat them, but it eats large insects in mid-air, holding them in its feet as it glides around, head bent down, biting off pieces as it goes.

DISPLAY AND VOICE
As you might expect from such a fine aerial acrobat, the Hobby displays with vigour and panache: pairs soar together, the male often diving at the slightly larger female or catching prey and passing it to her in the air. The female rolls over beneath him, stretches out a foot, and the gift is accepted. They also fly rapidly with deep, fast wing beats giving a great turn of speed. Calls are loud, nasal, quickly repeated bursts: *kew-kew-kew-kew*. Yet despite such vocal and aerial activity, Hobbies are notoriously difficult to observe around the nest once their eggs are laid.

BREEDING
Three eggs are laid in an old crow's nest or some similar structure in a tree, often a pine. They hatch after 28–31 days, after being incubated almost entirely by the female. The chicks fledge after 28–34 days. Breeding success depends to a large extent on escaping predation by crows, and on the weather: in wet summers they may rear few young.

MIGRATION
All Hobbies leave Europe between August and October to winter in southern and western Africa. They return in April and May.

Direct, fast flight.

Snatches dragonflies, then holds them in feet to eat while flying.

Adult male
Striking yellow feet and handsome head pattern.

Juvenile
Lacy pale feather edges above, but dark in flight; dull below with no rufous, thick stripes; pale tail tip but no other bars.

WHEN SEEN

Oct — April

April to October.

WHERE SEEN
S Britain, S and E Scandinavia, south to Mediterranean.

HABITAT AND INFO

SIMILAR SPECIES
Peregrine has broader shoulders, rump and tail; barred beneath; broader-based wings.

Heavier build

Barred beneath

Juvenile female
Young birds have pale tail tip; pale trailing edge to wing; browner edges above; duller head.

Adult male
Dark slaty, fades quite brown; not so pale on rump as Peregrine; narrower body.

Black hood, white neck patch striking.

Male's wings extend 25mm (1in) beyond tail, female's 10mm (⅜in).

First summer
Worn brown upperparts, develops dark grey on back.

Adult female
White neck/throat; rufous thighs; rather dark overall.

Adult female

Kestrel
Soaring with wings forward, tail spread.

Female Kestrel
Can be remarkably like Hobby, but has broader wings, rounder tail tip.

Juvenile
White neck side obvious; pale forehead; no rufous; dark underwing and body (compare with juvenile Red-footed Falcon).

Adult female

Hobby
More angular, wings sharper.

Adult male
Longer "arm", shorter tail than female.

FLIGHT PATTERN
Fast flight very precise, snappy, with deep beats of sharp wings; pursues large insects with fast chase, then strikes with slow, floating stall.

DID YOU KNOW?
Long associated with heathland, the Hobby has recently increased in ordinary farmland areas, but this is perhaps connected with the proliferation of flooded gravel pits in lowland river valleys. These have become valuable wetland habitats and attract dragonflies and also martins, the Hobby's favourite foods. Tall trees nearby remain essential for nesting.

Lesser Kestrel

SCALE v Woodpigeon

LENGTH / 29–32cm (11½–12½in)
WINGSPAN / 63–72cm (25–28½in)
WEIGHT / 90–200g (3¼–7oz)

■ **STATUS /** Endangered

Much scarcer than the Kestrel, it is very similar but with narrower wings. Its inner wing is much shorter and its outer wing is longer, giving a subtly different shape.

Although very like the Kestrel in appearance, the Lesser Kestrel is a much rarer bird, far more restricted to the warmer parts of Europe, and also a genuine migrant over the whole of its range. Owing to the effects of modern farming in its breeding range, with pesticides eliminating much of its insect food, the Lesser Kestrel is declining fast in Europe; in some areas where once it was common, it is now threatened with extinction. It prefers open, often cultivated countryside with scattered trees, old buildings, or cliffs.

FEEDING

This species is much more insectivorous than the Kestrel. It eats chiefly grasshoppers, beetles, crickets, and cockchafers; in Africa, it preys heavily on termites. It catches a few lizards, far fewer mammals such as voles, and very rarely small birds. It usually hunts from a perch, less often by hovering, and simply drops down to its prey like a shrike. This technique is most effective on very open ground, even places where sparse vegetation exposes a lot of bare earth. Such feeding areas offering an abundance of insect prey must be within easy reach of a town, cliff, or trees, where there are safe nest sites.

DISPLAY AND VOICE

Males reach the breeding territories earlier than females, searching for likely nest sites. When the females arrive, the males display with simple circling flights and dive toward their mates. Much more social than the Kestrel, the Lesser Kestrel is also more vocal, using hoarse *chay-chay-chay* notes and a more musical, wader-like *vivivivi*.

BREEDING

They nest in colonies, with as many as 100, or even 200, pairs breeding together in suitable areas. The 3–5 eggs are laid directly on a cliff ledge or in a deeper cleft inside a cave, a niche in a large town building or old ruin, or a cavity in a dead tree. Both sexes incubate for 28–29 days, and the chicks fly when 28 days old. Pairs stay together for just a single season.

MIGRATION

A very few adults spend the winter in the extreme south of Europe or in north Africa. The rest of the population moves on south in autumn, to the plains of Africa south of the Sahara and on down the east coast. Large groups forage over the migrating herds of big mammals in east Africa, preying on the many insects they disturb from the grass. Lesser Kestrels from western Asia reach South Africa, where many thousands roost together in large trees.

Kestrel, female
95 percent are dark on cheek.

Back unmarked.

Lesser Kestrel, female
Light cheek; moustache effect shown here at strongest, often paler.

Long wingtips nearer tail tip than on Kestrel's: wingtips reach black tailband at all ages and in both sexes.

Male
Richly coloured; bluish wing patches; plain flanks.

Juvenile
Buffer cheek than female (far right); pale chin; bars on upperparts duller, edged pale.

All have pale claws (black on Kestrel).

Female
More often grey on uppertail coverts and rump than Kestrel's.

Juvenile
Tail patterns vary in both sexes, as Kestrel's; tends to have narrower bars.

Lesser Kestrel   Kestrel
Coverts of Lesser Kestrel have narrower bands.

WHEN SEEN

Sept — March

March to September.

WHERE SEEN
Spain and Portugal, where declining fast; rare S France, Sardinia, S Italy, Greece; rare vagrant elsewhere.

HABITAT AND INFO

SIMILAR SPECIES
Male Kestrel is spotted on back; female very similar.

Spots on back

No grey in wing

RARE MIGRANT
Lesser Kestrels are declining, perhaps
because of problems in Africa.

Female
Underwing too variable
to help identification;
rear flank unmarked
(streaked on Kestrel).

Dark wingtips.

Male
Underwing entirely
white or variably dotted;
breast plain or dotted
dark on chest and sides.

Female

Slow descent.

Gliding

Fast glide when hunting.

Sailing on the wind.

Male, first summer
Barred tail sides;
no grey on wing;
mottled coverts.

Soaring.

Compare shapes with
Kestrel (pages 172–3):
note short "arm",
narrow tail often
with central feathers
extending (but beware
effects of moult).

Male
Adult has blue head,
blue tail, blue patch on
wing (but may be less
contrasted in some
lights and when worn).

Head plain bluish;
duskier around bill
but no moustache.

Soaring with wings
slightly raised, less
broad or pushed
forward than Kestrel's.

FLIGHT PATTERN
Wing beats shallow and
quick; hovers frequently;
also takes long, higher
patrolling flights after
insects over open ground,
with supple action more
like Hobby's.

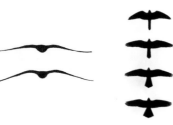

DID YOU KNOW?
Rodenticides caused serious declines of the Lesser Kestrel in
countries such as Israel a few decades ago, and intensive farming
with the use of insecticides has caused populations to crash
elsewhere. From being a common and widespread bird of
southern Europe, this bird has become a rare one with
serious concerns for its future. Similar factors in African
wintering grounds exacerbate the problems.

Kestrel

ORDER *Falconiformes*
FAMILY *Falconidae*
SPECIES *Falco tinnunculus*
COMMON NAME Kestrel

LENGTH / 33–39cm (13–15½in)
WINGSPAN / 65–80cm (25½–31½in)
WEIGHT / 190–300g (6¾–10½oz)

■ STATUS / Secure

SCALE v Woodpigeon

The everyday falcon almost everywhere, it is typical of farmland and roadsides as well as wilder areas and cliffs. Its persistent hovering is highly characteristic.

Although it is one of the smaller, less dramatic, and less powerful of the falcons, the Kestrel is capable of giving exciting aerial performances, especially given a strong wind swirling against a sheer cliff, in which it can soar and climb and stoop again almost in the manner of a Peregrine. Yet it is as a roadside hunter, perched on trees, wires, or telegraph poles, or most distinctively, hovering head-to-wind above a grassy road verge, that the Kestrel is most familiar.

FEEDING

The Kestrel preys mainly on small mammals: mostly voles and rather fewer mice. It can catch rats, but it usually avoids large prey. If it takes them by surprise a Kestrel can fly fast enough, briefly, to catch small birds including House Sparrows, finches, and starlings. A variety of grasshoppers, beetles, lizards, and the young of larger birds make up a smaller proportion of its varied diet. It has acute eyesight, and it is likely that a Kestrel can see well in a wavelength invisible to people; the prey that remains so well hidden to our eyes probably gives itself away more easily to a hunting falcon. When hovering, the Kestrel is able to keep its head still relative to the ground, absorbing the effects of the wind by moving its body and adjusting its wings and tail. It also detects a lot of prey when watching from a suitable perch, and Kestrels are frequently seen hunting at dusk.

DISPLAY AND VOICE

The display flights over breeding territories are low, fast, twisting circuits with rapid, almost flickering wing beats. The male also dives at the female as she perches. The calls used during displays, and often at other times, are high, nasal, rather weak repetitive notes: *kee-kee-kee-kee*.

BREEDING

No nest is made; the female lays her eggs on a bare ledge on a cliff, in a quarry, or on a tall building, inside a large cavity in a tree or in an artificial nest box. The usual clutch is 3–6, rarely as many as 9 eggs, which hatch after 27–29 days. The chicks fly after about 27–32 days. They remain dependent on their parents for a further month or more.

MIGRATION

Kestrels from north-east and northern Europe migrate, escaping the cold winter weather to travel south and west, some of them going as far as central Africa. Most other European Kestrels are more or less resident, but young birds in particular may move generally southward in winter.

Juvenile

Gliding.

Display flight fast, rolling, with very quick, shallow wing beats.

aSoaring.

Gliding away: very narrow tail; wings longer-tipped than Sparrowhawk's, which can look similar in this attitude.

Male **Female**
Often watches for prey from post, tree or wire; active, even hovering, until late dusk.

Adult male
Grey head; weak moustache; spotted back; blue-grey tail.

Adult female
Beautifully barred over back and tail.

WHEN SEEN

All year except in far north and east, where mostly April to October.

WHERE SEEN
All of Europe except Iceland and bleakest parts of Scandinavia.

HABITAT AND INFO

SIMILAR SPECIES
Sparrowhawk has squatter shape; squarer wings; shorter wingtip; does not hover.

Short wings

Barred beneath

Male has pale underwing, can look very white in sun or reflected light, but more marked than Lesser Kestrel's.

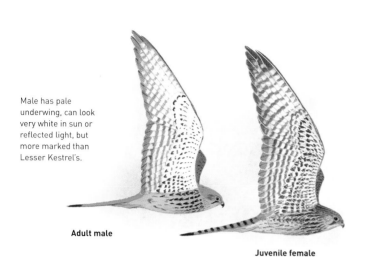

Adult male

Juvenile female

Classic hover.

Female
Gliding.

Male
Gliding; narrow wings.

Male
Gliding fast.

Female
Soaring.

Distinctive pale inner wing and dark outer wing in both sexes.

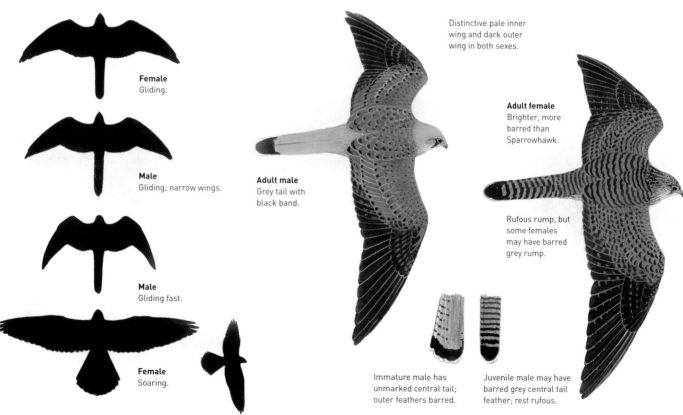

Adult male
Grey tail with black band.

Adult female
Brighter, more barred than Sparrowhawk.

Rufous rump, but some females may have barred grey rump.

Immature male has unmarked central tail; outer feathers barred.

Juvenile male may have barred grey central tail feather; rest rufous.

FLIGHT PATTERN
When hovering, head is stock-still; wings, tail, and body adjust positioning.

DID YOU KNOW?
Kestrels are associated with buildings in many areas. In European cities, they often nest close to the centre, on towers, cathedrals, or other high buildings. In suburban areas, they may choose industrial buildings, from power stations to quite small buildings. Outside Europe, they are familiar residents around such dramatic buildings as the ancient Egyptian temples and pyramids.

Eleonora's Falcon

LENGTH / 36–42cm (14–16½in)
WINGSPAN / 87–104cm (34–41in)
WEIGHT / 350–500g (12½–18oz)

STATUS / Vulnerable

SCALE v Woodpigeon

This large, elegant, long-winged falcon is a Mediterranean coast and island speciality, catching small migrant birds to feed to its young in autumn.

With its rakish silhouette, exceptional powers of flight, preference for Mediterranean cliffs and coastlines, and frequent occurrence in small groups, Eleonora's Falcon is a particularly exciting and appealing bird. It is a large falcon combining some of the characteristics of smaller species like the Hobby, but as well as being an insect-eater, it is a specialist predator of small birds. It is an unusual species, too, having two distinct colour forms.

FEEDING

Outside the breeding season, Eleonora's eat insects, often catching them in the air in the manner of a Hobby or Red-footed Falcon. The birds have a particularly elegant, fluent flight, swooping after dragonflies and butterflies as well as tiny fare such as flying ants. They also eat grasshoppers and beetles taken on the ground. In the breeding season, they turn to small birds, and their nesting period is delayed into late summer and autumn to ensure that they benefit from the constant supply of tired, night-flying migrant birds along the Mediterranean coasts and islands. Their victims vary from place to place: in one area, they may eat chiefly small warblers; in another, chats and shrikes, depending on what is available. Anything from Willow Warblers and Redstarts to Nightingales, Wheatears, and Red-backed Shrikes are caught on the wing, often out over the sea as they struggle toward land at dawn. Several falcons hang in the wind, facing the incoming migrants, stooping on them from a height. It is a sad end to the migration, which is over almost before it has begun for some of these songbirds, but a mighty efficient way for the falcons to feed their young.

DISPLAY AND VOICE

Breeding groups sometimes fly off to feed together, as if this has some special social function. Pairs perform fast, free-flowing aerobatics, playfully diving, soaring, and circling together. They do not call much unless disturbed at the nest, when they make a loud, typically falcon-like chatter, neither so powerful or nasal as a Peregrine nor so musical as a Hobby: *ke-ke-ke-ke*.

BREEDING

Always breeding in groups of 20–200 pairs, Eleonora's choose a cliff ledge for their 2–3 eggs. These hatch after four weeks, and the young fly when 35–40 days old.

MIGRATION

In autumn, Eleonora's Falcons fly east to the Red Sea (even those from north Africa and the Canaries), then down to Madagascar, where the whole population spends the winter.

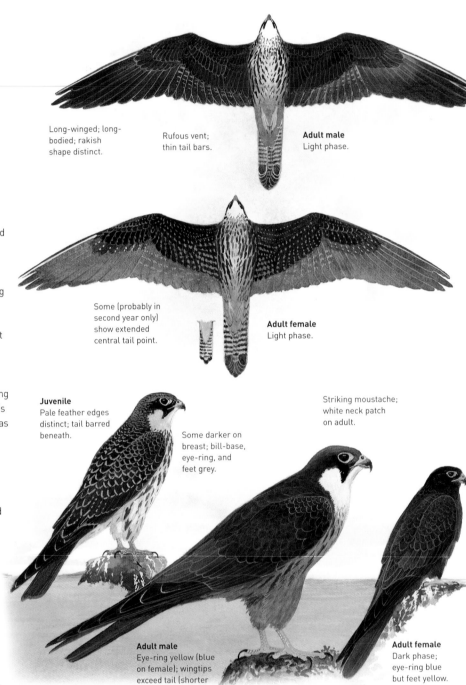

Long-winged; long-bodied; rakish shape distinct.

Rufous vent; thin tail bars.

Adult male
Light phase.

Some (probably in second year only) show extended central tail point.

Adult female
Light phase.

Juvenile
Pale feather edges distinct; tail barred beneath.

Some darker on breast; bill-base, eye-ring, and feet grey.

Striking moustache; white neck patch on adult.

Adult male
Eye-ring yellow (blue on female); wingtips exceed tail (shorter on female).

Adult female
Dark phase; eye-ring blue but feet yellow.

WHEN SEEN

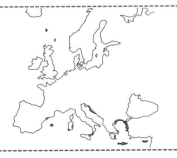

Late April to November.

WHERE SEEN

Balearics, Sardinia, islands off Italy, in the Adriatic and the Aegean Seas, Cyprus; vagrant in UK.

HABITAT AND INFO

SIMILAR SPECIES

Peregrine has broader wings, body, and tail; short-tailed; paler underbody.

Paler grey above

Barred beneath

MENACING BIRD CATCHER
Eleonora's Falcons watch patiently for
potential prey approaching over the sea.

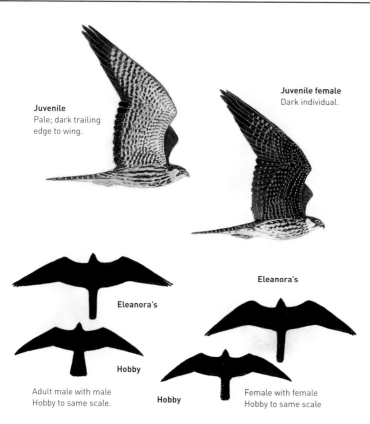

Juvenile
Pale; dark trailing
edge to wing.

Juvenile female
Dark individual.

Eleanora's

Eleanora's

Hobby

Adult male with male
Hobby to same scale.

Hobby

Female with female
Hobby to same scale

Soaring.

Sailing.

Adult female
Pale phase; underwing
dark; coverts darkest.

Adult
Dark phase; pale
underwing patch.

Female
Mixed grey/brown
above; looks quite
a brown bird.

Juvenile
Heavily scaled above.

FLIGHT PATTERN
Flight dashing, acrobatic;
marked changes of pace
recall Hobby; wing beats
soft, relaxed, become
deep, whippy at speed.

DID YOU KNOW?
Migration routes of many species may give clues to how their current
distribution developed. Eleonora's Falcons perhaps spread gradually
westward. All of them, even those breeding in Morocco, still use the
same migration route, moving through the Mediterranean region and
along the Red Sea to spend the winter in east Africa and
especially Madagascar.

?

Merlin

SCALE v Woodpigeon

LENGTH / 25–30cm (9¾–11¾in)
WINGSPAN / 60–65cm (23½–25½in)
WEIGHT / 140–230g (5–8oz)

■ **STATUS /** Vulnerable

A small, thickset, spirited falcon of open spaces, the Merlin is sometimes more like a Sparrowhawk than a Kestrel, swift and agile but without the aerial grace of a Hobby. In summer, it frequents moorland; in winter, farmland, marshes, and dunes, often sitting on the ground, a low rock, or a post.

Despite its small size, this is a fast-flying, tenacious, gritty little hunter, a bird of open spaces over which it is all too often little more than a fleeting shape, no sooner spotted than disappearing into the distance, low over the ground. This is its winter guise; in summer, it may mob intruders at the nest with great persistence and much noise, or simply slip away until the danger has passed. Those who know it well grow to like the little falcon of the moors for its unique character, no doubt enhanced by the wild environments in which it is usually to be found.

FEEDING

Although it eats a good many large moths and a few small mammals, the Merlin chiefly feeds on small birds. It watches from a low perch, then tries to take them by surprise and dash after them, rising above and stooping from a low elevation. If this doesn't succeed, it may simply try to fly them down in a long, tiring chase, but such attempts are generally less successful. If the prey is itself agile and determined to escape, the Merlin is tested to the full and puts on a real show, twisting and turning adroitly in pursuit of its meal. Meadow Pipits are favourite food; also Skylarks, Wheatears, Whinchats, and various tits and finches from the edges of pine plantations. A number of small birds such as young pipits are also taken from nests on the ground.

DISPLAY AND VOICE

Displays consist of low-level, rather inconspicuous flights and much calling from perches on the ground. Males have a sharp, very fast *ki-ki-ki-ki-ki*, while females have a whinnying, peevish, but slightly fuller *yee-yee-yee-yee*.

BREEDING

Many nests are simple scrapes on the ground, in thick heather with a view downhill from a steep slope. Other pairs choose old crows' or Rooks' nests in trees, especially hawthorns, pines, or larches, in isolated spinneys, in long windbreaks, in sheltered gullies, or on the moorland edge. Tree nests are the most common type in Scandinavia. After 3–5 eggs are laid, both sexes incubate them for 28–32 days. The chicks are ready to fly after a similar period.

MIGRATION

Most Merlins move at least downhill toward the coast in autumn. The majority are true short-distance migrants, going south. A few, even in Scandinavia and Iceland, remain in their breeding areas all year. Most British birds remain within Britain, but a few move to France.

Juvenile female

Broad-based wings and short tips tapered to point can recall fast, low-flying Sparrowhawk.

Male
Tiny; bluish-grey above, orange-buff below, quite vivid at close range in good light but tends to look dark and dull in typical view.

Spread tail reveals dark bars; black band.

Approaches prey fast, with wings withdrawn, tips flicked out in thrush-like action, or with wings below body level as if "flying on wingtips".

Adult female
Earthy-brown, not rufous like Kestrel; tail barred cream.

Adult male
Grey form.

Lacks heavy facial marks of Hobby or Peregrine.

WHERE SEEN
Breeds Iceland, Britain, Ireland, Scandinavia; widespread in winter but scarce south to Mediterranean.

HABITAT AND INFO

SIMILAR SPECIES
Sparrowhawk has broader wings tapered back to shorter or squarer tip; plainer tail; barred beneath.

Short wings

Barred below

Juvenile female

Adult male
Rufous form.

Spread tail of juvenile female.

Breast feather of adult female.

Breast feather of juvenile.

Flank feather of both.

Adult female
Pale form.

Adult male

Juvenile male

Adult male
Worn, darker.

Juvenile female

Chunkier, shorter-tailed, broader-winged than Kestrel; wingtips sharper than Sparrowhawk's.

FLIGHT PATTERN
Hunting flight: may stoop, or chase in rapid, level flight, often with tight, acrobatic twists and turns in final moments.

DID YOU KNOW?
The scientific name confirms a relationship between pigeons and the Merlin. In North America, it has long been called the Pigeon Hawk (or Falcon). Yet it is much too small to kill a pigeon: possibly, the inference is that it looks rather pigeon-like. The English name, Merlin, is of obscure origin, with no apparent link to the Arthurian wizard.

?

Peregrine

SCALE v Woodpigeon

LENGTH / 39–50cm (15½–19½in)
WINGSPAN / 95–115cm (37–45in)
WEIGHT / 600–1,300g (21–46oz)

■ STATUS / Vulnerable

A medium-large, stocky, sharp-winged falcon, broad-shouldered and powerfully built, the Peregrine is a superb flier but spends much of its time perched and inconspicuous. Its bold head pattern is an important identification clue.

Peregrine means wanderer: the name of the most dramatic of the falcons reflects its widespread dispersal outside the breeding season, when it is apt to turn up at a reservoir, lake, marsh, or flood to terrorize the local wildfowl for a few days before moving on. Few birds inspire such admiration as the Peregrine: for those who love wild places and nature in the raw, a Peregrine in full chase pricks up the hairs on the back of the neck. It is certainly a powerful bird, but also a glorious exponent of the art of flying. To many of us, the sight of a Peregrine in the air never palls. Others may not share this adoration of birds of prey, but even they have to agree that this one is a particularly handsome and genuinely impressive example of its kind.

FEEDING

This specialist bird hunter virtually ignores insects, mammals, and reptiles. Its preferred prey depends on local circumstances, but pigeons (Rock, feral, or racing pigeons; less often, Woodpigeons and Stock Doves) often dominate its diet. Thrushes of various kinds, starlings, and waders, including Snipe and Lapwings, make up much of its summer food; in winter, it kills more ducks. On moors, it regularly takes Red Grouse in small numbers. Many kills are simple chases in level flight. Others involve a precise upward swoop, rolling at the top of the climb to snatch the bird. More dramatic is the classic stoop: the Peregrine often having flown a long distance to get above its prey before diving headlong at great speed. The air rushing over its partly open wings can be heard easily at quite a distance. Many stoops fail, but a hungry Peregrine will circle, gain height, and stoop again and again if necessary.

DISPLAY AND VOICE

The displays involve high circling flights; the pair dive and twist together at speed. Calls are loud and raucous: basically a typical falcon chatter, higher-pitched from the male, like *kyee-kyee-kyee-kyee*, and a rougher, lower, rasping, and more nasal alarm from the female, *ehk-ehk-airhk-airrhk.*

BREEDING

The female lays her eggs on a cliff ledge, often with a bed of earth and some grassy vegetation at its lip, or in a quarry, or on a tall building. The usual clutch of 3–4 eggs hatches after 29–32 days, and the chicks fly at 35–42 days old.

MIGRATION

Northern populations move south in winter. Southern and western birds are more resident except for wandering immatures.

Adult female (right)
Striking head pattern; compare with smaller Hobby; compared with male, adult female often greyer, less blue above; pinker below, with less brilliant white on chest.

Juvenile
Compare dark lobe-shaped moustache with Gyr's.

Juvenile male
Note slim stance compared with Gyr's.

Adult　Juvenile

WHEN SEEN

All year.

WHERE SEEN
Breeds UK, Spain, Alps, Italy, Balkans, NE Europe, and N and W Scandinavia; widespread in winter.

HABITAT AND INFO

SIMILAR SPECIES
Hobby looks like small, slim, elegant Peregrine with similar head/neck pattern; absent in winter.

Narrower tail base　Streaked underside

Juvenile
Mediterranean race *brookei* at same scale as below; smaller, darker; note large tailband.

FEEDING PATTERN
Peregrines catch birds in flight, but feed on the ground.

Juvenile male
Streaked below.

Juvenile
Mediterranean race *brookei*.

Juvenile
Bold moustache; white throat and side of neck.

Adult female
Variable: N Russian *calidus* race much paler than this.

Adult male
Shape as female, but smaller; may be whiter on chest.

Adult
From above, broad, pale rump often distinctive (Hobby's narrower, darker); broad-based wings often swept back in smooth, tapered curve to point.

Short-tailed "anchor" shape; soars for long periods, dives at great speed, chases with deep, fast, whippy wing beats.

May look dark against bright sky but head/neck/throat contrast usually clear.

FLIGHT PATTERN
Flight shapes may recall widely differing species, from Hobby to Raven or Fulmar, depending on attitude and angle of view.

DID YOU KNOW?
At the top of a food chain, the Peregrine is vulnerable to contaminants in its diet. In the 1960s, it was wiped out from vast areas of its world range by the effects of pesticides such as DDT, which it gradually accumulated by eating birds that had fed on treated grain. High doses killed Peregrines; sub-lethal doses thinned their eggshells or made them infertile.

?

Gyr Falcon

LENGTH / 55–60cm (21½–23½in)
WINGSPAN / 110–130cm (43–51in)
WEIGHT / 1–2.1kg (2¼–4¾lb)

■ **STATUS /** Vulnerable

SCALE v Woodpigeon

A big, heavy, broad-winged falcon, with many plumage variations. White individuals are easily identified, others require great care – concentrate on the shape of the bird.

Even when compared with most Peregrines, the Gyr Falcon is enormously big and heavy. It is remarkably powerful, but often lacks the elegance and purpose of a Peregrine at its best: it is slower, sometimes even lumbering, and has none of the aerial skill of the smaller falcons. Yet, for all that, it is a picture of magnificence and a truly charismatic bird. The glorious white-phase adults, in particular, are hard to beat. While the Peregrine is a bird of the air – even though it spends long hours perched on cliffs – the Gyr is a bird of the ground, always poised on some rock or mound in the northern tundra, patiently watching for prey.

FEEDING

Big birds such as grouse and Ptarmigan form the bulk of its prey in most areas. In some years, when small mammals like lemmings or sousliks are abundant, it eats a great many of these. Gulls, ducks, divers, waders, and auks are all part of its varied diet to a greater or lesser extent; in winter, wildfowl may make up a fair proportion of the kills. The Gyr usually hunts from a perch, with a low chase that may continue over several kilometres until the prey is exhausted. The falcon's quarry may eventually try to gain height to escape, but the Gyr then rises above it in a series of circles and stoops, or sweeps up from beneath to take it with a sudden twist. Although the power and weight of the Gyr may make it look clumsy and even slightly slow, this is deceptive: in level flight, a Gyr Falcon is said to be capable of catching a Peregrine.

DISPLAY AND VOICE

Males begin to defend a territory early in the year and the females soon join them. They rise to a height and dive down noisily toward the nest. They call less often than some falcons. The calls follow a similar pattern, but are particularly deep, hoarse, and rhythmic: *krery-krery-krery* or *kerreh-kerreh-kerreh*.

BREEDING

The female lays her eggs on a ledge of a sheer cliff, often beneath an overhang which gives shelter and renders it inaccessible. Sometimes the pair use the nest of a Rough-legged Buzzard in a tree. The 3–5 eggs are incubated for 35 days. The chicks may not fly for about 7–8 weeks.

MIGRATION

Western Gyr Falcons are sedentary except for wandering immatures in winter. Russian birds move more regularly to the south and west. Icelandic Gyrs remain in Iceland all year, but are joined in winter by more from Greenland.

Juvenile male
White type.

Juvenile
Cheeks dark, but lacks elongated moustache of young Peregrine.

Juvenile (left) has bluish feet; adult's feet (right) are yellow.

Adult female

Juvenile male

Juvenile female
Compare stance with Peregrine; Gyr much heavier-footed, thickly feathered on thighs, more buzzard-like.

WHEN SEEN

All year; in W Europe more often early spring.

WHERE SEEN
Breeds Iceland, N and W Scandinavia; rare vagrant UK and elsewhere.

HABITAT AND INFO

SIMILAR SPECIES
Juvenile Peregrine has bolder black cheek patch; less contrast on underwing; paler thighs.

Longer, bolder black moustache

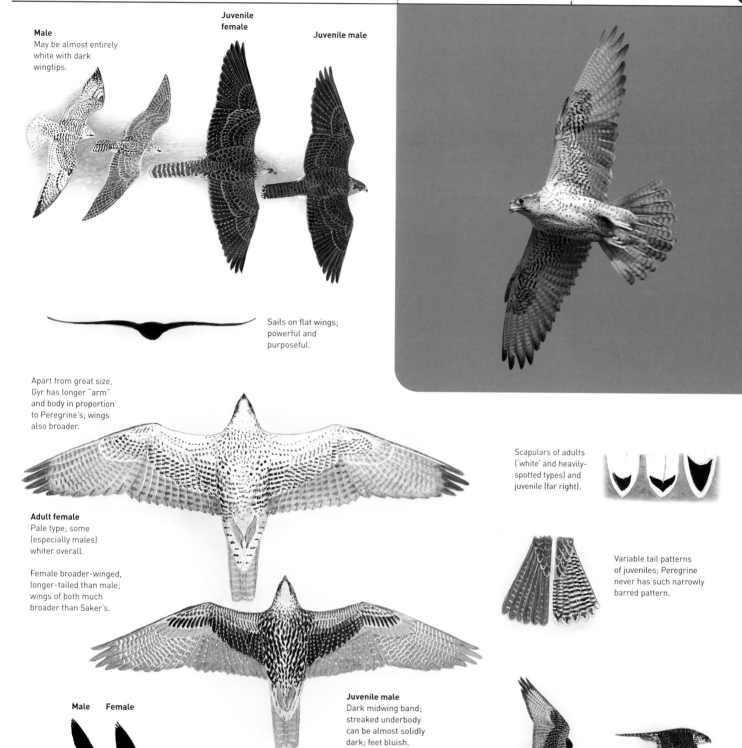

MUSCULAR BUILD
Of all the falcons, this has the broadest wings and tail, and heaviest body.

Male
May be almost entirely white with dark wingtips.

Juvenile female

Juvenile male

Sails on flat wings; powerful and purposeful.

Apart from great size, Gyr has longer "arm" and body in proportion to Peregrine's; wings also broader.

Scapulars of adults ('white' and heavily-spotted types) and juvenile (far right).

Adult female
Pale type; some (especially males) whiter overall.

Female broader-winged, longer-tailed than male; wings of both much broader than Saker's.

Variable tail patterns of juveniles; Peregrine never has such narrowly barred pattern.

Juvenile male
Dark midwing band; streaked underbody can be almost solidly dark; feet bluish.

Heavier, broader-winged than Peregrine, with bulky belly; more elastic, long-armed wing beats.

Male   **Female**

Juvenile female

Juvenile male

DID YOU KNOW?
White Gyr Falcons are fantastically spectacular birds. They have long been highly prized by royal falconers and were used to smooth many international dealings in the Middle Ages. Despite efforts to protect them in more recent times, they remain vulnerable to illegal trading and have reputedly fetched as much as $100,000 each on the oil-rich black market.

Lanner

ORDER
Falconiformes

FAMILY
Falconidae

SPECIES
Falco biarmicus

COMMON NAME
Lanner

SCALE v Woodpigeon

LENGTH / 43–52cm (17–20½in)
WINGSPAN / 95–105cm (37–41in)
WEIGHT / 500–900g (18–32oz)

■ **STATUS /** Vulnerable

A big, lanky, long-winged falcon, it has the shape of a big Kestrel, with Peregrine-like plumage but a paler head pattern and a darker midwing panel beneath.

A large and impressive falcon, the Lanner behaves rather like a 'desert Peregrine' – although it is seen perched on top of a post or rock as often as in full flight in pursuit of prey. Rare in Europe, it is largely a bird of Africa, where it inhabits semi-desert plains, savannahs with scattered trees, and the fringes of arid mountain regions. In Sicily, it tends to choose steep cliffs overlooking areas of pasture and rough hillsides near the coast.

FEEDING

This is essentially a bird-eater: it may take prey as large as a Mallard or Jackdaw, but concentrates on smaller birds such as larks and doves. Small mammals and reptiles are a minor part of its diet. Pairs hunt together, one flushing birds from cover while the other waits to take them by surprise, swooping in as the prey take flight.

DISPLAY AND VOICE

Calls are hoarse cries of varied rhythm and pace: *kyhek-kyhek-kyhek.*

MIGRATION

Most Lanners remain in their breeding areas all year. A few descend to lower areas in cold winter weather. Young birds disperse, but rarely stray far from the usual range.

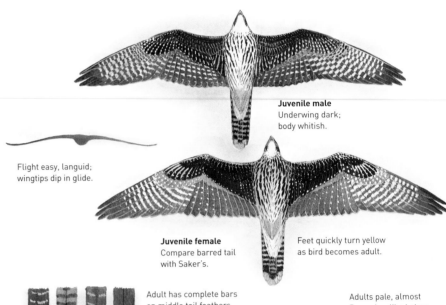

Juvenile male
Underwing dark; body whitish.

Flight easy, languid; wingtips dip in glide.

Juvenile female
Compare barred tail with Saker's.

Feet quickly turn yellow as bird becomes adult.

Juvenile   Adult   Juveniles

Adult has complete bars on middle tail feathers (never seen on Saker's) but variable juveniles difficult to separate.

Adults pale, almost Peregrine-like below; extent of rufous and of black moustache varies.

Adult female

Juvenile
Conspicuous pale stripe over eye.

Adult male
Some are whiter on cheeks.

Thighs more streaked, less solidly dark, than Saker's.

Adult is slate grey; wingtips darker.

Adult male

Adult
Rufous crown; thin moustache; flank barred, unlike Saker's.

Barred tail.

RUSTY CAP
The grey upperparts contrast well with the head pattern when seen closely.

WHEN SEEN

All year.

WHERE SEEN

Rare and threatened in Europe; just a few pairs in Italy (including Sicily), the Balkans, some Aegean islands.

HABITAT AND INFO

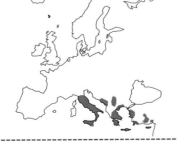

SIMILAR SPECIES

Peregrine has darker cap and broader black cheek patch; adult barred beneath.

Blacker cap

Whiter cheek

Saker

A massive falcon, nearly the size of a Gyr, the Saker is browner and blunter-winged than a Lanner or Peregrine.

LENGTH / 48–57cm (19–22½in)
WINGSPAN / 110–130cm (43–51in)
WEIGHT / 730–1,300g (26–46oz)

■ **STATUS /** Endangered

SCALE v Woodpigeon

This is one of the biggest falcons: a massively built and impressive bird. It is extremely rare in Europe, with just a handful of pairs west of the Ukraine. It is a bird of the steppe, inhabiting mixed forest and pasture, uncultivated grasslands, and the edges of marshes. It often perches on telegraph poles on plains.

FEEDING
Sakers are not bird-eaters like Peregrines or Lanners: they prefer to eat mammals, especially sousliks, but also a smaller number of rats, voles, moles, lemmings, marmots, and hares. Medium-sized birds, reptiles, amphibians, and large insects form a minor part of their diet. Sakers watch from a perch and take prey in short, sudden dashes to the ground, although they are powerful birds in flight.

DISPLAY AND VOICE
The hoarse, repetitive screeching calls resemble those of other large falcons and are often used near the nest.

MIGRATION
Eastern Sakers move to the Middle East and east Africa in winter; a few remain in the Mediterranean area.

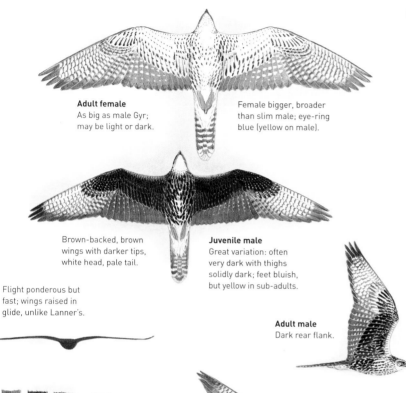

Adult female
As big as male Gyr; may be light or dark.

Female bigger, broader than slim male; eye-ring blue (yellow on male).

Brown-backed, brown wings with darker tips, white head, pale tail.

Juvenile male
Great variation: often very dark with thighs solidly dark; feet bluish, but yellow in sub-adults.

Adult male
Dark rear flank.

Flight ponderous but fast; wings raised in glide, unlike Lanner's.

Middle tail feathers: juvenile (far left) has incomplete bars; adults (two on right) either lightly marked or as juvenile.

Juvenile female
White on crown; moustache may be absent.

Adult female
White over eye, not rufous like Lanner.

Wings almost reach tail tip on some males.

Tail very pale, spots look like bars.

Adult
Pale form.

BOLD KILLER
Sakers are big, powerful and fearless falcons, able to tackle substantial prey.

WHERE SEEN
Extreme E Europe; rare in winter in Italy, Balkans, Sardinia.

HABITAT AND INFO

SIMILAR SPECIES
Lanner is greyer; stronger dark moustache; barred tail; often rufous cap.

Grey back

Barred tail

Levant Sparrowhawk

LENGTH / 33–38cm (13–15in)
WINGSPAN / 63–76cm (25–30in)
WEIGHT / 155–265g (5½–9½oz)

■ **STATUS /** Secure

SCALE v Woodpigeon

A rather short-tailed hawk with quite pointed wings, it is elusive when breeding but migrates in large flocks.

This large, slim hawk is usually seen in flight over wooded countryside. It is easiest to see on migration, when it forms large flocks. It tends to occupy lowland areas, while in south-east Europe the very similar Sparrowhawk is more commonly found in the mountains.

FEEDING

It catches mice, voles, squirrels, and many small birds in low, fast hunting flights, as well as reptiles and insects. Much of the prey is captured after long spells of careful watching from a perch.

BREEDING

Nests are usually built in deciduous trees, using slender sticks with a lining of finer material. The 3–5 eggs hatch after about 30–35 days. The young fly when 40–45 days old.

MIGRATION

In autumn, all Levant Sparrowhawks leave Europe, probably for Ethiopia. They cross the Bosphorus between August and mid-October and return in mid-April. Large, swirling flocks are seen over a period of just a few days each season.

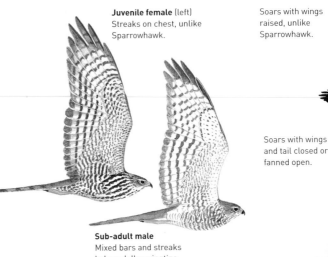

Juvenile female (left)
Streaks on chest, unlike Sparrowhawk.

Soars with wings raised, unlike Sparrowhawk.

Soars with wings and tail closed or fanned open.

Sub-adult male
Mixed bars and streaks below; duller wingtips than adult's.

Male
Pale below with sharp, dark wingtips; blue-grey above.

Male

Female
Slightly larger than male; slimmer than Sparrowhawk.

Sparrowhawk
Broader-winged than Levant Sparrowhawk.

Female
Dumpy, thick-necked shape; broad rufous bars below; dark head; dark eye, unlike female Sparrowhawk.

Male
Dark eye; grey hood.

Juvenile
Streaks/spots below; may have heavier bars on flanks.

PLAIN FACED HAWK
The grey face gives an unusual expression to this distinctive hawk.

WHEN SEEN

Oct — April

April to October.

WHERE SEEN
Breeds sparsely in Albania, Greece, Bulgaria, and Ukraine.

HABITAT AND INFO

SIMILAR SPECIES
Sparrowhawk has pale or orange-pink cheeks; pale eye; less obvious dark wingtip.

Paler cheeks

Black-winged Kite

A stocky, broad-winged but beautiful, unique bird of prey, it is often seen hovering expertly with fast wing beats.

LENGTH / 31–34cm (12–13½in)
WINGSPAN / 71–85cm (28–33½in)
WEIGHT / 230g (8oz)

■ **STATUS** / Vulnerable

SCALE v Woodpigeon

Juvenile
Brownish back; dark tail.

Adult
Very pale tail; sharp grey and black above; white head.

Adult male

Juvenile female

Sails on raised wings.

Hovers with fast, almost trembling wing action.

Adult male
Very white below except for bold black wingtips; short white tail often fanned.

Juvenile male
Brown marks, pale feather edges on back; buff chest; smudgy crown.

Adult female
Wingtips project beyond tail (equal in male).

A small, pale, thickset, but extremely buoyant bird of prey, the Black-winged Kite is more typical of the narrow green strip beside the Nile in Egypt than of Europe, but a small, rather isolated population thrives in Iberia. It is typically seen as a distinctive grey-and-white bird perched in a tree or wire, or hovering like a big, soft-winged, bulky Kestrel over a field or marsh. It favours flat countryside with scattered trees or planted with shelter belts.

FEEDING
Most of its prey consists of small animals such as insects, small reptiles, and small rodents, but it also catches some birds.

DISPLAY AND VOICE
Always elegant in flight, this species becomes a joy to watch in display: it flies up in high spirals, wings beating quickly, then dives or glides down with its wings raised in a V-shape, often with its legs dangling. It calls with whistling notes, like *kyu-it* or *kuee*.

BREEDING
It usually nests in flat-topped thorn trees, laying 3–4 eggs.

MIGRATION
Resident.

RED-EYED WATCHER
These birds frequently spend long periods watching for prey from an exposed perch.

WHEN SEEN

All year.

WHERE SEEN
S Portugal and, more rarely, SW Spain.

HABITAT AND INFO

SIMILAR SPECIES
Hen Harrier's upperwing is plainer except for black tip; white rump; does not hover.

Dark hindwing band

Greyer breast

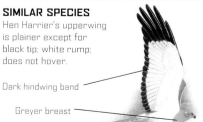

Corncrake

SCALE v Pigeon

LENGTH / 27–30cm (10½–11¾in)
WINGSPAN / 46–53cm (18–21in)
WEIGHT / 135–200g (4¾–7oz)

■ **STATUS /** Endangered

A remarkably secretive bird of dense vegetation, it is rarely seen but often heard on breeding grounds.

Since it spends much of its time concealed in dense, low vegetation, the Corncrake is hard to glimpse, but it is often heard. In spring, males may emerge into the open, calling from small clearings and running between iris beds or even along stone walls. However, once the grass grows Corncrakes are all but invisible. Early hay-cutting has led to a drastic decline almost everywhere and a huge reduction in range.

FEEDING
Corncrakes eat small insects, other invertebrates, and some seeds.

DISPLAY AND VOICE
Males sing with their heads raised and bills opening with each call, as if throwing the sound across the fields, making a loud, hard, rasping *crek-crek*. At a distance the sound has a light, dry quality. Close up, especially at night, it is a loud, ratchet-like, echoing rattle: *brrrp-brrrp*.

BREEDING
Laid in dense cover, the 8–12 eggs hatch after 16–19 days.

MIGRATION
Most arrive in their breeding areas and leave for Africa in autumn without being seen elsewhere.

Flies low on bowed, rufous wings, with legs trailed.

Grey-faced male sings with head raised.

Female
More orange than male.

Male
May look rather dark and grey, with well-barred flanks.

TERRITORIAL PROCLAMATION
Male Corncrakes sing for hours on summer nights.

WHEN SEEN

Oct
April

April to October.

WHERE SEEN
Locally W Ireland, W Scotland, France, W Norway, S Sweden, Russia, Poland, and central and E Europe.

HABITAT AND INFO

SIMILAR SPECIES
Grey Partridge is bulkier; less orange-brown on wings; rusty-orange face patch.

Orange face patch

Bolder flank bars

Water Rail

Not always shy, but it stays close to cover and runs into reeds or flooded willows if startled. It looks small, round in side view but very narrow end-on, with spiky bill, long toes. It is seen on salt marshes during winter.

LENGTH / 22–28cm (8³/₄–11in)
WINGSPAN / 38–45cm (15–17¹/₂in)
WEIGHT / 85–190g (3–6³/₄oz)

■ STATUS / Secure

SCALE v Pigeon

The classic Water Rail habitats are reed beds and freshwater marshes, but they can be found almost anywhere that is wet: a flooded ditch beneath willows and alders, for example, is good enough for a Water Rail or two to creep about in, quietly, during winter. Here they are elusive but not really shy: with patience, it is possible to get superb close-up views. From the side they look round and dumpy, especially in cold weather, but a typical tail-end view shows how remarkably thin and compressed this species is.

FEEDING
Water Rails eat a variety of insects, aquatic molluscs, and newts, plus berries, shoots, and even small birds in hard weather.

VOICE
Most calls are loud, screaming or whistling, rather pig-like squeals.

BREEDING
Nests are neat, just off the ground, in reeds or willows. Up to 11 eggs are incubated for 19–22 days.

MIGRATION
Northern birds move west and south in autumn, reaching the UK and Ireland from September to April.

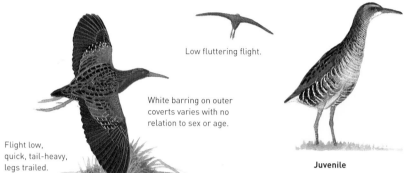

Low fluttering flight.

White barring on outer coverts varies with no relation to sex or age.

Flight low, quick, tail-heavy, legs trailed.

Juvenile

Male
Longer, thicker bill.

Female

Underneath tail variable, allowing identification of individuals.

Striking pale patch under tail shows as bird runs off.

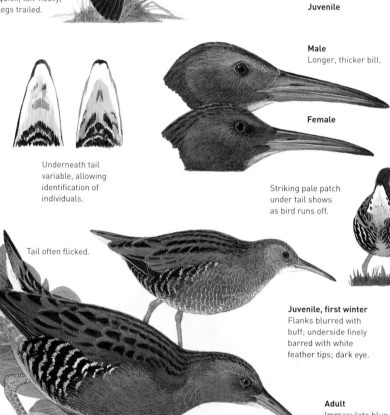

Tail often flicked.

Juvenile, first winter
Flanks blurred with buff; underside finely barred with white feather tips; dark eye.

Adult
Immaculate blue-grey below; sub-adults marked with buff; red on bill varies.

Males often much larger than females, but sizes overlap.

White flank bars vary; long, red-pink toes.

CREEPING IN THE SHALLOWS
Reeds at the water's edge provide cover for this secretive bird.

WHEN SEEN

All year; in most areas, mainly from August to April.

WHERE SEEN
Sparse breeder Iceland, UK and Ireland, much of W, central, and E Europe; more widespread in west in winter.

HABITAT AND INFO

SIMILAR SPECIES
Juvenile Moorhen is plainer brown with white flank stripe; white undertail; short bill.

Plain back

White stripe

Spotted Crake

ORDER / Gruiformes **FAMILY** / Rallidae **SPECIES** / *Porzana porzana* **COMMON NAME** / Spotted Crake

LENGTH / 22–24cm (8³⁄₄–9¹⁄₂in)
WINGSPAN / 35cm (14in)
WEIGHT / 70–80g (2¹⁄₂–2³⁄₄oz)

■ STATUS / Secure

SCALE v Pigeon

Secretive, shuffling, sometimes almost rat-like bird of water's edge. Good views reveal beautiful, richly barred, and spotted plumage. Its bill is short, pale with orange-red at base, and its legs are green.

This is a remarkably difficult bird to see, but like other crakes and rails it is not so much shy as elusive. At times it appears on open mud or at the edge of a reed bed and trots about in full view, just a few metres away; it will even feed on an angler's stock of worms. A quiet observer can then see the true beauty of its complicated, delicate plumage pattern, and the superb sheeny quality of its feathers. A more typical view is a brief glimpse of the bird in flight, often rising from almost underfoot, before it drops down to be lost for good in dense vegetation.

FEEDING
It eats insects, worms, seeds, and berries, mostly picking them from mud beneath reeds or from low stems.

VOICE
In spring, it repeats a rhythmic, whiplash-like or water-dripping *whit-whit-whit* at dusk. It also makes a hard ticking.

BREEDING
It nests in dense, wet vegetation in marshes, incubating two broods of 8–12 eggs for 18–19 days.

MIGRATION
In August and September, it moves south from N and E Europe through W Europe, returning in April.

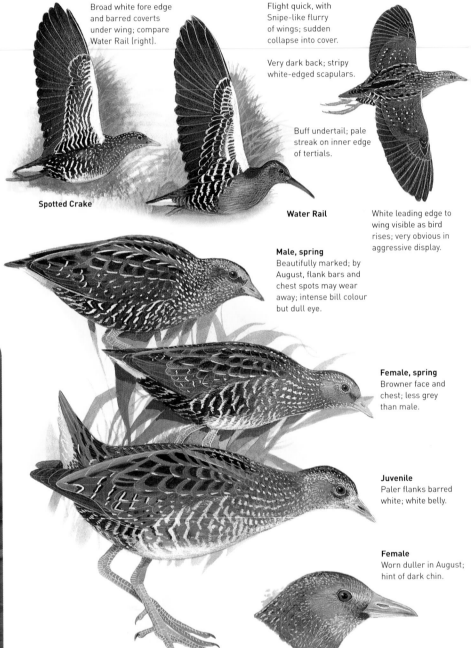

Broad white fore edge and barred coverts under wing; compare Water Rail (right).

Flight quick, with Snipe-like flurry of wings; sudden collapse into cover.

Very dark back; stripy white-edged scapulars.

Buff undertail; pale streak on inner edge of tertials.

Spotted Crake

Water Rail

White leading edge to wing visible as bird rises; very obvious in aggressive display.

Male, spring
Beautifully marked; by August, flank bars and chest spots may wear away; intense bill colour but dull eye.

Female, spring
Browner face and chest; less grey than male.

Juvenile
Paler flanks barred white; white belly.

Female
Worn duller in August; hint of dark chin.

DEEP-BODIED WADER
Crakes have deep, round bodies that are very narrow in cross-section.

WHEN SEEN

Nov / Mar / Apr / Aug

Mostly March–April and August–November in W Europe.

WHERE SEEN
Sparsely across Europe except extreme N and S; rare in UK.

HABITAT AND INFO

SIMILAR SPECIES
Water Rail has longer bill; narrower head and neck; plainer underside.

Long bill

Plain breast

ORDER
Gruiformes

FAMILY
Rallidae

SPECIES
Porzana parva

COMMON NAME
Little Crake

Little Crake

A tiny, sharp-tailed, sharp-winged crake, usually looking slim and neat despite very long, slim toes. The male typically has a lovely rich appearance.

LENGTH / 18–20cm (7–8in)
WINGSPAN / 34–39cm (13½–15½in)
WEIGHT / 40–65g (1½–2¼oz)

■ STATUS / Vulnerable

SCALE v Pigeon

Little Crake

Pale coverts like minute Little Bittern; much paler than Baillon's Crake (shown to same scale on page 190).

Baillon's Crake

Adult male
Rich blue-grey below; rusty-brown above with black streaks and two buff lines each side on tertials.

Bill of male has small red mark at base, often absent in winter (lower).

Adult female
The only sandy-buff crake with dark patches above.

Wingtips long, almost reach pointed tail tip; underside unmarked except at extreme edge of flank and under tail.

Green legs.

White throat; hint of red on bill; clean buff below.

Juvenile
Dark "shoulder"; whiter face/throat than juvenile Baillon's; see also larger Spotted Crake.

Long primary projection beyond tips of tertials.

IMMACULATE MALE
Small crakes have a handsome sheen to their plumage.

A patient watcher, concealed in a hide at a nature reserve in eastern Europe or the Middle East, may be lucky enough to see a Little Crake in full view as it forages along the edge of a dyke. It is a smart little bird, beautifully coloured, with a gloss-like polished stone. In western Europe, a rare vagrant may provide just the briefest glimpse as it crosses a gap between two clumps of reed, then vanishes for good – often leaving the observer wondering if it really was a Little Crake, or something similar but less rare.

FEEDING
Like other crakes and rails, it creeps about at the edges of reed beds, reed mace thickets, and reedy ditches or pools, picking tiny insects and molluscs from the mud.

VOICE
The song is a low croak that accelerates into a hard, staccato trill.

BREEDING
It nests irregularly in a few scattered sites in France and Iberia.

MIGRATION
A few from eastern Europe move west in autumn, but in western Europe it is a very rare bird everywhere.

WHEN SEEN

Nov

Aug

Most vagrants in late autumn and early winter in W Europe.

WHERE SEEN
Breeds in NE Europe and irregularly elsewhere in W Europe; rare vagrant outside breeding range.

HABITAT AND INFO

SIMILAR SPECIES
Baillon's Crake has no red on bill; black-edged white spots above; more white bars below.

Spotted back

Barred flank

189

Baillon's Crake

LENGTH / 17–19cm (6¾–7½in)
WINGSPAN / 33–37cm (13–14½in)
WEIGHT / 30–50g (1–1¾oz)

STATUS / Vulnerable

SCALE v Pigeon

A tiny, sparrow-sized, rounded, blunt-ended crake, its colours recall Spotted Crake but its rich brown back has bold black marks and flecks, with splashes and rings of white. The green bill has no trace of red.

Of all the crakes this is the tiniest, like a minute ball of animated feathers; quick, elusive, and hard to watch. A sure identification relies on checking a few fine details, but seeing them is a challenge. To most people in Europe, crakes are just impossible. In favoured places in eastern Europe and the Middle East, they can be watched at close range, but even vagrants in the west may be remarkably tame, as if totally oblivious to human presence.

FEEDING
The bird eats tiny aquatic invertebrates, seeds, and shoots as it forages beneath sedges, rushes, reeds, and other swamp vegetation. Quite small ditches and drainage channels are suitable for it while on migration.

VOICE
The song is a dry, rising and falling rattle that lasts two or three seconds, like the song of an Edible Frog. It is quiet, and carries less well than the calls of other crakes and rails.

MIGRATION
In autumn, breeding birds from central Europe move south into Africa for the winter. They are rare vagrants in western Europe, and very rarely seen in Britain.

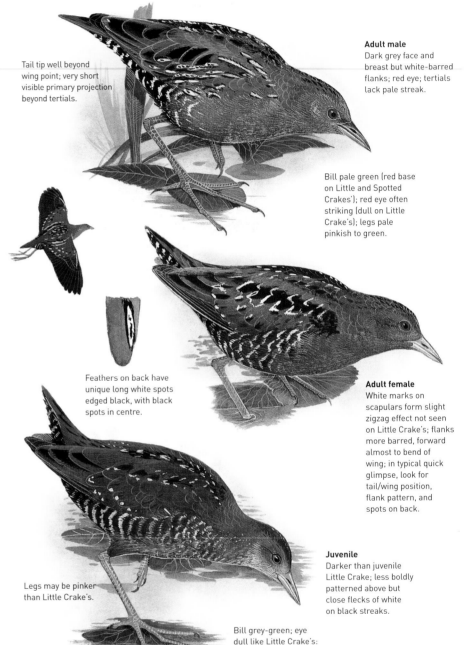

Tail tip well beyond wing point; very short visible primary projection beyond tertials.

Adult male
Dark grey face and breast but white-barred flanks; red eye; tertials lack pale streak.

Bill pale green (red base on Little and Spotted Crakes'); red eye often striking (dull on Little Crake's); legs pale pinkish to green.

Feathers on back have unique long white spots edged black, with black spots in centre.

Adult female
White marks on scapulars form slight zigzag effect not seen on Little Crake's; flanks more barred, forward almost to bend of wing; in typical quick glimpse, look for tail/wing position, flank pattern, and spots on back.

Juvenile
Darker than juvenile Little Crake; less boldly patterned above but close flecks of white on black streaks.

Legs may be pinker than Little Crake's.

Bill grey-green; eye dull like Little Crake's: try to check structure and tertial pattern.

RARE SIGHT
Although sometimes ridiculously tame, this crake is not often seen in the open.

WHEN SEEN

Oct — March

Spring and autumn.

WHERE SEEN
Extreme E Europe; very sparse in central Europe; vagrant elsewhere.

HABITAT AND INFO

SIMILAR SPECIES
Male Little Crake has neater flanks; pale stripe each side of rump; fewer white spots above.

Plainer flank

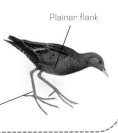

Greener legs

Coot

A squat, round-backed, low-tailed, duck-like water bird, with slaty-black and a bold white facial shield and bill. It is often in flocks on open water, especially in winter.

LENGTH / 36–38cm (14–15in)
WINGSPAN / 70–80cm (27½–31½in)
WEIGHT / 600–900g (21–32oz)

■ **STATUS /** Secure

SCALE v Pigeon

Pale trailing edge obvious; weak in immature birds.

Adult
Flight quick but heavy, little agility; wings paler than body; legs trail.

Female   **Male, breeding**

Large grey-green feet with broadly lobed toes.

First year has pale chin.

Grazing birds flee to water if disturbed.

Grazing birds walk forward, pulling head back and sideways to crop grass.

Juvenile has white face and chest, dull body; compare to smaller grebes.

Whether splashing about in quarrelsome groups on a town park lake or large reservoir, or feeding quietly on a grassy bank beside a river or – especially in winter – by the coast, Coots are among the most familiar of water birds. Except for their rather drab young, they are really quite unmistakable.

FEEDING
Coots graze on grass but also feed a lot in water, diving under regularly and popping back up like corks. They eat seeds, insects, snails, and tadpoles as well as aquatic plants.

DISPLAY AND VOICE
Coots often fight like Moorhens, using their feet as they lie back on the water. They make a short, squawking *kowk*, a higher *teuk* and *kt-towk,* and a sudden *ptik*!

BREEDING
Nests are large affairs at the water's edge, often in overhanging branches or reeds. The 6–9 eggs hatch after 21–24 days' incubation.

MIGRATION
Many move to larger lakes and reservoirs in winter. Eastern European birds move west in autumn.

CLUMSY IN THE AIR
Coots have little aerobatic ability, with their long, trailing feet and short wings.

WHEN SEEN

All year; in N and E Europe, mostly March to September.

WHERE SEEN
Breeds most of Europe except Iceland, N Scandinavia, but only local and widely scattered in much of S Europe.

HABITAT AND INFO

SIMILAR SPECIES
Moorhen has pointed tail often cocked; white flank stripe and white under tail.

Bright bill

Flank stripe

Moorhen

LENGTH / 32–35cm (12½–14in)
WINGSPAN / 50–55cm (19½–21½in)
WEIGHT / 250–420g (9–15oz)

■ **STATUS /** Secure

SCALE v Pigeon

A familiar riverside, farm pond, and lake bird, it is shy, quick to run or skitter across water into cover. It may even dive and stay underwater with only bill-tip protruding. Its white flank stripe and patches under tail help to identify it.

Many people know and admire the Moorhen when they see it on a town park lake or river backwater. Others perhaps wonder what manner of bird it is that skitters across the river with fluttering wings and disappears into the fringing vegetation at the least hint of disturbance. Although it is widespread, the Moorhen has declined where rivers have been straightened, deepened, and tidied up by clearing away the bankside rushes and sedges. Unlike Coots, Moorhens cannot survive in such scoured, open, bleak surroundings: they must have some dense vegetation cover. Yet they also feed out on open fields, often in pastures with horses or sheep, although always just a short, fast run from the nearest hedge. They venture into gardens and orchards and climb old, gnarled apple trees and hawthorns, surprisingly at home high off the ground. Sometimes they even nest in such elevated places. Moorhens are noisy, quite highly strung birds, very likely to pick fights with intruders of their own kind, especially in spring. It is not easy to overlook them.

FEEDING
The Moorhen's diet reflects its habitat: shoots, seeds, buds, and berries from water plants, water beetles and other aquatic invertebrates, snails, tadpoles, worms, and almost any edible bits and pieces gathered from the waterside. Much of its food is found on dry land. The Moorhen does not dive to feed, although it can and does submerge when pressed.

DISPLAY AND VOICE
Fights and chases are frequent, the birds using their long toes and sharp claws to good effect. The displays exploit the white flank stripes and white patches on each side of the raised tail. These can be expanded and flirted to maximize their impact. Calls include a sharp, sudden, metallic but rather deep *kurruck* or *kittik*, high *kik* or *kek* notes, and a rapid, stuttering *kik kik-ikikikik*.

BREEDING
Moorhen nests are small and neat; not huge, high platforms like the largest Coot nests. A nest is often made where an overhanging branch brushes the water of a pond or stream. A central cup of fine stems holds up to 11 buff eggs. These hatch after 21–22 days. The chicks are fed for 40–50 days until they can fly. In late summer, the young of second broods are often fed by those of earlier broods reared in spring.

MIGRATION
Some NW European birds move south to Britain in winter. Most W European Moorhens are resident.

Male
Upperparts rich brown, glossy in good light; immaculate.

Female
Duller, paler than male; paler on belly.

Sub-adult
Black-tipped bill.

Head and bill of juvenile grey by late October.

Juvenile
Browner than young Coot; no white on breast, but white line along side.

Chick
Red bill and wing; blue over eye.

White flank stripe unmistakable; adult has yellow-green legs with red "garter" at top; very long, slender toes.

WHEN SEEN

All year; in Scandinavia and NE Europe, only spring to autumn.

WHERE SEEN
Lakes, rivers, pools; most of Europe except N Scandinavia, Iceland, high Alps, and other mountainous, bleak, or dry areas.

HABITAT AND INFO

SIMILAR SPECIES
Coot is blacker; rounder back and tail held low; white facial shield.

White bill

Rounded tail

Constantly flicks tail up to reveal black and white beneath, on land or on water; walks easily, with springy rhythm.

Swims with head forward, bobbing rhythmically with tail/wingtips higher than back, unlike Coot's.

Adult male
Thickest bill, gleaming red and yellow.

Adult female
Slightly slimmer bill than male.

Juvenile
Bill dark, without frontal shield.

Flight quite swift and strong despite shallow flaps; usually low over water but may fly from trees or high over meadows.

Often flies about at night, even over towns, calling *kek kek*.

Adult male
Broader wings than female's; length from rear of wing to tail tip longer than on female's.

Adult female
Narrower wings than male's; rear body/tail length shorter.

Sooty grey underwing except for white leading edge; some birds have subtle paler barring.

DID YOU KNOW?

Moorhens are found on five continents, a near-worldwide distribution that few other species can match. In the UK, they are abundant in winter, second only to the Mallard among water birds, yet always spread rather thinly, rarely in groups of more than 20 at a time. Their success contrasts markedly with the many other rails that have suffered extinction on remote islands.

Purple Gallinule
Crested Coot

ORDER Gruiformes	**FAMILY** Rallidae	**SPECIES** *Porphyrio porphyrio*	**COMMON NAME** Purple Gallinule
ORDER Gruiformes	**FAMILY** Rallidae	**SPECIES** *Fulica cristata*	**COMMON NAME** Crested Coot

SCALE v Pigeon

	PURPLE GALLINULE	CRESTED COOT
LENGTH /	45–50cm (17½–19½in)	38–42cm (15–16½in)
WINGSPAN /	90–100cm (35½–39in)	75–85cm (29½–33½in)
WEIGHT /	720–1,000g (25–35oz)	770–990g (27–35oz)
■ **STATUS /**	Endangered	Endangered

Crested Coot resembles Coot but has a more prominent hump at rear end, triangular shield, and, in breeding season, red knobs.

Purple Gallinule is much bigger: it's a dramatically coloured but secretive bird of tall marsh vegetation.

The Purple Gallinule, also known as a Swamphen, is a truly magnificent bird of dense marsh vegetation. In Europe, it is rare and very localized, found beside shallow freshwater pools (but in Africa also beside large rivers). The Crested Coot is confined to marshes in the Seville area of southern Spain.

FEEDING
Purple Gallinules eat plant stems and roots (especially the soft pith from rushes), often uprooting and holding them in their huge feet while using their bills to rip them apart. Crested Coots dive for food like Coots.

VOICE
Purple Gallinules make many strange noises, including a sharp *chock-chock* and a remarkable booming or mooing. Crested Coots call like Coots, but they also have a groaning or moaning note.

MIGRATION
Both are essentially resident, but some wander with changes in temporary wetland habitat.

Purple Gallinule, immature
Dull, greyish beneath.

Purple Gallinules
Large, long-legged, long-toed; huge bright red shield and bill; white undertail.

Crested Coot (right)
Unlike Coot, no pale trailing edge nor whitish leading edge to underwing.

May swim with tail up.

Crested Coot, breeding
Red knobs on forehead; nape low, sloping.

Coot
Rounder head; less sloping nape.

Crested Coot, non-breeding
Lacks red knobs; bluish bill, white shield; shield more triangular than Coot's.

MASSIVE PRESENCE
The Purple Gallinule is a big, solid bird with a remarkable bill.

WHEN SEEN
All year.

WHERE SEEN
Purple Gallinule in extreme SW Spain, S Portugal, Sardinia; Crested Coot in SW Spain.

HABITAT AND INFO

SIMILAR SPECIES
Moorhen is much smaller, browner, dull legs, small bill with yellow tip; Coot has rounder head; whiter bill; no forehead knobs; pale trailing edge to wing.

Yellow on bill

White flank stripe

Great Bustard

Immense terrestrial bird, but a powerful flier, easily identified by its combination of large size and bold white wing patches.

LENGTH / 75–105cm (29½–41in)
WINGSPAN / 2.1–2.4m (6¾–7¾ft)
WEIGHT / 8–16kg (18–35lb)

■ STATUS / Endangered

SCALE v Pigeon

One of the truly great birds of Europe in every sense, this is also one of the most threatened. It is a big bird that needs big spaces, and it cannot tolerate modern, intensive farming. That leaves its future deeply uncertain in the face of agricultural pressure throughout its range.

FEEDING
Bustards stride open spaces in search of food, which they take from the ground: mostly plants, including seeds, but also insects, small rodents (which they eat in large numbers if they are abundant), and reptiles.

DISPLAY
When they display on open ground the males seem to turn themselves inside out as they fan their wings and tails and inflate their necks to reveal large areas of startling white plumage. They are silent birds.

BREEDING
The females incubate 2–3 eggs for 21–28 days, in shallow hollows.

MIGRATION
In the west, they gather into flocks in winter within their usual range. Eastern populations move south and west in winter.

Female

Little Bustard
(To scale.)

Male

Male

Male

Female

Female has narrower wing; immature male (far right) has white as female's, wing shape as adult male's.

Flight majestic, constant beats of "fingered" wings.

Female

Male

Female

Male much bigger than female; grey head and neck; ginger-brown shawl and back; white belly.

Male
Wispy "moustache" in spring; white often shows on closed wing; less orange, more buff as plumage fades.

Female
Less white on wing; both sexes can be blacker above when pale tips wear off.

Adult females, juveniles, and immatures not distinguishable on ground.

GIANT MALE
A heavy bird, the Great Bustard looks mighty impressive.

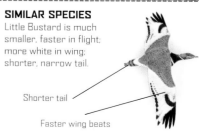

WHEN SEEN

All year; autumn/ winter vagrant in NW Europe.

WHERE SEEN
Breeds Iberia; very locally E Germany, Poland, E Europe.

HABITAT AND INFO

SIMILAR SPECIES
Little Bustard is much smaller, faster in flight; more white in wing; shorter, narrow tail.

Shorter tail

Faster wing beats

Little Bustard

SCALE v Pigeon

LENGTH / 40–45cm (15½–17½in)
WINGSPAN / 83–91cm (32½–36in)
WEIGHT / 600–900g (21–32oz)

■ **STATUS /** Vulnerable

A smallish terrestrial bird, long-legged and long-necked. In flight, it shows much white and moves surprisingly fast.

Although it is a true bustard, this species is much smaller and much quicker in its actions (especially in flight) than the Great Bustard. It often surprises people on first acquaintance. In winter, Little Bustards form flocks and behave more like smaller game birds. In flight they are almost pigeon-like, an effect enhanced by their piebald pattern. Although still much more common in places than Great Bustards, Little Bustards are also declining practically everywhere. The males' wing feathers make a loud whistle in flight.

FEEDING
It eats small rodents, insects, seeds, shoots, and berries, taking food from the ground or low plants in a slow, statuesque walk.

DISPLAY AND VOICE
Males inflate their necks and raise their black-and-white plumage as they give short calls and make quick, vertical leaps into the air.

BREEDING
The 3–4 eggs laid in a scrape are incubated for 20–22 days.

MIGRATION
Resident, but from France Little Bustards move south in winter.

Adult female
Some have two or three dark bars across white.

Spread tail shows white sides, white coverts.

Adult female

Inner primaries shorter than male's; narrow outer wing shape.

Adult male has more white on primary coverts; broader wingtip.

Adult male, breeding
Very short fourth primary (fourth equal to third in young males).

Short fourth primary creates high-pitched whistling sound in flight.

Adult male, breeding
Neck inflated in display; head pattern unique.

Winter male resembles female.

Immature male, winter   **Adult male, winter**

Displaying males puff out necks, flap, and leap.

Adult female
Shape and stance of both sexes unlike any other European species.

BANDED MALE
The black-and-white neck and chest have a unique pattern.

WHEN SEEN

All year in south; summer only in central and NE France.

WHERE SEEN
France, Spain; locally in Sardinia, Balkans.

HABITAT AND INFO

SIMILAR SPECIES
Great Bustard is much bigger; more rufous; broader, rounder tail.

Greyer head

Wide tail

Stone-curlew

A stocky, pale, sandy-brown bird with an obvious pale base to the bill and pale stripe under the eye. It is boldly marked in flight. Its habitat and range are useful clues. It is often hard to spot by day, more often heard than seen. Calls are at night in flight and on the ground.

LENGTH / 40-44cm (15½-17½in)
WINGSPAN / 77-85cm (31-33in)
WEIGHT / 370-450g (13-16oz)

■ **STATUS** / Vulnerable

SCALE v Pigeon

This peculiar, elusive "wader" of dry, sandy heaths and flinty fields is most active before dawn and at dusk, when its strange wailing and whistling calls, like a mixture of Curlew and Oystercatcher, may betray its presence. By day it stands or crouches near cover or in the shade of a tree, and even in full view it is difficult to spot against pale, dry grassland.

FEEDING
It feeds on large insects picked from the ground.

DISPLAY AND VOICE
Calls play a large part in the courtship displays, as do stiff bowing postures and wings spread to reveal their black-and-white patterns. The normal calls include a sharp *kit kit kit* and a liquid *cloo-ee*.

BREEDING
The nest is a shallow scoop in the soil. The two chicks fly when 36–42 days old and return to breed when three years old.

MIGRATION
Flocks form after breeding and fly to Spain and north Africa in October. They return in March or April.

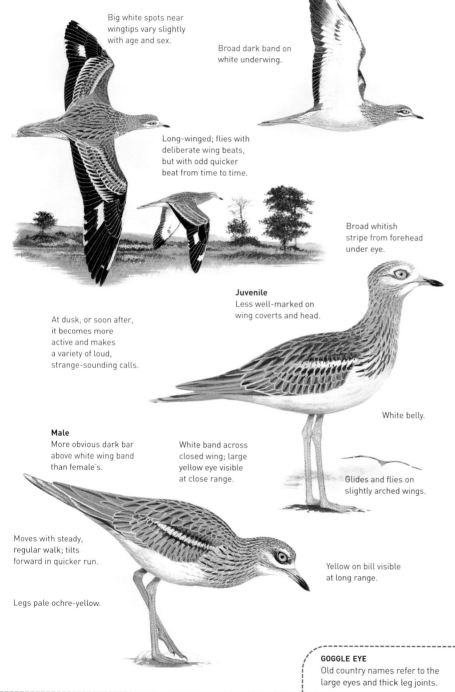

Big white spots near wingtips vary slightly with age and sex.

Broad dark band on white underwing.

Long-winged; flies with deliberate wing beats, but with odd quicker beat from time to time.

Broad whitish stripe from forehead under eye.

Juvenile
Less well-marked on wing coverts and head.

At dusk, or soon after, it becomes more active and makes a variety of loud, strange-sounding calls.

White belly.

Male
More obvious dark bar above white wing band than female's.

White band across closed wing; large yellow eye visible at close range.

Glides and flies on slightly arched wings.

Moves with steady, regular walk; tilts forward in quicker run.

Yellow on bill visible at long range.

Legs pale ochre-yellow.

GOGGLE EYE
Old country names refer to the large eyes and thick leg joints.

WHEN SEEN

Oct

March

All year in Spain; elsewhere March to October.

WHERE SEEN
Open farmland, heaths, stony steppe; southern England, east to southern Russia and south to the Mediterranean.

HABITAT AND INFO

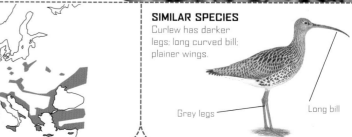

SIMILAR SPECIES
Curlew has darker legs; long curved bill; plainer wings.

Grey legs

Long bill

Collared Pratincole

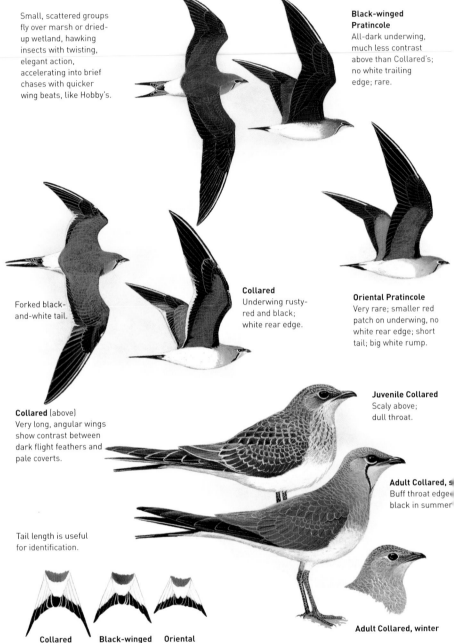

SCALE v Pigeon

LENGTH / 23–26cm (9–10¼in)
WINGSPAN / 60–70cm (23½–27½in)
WEIGHT / 50–80g (1¾–2¾oz)

■ **STATUS /** Endangered

A large-eyed, small-billed, short-legged wader with a bulky Swallow-like form, it is elongated when alert, more rounded when resting. Its flight is buoyant, with frequent twists, climbs, and steep dives. It has a harsh, tern-like, creaking call.

Although technically a wader, this elegant bird feeds almost like a big Swallow and calls like a tern. It has a rhythmic, powerful, tern-like action in direct flight. Individuals in small groups often stand a little apart, facing the same way, very inconspicuous on dried earth or grassland. They look much rounder than they do in flight.

FEEDING
It glides and weaves in the air, catching insects in its bill.

DISPLAY AND VOICE
Courtship begins in late winter flocks, and pairs then move to breeding areas where they perform rapid flights overhead and a bowing ceremony on the ground. The voice includes a rolling, vibrating spring song and various rasping calls in flight, like *kik kik* or *kikki-kirrik*.

BREEDING
The nest is on the ground near water. The three chicks fly when 25–30 days old. Parent birds draw predators away from nests and chicks with elaborate "injury-feigning" distraction displays.

MIGRATION
In autumn, Collared Pratincoles leave Europe for Africa.

Small, scattered groups fly over marsh or dried-up wetland, hawking insects with twisting, elegant action, accelerating into brief chases with quicker wing beats, like Hobby's.

Black-winged Pratincole
All-dark underwing, much less contrast above than Collared's; no white trailing edge; rare.

Forked black-and-white tail.

Collared
Underwing rusty-red and black; white rear edge.

Oriental Pratincole
Very rare; smaller red patch on underwing, no white rear edge; short tail; big white rump.

Collared (above)
Very long, angular wings show contrast between dark flight feathers and pale coverts.

Juvenile Collared
Scaly above; dull throat.

Adult Collared, s
Buff throat edge
black in summer

Tail length is useful for identification.

Collared **Black-winged** **Oriental**

Adult Collared, winter

ALERT AND UPRIGHT
Collared Pratincoles look slim in the air, but rather deep-bodied on the ground.

WHEN SEEN
Oct
April

April to October.

WHERE SEEN
Extensive muddy plains, wetland fringes: Spain, Camargue, Balkans.

HABITAT AND INFO

SIMILAR SPECIES
Black Tern is greyer; lacks white rump and white trailing edge to wing.

Grey back

Grey tail

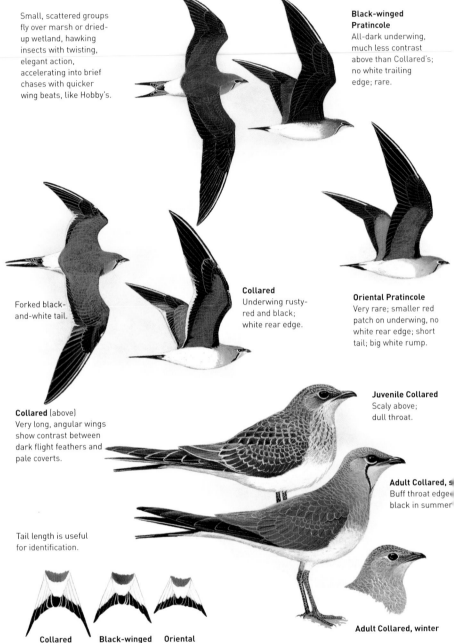

Black-winged Stilt

Unmistakable, with immensely long, vivid red-pink legs. It is black above, with white neck, body, and tail. Its head is variably marked darker.

LENGTH / 35–40cm (14–15½in)
WINGSPAN / 70cm (27½in)
WEIGHT / 250–300g (9–10½oz)

■ STATUS / Secure

SCALE v Pigeon

Juvenile (above)
Pale feather edges; white trailing edge to wing.

Flight fast with quick, flicked wing beats.

Underwing black except for white triangle at base.

Long white V up back.

Feet often crossed in flight.

Variable black on head in summer: both sexes may have extensive or little black.

Whiter heads in winter with grey on crown and cheeks.

Adult, summer

Extremely long, deep pink legs; stands on one leg for long spells.

Juvenile

Typically wades deeply, picks from surface, using long legs to range far from shore.

Adult, winter
Upperside more strongly glossed green-black on male.

Fine, black bill is straight or slightly upcurved.

Grotesquely long legs stamp an unmistakable character on the Stilt and everything it does. It is a slender, elegant bird, with a fine bill that adds a beautifully refined touch to its appearance, yet the length of its legs is evident whether it stands motionless on a sandbank, wades into water, or flies overhead calling noisily, its legs trailing and feet crossed for support.

FEEDING
The Stilt picks tiny aquatic invertebrates from the surface of fresh or salty water, bending forward or wading belly-deep to take food that is out of reach of most shoreline waders.

DISPLAY AND VOICE
Courtship involves noisy aerial chases, "butterfly flights" on raised wings, and elegant mating rituals with stereotyped preening. Stilts call with a sharp, Coot-like _kek_ and longer, harsh, tern-like sounds.

BREEDING
The nest is typically a scrape on dried waterside mud. The four chicks fly when 30 days old, and breed at two years old.

MIGRATION
Almost all migrate in autumn to central Africa.

AMAZING GRACE
The extraordinarily long legs are always a surprise, however often they are seen.

WHEN SEEN

Oct — March

March to October.

WHERE SEEN
S Europe, UK, very sporadic on shallow lagoons.

HABITAT AND INFO

SIMILAR SPECIES
Avocet is whiter overall; dull legs; white wings with black tips in flight.

White shoulder

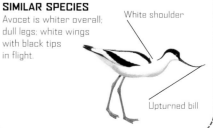

Upturned bill

Avocet

LENGTH / 42–45cm (16½–17½in)
WINGSPAN / 67–77cm (26½–30½in)
WEIGHT / 250–400g (9–14oz)

■ **STATUS /** Vulnerable

SCALE v Pigeon

This is a round-bodied, small-headed wader with stark black-and-white patterning and an upcurved, black bill.

An Avocet feeding on a muddy shore among scattered gulls can be overlooked, but a good view reveals its startlingly white body with neat black markings, and its unique upswept bill. In summer, Avocets are restricted to areas of shallow, brackish water with islands, often on estuaries.

FEEDING
It tilts forward and sweeps its upcurved bill sideways through water or glistening ooze to capture tiny shrimps and other invertebrates of saline lagoons and estuarine mud.

DISPLAY AND VOICE
Courtship involves ritualized displays with rhythmic preening and drinking movements. Avocets are noisy and draw attention by their loud, liquid *quilp* calls.

BREEDING
The nest is a mere scrape on mud or sand. Four chicks fly when 35–42 days old. They breed at two, sometimes three, years of age.

MIGRATION
Most move south and west in winter, to sheltered estuaries of western Europe or even south into Africa. They are then very gregarious, feeding and flying in tight-knit flocks.

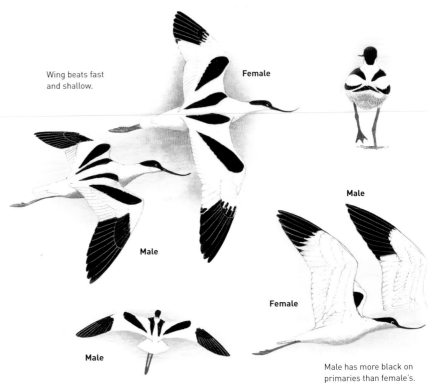

Wing beats fast and shallow.

Female

Male

Male

Female

Male

Male has more black on primaries than female's.

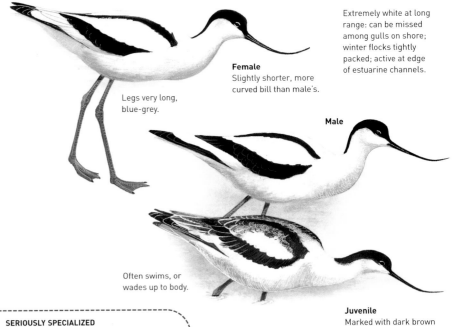

Legs very long, blue-grey.

Female
Slightly shorter, more curved bill than male's.

Extremely white at long range: can be missed among gulls on shore; winter flocks tightly packed; active at edge of estuarine channels.

Male

Often swims, or wades up to body.

Juvenile
Marked with dark brown and smudged greyish.

SERIOUSLY SPECIALIZED
The upturned bill is perfect for a sideways sweep through water and wet mud.

WHEN SEEN

All year; March to September at colony.

WHERE SEEN
Brackish water, estuaries; erratically south from Denmark and the Baltic.

HABITAT AND INFO

SIMILAR SPECIES
Black-headed Gull is similar only as "white bird" at great range, when shorter legs and bill may be visible.

Short bill

Short legs

Oystercatcher

A spectacular, stockily-built, large wader, strikingly pied. Adults have an unmistakable vivid orange bill.

LENGTH / 40–45cm (15½–17½in)
WINGSPAN / 80–85cm (31–33in)
WEIGHT / 400–700g (14–25oz)

■ **STATUS /** Secure

SCALE v Pigeon

Dazzling flight pattern: flocks confuse predators with sudden mass takeoff.

First winter
White collar.

Immature
Widest white collar; dull bill.

Adult, winter
White collar.

Adult, summer
Striking orange bill; red eye with red ring; no white collar in breeding plumage.

Juvenile
Dull, marked with buff-brown; no white collar at first.

Legs clear pink on summer adult, dusky on immatures.

On northern coasts, along stony rivers and in farmed valleys, Oystercatchers nest in pairs that probably last for life. After breeding, however, they are more familiar in the south and west as birds of estuaries and sandy beaches, or rocky places with an abundance of mussels and limpets.

FEEDING
Inland breeders eat mostly caterpillars and earthworms. On the coast they take cockles from soft mud and mussels prised from rocks. Some slip their blade-like bills between the shells to cut the shell-closing muscles; others simply hammer them to pieces.

DISPLAY AND VOICE
Noisy piping displays in small groups are frequent, often leading to whirring display flights. Calls include loud, strident *kleep*, *kwik*, *k-peep* and variations.

BREEDING
Oystercatcher nests are scrapes in the ground, sometimes on stumps or rocks. Three eggs are usual, hatching after 24–27 days.

MIGRATION
Northern, eastern, and inland breeders all move south and west in winter, some as far as Africa.

Small groups bend forward and call in strident, earsplitting piping display with open bills pointing down.

Broad white wingbar and white V on back, bolder than on Black-tailed Godwit's.

ASSORTED COLLARS
Non-breeding adults and immatures have variable white bands on the throat.

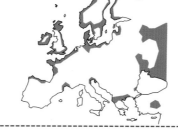

WHEN SEEN

All year.

WHERE SEEN
All UK and NW European coasts; inland in N Britain and Low Countries.

HABITAT AND INFO

SIMILAR SPECIES
Black-tailed Godwit is much slimmer, with longer bill and neck; long trailing legs; no dark chest band.

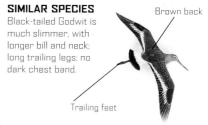

Brown back

Trailing feet

Ringed Plover

LENGTH / 18–20cm (7–8in)
WINGSPAN / 48–57cm (19–22½in)
WEIGHT / 55–75g (2–2¾oz)

■ **STATUS /** Secure

SCALE v Pigeon

A round-faced, neat, Starling-sized shorebird, clean white beneath. Adults have crisp black-and-white head patterns and brightly coloured bill and legs. Its pleasant, fluty call is distinctive.

The Ringed Plover is often to be seen on a beach of sand, shingle, or mud, running nimbly for a few steps, then stopping – taut, alert – looking around or searching for prey. In summer, pairs are widely spaced along the beaches, or around flooded gravel pits inland. In autumn and winter, they join together in flocks, gathering at high tide in their hundreds.

FEEDING
The Ringed Plover feeds mainly on tiny beach crustaceans and insects picked from the ground.

DISPLAY AND VOICE
An aggressive bird runs toward others intruding on its territory in a forward-leaning hunch, its wings slightly open to make itself look larger and show off its bold chest patterning. It may also fan its tail and tilt it toward the adversary. Courtship involves a song flight by the male, using a slow, flicked wing action while tilting side to side, singing a rich, fluty *teelew teelew teelew d'loo d'loo d'loo*. Normal calls are bright, mellow, liquid notes emphasizing the second syllable: *toolee* or *keeip*, with variations used to convey alarm, threats, or warnings to young chicks if danger threatens.

BREEDING
While most Ringed Plovers in the UK nest on or near the coast, increasing numbers use flooded gravel workings inland, where they may arrive earlier than Little Ringed Plovers and take the best territories. The nest is a shallow dish-shaped hollow scraped in sand or shingle, and lined with tiny shell fragments or stones. Both parents incubate the 3–4 well-camouflaged eggs, with frequent changes, for 23–25 days. The irresistibly attractive downy chicks are quickly active. They fly after 24 days, soon become independent, and breed when one year old. As so many pairs nest on popular beaches, with considerable human disturbance, failures are frequent. Even inland, or on islands, eggs and chicks are often taken by predators as varied as hedgehogs, gulls, and crows.

MIGRATION
Some British birds are resident, but most Ringed Plovers migrate. Those from the far north of Europe, Asia, Greenland, and the Canadian Arctic move farthest south, as far as South Africa, while those breeding farther south in Britain, Ireland, France, and the Low Countries tend to remain in western Europe or the Mediterranean area in winter.

Adult　　Juvenile　　Adult, summer

Adult male, summer
Brightly patterned with bold black bands on face and chest; colourful legs and bill.

Adult, winter
Note slightly less crisp black band; duller bill; grey eye-ring.

Tail tip of male extends beyond closed wingtips.

Juvenile has blackish bill with trace of yellow at base, and dull, yellowish legs.

Typical plover stance: alert "stop and look", then forward-leaning run and dip to pick food from ground – "run, stop, tilt".

Juvenile female
Crown dull brown; white forehead extends as stripe over eye; breast band narrow, brown, barely complete in centre; back scaly.

Adult female, winter
Wingtips and tail tips equal length, unlike male's; reduced black on top of head in winter plumage.

WHEN SEEN

All year in most of NW Europe; March to September in the north and August to May in the south-west.

WHERE SEEN
Estuaries, exposed beaches of sand, shingle or rock; lakesides and some sandy grassland areas inland (Breckland).

HABITAT AND INFO

SIMILAR SPECIES
Little Ringed Plover is slimmer; dull legs; darker bill; yellow ring round eye; plain wings.

Yellow eye-ring

Duller legs

BREAKING OUTLINES
The seemingly obvious pattern breaks up the shape and acts as camouflage on a stony beach.

Juvenile

Adult

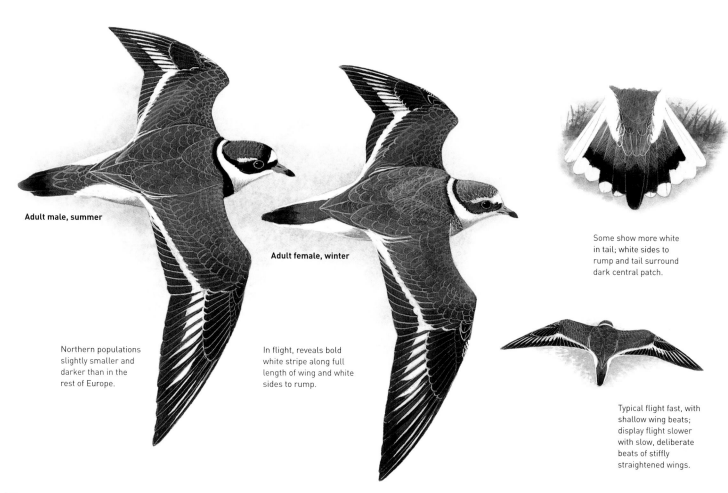

Adult male, summer

Adult female, winter

Some show more white in tail; white sides to rump and tail surround dark central patch.

Northern populations slightly smaller and darker than in the rest of Europe.

In flight, reveals bold white stripe along full length of wing and white sides to rump.

Typical flight fast, with shallow wing beats; display flight slower with slow, deliberate beats of stiffly straightened wings.

DID YOU KNOW?
Plovers typically find food by sight in a run-stop-look-tilt action; Ringed Plovers do so more quickly where food is abundant. They also use a "foot trembling" action, vibrating the toes of one foot against the surface of sand or mud, to stimulate a response from hidden prey such as minute worms and crustaceans.

?

Kentish Plover

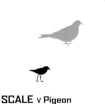

LENGTH / 15–17cm (6–6³⁄₄in)
WINGSPAN / 50cm (19¹⁄₂in)
WEIGHT / 40–60g (1¹⁄₂–2oz)

SCALE v Pigeon

■ **STATUS /** Vulnerable

A small, very pale plover, with dark only at the sides of the breast, slender black legs, and a relatively thick black bill.

With its long legs, rounded body, and often upright stance, this neat, lively, very pale little plover looks almost like the small chick of a larger species. It is typical of warm, sandy shorelines and saline lagoons, especially on flat areas of hard, salty mud or sand, but sometimes it finds temporary nesting habitats around gravel pits, or even on building sites.

FEEDING
It employs the fast run, stop, tilt-over feeding method typical of plovers, using its black bill to pick mainly small crustaceans and molluscs from the sand and shingle.

DISPLAY AND VOICE
Its display flights over nesting areas are accompanied by grating, trilling calls. More normal calls include a sharp *kip* and a quiet, short, fluty whistle.

BREEDING
It nests on the beach in a shallow scrape. The four eggs hatch after an incubation of 24–27 days.

MIGRATION
Most leave Europe for Africa in winter. A few reach the UK in spring and autumn.

Long white wingbar and distinctive white sides to tail.

White sides to tail, unlike other ringed plovers.

Nervous and rather shy; wingtips slender, but may look quite dumpy and short-tailed, almost chick-like.

Male, breeding
Rusty nape in spring.

Black marks on head and sides of breast.

Cool spring posture.

Juvenile
Duller with no black; black/grey legs unlike young Ringed Plover's.

Very rarely has paler legs.

Hot summer posture.

Legs typically dark grey.

Female
Pale sandy; no black on head; the palest of the ringed plovers.

In southern Europe. may look quite frayed and bleached by mid-year.

MEDITERRANEAN PLOVER
The plover with a broken breast band is a familiar shorebird of southern Europe.

WHEN SEEN

Oct — March

Mostly March to October, a few in winter.

WHERE SEEN
Sandy coasts, lagoons, salt pans; mostly S European and S North Sea coasts.

HABITAT AND INFO

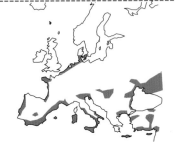

SIMILAR SPECIES
Juvenile Ringed Plover is stockier; darker cheek and more extensive breast patch.

Deeper breast patch

Pale legs

Little Ringed Plover

A small plover, with a low-slung, long-tailed shape when standing. The eye-ring, bill colour, and wing pattern are distinctive.

LENGTH / 14–15cm (5½–6in)
WINGSPAN / 42–48cm (16½–19in)
WEIGHT / 30–50g (1–1¾oz)

■ **STATUS /** Secure

SCALE v Pigeon

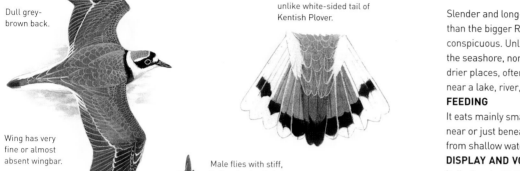

Dark band across tail, unlike white-sided tail of Kentish Plover.

Dull grey-brown back.

Wing has very fine or almost absent wingbar.

Male flies with stiff, jerky wing beats in display flight.

Slender and long-winged, this species looks less dumpy than the bigger Ringed Plover. Its yellow eye-ring is usually conspicuous. Unlike the Ringed Plover, it is not a bird of the seashore, nor is it found in Europe in winter. It prefers drier places, often waste ground or bare earth and gravel, near a lake, river, or flooded pit.

FEEDING
It eats mainly small insects, usually picking them from near or just beneath the surface of damp ground or from shallow water.

DISPLAY AND VOICE
It displays in flight above its territory, rolling on stiff, fully stretched wings while the male produces a rhythmic, grating song: *grria-grria-grria*. The typical call is an abrupt *piw* or *pew* without the fluty, musical quality of a Ringed Plover.

BREEDING
The four large eggs are laid directly on the ground. Incubated by both parents, they hatch after 24–25 days.

MIGRATION
All Little Ringed Plovers leave Europe in autumn, heading for Africa south of the Sahara. They return early, reaching the UK in March.

White band over front of crown.

Yellow ring around eye.

Bill all-black or with tiny pale patch.

Female has narrower eye-ring.

Breeding male

More horizontal than Ringed; looks slimmer, longer-legged, more tapered to wingtips.

Narrow black band on breast.

Breeding female

Juvenile
Lacks white over eye, so has hooded look; thin yellow eye-ring.

Breast band typically narrower than on Ringed Plover.

Dull pinkish-ochre legs.

STRIKING EYELIDS
The yellow orbital ring around the eye is always distinctive.

WHERE SEEN
Scattered throughout Europe in suitable habitat.

HABITAT AND INFO

SIMILAR SPECIES
Adult Ringed Plover is stockier; brighter bill and legs; dark eye without yellow ring; broad white wing stripe.

Orange bill base

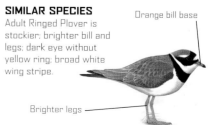

Brighter legs

Dotterel

LENGTH / 20–22cm (8–8¾in)
WINGSPAN / 57–64cm (22½–25in)
WEIGHT / 90–145g (3¼–5oz)

■ STATUS / Vulnerable

SCALE v Pigeon

A rounded, long-legged, short-billed terrestrial bird with a striking white V on the head and a white band (sometimes faint) around the breast. It is often in small groups, especially on spring migration.

Dotterels breed on broad, rolling mountain slopes and northern hills, on the highest tops in the Highlands of Scotland but at lower altitudes farther north. In spring, small groups, or trips, appear on lowland fields in traditional areas, staying for a few days before moving north.

FEEDING
Dotterels eat mainly insects and spiders, picking them from the ground or from clumps of moss.

DISPLAY AND VOICE
In a reversal of the normal roles, females take the initiative and chase individual males from spring groups, forming pairs before arrival on the nesting areas. Each female may pair with two or more males. Calls include a soft, penetrating *pweet pweet*.

BREEDING
Three eggs are incubated mostly or wholly by the male for 24–28 days, in a hollow on open ground. The chicks fly at 25–30 days. A female may lay more than one clutch to be incubated by several males. Females help incubate second clutches.

MIGRATION
All breeders move south to north Africa for the winter.

Breeding male
Duller, paler than female.

White underwing.

Upperside plain in flight; white vent may catch the eye.

Fine, pointed, black bill.

Breeding female
Brighter, darker than male with stronger underpart pattern.

Female, winter
Duller, more buff, with ghost of breast band and obvious white V around dark cap.

Tail of female projects beyond wingtips.

Pale ochre-yellow legs.

Juvenile, autumn
Beautifully patterned with lacy feather edgings, breast band, and cap.

Male, winter
Upright when alert; round and dumpy when resting.

REVERSE ROLES
This female Dotterel is a handsome bird, more strikingly patterned than the male.

WHEN SEEN

Sept — April

April to September.

WHERE SEEN
Breeds in Scotland and upland Scandinavia; rarely England, on high moorland; scarce on passage in W Europe.

HABITAT AND INFO

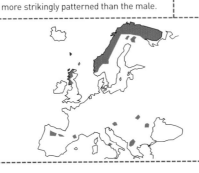

SIMILAR SPECIES
Golden Plover is more spangled above and in winter has less defined pale stripe over eye; whitish wingbar.

Spangled back

Black legs

Turnstone

A dark, busy, shuffling wader of weedy rocks and stony beaches, it is well-camouflaged among seaweed but striking when it flies up, flashing unique patterns of white and calling with sharp, staccato notes.

LENGTH / 22–24cm (8¾–9½in)
WINGSPAN / 44–49cm (17½–19in)
WEIGHT / 80–110g (2¾–3¾oz)

■ STATUS / Secure

SCALE v Pigeon

Adult, winter

Adult, spring

Adult, winter
Dark back; head variable but always a bold black band across chest, above white belly.

Juvenile
At all ages unique bold white band across base of tail; white back and white triangle on inner wing.

Flight usually low, twisting at first, then direct and powerful.

Forehead sometimes white.

Leans forward to pick up food with short, slightly upswept bill.

Short, thick, vivid orange legs at all seasons mark it out from other small waders.

Adult, breeding
Male generally whiter-headed than female, but some racial variation.

Always close to the water's edge, Turnstones search busily for food among rocks, seaweed, and the strandline of debris thrown up by the tides on sandy or shingle beaches. At high tide, they fly to secluded places to roost with other waders, often mixing with Ringed Plovers and Dunlins.

FEEDING
Turnstones search for small crustaceans and molluscs by riffling through (and really turning over) stones, shells, and bits of weed, or poking about at the edges of rock pools. In the breeding season, they eat insects, spiders, and some seeds.

DISPLAY AND VOICE
Calls are quick, staccato repetitions: *kitititit*, *tuk-i-tuk*, or a rolling *titwoootitwoooorit-it-ititititit*. These birds may chase each other while calling loudly, and posture with hunched backs and spread tails.

BREEDING
It breeds in the far north on coasts and islands, laying four eggs in a simple scrape on the ground.

MIGRATION
It moves south to North Sea and Atlantic coasts in autumn.

Juvenile
Like winter adult but more even V-shaped feather edges above; paler cheeks and throat.

Dark tortoiseshell effect much brighter in spring with large rufous patches above.

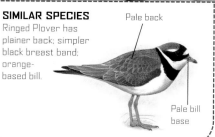

TIDE-LINE SCAVENGER
Turnstones are likely on almost any beach and can become tame.

WHEN SEEN

Almost all year in non-breeding areas; May to September in north.

WHERE SEEN
Coasts of Scandinavia; migrates to NW European and African shores; scarce inland.

HABITAT AND INFO

SIMILAR SPECIES
Ringed Plover has plainer back; simpler black breast band; orange-based bill.

Pale back
Pale bill base

Broad-billed Sandpiper

LENGTH / 16–17cm (6¼–6¾in)
WINGSPAN / 30–34cm (11¾–13½in)
WEIGHT / 50–65g (1¾–2¼oz)

■ STATUS / Vulnerable

SCALE v Pigeon

This is a short-legged, thick-billed, dark wader with a striped head, smaller than a Dunlin.

Compared with most of the small sandpipers, this is a dark, swarthy, almost Snipe-like bird. In spring, its fresh feathers are pale, giving it a hoary appearance, but the edges wear away to reveal darker centres.

FEEDING
It feeds in shallow water with delicate probing and occasional short, quick runs, taking small insects and seeds. It may feed with Dunlins, or in small groups. In the Middle East, it often forms much larger flocks.

DISPLAY AND VOICE
The male gives a rhythmic, buzzing song in flight. If flushed it has a short, rising, dry trill, *chr-e-e-et* or *trrhuit*, more trilling than a Dunlin flight call and less musical than a Curlew Sandpiper's.

BREEDING
It breeds in loose colonies. Females lay 3–4 eggs in a grassy cup in a tussock of grass.

MIGRATION
It is a rare bird in western Europe, but breeds in Scandinavia and migrates to the Middle East and India in winter. In the UK, it appears mostly between May and July.

Adult, non-breeding

Adult, breeding

Sides of rump white.

Head marks least obvious in winter.

Thin white wingbar.

Head striped with black crown, double pale lines over eye; best seen head-on.

Bill slightly kinked down at tip.

Split eye stripe.

Breeding
Late spring plumage dark and rich as pale fringes wear off; dark V-shapes on flanks.

Juvenile
Upperparts more stint-like than those of adult.

Belly and flanks white; legs dark greenish.

Early spring plumage frosted with paler feather edges.

Dark shoulder recalls Sanderling, unlike Dunlin; often hidden under flank feathers; note lace pattern.

Non-breeding
Dull, pale, with white belly, dark shoulder; head stripes dull but important clues.

TRICKY CHALLENGE
Care and close observation is needed for correct identification.

WHEN SEEN

 Sept April

April to September.

WHERE SEEN
N Scandinavia; on migration, very rare elsewhere on coastal lagoons and marshes.

HABITAT AND INFO

SIMILAR SPECIES
Dunlin has plainer head; more evenly tapered and curved bill; less contrast on wing.

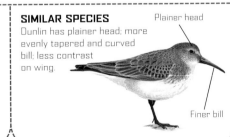

Plainer head

Finer bill

Temminck's Stint

A short-legged, small-billed, dull grey-brown sandpiper with pale legs, white sides to tail and short, trilling call. This is a freshwater bird, with a slow, deliberate walking action when feeding and distinctive at long range.

LENGTH / 13–15cm (5–6in)
WINGSPAN / 34–37cm (13½–14½in)
WEIGHT / 20–40g (¾–1½oz)

■ STATUS / Vulnerable

SCALE v Pigeon

This is a rather rare bird in western Europe: a scarce passage migrant. In the UK, it occurs in threes and fours in May. It breeds in Scandinavia (with a very few in Scotland) and northern Asia, and moves to Africa and southern Asia in winter.

FEEDING
It feeds less actively than most small sandpipers, creeping and shuffling over wet grass or mud to pick up insects, worms, and molluscs.

DISPLAY AND VOICE
The song is a rising and falling trill, *sirrrrr* or *kilililili* given in flight. The usual call when flushed is a valuable clue – a short, hard *tr-r-r-r*.

BREEDING
The nest is built on the ground in low vegetation, often near willow scrub, or in an open space near water, close to Arctic inlets, deltas, and rivers. The four eggs hatch after 21–22 days. Sometimes one parent incubates a clutch each, or two males and one female may incubate three clutches.

Thin white wingbar; white sides to tail; broader, less angled wings than Little Stint's in typical flight.

Towers up in erratic flight when flushed, often calling.

Underwing distinctive in flight or wing stretching.

Wingtips equal tail on male.

Greyish; white belly; grey breast band.

Male, non-breeding

Male, breeding Irregular dark blotches on back; these appear slowly in spring.

Tail projects on female.

Juvenile female Upperpart feathers edged with yellow-buff and thin dark crescent; white mark between wing and breast recalls Common Sandpiper.

Legs pale yellow-ochre to greenish-yellow.

Wide white sides to tail unlike other small sandpipers.

NOT SO DULL Although seemingly unexciting, this scarce bird is always a good find.

WHEN SEEN

May to September; some winter in Italy, Greece.

WHERE SEEN Breeds along Scandinavian spine and north coast of Europe; scarce migrant on muddy lake edges and coastal lagoons but not estuary mud or beaches.

HABITAT AND INFO

SIMILAR SPECIES Dunlin is bigger, heavier; blacker legs; longer bill; different call.
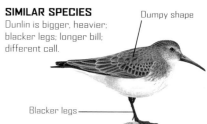
Dumpy shape
Blacker legs

Little Stint

LENGTH / 12–14cm (4³⁄₄–5¹⁄₂in)
WINGSPAN / 34–37cm (13¹⁄₂–14¹⁄₂in)
WEIGHT / 20–40g (³⁄₄–1¹⁄₂oz)

■ **STATUS /** Secure

SCALE v Pigeon

A tiny, neat wader, of both salt- and freshwater, it is active, quick, black-legged, and white-bellied at all times. A prominent white V is on the back of juvenile and breeding adult.

In most of western Europe, Little Stints are usually seen in late summer and autumn, with a small number of migrating adults followed by larger numbers of juveniles. There are far fewer seen in spring. They usually travel and feed with Dunlins and sometimes Curlew Sandpipers, and often they are absurdly tame.

FEEDING
A Little Stint usually feeds at the water's edge, using short runs and quick-picking from the surface with its bill.

DISPLAY AND VOICE
Little Stints have a typical sandpiper/stint song flight. Autumn migrants twitter in flocks and call with a short, sharp *pit*, *chit*, or *pit-it*.

BREEDING
Nesting areas are in High Arctic tundra and islands.

MIGRATION
Each autumn they move south to spend the winter in Africa and India, visiting many west European coasts and inland waters, but they are much more frequently seen in south-east Europe in spring.

Narrow wings, white below.

Thin, short black bill; black legs; white belly at all times. With Dunlins, looks small; bright; active; white-bellied.

Adult, winter
Greyish above.

Wingtips project more on juvenile.

Thin white wingbar; white sides to rump; flight fast, flickering with sideways tilts.

Juvenile, autumn
Pale V on back.

Juvenile, autumn
Strong V on back; rusty feather edges above; pale breast band streaked at sides.

Juvenile has streaked cap; pale line over eye.

Dark centre and white sides to rump like Dunlin's; grey sides to tail unlike Temminck's Stint's.

Very short wingtip projection on adult.

Breeding
Bright rusty-brown above with cream feather tips; hint of pale V; white belly.

Rufous breast.

Non-breeding
Plain grey above, white below; slight greyish breast band; plain head.

Adult, early spring

SPARROW-SIZED WADER
Often seen with Dunlins, this bird attracts attention by its tiny size.

WHEN SEEN

Oct
May

May to October; mostly August-September in NW Europe.

WHERE SEEN
Breeds in extreme N Norway and Siberia; widespread on migration, especially in coastal areas.

HABITAT AND INFO

SIMILAR SPECIES
Juvenile Dunlin is bigger; less clean below with smudgy flanks; different call.

Blotchy flanks   Curved bill

Sanderling

A neat wader, just bigger than a Dunlin and with a shorter, straighter bill, black legs, and a gleaming white belly at all times.

LENGTH / 20–21cm (8in–8¼in)
WINGSPAN / 36–39cm (14–15½in)
WEIGHT / 50–60g (1¾–2oz)

■ **STATUS /** Secure

SCALE v Pigeon

Blackish wings have broad white stripe.

Adult, early spring (left)
Grey wears off: see bird at far right.

Upperpart feathers have white tips in spring, giving marbled effect that wears off by late summer.

Head plain, without strong stripe over eye.

Adult, breeding
Mottled black and rust-red in spring; lacks pale V on back of Little Stint; looks more mealy.

Black legs; no hind toe.

Adult, non-breeding (below)
Very grey and white; gradually darkens toward spring.

Juvenile
Spotted black above; dark cap.

Black bill straighter and shorter than that of Dunlin.

Dark shoulder patch often hidden.

Usually runs on clean sand, tripping along water's edge and following waves; may feed on muddier or algae-covered beaches and flat rocks; often inland in May.

SHARP FEATURES
Black, silver-grey, and a bold white wingbar create a striking effect in flight.

Outside the breeding season the Sanderling is a bird of the open seashore, tripping across sandy beaches, chasing receding waves, or sitting out the high tide in tight-knit, motionless flocks. It is best known as a pearly grey and white wader, with black legs and bill. In May, small numbers appear beside reservoirs inland, moving on quickly northward.

FEEDING
It picks small invertebrates – flies, crustaceans, and occasional small marine worms – from the beach with quick, deft movements and frequent shallow probes of its bill.

DISPLAY AND VOICE
It makes a peculiar frog-like sound during its song flight over the nesting territory. At other times its usual call is a short, hard, dry *twick*. Flocks twitter when feeding.

BREEDING
In summer, it breeds on the High Arctic tundra, laying its four eggs on bare earth or stones.

MIGRATION
After breeding in the Arctic, it winters on suitable beaches as far as the southern tips of Africa and South America, and Australasia.

WHEN SEEN

Aug   May
August to May.

WHERE SEEN
Migrant on all coasts mostly on sandy beaches, scarce inland but regular by some reservoir edges in May.

HABITAT AND INFO

SIMILAR SPECIES
Dunlin is drabber, less pure grey; bill faintly curved; less bold contrast on wing.

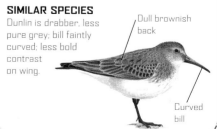

Dull brownish back

Curved bill

Dunlin

LENGTH / 16–20cm (6¼–8in)
WINGSPAN / 35–40cm (14–15½in)
WEIGHT / 40–50g (1½–1¾oz)

SCALE v Pigeon

■ STATUS / Secure

A small, short-legged, medium-billed, hunch-backed wader. It is grey-brown in winter, chestnut in summer with distinctive black belly. It is sometimes in huge flocks.

On almost any smooth coastline, whether of mud or sand, small, short-legged waders scuttle about at low tide. They are usually Dunlins, and these are the most widespread and numerous of the smaller seashore waders. They are also often seen inland in spring and autumn, beside muddy lakes and reservoirs. If the water levels remain low and shores stay muddy, groups of Dunlins may stay around reservoirs all winter. This frequency makes the Dunlin the benchmark against which to judge scarcer waders such as the Little Stint or Curlew Sandpiper, as well as more local coastal species such as the Knot.

The Dunlin is a small wader, with a medium-length bill, short legs, and a broad-bodied, round-shouldered shape. It is not as elegant as a Curlew Sandpiper, or as quick and nimble as a Little Stint. Yet Dunlins are enchanting little birds, and in full breeding plumage they can be handsome. They illustrate the plumage sequences shown by all the *Calidris* sandpipers. In early spring, they moult into new body plumage with broad, pale feather edges; these pale edges wear away to reveal the brighter, darker colours beneath, creating a rich breeding plumage. The extent of the moult and abrasion varies. One bird's upperparts may retain some grey winter feathers, while another still has pale edges on its bright summer feathers – this creates a lot of variation. The birds moult their larger wing and tail feathers in late autumn, so by spring these are only slightly worn; by late summer they are faded and abraded at the tips. The breeding plumage of different races varies, too. British breeders have big, black feather centres, creating a boldly mottled upperpart pattern, while northern birds have smaller black spots in more extensive chestnut, once the broad pale grey fringes wear away.

FEEDING
In summer, on bogs and moors, Dunlins eat insects. At other times they eat a variety of tiny worms and molluscs. They are equally at home feeding on soft mud and weed-covered rocks. On soft mud they probe quickly with a "stitching" action, but on harder ground they locate more prey by sight and pick it up with more precision.

DISPLAY AND VOICE
Outside the breeding season Dunlins are sociable and may feed in groups of hundreds, roosting in flocks of several thousands. In spring, the Dunlin flocks separate into pairs, and the males advertise their territories in display flights. These begin with a fast, steep rise, followed by a hovering or switchback flight into the wind, with a prolonged, whinnying trill: *chrrii-i-i-i-i-ri-ri-ri-ri*. This can often be heard from roosting flocks on beaches in spring. The typical call is a low, drawn out, slightly grating, reedy *tr-reeee* or slurred *treep*.

BREEDING
Dunlin nests are slight scrapes on the ground, usually concealed in tussocks of vegetation. The four eggs are incubated by both parents and hatch after 21–22 days. The chicks leave the nest quickly and fly at 19–21 days old.

MIGRATION
Breeders from the north and inland move to the coast and head south to spend the winter throughout Europe to north and west Africa. Small parties often appear inland.

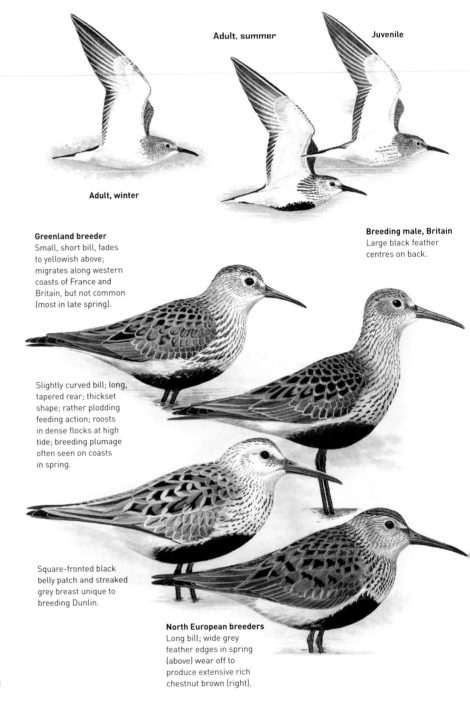

Adult, summer

Juvenile

Adult, winter

Greenland breeder
Small, short bill, fades to yellowish above; migrates along western coasts of France and Britain, but not common (most in late spring).

Breeding male, Britain
Large black feather centres on back.

Slightly curved bill; long, tapered rear; thickset shape; rather plodding feeding action; roosts in dense flocks at high tide; breeding plumage often seen on coasts in spring.

Square-fronted black belly patch and streaked grey breast unique to breeding Dunlin.

North European breeders
Long bill; wide grey feather edges in spring (above) wear off to produce extensive rich chestnut brown (right).

WHEN SEEN

All year; in N Europe mostly April to September.

WHERE SEEN
All year; in N Europe mostly April to September; breeds Iceland, Scotland, N England, scarce Wales and Ireland, Norway, locally Sweden and Finland, Baltic states, and Germany; widespread at other times.

HABITAT AND INFO

BASIC REFERENCE
Learning the Dunlin is an essential step
before identifying scarcer waders.

Typical small sandpiper;
thin white wingbar and
white sides to dark-
centred rump and tail.

Winter adults and juveniles

Adult, winter

Juvenile (right)
Shares basic flight
pattern but much
brighter above; hint
of pale V on back.

Adult, autumn
Transitional plumage
shows scattered, dark
chestnut summer
feathers among
winter grey.

Juvenile
Moulting into winter
plumage with scattered,
very dark summer
feathers and old,
brown tertials.

Adult, autumn
Transitional plumage.

Little Stint, winter
Shorter, straighter bill.

Juvenile
Rich chestnut with black
and cream on back;
scaly on wings; flanks
streaked and blotched.

Tail length varies
with individuals and
discrete populations
within Europe.

Adult, winter
Complete non-breeding
plumage, wholly pale
brownish-grey above
with dark shaft streaks.

SIMILAR SPECIES
Sanderling is more
spotted than streaked on
chest; clean white below;
sharp call.

Straight bill

Bright white below

DID YOU KNOW?
Dunlins use several similar feeding methods, pecking from the surface
around 15-25 times a minute, probing while walking and using a rapid
"stitching" action - with short, fast bursts - often moving forward less
than 1m (3ft) in 30 minutes. Of the 15-25 pecks a minute, only 1 or 2 of
these catch food. Most prey is swallowed as the bill is being
withdrawn from the mud.

?

Curlew Sandpiper

LENGTH / 18–23cm (7–9in)
WINGSPAN / 38–41cm (15–16in)
WEIGHT / 45–90g (1½–3¼oz)

■ STATUS / Secure

SCALE v Pigeon

A slender, elegant, long-legged, and long-billed wader, marginally larger than a Dunlin.

Of the several sandpipers with a general resemblance to the Dunlin, this is the most elegant. Like larger species such as the Knot, it sports rich red breeding plumage in spring, but at that time it is common only in south-east Europe. Small numbers appear in the west in autumn, with Little Stints and Dunlins.

FEEDING
It wades in water, probing for small molluscs and crustaceans.

DISPLAY AND VOICE
Although it lacks the vibrant effect of the Dunlin's, the flight call is distinctive: a soft, chirruping or slightly rippling *chirrrip* or *kil-l-lee*.

BREEDING
It breeds in extreme north of Siberia. Four eggs are incubated for 21 days.

MIGRATION
In spring, large flocks occur in eastern Europe. In autumn, a few scores to thousands stop off in Britain and the Low Countries, on estuaries or shallow coastal lagoons, or beside lakes inland. Adults move in July and early August, juveniles in August and September. Good years for autumn migration occur when lemming numbers are high, because predators eat them in preference to Curlew Sandpipers.

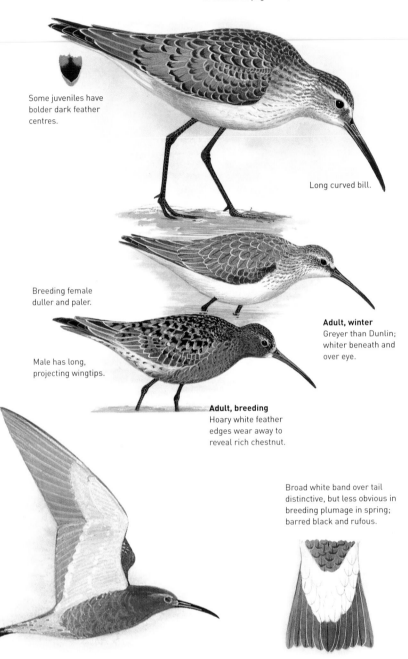

Juvenile
Beautiful scaly effect: grey, washed yellow-buff; bright orange-buff to yellow-peach chest; white over eye. (Same scale as Dunlin on page 212.)

Some juveniles have bolder dark feather centres.

Long curved bill.

Breeding female duller and paler.

Male has long, projecting wingtips.

Adult, winter
Greyer than Dunlin; whiter beneath and over eye.

Adult, breeding
Hoary white feather edges wear away to reveal rich chestnut.

Broad white band over tail distinctive, but less obvious in breeding plumage in spring; barred black and rufous.

White rump and wingbar; projecting feet.

WHEN SEEN

Oct / March
July / May

March to May; July to October or November; rare in winter.

WHERE SEEN
Most of Europe on migration.

HABITAT AND INFO

SIMILAR SPECIES
Juvenile Dunlin is stockier; shorter legs and bill; smudgy flanks; more streaked, less scaled, above; black-centred rump.

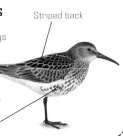

Striped back

Smudgy underside

DID YOU KNOW?
Like many other waders, Curlew Sandpipers migrate south from the
Arctic at a leisurely pace in autumn, adults ahead of the juveniles. The
latter will be encountering humans for the first time and, in suitable
places such as the edge of a reservoir, may sometimes be
approached to within arm's length without causing any
apparent alarm.

?

Knot

LENGTH / 23–25cm (9–9¾in)
WINGSPAN / 47–54cm (18½–21in)
WEIGHT / 125–215g (4½–7½oz)

■ **STATUS /** Vulnerable

SCALE v Pigeon

A dumpy, medium-sized wader with a medium-short bill and legs, and distinctive grey rump. It is very quiet for a wader, lacking loud alarm calls. It is typically very gregarious and individuals can be extraordinarily tame.

Even among the waders – a group that boasts many long-distance travellers – the Knot is a remarkable globetrotter, flying vast distances each spring and autumn. Knots have been intensively studied because of this hugely demanding way of life, which must bring great benefits to offset its stresses. The 24-hour daylight and abundant food of the Arctic summer clearly outweigh the problem of escaping the dark, cold Arctic winter by undertaking long, dangerous flights over the sea. Knots are especially sociable, feeding in dense flocks on open mud flats. They advance like a grey carpet: even if there are only a hundred or so they jostle almost shoulder-to-shoulder. When disturbed, or moving to their roosts as the tide rises, airborne flocks are wonderfully impressive as they twist and turn like columns of smoke in turbulent air.

FEEDING
In the Arctic, Knots feed on insects and seeds. On coasts outside the breeding season, they prefer muddy, or less often sandy or shingly areas, where they pick small molluscs from the surface or just below.

DISPLAY AND VOICE
Many Knots return to their breeding areas already paired. Other males and females arrive singly, but ready to court and claim a territory as soon as the ground thaws in the summer sun. The male flies slowly over the territory, circling on rapidly vibrating wings, then glides down on wings held stiffly in a V, levels out on flat wings, and rises again with wings quivering. During this display he sings: *whip-poo-mee* and *poo-mee*, the song changing with his style of flight. At other times, the usual call is a low, hoarse note, often from feeding flocks, creating a jumbled, unmusical chorus. A liquid double note is occasionally used in flight.

BREEDING
The 3–4 eggs are laid on the ground in a slight hollow with a flimsy lining of leaves, stems, and lichen. They hatch after 21–22 days, and the chicks quickly move to feed beside nearby stretches of water. They fly after just 18–20 days.

MIGRATION
Knots from the extreme north of Canada and Greenland winter in western Europe (from farther south in Canada, they go to South America). Those from central Siberia migrate through Europe to west and south Africa, while Knots from farther east go to Australia and New Zealand. They can lose as much as 80 per cent of their body weight during these long flights.

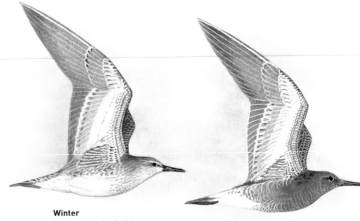

Winter
Dull, grey, pale; lacks striking features.

Breeding
Underside pale to deep rufous; white vent.

Huge flocks in distance look like smoke.

Adult, winter
Grey above; pale line over eye.

Clean grey in autumn, fading duller and browner by spring.

Legs short, pale, grey-green.

Juvenile
Grey with neat, lacy, scalloped feather edges above; breast flushed pale orange-buff. Greyer, dumpier than Ruff, bigger than Dunlin, paler than Redshank.

Wingtip equal to tail on Siberian breeders.

WHEN SEEN

All year; in W Europe, most late July or August to early May.

WHERE SEEN
Winters mostly on a few estuaries around North Sea, Irish Sea, English Channel, and Biscay coasts; widespread on migration.

HABITAT AND INFO

SIMILAR SPECIES
Female Ruff has longer, paler legs; less grey; dark-centred rump.

Scaly back

Longer legs

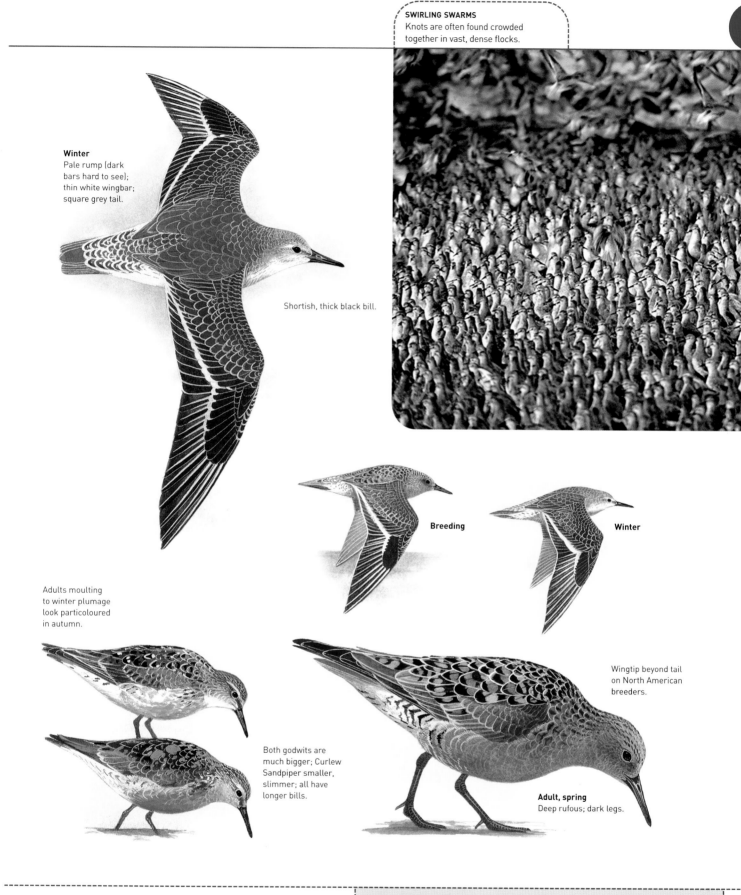

Winter
Pale rump (dark bars hard to see); thin white wingbar; square grey tail.

Shortish, thick black bill.

Breeding

Winter

Adults moulting to winter plumage look particoloured in autumn.

Wingtip beyond tail on North American breeders.

Both godwits are much bigger; Curlew Sandpiper smaller, slimmer; all have longer bills.

Adult, spring
Deep rufous; dark legs.

DID YOU KNOW?
Freshly arrived Knots on Arctic breeding grounds eat shoots, seeds, and flowers of grasses and sedges and other plant matter until insects become more active by midsummer, but vegetable matter remains around half of their diet throughout their stay in the region. In winter, they eat various species of tiny shellfish, depending on availability.

Purple Sandpiper

LENGTH / 20–22cm (8–8¾in)
WINGSPAN / 40–44cm (15½–17½in)
WEIGHT / 60–75g (2–2¾oz)

■ STATUS / Vulnerable

SCALE v Pigeon

A small, neat, round-bodied wader, looking dark unless seen against very dark seaweed of typical rocky shore habitat. Subtly beautiful plumage is combined with yellow bill and orange-yellow legs.

Purple Sandpipers live at the very edge of the sea, where they often have to leap clear of breaking waves. They are typical of really rocky shores, where they feed among the barnacles and seaweeds. They often occur with Turnstones, when they are less easy to approach than when alone.

FEEDING
They feed where the sea is in constant motion, using their slim bills to pick up invertebrates momentarily exposed by the waves.

DISPLAY AND VOICE
Typical winter calls are short and sharp, such as *pwit* or *wit*. The song is a series of fast trills. Pairs seem to form in the winter flock, without obvious displays on the breeding areas. The white underwing is important in communication.

BREEDING
They nest from about mid-May, the female selecting one of several scrapes made by the male. Four eggs hatch after 21 days.

MIGRATION
In autumn, after the breeding season, birds move to adjacent coasts or farther south to Britain, France, and northern Spain.

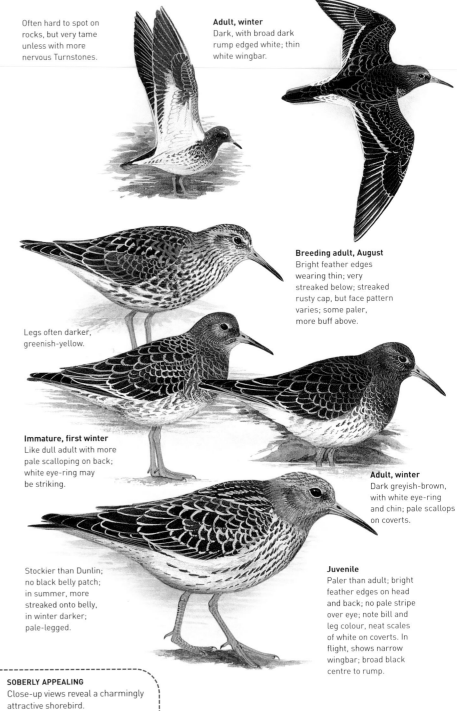

Often hard to spot on rocks, but very tame unless with more nervous Turnstones.

Adult, winter
Dark, with broad dark rump edged white; thin white wingbar.

Breeding adult, August
Bright feather edges wearing thin; very streaked below; streaked rusty cap, but face pattern varies; some paler, more buff above.

Legs often darker, greenish-yellow.

Immature, first winter
Like dull adult with more pale scalloping on back; white eye-ring may be striking.

Adult, winter
Dark greyish-brown, with white eye-ring and chin; pale scallops on coverts.

Stockier than Dunlin; no black belly patch; in summer, more streaked onto belly, in winter darker; pale-legged.

Juvenile
Paler than adult; bright feather edges on head and back; no pale stripe over eye; note bill and leg colour, neat scales of white on coverts. In flight, shows narrow wingbar; broad black centre to rump.

SOBERLY APPEALING
Close-up views reveal a charmingly attractive shorebird.

WHEN SEEN

Aug — May
August to May in south.

WHERE SEEN
Breeds Iceland; central spine of Scandinavia; winters on nearby coasts and south to Spain; rare inland.

HABITAT AND INFO

SIMILAR SPECIES
Dunlin is paler; browner; without white feather edges above; black legs.

Whiter underside

Dark legs

Terek Sandpiper

A broad-winged, short-tailed, short-legged wader with an upcurved bill and pale hindwing band. It is much smaller than a Greenshank.

LENGTH / 22–24cm (8¾–9½in)
WINGSPAN / 38–40cm (15–15½in)
WEIGHT / 60–120g (2–4¼oz)

■ STATUS / Vulnerable

SCALE v Pigeon

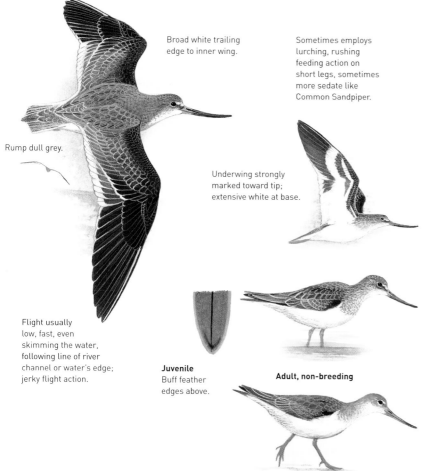

Broad white trailing edge to inner wing.

Rump dull grey.

Sometimes employs lurching, rushing feeding action on short legs, sometimes more sedate like Common Sandpiper.

Underwing strongly marked toward tip; extensive white at base.

Flight usually low, fast, even skimming the water, following line of river channel or water's edge; jerky flight action.

Juvenile
Buff feather edges above.

Adult, non-breeding

Its curious dumpy body, short legs, and long, upswept bill make this smallish sandpiper quite unique. It has a peculiar, almost drunken action at times, dashing to and fro or twisting from side to side with sudden stops and starts, its head pushed forward and breast held low. It is a rarity in Europe, and always an exciting find.

FEEDING
It uses its long bill to probe for invertebrates in exposed mud, often washing its food before swallowing it. It also eats seeds and even insects caught in the air.

DISPLAY AND VOICE
Little is known about its breeding displays, but it has a rich, melodious, whistling song. The flight call is a soft, rippling trill, like a shorter, softer, more melodious version of the Whimbrel's call.

BREEDING
It breeds in northern marshy valleys, laying four eggs on the ground. They hatch after 23 days.

MIGRATION
The Terek Sandpiper's wintering grounds are on the coasts of Africa, Asia, and Australasia. Very few migrants reach western Europe.

Bobs rear of body like a Common Sandpiper.

White patch in front of eye.

Yellow base to long, upcurved bill.

Adult, breeding
Upperparts grey, striped black in spring; white belly.

Yellow legs.

EASTERN RARITY
This is a real prize anywhere in Europe.

WHEN SEEN

Aug — May

May to August.

WHERE SEEN
East from Finland; rare migrant, chiefly on muddy or sandy coasts and shallow water at lake edges.

HABITAT AND INFO

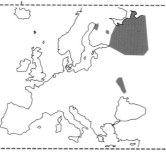

SIMILAR SPECIES
Redshank is larger, browner; straight bill; red legs; bolder wing pattern.

Straight bill

Redder legs

Green Sandpiper

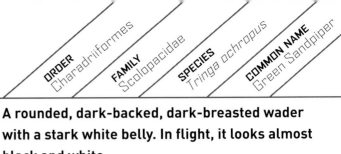

LENGTH / 21–24cm (8¼–9½in)
WINGSPAN / 41–46cm (16–18in)
WEIGHT / 70–90g (2½–3¼oz)

STATUS / Secure

SCALE v Pigeon

A rounded, dark-backed, dark-breasted wader with a stark white belly. In flight, it looks almost black and white.

This small sandpiper looks dark on the ground, yet boldly pied in flight as it displays its blackish underwing and striking white rump patch. As it walks, it bobs its head and swings its rear up and down. When disturbed it tends to rise high and flies far away before settling again.

FEEDING
It pecks tiny items of food from mud or shallow water, often wading but rarely venturing far out onto open mud. It is often to be seen feeding in small ditches or muddy creeks at the edge of salt marsh.

DISPLAY AND VOICE
Display flights are accompanied by rich, rippling songs. The normal call is full, throaty, and liquid, a slurred *kluw-w-it-wit-wit*.

BREEDING
It breeds in swampy places with scattered pines and birches, laying its eggs in old nests of pigeons or thrushes, or even in squirrel dreys.

MIGRATION
Most move south to Africa but some regularly spend the winter in Britain and France.

Feet scarcely show beyond tail; tends to fly off with sharp twists and fast climb, with rich, throaty, startling calls.

Underwing very dark: looks very black and white in flight.

Upperwing all dark.

Short white line from bill to eye; white eye-ring.

Straight, dark bill.

Descends in rapid, steep glide with final flurry.

Adult, breeding
Upperparts finely spotted.

Breast streaked grey.

Pristine white underside; dull greenish legs.

Rump vivid white; few broad bars on tail.

Juvenile
Upperparts spotted with dull buff.

STRONG CONTRASTS
In many situations, this species looks almost black and white.

WHEN SEEN

Oct

April

April to October.

WHERE SEEN
Breeds from Scandinavia eastward; throughout Europe on migration, in marsh creeks, by lakes, even small wet ditches and ponds.

HABITAT AND INFO

SIMILAR SPECIES
Wood Sandpiper is paler, browner; paler underwing; long pale stripe over eye; different call.

Longer legs

Smaller rump patch

Wood Sandpiper

A neat, pretty wader with medium-length bill, long legs, and a distinctly spotted pattern on upperparts. It has a white rump but plain wings.

LENGTH / 19–21cm (7½–8¼in)
WINGSPAN / 36–40cm (14–15½in)
WEIGHT / 50–90g (1¾–3¼oz)

■ STATUS / Vulnerable

SCALE v Pigeon

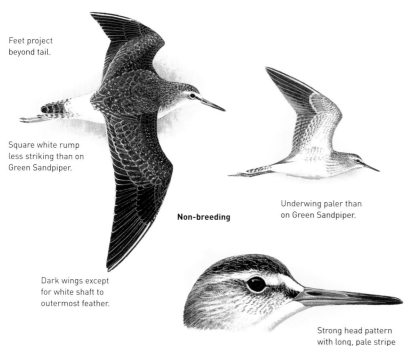

Feet project beyond tail.

Square white rump less striking than on Green Sandpiper.

Non-breeding

Underwing paler than on Green Sandpiper.

Dark wings except for white shaft to outermost feather.

Strong head pattern with long, pale stripe from bill over eye and ear coverts.

Adult, breeding
White speckling strongest in summer.

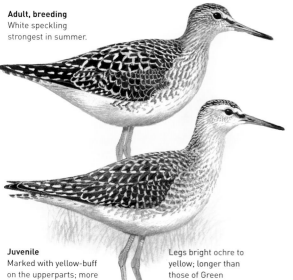

Tail finely barred.

Juvenile
Marked with yellow-buff on the upperparts; more spangled than Ruff or larger, darker Redshank.

Legs bright ochre to yellow; longer than those of Green Sandpiper's.

A flighty, noisy wader, the Wood Sandpiper has a round body, slim neck, long legs, and a high-stepping, elegant appearance. Like other sandpipers, it bobs its head and tail, but less obviously than the Common Sandpiper. It tends to fly erratically and fast to a great height, giving sharp calls that are unlike the more liquid notes of a Green Sandpiper.

FEEDING
It feeds on the edge of shallow, freshwater or in marshes, taking small worms and insects. It likes marshes and patches of wet mud, and is rarely seen far out on open mud or on beaches.

DISPLAY AND VOICE
Both sexes circle over their nesting area with rhythmic, whistling songs. The normal call is a loud, thin *chiff chiff chiff*.

BREEDING
Nests are on the ground among scattered trees or on open bogs, often on a slight rise. The usual clutch of four eggs hatches in 22–23 days.

MIGRATION
In autumn, it moves south to Africa, appearing in most of Europe on passage. It is scarcer in spring, but seen in western Europe in May.

MARSHY HABITAT
Wood is a misnomer: you will see this bird in watery places.

WHEN SEEN

Oct
April

April to October.

WHERE SEEN
Breeds north and east from Denmark; widespread on migration but scarce by freshwater lakes and marshes.

HABITAT AND INFO

SIMILAR SPECIES
Green Sandpiper is darker, with smaller spots; pale stripe finishes at eye; blacker underwing.

Short legs

Bolder contrast

Common Sandpiper

LENGTH / 19–21cm (7½–8¼in)
WINGSPAN / 32–35cm (12½–14in)
WEIGHT / 40–60g (1½–2oz)

■ STATUS / Secure

SCALE v Pigeon

An olive-brown and bright white wader with short, dull legs and a medium length, straight bill. Its flight and feeding action is distinctive.

This wader is easily identified by the constant up-and-down, rhythmic swing of its rear body and bobbing head. In flight, it is equally distinctive, keeping low and using a stiff, bow-winged, flickering action.

FEEDING
It feeds along streams and the edges of lakes, picking insects from mud, stones, and the water surface. It rarely probes in mud or wades deeply.

DISPLAY AND VOICE
Its display involves rapid flights above clear, stony streams, making good use of the white underwing pattern, as well as frequent vocal contact with loud trilling and rhythmic songs. The normal call is a high, ringing *tswee-wee-wee*.

BREEDING
It lays four large eggs on the ground, usually on a bank near a stony river or shingly lakeside. They hatch in 21–22 days, and the chicks fly after 28 days.

MIGRATION
Most spend the winter in Africa, but a tiny number remain in western Europe, usually on sheltered estuaries or lakesides.

Broad white wingbar.

Bowed, stiff wings flicker in flight in shallow down beats.

Underwing well-marked but usually hard to see.

Sides of tail white; centre creates dark blob.

Wings held stiff, arched, and rather straight.

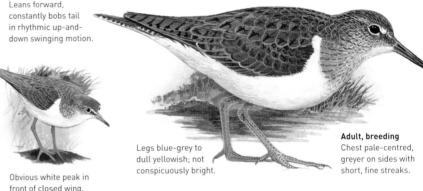

Upperside marked blackish in summer.

White patch in front of eye.

Leans forward, constantly bobs tail in rhythmic up-and-down swinging motion.

Legs blue-grey to dull yellowish; not conspicuously bright.

Adult, breeding
Chest pale-centred, greyer on sides with short, fine streaks.

Obvious white peak in front of closed wing.

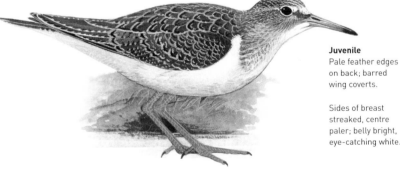

Juvenile
Pale feather edges on back; barred wing coverts.

Sides of breast streaked, centre paler; belly bright, eye-catching white.

HIGH-STEPPING WALK
Sandpipers move with springy steps, bobbing both head and tail.

WHEN SEEN

Oct   April

April to October.

WHERE SEEN
All Europe, scarce in south; breeds beside small rivers and shingly lakes but visits all kinds of watersides when on migration.

HABITAT AND INFO

SIMILAR SPECIES
Dunlin is less contrasted, drabber, more streaked; dark legs; different call.

Duller breast sides

Blackish legs

Redshank

A long-legged, long-billed wader, dark on the ground but revealing broad white bands on wings and vivid white rump in flight. Rarely flies without fast, loud yelping or clear, ringing calls. A waterside or mud-flat bird outside the breeding season, often in salt-marsh creeks.

LENGTH / 27–29cm (10½–11½in)
WINGSPAN / 45–52cm (17½–20½in)
WEIGHT / 85–155g (3–5½oz)

■ **STATUS /** Vulnerable

SCALE v Pigeon

On beaches of rocks, shingle, sand, or mud, around reservoir edges and beside winter floods or freshwater marsh, it is likely there will be Redshanks probing in wet mud and shallow water for food. At the merest hint of danger, they raise their voices in almost hysterical, wild yelping whistles.

FEEDING
Redshanks delve rather sluggishly for worms, crustaceans, and other small invertebrates.

DISPLAY AND VOICE
Displays include wing-raising to reveal sparkling white undersides and stiff-winged flights with yodelling *tyoo* notes that become excited *tuleeu tuleeu tuleeu* choruses on landing. Usual calls are a mournful, squealing or yelping *tyuuuuu*, and a quick, bouncy *teu-huhu*, *tyu*, and *tui*.

BREEDING
Nests are on the ground, by a grassy tussock or under a canopy of long grass. Four eggs hatch after 24 days. The chicks fly 25–35 days later.

MIGRATION
After breeding, Redshanks move to coastal areas of the British Isles, western Europe, and the Mediterranean.

White rump and bold white panels at rear of wing give unique pattern.

Jerky wing beats and stiff-winged glides in display flight.

Adult, breeding

Vivid white underwing raised in display.

Adult, breeding
Heavily streaked on breast; bright red on bill and legs.

Females generally less streaked on breast, but much variation.

Dark brown, marked blacker above.

Juvenile
Bright ochre feather edges above; grey bill (compare Ruff).

Orange legs in winter.

Adult, winter
Plainer, greyer than in summer; no blackish bars above or breast streaks; thin white eye-ring.

Orange legs.

SPLASHES OF WHITE
Broad white bands on back and wings are distinctive.

WHEN SEEN

All year in Britain, Ireland, France; April to October N and central Europe.

WHERE SEEN
Widespread in N Europe, British Isles; sparse, localized in central and SW Europe.

HABITAT AND INFO

SIMILAR SPECIES
Winter Ruff is more sandy-brown; plainer head; faintly curved bill; plainer wings; much quieter.

Faintly curved bill

Scaly upperparts

Greenshank

LENGTH / 30-33cm (11¾-13in)
WINGSPAN / 53-60cm (21-23½in)
WEIGHT / 140-270g (5-9½oz)

■ **STATUS /** Vulnerable

SCALE v Pigeon

A supremely elegant, long-legged wader with a faintly upswept bill. In flight, its dark wings contrast with a white V on its back.

Unlike the Redshank, this is a breeding bird of wild moors and boggy clearings in northern forests. On migration, it appears beside freshwater almost anywhere, staying for a few days in autumn in favoured spots with soft mud and shallow lagoons. Most are rather wild and unapproachable.

FEEDING
Catches small fish and tiny crabs and probes for worms and molluscs. Sometimes very quick in its actions.

DISPLAY AND VOICE
Display flights over moorland territories are long and high, with quick, liquid *too-hoo-too-hoo* notes. Typical clear, ringing, three-syllable *tew tew tew* calls have a more even emphasis than the Redshank's call.

BREEDING
Nests on the ground, often beside an old stump or rock. The four eggs hatch within 24–25 days.

MIGRATION
All breeding birds move south in autumn, mostly to Africa. A few spend the winter in south-west England, southern Ireland, western France, and Iberia. They return north in April and May.

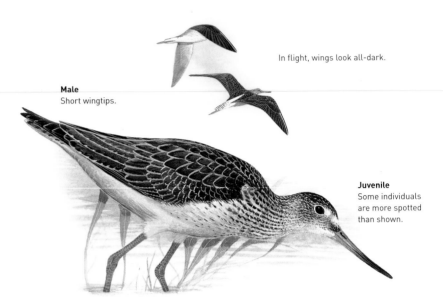

In flight, wings look all-dark.

Male
Short wingtips.

Juvenile
Some individuals are more spotted than shown.

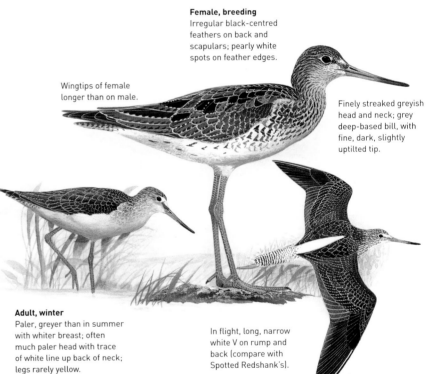

Female, breeding
Irregular black-centred feathers on back and scapulars; pearly white spots on feather edges.

Wingtips of female longer than on male.

Finely streaked greyish head and neck; grey deep-based bill, with fine, dark, slightly uptilted tip.

Adult, winter
Paler, greyer than in summer with whiter breast; often much paler head with trace of white line up back of neck; legs rarely yellow.

In flight, long, narrow white V on rump and back (compare with Spotted Redshank's).

Juvenile
Speckled head greyer than winter adult's.

ALMOST MONOCHROME
Greenshanks often look grey and white with darker markings.

WHEN SEEN

Oct — April

Mostly April to October; fewer winter in W Europe.

WHERE SEEN
Breeds on remote moors and bogs of Scotland, Scandinavia; widespread on migration, local on estuaries in winter in UK, Ireland, France, Iberia.

HABITAT AND INFO

SIMILAR SPECIES
Redshank is browner, less grey; shorter bill and legs; red legs; white bands on upperwing.

Browner overall

Red legs

Spotted Redshank

A lively feeder, often wading deeply, up-ending or swimming, snatching food with its straight, fine bill. In flight, its call and the white patch on its back are distinctive.

LENGTH / 29–31cm (11½–12in)
WINGSPAN / 48–52cm (19–20½in)
WEIGHT / 135–250g (4¾–9oz)

■ **STATUS /** Vulnerable

SCALE v Pigeon

In its breeding plumage, a Spotted Redshank is a spectacular bird. Such adults may be seen far south of their nesting areas in mid- or late summer, but most birds seen in western Europe are paler winter birds or dull juveniles, identifiable by their lively feeding action, thin bills, long legs, and calls.

FEEDING
Typically fast and energetic, they chase fish or probe underwater, often in small groups.

DISPLAY AND VOICE
Circling, dipping, or diving display flights are accompanied by creaky, whistling calls: *kurrevi-kurrevi-kurrevi*. The usual call is a very clear, sharp, loud *chew-it* or *tee-veet*, lacking the ringing quality of Redshank's or Greenshank's.

BREEDING
Nests are on the ground in wooded tundra. The 3–4 eggs may be incubated wholly by the male.

MIGRATION
Arctic breeders migrate to Africa just south of the Sahara. A few winter in western Europe, including southern Britain and Ireland.

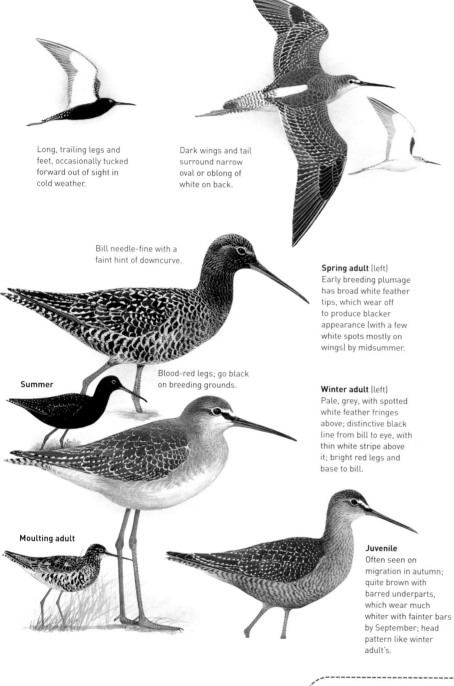

Long, trailing legs and feet, occasionally tucked forward out of sight in cold weather.

Dark wings and tail surround narrow oval or oblong of white on back.

Bill needle-fine with a faint hint of downcurve.

Spring adult (left)
Early breeding plumage has broad white feather tips, which wear off to produce blacker appearance (with a few white spots mostly on wings) by midsummer.

Summer

Blood-red legs; go black on breeding grounds.

Winter adult (left)
Pale, grey, with spotted white feather fringes above; distinctive black line from bill to eye, with thin white stripe above it; bright red legs and base to bill.

Moulting adult

Juvenile
Often seen on migration in autumn; quite brown with barred underparts, which wear much whiter with fainter bars by September; head pattern like winter adult's.

AUTUMN JUVENILE
Young birds in autumn are browner than adults.

WHEN SEEN

Oct
April

Mostly April to October in UK, a few in winter; some remain all summer in southern England.

WHERE SEEN
Shallow freshwater lagoons, coastal marshes, muddy estuary creeks of W Europe; breeds N Scandinavia.

HABITAT AND INFO

SIMILAR SPECIES
Greenshank has thicker bill faintly upturned; paler legs; different call.

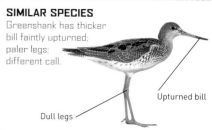

Upturned bill

Dull legs

Marsh Sandpiper

LENGTH / 22–24cm (8¾–9½in)
WINGSPAN / 50cm (19½in)
WEIGHT / 80–90g (2¾–3¼oz)

STATUS / Vulnerable

SCALE v Pigeon

A rather small-bodied but long-legged, upstanding waterside bird with a thin, straight bill, dull legs, and dark wings. It has a Greenshank-like white triangle on its back.

A rarity in Europe, this is a bird of central Asia that sometimes strays westward on migration. It resembles a smaller, more dainty Greenshank but its very thin, straight bill identifies it at once. It is often unusually tame.

FEEDING
The Marsh Sandpiper picks worms and insects from shallow water in ditches or pools.

DISPLAY AND VOICE
Breeding behaviour is little known, but it produces a melodious, far-carrying song. The usual calls from migrants are short, sharp, and metallic, such as *kew* or *tew*.

BREEDING
Pairs or small groups nest on the ground in wet river valleys, flooded meadows, or shallow marshes. The usual clutch is of four eggs.

MIGRATION
Marsh Sandpipers move south from eastern Europe and central Asia through the Middle East. A few winter in Egypt and the Arabian Gulf, but most go to Africa and India. In spring, some straggle west as far as Britain and the Netherlands.

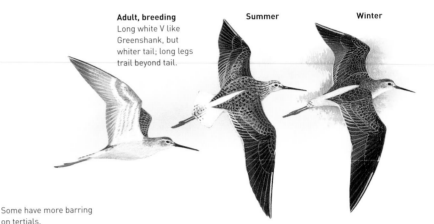

Adult, breeding
Long white V like Greenshank, but whiter tail; long legs trail beyond tail.

Summer

Winter

Some have more barring on tertials.

Adult, winter
Upperparts pale grey, becoming browner with wear; very white below, on forehead, and over eye.

Bill fine, straight, rather long; legs long, slender, dark or pale olive-green (compare with heavier, thicker-billed, larger Greenshank).

Head of adult often white by July.

Needle-like bill.

Juvenile wing covert.

Adult, breeding
Full breeding plumage; many retain some grey winter feathers, with fewer black diamonds on back; some, probably female, are less marked on chest.

Fresh juvenile (above)
By July, buff/brown patterning often lost to give adult grey on back, but pale-edged wing feathers remain.

NEEDLE BILL
The fine bill and white appearance pick out this rare bird.

WHEN SEEN

Aug   May

Mostly May to August in W Europe, but sporadic breeders in north and east; a few regularly winter in Spain.

WHERE SEEN
Rare in shallow lagoons and freshwater marshes of S and W Europe.

HABITAT AND INFO

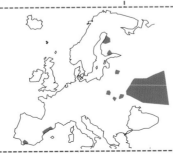

SIMILAR SPECIES
Greenshank is bigger, more thickset, with thicker, pale-based, slightly upcurved bill.

Thicker bill

Thicker legs

Grey Phalarope

A small, long-billed, swimming bird, normally seen in non-breeding grey, white, and black plumage. It looks gleaming white underneath, with contrasted dark mask and wingtips. It is usually at sea, but it can be storm-blown onto shore or far inland.

LENGTH / 20–22cm (8–8³⁄₄in)
WINGSPAN / 37–40cm (14¹⁄₂–15¹⁄₂in)
WEIGHT / 50–75g (1³⁄₄–2³⁄₄oz)

■ STATUS / Secure

SCALE v Pigeon

Such a tiny, dainty bird seems ill-fitted to a life at sea, yet for much of the year it rides the waves in mid-ocean, buoyant as a cork and as resilient as a bird several times its size.

FEEDING
Phalaropes mostly eat small invertebrates, but they also take seeds, especially in the breeding season. They pick most of their food from the water while swimming. In winter, they eat crustaceans, gathering them from mats of floating weed and even from the backs of whales, or from the disturbed water around pods of whales.

DISPLAY AND VOICE
The usual sex roles are reversed, with females being larger and brighter and making circling display flights. Calls are short, shrill, and clipped monosyllables: *pit* or *wit*.

BREEDING
Nests are shallow cups of plant material on the ground, in small, loose colonies. Males incubate the eggs and care for the young.

MIGRATION
Most spend the winter at sea off the coasts of west Africa. Some are blown ashore by gales in autumn.

Grey
Bill relatively thick and blunt-tipped.

Red-necked
Bill finer, more pointed.

Adult, autumn

Red-necked, bill from above.

Grey, bill from above.

Adult, winter

Male is duller, with more black on bill.

Juvenile, late autumn

Female, breeding
Bright with mostly yellow bill; crisp white face patch.

Juvenile, summer
(Rarely seen in Europe.)

Grey feathers appear more quickly than on Red-necked Phalarope.

Buff-edged black-brown back and wing feathers on juvenile are replaced by grey.

Juvenile, autumn

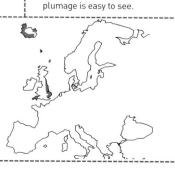

AUTUMN JUVENILE
The transition to grey winter plumage is easy to see.

WHEN SEEN

Dec

Sept

Mostly late autumn in W Europe.

WHERE SEEN
Breeds in Iceland and the Arctic; migrants scarce off W European seaboard, sometimes blown into coastal lagoons or lakes inland.

HABITAT AND INFO

SIMILAR SPECIES
Red-necked Phalarope has finer bill; darker upperside.

Fine bill

Grey breast

Red-necked Phalarope

LENGTH / 18–19cm (7–7½in)
WINGSPAN / 30–34cm (11¾–13½in)
WEIGHT / 25–50g (1–1¾oz)

■ **STATUS /** Secure

SCALE v Pigeon

A tiny aquatic wader with a needle-fine bill and bold flight patterns. It is colourful in summer. In winter, it is at sea, but juveniles are occasionally near coasts.

Red-necked Phalaropes are slightly less northerly breeders than Grey Phalaropes, but scarcely more familiar to European bird-watchers: of the two, the Grey is more frequently seen ashore in autumn. However, Red-necked Phalaropes can be found in remote parts of north-west Europe in summer.

FEEDING

Typically for a phalarope, the Red-necked swims while searching for food, often spinning on one spot to pick tiny insects and other creatures from the water.

DISPLAY AND VOICE

As with other phalaropes, the female takes the lead, flying over the territory, calling and whirring her wings. Calls are mostly short, sharp *kirk* or *cherrp* notes.

BREEDING

Nesting areas are wet marshes beside lakes, where single pairs or small groups nest on the ground. The male incubates 3–4 eggs for 17–21 days.

MIGRATION

Most Red-necked Phalaropes winter at sea off Arabia. Rare migrants reach western Europe.

Bold white wingbar recalls Sanderling.

Grey, first winter

Red-necked, winter

Red-necked juvenile

Grey juvenile

Male, breeding

Female, breeding

Juvenile
Strong buff back stripes; often white patch at front of flank.

Grey, breeding

Male, breeding

Black mask and cap rule out Sanderling.

Adult, winter
Slightly darker than Grey, with finer bill.

Immature, autumn
Darker than Grey, with finer bill.

SEXUAL REVERSAL
It is the male (left) that is relatively dull and streaky.

WHERE SEEN
Breeds in Iceland, Faeroes, Scandinavia, N Scotland (rare); on migration rare on coasts.

HABITAT AND INFO

SIMILAR SPECIES
Grey Phalarope has thicker bill with yellow at base; paler upperside.

Thicker bill

Paler back

Spur-winged Plover

A strikingly contrasted wader of rather dry, open, waterside habitats. The bold black cap, white neck patch, and broad white band along the upperwing help identify it. Sharp, agitated calls draw attention to its presence.

LENGTH / 25–27cm (9¾–10½in)
WINGSPAN / 70–80cm (27½–31½in)
WEIGHT / 130–160g (4½–5¾oz)

■ **STATUS /** Secure

SCALE v Pigeon

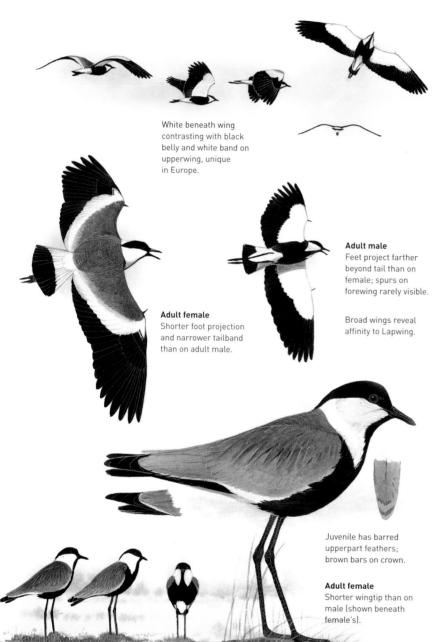

White beneath wing contrasting with black belly and white band on upperwing, unique in Europe.

Adult female
Shorter foot projection and narrower tailband than on adult male.

Adult male
Feet project farther beyond tail than on female; spurs on forewing rarely visible.

Broad wings reveal affinity to Lapwing.

Juvenile has barred upperpart feathers; brown bars on crown.

Adult female
Shorter wingtip than on male (shown beneath female's).

This splendid lapwing is found in the Middle East and Africa in a broad band from west Africa to Kenya, and only just makes Europe with a sparse population in Greece. Where it is common, it forms large, loose parties. Everywhere the pairs are eye-catching, bold, and noisy.

FEEDING
Mostly insects, picked from the ground in areas with dried mud or bare patches on grassy banks.

DISPLAY AND VOICE
The birds typically display on the ground, showing off the head and breast pattern in forward-leaning runs. They also stand upright with opened wings to reveal their vivid undersides. Calls include a strident, screeching *did-he do-it* and sharp, metallic *hik* or *zik zik* alarm notes.

BREEDING
Four eggs are laid on the ground. Incubation lasts 22–24 days.

MIGRATION
The small numbers breeding in Greece and Turkey move south to northern Africa in September, returning in March and April.

EYE-CATCHING CONTRAST
Black, white, and brown look striking in strong light and shade.

WHEN SEEN

Sept — March

Mid-March to late September.

WHERE SEEN
Sandbanks, grassy flats, and embankments beside lagoons, marshes, and rivers; in Europe, only in Greece.

HABITAT AND INFO

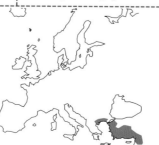

SIMILAR SPECIES
Lapwing is much darker, less brown above; plain upperwing.

Less brown

Plain upperwing

Golden Plover

SCALE v Pigeon

LENGTH / 26–29cm (10¼–11½in)
WINGSPAN / 67–76cm (26½–30in)
WEIGHT / 140–250g (5–9oz)

■ **STATUS** / Secure

A short-billed, round-headed terrestrial bird, it is inconspicuous on ground. Its yellow spangled upperparts are clear at close range, but uniform golden-brown at distance.

In summer, this is a colourful bird of upland moors and mountains, but in winter it becomes much more subdued and lives in flocks in the lowlands. In its breeding areas, it is a wild, solitary bird with far-carrying calls that make it difficult to locate, but on its wintering grounds it is often mixed with Lapwings and Black-headed Gulls on pastures or ploughed fields.

FEEDING
It has a run-and-tilt action, picking worms and insects from the ground. It is often robbed by gulls.

DISPLAY AND VOICE
Breeding males fly over their territories with a slow, butterfly-like wing action and a plaintive, wailing song. Flight calls are liquid *too-ee* and *tloo* notes.

BREEDING
Nests are shallow scrapes on the ground, on limestone grassland, heathery moors, or low tundra in the far north. Four eggs hatch after 28–31 days. The young fly 30 days later.

MIGRATION
A general movement to the south and west in winter.

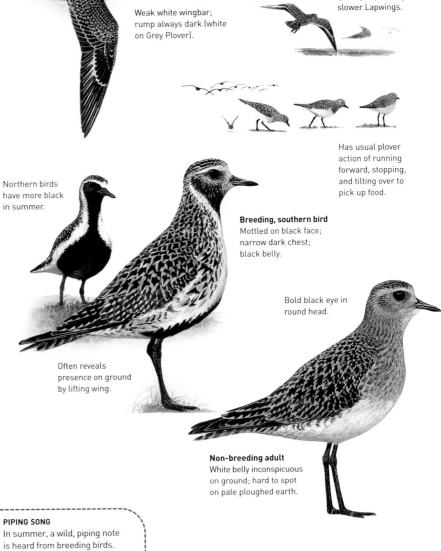

Striking white underwing flashes in flight and as it catches the light on landing.

Weak white wingbar; rump always dark (white on Grey Plover).

Winter flocks fly fast, with rapid wing beats, quickly separating from slower Lapwings.

Has usual plover action of running forward, stopping, and tilting over to pick up food.

Northern birds have more black in summer.

Breeding, southern bird
Mottled on black face; narrow dark chest; black belly.

Bold black eye in round head.

Often reveals presence on ground by lifting wing.

Non-breeding adult
White belly inconspicuous on ground; hard to spot on pale ploughed earth.

PIPING SONG
In summer, a wild, piping note is heard from breeding birds.

WHEN SEEN

All year; March to August on breeding areas.

WHERE SEEN
Iceland, Britain, Scandinavia; in winter NW France, Low Countries, locally south to Mediterranean.

HABITAT AND INFO

SIMILAR SPECIES
Juvenile Grey Plover has bigger head, eye, and bill; less brown; white rump; black wingpit.

Bigger bill

Greyer breast

Grey Plover

A stocky, thick-billed, large-eyed wader, it usually looks rather dark out on an estuary, but close views reveal spangling. It has unique black "armpits" in flight.

LENGTH / 27–30cm (10½–11¾in)
WINGSPAN / 71–83cm (28–32½in)
WEIGHT / 200–250g (7–9oz)

■ STATUS / Vulnerable

SCALE v Pigeon

A larger, more northerly counterpart of the Golden Plover, the Grey Plover is a bird of High Arctic tundra in the brief northern summer, and of estuaries for the rest of the year. It is a coastal wader in winter, not usually found inland or on farmland habitats used by Golden Plovers and Lapwings.

FEEDING
In winter, it pulls most of its food from soft mud: small worms, crustaceans, and molluscs. It usually pecks from the surface, stands still for several seconds, then moves to a new spot and repeats the process.

DISPLAY AND VOICE
Grey Plovers are easily detected on estuaries by their far-carrying boyish whistle, a three-note *tlee-oo-ee*, with the middle note lower.

BREEDING
This is a bird of the northern tundra, beyond the tree limit, nesting on drier, stony ridges above rolling ground with patches of snow. The four eggs hatch after 26–27 days.

MIGRATION
Many spend the winter in north-west Europe. Others fly to southern Africa and Australia.

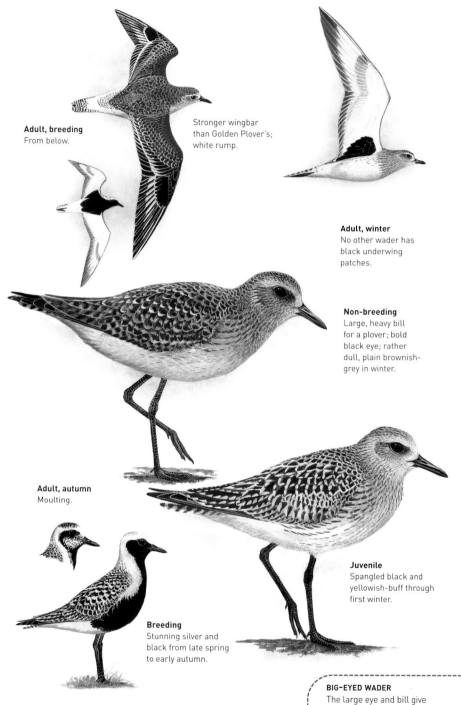

Adult, breeding
From below.

Stronger wingbar than Golden Plover's; white rump.

Adult, winter
No other wader has black underwing patches.

Non-breeding
Large, heavy bill for a plover; bold black eye; rather dull, plain brownish-grey in winter.

Adult, autumn
Moulting.

Juvenile
Spangled black and yellowish-buff through first winter.

Breeding
Stunning silver and black from late spring to early autumn.

BIG-EYED WADER
The large eye and bill give a distinctive expression.

WHEN SEEN

All year; only a few remain in Europe in summer.

WHERE SEEN
Most W European coasts; locally in Mediterranean.

HABITAT AND INFO

SIMILAR SPECIES
Winter Knot is smaller; paler; paler legs; finer, longer bill.

Grey rump

Longer bill

Ruff

LENGTH / Male 26–32cm (10¼–12½in); female 20–25cm (8–9¾in)
WINGSPAN / 46–58cm (18–23in)
WEIGHT / 70–230g (2½–8oz)

SCALE v Pigeon

■ **STATUS /** Vulnerable

Ruffs are medium-sized, round-bodied waders with shortish bills and long legs, typically buff with scaly feather edges. Males in spring are extraordinarily ornamented.

In its spring plumage, the male Ruff is one of the most remarkable and eye-catching of all European birds, yet it is best known as a relatively dull, brown bird of the autumn. Most Ruffs seen in Britain are juveniles on autumn migration: not so dramatic as their fathers, but subtly beautiful and exceptionally neat. Ruffs are variable in all other plumages, and also in their size: adult females are much smaller than males, and juveniles smaller still. They occupy a place between small waders such as sandpipers and large waders like godwits, and to match their medium size they have medium-length bills and legs. This gives them an ordinariness – outside the breeding season – that is in itself characteristic, lacking extremes of shape or structure.

FEEDING
Ruffs like freshwater, not saltwater, and feed in muddy places at the edges of reservoirs, on flooded fields, or on damp grass in the kind of old-fashioned, rough, poorly drained meadowland that has become a rarity in western Europe. At times, they join plovers on ploughed fields. They pick small worms and insects from the surface, occasionally taking frogs or small fish and sometimes seeds.

DISPLAY AND VOICE
No two males are quite alike in their spring adornments. Those with white ruffs help to attract others to a display ground, or lek, but it is often the dark-ruffed birds that are chosen as mates by watching females. The males spar and chase, performing mock fights intended to show off their fitness rather than to do real damage. Each female mates with a chosen male, which then plays no further part in family matters. Ruffs are strangely silent birds. They occasionally make a low *wek* call, but unlike most waders, they have no distinctive flight note.

BREEDING
Once mated, the female leaves the lek and the posturing males and moves off to a secluded area, making a well-hidden nest in long grass and laying four eggs. These hatch after 20–21 days' incubation. The chicks soon leave the nest and fledge after 25–28 days. Each female rears one brood, but males may father several.

MIGRATION
Most European Ruffs move to Africa in winter, but there are a number of places on the coast (and a few inland) where groups remain all winter in western Europe, including Britain and Ireland.

Males look masculine, slightly brutal; females look more delicate.

Breeding female
Heavily blotched.

Male
Moulting ruff in late spring.

Breeding male, spring
Extraordinary variety in colours of ruff, tippets, and legs.

Male

Male

Male

Male

Female

Mantle feathers lift in wind like a shield.

Winter female
Much plainer than breeding bird; winter male larger, often red-legged, whitish around head and neck.

Male

WHERE SEEN
Breeds Scandinavia, NE Europe and very locally Netherlands, Denmark, Germany, sporadic France and Britain; widespread migrant; winters Britain, North Sea coast, locally France, Iberia, Italy.

HABITAT AND INFO

SIMILAR SPECIES
Redshank is darker, with whiter belly; longer bill; red legs; white bands on wings.

Plainer brown　　Longer bill

BLACK IS BEST
Black ruffs are often most attractive to
watching females at spring displays.

Plain head; thick,
shortish, slightly
curved bill.

Juvenile female
Small; greenish legs.

Back feathers
are variable.

Feathers vary
on upperparts.

Juvenile male
Large; bright buff
V-shapes on back
feathers; greenish legs.

White underwing.

Juvenile male
Large wings of
male give powerful
impression in flight.

Juvenile female
Note feet project
beyond tail in
both sexes.

Juvenile
Buff breast.

White sides to rump
meet in long U-shape or
create separate ovals.

Narrow wingbar; long,
broad wings give slow,
gentle flight action over
short distance.

DID YOU KNOW?
Many Ruffs' lekking sites, at which they display each spring, have
been known for 60 or 100 years. These old sites attract the largest
numbers of Ruffs. The factors that influence the females' choice of
mates, the behaviour of males according to their plumage types and
social status, and even the ratio of males to females have
proved complex and variable.

?

Bar-tailed Godwit

LENGTH / 37–39cm (14½–15½in)
WINGSPAN / 61–68cm (24–27in)
WEIGHT / 280–450g (10–16oz)

■ STATUS / Secure

SCALE v Pigeon

A Curlew-like wader but much smaller and paler. It is very long-billed but with medium-length legs. It looks much like Black-tailed Godwit at rest, but plainer wings and white V above pale tail are very different.

This is one of a number of wading birds that have predominantly coppery-red plumage in summer, when they breed in the Arctic. They become essentially dull brown birds outside the breeding season, but the juveniles show a warmth of plumage colour that echoes the breeding adults. Unlike the Black-tailed Godwit of more temperate regions, the Bar-tailed Godwit migrates far to the north in late spring, although most breed in the Low Arctic rather than High Arctic. The birds do not need to move north early, despite the length of the journey, because only in June do conditions on the tundra become feasible for nesting and rearing chicks. In winter, Bar-tailed Godwits like muddy estuaries, often mixing with other waders such as Redshanks and Curlews when feeding. They fly to their high-tide roosts, often with exciting, aerobatic manoeuvres and sudden, twisting dives to the roost from a great height. At the roost they tend to form dense groups a little aside from the smaller Redshanks and Knots, and the larger Curlews.

FEEDING

Bar-tailed Godwits are typically active feeders, using their long, sensitive bills to probe into wet sand and soft mud in search of lugworms, molluscs, and crustaceans. They rotate their heads slightly during shallow or full-depth probes, often immersing them in shallow water.

DISPLAY AND VOICE

Males fly high over territories, using a range of calls. Away from the breeding area the usual call is a rather sharp, low *kirruk* or nasal *yak*.

BREEDING

The nest is a scrape on a slightly raised, and therefore drier, ridge surrounded by swampy ground. Typical breeding habitat is damp, peaty terrain close to the coast, although the adults perch freely on scattered trees. The 3–4 eggs are incubated for three weeks. The chicks fly when around four weeks old, although the exact period is uncertain.

MIGRATION

Bar-tailed Godwits breeding in northern Europe and western Siberia move to the estuaries of western Europe and down to west Africa in autumn, fewer reaching Mediterranean shores, the Red Sea, and the Arabian Gulf. The great majority winter in Mauretania. A few find their way far into mainland Europe, or even inland Britain. There is a marked migratory movement along the southern side of the North Sea and through the Baltic in spring.

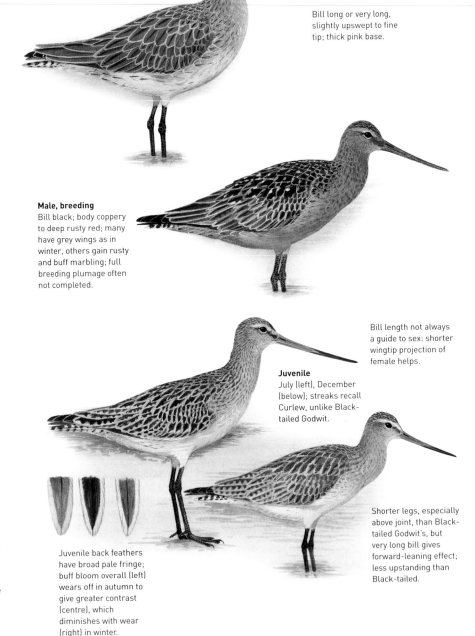

Winter adult
Grey back feathers with dark streak.

Bill long or very long, slightly upswept to fine tip; thick pink base.

Male, breeding
Bill black; body coppery to deep rusty red; many have grey wings as in winter, others gain rusty and buff marbling; full breeding plumage often not completed.

Bill length not always a guide to sex: shorter wingtip projection of female helps.

Juvenile
July (left), December (below); streaks recall Curlew, unlike Black-tailed Godwit.

Juvenile back feathers have broad pale fringe; buff bloom overall (left) wears off in autumn to give greater contrast (centre), which diminishes with wear (right) in winter.

Shorter legs, especially above joint, than Black-tailed Godwit's, but very long bill gives forward-leaning effect; less upstanding than Black-tailed.

WHEN SEEN

All year; in W Europe mostly September to May.

WHERE SEEN
Breeds extreme N Norway, Sweden, Finland, and Russia; most in winter in Low Countries, Britain, Ireland, France, and W Iberia.

HABITAT AND INFO

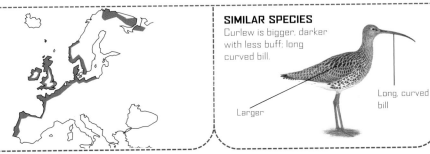

SIMILAR SPECIES
Curlew is bigger, darker with less buff; long curved bill.

Larger

Long, curved bill

DRAMATIC BILL
The very long bill equips a Bar-tailed
Godwit for deep probing in soft mud.

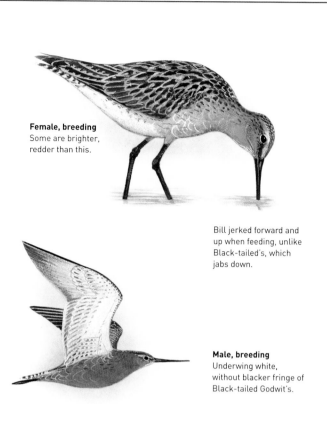

Female, breeding
Some are brighter,
redder than this.

Bill jerked forward and
up when feeding, unlike
Black-tailed's, which
jabs down.

Male, breeding
Underwing white,
without blacker fringe of
Black-tailed Godwit's.

Male, breeding

Juvenile
Fresh feathers with
broad pale fringes.

Very short foot
projection, unlike
Black-tailed Godwit's;
white V on back, but
tail and wings dull.

Female, winter

DID YOU KNOW?
Bar-tailed Godwits, like most northerly waders, are long-distance
migrants. Those breeding in Alaska spend the winter in New Zealand,
and make the 11,000km (6,000 mile) journey without stopping.
Astonishingly, this takes around seven days, and is probably the
longest non-stop journey made by any bird.

Black-tailed Godwit

LENGTH / 40–44cm (15½–17½in)
WINGSPAN / 62–70cm (24½–27½in)
WEIGHT / 280–500g (10–18oz)

■ **STATUS /** Vulnerable

SCALE v Pigeon

Large, but much smaller than a Curlew, it is elegant and upstanding. It is particularly long-legged and long-billed, even for a wader. Essentially dark at rest, it reveals a dramatic pattern of white when it spreads its wings.

In a bird family marked by elegance and grace, the Black-tailed Godwit stands out as a particularly upstanding, long-legged, and long-billed bird, although it does not have quite the sinuous ease of movement displayed by some of its smaller relatives. In flight, its legs trail well beyond its tail. On the ground, it tends to feed with its bill pointing vertically down to probe close to its toes. It has declined substantially over much of its former breeding range in western Europe because of changes in agriculture, especially the drainage and improvement of wet pasture. In most countries, it is most familiar as a wintering species, on sheltered, muddy, mild estuaries.

FEEDING
It locates prey by sight and by touch, immersing the sensitive tip of its long bill into shallow water or soft mud. The bird probes almost vertically and quite vigorously, with sudden rapid, deep probes once it has detected prey. The unfortunate worm or mollusc is then hauled out and usually swallowed instantly.

DISPLAY AND VOICE
The display flights by the male are varied, rising and falling and often employing half-rolls onto one side before the bird nosedives steeply to the ground. The display shows off the bold white wing stripes and strong contrast between the white underwings and dark belly. The song during these flights is far-carrying, high-pitched, and ringing, although with a Lapwing-like nasal quality. Other calls are a strident *weeka-weeka-weeka*, *kip kip*, and *chut*.

BREEDING
In Iceland, Black-tailed Godwits occupy vast areas of marshy moorland, drier hummocks, and damp meadows. Elsewhere some use moorland sites and even heathland, but most breed on farmland, particularly in waterlogged areas that may be prone to flooding. This can cause a failure to rear chicks in some years. The 3–4 eggs are laid in a shallow hollow in the ground, either exposed or more hidden in short vegetation, and incubated for 22–24 days. The chicks leave the nest soon after hatching, like those of other waders. They feed easily from the start and fly after 25–30 days.

MIGRATION
They mainly breed in Iceland and spend the winter in western Europe. Others breed in Denmark, the Netherlands, and across north-eastern Europe, then migrate in autumn to southern Europe and the Middle East and on into west Africa along the southern edge of the Sahara.

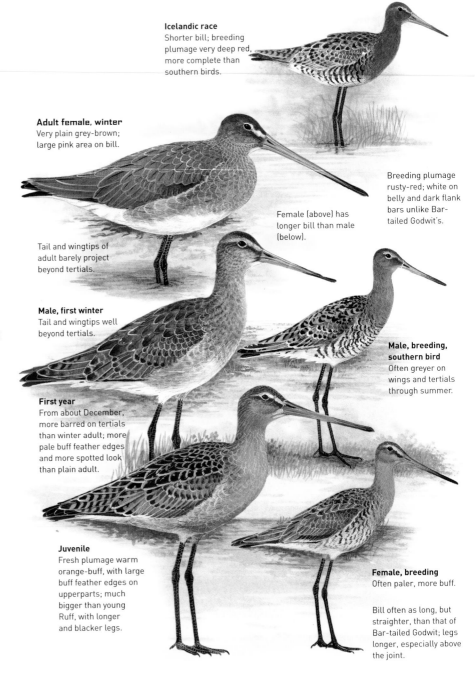

Icelandic race
Shorter bill; breeding plumage very deep red, more complete than southern birds.

Adult female, winter
Very plain grey-brown; large pink area on bill.

Female (above) has longer bill than male (below).

Breeding plumage rusty-red; white on belly and dark flank bars unlike Bar-tailed Godwit's.

Tail and wingtips of adult barely project beyond tertials.

Male, first winter
Tail and wingtips well beyond tertials.

First year
From about December, more barred on tertials than winter adult; more pale buff feather edges and more spotted look than plain adult.

Male, breeding, southern bird
Often greyer on wings and tertials through summer.

Juvenile
Fresh plumage warm orange-buff, with large buff feather edges on upperparts; much bigger than young Ruff, with longer and blacker legs.

Female, breeding
Often paler, more buff.

Bill often as long, but straighter, than that of Bar-tailed Godwit; legs longer, especially above the joint.

WHEN SEEN

All year.

WHERE SEEN
Breeds Iceland; very locally Norway and Sweden, Britain and France; more widely Denmark and the Netherlands; Germany, Poland, and scattered across E Europe.

HABITAT AND INFO

SIMILAR SPECIES
Bar-tailed Godwit has shorter legs, especially above joint; plainer wings.

Streaked back

Shorter legs

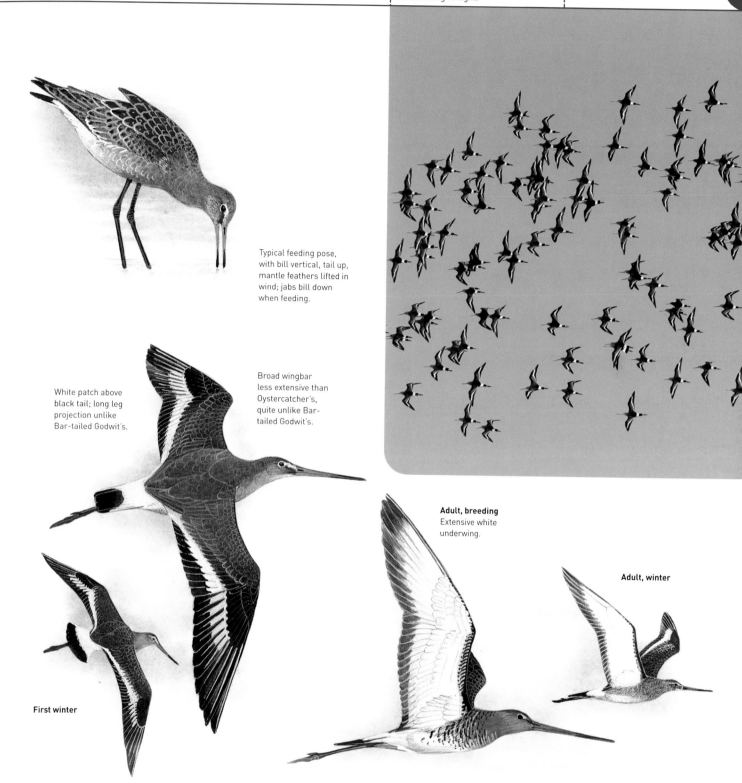

EYE-CATCHING EFFECTS
The bold white wing stripes
are striking in flight.

Typical feeding pose,
with bill vertical, tail up,
mantle feathers lifted in
wind; jabs bill down
when feeding.

White patch above
black tail; long leg
projection unlike
Bar-tailed Godwit's.

Broad wingbar
less extensive than
Oystercatcher's,
quite unlike Bar-
tailed Godwit's.

Adult, breeding
Extensive white
underwing.

Adult, winter

First winter

DID YOU KNOW?
Mainland European breeders spend the winter in Africa where they
may face problems with climate change. Mud flats around Lake Chad
have traditionally been important for tens of thousands of godwits, but
lakes south of the Sahara have an uncertain future and are now
frequently dry for most of the year.

Lapwing

SCALE v Pigeon

LENGTH / 28–31cm (11–12in)
WINGSPAN / 70–76cm (27½–30in)
WEIGHT / 150–300g (5¼–10½oz)

■ **STATUS /** Vulnerable

A sociable, short-billed, thickset, black-and-white bird with a unique wispy crest. Its black breast band contrasts with its white belly and underwing, while its green upperside looks dark at long range or in flight. It has an unmistakable broad-winged shape in the air. Solitary birds are not infrequent.

Despite a widespread decline with changing farming practices, the Lapwing remains a familiar and much-loved bird in Europe. In spring, males perform exciting display flights, while in winter Lapwings gather into large flocks, often of hundreds and sometimes thousands, in lowland fields and flooded pastures. In the past, its eggs were gathered as a spring delicacy. Today, though, so few remain in most areas that it would be difficult to find them.

FEEDING
Lapwings frequently feed sociably, even in summer, but they inevitably compete for food with each other and face competition from Golden Plovers and gulls in winter. They eat small invertebrates and worms, sometimes pulling them from the ground with much effort. Lapwings are often seen pattering the ground with their feet, to soften it and gain access to buried prey. Occasionally, they feed on moonlit nights.

DISPLAY AND VOICE
The song flight of the Lapwing is a memorable feature of the countryside in early spring: males fly up, twist and tumble, and dive apparently out of control toward the ground, only to rise again with loudly beating wings. The throb of the wing feathers combines with a loud, nasal, rhythmic song: *airr, willuch-o-weep*. Other calls include notes that give rise to several local names, such as *peewit, peer-wit, pee-wee, weep*, and similar variants on the theme.

BREEDING
The nest is little more than a shallow scrape on the ground, in an open space with a good view of potential dangers. Lapwings like a patchwork of bare earth and short grass: the change to autumn-sown cereals has made life difficult for them, as the crop is usually too tall and dense for small chicks by the time the Lapwing eggs hatch. Four eggs are laid, hatching after 28 days. The chicks fly when they are about 35–40 days old.

MIGRATION
Lapwings are present all year in parts of southern and western Europe, but even there they make local movements, or leave the hills and gather on lowland farmland. They are joined by many more from northern and eastern Europe, which move west and south each autumn to escape the icy winters. Cold spells and especially snow in winter frequently cause mass movements to the south and west of Britain and Ireland, and into France and Spain.

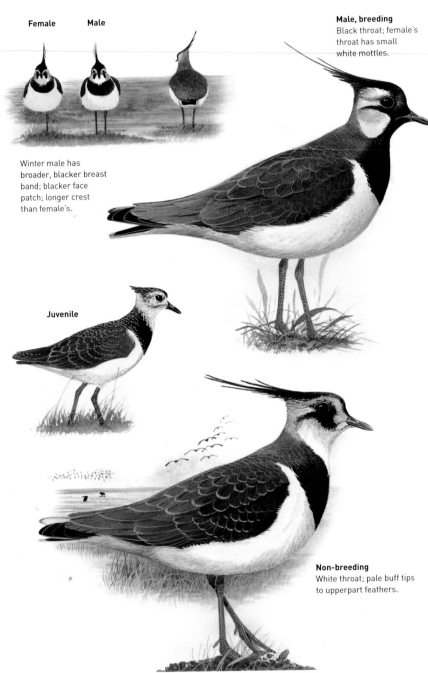

Female   Male

Winter male has broader, blacker breast band; blacker face patch; longer crest than female's.

Male, breeding
Black throat; female's throat has small white mottles.

Juvenile

Non-breeding
White throat; pale buff tips to upperpart feathers.

WHEN SEEN

All year.

WHERE SEEN
Almost all of Europe in summer, on farmland and moors; south from Britain and Low Countries in winter, chiefly on pastures, ploughed land, and also coastal grazing marshes.

HABITAT AND INFO

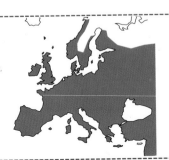

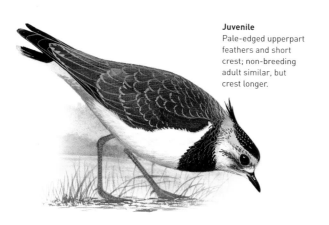

Juvenile
Pale-edged upperpart feathers and short crest; non-breeding adult similar, but crest longer.

Recognizable at great distance.

White rump contrasts with black tailband.

Raises wings as it settles and also to ward off intruders at nest.

Male

Female

Striking white underwing coverts contrast with black quills.

Male has broader, rounder outer wing than female's.

FLIGHT PATTERN
Distinctive jerky action in flight; flight often highly aerobatic when coming in to land.

DID YOU KNOW?
Lapwings are often active well into dusk and will feed on moonlit nights, although most food is located by sight. They use foot-pattering to make hidden prey move. In some areas, flocks of Lapwings have recently taken to roosting at night and resting by day on flat roofs of industrial and retail buildings in urban areas.

Curlew

SCALE v Pigeon

LENGTH / 50–60cm (19½–23½in)
WINGSPAN / 80–100cm (31½–39in)
WEIGHT / 575–950g (20–34oz)

■ **STATUS /** Vulnerable

The largest wader, it is rather dark on mud flats at a distance, yet it looks pale on heather moorlands in summer. It roosts in flocks, but often feeds in isolation or very loose groups.

Large, stately and blessed with a wonderful voice, the Curlew is also remarkable for its long, smoothly down-curved bill. It is a widespread bird with a range of habitats, familiar both inland and on the coast, on remote hills and in grassy meadows, on wild marshes and beside busy seaside promenades. Throughout most of the year it is the distinctive voice of the salt marsh and muddy estuary, and in spring it is the chief glory of the heather moor and blanket bog. Curlews are sociable outside the breeding season and form large flocks at high tide. Yet they often keep separate from the godwits, Redshanks, Grey Plovers, and smaller waders that roost nearby, forming long lines of bigger, hunched, dark-looking birds that might almost be taken for young gulls.

FEEDING

The benefit of the Curlew's curved bill is still debated. It may give the bird a better view of its bill tip for more precise probing. It probably allows easier withdrawal of worms from deep within sand and mud in one long, backward-leaning pull. If it can be rotated in wet mud or sand, it could also let the Curlew detect prey in a wider area than a simple probe with a straight bill. It is certainly sensitive at the tip and can both feel and grasp worms, crabs, shellfish, and similar prey hidden in mud or sand, beneath seaweed, in rock pools, or under clumps of heather, grasses, or rushes. The bird shakes crabs to break off their legs, and usually washes lugworms before swallowing them whole.

DISPLAY AND VOICE

In spring, Curlews fly over their breeding territories, rising with slow wing beats and then gliding slowly down, with a song that begins with long, slow, melancholy notes and develops into a fast, liquid, throbbing or bubbling ecstatic trill. The song may be heard at other times of the year in a more or less developed form, with a variety of loud calls: a hoarse, throaty *whaup*, a repeated *lee lee lee*, and a liquid, sad *cour-li*. These calls echo around salt-marsh creeks and estuaries, and are an essential part of their atmosphere.

BREEDING

The nest is a grass-lined hollow in heather, grass, or rushes, on a quiet moor or in a rough field. Four eggs hatch after 27–29 days. The chicks fly when about five weeks old.

MIGRATION

Many Curlews simply move to the coast in autumn, but some western European breeders go south to Iberia. Northern and eastern European nesters move south and west.

Display flight starts with steep rise, then glides with wings raised.

Adults have thin black bars across tertials (see dogtooth pattern on juvenile).

Male, spring
Rich tawny-brown, heavily marked black-brown; legs blue-grey.

Female
Long bill may rule out male, but some are difficult to tell.

Tail projects beyond wingtips in female (reverse in male).

Juvenile
Note dogtooth dark barring at rear.

Pale feather fringes wear away, leaving notches in feather edges.

WHEN SEEN

All year.

WHERE SEEN
Breeds Ireland, Britain, NW France, east across Europe to Siberia, north to N Norway, south to S France and parts of S Germany; widespread migrant.

HABITAT AND INFO

SIMILAR SPECIES
Juvenile Herring Gull has more contrasted upperwing and tail; slower, more varied wing beat.

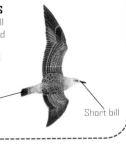

Dark tailband   Short bill

Flocks move rather gull-like.

Performs exhilarating, ecstatic song during display flight.

Female

Western breeders have brown-spotted underwing; becomes whiter farther east (such birds move west in winter).

Long head, neck, and bill compared with chunkier, shorter-billed, darker-looking Whimbrel's.

Dark with wide white V on rump: compare with Bar-tailed Godwit and Whimbrel.

Female (above) longer-billed than male (below).

Male

Underparts may be much whiter.

FLIGHT PATTERN
Flocks moving to or from roosts often form long lines or V-shapes.

DID YOU KNOW?
The long, curved bill is a versatile tool, used for pecking, probing, and inserting sideways under tussocks of grass and into mudbanks, for breaking up crabs, and even for catching flying insects. The preferred food depends on the length of the bill, so there tends to be a difference in diet between males and longer-billed females.

Whimbrel

LENGTH / 40–42cm (15½–16½in)
WINGSPAN / 71–81cm (28–32in)
WEIGHT / 270–450g (9½–16oz)

■ STATUS / Secure

SCALE v Pigeon

Very Curlew-like, the Whimbrel is smaller, darker, more stripy-headed, with a slightly shorter bill. In flight, it is more compact, quick, and dark-looking.

While Curlews are present in Europe all year round, Whimbrels are welcome visitors in spring, sometimes moving north in flocks of several dozen together. In autumn, they make a more leisurely return southward, their frequent flight calls drawing attention to small parties flying high overhead.

FEEDING
Whimbrels probe for worms and take various insects and molluscs.

DISPLAY AND VOICE
The song is a beautiful repetition of low, fluty notes, accelerating into a more rapid trill than the very similar Curlew song. The call is a quick series of sharp notes in an evenly-pitched trill: *pip ip ip ip ip ip ip*.

BREEDING
Whimbrels breed on northern moors and wild heath, from sea level to high tundra and hills above the tree line, nesting on the ground. The 3–4 large eggs hatch after 27–28 days.

MIGRATION
European populations migrate south to the coasts of Africa each winter.

Adult
Long, dark wings and clean white V on lower back and rump; long, flat crown, shortish bill.

Slightly darker, quicker, chunkier, and deeper-chested than Curlew in flight.

Adult
On average, bill longer on female, but some overlap.

Note head stripes.

Both sexes deep pink on bill outside breeding season.

Female

Male, breeding

Wingtips equal tail tip on female (top); shorter on male.

Breeding birds have pale notches on fresh feathers.

Juvenile
Fresh feathers have neat buff edges.

Upperparts look darker by midsummer as pale spots wear away.

DARK AND STOCKY
Very like a Curlew in flight, the Whimbrel has a darker, deeper body.

WHEN SEEN

Oct
April

April to October.

WHERE SEEN
Moors and islands of Iceland, N Scotland, Scandinavia; widespread on migration on W European coasts.

HABITAT AND INFO

SIMILAR SPECIES
Curlew is bigger, slimmer, slightly paler; slower flight, different call.

Paler body

Longer bill

Woodcock

A stocky, long-billed, barrel-chested bird with complex patterns, it is rarely seen on the ground. If disturbed, it flies off fast and low with noisy wing beats.

LENGTH / 33–35cm (13–14in)
WINGSPAN / 55–65cm (21½–25½in)
WEIGHT / 250–420g (9–15oz)

■ STATUS / Vulnerable

SCALE v Pigeon

Dark silhouette over woods at dusk.

Wings angled back to short point.

Bill points down in flight.

Many shorter-billed birds now found; the reason is not known.

Note white tailband.

Fast, noisy takeoff if disturbed.

Unusually for a wading bird, the Woodcock is active between dusk and dawn and lives in woodland, not on the shore. More heavily built than a Snipe, with broader wings and a thicker bill, it is associated with deep leaf mould on the forest floor, beneath brambles, or sometimes under thick bracken on open slopes.

FEEDING
It probes for earthworms in soft earth, its flexible bill detecting and grasping them deep underground.

DISPLAY AND VOICE
Males display at dusk, flying at tree-top height and alternating sharp whistles with throaty croaks. Some people hear the high *tswik* more easily than the deep, double *grrk grrk*; others find the opposite.

BREEDING
Four eggs are laid on the ground. The chicks fly when just 15–20 days old. Females breed at one year old, males at two.

MIGRATION
Most birds breeding in continental Europe migrate west or south in winter to areas bordering the North Sea and Mediterranean.

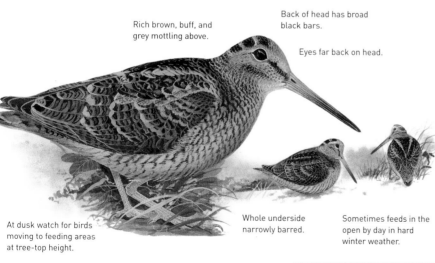

Rich brown, buff, and grey mottling above.

Back of head has broad black bars.

Eyes far back on head.

At dusk watch for birds moving to feeding areas at tree-top height.

Whole underside narrowly barred.

Sometimes feeds in the open by day in hard winter weather.

THREATENING WEATHER
Deep snow or hard frost prevent Woodcocks from reaching their food.

WHEN SEEN

Aug — March

Breeds March to August.

WHERE SEEN
Mixed and deciduous woods, meadows, and field edges in winter; Ireland eastward to Russia; sparse in south.

HABITAT AND INFO

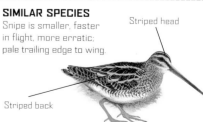

SIMILAR SPECIES
Snipe is smaller, faster in flight, more erratic; pale trailing edge to wing.

Striped head

Striped back

Great Snipe

LENGTH / 27–29cm (10½–11½in)
WINGSPAN / 43–50cm (17–19½in)
WEIGHT / 170–260g (6–9oz)

STATUS / Vulnerable

SCALE v Pigeon

This dark snipe has three white lines along its open wings, relatively weak back stripes, and heavily barred underparts. Its tail and upperwing patterns are useful for identification.

A heavy-bodied snipe with a rather thick bill, this rare bird should not be confused with the common Snipe. It is much heavier, has broader wings, and a slower, more Woodcock-like flight. Usually seen in the air, its bold wing pattern and white tail sides are its most distinctive features. If flushed at close range, its flight is low and straight, lacking the fast zigzags of the Snipe.

FEEDING
It feeds in typical snipe fashion, probing for worms in soft earth and wet mud.

DISPLAY AND VOICE
Groups gather on the ground where males puff out their plumage and perform low, fluttering leaps and complex posturings, along with gurgling and rasping sounds.

BREEDING
It breeds in areas of mixed bog and open woodland: marshy mountain slopes and drier places in the north, extensive marshes in the east. The four eggs hatch in 22–24 days.

MIGRATION
The whole population migrates to Africa for the winter.

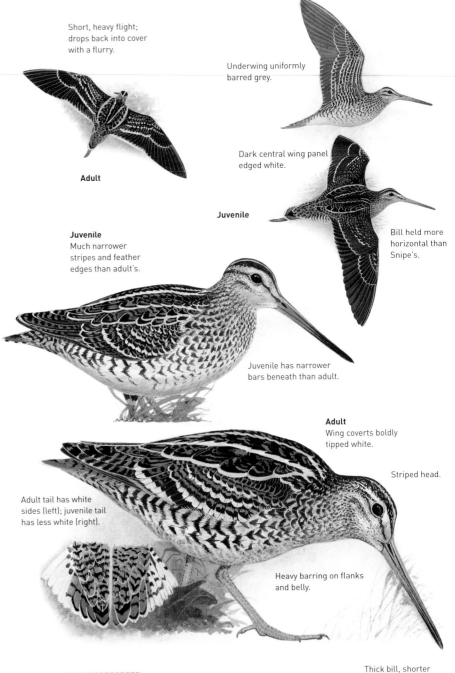

Short, heavy flight; drops back into cover with a flurry.

Adult

Underwing uniformly barred grey.

Dark central wing panel edged white.

Juvenile

Bill held more horizontal than Snipe's.

Juvenile
Much narrower stripes and feather edges than adult's.

Juvenile has narrower bars beneath than adult.

Adult
Wing coverts boldly tipped white.

Striped head.

Adult tail has white sides (left); juvenile tail has less white (right).

Heavy barring on flanks and belly.

Thick bill, shorter than Snipe's.

IDENTIFICATION CHALLENGE
Away from its breeding grounds, this bird is a difficult one to identify.

WHEN SEEN

Oct
April
April to October.

WHERE SEEN
Wild and remote marshes in central Scandinavia, NE Europe; on migration very rare in rough, often drier ground in W Europe.

HABITAT AND INFO

SIMILAR SPECIES
Snipe has plainer upperwing with double pale midwing bars; less barred on underside.

Longer bill
Whiter belly

Snipe

A marshland wader that flies up almost underfoot with a loud rasping call. Its striped back and dark wings are distinctive but hard to see in sudden, fast zigzag takeoff.

LENGTH / 25–27cm (9¾–10½in)
WINGSPAN / 37–43cm (14½–17in)
WEIGHT / 80–120g (2¾–4¼oz)

STATUS / Vulnerable

SCALE v Pigeon

Favouring overgrown mud and shallow water, the Snipe is hard to see when on the ground. It flies away high and fast if disturbed, sometimes in small groups or "wisps". Unlike most waders, it does not normally associate with other species.

FEEDING
It needs soft ground so it can probe for earthworms with its sensitive bill. Hard frost is a threat.

DISPLAY AND VOICE
Snipe are easiest to see in spring when the males display in high switchback flights, producing a buzzing whirr (known as drumming) from their stiff tail feathers. They also stand on wires or telegraph poles calling with repetitive *chip-per* notes. When flushed from cover they call with a hard tearing or rasping note.

BREEDING
Snipe typically breed on wet meadows or moors. Four eggs laid on the ground hatch in 18–20 days.

MIGRATION
Most European Snipe move west or south in winter to Britain and Ireland, France, Spain, Greece, and Turkey.

Adult
Grey-and-white underwing.

Flight fast, flickering, often rolling; bill angled down.

Juvenile
Narrowly barred underwing.

Juvenile
Narrower buff stripes on back.

Lesser coverts near front of wing: juvenile (left); adult (right).

Rufous patch across tail.

Adult
Head striped bright buff and black; broader stripes and feather edges than juvenile.

Legs short, often flexed; usual walk a creeping shuffle.

Bill long and straight.

Prefers wet places with mud, grass, sedges, and rushes to open shorelines, but may feed on expanses of mud at lake or reservoir edge; often feeds on damp pasture in winter.

A TIGHT BUNDLE
Snipe often rest in small, close groups but feed a little apart.

WHEN SEEN

All year; March to August in north and east of range.

WHERE SEEN
Breeds Iceland, Britain, Netherlands eastward, in marshes and on upland moors; scattered farther south.

HABITAT AND INFO

SIMILAR SPECIES
Female Ruff is less striped; much plainer head; longer legs, but shorter bill.

Scaly back

Plain underside

Jack Snipe

LENGTH / 17–19cm (6¾–7½in)
WINGSPAN / 30–36cm (11¾–14in)
WEIGHT / 35–70g (1¼–2½oz)

SCALE v Pigeon

■ **STATUS** / Vulnerable

A small, short-billed, dark-backed snipe, it is restricted to grassy or rushy vegetation in wet places. It is typically seen only when flushed at very close range.

A skulking bird of dense marsh vegetation, the Jack Snipe is even more secretive than the common Snipe and extremely hard to spot on the ground. It is usually seen as it flies up when almost trodden on, quickly dropping back into the marsh. Even if there are several in a small marsh, they usually rise singly and rarely join up in the air, unlike the common Snipe.

FEEDING
The typical snipe probing for worms is accompanied by a characteristic springy bobbing action.

DISPLAY AND VOICE
When flushed it is usually silent, unlike the common Snipe, but in display it produces muffled sounds like a distant cantering horse.

BREEDING
Jack Snipe breed in open spaces in northern forests, laying four eggs in a nest on the ground and incubating them for 17–24 days.

MIGRATION
The species winters in Britain and Ireland, the Low Countries, and parts of southern Europe, arriving there in September and October and leaving in late March.

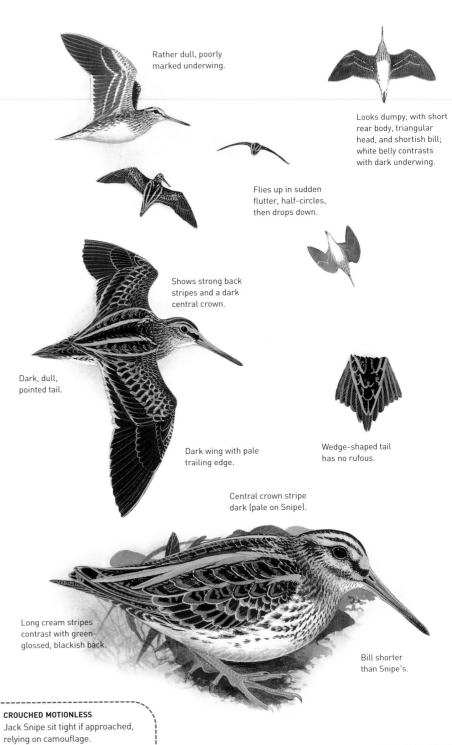

Rather dull, poorly marked underwing.

Looks dumpy, with short rear body, triangular head, and shortish bill; white belly contrasts with dark underwing.

Flies up in sudden flutter, half-circles, then drops down.

Shows strong back stripes and a dark central crown.

Dark, dull, pointed tail.

Dark wing with pale trailing edge.

Wedge-shaped tail has no rufous.

Central crown stripe dark (pale on Snipe).

Long cream stripes contrast with green-glossed, blackish back.

Bill shorter than Snipe's.

CROUCHED MOTIONLESS
Jack Snipe sit tight if approached, relying on camouflage.

WHEN SEEN

Sept — April

April to September in north; September to May in west.

WHERE SEEN
Densely vegetated muddy or waterlogged marshes; breeds NE Scandinavia; winters in W Europe.

HABITAT AND INFO

SIMILAR SPECIES
Snipe is bigger; longer bill; faster, more erratic, higher flight.

Cream crown stripe

Long bill

Great Skua

A dark, powerful, gull-like bird with large white wing patches, it looks heavy-bodied and broad-winged. It usually flies low over the sea singly or in pairs. Size, bulky body, and long, ample wings (especially "arm" length) distinguish it from other skuas.

LENGTH / 53–58cm (21–23in)
WINGSPAN / 125–140cm (49–55in)
WEIGHT / 1.2–2kg (2½–4½lb)

■ **STATUS /** Vulnerable

SCALE v Woodpigeon

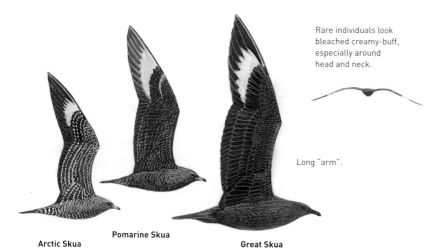

Rare individuals look bleached creamy-buff, especially around head and neck.

Long "arm".

Arctic Skua

Pomarine Skua

Great Skua

The largest and heaviest of the skuas, with the broadest wings and slowest direct flight, the Great Skua can be powerful and fast when necessary. It is able to tip a Gannet into the sea by grabbing its wing in flight. It is often an exciting bird to watch.

FEEDING
This big skua is a pirate, chasing gulls, terns, Fulmars, and Gannets to steal fish. It also kills many auks, Kittiwakes, and other birds.

DISPLAY AND VOICE
Its displays include raising its wings while on the ground to show off the big white patches to best effect. Its vocal repertoire is restricted to short, low, gruff notes and deep *tuk tuk* calls.

BREEDING
Nests are shallow scrapes in loose colonies on remote islands and coastal moors. The birds are fiercely protective of their eggs and chicks.

MIGRATION
In autumn, all Great Skuas move south, many through the North Sea and English Channel, to winter at sea in the South Atlantic.

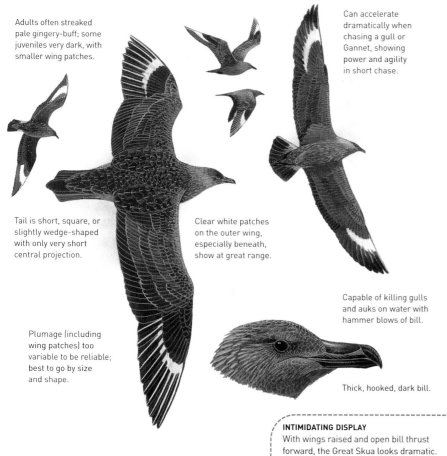

Adults often streaked pale gingery-buff; some juveniles very dark, with smaller wing patches.

Can accelerate dramatically when chasing a gull or Gannet, showing power and agility in short chase.

Tail is short, square, or slightly wedge-shaped with only very short central projection.

Clear white patches on the outer wing, especially beneath, show at great range.

Capable of killing gulls and auks on water with hammer blows of bill.

Plumage (including wing patches) too variable to be reliable; best to go by size and shape.

Thick, hooked, dark bill.

INTIMIDATING DISPLAY
With wings raised and open bill thrust forward, the Great Skua looks dramatic.

WHEN SEEN

Oct — March

March to October.

WHERE SEEN
Breeds on peaty and moorland hills and islands from N Scotland north to Faeroes, Iceland; on migration, seen off many western headlands; rare in winter.

HABITAT AND INFO

SIMILAR SPECIES
Immature Herring Gull has more variegated plumage; white on rump but no white wing patch.

White on head

White rump

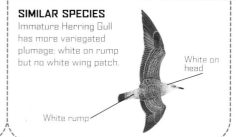

Pomarine Skua

LENGTH / 46–51cm (18–20in)
WINGSPAN / 113–125cm (40–49in)
WEIGHT / 550–900g (19–32oz)

■ **STATUS /** Vulnerable

SCALE v Woodpigeon

A big, bold skua, heavier than the Arctic Skua, with broad, blunt central tail feathers when adult.

A big skua, the Pomarine has the variable colour phases of the Arctic Skua but almost matches the Great Skua in bulk and power. It is generally the scarcest of the three, although it can be seen from many headlands in May and may be relatively numerous in late autumn.

FEEDING
Like other skuas, it harries seabirds until they drop fish, and also kills a number of gulls and auks. On the tundra, it eats mainly lemmings.

DISPLAY AND VOICE
Exciting aerial displays take place over breeding sites. It is silent at sea.

BREEDING
It nests on northern tundra and lays two eggs in June. Like other skuas, it attacks intruders – animal or human – at the nest.

MIGRATION
Spring movement to the north is often concentrated in May, through the English Channel and North Sea or around western Scotland. Return movements take place from August to November. A few spend the winter in western Europe, but most move far south.

Adult
Full tail (right).

Broader wing, with longer "arm", and deeper belly than Arctic Skua's.

Birds gradually attain full adult tail length in 3–4 years.

Pale adult (above)
(Dark ones scarce)
Blunt tail projection.

Juvenile
Like young Arctic; barred rump often paler.

Sub-adult
Shorter tail than adult's.

Juvenile's tail may be round or with variable short, blunt central projection.

Double pale crescent on underwing is useful clue.

Bill heavier than Arctic Skua's; pale base more obvious.

HORIZONTAL STANCE
This typical skua is often barred on the flanks.

WHEN SEEN

Nov
May

In W Europe mostly May to November.

WHERE SEEN
Off headlands, in northern estuaries.

HABITAT AND INFO

SIMILAR SPECIES
Arctic Skua is slimmer, less deep-chested; more varied flight on narrower wings.

Lightweight body

Pointed tail

Arctic Skua

An exciting, ocean-going buccaneer with long, slim, pointed wings and a pointed tail spike when adult. It flies low over the sea in a steady, relaxed flight, accelerating to chase terns or gulls in acrobatic attack.

LENGTH / 41–46cm (16–18in)
WINGSPAN / 97–115cm (38–45in)
WEIGHT / 380–600g (13½–21oz)

■ **STATUS /** Vulnerable

SCALE v Woodpigeon

An agile, elegant, fast-flying pirate of the seas, the Arctic Skua lives by forcing other birds to give up the prey they have caught. On migration it flies low over the ocean, moving easily in relaxed, supple flight. It is unusual in that it can be seen in 2–3 different colour varieties.

FEEDING
Arctic Skuas chase gulls, terns, and auks until they disgorge fish. They often harry their victims in pairs.

DISPLAY AND VOICE
At the breeding grounds, loud, nasal, wailing *ya-woh* or *gee-ah* calls accompany wild, dashing display flights which include steep climbs and fast, roaring dives.

BREEDING
Nests are on the ground on wild coastal moorland, close to other seabird colonies.

MIGRATION
Arctic Skuas move south in autumn, passing most European coasts on their way to the South Atlantic. They are less commonly seen on their return in spring.

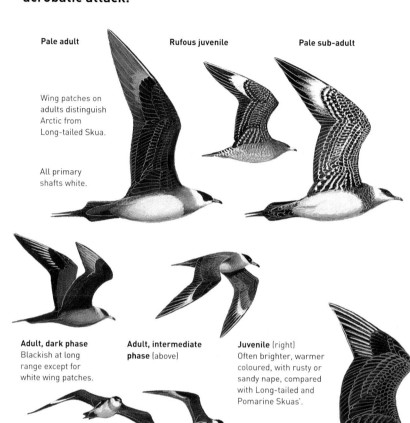

Pale adult

Wing patches on adults distinguish Arctic from Long-tailed Skua.

All primary shafts white.

Rufous juvenile

Pale sub-adult

Adult, dark phase
Blackish at long range except for white wing patches.

Adult, intermediate phase (above)

Juvenile (right)
Often brighter, warmer coloured, with rusty or sandy nape, compared with Long-tailed and Pomarine Skuas'.

Adult, pale phase (above)
Dusky breast band (unlike Long-tailed Skua's); dark underwing and upperparts; often pale base to tail.

Rump of juvenile appears as dark or darker than nape (paler on Pomarine).

Juvenile has short pointed tail projections.

Bill longer than Long-tailed Skua's, slimmer than Pomarine Skua's.

TWO EXTREMES
Pale and dark forms may pair up and interbreed freely.

WHEN SEEN

Oct
April

April to October.

WHERE SEEN
Breeds in Iceland, Scandinavia, N Scotland on coastal moors and islands, inland on peat bogs; migrates through North Sea and along Atlantic coasts to South Atlantic.

HABITAT AND INFO

SIMILAR SPECIES
Immature Herring Gull is bigger; broader-winged; shorter-tailed.

Pale crown

Whiter body

Long-tailed Skua

SCALE v Woodpigeon

LENGTH / 35–58cm (14–23in)
WINGSPAN / 105–112cm (41–44in)
WEIGHT / 250–450g (9–16oz)

■ STATUS / Vulnerable

A small, tern-like skua with a short bill and long narrow wings that make it look larger in flight. Adults have long, whippy tail projections. Flight is easy at sea: its light body gives it a more floating action than the heavily laden Arctic Skua. It can look similar to a brown tern.

Long-winged, slender, and distinctly tern-like, with exceptionally long tail streamers on adults, this is a predatory bird in summer and less piratical than the Arctic Skua. Of all the European skuas, it is the least common off western European headlands in spring and autumn, although in some years large numbers are seen at favoured sites.

FEEDING
It preys upon lemmings and other small mammals, small birds, eggs, and fish. It rears more young in good lemming years than in poor years, when many pairs fail to breed.

VOICE
It calls with high-pitched squeals near the nest. Otherwise it is silent.

BREEDING
The Long-tailed Skua nests on the ground, on high arctic-alpine hills and coastal tundra. It lays two eggs, which hatch after 23–25 days.

MIGRATION
Long-tailed Skuas move south in autumn, but are scarce off most coasts. They winter in the South Atlantic. In some years, there is a marked spring movement off the Western Isles of Scotland.

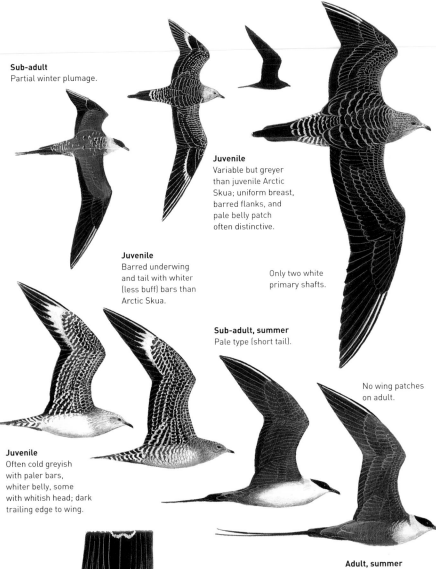

Sub-adult
Partial winter plumage.

Juvenile
Variable but greyer than juvenile Arctic Skua; uniform breast, barred flanks, and pale belly patch often distinctive.

Juvenile
Barred underwing and tail with whiter (less buff) bars than Arctic Skua.

Only two white primary shafts.

Sub-adult, summer
Pale type (short tail).

No wing patches on adult.

Juvenile
Often cold greyish with paler bars, whiter belly, some with whitish head; dark trailing edge to wing.

Juvenile has blunt central tail projection, longer than that of juvenile Arctic Skua's.

Adult, summer
Long, whippy tail projection; dusky belly of variable extent, but no dark breast band.

Bill rather short and thick.

WHIPPY TAIL
The long tail projection is flexible, especially in flight.

WHEN SEEN

Sept
May

May to September.

WHERE SEEN
Breeds on tundra in Scandinavia; rare on migration along North Sea and Atlantic coasts.

HABITAT AND INFO

SIMILAR SPECIES
Arctic Skua is similar; look for tail shapes and varying plumage patterns.

Large white wing patch

Short tail point

COMMON NAME
Slender-billed Gull

SPECIES
Larus genei

FAMILY
Laridae

ORDER
Charadriiformes

Slender-billed Gull

An elegant, forward-leaning, long-necked gull with a pattern like Black-headed's, but with no dark hood in summer.

LENGTH / 42–44cm (16½–17½in)
WINGSPAN / 90–102cm (35½–40in)
WEIGHT / 250g (9oz)

■ **STATUS /** Vulnerable

SCALE v Pigeon

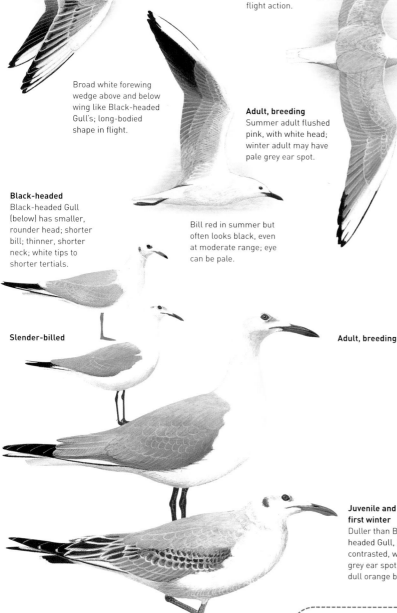

Longer tail, longer neck than Black-headed Gull's; longer inner wing gives less snappy flight action.

Broad white forewing wedge above and below wing like Black-headed Gull's; long-bodied shape in flight.

Adult, breeding
Summer adult flushed pink, with white head; winter adult may have pale grey ear spot.

Black-headed
Black-headed Gull (below) has smaller, rounder head; shorter bill; thinner, shorter neck; white tips to shorter tertials.

Bill red in summer but often looks black, even at moderate range; eye can be pale.

Slender-billed

Adult, breeding

Juvenile and first winter
Duller than Black-headed Gull, less contrasted, with grey ear spot, plain dull orange bill.

ERECT HEAD AND NECK
The slender, upright neck is more obvious than the bill shape.

This is effectively a "hooded gull" without a hood: in other respects, its plumage looks very like that of a Black-headed Gull. It is very much rarer, though, being restricted to Mediterranean lagoons, salt pans, and marshes in summer. Even in winter it remains scarce and essentially coastal.

FEEDING
It catches fish and insects by plunge-diving, up-ending, surface-dipping from the air, picking from the surface while swimming, or by foot-paddling and probing on the shore.

DISPLAY AND VOICE
A sociable breeder, its behaviour resembles that of the Black-headed Gull. Its calls are deeper and more nasal.

BREEDING
Most colonies are small, on the ground in open places near lagoons or on low islands. The 2–3 eggs hatch after 22 days' incubation.

MIGRATION
It is mostly resident, moving within the Mediterranean or to west Africa. Eastern breeders move to the Red Sea in winter.

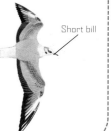

WHEN SEEN
Oct — March

At breeding sites spring to autumn; in Mediterranean sparsely all year.

WHERE SEEN
Breeds S Spain, S France, Sardinia, N Italy, N Greece; scarce in Mediterranean and very rare farther north.

HABITAT AND INFO

SIMILAR SPECIES
Winter Black-headed Gull has shorter bill and neck; shorter body; blacker ear patch.

Short bill

Shorter tail

Black-headed Gull

LENGTH / 34–37cm (13½–14½in)
WINGSPAN / 100–110cm (39–43in)
WEIGHT / 225–350g (8–12½oz)

SCALE v Pigeon

■ **STATUS /** Secure

A familiar, very pale, small gull with a dark hood in summer. It is social and noisy, often beside rivers and park ponds in towns. It is common on farmland, but equally abundant at the coast.

Few gulls are really restricted to the sea. The Black-headed Gull never has been, and flocks of these gulls seen inland are no indication of conditions at sea. They breed inland as often as they breed near the coast, favouring sites beside lakes both in the lowlands and on hills and moors. In autumn, they follow the plough, gleaming white against the dark, freshly turned earth. In winter, they are still on the fields, finding worms or chasing Lapwings to steal theirs. Flocks forage along riversides even in city centres, while groups stand around on shop roofs or dive briefly into gardens to pick up scraps. In short, they are everywhere: easy to see, easy to learn, and thoroughly enjoyable. They squabble and scrap, adding life and movement wherever they are. If your interest lies in more unusual species, Black-headed Gulls still have appeal, because their flocks are likely to attract wandering rarities such as a Mediterranean Gull.

FEEDING
They catch insects and other small invertebrates, including a great many earthworms, on grass or ploughed land. They snatch insects from the air, especially flying ants, and pick caterpillars and even fruit from leafy trees. They also capture small fish and other aquatic creatures, picking them from the surface in flight or grabbing them in shallow plunges.

DISPLAY AND VOICE
In summer, the birds use their dark hoods as signals of aggression or dominance, showing their pale napes as they turn their heads in a head-flagging display. Calls are equally important in displays. Most have a high-pitched, squealing or grating quality: *kwarrr*, an angry, emphatic *kee-earr*, *kwuk*, *kuk-uk*, *orr*, and variations. Feeding groups make a quiet, babbling, yapping chorus.

BREEDING
They nest in colonies of anything from two pairs to several hundred. The nests vary from small scrapes in mud or peat to substantial structures in reeds and rushes. The 2–3 eggs hatch after 23–26 days. The chicks fly when they are about 35 days old.

MIGRATION
Many move inland to exploit feeding areas and safe roosts on reservoirs in winter. Northern European breeders move south and west in autumn. The adults move back to their breeding colonies suddenly and quickly in early spring. Immatures remain on their wintering grounds later into spring and summer.

Dark grey toward underside of wingtip with sharp white stripe.

Bill bright red with dark tip; legs pale bright red in winter.

White head with soft grey wash on crown; dusky spot on ear coverts.

Adult, non-breeding

Male has long tail, short primary projection; female (lower) has shorter tail.

Adult, breeding
Black head; bill plum-red; legs crimson to deep maroon in summer.

Immature male, first winter
Bill and legs orange to ochre; pale brown band across wing; dark band on tail.

WHEN SEEN

All year; mostly April to September in north and east.

WHERE SEEN
Breeds Iceland, Britain, and Ireland, France eastward, local in extreme north and absent from most of S Europe; widespread in winter, mostly coastal in Mediterranean region.

HABITAT AND INFO

SIMILAR SPECIES
Mediterranean Gull is slightly stockier with bulkier head; thicker bill; white crescent below eye; stiffer flight.

Thicker bill

Longer legs

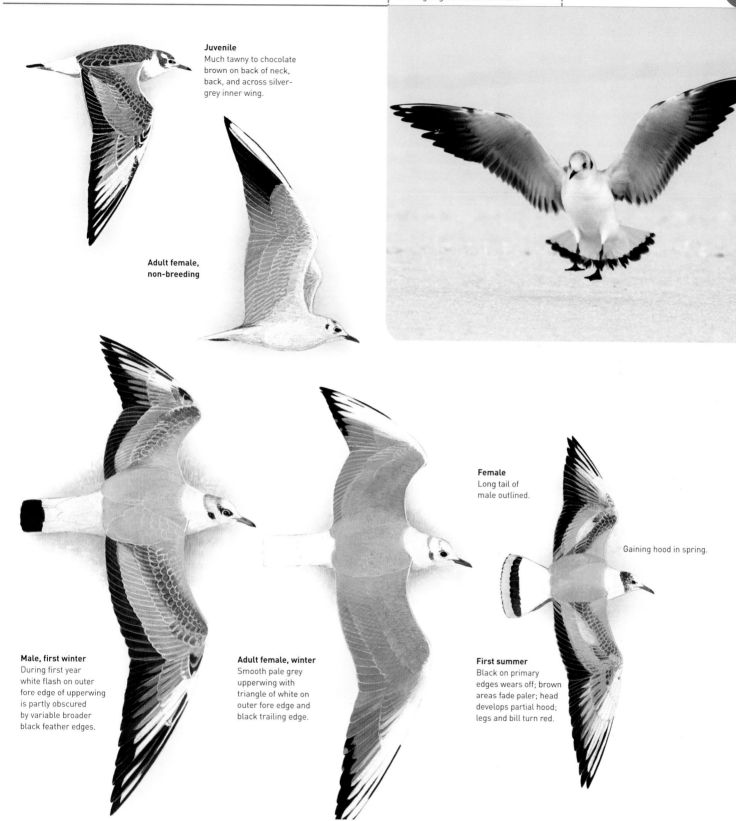

DISTINCTIVE UNDERWING
The dark primaries with a white
leading edge are characteristic.

Juvenile
Much tawny to chocolate
brown on back of neck,
back, and across silver-
grey inner wing.

**Adult female,
non-breeding**

Female
Long tail of
male outlined.

Gaining hood in spring.

Male, first winter
During first year
white flash on outer
fore edge of upperwing
is partly obscured
by variable broader
black feather edges.

Adult female, winter
Smooth pale grey
upperwing with
triangle of white on
outer fore edge and
black trailing edge.

First summer
Black on primary
edges wears off; brown
areas fade paler; head
develops partial hood;
legs and bill turn red.

DID YOU KNOW?
Breeding Black-headed Gulls are often faithful to traditional sites,
even if these change quite dramatically over many years, but they
are also quick to adapt to sudden changes. On rare occasions,
they may even switch from rapidly flooding marshes to nest in
trees above the rising waters.

?

Mediterranean Gull

LENGTH / 36–38cm (14–15in)
WINGSPAN / 98–105cm (39–41in)
WEIGHT / 200–350g (7–12½oz)

SCALE v Pigeon

■ **STATUS /** Vulnerable

Stocky in build, with a heavy bill and frowning expression, long legs, and a strutting walk. It has rather straight, stiff, blunt wings in flight. Its beautifully ghostly, pearly-white plumage makes it an exceptionally handsome gull.

With its inky-black hood, big white eyelids, vivid red bill, pearly upperwings, and spotless white underwings, a Mediterranean Gull in breeding plumage is a stunningly beautiful bird. Even those who maintain that gulls are boring cannot fail to be impressed. At other times this is a bird with real character: a bully, aggressive and confident in a mixed flock, its "pirate patch" often completing the impression. Mediterranean Gulls were once thought to be declining in a sorry spiral toward extinction, but in recent years they have increased and spread. Before their numbers built up sufficiently to establish a small, pure population, they were so scarce in parts of western Europe that single birds sometimes formed mixed pairs with Black-headed Gulls. Now there are substantial numbers in autumn and winter at some coastal locations along both sides of the English Channel, although nesting pairs remain few and erratic over much of the species' range.

FEEDING
Less likely to turn up on fields and tips inland than other gulls (although it sometimes does so), the Mediterranean Gull feeds chiefly on beaches, at sewage outfalls, and over the sea, finding all kinds of offal and scraps, invertebrates, small fish, and molluscs. On its summer breeding grounds, it feeds mainly on insects, snails, and earthworms.

DISPLAY AND VOICE
Like other hooded gulls, the Mediterranean uses its bold black hood in courtship and territorial displays. It is mostly silent in winter, but in spring its calls have a nasal, throttled quality, with a piercing *whaa-whaa-whaa-whaa-oo-ah* and a more tern-like *kee-er*.

BREEDING
Isolated pairs nest among Black-headed Gulls, but larger colonies in eastern Europe are usually pure. Three eggs are laid in a grassy nest on the ground. They hatch after 23–25 days, and the young fledge after another 35–40 days.

MIGRATION
Black Sea breeders mostly move to the Mediterranean in winter. Increasing numbers move west to the North Sea and Atlantic coasts and some remain to breed in these regions. Most adults return east in March while immatures remain in the west all year.

Second year

Both first and second years can look like this; much individual variation.

Variable amount of black across outer primary tips in second year.

Juvenile (below)
Pale head; gingery neck; black bill; bold black marks on back.

First winter (right)
Head rounded or angular with peaked crown; black smudge through eye curves up into grey nape; white eyelids obvious; grey of back cold, hard, silvery, not bluish.

During first winter bill varies from ochre-buff to dull red with black tip.

Adult, breeding
Jet black hood extends over nape; big white eyelids; scarlet bill with variable black band and yellow tip.

Adult, non-breeding
Variable black on head may form mask and turn up into grey wash across nape; bill red or black; legs red, purple-red, or black.

Wingtip of adult pure white: may contrast with grey back, or blend in according to light; thin black outer line at close range; underwing spotless white.

Male (upper) longer-tailed than female (lower).

WHEN SEEN

All year; in NW, adults typically winter and spring; immatures spring to autumn. Small breeding population in W Europe.

WHERE SEEN
Breeds very locally, often erratically, in Greece, central Europe, Baltic and North Sea coasts, rarely England, France, E Spain; in winter, more widespread on coasts.

HABITAT AND INFO

SIMILAR SPECIES
Juvenile Common Gull is longer-winged; darker back; broader tailband; plainer head; less contrast on upperwing.

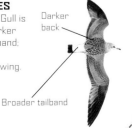

Darker back

Broader tailband

PIRATE PATCH
White wingtips and dark eye-patch are a unique combination.

Fades to much paler in spring.

First winter
Pale, pearly-grey back and panel across midwing (darker on Common's); outer primaries blackish, inner ones pale; tail of female shorter.

Female, first winter
Outer primaries show white lines when fully spread; pale midwing panel blends into patch behind bend of wing; narrow dark trailing edge and tailband.

Second year
Adult and second year have clean white underwing, unlike Black-headed Gull's.

Male, breeding

DID YOU KNOW?
Early colonization of the UK in the 1980s often involved individuals pairing with Black-headed Gulls, producing hybrid young, but, as the population increased, so pure pairs dominated. Colonies on the English Channel coast grew to more than 100 strong early in the 21st century.

Little Gull

SCALE v Pigeon

LENGTH / 25–27cm (9¾–10½in)
WINGSPAN / 70–77cm (27½–30½in)
WEIGHT / 90–150g (3¼–5¼oz)

■ **STATUS** / Vulnerable

A rather tern-like, delicate gull, but adults are blunt-winged, short-tailed, and short-billed. Juveniles have sharper wings, but similar gentle-faced character. It flies head-to-wind, low over water, dipping to take food from the surface.

This is the smallest and most tern-like gull: an elegant, light, airy creature that seems to be at the mercy of the winds and waves. Yet it is quite capable of riding out storms on the open sea and is often to be seen at the coast – dipping, twisting, and turning over surf crashing against a breakwater, or in the melée of assorted gulls fighting for scraps at a sewage outfall. Flocks migrate along coasts, but small groups are equally likely to be seen over large reservoirs inland where they behave quite like Black Terns, beating into the wind, low over the surface, and dipping, rather than diving, to pick morsels from the water.

FEEDING

Most of the Little Gull's diet consists of insects and other aquatic invertebrates, especially in summer, when it takes flies in the air and from the surface of shallow floods and lakes. It also catches small fish, chiefly tiny fry from the surface, particularly when wintering at sea. It searches by flying low, head-to-wind, its bill angled downward. When it dips it usually makes a clean snatch with its bill, but it may settle for a moment, submerge its head, or patter along the surface with its feet before rising steeply again. This feeding behaviour helps to identify Little Gulls even at very long range. When feeding they often mix with small groups of terns.

DISPLAY AND VOICE

Compared to most gulls, Little Gulls are relatively quiet birds, except near the nesting colony. The usual call is a low *kek-kek-kek*; in alarm this develops into a harsher, tern-like or squeaky chatter. Territorial calls also have a chattering, squeaky quality. The courtship displays are like those of the Black-headed Gull. The birds show off their jet black hoods by posturing with their heads stretched forward or raised. A pair will walk side by side and tilt their heads away from each other to reduce the amount of black visible. This seems to be a way of reducing the "threat" posed by the dark hood. The birds threaten intruders by raising their heads vertically to show off their hoods.

BREEDING

They nest colonially, in hollows in wet vegetation beside freshwater lakes and close to water in marshes. Pairs incubate 2–3 eggs for 23–25 days. The chicks fly after about three weeks.

MIGRATION

Movements are complicated, but most eastern European breeders move west to the North Sea and Atlantic or south into the Mediterranean in winter.

Juvenile
Dark brown above at first; quickly loses brown on hind neck and sides of breast; gains grey on back during autumn as first winter plumage develops; pale pink legs.

Second year
In early spring, hood develops quickly from rear edge forward; may be complete in summer; dark wingtips on perched or swimming bird may confuse identification.

Closed wingtips white, but dark underside of far wing often shows.

Adult, summer
Jet black hood; bill dark or bright red.

Adult, winter
Grey cap; blacker ear spot; black bill.

Late juvenile
During transition to first winter dark upper back extends as lobe onto sides of breast.

WHEN SEEN

Aug — May

Mostly August to May in W Europe, a few in summer.

WHERE SEEN
Breeds from Finland eastward; a few scattered in W Europe.

HABITAT AND INFO

SIMILAR SPECIES
Black Tern is greyer on back, rump, and tail; pale underwing.

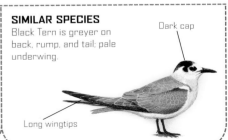

Dark cap

Long wingtips

IMMACULATE EFFECT
Breeding plumage is remarkably neat and smart.

Second summer
Dark underwing may be similar to adult, but coverts often much paler.

Adult, summer
At all seasons shows very dark underwing with white rear edge broader at tip; unique dark-light twinkling contrast as it flies low over water, visible at great range.

First summer
Like first winter but variable dark hood; wing markings gradually fade paler and browner; often more obvious white streaks along inner webs of outer primaries.

Adult, winter
Clean grey above with even, broad white rim around hindwing to small spot at tip; no black on upperwing at all.

First winter
Black zigzag above; black on tail; dark cap and ear spot.

First autumn
Juvenile plumage replaced by first winter feathers, giving clear grey back; dark wingbars often joined across rump at this stage, never seen on young Kittiwake; also darker marks on hindwing.

Second year
Some look adult; others have variable amount of black on outer primaries (often less than shown), more rarely on primary coverts.

DID YOU KNOW?

Sometimes huge movements take place along North Sea coasts and occasionally thousands may be seen together for a short time on coastal lakes in north-east England and the Low Countries. Small numbers often associate with migrant flocks of Black Terns on lakes inland, quickly moving on after a day or two, or even just a few hours.

Kittiwake

SCALE v Pigeon

LENGTH / 38–40cm (15–15½in)
WINGSPAN / 95–110cm (37–43in)
WEIGHT / 300–500g (10½–18oz)

■ **STATUS /** Secure

A small gull of the open sea, but it forms spectacular, noisy sea cliff breeding colonies in summer. It flies with steeply banking, shearwater-like action in gales. Adults have matt-grey across back with prominent long white head, white tail, and dipped-in-ink wingtips.

In winter, Kittiwakes forage around fish docks and ferry terminals, and in spring and autumn they are not infrequent over inland waters. Yet the Kittiwake is most at home far offshore, over the open ocean – of all the gulls the Kittiwake is the most truly marine. Its mastery of the elements, even in a North Atlantic gale, matches that of large shearwaters and petrels: it rides the wind in a series of high, bounding arcs, now on one wingtip, now on the other, travelling effortlessly over huge distances. Few people get to see it at sea, though, and to most of us it is best known as a bird of sheer, rocky sea cliffs, where it forms summer nesting colonies along with Guillemots and Razorbills. The massed Kittiwakes make the cliffs ring to their clamour as they endlessly call their name from the ledges. They can be seen at close range at the nest, revealing that they are delightful creatures, immaculate in full breeding plumage, and with a gentle, dove-like facial expression.

FEEDING

The bulk of a Kittiwake's food is fish, especially sandeels in summer, supplemented by a variety of marine invertebrates caught at sea. Kittiwakes do not scavenge at tips or feed on the shore: they dip to the surface of the open sea, plunge from a low height to reach deeper-swimming fish, or join in the general melée around trawlers, snapping up whatever bits of offal they can reach. They also forage at sewage outflows, although rarely form more than a small minority of the gull flocks at such sites. In the Arctic, upwelling water masses bring enormous quantities of shrimps to the surface (as do feeding whales in places) and huge flocks of Kittiwakes take advantage of the abundance of food.

DISPLAY AND VOICE

Kittiwakes call repeatedly at their breeding colonies: a loud, ringing, nasal *kitt-i-awa-ake* or *k-wake*. They also make quieter, whining, mewing, or wailing sounds. Away from the colony they are silent. Displays involve posturing on the nest, head-bobbing, choking motions, and feeding of the female by the male.

BREEDING

Nests are small masses of weed, grass, and mud on minute cliff ledges. Two eggs hatch after 27 days. The young fly when 42 days old.

MIGRATION

Most move far into the North Atlantic in winter. Small groups cross inland Britain in spring, but rarely stay long at reservoirs or lakes. A few penetrate into the Mediterranean, but they do not enter the Baltic Sea.

Adult, breeding
White head; red eye-ring; red gape.

Adult, winter
Dusky ear patch, smoky-grey nape; black legs, often tinged red-brown in summer, webs of feet paler.

Second winter
Bill has variable dark patches, often at base.

Juvenile
Black legs and bill; black-streaked tertials show at rest (hidden in flight); long wings; short legs.

Adult, winter
Dusky around eye; bill tinged green at base.

WHEN SEEN

All year, but most March to September on coasts.

WHERE SEEN
Breeds NW European coasts from N Scandinavia and Iceland to Portugal; widespread at sea in winter.

HABITAT AND INFO

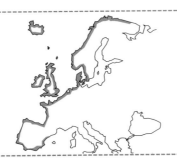

SIMILAR SPECIES
Common Gull has broader wing with large white spots on black tips; longer pale legs.

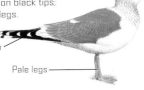

White wingtip spots

Pale legs

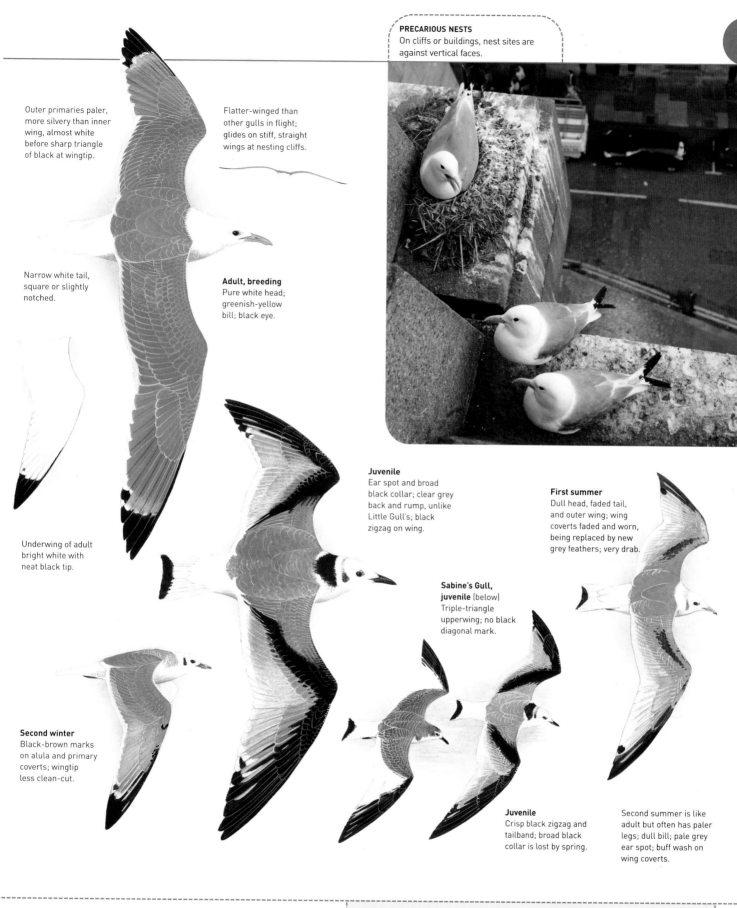

Outer primaries paler, more silvery than inner wing, almost white before sharp triangle of black at wingtip.

Flatter-winged than other gulls in flight; glides on stiff, straight wings at nesting cliffs.

PRECARIOUS NESTS
On cliffs or buildings, nest sites are against vertical faces.

Narrow white tail, square or slightly notched.

Adult, breeding
Pure white head; greenish-yellow bill; black eye.

Underwing of adult bright white with neat black tip.

Juvenile
Ear spot and broad black collar; clear grey back and rump, unlike Little Gull's; black zigzag on wing.

First summer
Dull head, faded tail, and outer wing; wing coverts faded and worn, being replaced by new grey feathers; very drab.

Sabine's Gull, juvenile (below)
Triple-triangle upperwing; no black diagonal mark.

Second winter
Black-brown marks on alula and primary coverts; wingtip less clean-cut.

Juvenile
Crisp black zigzag and tailband; broad black collar is lost by spring.

Second summer is like adult but often has paler legs; dull bill; pale grey ear spot; buff wash on wing coverts.

DID YOU KNOW?
In recent years, breeding Kittiwakes on the North Sea coast have faced difficulties feeding their young as cold water plankton, and the sandeels that feed on it, have moved north. Kittiwake chicks have starved to death despite being surrounded by piles of tough, indigestible pipefish, brought in place of sandeels by desperate parents.

?

Glaucous Gull

LENGTH / 63–68cm (25–27in)
WINGSPAN / 1.4–1.6m (4½–5¼ft)
WEIGHT / 1–2kg (2¼–4½lb)

■ **STATUS /** Secure

SCALE v Pigeon

A big, heavy-billed, pale gull with no black on the wingtips, secondaries, or tailband at any age.

Breeding around the Arctic, this is a charismatic, scarce winter visitor to north-west Europe. It is a large, powerful bird between a Herring Gull and Great Black-backed Gull in size: a handsome bird with a suitably frosty, Arctic look. It forages at refuse tips, outfalls, and fish quays, and often roosts on reservoirs inland with other gulls.

FEEDING
It eats mostly fish, some birds, and offal or refuse at tips. It finds dead animal matter on the tide line and steals food from other birds.

DISPLAY AND VOICE
Displays are like those of other large gulls, with long calls with head raised. Calls are like a Herring Gull's, but hoarser.

BREEDING
A shallow grassy nest is made on a rocky pinnacle, cliff ledge, or bank. Three eggs are incubated for 27–28 days. The chicks fly in seven weeks.

MIGRATION
East Greenland birds reach Iceland in winter. Variable numbers reach Britain and Ireland. Iceland breeders are resident. North European birds move south with the winter ice. Some reach the North Sea.

First winter
Beautifully patterned with pale flight feathers; underwing coverts and belly often quite dark; tail barred but no very dark band.

First winter
Beware confusion with shiny pale underwing tips of some young Herring Gulls.

Iceland Gull
To same scale as Glaucous (left): dark bill; paler underwing; slimmer rear body; shorter-tailed effect.

Adult
White and silvery-grey; broad secondary and primary tips make bold white triangle at rear; head pure white in summer, streaked autumn to spring.

Bill may be heavy, or rather slim but long; small eyes; head quite round or flat-topped.

Third/fourth year

First summer

Primary tips extend beyond tail, but less so than on Iceland Gull; legs longer; bill longer and pale pink with small, sharp, black tip; despite size and bulk, can be shapely and elegant.

Older immatures become more uniformly pale, gain grey on back; bill has narrower dark band near tip.

First winter
Some first winters much darker below; juvenile darker; first summer blotched and faded much paler.

Adult, summer

OATMEAL PATTERN
Year-old birds are pale, with black-tipped bills.

WHEN SEEN

Oct — April

In Iceland all year; Faeroes and NW Europe mostly October to April.

WHERE SEEN
Breeds Iceland, Spitsbergen, extreme N Russia; winters Atlantic and North Sea south to France.

HABITAT AND INFO

SIMILAR SPECIES
Juvenile Herring Gull is darker on hindwing, wingtip, and tailband; whiter on rump.

Dark wingtip

Dark tailband

Iceland Gull

A large gull with long wingtips, a rounded head, and a short bill. There is no black on its wingtips.

LENGTH / 52–60cm (20½–23½in)
WINGSPAN / 130–140cm (51–55in)
WEIGHT / 750–1,000g (26–35oz)

■ STATUS / Secure

SCALE v Pigeon

First winter

Iceland (top) has slimmer belly, shorter "arm" than Glaucous'.

Short body of Iceland gives short-tailed look in flight.

Inner wing proportionately shorter than on Glaucous, giving broad-winged effect.

Adult, summer

Glaucous
Same scale.

Eye-catching white wingtips separate these two species from Herring Gull group.

Adult, winter

Wingtip projection variable but can be very long; when swimming may be steeply angled upward.

May droop primaries to reveal more grey.

Adult's pale eyes often look dark at distance.

Second winter

Immature
Older immatures difficult to age; become very pale overall before gaining grey back.

Male

Female

Male's bill (inset above) heavier than female's; juvenile has dark bill with dark tip extending back as wedge – loses dark with age.

First winter
Long pale primaries extend well past tail; small, thick or slender bill less hooked than Glaucous's; steep forehead; rounded crown and nape; shortish legs rather dark pink; underparts never very dark.

Gentler, more dove-like, with larger, more central eye than Glaucous Gull; lacks brutal look.

GHOSTLY WINGS
The pale wingtips and tail catch the eye in flight.

Scarcer than the Glaucous Gull in Europe, the Iceland Gull breeds around Greenland and Arctic islands north of Canada. It visits Iceland in some numbers in winter, and variable numbers, some following fishing fleets, reach north-west Europe each winter. A few regularly move inland in Britain, roosting on reservoirs early in the year.

FEEDING
It eats mainly fish, catching them in shallow dives. It also eats eggs and young birds in summer, and refuse from beaches and tips in winter.

DISPLAY AND VOICE
The social behaviour is generally like that of the Herring Gull, but its calls are shriller.

BREEDING
Most nests are on flat cliff ledges beside the sea. The 2–3 eggs hatch after 28–30 days.

MIGRATION
West Greenland breeders disperse locally in winter, but some move farther. East Greenland breeders move to Iceland. Numbers reaching Britain and Ireland vary from a few score to a few hundred in exceptionally good years.

WHEN SEEN

Nov

April

November or December to April.

WHERE SEEN
Iceland, locally Ireland, Scotland, England, Norway in winter.

HABITAT AND INFO

SIMILAR SPECIES
Glaucous Gull has longer, thicker bill; shorter, broader wingtips.

Longer bill

Shorter wings

261

Common Gull

LENGTH / 40–43cm (15½–17in)
WINGSPAN / 105–125cm (41–49in)
WEIGHT / 300–500g (10½–18oz)

■ STATUS / Secure

SCALE v Pigeon

An elegant gull with basic pattern of a Herring Gull, but smaller, neater, more gentle-looking, never with pink legs, red bill spot, or yellow eyes. It is long-winged, but it rarely glides as masterfully as the larger gulls. It is typically seen foraging in flocks on fields or loafing on beaches.

Resembling a small Herring Gull, the Common Gull is a less familiar bird and certainly not the most common gull in many parts of Europe. Its distribution is curiously patchy: in Britain there are places where hundreds of Common Gulls march steadily across the fields looking for food in winter, while not far away they are rarely seen. In most wintering areas inland, they are far outnumbered by Black-headed Gulls. Most of them withdraw to the north in spring, to nest in pairs, groups, or small colonies. In summer, Common Gulls like boggy moors and sheltered coasts. They prefer little beaches and bays between rocky headlands and islands to open, windswept cliffs. In winter, they are found on broad, sandy beaches and estuaries, and on farmland with long-established grassy meadows or freshly ploughed fields. Like other gulls, they fly to large reservoirs or lakes each evening to roost.

FEEDING

Favoured food includes earthworms, insect larvae, and other invertebrates, pulled from the ground or stolen from other gulls or Lapwings. Common Gulls are chiefly ground-feeders, but they also pick scraps and occasional fish from water, take berries from shrubs, and catch insects in the air. It is only in recent years that Common Gulls have taken to urban feeding or visiting gardens.

DISPLAY AND VOICE

Most calls have a recognizable high, nasal, squealing quality, although with a pattern much like the calls of Herring Gulls. Their displays are also similar to those of Herring Gulls: the female begs and is fed by the male, and both birds toss their heads and call with their bills stretched vertically upward. There is also a good deal of posturing with heads stretched forward or downward and the wings pushed half-open at the carpal, or "wrist", joints.

BREEDING

Nests are made of seaweed, grasses, and plant stems, and placed in shallow depressions in rocks, on stumps or earth banks, on fence posts or drystone walls, on piers, or even on the roof ridges of disused buildings. Typically three eggs are laid. They hatch after 22–28 days.

MIGRATION

Most are migratory, moving south and west in autumn, but not penetrating far into continental Europe. This is a species of coastal countries in the main.

Adult, breeding
Green-yellow bill.

First year
Bill clear-cut pink and black.

Second winter
Closed wingtip looks all-black; bill often with broad black ring.

Adult, winter
Large white crescent between grey back and black of wingtip; bill may have thin black ring; legs blue-green or grey.

First winter
Grey saddle; neat covert pattern; pinkish legs and bill base.

WHEN SEEN

All year; September to April where it does not breed.

WHERE SEEN
Breeds on moors, islands; Britain and Ireland, Low Countries, and Scandinavia, sparsely N Europe; widespread in North Sea countries in winter, but not Iberia or Mediterranean.

HABITAT AND INFO

SIMILAR SPECIES
Herring Gull is larger; paler; large-billed; has pale eyes; pink legs.

Heavy bill

Pink legs

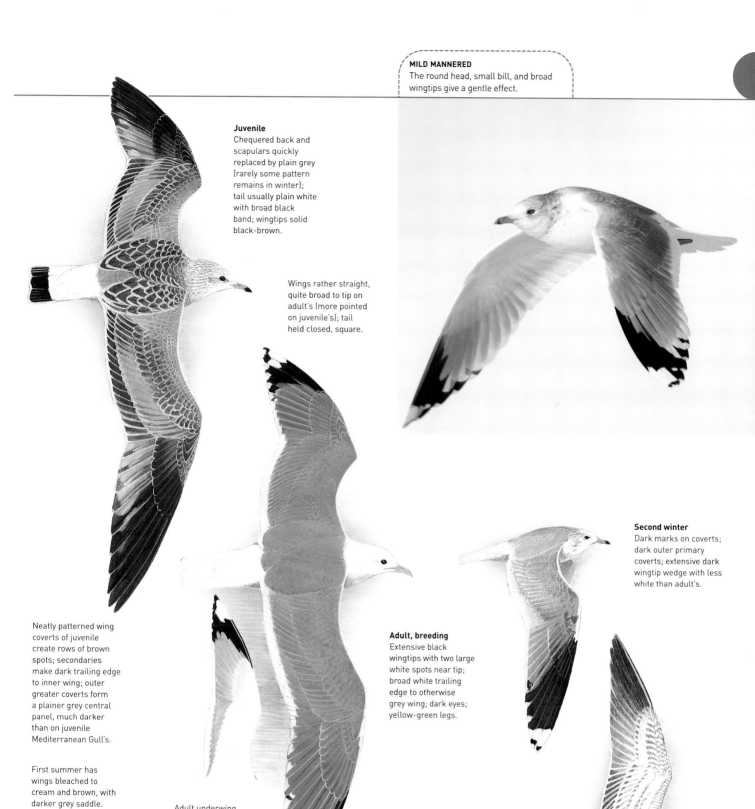

Juvenile
Chequered back and scapulars quickly replaced by plain grey (rarely some pattern remains in winter); tail usually plain white with broad black band; wingtips solid black-brown.

Wings rather straight, quite broad to tip on adult's (more pointed on juvenile's); tail held closed, square.

Second winter
Dark marks on coverts; dark outer primary coverts; extensive dark wingtip wedge with less white than adult's.

Neatly patterned wing coverts of juvenile create rows of brown spots; secondaries make dark trailing edge to inner wing; outer greater coverts form a plainer grey central panel, much darker than on juvenile Mediterranean Gull's.

First summer has wings bleached to cream and brown, with darker grey saddle.

Adult, breeding
Extensive black wingtips with two large white spots near tip; broad white trailing edge to otherwise grey wing; dark eyes; yellow-green legs.

Adult underwing.

Juvenile
Variable but typically with neat lines of brown spots on underwing coverts; white tail with clean black band.

DID YOU KNOW?
Smaller, lighter, and more delicate than a Herring Gull, the Common Gull can use more varied feeding techniques when the opportunity arises. It will pick insects from vegetation, including caterpillars from heather and flies from flowers, and catch flying ants high in the air along with Black-headed Gulls and starlings. Its lifespan is typically 10 years, but the oldest known is 22 years and 6 months.

Ring-billed Gull

LENGTH / 43–47cm (17–18½in)
WINGSPAN / 112–124cm (44–49in)
WEIGHT / 450–500g (16–18oz)

■ STATUS / Secure

SCALE v Pigeon

A rare visitor from North America, it is slightly larger than the Common Gull, with a paler back and thicker bill.

Unknown in Europe until late in the 20th century, this common American gull is now a regular visitor, in small numbers, to north-west Europe. It mixes with Common and Herring Gulls in estuaries and around coastal lakes, roosting with them on beaches and feeding on fields, at sewage outflows, and along the tide line.

FEEDING
Like other larger gulls, it eats almost anything, from fish and molluscs to rubbish and waste food around quays and seaside resorts.

DISPLAY AND VOICE
Calls resemble a Herring Gull's but tend to be higher in pitch and more nasal.

MIGRATION
Adults appear on the coasts of north-west Europe in late autumn and remain through the winter. There is often an increase in records around March and April, when Common Gulls are moving north. Immatures tend to move later in spring and may be seen during the summer.

Adult, summer
Black wingtip usually has smaller white spots than Common Gull's.

First winter (below, both)
Back paler than Common Gull's; tail has more complex pattern; compare immature Herring Gull.

Second winter
Dark spots on tail, often also on hindwing and outer wing coverts.

Paler grey than Common Gull; narrower, less striking white trailing edge.

Juvenile tail feathers, showing variation; Common Gull has sharper, straight black band.

Adult, winter (below)
Paler than Common Gull; less white between grey back and black wingtip.

Pale eye.

Bills of juvenile (top) and juvenile Common Gull (below).

Bill yellow (greener in winter), pale tip, broad black band.

STARING EYE
The pale eye is not always easy to see but is an important pointer.

WHEN SEEN

All year; most October to April.

WHERE SEEN
Annual in Ireland, Britain (mostly SW), and rare vagrant in many other countries from Iceland to Spain.

HABITAT AND INFO

SIMILAR SPECIES
Herring Gull is bigger; broader winged; less contrasted upperwing pattern.

Bigger bill

Larger size

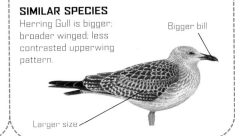

ORDER
Charadriiformes

FAMILY
Laridae

SPECIES
Larus audouinii

COMMON NAME
Audouin's Gull

Audouin's Gull

A rare gull of the Mediterranean, it is dark-billed and dark-legged.

LENGTH / 48–52cm (19–20½in)
WINGSPAN / 117–128cm (46–50in)
WEIGHT / 600–700g (21–25oz)

■ **STATUS /** Vulnerable

SCALE v Pigeon

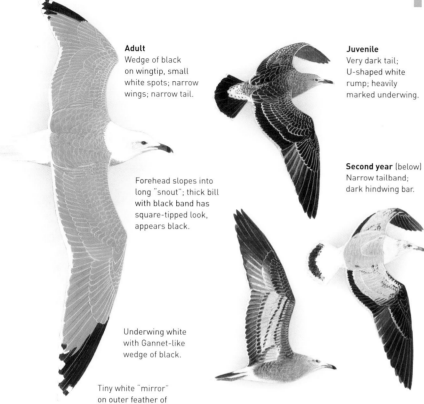

Adult
Wedge of black on wingtip, small white spots; narrow wings; narrow tail.

Juvenile
Very dark tail; U-shaped white rump; heavily marked underwing.

Second year (below)
Narrow tailband; dark hindwing bar.

Forehead slopes into long "snout"; thick bill with black band has square-tipped look, appears black.

Underwing white with Gannet-like wedge of black.

Tiny white "mirror" on outer feather of upperwing.

One of the most specialized of gulls, and until recently one of the rarest, Audouin's Gull is showing signs of a wider range of feeding methods and is increasing in numbers. In the 1960s, only around 1,000 pairs remained. By the end of the 20th century, single colonies numbered several thousand pairs.

FEEDING
Since they specialize in snatching fish from the surface of the sea, Audouin's Gulls rarely feed on beaches, but some may now be seen inland. Typically, fish are caught in the bill without any other part of the bird touching the water.

DISPLAY AND VOICE
Displays are similar to those of the Yellow-legged Gull. Calls are particularly hoarse and deep.

BREEDING
Colonies occupy rocky islands. The 2–3 eggs are laid in a scantily lined nest on the ground.

MIGRATION
Most disperse within the Mediterranean and along the west coast of Africa after breeding. A few reach the west coast of Iberia.

Juvenile
Dark, blotched; very long wings.

Adult has dark eye.

Wingtip spots wear off by summer.

Adult
White head; bill with variable yellow tip, looks very dark unless seen closely; body washed palest grey; legs dark grey-green.

Adult

Juvenile

STRIKING ADULT
The dark eye, bill, and legs help generate a unique impression.

WHEN SEEN

All year.

WHERE SEEN
Breeds locally E Spain, Balearics, Corsica, Sardinia, S Italy, Greece; widespread in W Mediterranean in autumn.

HABITAT AND INFO

SIMILAR SPECIES
Herring Gull is bigger, broader-winged; pale eyes, bill, and legs.

Larger size

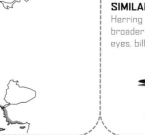

Paler legs

Yellow-legged Gull

LENGTH / 59–67cm (23–26½in)
WINGSPAN / 1.3–1.5m (4¼–5ft)
WEIGHT / 0.75–1.2kg (1¾–2½lb)

■ **STATUS /** Secure

SCALE v Pigeon

A large, handsome gull of the familiar white-headed, grey-backed, black-wingtipped type, adults having strikingly yellow legs and thick, bright bills. Immatures are not so easy, but tend to be white-headed, dark-backed, and dark-tailed.

Not long ago "Herring Gulls" were Herring Gulls, and that was that as far as ordinary bird-watchers were concerned. It was, nevertheless, obvious that those in southern Europe looked different from the ones breeding in the north-west – but then, so did those in North America, others in the Middle East, and still more in northern or central Asia. It is still not entirely certain how many of these variations represent local races or different species, but the Yellow-legged Gull has clearly emerged as a separate species in its own right. In Britain, the Netherlands, and France this is a regular, indeed increasing visitor. Most arrive after the breeding season, but a few remain all winter. Superficially, they look like Herring Gulls, but with practice they are easily picked out. Summer adults are really handsome birds, their relatively dark backs and strong leg and bill colours most striking in a good view. In some towns they are tame, but in many Mediterranean areas they are rather sparse, not so easy to approach and difficult to see well in the prevailing heat shimmer over sandy beaches, estuaries, and salt pans.

FEEDING
Like the Herring Gull this species takes fish, offal, and all manner of other material, feeding extensively on refuse tips.

DISPLAY AND VOICE
Their displays are like those of the Herring Gull, with some details more like those of the Lesser Black-backed Gull. Their calls resemble the Lesser Black-back's, with a deep, guttural, nasal quality. The long call is faster, longer, and more guttural than a Herring Gull's.

BREEDING
They breed in colonies, usually on rocky islands and much less often on buildings or other man-made structures than Herring Gulls. The nest is a similar shallow dish or pad of grasses but may be much more scanty, or absent altogether. Two or three eggs are incubated for 27–31 days. The chicks fly when 35–40 days old.

MIGRATION
After breeding a proportion of the population evidently moves north, reaching North Sea coasts and penetrating central Europe along major rivers. This pattern seems to have developed since the 1970s, prior to which the species was more or less sedentary. Populations in Morocco are still resident all year round, and elsewhere in the Mediterranean many remain throughout the year.

Adult male
Head white, variably marked with soft streaks around and behind the eye in late summer and autumn, but strikingly white in winter; legs rich yellow.

Juvenile (below)
Solid dark tertials with pale tips; whitish head; dark back; blackish bill; some darker-chested like Lesser Black-backed Gull.

Wingtips of adult female shorter than male's, but still a long-winged bird.

Some juveniles obvious rusty-brown.

Fourth year
Like adult, but often has black bill ring.

Second year
Grey on back, still much dark brown on wings; legs pinkish.

First winter
Head pale, streaked; dark, neat tailband and pale rump; dark bill; much grey on back; dark tertials.

Third year
Legs yellowish.

WHEN SEEN

All year; in North Sea area mostly August to November.

WHERE SEEN
Breeds coasts of Spain, Portugal, S France, Italy, Balkans; also locally N Italy, Switzerland, Romania, Bulgaria.

HABITAT AND INFO

SIMILAR SPECIES
Herring Gull is very alike but usually has pink legs.

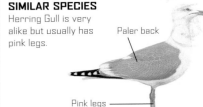

Paler back

Pink legs

Adults in Portugal show grey primary coverts beneath wing.

Juvenile
Darker underwing than Herring Gull's; neat tailband often edged white.

Striking white rump, dark band on tail.

Juvenile
White head; dark upperwing with weak paler patch behind bend of wing (more like Lesser Black-backed than Herring Gull).

Second winter
Still marked tailband; plain grey back same shade as adult's.

Third winter
Blackish wingtips show little white; some dark on tail.

Upperparts darker than British race of Herring Gull; obviously paler than Lesser Black-backed Gull's.

Wings long, narrower than Herring Gull's; held flatter.

Male (right) longer-tailed than female (left).

Adult (right)
Typically large areas of white on outermost two primaries give big wingtip patch; white tips wear off in summer leaving extensive black.

Black/grey wing contrast much stronger than Lesser Black-backed Gull's.

DID YOU KNOW?

Only many years of study, plus lobbying by bird-watchers, persuaded taxonomists that this bird should be separated from the Herring Gull as a distinct species. The situation is remarkably complex, with different races of "yellow-legged" gulls in various parts of Europe, including a small race in western Iberia and a darker one on the Atlantic islands.

Herring Gull

LENGTH / 55–64cm (21½–25in)
WINGSPAN / 1.3–1.6m (4¼–5¼ft)
WEIGHT / 0.75–1.2kg (1¾–2½lb)

■ STATUS / Secure

SCALE v Pigeon

One of the most familiar gulls, white-headed in summer but streaked in autumn and winter, with a pale grey back, black-and-white wingtips, and pale pink legs. Northern birds are bigger and darker-backed, but with less black in the wing.

To most of us this bird is the quintessential "seagull": yet it is a controversial and complex species with a range of variations that leave scientists (and bird-watchers) in disagreement and confusion. One way to treat the species complex in Europe is to separate the Yellow-legged Gull (chiefly of the Mediterranean) as *Larus michahellis*, and a more eastern form, the Caspian (or Steppe) Gull, as *Larus cachinnans*, leaving the pink-legged birds breeding in northern and western Europe as "Herring Gulls". The situation is more complicated than this, however, especially once the variety of forms breeding in Asia and wintering through the Middle East, into Africa, and eastward to south-east Asia are taken into account. In Europe, the Scandinavian race *argentatus* is bigger than the race *argenteus* of Britain and Iceland. They mix in winter, the most extreme examples being quite strikingly different. Herring Gulls as seen in summer beside the sea in Britain and most of north-western Europe are big, bold, noisy birds. In seafront towns, they wake people at an unearthly hour with their calls, frighten children by swooping down to steal their sandwiches, and make a mess over buildings, statues, and parked cars. Yet on sea cliffs these dramatic birds add immeasurably to the coastal atmosphere with their strident calls and mastery of flight. In winter, hundreds roost on reservoirs far inland.

FEEDING
Herring Gulls eat whatever they can get, on beaches, at fish quays, on the promenade, on refuse tips, from ploughed fields and pastures, and along built-up estuaries. Fish, earthworms, small mammals, eggs, grain, and waste human food are all eaten with relish.

DISPLAY AND VOICE
Gull displays are complex. The most familiar is the "long call", given as the head is bowed deeply, then raised with bill wide open. Aggressive displays involve standing upright with the bill pointed down and wings pushed away from the body. Birds also peck at the ground or tug at grass stems. The calls include the long, loud, clear, yelping *au-kyee-kau-kau-kau-kau-kau-kau-au-ow*, a barked *gagagag*, and an explosive, yelped *kyow*!

BREEDING
Nests are grassy pads on rock ledges, islets, or roofs. Three eggs hatch within 28–30 days and the young fly at about five weeks old.

MIGRATION
Northern birds move south and west in winter.

First summer *argenteus*
Pale, but still marked over head and chest, little clear grey above; tertials markedly pale, unlike Yellow-legged Gull's; bill pale at base.

Second summer *argenteus*

Scandinavian race *argentatus* (below) is immaculate in summer, but head and chest dark in winter (detail); big, thick bill largest on male.

Juvenile *argenteus*
British race: small, pale, lacy buff feather edges on back; pale base to bill; notched tertials.

Juvenile *argentatus* (above)
Scandinavian race: big; bulky; broad white tertial tips.

Adult *argentatus* (above right)
Bigger, bulkier than *argenteus*; back darker; broader white tertial tips, more white, less black at wingtip (exceptionally much reduced); legs greyish-pink.

Adult *argenteus*
Smaller than *argentatus*; neat, pale silvery-grey, wingtips with much black, bold white spots (white tips wear off in summer).

Second summer/ third winter *argenteus*
Rate of development toward adulthood varies.

Adult, winter *argenteus*
Some are much more heavily clouded and streaked grey-brown.

WHEN SEEN

All year.

WHERE SEEN
Breeds Iceland, coasts of Norway, widely Sweden, Finland, Baltic states, locally Germany; North Sea coasts, Britain, Ireland, NW France; winters south to N Spain.

HABITAT AND INFO

SIMILAR SPECIES
Juvenile Lesser Black-backed gull is darker, with darker bands on upperwing; darker tail; blacker bill base.

Blacker bill

Darker wing coverts

Second summer
argentatus

Juvenile
Mottled rump and
tail base blend into
tailband; pale patch
behind angle of wing.

Brown on juvenile fades
to creamy-buff in late
spring to summer;
pale patch on inner
primaries often obvious.

Juvenile
Pale underwing,
especially behind
bend of wing.

BROWN JUVENILE
Young gulls are much browner than the
adult birds.

Adult *argenteus*
Small, pale, sharp
wingtip contrast.

Third year
Retains traces
of immaturity.

Adult *argentatus*
Big, broad-winged;
some enormous
compared with
small *argenteus*.

Adult flight feathers
much paler from
below than Lesser
Black-backed Gull's.

Race *argentatus* has
smaller band of grey-
black under wingtip,
sometimes reduced
almost to nothing;
large white tips to
outer primaries.

DID YOU KNOW?

Herring Gulls often drop shellfish onto a hard surface to crack them
open: a risky strategy, as other gulls will swoop in to try to steal the
food. It seems that the bird that drops the shell has an advantage
through being able to predict the place where it will land more
accurately, giving it a good chance to retrieve its meal.

?

Great Black-backed Gull

LENGTH / 64–78cm (25–30½in)
WINGSPAN / 1.5–1.7m (5–5½ft)
WEIGHT / 1–2.1kg (2¼–4¾lb)

■ **STATUS /** Secure

SCALE v Pigeon

The biggest gull, always thickset and heavy-billed, it is typically pale-headed and contrasted at all times. Previously it was mostly coastal, but increasing numbers winter inland in Britain.

The largest of the world's gulls, the Great Black-back is a fearsome, yet handsome bird. The adult is one of the most contrasted of the gulls, really black-and-white in fresh plumage. Immatures are boldly chequered, but often best distinguished by their size and especially the weight of their bills. The Great Black-backed Gull has a more restricted breeding habitat than the more widespread Herring Gull. Where nesting, Herring Gulls are often numerous along the upper edges of sea cliffs on wide, grass-fringed ledges or steep crags, Great Black-backs are typically more scattered, with each pair occupying some prominence, such as the top of an offshore stack, or the end of a rocky promontory. Pairs may nest on ledges or even on flatter ground, but their first choice is a more obvious feature – as befits the biggest, most dominant of the gulls. Outside the breeding season they move to all kinds of shores, including harbours and flat, sandy beaches. Many go inland: in England the numbers at winter roosts on reservoirs greatly increased in the late 20th century as more birds took advantage of the food available on refuse tips. In some areas, Herring Gulls did this much earlier but then declined, so Great Black-backed Gulls now outnumber them.

FEEDING
Great Black-backs kill many more birds and animals than most other gulls. Some specialize in taking Puffins, or various shearwaters and petrels, at their breeding colonies. They kill Manx Shearwaters on the ground, but grab Puffins by the neck in mid-air. In winter, they may even attack wildfowl. They eat a lot of fish, and large flocks follow trawlers, seizing discarded fish and offal. They also scavenge for all kinds of dead animal matter and scraps on beaches and at rubbish tips.

DISPLAY AND VOICE
Their displays resemble those of the Herring Gull. Calls, however, are mostly distinctive, with a deep, barking, throaty quality. A deep, abrupt bark, *aouk*, is frequent, as is a throaty *uh-uh-uh*.

BREEDING
The nest is a mound of seaweed, grass, and other vegetation, usually placed on top of a rock outcrop or offshore stack, or beside some prominent feature on the cliff edge. The 2–3 eggs are incubated for 27–28 days. The young are able to fly when 7–8 weeks old.

MIGRATION
Northern breeders move south-west in winter.

First winter
Massive bill blacker at first, paler by spring; upperparts very chequered.

Second summer
Black back; wings develop black at varying rate.

Third winter

Second summer bird has all-black wingtips and black saddle, but brown wing coverts, fading paler, and white tertial tips.

Birds with larger white tip to wing probably male.

Adult female, summer
Very black (fades browner); legs pale pink to whitish.

Adult, summer

Third/fourth summer
Near-adult has dark billband; uneven wing colour.

Adult, winter
Head much whiter than most Lesser Black-backs'.

WHEN SEEN

All year.

WHERE SEEN
Breeds on coasts of Iceland, Ireland, Britain, Sweden, Norway, Denmark, Finland, locally NW France.

HABITAT AND INFO

SIMILAR SPECIES
Lesser Black-backed Gull is smaller, greyer, smaller-billed; has yellow legs.

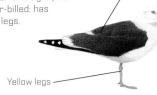

Paler back

Yellow legs

Juvenile
Dark back (paler, more chequered in first winter); dark trailing edge to wing, slight pale "window" beyond the bend of the wing; quite narrow tailband broken at basal edge.

Looks large and long-winged in flight, with protruding head, obvious heavy bill, and deep belly; wings often markedly arched.

Second summer
White head and body; blackness of saddle useful clue; some black wing coverts appear; dark band on yellow bill.

Third summer
Wings become blacker with white spots at tip; tail whiter.

Adult, summer
Large white wingtip spots.

Adult, summer
Bright white head and body; much dark grey under flight feathers.

DID YOU KNOW?
Many people realize gulls are likely to take whatever they can, alive or dead, but the predatory nature of this giant species is not so widely appreciated. Some live on smaller seabirds, from auks to shearwaters, all summer, and they are capable of the occasional capture of birds such as Teals and Coots on wetlands in winter.

Lesser Black-backed Gull

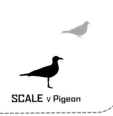

LENGTH / 52–64cm (21–25in)
WINGSPAN / 128–148cm (50–58in)
WEIGHT / 650–1,000g (23–35oz)

■ **STATUS /** Secure

SCALE v Pigeon

A large gull, white-headed in summer, with a mid-grey to dark grey or black back, black-and-white wingtips, red-spotted yellow bill, and bright yellow legs when adult.

A Lesser Black-backed Gull in early summer is a beautiful bird by any standards, its slate-grey back contrasting with its immaculate white head and underparts, and set off by yellow legs and a really vivid, waxy yellow bill. These gulls are less attractive in their feeding habits, however, since they kill a great many smaller seabirds, including Puffins, Manx Shearwaters, and Storm Petrels. Lesser Black-backs like to breed on flatter ground than Herring Gulls, on moors and on the tops of broad islands. In south-west Wales, they nest on islands that are clothed in drifts of bluebells and red campion: surely some of the most beautiful seabird colonies anywhere in the world. In the past, nearly all the British breeders of the western European race *graellsii* migrated to Africa in winter, but since the mid-20th century more and more have been remaining in Britain all year. They are probably encouraged by the greater availability of food inland, especially at refuse tips, combined with the security of safe night roosts on reservoirs. Scandinavian birds of the race *fuscus* – now proposed as a separate species, the Baltic Gull – move south-east in winter and are rare in western Europe at any time. A third group, *intermedius*, which breeds in Denmark and the Low Countries, is relatively frequent in Britain and France.

FEEDING

Fish form a large proportion of their diet, but Lesser Black-backs take other seabirds in summer where they are available. At other times they forage widely for all kinds of animal and vegetable food, and often scavenge from refuse tips.

DISPLAY AND VOICE

Their displays are generally like those of the Herring Gull, but their calls have a throaty, sometimes strangled but typically deeper quality. These deep calls are easily identifiable in winter at a mixed roost. In spring, the long call is often heard from birds migrating over land, or loafing about near feeding sites.

BREEDING

Lesser Black-backs typically nest on the ground, often in vegetation, but increasingly they nest on roof tops. Three eggs hatch after 24–27 days. The chicks fly at 30–40 days old.

MIGRATION

Most Lesser Black-backs are migratory, but in Britain many now remain inland all winter.

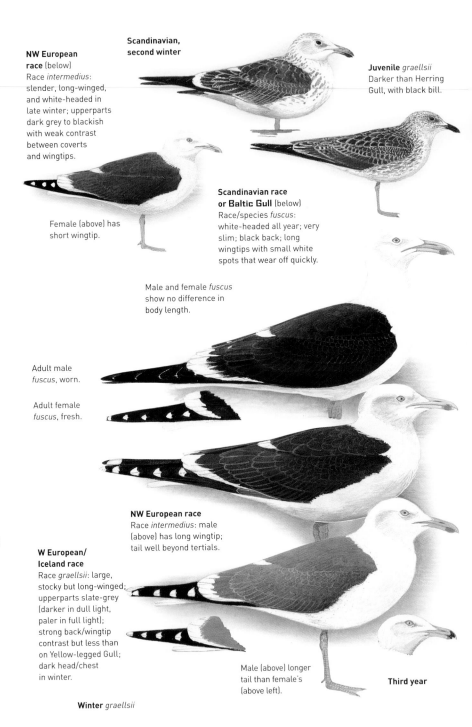

NW European race (below)
Race *intermedius*: slender, long-winged, and white-headed in late winter; upperparts dark grey to blackish with weak contrast between coverts and wingtips.

Scandinavian, second winter

Juvenile *graellsii*
Darker than Herring Gull, with black bill.

Female (above) has short wingtip.

Scandinavian race or Baltic Gull (below)
Race/species *fuscus*: white-headed all year; very slim; black back; long wingtips with small white spots that wear off quickly.

Male and female *fuscus* show no difference in body length.

Adult male *fuscus*, worn.

Adult female *fuscus*, fresh.

NW European race
Race *intermedius*: male (above) has long wingtip; tail well beyond tertials.

W European/Iceland race
Race *graellsii*: large, stocky but long-winged; upperparts slate-grey (darker in dull light, paler in full light); strong back/wingtip contrast but less than on Yellow-legged Gull; dark head/chest in winter.

Male (above) longer tail than female's (above left).

Third year

Winter *graellsii*

WHEN SEEN

All year; in N Europe, summer only.

WHERE SEEN

Breeds locally Iceland, widely throughout Scandinavia and Russia, locally N Germany, Low Countries, NW Ireland, and mostly N and W Britain.

HABITAT AND INFO

SIMILAR SPECIES

Yellow-legged Gull is paler above; much more contrasted black wingtips.

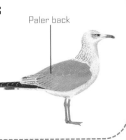

Paler back

Contrasted wingtips

DUSKY HEAD
Winter plumage is characterized by a streaked head and neck.

First year *fuscus*
Dark tail, whiter rump; all-dark flight feathers (unlike Herring Gull's); all-dark greater coverts, alula, primary coverts.

First year *graellsii*
Underwing.

Adult *intermedius*
Underwing of all three forms has darker flight feathers than Herring Gull's or Yellow-legged Gull's.

First year *graellsii*
Longer tail than *fuscus*'s, with less black; pale tips to greater coverts, alula, and primary coverts.

Upperwing of first-year bird lacks pale inner primary patch of Herring Gull.

Female *graellsii* has shorter tail (inset).

Adult male *graellsii*
(right)

Note wingtip contrast on adult *graellsii* (left) compared with *intermedius* (right); both darker than Yellow-legged Gull's.

Adult *intermedius* (right)
Broader wings than *graellsii*'s.

Adult *fuscus* (right)
No wingtip contrast; wings long and slender; compare larger Great Black-backed Gull, which has broad wings with much more white at tip.

DID YOU KNOW?
With Herring Gulls, Lesser Black-back Gulls have colonized many city roofscapes in recent years, including unexpected places such as railway station canopies far inland. In the UK, a mixed colony has reached almost 2,500 pairs, more than 2,000 of them Lesser Black-backs. The early-morning noise and mess have frequently caused controversy and calls for elimination of the gulls.

?

Common Tern

SCALE v Pigeon

LENGTH / 31–35cm (12–14in)
WINGSPAN / 82–95cm (32–37in)
WEIGHT / 90–150g (3¼–5¼oz)

■ STATUS / Secure

A typical grey sea tern with black cap in summer, it is greyer than Roseate and Sandwich Terns. It is fractionally broader-winged and shorter-tailed than the Arctic Tern, with a longer head and longer bill.

Terns are generally smaller, neater, more streamlined, longer-winged, and longer-tailed than gulls. The *Sterna* terns, which include the Common and Arctic Terns, are distinguished by pale grey wings, paler grey underparts, long, streamered white tails, and jet black caps in summer. Their bills are sharp and red, their legs very short. Near the sea, Common Terns like shallow lagoons in sandy or shingly places, or even quite small shingle beaches. Inland they have increased in recent years by colonizing flooded gravel pits with gravelly or sandy islands. In central Europe, they nest on riverside shingle. In places, they mix with Arctic Terns, but are typically not such northerly birds, less associated with rocky islands off wild coasts.

FEEDING
Although they often eat crustaceans or insects, Common Terns are essentially fish-eaters, catching them after a headlong plunge from the air and bringing them to the surface to swallow them. The plunge is often preceded by a Kestrel-like hover. Inland, Common Terns frequently feed on tiny fish fry or insects scooped from the surface, diving much less than they do at sea.

DISPLAY AND VOICE
Common Terns are colonial breeders. Pairs may be seen flying high over their territories in beautifully synchronized flight, swaying from side to side. Males often feed fish to females during the egg-laying period. Their calls are mostly harsh, with an irritating screechy or rasping quality, mostly slightly lower than the calls of an Arctic Tern. A grating *kee-yah* (the emphasis on the first syllable) is distinctive; also *kek-kek* and *karrr*. Yet whole colonies may suddenly fall silent and fly away in what is known as a "dread".

BREEDING
The 2–3 eggs are laid in a bare, shallow scoop in sand or shingle, or often now on specially provided rafts. The eggs hatch after 21–22 days. The chicks fly when they are 25–26 days old.

MIGRATION
Common Terns move south in autumn, becoming quite widespread inland and around many coasts where they do not breed. They spend the winter in Africa, chiefly off the west coast. A few fly round the Cape and head north along the east coast of Africa.

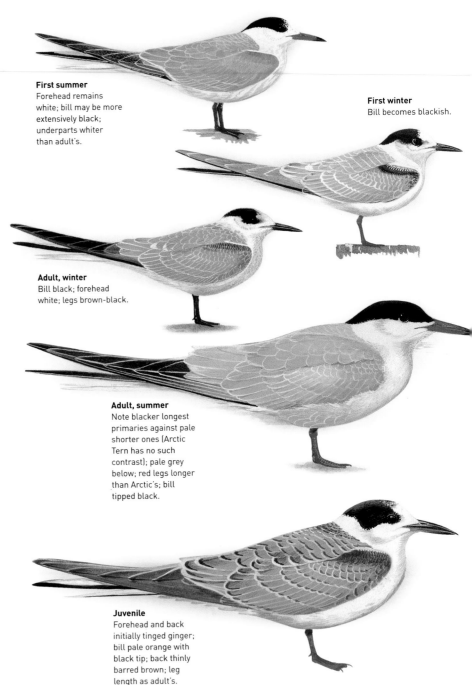

First summer
Forehead remains white; bill may be more extensively black; underparts whiter than adult's.

First winter
Bill becomes blackish.

Adult, winter
Bill black; forehead white; legs brown-black.

Adult, summer
Note blacker longest primaries against pale shorter ones (Arctic Tern has no such contrast); pale grey below; red legs longer than Arctic's; bill tipped black.

Juvenile
Forehead and back initially tinged ginger; bill pale orange with black tip; back thinly barred brown; leg length as adult's.

WHEN SEEN

Oct — March

March to October.

WHERE SEEN
Widespread on all coasts except Iceland on migration. Breeds locally inland and around coasts of Ireland, Britain, Norway; most of Sweden and Finland east into Russia; south locally to Mediterranean, but rare in Iberia.

HABITAT AND INFO

SIMILAR SPECIES
Arctic Tern is greyer below but paler on narrower, more tapered wing; see-through flight feathers.

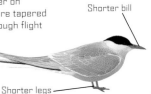

Shorter bill

Shorter legs

Juvenile
Rump pale grey in centre; hindwing grey (midwing paler); forewing blackish; underwing like adult's.

Adult, summer
Outer primaries darker than inner ones; often a small dark wedge on fourth/fifth outermost (compare Arctic Tern).

Compared with Arctic Tern, head/bill projects more, tail less; longer inner wing ("arm") and shorter outer wing.

Underwing shows broad, slightly diffuse, dusky tips to outer primaries; only inner few primaries look translucent.

Cap rather flat; bill scarlet or orange-red with black tip.

DID YOU KNOW?
Like the quite different Hobby, Ringed Plover, and Tufted Duck, the Common Tern has benefited greatly from the spread of flooded gravel and sand pits in lowland areas. These provide the low-lying islands that offer secure breeding sites, but terns inland seem to eat more aquatic insects than their fish-eating counterparts on the coast.

?

Arctic Tern

LENGTH / 33–35cm (13–14in)
WINGSPAN / 80–95cm (31½–37in)
WEIGHT / 80–110g (2¾–3¾oz)

■ **STATUS /** Secure

SCALE v Pigeon

The most delicate and lightweight sea tern, with very pale, clean wings, and a very long tail. Its rounded head and short bill project much less than the Common Tern's.

While the Common Tern is slim and elegant, the Arctic Tern is even more so: it is beautifully turned out at all times, shorter in the bill but longer in the tail, and has long, slender, attenuated wingtips. Arctic Terns are generally far less common inland, although a number visit reservoirs on migration (sometimes even large flocks for a few hours in spring). They like rocky islets and lonely, undisturbed shingle or sand beaches, especially on more remote coasts. In spring and autumn, small numbers can be identified moving past headlands or pausing on low-lying coasts south of their breeding range. Since they spend the summer so close to the Arctic and the winter at sea in the Antarctic, these terns are said to experience more constant daylight than any other species.

FEEDING
Small fish such as sandeels form the staple diet of Arctic Terns. In some years, the fish supply is limited, probably because of overfishing by trawlers, and large numbers of Arctic Tern chicks starve in the nest. In these circumstances, the adults turn to crustaceans; they survive but they rear fewer young. They catch fish in vertical dives, each tern usually just immersing itself and rarely going deeper.

DISPLAY AND VOICE
Displays are very much like those of the Common Tern. The voice may be useful, since most calls are higher in pitch. A sharp alarm note, *keearr*, with the emphasis on the second rather than the first syllable, is most characteristic. Other notes include a scolding *kit-it-it-aarr* and a squeaky *kee* and *peet*. Scolding notes should be taken seriously, as Arctic Terns at their colony are quite capable of striking an intruder's head and drawing blood.

BREEDING
Up to three eggs are laid on the ground, in sand or shingle, or in a small depression on a rocky island. They are incubated for 20–24 days. The young fly at 21–24 days old.

MIGRATION
In autumn, small numbers visit lakes and reservoirs inland, often staying a little later than Common Terns. In spring, scores or even hundreds appear at such sites in occasional "rushes". In winter, Arctic Terns move south along the west African coast and then on to the Antarctic pack ice. In summer, some breed on islands far to the north of the Arctic Circle.

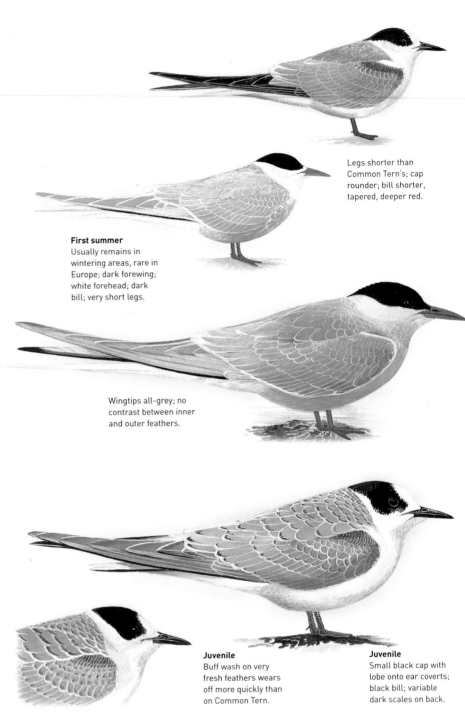

Legs shorter than Common Tern's; cap rounder; bill shorter, tapered, deeper red.

First summer
Usually remains in wintering areas, rare in Europe; dark forewing; white forehead; dark bill; very short legs.

Wingtips all-grey; no contrast between inner and outer feathers.

Juvenile
Buff wash on very fresh feathers wears off more quickly than on Common Tern.

Juvenile
Small black cap with lobe onto ear coverts; black bill; variable dark scales on back.

WHEN SEEN

April to November.

WHERE SEEN
Breeds Iceland, Spitsbergen and other Arctic islands, Faeroes, Scotland, Ireland, very locally England; many more inland in N Scandinavia; also Baltic and North Sea coasts south to Low Countries.

HABITAT AND INFO

SIMILAR SPECIES
Juvenile Common Tern has longer bill, neck, and head; longer legs; darker grey hindwing bar.

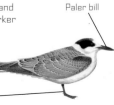

Paler bill

Longer legs

Juvenile
Rump white; hindwing has triangle of very pale grey and white, paler than midwing; forehead pure white; bill black, at most only slight deep red at base.

Adult, summer
Outer wing all pale grey with no contrast between feathers; wingtip long, drawn into thin, tapered tip; inner wing ("arm") shorter than Common Tern's.

Long tail streamers; very white rump; back silvery; underside grey, leaving narrow white cheeks; round black cap; short, spiky, blood-red bill.

Common   Arctic
First summer upperwings.

Underwing at all ages very white with a long, tapered, sharp dark grey line along primary tips; all flight feathers translucent.

Body greyer than Common Tern's, but beware variations of light and shade.

DID YOU KNOW?
As the temperature of the North Sea rises with climate change taking effect, so the plankton that live in cold water move north, and, with them, the sandeels that eat the plankton. This has removed the food from the terns, with a disastrous effect. Some colonies that used to have 2,000 successful breeding pairs have reared no young birds in recent summers.

Roseate Tern

LENGTH / 33–38cm (13–15in)
WINGSPAN / 75–80cm (29½–31½in)
WEIGHT / 95–130g (3½–4½oz)

■ STATUS / Endangered

SCALE v Pigeon

Typically extremely pale, recalling Sandwich Tern, but with red on the bill for much of the year, relatively long red legs, and very long white tail streamers in spring. Its flight is slightly stiff-winged and fast except during graceful display.

Unaccountably rare throughout its large world range, this is a superb tern. It is ghostly pale, especially in summer when the pink of spring has faded to leave its underside gleaming white. It is a marine species, and exceptionally scarce inland.

FEEDING
Dives for fish after a rapid hover, almost flying into the water.

DISPLAY AND VOICE
The extraordinarily long tail feathers look wonderfully elegant in the slow-winged, springy display flights. The tern also raises them in displays on the ground. By contrast the calls are harsh: a deep, grating *aahrk* and a sharper, bright *chu-vee*, often used around colonies.

BREEDING
Nests are often hidden in long vegetation on rocky islets. At some colonies these rare terns are also provided with nest boxes as a conservation measure. The 1–2 eggs are incubated for 21–26 days.

MIGRATION
The western European population spends the winter off west African coasts.

Underwing differs from that of Common or Arctic Tern's: thin black line on leading edge but no complete dark trailing edge to wingtip; white lines along feathers reach to the tip.

Adult
Upperwing pale except for black on outer two or three feathers.

Juvenile
Dark bar on secondaries; rather plain outer wing; underwing as adults.

Wingtip darkens as summer progresses.

Adult, early summer
Long tail; bright pink flush; dark bill; note long legs.

Adult, summer
Bill gains more red by late summer.

Adult, winter

Juvenile
In August.

Juvenile has bright buff feather edges over whole upperparts; by autumn departure back is plain grey but wings remain the same.

First winter
Juvenile replaces bar feathers with grey.

Fresh juvenile
All-dark forehead; dark bill and legs; scaly back.

SLENDER SEABIRDS
Roseate Terns look slim, long-legged, and long-billed on the ground.

WHEN SEEN
Oct
April

In W Europe from April to October.

WHERE SEEN
Very few colonies in the Irish Sea, Brittany, NE Britain; rare elsewhere and very rare inland.

HABITAT AND INFO

SIMILAR SPECIES
Common Tern is darker grey below; bill usually with more red, less black.

Darker grey

Shorter tail

278

Gull-billed Tern

A relatively stocky, long-winged, short-billed, long-legged tern. In summer, its smooth, rounded black cap and all-black bill are distinctive. In winter, it looks extremely pale despite its grey rump and variable grey or black eye-patch.

LENGTH / 35–38cm (14–15in)
WINGSPAN / 76–86cm (30–34in)
WEIGHT / 200–250g (7–9oz)

■ STATUS / Vulnerable

SCALE v Pigeon

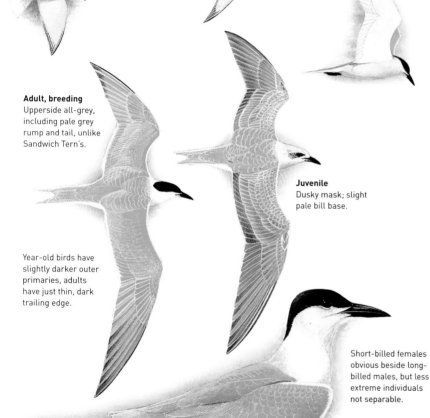

Adults, breeding
White below; black cap and bill; male has longer bill than female's and juvenile's.

Adult, winter
Extremely pale.

Adult, breeding (below)
Typical side view of foraging bird: can look quite dumpy, yet very slender from other viewpoints.

Adult, breeding
Upperside all-grey, including pale grey rump and tail, unlike Sandwich Tern's.

Juvenile
Dusky mask; slight pale bill base.

Year-old birds have slightly darker outer primaries, adults have just thin, dark trailing edge.

Male

Short-billed females obvious beside long-billed males, but less extreme individuals not separable.

Adult, breeding
May look quite grey when standing; note black legs, thick bill, deep chest.

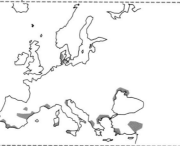
SMOOTH CAP
The thick bill and rounded black cap distinguish this species.

Unlike most terns, Gull-billed Terns feed mainly over pastures and marshland, as well as on shallow lagoons near the coast, and are less likely to be seen fishing.

FEEDING
They take insects, lizards, even voles and small chicks from other birds. In winter, they migrate to the plains of east Africa, where they forage around the great herds of grazing wildebeest, gazelles, and zebras.

DISPLAY AND VOICE
Displays are much the same as those of other terns, but the calls are distinct: a nasal *chuvek* and a croaking *kway kway kway*.

BREEDING
Small breeding colonies are widespread through the Mediterranean region. The nests are hollows on the ground on grassy banks and dunes near coastal lagoons or estuaries; less often on open beaches. The 2–3 eggs are incubated for 22–23 days.

MIGRATION
European birds move south into Africa from August to October and return in March and April.

WHEN SEEN

Oct — March

March to October.

WHERE SEEN
Mostly freshwater and brackish marshes and wet meadows around the Mediterranean, also interior of Spain; only a vagrant in NW Europe, usually on the coast.

HABITAT AND INFO

SIMILAR SPECIES
Sandwich Tern has longer black bill with pale tip; longer, whiter tail.

Slim bill
White rump

Sandwich Tern

LENGTH / 36–41cm (14–16in)
WINGSPAN / 95–105cm (37–41in)
WEIGHT / 210–260g (7½–9oz)

■ **STATUS /** Vulnerable

SCALE v Pigeon

A large, long-winged, dagger-billed tern: angular, lively, and expressive compared with smaller terns. Beside Common or Arctic Terns, it looks extremely pale, with much brighter white underparts. Black legs and bill are useful clues.

This is the largest tern in most of Europe (Gull-billed Terns are much more restricted and the huge Caspian Tern is mostly very rare). It is a rather lanky, angular, bony-looking tern – but its pale plumage, set off by a black crest and a long, spiky, black bill, give it a refined, clean, and handsome character. It is a lovely bird when seen close up, especially early in spring when it is at its best, with a full black cap. (It is also one of the first welcome signs of summer.) At long range over the sea it has a whiteness that marks it out from the greyer Common Tern, and because of its fishing technique – a faster dive from a greater height giving a bigger splash as it plunges headlong into the sea – it can often be discerned right out on the far horizon. Its extra whiteness is perhaps less obvious on a sunny day, when all gulls and terns tend to gleam in the bright light reflected from the sea, but on a dull day it can shine out from the gloom.

FEEDING
It catches mainly small fish, especially sandeels, sprats, and herrings, after a vertical plunge into the sea.

DISPLAY AND VOICE
Its displays are much like those of other terns, involving pursuit flights over the nesting colony and posturing on the ground. It often crosses its angular wings over its raised tail, pushing their joints out from its body at the shoulders, while raising its head and expanding its pointed crown feathers into a spiky crest. During courtship males feed females with fish, both to cement the pair bond and to give her much-needed extra nutrition to build a clutch of large eggs. Calls are harsh, loud, far-carrying, and characteristically rhythmic, including *kier-ink* and *kirrik*.

BREEDING
Sandwich Tern colonies are notoriously fickle, the birds deserting easily if disturbed and moving from place to place in different years. They usually nest on dunes, or sandy or shingly islands in coastal lagoons; some contain hundreds of pairs. The nest is a mere scrape. The 1–2 eggs hatch in 21–29 days and the chicks fledge in 28–30 days. Adults are aggressive, but fall easy prey to foxes, hedgehogs, even badgers, and predatory birds.

MIGRATION
In spring, they arrive in Europe early, often in March, but most birds move south back to west Africa in August and September. Occasionally, one or two are seen in winter in south-west Europe, or rarely in Ireland, Britain, or the Netherlands.

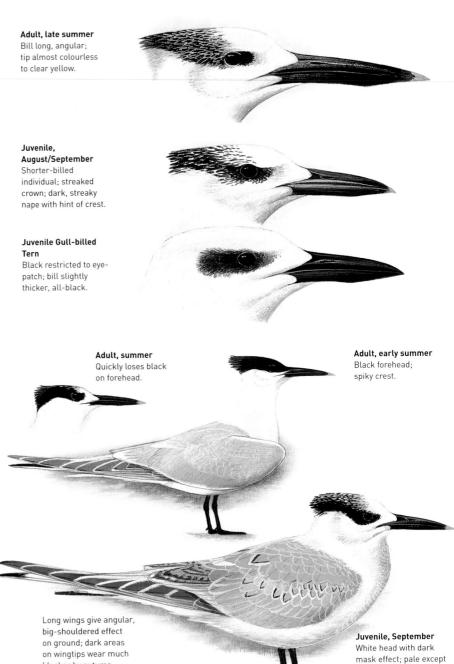

Adult, late summer
Bill long, angular; tip almost colourless to clear yellow.

Juvenile, August/September
Shorter-billed individual; streaked crown; dark, streaky nape with hint of crest.

Juvenile Gull-billed Tern
Black restricted to eye-patch; bill slightly thicker, all-black.

Adult, summer
Quickly loses black on forehead.

Adult, early summer
Black forehead; spiky crest.

Long wings give angular, big-shouldered effect on ground; dark areas on wingtips wear much blacker by autumn.

Black legs at all ages and seasons.

Juvenile, September
White head with dark mask effect; pale except for dark outer wing, darker hindwing and dark corners to tail.

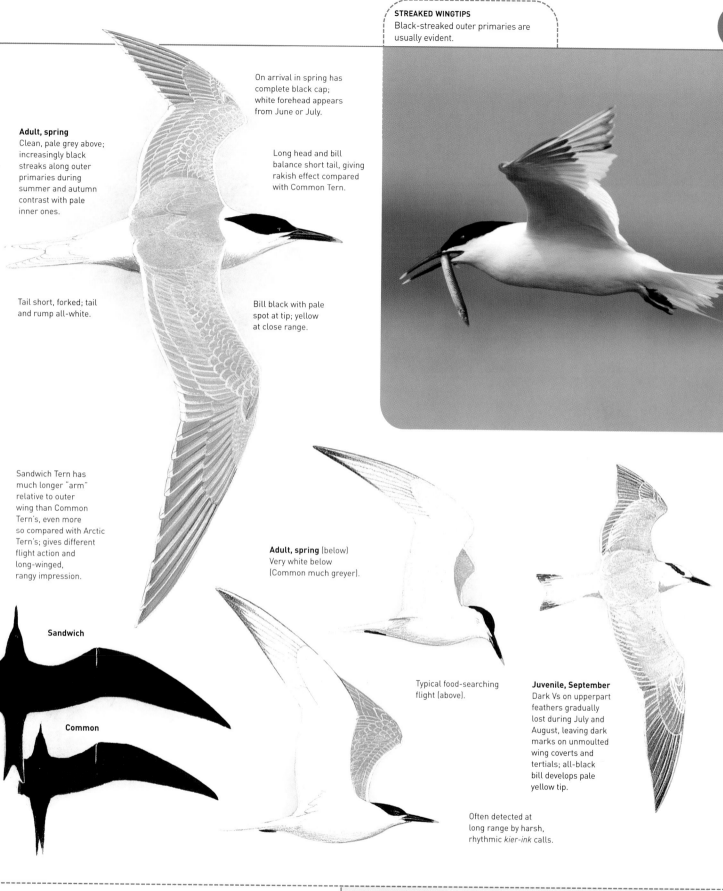

Adult, spring
Clean, pale grey above; increasingly black streaks along outer primaries during summer and autumn contrast with pale inner ones.

On arrival in spring has complete black cap; white forehead appears from June or July.

Long head and bill balance short tail, giving rakish effect compared with Common Tern.

Tail short, forked; tail and rump all-white.

Bill black with pale spot at tip; yellow at close range.

Sandwich Tern has much longer "arm" relative to outer wing than Common Tern's, even more so compared with Arctic Tern's; gives different flight action and long-winged, rangy impression.

Adult, spring (below)
Very white below (Common much greyer).

Sandwich

Common

Typical food-searching flight (above).

Juvenile, September
Dark Vs on upperpart feathers gradually lost during July and August, leaving dark marks on unmoulted wing coverts and tertials; all-black bill develops pale yellow tip.

Often detected at long range by harsh, rhythmic *kier-ink* calls.

DID YOU KNOW?
This species has a vast range, from the Americas to the Indian Ocean, and migrates over great distances. Yet its English name is based on its discovery in 1784 in Sandwich, Kent, in south-east England. The Dartford Warbler and Kentish Plover (no longer a breeding bird in Britain) have equally inappropriate Kentish names.

Black Tern

SCALE v Pigeon

LENGTH / 22–24cm (8³/₄–9¹/₂in)
WINGSPAN / 63–68cm (25–27in)
WEIGHT / 50–75g (1³/₄–2³/₄oz)

■ **STATUS /** Vulnerable

A small, delicate, short-legged tern, with a fine, spiky bill, round head, and long wings. In spring, its sooty-black appearance is obvious. In autumn, its dark shoulder smudge is characteristic.

The three small *Chlidonias* terns are often called "marsh terns" because they are associated with shallow, reed-fringed freshwaters, overgrown lake shallows, riversides, and similar wetlands far more than with the open waters and coasts frequented by the *Sterna* terns. They have an easy, lazy flight over such places, quite distinct from Common Terns. On migration, however, Black Terns are just as frequent on large reservoirs, where groups of 10, 20, or sometimes a few hundred may appear in spring and autumn. They also pass by coastal headlands over the sea. In winter, they form flocks, fly faster, and even hover more, resembling Common Terns in their behaviour. They are nevertheless delicate birds, usually dipping to the surface rather than diving for food (but migrating Common Terns, Arctic Terns, and Little Gulls do this, too).

FEEDING

In summer, they eat mainly insects and small aquatic creatures, but on migration and in winter they turn to fish. They typically feed in groups, flying head-to-wind, rising and falling – but not hovering – between swoops to the surface to snatch food in their bills. Black Terns also catch insects in the air like overgrown Swallows.

DISPLAY AND VOICE

In spring, groups of pairs fly over the breeding colony in a high, jerky flight followed by a downward glide, in which the leading pair are followed at a distance by the rest. Males feed females with fish once they are paired. Calls are relatively quiet and simple, with a slight squeaky quality: *kik-kik*, *teek-teek*, and *teeuw*.

BREEDING

The birds breed in colonies of perhaps 20–30 nests together at the edge of a marsh, often close to (but not mixed with) other species of tern or Black-headed Gulls. The nests are built on floating vegetation or heaps of weed. They are little more than piles of damp waterweed. The 2–4 eggs are incubated for 21–22 days.

MIGRATION

Black Terns winter in Africa. In autumn, huge numbers gather in the Netherlands before moving south over the sea; adults move a month or so before juveniles. Many stop at inland reservoirs and lakes for a few days. In spring, the northward movement tends to be more urgent and some cross the Sahara direct rather than going around to the west. Large groups that arrive at reservoirs may be gone within a few hours. Black Terns may migrate at night, at a considerable height, as well as by day.

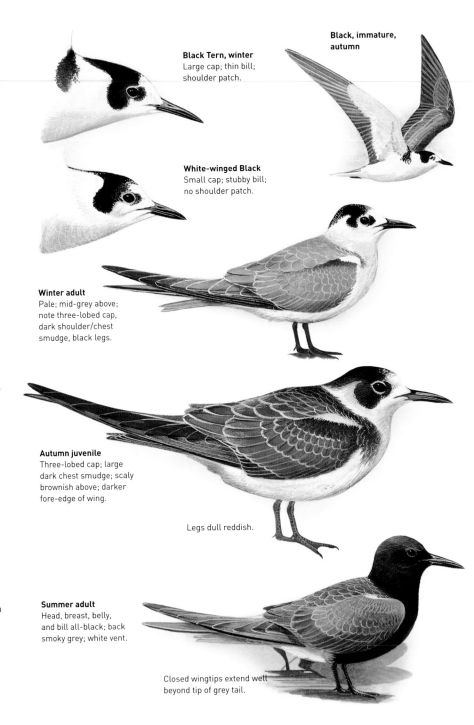

Black Tern, winter
Large cap; thin bill; shoulder patch.

Black, immature, autumn

White-winged Black
Small cap; stubby bill; no shoulder patch.

Winter adult
Pale; mid-grey above; note three-lobed cap, dark shoulder/chest smudge, black legs.

Autumn juvenile
Three-lobed cap; large dark chest smudge; scaly brownish above; darker fore-edge of wing.

Legs dull reddish.

Summer adult
Head, breast, belly, and bill all-black; back smoky grey; white vent.

Closed wingtips extend well beyond tip of grey tail.

WHEN SEEN

Oct — April

April to October.

WHERE SEEN
Breeds very locally south from S Sweden and Finland, most in E Europe; commoner south of Baltic than in Mediterranean region; widespread migrant.

HABITAT AND INFO

SIMILAR SPECIES
Juvenile White-winged Black Tern has paler inner wings and dark back giving saddle effect; white breast sides.

Dark back

White rump

Autumn juvenile (right)
Front edge of wing dark; washed brown above; rump pale grey; tail grey, only slight fork.

Summer adult
(above and right)
Smoky grey above includes tail; black on head and body; bright white undertail.

MARSH SPECIALIST
Shallow floods and extensive marshlands are necessary habitats.

Black, immature, autumn

Whiskered, immature, autumn
Scaly saddle; no white collar; rump normally grey; odd individual with white rump.

White-winged Black, breeding
White tail and forewing.

FLIGHT PATTERN
Flight is buoyant, erratic, sometimes rising high over water before departure, returning in fast, sweeping dive.

DID YOU KNOW?
Black, Whiskered, and White-winged Black Terns are collectively known as "marsh terns" and in parts of Europe and Africa may be seen over the same marsh or lake. The complexities of their juvenile, transitional, and winter plumages offer identification challenges that are soon removed by the appearance of their striking and distinctive breeding plumages in spring.

White-winged Black Tern

LENGTH / 20–23cm (8–9in)
WINGSPAN / 50–56cm (19½–22in)
WEIGHT / 60–80g (2–2¾oz)

■ STATUS / Vulnerable

SCALE v Pigeon

A small tern, slightly chunkier, dumpier, and less graceful than the Black Tern to the experienced eye. It has a slightly stouter bill, steeper forehead, and longer legs.

In summer, the adult White-winged Black is a really stunning tern. In western Europe, it is a rare visitor to shallow floods, swamps, and reed-fringed lakes, often among flocks of commoner Black Terns. These exciting finds are typically autumn juveniles: a spring adult is a real treat.

FEEDING
The tern picks insects and tiny fish from the water surface.

DISPLAY AND VOICE
Courtship displays are similar to those of Black Terns. The calls are more slurred, less piercing. The *kerr*, *keek*, or *kek* alarm notes are rarely heard outside the breeding season.

BREEDING
Like the Black Tern, it breeds in waterside colonies, often close to those of other water birds. The nests are built on floating weed, less often on the solid shore. The 2–3 eggs are incubated for 18–22 days.

MIGRATION
Most breeders move south through the Balkans in autumn, to winter in Africa (often in large flocks on east African lakes). They pass back through eastern Europe in spring.

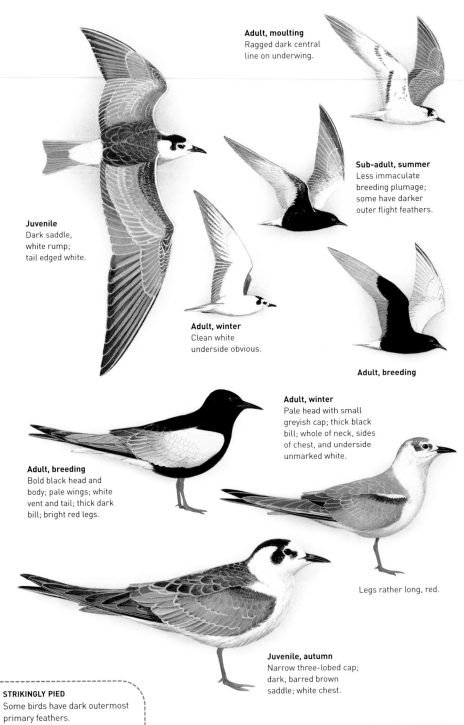

Adult, moulting Ragged dark central line on underwing.

Sub-adult, summer Less immaculate breeding plumage; some have darker outer flight feathers.

Juvenile Dark saddle, white rump; tail edged white.

Adult, winter Clean white underside obvious.

Adult, breeding

Adult, breeding Bold black head and body; pale wings; white vent and tail; thick dark bill; bright red legs.

Adult, winter Pale head with small greyish cap; thick black bill; whole of neck, sides of chest, and underside unmarked white.

Legs rather long, red.

Juvenile, autumn Narrow three-lobed cap; dark, barred brown saddle; white chest.

STRIKINGLY PIED Some birds have dark outermost primary feathers.

WHEN SEEN

Oct
April

April to October.

WHERE SEEN
Breeds E Europe, rare west to Poland; regular in very small numbers west to Britain, mostly in autumn.

HABITAT AND INFO

SIMILAR SPECIES
Juvenile Whiskered Tern is bigger, duller, less contrasted once brown back moults to grey; greyer rump.

Scaly back

Long legs

Whiskered Tern

The largest of the marsh terns, but still remarkably light, buoyant, and elegant. Its broader wings and relatively shorter tail give it a distinctive appearance in flight.

LENGTH / 23–25cm (9–9¾in)
WINGSPAN / 57–63cm (22½–25in)
WEIGHT / 70–80g (2½–2¾oz)

■ **STATUS /** Vulnerable

SCALE v Pigeon

Of the marsh terns, this is the largest. It is also the most like a Common or Arctic Tern in appearance and behaviour, especially in winter or juvenile plumage. It breeds in warmer regions than either of the black terns, in marshy areas with plenty of shallow, still water and the mats of floating vegetation that it needs for nesting.

FEEDING
It picks insects and small fish from the water surface in a slow, swooping flight, head-to-wind.

VOICE
Whiskered Terns are more vocal than Black Terns, with louder, more rasping calls at the colony: *kyick*, *cherk*, and a strident *kerch*.

BREEDING
The nest is small heap of vegetation anchored to reeds or rushes. The 2–3 eggs hatch after 18–20 days' incubation.

MIGRATION
Whiskered Terns spend the winter in west Africa. They are rarely seen inland once the central European breeders have migrated south-west along major rivers.

Whole upperside pale grey; lack of white collar helps identify it.

Winter

Summer

Summer

Winter

Breeding adult, summer
Black cap; white throat; grey underside almost black on belly.

Bill relatively long and thick.

Large cap; rear crown broadly black; central crown slightly streaked.

Compared with Arctic and Common Tern in winter (unlikely in Europe), grey (not white) short tail, shallow fork, and no white collar.

Autumn juvenile
Back ginger-brown with scaly black bars and white fringes; quickly becomes more uniform grey.

Legs reddish, long.

STRIKING CHEEKS
White on the throat and cheeks contrasts with the black cap.

WHEN SEEN

Oct
April

April to October.

WHERE SEEN
Very local across Europe south of the Baltic, most occur in Iberia and E Europe; rare vagrant north of this range.

HABITAT AND INFO

SIMILAR SPECIES
Arctic Tern has white rump and tail; simpler black nape pattern; very short legs.

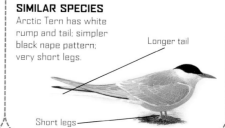

Longer tail

Short legs

Little Tern

LENGTH / 22–24cm (8³⁄₄–9¹⁄₂in)
WINGSPAN / 48–55cm (19–21¹⁄₂in)
WEIGHT / 50–65g (1³⁄₄–2¹⁄₄oz)

SCALE v Pigeon

■ **STATUS /** Endangered

A small, dynamic tern with fast, flickery wing beats. It has a white forehead at all seasons and is identified by a yellow bill when adult.

The smallest, nimblest, fastest tern, the Little Tern looks too small and delicate for a seabird, yet it flies with a determination and energy that fit it well for its life over inshore waters, and for its long migrations at sea. When nesting it is particularly attracted to shingle beaches right at the edge of the waves, and prone to having its nest and eggs washed away by high tides, or buried in windblown sand. It also needs protecting from disturbance on popular holiday beaches.

FEEDING
It catches small fish in quick dives that end with a sharp smack into the waves.

DISPLAY AND VOICE
Little Terns make noisy display flights and posture beside the nest. Calls are typically quick, sharp, and harsh: *kirree-ik kirree-ik.*

BREEDING
The 2–3 eggs are laid on sand or shingle, rarely on old concrete buildings or rafts.

MIGRATION
Many gather on estuaries in autumn before heading for Africa.

Tail fork varies: longer on breeding males.

Flickering hover, looking down for fish, before dive.

Mainly silvery-grey above, always looks very pale.

Outer primary feathers make black wedge on wingtip.

Juvenile

Flies with fast action; dives hurriedly with loud smack into waves.

Juvenile
Black bill; mottled crown; dark forewing band and scaly upperpart pattern.

Non-breeding

Breeding

Yellow legs and bill (usually with black bill tip).

Small, short body, but long wingtips stretch well beyond tail.

Some adults lose black bill tip in summer.

YELLOW BILL
Extensive yellow on the bill identifies this small tern.

WHEN SEEN

Sept   April

April to September.

WHERE SEEN
Mostly low-lying W European and Mediterranean coasts, also inland in S and E Europe; on migration off estuary mouths, sandy beaches, shingle banks, rare inland.

HABITAT AND INFO

SIMILAR SPECIES
Common Tern is bigger; greyer below; red legs and bill.

Red on bill

Darker legs

Caspian Tern

A dramatic, red-billed tern with black legs, it is identifiable by its large size, stout bill, and black under the wingtips.

LENGTH / 47–54cm (18½–21in)
WINGSPAN / 96–111cm (38–44in)
WEIGHT / 200–250g (7–9oz)

■ STATUS / Endangered

SCALE v Pigeon

This very large tern approaches the size of a Lesser Black-backed Gull, although it stands lower and is less bulky. Its powerful bill and large size are usually very obvious, allowing immediate identification, but it can be overlooked at long range if there are no smaller species nearby for comparison. Its long, angular wings with prominent black patches under the tips give an almost Gannet-like impression.

FEEDING
These terns take fish in dramatic headlong dives. They fly from their offshore colonies to feed in fresh or brackish lagoons rather than the sea.

DISPLAY AND VOICE
Displays involve showing off the black cap and crest and large, red bill. Calls include several rasping notes, such as *kak-ra-racha*.

BREEDING
Colonies occupy remote or secluded islands. The nest is a simple scrape in the sand. The 2–3 eggs hatch after 20–25 days' incubation.

MIGRATION
Most spend the winter in Africa, migrating along the western European coast. Rarely seen in Britain.

First year has thin tailband.

Black underwing tip conspicuous.

Breeding

Juvenile has dusky tailband and orange bill.

Size of bill not always obvious in flight.

Juvenile

First year
Dark wing covert band; dark secondaries.

Striking, heavy red bill with blackish marks near tip.

First summer
Streaked cap; often dark bill tip.

Breeding
Adult has flat, bushy crest and black forehead until midsummer.

Adult, winter
Pale-streaked cap.

Black legs.

MASSIVE APPEARANCE
The large bill is in proportion to this big tern's heavy build.

WHEN SEEN

Oct
May

May to October.

WHERE SEEN
Scarce breeding bird on beaches and coastal marshes in the Baltic; rare migrant on most coasts.

HABITAT AND INFO

SIMILAR SPECIES
Common Tern is much smaller; smaller bill and shorter red legs.

Slimmer bill

Red legs

Little Auk

LENGTH / 17–19cm (6¾–7½in)
WINGSPAN / 40–48cm (15½–19in)
WEIGHT / 140–170g (5–6oz)

■ **STATUS /** Secure

SCALE v Pigeon

This is a round-bodied, narrow-winged, short-billed, black-and-white seabird. Although tiny, it rides out most winter storms. Prolonged gales bring some inshore and even onto inland lakes.

Although remarkably abundant around some far northern islands, Little Auks are usually scarce in the southern North Sea and much rarer still in the eastern Atlantic. Sometimes northerly gales bring much bigger numbers farther south in late autumn. They are tiny, round-bodied, small-winged relatives of the larger Puffin.

FEEDING
Little Auks dive easily and frequently to catch tiny crustaceans and occasional fish fry.

DISPLAY AND VOICE
Courtship displays involve much bowing and mutual head-wagging. Flocks form mass flights above breeding cliffs, and larger flocks call with prolonged, rippling trills. They also give these calls on the water and from cliff ledges.

BREEDING
Nests are high on cliffs. The single egg hatches after 29 days. The chick flies at 27–28 days old.

MIGRATION
Arctic breeding sites are occupied in April and May, and vacated in August. Oceanic wintering areas are mostly occupied by November.

Flight fast, low, rolling, plover-like.

White trailing edge to wing (absent on juvenile).

Underwing very dark with thin white bar.

Non-breeding

White tracery on shoulders.

Breeding
Face and throat black in summer.

Peculiar frog-like profile.

Non-breeding
Black face; white rear cheeks and neck in winter.

Looks squat, neckless when exhausted; more alert when fit.

Dives frequently, with flick of tail and wingtips.

DUMPY SEABIRD
Typically, this Little Auk swims with its head withdrawn.

WHEN SEEN

Oct — March

October to March.

WHERE SEEN
Arctic Ocean, North Sea.

HABITAT AND INFO

SIMILAR SPECIES
Puffin in winter has dusky facial disk; dark wing without white edge; bigger bill.

Bigger bill

Dark trailing edge

Puffin

A small, sharply black-and-white auk with a colourful triangular bill in summer.

LENGTH / 26–29cm (10¼–11½in)
WINGSPAN / 47–63cm (18½–25in)
WEIGHT / 310–500g (11–18oz)

■ STATUS / Vulnerable

SCALE v Pigeon

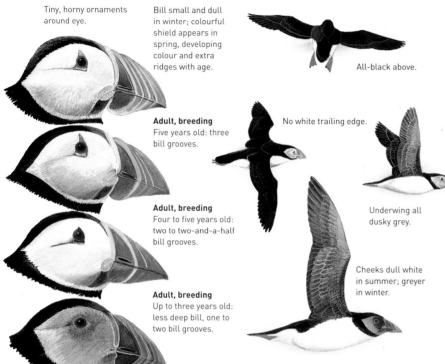

Tiny, horny ornaments around eye.

Bill small and dull in winter; colourful shield appears in spring, developing colour and extra ridges with age.

All-black above.

No white trailing edge.

Adult, breeding
Five years old: three bill grooves.

Adult, breeding
Four to five years old: two to two-and-a-half bill grooves.

Underwing all dusky grey.

Adult, breeding
Up to three years old: less deep bill, one to two bill grooves.

Cheeks dull white in summer; greyer in winter.

Adult, winter

Breeding

Cap silky black, often looks paler than back.

No white on back.

Most seabird colonies have some Puffins, but they are common only in the far north and west of Europe. For most of the year they live far out at sea.

FEEDING
They feed mainly on small fish, but also take crustaceans and other small marine creatures. They dive frequently to search for food, using their wings vigorously underwater.

DISPLAY AND VOICE
Most Puffin displays involve their big, colourful bills. Courting pairs attract the attention of nearby birds, which cannot resist joining in: they are the original nosy neighbours. Calls at the colony are deep growling and crooning notes.

BREEDING
Puffins nest in burrows or crevices in clifftop earth or fallen boulders, in a colourful world of sea campion, thrift, lichens, and blue sea. The single egg hatches after 39 days. The chick flies when about 38 days old. It will breed after five years at sea.

MIGRATION
The colonies are occupied from March to August or September. The birds then disperse to sea.

Juvenile/first winter
Grey-faced; small dark bill.

Swims buoyantly; rarely driven ashore in gales.

Vivid orange legs.

RITUALIZED DISPLAYS
Courtship and territorial displays follow rigid rules.

WHEN SEEN

Oct / March

October to March.

WHERE SEEN
Islands and mainland cliffs, Iceland, Britain, Ireland, Scandinavia, NW France; scarce offshore elsewhere; very rare waif inland.

HABITAT AND INFO

SIMILAR SPECIES
Little Auk is smaller; tiny blunt bill; sharper black-and-white face pattern; white on inner wing.

Tiny bill

Dumpy shape

Guillemot

LENGTH / 38–41cm (15–16in)
WINGSPAN / 64–73cm (25–28½in)
WEIGHT / 0.85–1.1kg (1¾–2½lb)

■ **STATUS /** Secure

SCALE v Pigeon

A sleek, elegant auk, the guillemot is brown above with a white front. It stands upright, resting on the full length of its leg; swims low with head raised, tail short and square; and flies fast with a whirring wing action.

Guillemots are individually fascinating, elegant creatures, but they are best seen *en masse* at the breeding colonies, where they add life, noise, and spectacle to a seabird cliff.

FEEDING
Guillemots catch fish in very deep dives, using their wings to "fly" underwater.

DISPLAY AND VOICE
Displays are relatively simple bowing and bill-fencing bouts, which reinforce pair bonds and confirm ownership of a tiny territory on a ledge. The calls at the nest are loud, whirring, rising growls.

BREEDING
Guillemots lay on open ledges on sheer cliffs, in the most precarious positions imaginable. A single egg is incubated for 28–37 days. The chick jumps from the ledge when barely half grown, encouraged and accompanied by a parent.

MIGRATION
The colony is occupied from March to August, then most move well out to sea, wintering from the Arctic south to Iberia.

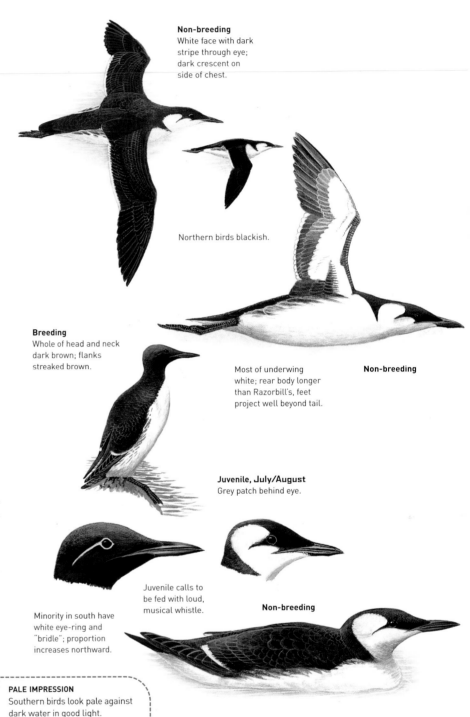

Non-breeding
White face with dark stripe through eye; dark crescent on side of chest.

Northern birds blackish.

Breeding
Whole of head and neck dark brown; flanks streaked brown.

Most of underwing white; rear body longer than Razorbill's, feet project well beyond tail.

Non-breeding

Juvenile, July/August
Grey patch behind eye.

Minority in south have white eye-ring and "bridle"; proportion increases northward.

Juvenile calls to be fed with loud, musical whistle.

Non-breeding

PALE IMPRESSION
Southern birds look pale against dark water in good light.

WHEN SEEN

All year.

WHERE SEEN
Breeds around coasts of Britain and Ireland, Iceland, Scandinavia, NW France, W Iberia; widespread offshore in winter; extremely rare inland even in autumn storms.

HABITAT AND INFO

SIMILAR SPECIES
Razorbill is blacker; more bull-necked, with thicker bill; longer, more pointed tail.

Pointed tail

Blacker back

Brünnich's Guillemot

A northern auk, it is heavier, thicker-billed and broader-winged than the Guillemot but hard to distinguish at sea.

LENGTH / 39–43cm (15½–17in)
WINGSPAN / 64–75cm (25–29½in)
WEIGHT / 810–1,200g (29–42oz)

■ STATUS / Vulnerable

SCALE v Pigeon

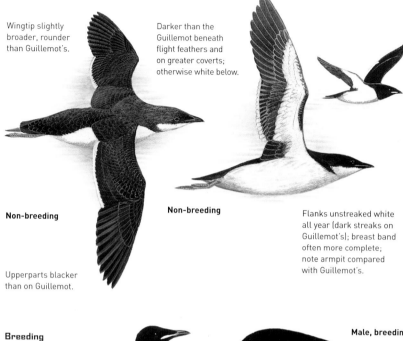

Wingtip slightly broader, rounder than Guillemot's.

Darker than the Guillemot beneath flight feathers and on greater coverts; otherwise white below.

Non-breeding

Non-breeding

Flanks unstreaked white all year (dark streaks on Guillemot's); breast band often more complete; note armpit compared with Guillemot's.

Upperparts blacker than on Guillemot.

Breeding
Thick white streak along gape in summer; white extends up throat as point (round on Guillemot's).

Male, breeding

Non-breeding

Guillemot

Thick white tips to secondaries; long tail extends well beyond wingtips.

Non-breeding
In winter, dark cap extends down to speckled cheeks, unlike Guillemot's with its whiter face and dark eye stripe.

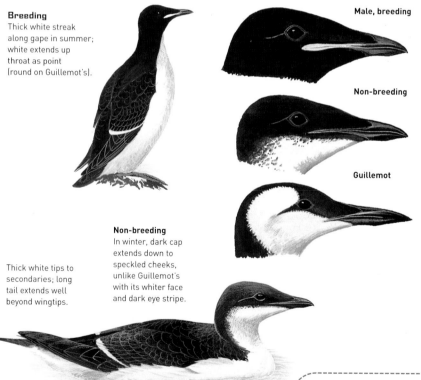

This is a northerly counterpart of the Guillemot, slightly larger and thicker-billed but similar and with much the same lifestyle. It breeds in huge, dense colonies on cliffs and otherwise spends its life at sea.

FEEDING
It catches fish and some marine invertebrates during deep dives from the surface, after searching for prey by swimming with its head held underwater.

DISPLAY AND VOICE
Its aggressive behaviour at nesting ledges is much the same as in Guillemots, but the pair-bonding activity is less obvious, with little bill-fencing and no upright, stretched poses adopted by pairs.

BREEDING
Brünnich's Guillemots nest on narrow ledges, but not the flat tops of sea stacks sometimes used by Guillemots. Some colonies total hundreds of thousands of pairs.

MIGRATION
Colonies are occupied from April to August. Otherwise the birds are at sea, mostly in the Arctic, in less saline water than Guillemots.

BOLD PATTERN
The clean half-dark, half-white body is sharply divided.

WHEN SEEN

All year; rare vagrant in NW Europe, mostly in winter.

WHERE SEEN
Breeds in Iceland, extreme N Norway and the Arctic; very rare elsewhere.

HABITAT AND INFO

SIMILAR SPECIES
Guillemot has slimmer bill without white streak; dark streaks on side.

Slim bill

Dusky flank

Razorbill

LENGTH / 37–39cm (14½–15½in)
WINGSPAN / 63–67cm (25–26½in)
WEIGHT / 590–730g (21–26oz)

STATUS / Secure

SCALE v Pigeon

A heavy-bodied, deep-billed auk that is black above, with a white front. The Razorbill stands upright on its full length of leg. It swims low, with head raised, tail pointed and often raised, and flies fast on short, whirring wings.

Razorbills are quite extraordinary seabirds, being among the deepest-diving birds in the world. They are usually less numerous than Guillemots at seabird colonies, where several species cram together to nest on the sheer cliffs.

FEEDING
Most of their food is fish, with a few other marine creatures. They usually catch several fish during each dive from the surface.

DISPLAY AND VOICE
Pairs indulge in bowing and preening, and also fly off the ledge in a beautiful downward flight with deep, slow beats of fully stretched wings. Their calls are gruff, rattling growls and short grunts.

BREEDING
They prefer more sheltered nesting sites than Guillemots, laying their eggs in cavities or crevices rather than open ledges. The single egg hatches after 36 days. The young flutters down to the sea after 18 days.

MIGRATION
Colonies are occupied from March to August or September.

Breeding

Non-breeding
Thick black cap to eye; black crescent on sides of neck and chest.

Shows narrow, dark rump with broad white sides in flight, like Guillemot's.

Underwing largely white; upperside black with obvious white trailing edge to inner wing.

Non-breeding

Most of underwing white; rear body shorter than Guillemot's; feet do not project beyond tail.

Breeding
Penguin-like form and colour on land; white line in front of eye.

Breeding

Juvenile
Stubby bill; dusky cheeks.

Breeding

Non-breeding

SEA CLIFF NESTER
Razorbills are usually in smaller numbers than Guillemots.

WHEN SEEN

All year.

WHERE SEEN
Breeds around Iceland, Scandinavia, Britain, Ireland, and NW France; in winter, south to W Mediterranean; more often in mouths of estuaries and shallow bays than other auks.

HABITAT AND INFO

SIMILAR SPECIES
Guillemot has more pointed bill; slimmer neck; shorter, squarer tail.

Pointed bill

Squarer tail

Black Guillemot

A stocky black-and-white seabird, it is usually seen
bobbing on waves offshore or flying low over the sea.

LENGTH / 30–32cm (11¾–12½in)
WINGSPAN / 52–58cm (20½–23in)
WEIGHT / 340–450g (12–16oz)

■ STATUS / Vulnerable

SCALE v Pigeon

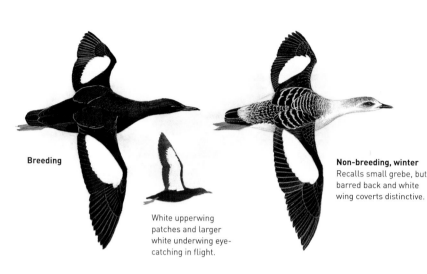

Breeding

White upperwing
patches and larger
white underwing eye-
catching in flight.

Non-breeding, winter
Recalls small grebe, but
barred back and white
wing coverts distinctive.

Immature

Juvenile

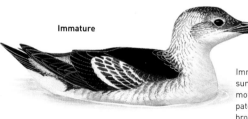

Juvenile dusky above,
white below, wing
patches barred; winter
adult cleaner, wing
patches white.

Immature

Immature in
summer has
mottled white
patch on
browner wings.

Breeding, summer
Unmistakable: smoky
black with oval white
wing patch; red legs.

Non-breeding, winter

While other guillemots breed on sheer cliff faces in large
colonies and may be seen floating on the water beneath the
cliffs in their hundreds, Black Guillemots are usually seen
in ones and twos near low, rocky islands, or in sheltered
bays along indented rocky shorelines.

FEEDING

They eat mainly fish in the south of their range, with more
marine crustaceans in the far north.

DISPLAY AND VOICE

The birds display using their red legs and mouths, and the
white wing patches above and below their wings. Pairs also
display on land by walking in an upright posture. They call
with a thin, shrill piping.

BREEDING

Nests are generally in crevices between boulders and
in scree slopes under cliffs. They are also under debris
such as driftwood and fish boxes.

MIGRATION

There is little southward movement in winter and all the
breeding areas remain occupied, although some birds
move well out to sea, even in Arctic waters.

SHORELINE CHARACTER
This bird is typical of rocky
coasts and islets.

WHEN SEEN

All year.

WHERE SEEN
Breeds from Ireland and
Scotland northward, and in
the Baltic; rare farther south.

HABITAT AND INFO

SIMILAR SPECIES
Guillemot has plain
dark upperwing;
browner above.

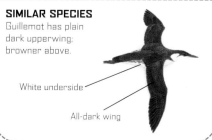

White underside

All-dark wing

Black-bellied Sandgrouse

LENGTH / 33–35cm (13–14in)
WINGSPAN / 60–63cm (23½–25in)
WEIGHT / 400–550g (14–19oz)

■ **STATUS /** Endangered

SCALE v Pigeon

Sandgrouse are fast-flying, long-winged, short-legged birds, somewhat dove-like but with complex, camouflaged patterns.

Arid or semi-arid steppe – poor pasture with areas of almost bare, dry earth and stones, rocky plateaux, and salt flats – is the preferred habitat of this localized bird. It is best seen in the morning when small flocks fly to lakes or even tiny pools to drink. Sandgrouse can tolerate extremely dry habitats, but they must have regular access to water, which they visit in a daily, rigid routine.

FEEDING
They pick seeds from the ground, or less often from the stems of plants, with a precise, pigeon-like action of the head and small bill.

VOICE
The flight call resembles that of a Turtle Dove or Black Grouse: a rolling or gurgling *ch-llll* or *churrr*.

BREEDING
The 2–3 eggs are laid in a bare or scantily lined hollow. They hatch after 23–28 days. The male brings water to the chicks by soaking his belly feathers in a pool. The chicks strip water from the feathers by drawing them through their bills.

MIGRATION
Resident.

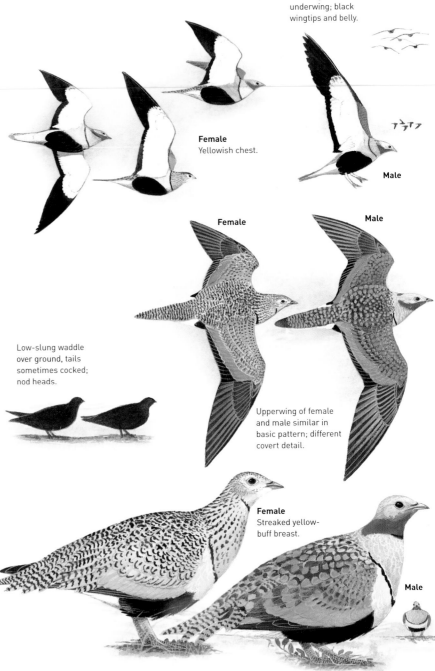

Flashing white underwing; black wingtips and belly.

Female Yellowish chest.

Male

Female

Male

Upperwing of female and male similar in basic pattern; different covert detail.

Female Streaked yellow-buff breast.

Male

Low-slung waddle over ground, tails sometimes cocked; nod heads.

BRILLIANT CAMOUFLAGE
Sandgrouse are always hard to see on the ground.

WHEN SEEN

All year.

WHERE SEEN
Locally in Portugal and widespread but scattered through Spain; also Turkey, Russia, N Africa.

HABITAT AND INFO

SIMILAR SPECIES
Pin-tailed Sandgrouse has white belly; long, pointed tail spike.

Long tail

White belly

Pin-tailed Sandgrouse

An exceptionally beautiful sandgrouse with a satin-white belly and long central tail point.

LENGTH / 31–39cm (12–15½in)
WINGSPAN / 55–63cm (21½–25in)
WEIGHT / 250–290g (9–10oz)

■ STATUS / Endangered

SCALE v Pigeon

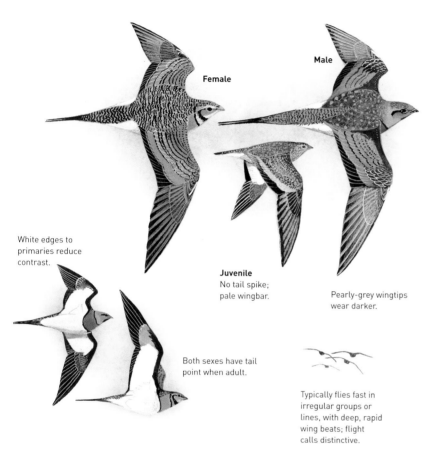

Female

Male

White edges to primaries reduce contrast.

Juvenile
No tail spike; pale wingbar.

Pearly-grey wingtips wear darker.

Both sexes have tail point when adult.

Typically flies fast in irregular groups or lines, with deep, rapid wing beats; flight calls distinctive.

Juvenile
Pale primary tips.

Female
Double black throat band.

Male
Unique pattern.

Juvenile (A) moults to barred pattern (B) like female's but without grey or head/breast pattern.

Non-breeding adults may have some barred feathers (B) above.

Although it may live on dry steppe like the Black-bellied Sandgrouse, the Pin-tailed Sandgrouse is often found on the dried-out edges of low-lying grassy marshland, on hard-baked mud flats and dunes, among scattered bushes, and on dry, flat arable fields. Where it is still common it gathers in larger flocks than the Black-bellied, sometimes of hundreds. These typically fly to their drinking sites in the morning, less often at dusk.

FEEDING
Virtually all its diet consists of seeds taken from the ground, supplemented by occasional green shoots and buds.

VOICE
Pairs may perform courtship flights at a great height. The flight call carries far, announcing the sudden arrival of a flock at a drinking pool: a slightly ringing *catarr-catarr*.

BREEDING
The 2–3 eggs hatch after 19–20 days, in an unlined nest on the ground, sometimes in a tuft of grass. The chicks fly when about four weeks old. Several pairs may nest close together, while others are solitary.

MIGRATION
Resident.

INTRICATE PATTERNS
The cryptic plumage is beautifully marked.

WHEN SEEN

All year.

WHERE SEEN
Rare S France; widely scattered but localized in Spain; also N Africa and Middle East.

HABITAT AND INFO

SIMILAR SPECIES
Black-bellied Sandgrouse is stockier, shorter-tailed; black belly.

Stocky shape

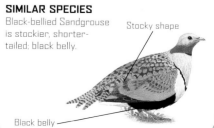

Black belly

Laughing Dove

LENGTH / 25–27cm (9³⁄₄–10¹⁄₂in)
WINGSPAN / 40–45cm (15¹⁄₂–17¹⁄₂in)
WEIGHT / 80–135g (2³⁄₄–4³⁄₄oz)

■ STATUS / Secure

SCALE v Pigeon

A rather dark, variable, pink-brown and slate-blue dove of extreme south-east Europe. It is long-tailed, round-winged. It may be very tame in towns, where often darkened by urban grime.

This is really a dove of the Middle East, Africa, and eastward through southern Asia, but it is a vagrant in the extreme south-east of Europe. In many places, it is extremely tame, even feeding beneath occupied tables at streetside tavernas. It is associated with cultivation, towns, and villages everywhere, but also lives in open woodland in quite wild regions.

FEEDING
It feeds in typical dove fashion, picking seeds, a few insects, spiders, small snails, and other such small items from the ground.

VOICE
Males identify their territory and attract mates with gliding display flights. Their call has a rolling, bubbling, laughing quality: *ha-ha-hoo-hoo-hoohoo-hoo*.

BREEDING
The nest is a frail, flat structure of twigs, typically in a tree or bush, but often on a building. Two eggs are incubated for 12–14 days. The squabs fly when two weeks old.

MIGRATION
Resident.

Compare plain red-brown back and blue-patched wings with paler (but chequered) Turtle Dove's; tail less white at tip than Turtle Dove's.

Flies on arched wings with jerky but rhythmic wing beats; flight swift and energetic, wings usually bent back and blunt.

Underwing very dark; belly, vent, and most of underside of tail pale grey to white.

Turtle Dove
Slimmer, with narrower wings.

Feeds inconspicuously on ground but may enter streetside cafes to forage under tables; open country individuals brighter than this.

Doves and pigeons shown to same scale (main and flight images).

Female
Male has more extensive black speckling on pink chest.

Juvenile
No necklace or half collar.

RUFOUS DOVE
An overall pinkish-rufous colour is characteristic of this small dove.

WHEN SEEN

All year.

WHERE SEEN
Istanbul; also N Africa and the Middle East.

HABITAT AND INFO

SIMILAR SPECIES
Collared Dove is paler, sandier; black base to tail.

Dark collar

Paler back

ORDER
Columbiformes

FAMILY
Columbidae

SPECIES
Columba livia

COMMON NAME
Rock Dove

Rock Dove

Pure north-west European Rock Doves are handsome birds with a white rump, white underwing, and two black bars across each wing. Domestic descendants (the basis of many feral populations) are varied, typically with a thicker bill and fatter white cere. Racing pigeons have longer head and neck, and swept-back wings are set farther back.

LENGTH / 31–34cm (12–13½in)
WINGSPAN / 63–70cm (25–27½in)
WEIGHT / 250–350g (9–12½oz)

■ **STATUS /** Secure

SCALE v Pigeon

The true Rock Dove is a handsome wild pigeon, but centuries of domestication, and the subsequent escaping of pigeons of varied form and colour back into the wild, have created a confusion of hybrid forms. The pigeons found in most areas are pretty much a mixture of domestic breeds, although those on coastal cliffs tend to revert to the true type. Only on wilder coasts and mountain ranges are pure Rock Doves still found.

FEEDING
They feed mainly on grain and smaller seeds, supplemented by a good deal of green matter such as shoots, buds, and soft leaves of herbs.

VOICE
Displays are the same as those of the familiar town pigeon, as is the call: a deep, moaning *ooorr* or *ooh-oo-oor*.

BREEDING
Rock Doves nest on cliff ledges in sea caves and high crags. Two eggs are incubated for 16–19 days.

MIGRATION
Resident.

Black wingbars, white rump.

Slim head.

Rock
Slim bill, tiny cere.

White underwing patch (unlike Stock Dove but like most feral pigeons); dark beneath tail.

Adult Rock Dove
Classically clean, pale grey with large white rump; black bar and trailing edge to inner wing; glossed neck with no white.

Domestic
Thick bill, fat cere.

BLUE ROCK
The wild rock dove has the basic "blue rock" pattern of domestic birds.

WHEN SEEN

All year.

WHERE SEEN
Locally N Scotland, Ireland, Iceland, Scandinavia, mountain regions; domestic pigeons gone wild established almost everywhere except much of Scandinavia.

HABITAT AND INFO

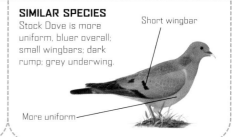

SIMILAR SPECIES
Stock Dove is more uniform, bluer overall; small wingbars; dark rump; grey underwing.

Short wingbar

More uniform

Stock Dove

SCALE v Pigeon

LENGTH / 32–34cm (12½–13½in)
WINGSPAN / 63–69cm (25–27in)
WEIGHT / 290–330g (10–11½oz)

■ **STATUS /** Secure

A rather large, compact, round-headed pigeon, often found with larger Woodpigeon but more like some domestic/feral pigeons. Its greyness, including underwing, is distinctive. It may flock, but is often in pairs.

While Woodpigeons are large, long-winged, broad-tailed, slim-headed birds, and usually abundant, Stock Doves are generally much less common and distinguished in flight by their smaller size, shorter wings and tail, and rounder heads. They are more likely to be mistaken for feral pigeons, but their much greater partiality to trees (especially when roosting) is a helpful guide. Feral (and especially racing) pigeons tend to look longer-necked, and have more swept-back wings. Stock Doves are not just woodland and farmland birds: they also like cliffs and crags, inland rather than at the coast, and they often occupy quarries. They fly out with a noisy clatter if disturbed. Lowland farms with plenty of trees and woodland edges are typical places for Stock Doves, especially where there are old trees with big holes for nesting in. The birds move out from the trees to feed on open fields. They often mix with Woodpigeons, Rooks, and Jackdaws, but sometimes form pure flocks of a few scores.

FEEDING
Their main foods are seeds, leaves, shoots, and buds. Stock Doves feed in typical pigeon fashion on the ground, walking slowly or standing almost still as they forage. They prefer more or less bare ground and feed close to water, which they need for frequent drinking. They also take some food directly from trees.

DISPLAY AND VOICE
A displaying male will fly with slow, deep wing beats, clapping its primary tips together over its back. It then glides with spread tail and raised wings, often from tree to tree or circling back to the same perch. Its song is characteristic. It is deeper than a Woodpigeon's, simpler in pattern and repeated several times: a rhythmic, almost booming *ooo-rooh* or *ooo-er*.

BREEDING
The nest is built in a tree cavity, on a shady ledge on a cliff, or inside an old, derelict building. It is a scanty construction of a few twigs and stems, on which two eggs are laid. They are incubated for 16–18 days. The chicks fly when 20–30 days old.

MIGRATION
Western birds are resident. Northern and eastern populations (north of the Baltic and east from Denmark and eastern France) migrate south and west in winter.

Display glide with upward-angled wings unlike any other pigeon.

Midwing very pale when fresh but feathers wear much duller.

Bluish head; green on neck; dull pink chest.

Woodpigeon
Flatter glide profile.

Dull black tailband; white on tail sides.

Tiny dark bars at base of wing: compare Rock Dove or town pigeon.

Often rather upright on ground; small dark wing spots.

Woodpigeon (above)
To same scale as Stock Dove at left; more horizontal.

Long tail beyond wingtips in first year, until July; in adult male, wingtip almost reaches tail, which projects further in female.

Typically deep, bright coral-red legs.

Round blue-grey head with bold, dark eye; pale-tipped bill dark at base, no white.

WHEN SEEN

All year in west; March to October in N and E Europe.

WHERE SEEN
Breeds Ireland, Britain (except far N Scotland), S Finland, S and E Scandinavia, and most of mainland Europe; scarce in Mediterranean region and absent from most Mediterranean islands.

HABITAT AND INFO

SIMILAR SPECIES
Rock Dove is typically paler above, with bold black wingbars; white rump; whiter underwing.

Bolder wingbars

Usually glides in to land
with curved wings;
lands with flutter.

**Juvenile to
first summer**
Longer tail than
adult's; less stocky,
more like Woodpigeon.

Display begins with
deliberate flaps before
long, sailing, curving
glide up to 1km (½ mile)
long; slowly raises tail
on landing in a tree.

Woodpigeon
Note pot belly, longer
wings and tail.

White outer web
on tail shows best
when landing.

Stock Dove
Relatively slim, sleek,
with more bulbous
head; no white.

Woodpigeon
White on neck;
broad tailbands; long
wings, long head.

Stock Dove
Narrow, pale
central tailband.

Stock Dove
Dull black wingtip and
hindwing outline pale
midwing panel.

FLIGHT PATTERN
Typically glides on bent
wings, unlike Woodpigeon;
angled wings beat deeply
in normal flight.

DID YOU KNOW?
Nest sites are remarkably varied within the context of a hole- or
cavity-nester. They include holes in trees and the tangled suckers of
old trees to cavities in buildings such as church towers, between bales
in hayricks, ledges on the cliffs of quarries, inland crags and sea cliffs,
and rabbit holes at ground level. Others have nested deep
inside wells.

Woodpigeon

LENGTH / 40–42cm (15½–16½in)
WINGSPAN / 75–80cm (29½–31½in)
WEIGHT / 480–550g (17–19oz)

■ **STATUS /** Secure

SCALE v Pigeon

A big, striking, heavyweight pigeon with boldly contrasted wings. In flight, it appears heavy, deep-chested, small-headed, with long, rather broad wings and a broad tail. It flies up from ground or trees with a loud clatter. It may sweep upward, clap its wings, and descend in a shallow glide.

Woodpigeons evoke mixed reactions: most people probably ignore them or dismiss them as just "pigeons". Sometimes, even in town parks where they are tame, they are regarded as pests. To farmers – and to many gardeners – they are undoubted pests: the enemies of greens and young shoots. To anyone with an eye to see, however, they really are splendid birds. Close up, even on bird tables in some areas, they are beautiful creatures: plump and shiny, their plumage patterns full of subtle variations on basic blue-greys, brownish-greys, and soft pinks. Distant flocks may number hundreds, even thousands, making a welcome sight in many open farming landscapes where there are relatively few birds, or against a winter sunset as they fly off to roost. Where they are shot relentlessly, on farmland and in nearby woods where they roost, Woodpigeons are generally wild and understandably difficult to approach. In gardens and towns, they may become quite tame, always wary but daring to let people get close unless they are given a fright, in which case their fragile relationship with people explodes in a clatter of alarmed wing beats as they dash away.

FEEDING

Woodpigeons eat seeds, grain, shoots, leaves, acorns, and many kinds of berries.

DISPLAY AND VOICE

Rival birds may fight quite dramatically, with feathers and white down spilling from the trees, but their most obvious displays are the special flights over tree tops in their breeding areas. These involve a steady climb followed by a sharp wing clap and a shallow glide on spread wings. The Woodpigeon's song is a lovely, lazy, relaxing summer sound: a rhythmic coo, typically *cu-COO coo, coo-coo, cu-COO coo*.

BREEDING

Nests are shallow and flimsy, see-through platforms of sticks in hedgerows and scrubby trees. Two pure white, shiny eggs are incubated for 17 days. Their empty shells are often found later, dropped away from the nest by the parents. The young, or squabs, are fed on special "milk" – a secretion from the parent's crop. They fly after 20–35 days.

MIGRATION

Most British breeders are sedentary, moving around in winter to find the best sources of food. Some winter visitors from the Continent swell their numbers. In Scandinavia and eastern Europe, Woodpigeons are summer migrants. Large numbers migrate over southern Europe in September to October and April.

Broad body, narrow head.

When perched, small head and full chest obvious; quite long, broad, square tail.

Juvenile
Duller, smokier grey than adult with pale scaly feather edges; white on wing but not on neck; very young ones untidy, fluffy, weak-looking.

Adult
Well-fed adults look immaculate, smooth, glossy, and colourful with bright bill and eye; rich pink breast; back wears slightly browner.

WHEN SEEN

All year.

WHERE SEEN
In farmland and mixed woods, town parks, large gardens; almost all Europe.

HABITAT AND INFO

SIMILAR SPECIES
Stock Dove is smaller, dumpier, darker blue-grey overall; no white on wing.

No white on neck

No white on wing

STRIKING COLLAR
Adults have bold white patches each side of the neck.

Typically flies up with loud clatter.

Striking flash of white across wing always obvious and instantly identifiable.

Large, long-tailed; wings often slightly angled back to blunt, slightly indented tips; at full stretch, wings look long and quite straight, with slightly notched tips.

Stock Dove
Same scale as Woodpigeon above.

Tail with broad, whitish central band, the black tailband always obvious as bird flies off.

Display flight includes steep climb and stall, with sharp, snapped wing-clap.

FLIGHT PATTERN
As it flies up it twists sideways, then dashes off with deep, fast wing beats.

DID YOU KNOW?
Many people who feed garden birds resent the attentions of Woodpigeons, which eat vast amounts of expensive bird food given the chance. They have greatly increased in gardens and town parks in recent years and, in the UK, have become perhaps the most obvious birds in the countryside, being so large and intensely sociable at all times.

Collared Dove

LENGTH / 31–33cm (12–13in)
WINGSPAN / 47–55cm (18½–21½in)
WEIGHT / 150–220g (5¼–7¾oz)

■ **STATUS /** Secure

SCALE v Pigeon

A large, long-tailed dove, its small head and short legs are typically dove-like and delicate, and its wings are broad and curved back in flight. Generally pale and lacking in contrast, with greyer areas on wing, silky-grey underwings and wide, dull whitish band beneath tail tip.

This ordinary-looking dove – although with an appeal and refinement of its own when seen at close range – is actually one of Europe's most remarkable birds. From the 1930s, it spread north and west from the Middle East, crossing the whole of Europe within a few decades and reaching Britain in the 1950s. Its phenomenal expansion more or less stopped in the 1970s, but it is now one of the most widespread species in the UK. Much of Scandinavia and Spain are still Collared Dove free.

FEEDING

The dove's spread and subsequent increase in numbers throughout its new range was largely made possible by the availability of spilled grain around the places where grain is handled, from backyard chicken runs, farms, and stockyards to railway sidings and distilleries. Few such places now spill significant quantities of grain, and few people now keep hens in the suburbs, so Collared Doves tend to feed more in gardens, parks, and horse pastures. They eat a variety of small insects and vegetable matter, and in many areas they frequently feed at bird tables. In town parks and gardens, they are particularly tame and approachable.

DISPLAY AND VOICE

The most obvious displays are steeply-climbing flights and long, flat, circling glides. These develop into rapid chases between pairs with more frenetic calling. The song is familiar: a loud, hollow, rather quick triple coo. The emphasis is on the second note, with the third more clipped: *coo-COO-cuk*. Excited males call with their necks inflated and an exaggerated bobbing of the whole body. Their frequently-heard flight call is a slurred, nasal, or sometimes more rasping *kwurrr*.

BREEDING

The nest is a typical, flimsy, and lightweight dove platform of thin sticks. It is usually in a dense conifer or shrub. Two pure white eggs are incubated for just 14–16 days. The young fly at only 17–18 days old.

MIGRATION

A few are still seen in out-of-the-way places north and west of the main range, but most are resident. The reasons for the dove's initial spread are still not fully understood, since although suitable food made it possible, such food had been available for hundreds of years before the Collared Dove took advantage of it.

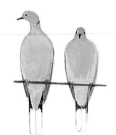

Looks slim and often erect when alert, but much more dumpy, small-headed when relaxed; frequently on wires, aerials, chimneys.

Spread tail reveals pale grey corners, lacking the white of Turtle Dove's.

Pale head and breast marked by thin, black, white-edged collar on adults; red eye often looks almost black.

Female
Face more buff than male's, but difficult to separate.

Male

Wingtips of female (above) reach almost to tip of tail coverts; those of male (below) fall short.

Juvenile is slightly scaly above with pale feather edges, and lacks dark collar.

WHEN SEEN

All year.

WHERE SEEN
Suburbs, farmland, pinewoods throughout Britain and Ireland except for most remote coasts and islands, mountains, and moors. From N Iberia to Norway, east throughout Europe and Middle East.

HABITAT AND INFO

SIMILAR SPECIES
Turtle Dove is spotted above; dark tail has narrower, more V-shaped white tip.

Chequered back

Narrow white band

Distinctive jerky, angle-winged flight action; loud flight call, unlike other doves and pigeons.

Upperwing shows little contrast, but blue-grey panel catches the eye in certain lights.

Wings broad, bent back toward tip, slightly rounded.

Silver-grey underwing, often looking very dark; characteristic pattern beneath tail.

Male

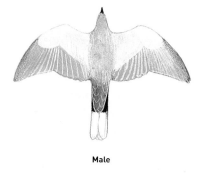

Male

These three views to scale with those of Turtle Doves (see pages 304–5).

Female

These three views to scale with those of Turtle Doves (see pages 304–5).

FLIGHT PATTERN
Frequently rises at steep angle, then sails in wide arc on depressed wings (compare with raised wings of Turtle Dove in display flight).

DID YOU KNOW?
The triple-note song is described as monotonous and unvarying, with the second note emphasized, rising slightly, and three times the length of the first. Yet careful attention reveals considerable variation, with different rhythms and emphasis and some strangled, strained, almost whining performances at times. Nevertheless, it remains highly distinctive and practically unmistakable throughout Europe.

?

Turtle Dove

LENGTH / 26–28cm (10¼–11in)
WINGSPAN / 47–53cm (18½–21in)
WEIGHT / 130–180g (4½–6½oz)

SCALE v Pigeon

■ **STATUS /** Vulnerable

Beautiful and delicate, this small, bright dove looks alert, quick, and lightweight. It spreads its tail on landing to reveal a broad, pure white band across the tip.

The Turtle Dove used to be a familiar and popular part of the English country scene, but for whatever reason – and probably there are several – the population has suffered a catastrophic decline. It has always been scarce or absent from most of Wales, Scotland, and Ireland. Indefensible spring shooting in southern Europe and France places excessive pressure on the diminished breeding population. There may also be problems in Africa, where the Sahel droughts of the 1960s and 1970s affected Turtle Doves, along with other species such as the Whitethroat and Sand Martin, and where pesticides might be doing damage now. There are also problems in England. These include the destruction of old hedges and especially the loss of farmland weeds: wild plants upon which many birds (not to mention insects) depend. As a result of all this, the Turtle Dove is now rather scarce, but its populations fluctuate; in favoured spots, there may still be small groups (often threes in summer, but larger flocks in late summer and autumn) to enjoy.

FEEDING
It eats mainly green shoots and seeds. In late summer, flocks of Turtle Doves may line overhead wires (sometimes mixed with Collared Doves) above the cereal fields, waiting to feed on the spilt grain after harvest.

DISPLAY AND VOICE
The display flight is similar to that of the Collared Dove but rather less obvious, and it ends in a glide on raised, rather than lowered, wings. The soporific summer song is a low, soft, purring coo: *toorrr toorrrr*. Like other pigeons, it has no alarm note or other call.

BREEDING
Typical nesting habitat is the edge of a mixed wood with dense shrubbery, or an old, overgrown, dense hedgerow with tall, spreading hawthorns and odd trees overwhelmed by tangles of ivy. A thin dish of fine twigs holds two pure white eggs. These are incubated for 13–14 days. The young birds fly when they are only 19–21 days old.

MIGRATION
Arrivals in spring reach north-west Europe in April and May. Flocks or small parties may be seen heading north along coastlines. They leave again between August and September, although occasional individuals hang on into winter. Turtle Doves spend the winter in west Africa.

Upperpart pattern more contrasted than Collared Dove's, with much richer colouring and brighter, bluer midwing panel.

Normal flight speed 95km/h (60mph); seems to fly at this speed wherever it goes.

Compare flight shapes and patterns with those of Collared Dove (to same scale on pages 302–3); wings taper to narrower tip, usually swept back.

Adult
Neck patch neatly striped.

Alarmed adults fly off with spread tails revealing white band.

WHEN SEEN

Sept — April

April to September.

WHERE SEEN
Typically in wooded farmland and tall hedgerows, England and E Wales; widespread in Europe except for Scandinavia and higher mountains.

HABITAT AND INFO

SIMILAR SPECIES
Collared Dove is plainer; longer tail has dark base, broad pale tip beneath.

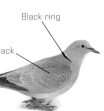

Black ring

Uniform back

Underside of tail largely white with narrow black base.

Unlike Collared Dove's flight; silent in flight.

Turtle Dove

Collared Dove
Display flight: note paler underwing, different tail pattern.

Adult
Crown grey; breast pink; much whiter belly than Collared Dove's; upperparts chequered.

Juvenile
Head grey' breast sandy, less pink than adult; upperside duller, less crisply marked; compare with plainer Laughing Dove in SE Europe.

FLIGHT PATTERN

Flies with occasional sideways rolls and flicked backward wing beats. Display flight ends with glide on raised wings.

DID YOU KNOW?

The French word, *tourterelle*, resembles the rolling purr of the Turtle Dove, which is altogether lost in the Anglicized version, turtle. It used to be an abundant species, with winter roosts of up to a million in west Africa, but desertification there, intensified agriculture in Europe, and centuries of undiminished shooting pressure in Mediterranean countries have seen a massive decline in recent years.

Cuckoo

LENGTH / 32–34cm (12½–13½in)
WINGSPAN / 55–65cm (21½–25½in)
WEIGHT / 105–130g (3¾–4½oz)

■ STATUS / Vulnerable

SCALE v Pigeon

Instantly identified by its unique call, yet unseen or unrecognized by many. It often perches on the side of a tree, fence post, or overhead wire. It resembles a small bird of prey in flight, but it flies with heavy, head-up, low-winged attitude.

It is remarkable how many people say that they frequently hear Cuckoos, but have never actually seen one. Yet they probably have seen one without knowing it, for Cuckoos are simply not recognized for what they are. They are not especially difficult to see. Indeed, they perch freely on open wires and on the outer twigs of tall trees, as well as on fence posts overlooking rough grassland, pastures, or marshy places. In summer, they need to find small birds' nests to parasitize, so they are often to be seen on bushy moorland looking for Meadow Pipits, beside marshes where they can find Reed Warblers, or near woods, hedges, and parks with breeding populations of small birds such as Wrens or Dunnocks.

FEEDING

The Cuckoo is unusual in that it eats hairy caterpillars, which are strongly distasteful or very irritating to small birds. It even expels much of its stomach lining periodically to rid itself of caterpillar hairs. It also eats a variety of other insects. It catches them on the ground or picks them off bushes, often after a steep dive from a perch.

DISPLAY AND VOICE

Cuckoos often droop their wings and raise and spread their tails in aggression to other Cuckoos, or in courtship when close to potential mates. The male's song is the familiar double note: *cuc-coo*, or *u-oo* at close range, given with the bill almost closed. It often becomes *cu-cuc-coo* and may sound remarkably hoarse from some birds. They call to each other with a low, quick dirty laugh sound, *kwak-ak-ak-ak*. Females have a quick, clear, throaty bubbling call with a remarkably liquid quality.

BREEDING

A female may lay 1–25 eggs. She watches small birds from a perch, or from overhead in open areas, until she locates a nest with fresh eggs. She then flies to the nest when it is left unguarded, removes an egg in her bill, and quickly lays one of her own directly into the nest (even into a difficult nest with a side entrance such as a Wren's nest in a cavity). The Cuckoo egg, incubated by its foster parents, hatches in 11–12 days. The chick devotes much energy to evicting the rightful occupants of the nest, hoisting both eggs and chicks to the nest rim and pushing them over the edge. The foster parents then feed it until it flies at 19 days old, by which time it is much bigger than they are.

MIGRATION

Cuckoos spend the winter in Africa, mostly south of the equator. Adults go south before the juveniles.

Adult female
Tinge of tawny-brown on chest.

Male often raises and fans tail when it lands, and looks from side to side.

Male, spring
Clean grey chest.

Juvenile
May be rufous type (below) or grey type (far below).

Juvenile, rufous type

Juvenile is heavily barred; broad bars beneath unlike Kestrel's, barred back unlike Sparrowhawk's.

Juvenile, grey type

Bold white spots on tail unlike hawks and falcons.

Juvenile has pale nape spot.

WHEN SEEN

Sept — April

April to September.

WHERE SEEN
Breeds throughout Europe except for Iceland and the northern tundra.

HABITAT AND INFO

SIMILAR SPECIES
Kestrel has narrow, square-tipped tail; shorter, squarer head; less triangular wings.

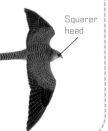

Squarer head

Squarer tail

Adult female, red phase
A rare form in Britain.

Juvenile

Adult

Flies with wings below horizontal; head looks thin, raised.

Pale band along midwing with dark patch each side in all plumages.

Female, first summer
Retains brown-barred inner flight feathers of juvenile.

Male, adult
Broad-based, pointed wings unlike Sparrowhawk's, grey unlike Kestrel's; thin head and curved bill.

Female has slightly shorter, blunter wing, but not distinguishable in field.

Male makes angry growling noises when approached.

FLIGHT PATTERN
Usually flies with shallow wing beats below the horizontal, almost quivering as it lands in a tree. Typical flight shapes: wings back, tail closed or fanned in diamond-shape, head raised.

DID YOU KNOW?
Cuckoos fresh from Africa in spring require an instant supply of nutritious food. They eat large, hairy caterpillars, giving their stomachs a furry lining. Climate change has affected the synchrony of caterpillar and Cuckoo, while intensified farming has reduced the number of moths and their caterpillars over vast areas of countryside, with a consequent dramatic decline in Cuckoo numbers everywhere.

Great Spotted Cuckoo

SCALE v Pigeon

LENGTH / 38–40cm (15–15½in)
WINGSPAN / 55–65cm (21½–25½in)
WEIGHT / 150–190g (5¼–6¾oz)

STATUS / Vulnerable

A large, rangy, long-tailed, southern European cuckoo, often difficult to watch.

This wonderful large, long-winged, long-tailed cuckoo is a bird of warm Mediterranean regions with heath, scrub, and scattered trees in which Magpies nest. It also likes olive and almond groves and cork oak, pine, or mixed woodland with plenty of open, airy, sunny spaces.

FEEDING
It favours hairy caterpillars but wipes off the hairs before eating them. It also catches and eats various other insects and spiders.

DISPLAY AND VOICE
A male has a dove-like display flight, rising quickly and gliding down. The pair then defend a territory that may contain up to 40 Magpie nests. The song is a chatter, becoming a gobbling sound: *kittera kittera kee-ow kee-ow -wow-wow-woh.*

BREEDING
The female lays one egg, occasionally 2–3, in the nest of a Magpie or other crow. Each female lays up to 18. The chick hatches after 12–14 days, and does not evict other eggs or chicks. It flies after 24 days.

MIGRATION
Most winter in Africa, south of the Sahara.

Adult
Long tail is characteristic; pale peachy flush on neck.

Juveniles and first winter birds have unique rufous primaries.

Flight quick, rolling, slightly laboured, small head raised.

First winter

Often a flight view is puzzling: this is a peculiar bird, unlike anything else.

Adult
Pale spots in rows across wing; grey outer wing.

Adult
All-grey crown; larger tail spots than juvenile's.

Adult

Some first winter birds have grey crown and mostly dark primaries, but usually retain a few rufous feathers.

Juvenile
Rufous on wing; black crown and cheeks.

ODD CUSTOMER
This species is often a bit of a puzzle at first sight.

WHEN SEEN

Feb
Sept

February to September.

WHERE SEEN
Breeds Portugal, Spain, S France, W Italy, very locally Balkans; rare vagrant outside this range, mainly in spring.

HABITAT AND INFO

SIMILAR SPECIES
Kestrel has squarer tail; much shorter head; narrower wings.

Narrow tail

Sharper wings

ORDER
Strigiformes

FAMILY
Strigidae

SPECIES
Surnia ulula

COMMON NAME
Hawk Owl

Hawk Owl

An exciting, long-tailed owl, often seen perching prominently on a high perch. It has a unique combination of shape, pattern, and character. It may attack people fiercely near its nest.

LENGTH / 36–39cm (14–15½in)
WINGSPAN / 69–82cm (27–32in)
WEIGHT / 250–380g (9–13½oz)

STATUS / Vulnerable

SCALE v Woodpigeon

Sparrowhawk-like flight profile.

Tail quite broad, but long, with obvious wedge-shaped tip.

Pale "braces" and dark stripes on sides of head.

Underpart barring varies individually.

Adult male
Female has shorter tail.

Characteristic fierce expression with white cheeks, black lines, and striking yellow eyes.

Ranging from the tundra in the north to the fringe of open steppe in the south, this is an owl of forests and forest edges. It likes clearings in birch and mixed woodland, but usually avoids solid conifer woods.

FEEDING
In summer, it eats mainly small voles. In winter, it varies its diet with some small birds. It hunts by day, even in sunshine, but also at dusk when it is feeding young.

VOICE
Males advertise their territories for some weeks before they begin nesting. They call in a display flight or from a perch: a bubbling, rising trill lasting up to 14 seconds. They also give a wheezy *aaaa-ik*.

BREEDING
Nests are unlined tree holes, old crow nests, or nest boxes. Up to 10 eggs hatch after 25–30 days. The chicks scramble into nearby branches before flying at 25–35 days.

MIGRATION
These owls are essentially nomadic, dispersing in winter. Large numbers sometimes move south when voles are unusually scarce.

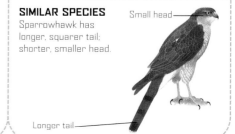

NORTHERN HUNTER
Hawk Owls can hear potential prey even under snow.

WHEN SEEN

All year.

WHERE SEEN
Breeds over most of Norway, Sweden (except south), Finland, and east through Russia. Very rare vagrant farther south.

HABITAT AND INFO

SIMILAR SPECIES
Sparrowhawk has longer, squarer tail; shorter, smaller head.

Small head

Longer tail

Tawny Owl

LENGTH / 37–43cm (14½–17in)
WINGSPAN / 94–104cm (37–41in)
WEIGHT / 330–590g (11½–21oz)

■ STATUS / Secure

SCALE v Woodpigeon

A big, large-headed, black-eyed owl of woods and parks, it is strictly nocturnal and usually difficult to see unless discovered at its daytime roost in a tree.

Tawny Owls really hoot in classic owl fashion, although their other calls are more common. They are responsible for the *tu-whit-tu-woo* known to every child, actually a duet between the female's *ke-wick!* and the male's hoot. Seldom seen, the bird waits until dark before emerging to call and hunt. By day it sits motionless in dense ivy, a tall tree, or, rarely, low down in dense cover, given away only by a splash of white droppings below. It may, however, be betrayed by small birds mobbing it from a safe distance.

FEEDING
It catches most of its prey on the ground, typically mice, voles, rats, earthworms, and beetles, but it also catches many birds at night.

DISPLAY AND VOICE
The song is a breathy, wavering hoot: *hooh! hu hu ho-ooooo*. Other calls are loud, wheezy, yelping notes: *ke-wick* or *ki-eer*.

BREEDING
The female lays 2–5 eggs in an unlined cavity in a tree or building, or in an old Magpie nest, and incubates them for 28–30 days.

MIGRATION
Resident.

Hunts from perch; listens for prey, then dives onto it.

Bulky; heavy-headed; short-winged.

Black eyes; high brows above round face.

Usually rich brown above; line of white spots on wing coverts; grey and rufous forms occur, ranging from extremely rufous to light and dark grey.

HOLE LIFE
These large owls need big tree holes for nesting.

WHEN SEEN

All year.

WHERE SEEN
Absent from Iceland, Ireland, most of Scandinavia and Sardinia, but otherwise widespread in Europe.

HABITAT AND INFO

SIMILAR SPECIES
Short-eared Owl is similarly brown, but longer-winged and rarely in trees.

Yellow eyes

Whiter underside

Barn Owl

This is a large, big-headed owl with tapered wings and white, heart-shaped face with small black eyes. It hunts at dusk and by day in cold weather.

LENGTH / 33–39cm (13–15½in)
WINGSPAN / 85–93cm (33½–37in)
WEIGHT / 290–460g (10–16oz)

■ STATUS / Vulnerable

SCALE v Woodpigeon

Light hunting flight with floating glides and quick wing beats; dives onto prey.

Male has paler wings than female's; less barred, but much variation.

Pale-breasted race
W and S Europe: striking white underwing and white body.

Dark-breasted race
Underwing can be darker.

Wingtip shape variable.

Few birds match the extraordinary beauty of a Barn Owl. At a distance it looks bright yellow-buff and white, while a close view reveals an intricate peppering of grey. It is easier to see than many owls. In summer, when it has young to feed, it hunts quite early in the evening; in a hard winter, when it risks starvation, it may be forced to hunt by day. In arable farming areas, Barn Owls are often restricted to hunting over roadside grass, where they are vulnerable to traffic.

FEEDING
It eats mainly small rodents, especially voles, mice, and rats, which it locates by flying low and slowly over the ground, often hovering before diving headlong into the grass.

VOICE
The adults make a strangled shriek. A hoarse snoring sound may betray young at the nest.

BREEDING
Up to seven eggs are laid in barns, bell towers, or other roof spaces, in hollow trees, and among hay bales. They hatch after 30–32 days. The young fly at 8–9 weeks old.

MIGRATION
Resident.

Dark-breasted race
N and E Europe: breast dark; upperparts much greyer (see also above centre).

Thin-legged, knock-kneed effect.

RODENT SPECIALIST
This is the supreme predator of mice, voles, and rats.

WHEN SEEN

All year.

WHERE SEEN
Widespread, but absent from Iceland, Scandinavia, E Europe, high altitude regions.

HABITAT AND INFO

SIMILAR SPECIES
Short-eared Owl has longer wings with dark wrist patches; yellow eyes in blacker sockets.

Mottled brown

Yellow eyes

Short-eared Owl

SCALE v Woodpigeon

LENGTH / 34–42cm (13½–16½in)
WINGSPAN / 90–105cm (35½–41in)
WEIGHT / 260–350g (9–12½oz)

■ **STATUS** / Vulnerable

A large, long-winged, fierce-eyed owl with distinctive dark wrist patches in front of bold pale orange-buff areas on primaries. It spends much time on the wing, often seen by day.

Unlike most owls, this species hunts by daylight, flying low over open ground. In summer, it is usually seen over moors, with or without small conifers, or over extensive marshes. In winter, it visits a surprising range of habitats, from land cleared for building to rough, semi-urban heaths, as well as open farmland and reed beds.

FEEDING
Its main victims are field voles. When these are abundant, several owls may concentrate in a small area.

DISPLAY AND VOICE
During summer display flights, it makes a deep, hollow *boo-boo-boo* and loud wing claps. In winter, it has a rare nasal, yapping, whip-like bark.

BREEDING
The 4–8 eggs are laid on the ground in a simple shallow scoop, usually among tall heather or rushes. They hatch after 24–29 days. The young fly when 24–27 days old.

MIGRATION
Many northern breeders move south and west in autumn. They also make erratic, nomadic movements, mostly connected with the varying abundance of small rodent prey.

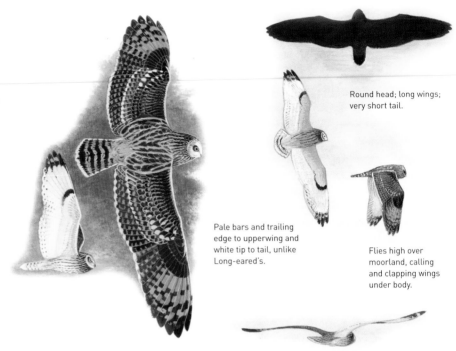

Round head; long wings; very short tail.

Pale bars and trailing edge to upperwing and white tip to tail, unlike Long-eared's.

Flies high over moorland, calling and clapping wings under body.

Bowed wings in glide.

Underwing pale with small, crisp dark marks.

Yellow eyes set in black against white face; rich tawny body marbled with black and buff.

Perches on ground, rock, or fence post in angled pose; may roost in bushes or in ivy in trees.

Small ear tufts may be raised.

FLUENT GLIDER
The typical hunting flight is low and graceful.

WHEN SEEN

All year, but unpredictable.

WHERE SEEN
Widespread in Europe as a wanderer or winter visitor; breeds mainly in N Britain, Iceland, Scandinavia, and NE Europe.

HABITAT AND INFO

SIMILAR SPECIES
Long-eared Owl is darker, more streaked below; more bars on wingtip and tail; longer ear tufts.

Darker body

Narrow tail bars

Long-eared Owl

A richly coloured, beautifully patterned, elusive owl of conifers and dense thickets near open moor or heath. Its long ear tufts are characteristic if raised, but less obvious when relaxed. It is strictly nocturnal except in very cold weather.

LENGTH / 35–37cm (14–14½in)
WINGSPAN / 84–95cm (33–37in)
WEIGHT / 210–330g (7½–11½oz)

■ **STATUS /** Secure

SCALE v Woodpigeon

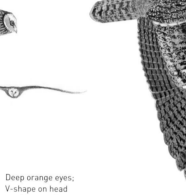

Underwing has more broken bars on tip than Short-eared's.

Tail all dark, barred, no white tip; longer than Short-eared Owl's.

Flattish wings in glide.

Deep orange eyes; V-shape on head continues up into raised ear tufts.

Rear of wing barred with narrow bands, giving more uniform appearance than bold pattern of Short-eared Owl; pale trailing edge less distinct.

Some individuals more creamy-buff, some more tawny.

Grey area on wing.

Occasionally discovered roosting in thorn or willow thicket in winter.

Where discovered by day, can be remarkably confiding, but vulnerable to repeated disturbance.

UPRIGHT ALARM
Mild alarm or curiosity is shown by the raised ear tufts.

Breeding Long-eared Owls are extremely elusive, since they are nocturnal and nest in forest edges, shelter belts, and copses with conifers where they are hard to see. The calls of young, demanding food, may give them away. In winter, however, groups of owls roost together in thickets and tree tops. It is sometimes possible to watch these over several weeks, so long as they are not scared off by anyone approaching too closely.

FEEDING
Hunting mainly at night, Long-eared Owls catch small rodents, plus many small birds in winter.

VOICE
In early spring, the owl gives a deep, moaning or cooing hoot: *oo oo oo*. The young call like squeaky gate hinges: *peee-oo*. It is silent in winter.

BREEDING
Nesting owls take over old nests of crows, pigeons, Magpies, Sparrowhawks, or squirrels. The 3–5 eggs hatch within 25–30 days and the young fly when 30 days old.

MIGRATION
Northern breeders move west and south in autumn, and some cross the North Sea.

WHEN SEEN

All year.

WHERE SEEN
Absent from Iceland and N Scandinavia; breeds in Britain, Ireland, and N Europe; widespread in winter.

HABITAT AND INFO

SIMILAR SPECIES
Tawny Owl is thickset; more rufous or grey-brown, less yellowish; dark eyes.

Broader head

Shorter wings

Scops Owl

LENGTH / 19–20cm (7½–8in)
WINGSPAN / 47–54cm (18½–21in)
WEIGHT / 150g (5¼oz)

■ STATUS / Vulnerable

SCALE v Woodpigeon

A small nocturnal owl, easily located by its persistent whistling call but often seen merely as a roof-top silhouette. It is very elusive by day.

Of the owls, only the Tawny forces itself upon our attention as often as the Scops, which calls so frequently in the wooded parks, gardens, and squares in and around Mediterranean towns and villages. It is extremely difficult to locate by day and often hard to see at night, but persistence is sometimes rewarded by an excellent view at dusk, or of a bird caught in the beam of a torch or a nearby street light.

FEEDING
The Scops Owl eats insects and spiders, plus a few reptiles, frogs, and small birds. It seizes them in its feet after flying down from a perch, but it sometimes catches moths in flight.

VOICE
It repeats a slightly ringing, whistled, unvaried *peu* or *tyuu*, at a rate of about 22–26 notes per minute. It also has a shrill, squealed alarm call.

BREEDING
Nests are in holes in trees or walls. The clutch of 4–5 eggs hatches after 24–25 days' incubation.

MIGRATION
European Scops Owls winter in Africa, except for a few in southernmost Spain, Italy, and Greece.

Can be called and seen by lights of street lamps.

Often seen on roof-tops at dusk; dives away if approached.

Ears raised or flat.

Very rufous on forewing close to body.

Strongly barred underwing.

Female will duet with male at different pitch.

Grey and rufous phases: some greyer than shown.

Long, narrow wings make it look much larger in flight.

Very variable facial shapes and postures; yellow eyes show when fully open, alert.

ACTIVE AFTER DARK
Scops owls are rarely encountered in daylight.

WHEN SEEN

Sept ◐ March

Mostly March to September; all year in far south of Europe.

WHERE SEEN
Iberia, France, Italy, locally Austria, Balkans, E Europe north to W Russia; rare vagrant elsewhere.

HABITAT AND INFO

SIMILAR SPECIES
Little Owl is thicker set, with larger, flatter head; different calls.

Flatter head

Shorter tail

Pygmy Owl

A very small, round owl of thick forest, it is active at dusk, often bold and likely to approach if its call is imitated.

LENGTH / 16–17cm (6¼–6¾in)
WINGSPAN / 32–39cm (12½–15½in)
WEIGHT / 50–80g (1¾–2¾oz)

■ STATUS / Secure

SCALE v Woodpigeon

Alert, often with tail raised; pale face marks on back of head.

Great Tit prey shows small size.

Barred tail; some more marked on back and wings.

Pygmy   Scops   Little

Head has distinctive shape when feathers are raised.

Barred flight feathers beneath, but very clean coverts.

Small, rounded (same scale as Scops page 314).

Yellow eyes; white brows.

Undulating flight, like Woodpecker's.

Male Pygmy Owls sit in tree tops at dawn and dusk, at the edges of glades and boggy areas in mixed or coniferous woods, calling repeatedly for minutes on end. They often cock or wave their tails and generally have an active, fidgety character. Pygmy Owls are frequently active by day, and in winter they may come close to farms and villages in search of prey.

FEEDING
They catch voles, mostly at dawn and dusk, and take small birds from perches or even on the wing. The owls store food in holes, including nest boxes, especially in winter when dead prey is preserved by frosts.

VOICE
Males defend their territories all year, using a flute-like call like that of a Bullfinch: *du*, *pyuh*, or *pyuk*. The note is given 30–60 times a minute for several minutes.

BREEDING
The nests are in tree holes or nest boxes. The 4–7 eggs hatch after 28–30 days. The young fly at 27–34 days old.

MIGRATION
Resident, dispersing in far north of Europe if food is short.

HOLE NESTER
Tree holes are essential for roosting and nesting.

WHEN SEEN

All year.

WHERE SEEN
Scandinavia, east and south to Russia, Poland; S Germany and the Alps; locally in E Europe.

HABITAT AND INFO

SIMILAR SPECIES
Little Owl is larger-headed, shorter-tailed; flatter crown with frowning expression.

Low brows

Short tail

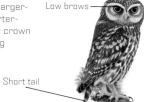

Little Owl

LENGTH / 21–23cm (8¼–9in)
WINGSPAN / 50–56cm (19½–22in)
WEIGHT / 140–200g (5–7oz)

SCALE v Woodpigeon

■ STATUS / Vulnerable

A small, dumpy, rather flat- or square-headed owl with bright yellow eyes and white eyebrows. It is typically upright on short, slim legs. It is often seen by day but hunts at dusk, from trees, poles, and fence posts. When curious, it bobs its whole body and twists its head.

The Little Owl's alert expression became familiar in southern Britain after it was introduced from Europe in the late 19th century. It took well to the mixed farmland of England and even spread to remote, bleak islands and coastal cliffs. Yet it remains a bird of warmer habitats in much of southern Europe and north Africa: anywhere from Egyptian temples to the terracotta tiles of barn roofs and stony yards of old Spanish farmsteads.

FEEDING
Although often obvious by day, the Little Owl hunts chiefly after dark, catching beetles, moths, worms, small voles, and small birds.

VOICE
Most of its calls are far-carrying whistles, including a clear, mellow *gooeek* and a sharper *k-weeew*.

BREEDING
Nests are typically in rather long, deep holes, in hollow branches, among rocks, or in earth banks. The 2–5 eggs hatch after 27–28 days. The chicks fly five weeks later.

MIGRATION
Resident.

Female has longer tail than male.

Female

Barred underwing.

Males

Quick, bounding flight with frequent wing closures; sweeps up to perch.

Upperparts brown, white-spotted.

Yellow eyes set in dark sockets; fierce look.

The only small, white-spotted owl in Britain; Tengmalm's occupies different habitat in mainland Europe.

Male

Female

EVER ALERT
Bright eyed and upright, the Little Owl is often seen by day.

WHEN SEEN

All year.

WHERE SEEN
England and Wales, widespread over most of mainland Europe north to Denmark, Latvia, and Russia.

HABITAT AND INFO

SIMILAR SPECIES
Tawny Owl is bigger, browner, rounder-faced; dark eyes.

Black eyes

Longer wings and tail

Tengmalm's Owl

A highly nocturnal forest owl, rarely seen except in high latitudes in summer. It is warmer brown than Little Owl, more rufous-buff below. Its raised eyebrows give a questioning or surprised look, less frowning.

LENGTH / 24–26cm (9½–10¼in)
WINGSPAN / 50–62cm (19½–24½in)
WEIGHT / 150–200g (5¼–7oz)

■ STATUS / Secure

SCALE v Woodpigeon

This is a curiously large-headed, high-browed owl with a look of constant surprise or inquiry. It is difficult to see, being strictly nocturnal in its behaviour. It has some preference for spruce forest, but is also widespread in mixed stands of pine, birch, and poplar in mountain forest and in the northern taiga.

FEEDING
Its staple prey is small voles, although it also catches some mice, shrews, and small birds. It hunts from a perch within woodland.

VOICE
The usual call is a soft, repetitive *po-po-po-po-po*, with up to 25 notes in succession, which carries for 2km (1¼ miles). The rhythm of the hollow, barking hoots varies individually from male to male.

BREEDING
Tengmalm's Owls nest in holes in trees, but also use nest boxes. The 3–7 eggs hatch after 25–32 days' incubation. The chicks fly when about 4–5 weeks old.

MIGRATION
Mostly resident. Some dispersal when food is short.

Underside varies, may be more or less barred or paler on belly; smaller white upperwing spots than Little Owl's.

Degree of spotting variable.

Juvenile leaves nest in all-dark down; gradually develops adult pattern.

Spotted crown; white V-shape between eyes; high points to white cheeks; line of white spots on coverts.

Flight quite direct with short glides; prefers to keep within canopy, using well-concealed perches. (Pygmy Owl often uses tree-top perch; Little Owl perches in the open.)

PERMANENT SURPRISE
This owl has a distinctively questioning expression.

WHEN SEEN

All year.

WHERE SEEN
Most of Norway, Sweden, Finland, Baltic states, and Russia; scattered through central Europe, rare and local in Pyrenees, Balkans, E Europe.

HABITAT AND INFO

SIMILAR SPECIES
Tawny Owl is bigger; bulkier; browner on face; dark eyes.

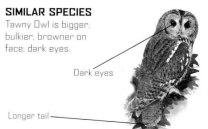

Dark eyes

Longer tail

Ural Owl

LENGTH / 60–62cm (23½–24½in)
WINGSPAN / 103–124cm (41–49in)
WEIGHT / 500–1,300g (18–46oz)

SCALE v Woodpigeon

■ STATUS / Vulnerable

A unique round-headed, grey owl with a barred and streaked look. It has a mild facial expression with small, beady eyes.

This is an aggressive owl that chases other owls and birds of prey from its territory – and is liable to strike human intruders in the face. It needs mature, undisturbed forest, and pressure on its habitat has reduced numbers over most of its range.

FEEDING
It captures rodents in forest clearings and bogs, but it also eats medium-sized or large birds such as Jays and Willow Grouse, especially in years when small rodents are scarce.

VOICE
The owl's territorial call carries up to 2km (1¼ miles): a soft, deep *VOOhoo–voohoo-oVOOho*. Various other gruff hoots and barks are heard near the nest.

BREEDING
Ural Owls nest in big holes in tree stumps, rarely in old stick nests, and increasingly in nest boxes. The 2–4 eggs hatch after 27–34 days. The young leave the nest after about four weeks, but do not fly until they are 40 days old.

MIGRATION
Resident. It requires an all-year round territory to ensure survival.

Tawny Owl (left) at same scale and showing shorter tail.

Large head distinctive.

Adult
Pale patch near wingtip; juveniles have narrower bars.

Long wedge-shaped tail distinctive.

Adult (left)
Pale underwing; darker breast.

Adult

Tail of some juveniles less heavily barred.

Round head; small, round, dark eyes.

Adult

Note long tail beyond wingtips.

TINY EYES
Small dark eyes in a wide, bland face are distinctive.

WHERE SEEN
Sweden, Finland, Russia, Belarus, and locally south to N Germany; Romania; rare and local Carpathians and Balkans.

HABITAT AND INFO

SIMILAR SPECIES
Great Grey Owl has even bigger head; small yellow eyes; back chin streak.

Huge head

Pale eyes

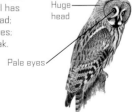

Great Grey Owl

A massive, rare, elusive owl, with an enormous head and facial disc, but small, piercing yellow eyes. It has very variable plumage.

LENGTH / 64–70cm (25–27½in)
WINGSPAN / 1.3–1.5m (4¼–5ft)
WEIGHT / 0.5–1.9kg (1–4¼lb)

■ **STATUS /** Vulnerable

SCALE v Woodpigeon

A truly extraordinary giant owl of northern forests, the Great Grey is one of Europe's most dramatic birds. It may be seen by day in mixed or coniferous forests, as well as adjacent clearings and boggy areas. It is famous for its dangerous aggression toward humans at the nest, and for its ability to detect (by sound) and catch small rodents hidden under deep snow. Yet it is often extremely hard to find. In years when food is scarce, especially, it can be most unobtrusive for such a huge bird.

FEEDING
Small voles make up the bulk of its prey, supplemented by shrews and small to medium-sized birds.

VOICE
The territorial call is a deep, muffled, pumping boom of 10–12 hoots. Given only in the darkest hours of the night, it carries barely 400m (¼ mile). Other feeble notes are given by the female.

BREEDING
Great Grey Owls nest on broken stumps or in the stick nests of hawks and buzzards. Up to six eggs are usual. They hatch in 28–30 days.

MIGRATION
Resident, but may roam in search of food if vole numbers crash.

Diving to catch prey in snow.

Adult
Pale wingtip patch rich buff (compare Ural Owl); juvenile paler overall on wingtip, with more uniform bars.

Juvenile
Less strongly barred than adult.

Note shoulder straps.

Black eye-rings inside white crescents; black around small, pale bill.

Adult

Adult
Bold bars on wing (juvenile has narrower, weaker bars).

Will perch on tree top looking slim, tapered.

LOW SWOOP
This huge owl prefers quite small prey.

WHEN SEEN

All year.

WHERE SEEN
NE Sweden, sporadic N Norway, more commonly Finland; rare Belarus, Russia, Ukraine.

HABITAT AND INFO

SIMILAR SPECIES
Ural Owl has longer tail; plain face; dark eyes.

Dark eyes

Longer tail

Eagle Owl

SCALE v Woodpigeon

LENGTH / 60–75cm (23½–29½in)
WINGSPAN / 1.4–1.7m (4½–5½ft)
WEIGHT / 1.5–3kg (3¼–6½lb)

■ **STATUS** / Vulnerable

A huge eared owl, it is heavily built, broad-winged, but usually elusive. It is inactive and well-hidden by day.

The size and intensity of colour of Eagle Owls varies from region to region. Pale Siberian birds are truly giant owls, while darker, more richly coloured western ones are somewhat smaller. Eagle Owls are 10 times the weight of Long-eared Owls, giving an idea of their real bulk and great power.

FEEDING
They take a great range of prey, regularly killing gulls, ducks, grouse, crows, other owls, and birds of prey, as well as rabbits, hares, and even young deer. They take most of their prey at night, except in the far north in summer, when Eagle Owls hunt over the tundra in daylight.

VOICE
Just after sunset in late winter males call with deep, short, booming hoots which carry up to 5km (3 miles): *HOO-o*. Hoarse notes and a sharp *ke-ke-kekayu* in alarm can also be heard near the nest.

BREEDING
They nest on cliff ledges, in caves or in large holes in old trees. The 2–4 eggs hatch after 32–34 days.

MIGRATION
Resident.

Short, square tail; long, broad wings; easy flight.

Juvenile
Much like adult except for weaker wingtip barring.

Adult
Note ample wings; buff below; well marked at tip.

Ear tufts tend to be flattened outward or raised in wide V; deep orange eyes.

Glides on flat wings.

Adult
Ear tufts raised.

Adult
Variable but typically very dark on forewing, some almost solidly blackish.

INTENSE GAZE
Eagle owls have huge eyes, giving them exceptional vision.

WHERE SEEN
S and W Norway, S and central Sweden, Finland and east into Siberia; Denmark, very locally central Europe to Balkans, Italy, S France, Iberia.

HABITAT AND INFO

SIMILAR SPECIES
Common Buzzard has bold underwing pattern, smaller dark eyes, smaller head.

Small head

Longer tail

Snowy Owl

A unique, massive, rounded, white or heavily barred owl of wild, open regions.

LENGTH / 55–65cm (21½–25½in)
WINGSPAN / 1.2–1.5m (4–5ft)
WEIGHT / 1.2–2.5kg (2½–5½lb)

■ **STATUS /** Endangered

SCALE v Woodpigeon

Big, round, with pure white males, Snowies are tremendous birds. Females are bigger still, but not quite so pristine. These are owls of open, cold, windswept moors, high mountain plateaux, and stony, snow-covered ridges on remote tundra. They are highly nomadic and settle wherever there is a good supply of food.

FEEDING
Lemmings and small rodents make up the bulk of their diet. If these are not available the owls catch rabbits, Arctic hares, and a variety of birds, ranging from Oystercatchers to skuas.

VOICE
The territorial hoot is a rather weak, soft *gawh* or a rougher, more drawn-out *hoo*. The alarm is a harsh, quacking *kraik-kraik-kraik*.

BREEDING
Snowy Owls lay their eggs on a raised hummock or rock, often protruding from surrounding snow. The clutch of 3–9 eggs is incubated for 30–33 days. The chicks fly when 45–50 days old.

MIGRATION
Nomadic; rare far to the south of the usual breeding range.

Yellow eyes look dark at distance.

Much bigger than Barn Owl, which is very white below in UK; European Barn Owls have all or partly buff underwings.

Barn Owl

Juvenile male

Adult male
Whitest plumage.

Adult female
Variable but evenly barred over body and upperwings; barred tail.

Juvenile
(left and right)
Great variation; males (left) less barred than females (right) but some overlap; some look dark with bold white face.

Adult male
Smaller than female.

Adult female
Piercing yellow eyes at close range.

APPEALING SNOWMAN
Females are barred, but older males become practically unmarked white.

WHERE SEEN
Locally N and W Norway, N Sweden, N Finland, N Russia; very few breed Iceland. Has bred Shetland, but now rare vagrant in Britain.

HABITAT AND INFO

SIMILAR SPECIES
Barn Owl is size of pigeon, not huge; buff and grey above; small dark eyes.

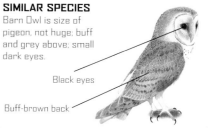

Black eyes

Buff-brown back

Alpine Swift

LENGTH / 20–22cm (8–8³⁄₄in)
WINGSPAN / 51–58cm (20–23in)
WEIGHT / 75–100g (2³⁄₄–3¹⁄₂oz)

■ **STATUS /** Secure

SCALE v Woodpigeon

This is a big swift with a white underside. It has typical scythe-like wings and a tapered body. The broad wing bases give it a muscular, yet elegant, action.

Although every inch a swift in its shape and actions, the Alpine Swift is a big, powerful species that flies with strong, deep wing beats and purposeful glides. It is characteristic of southern European mountain ranges and gorges, especially with limestone cliffs full of cavities in which it can nest, but it also mixes with Swifts and Pallid Swifts over southern towns.

FEEDING
Insects caught in the air are the standard prey of all swifts. Alpine Swifts eat large insects, including moths attracted to lights at night.

DISPLAY AND VOICE
Small groups dash around cliff faces and fly up to nesting cavities with noisy, chattering or trilling calls. They sometimes fight.

BREEDING
Each pair rears three chicks that fly when 45–55 days old. They will not breed until 2–3 years old. As with other swifts, they spend their immaturity entirely on the wing.

MIGRATION
They all move to Africa in the autumn. A few overshoot in spring and turn up unusually far north.

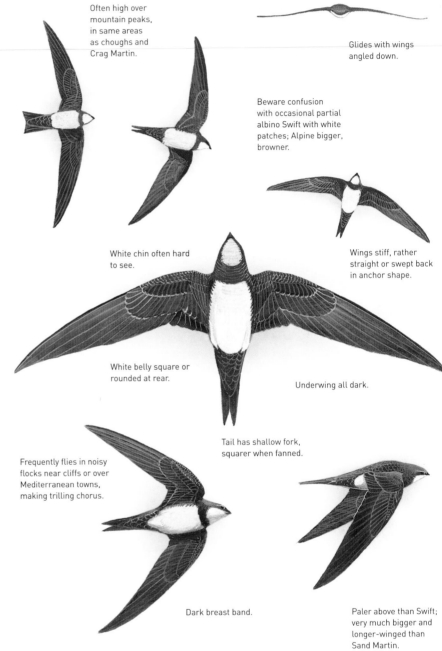

Often high over mountain peaks, in same areas as choughs and Crag Martin.

Glides with wings angled down.

Beware confusion with occasional partial albino Swift with white patches; Alpine bigger, browner.

White chin often hard to see.

Wings stiff, rather straight or swept back in anchor shape.

White belly square or rounded at rear.

Underwing all dark.

Tail has shallow fork, squarer when fanned.

Frequently flies in noisy flocks near cliffs or over Mediterranean towns, making trilling chorus.

Dark breast band.

Paler above than Swift; very much bigger and longer-winged than Sand Martin.

DRAMATIC APPEARANCE
This is a large and dynamic swift with a powerful action.

WHEN SEEN

 Oct March

March to October.

WHERE SEEN
Mostly in mountains in S Europe north to Alps; often in high altitude towns and villages.

HABITAT AND INFO

SIMILAR SPECIES
Hobby has longer, square tail; broader-based wings; bold head pattern.

Broader wings

White neck patch

| ORDER Apodiformes | FAMILY Apodidae | SPECIES Apus caffer | COMMON NAME White-rumped Swift |
| ORDER Apodiformes | FAMILY Apodidae | SPECIES Apus affinis | COMMON NAME Little Swift |

White-rumped Swift

Little Swift

White-rumped Swift is blackish, thin-winged, with long, tapered tail (deeply forked when spread) and crescent-shaped white rump. It often flies with its tail closed to a point. Little Swift is blackish, stiff-winged, with a short, square tail and a broad, square white rump.

WHITE-RUMPED
LENGTH / 14cm (5½in)
WINGSPAN / 33–37cm (13–14½in)
WEIGHT / 20–30g (¾–1oz)
■ STATUS / Vulnerable

LITTLE SWIFT
12cm (4¾in)
32–34cm (12½–13½in)
20–30g (¾–1oz)
■ Rare

SCALE v Woodpigeon

These two small, white-rumped swifts are essentially African species, rare in Europe. Both are fast fliers. The Little Swift is typical of town and city skies, twinkling on stiff, straight wings. The White-rumped Swift is a bird of more remote areas and villages, and rather more elegant.

FEEDING
Both catch small insects on the wing, usually high up.

DISPLAY AND VOICE
Parties fly over their nesting areas, White-rumped Swifts calling with low twittering notes, Little Swifts with high, screeching, rippling calls.

BREEDING
Pairs of Little Swifts make globular nests of straw, feathers, and saliva on buildings. White-rumped Swifts use old Red-rumped Swallow nests under eaves, and also beneath bridges and even roadside culverts.

MIGRATION
White-rumped Swifts migrate to central Africa from Spain and Morocco. Little Swifts are resident in north Africa and a few places in the Middle East, and sporadic elsewhere.

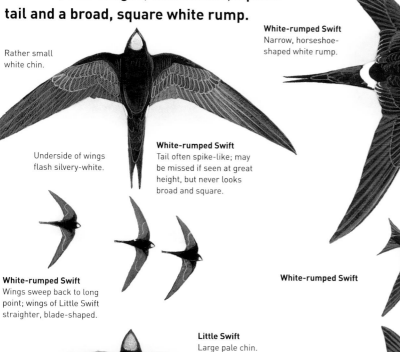

Rather small white chin.

Underside of wings flash silvery-white.

White-rumped Swift
Tail often spike-like; may be missed if seen at great height, but never looks broad and square.

White-rumped Swift
Narrow, horseshoe-shaped white rump.

White-rumped Swift

White-rumped Swift
Wings sweep back to long point; wings of Little Swift straighter, blade-shaped.

Little Swift
Large pale chin.

Black, with greyer wings from below; tail always square-cut.

Little Swift
Broad, obvious white rump.

Little Swift makes high, rippling trill.

SHARP FEATURES
Both wing and tail are tapered to points.

WHEN SEEN

Oct — May

May to October.

WHERE SEEN
White-rumped breeds S Spain near coast; Little is rare vagrant in Europe, rare UK, mostly on coasts, islands.

HABITAT AND INFO

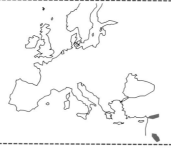

323

Swift

LENGTH / 16–17cm (6¼–6¾in)
WINGSPAN / 42–48cm (16½–19in)
WEIGHT / 36–50g (1¼–1¾oz)

SCALE v Woodpigeon

■ **STATUS /** Secure

A slim, dark, scythe-winged bird of the air, it is never seen perched. It is often in noisy groups, flying between buildings.

Spending most of its life on the wing, the Swift circles high in the air to feed and even sleep, but swoops low around the roof tops in noisy displays, especially towards dusk.

FEEDING
It feeds entirely on flying insects and small airborne spiders, which it catches in its gaping mouth.

DISPLAY AND VOICE
Parties career over breeding sites, females screaming a high *swee*, males a loud, slightly lower *sree*, in a prolonged duet of *swee-ree* sounds. They fight and display in the dark of the nest cavity, recognizing each other by sexual and individual variations in voice.

BREEDING
The Swift collects feathers, bits of grass, and other material in the air and builds a nest in a roof or church tower, although some use natural holes in cliffs. The two chicks fly after 37–56 days, depending on the availability of food. They do not breed until four years old.

MIGRATION
Immatures may spend three years aloft in Africa. Adults arrive in Europe late in spring and leave early, heading for southern Africa.

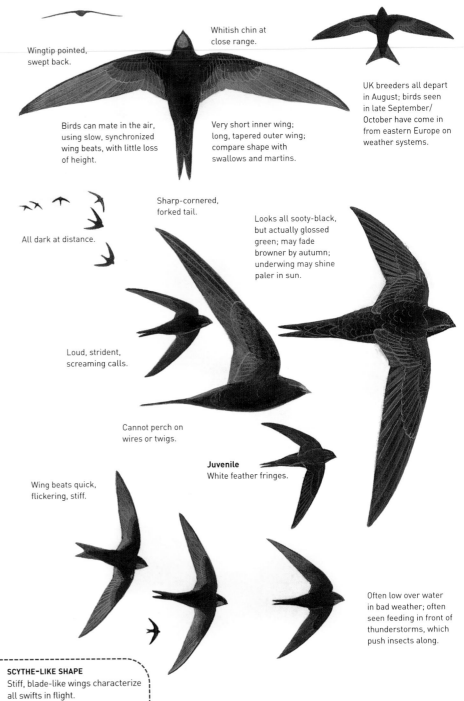

Wingtip pointed, swept back.

Whitish chin at close range.

UK breeders all depart in August; birds seen in late September/October have come in from eastern Europe on weather systems.

Birds can mate in the air, using slow, synchronized wing beats, with little loss of height.

Very short inner wing; long, tapered outer wing; compare shape with swallows and martins.

Sharp-cornered, forked tail.

Looks all sooty-black, but actually glossed green; may fade browner by autumn; underwing may shine paler in sun.

All dark at distance.

Loud, strident, screaming calls.

Cannot perch on wires or twigs.

Juvenile
White feather fringes.

Wing beats quick, flickering, stiff.

Often low over water in bad weather; often seen feeding in front of thunderstorms, which push insects along.

SCYTHE-LIKE SHAPE
Stiff, blade-like wings characterize all swifts in flight.

WHEN SEEN

Sep   April

Late April to September (most leave Britain in August).

WHERE SEEN
Over almost any open landscapes and freshwater, in all but extreme N Europe.

HABITAT AND INFO

SIMILAR SPECIES
Swallow has pale underside; white tail spots; more fluid flight with flexed wings.

Pale underside

Tail streamers

Pallid Swift

A dull, muddy-brown swift, with slightly blunter wings and a shorter tail than the Swift's.

LENGTH / 16–17cm (6¼–6¾in)
WINGSPAN / 39–46cm (15½–18in)
WEIGHT / 50g (1¾oz)

■ STATUS / Secure

SCALE v Woodpigeon

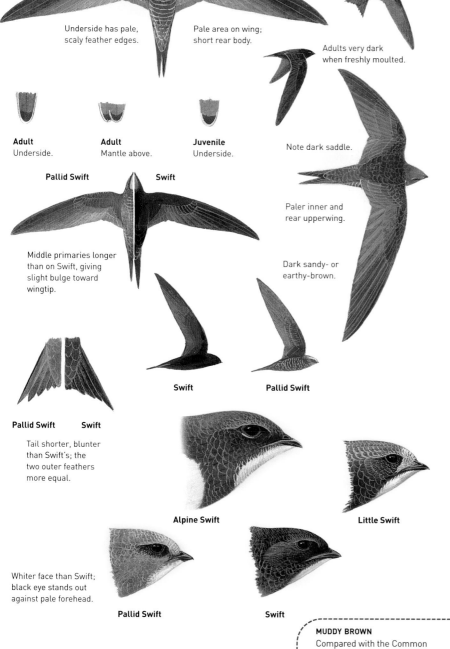

Flight fractionally less rapid and agile than Swift's; more slow turns and flat glides.

Underside has pale, scaly feather edges.

Pale area on wing; short rear body.

Adults very dark when freshly moulted.

Adult Underside.

Adult Mantle above.

Juvenile Underside.

Pallid Swift

Swift

Note dark saddle.

Paler inner and rear upperwing.

Dark sandy- or earthy-brown.

Middle primaries longer than on Swift, giving slight bulge toward wingtip.

Pallid Swift

Swift

Swift

Pallid Swift

Pallid Swift   Swift

Tail shorter, blunter than Swift's; the two outer feathers more equal.

Alpine Swift

Little Swift

Whiter face than Swift; black eye stands out against pale forehead.

Pallid Swift

Swift

This is the Mediterranean swift, a bird of ancient towns and villages with plentiful cavities beneath roof tiles or wooden eaves. It is just as gregarious as the Swift, and the two species are often seen together. When seen apart they are harder to identify: Pallid Swifts can look dark in poor light while Swifts may look browner in strong sun, but a good view of a Pallid in clear conditions usually reveals its distinctive muddy-brown appearance.

FEEDING
It eats airborne insects, caught in high, swooping flight.

DISPLAY AND VOICE
Its screaming calls are not quite so shrill as those of the Swift, but it chases around the houses and roof tops in similar fast-flying, noisy parties.

BREEDING
It nests in dark spaces, like the Swift, under eaves, or in ancient towers and walls. Each pair rears two chicks, which fly after about 46 days.

MIGRATION
It arrives in southern Europe earlier than the Swift and is occasionally seen in winter, but it is extremely rare north of its usual range.

MUDDY BROWN
Compared with the Common Swift, this one is much browner.

WHEN SEEN

Oct   March

March to October.

WHERE SEEN
Towns, villages, cliffs near Mediterranean coastal strip.

HABITAT AND INFO

SIMILAR SPECIES
Swift is generally darker; fine white feather edges on juvenile; sharper wings.

Narrower head

Blacker body

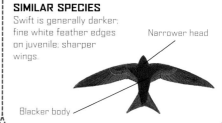

Nightjar

LENGTH / 26–28cm (10¼–11in)
WINGSPAN / 54–60cm (21–23½in)
WEIGHT / 75–100g (2¾–3½oz)

■ STATUS / Vulnerable

SCALE v Woodpigeon

A strange, mysterious bird, it is active at dusk and dawn. It is revealed by distinctive calls and a unique, mechanical song.

Few birds exercise the imagination in quite the same way as the Nightjar: a strange voice of the short summer nights, a shadowy shape at twilight. It becomes active around sunset and is not easy to see, although at times it seems to be remarkably inquisitive. By day it hides, either on the ground among dead leaves and bracken stems, or by sitting still and invisible along a horizontal branch.

FEEDING
It catches moths and large beetles in the air, snapping them up in its wide, bristle-fringed gape as it hawks over heaths, around bushes, and in woodland clearings.

DISPLAY AND VOICE
The male sings from a perch at dusk, with a prolonged, even, mechanical churr or rattle, with occasional changes in pitch, like a distant motorbike. He flies from the perch with 2–3 loud wing-claps. The flight call is a nasal *goo-ik*.

BREEDING
Two eggs are laid on bare ground. They hatch after 17–18 days.

MIGRATION
Nightjars fly to Africa in August–September. They return in May.

Flight extremely agile, light, manoeuvrable with skipping twists and turns, hovers, glides.

Wings long, tapered, broadest in middle; tail full, long, often fanned.

Female has all-brown tail.

First summer male has buff tail corners.

Adult male.

Sits along open, dead branches; sometimes silhouetted at dusk.

Adult male
Striking white wing spots and tail corners, visible late into dusk.

Female
Buff wing spots.

Male
Can be lured by giving the *goo-ik* call.

GREAT CAMOUFLAGE
On a dead stick or leaves it is remarkably hard to see.

WHEN SEEN

Sept
May

May to September.

WHERE SEEN
Locally through Europe except Iceland, N and W Scandinavia, high mountain regions.

HABITAT AND INFO

SIMILAR SPECIES
Juvenile Cuckoo is active by day; longer bill; pale spot on back of neck.

Pale nape spot

Whiter underside

Red-necked Nightjar

A typical nightjar, it is active very late or after dark. It has a distinctive repetitive song. In Europe, it is restricted to Iberia.

LENGTH / 30–32cm (11¾–12½in)
WINGSPAN / 60–65cm (23½–26in)
WEIGHT / 75–100g (2¾–3½oz)

■ **STATUS /** Vulnerable

SCALE v Woodpigeon

A speciality of Iberia and north Africa, the Red-necked Nightjar is a fraction bigger and brighter than a Nightjar, but nine times out of ten it is identified by its distinctive voice. Like the Nightjar, it has a superb light, airy, acrobatic flight, with springy wing beats, long glides on raised wings, and rapid spins and turns in pursuit of flying insects. It prefers open, flat areas with dry sandy soil and scattered bushes or trees, thickets, or groves of olive, cork oak, and eucalyptus.

FEEDING
It captures moths and beetles in the air. More rarely it picks insects from the ground.

VOICE
The song is a hollow sounding, monotonous, rhythmically repeated double note, like a blow on a piece of wood: *ku-TOK, ku-TOK, ku-TOK,* with a slightly squeaky effect at close range.

BREEDING
Two eggs are laid on the ground among low bushes.

MIGRATION
The whole population winters in west Africa, mostly in Mali.

Female has no white on outer tail feathers.

Agile, gliding flight, often with wings raised in a V-shape.

Both nightjar species have the smallest ratio of body weight to wing area of any European bird, which accounts for their floating, bouncing flight.

Rufous collar and white throat marks rarely seen.

Both sexes have clear white wing spots.

Like all nightjars, superbly camouflaged when roosting, either on the ground or on a branch.

HUGE EYE
Nightjars have big eyes, ideal for good vision at dusk.

WHEN SEEN

Oct — March

March to October.

WHERE SEEN
S Portugal, central, E, and S Spain; very rare vagrant elsewhere.

HABITAT AND INFO

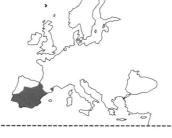

SIMILAR SPECIES
Nightjar is darker, duller; different song.

Greyer brown

Kingfisher

LENGTH / 16–17cm (6¼–6¾in)
WINGSPAN / 24–26cm (9½–10¼in)
WEIGHT / 35–40g (1¼–1½oz)

■ **STATUS /** Vulnerable

SCALE v Pigeon

A uniquely large-headed, long-billed, short-tailed bird of watersides, it is smaller than most people imagine. It is typically seen flying low and fast over water, giving a sharp call, when its electric-blue rump is most obvious. It is far less conspicuous when perched, despite colours.

Despite its genuinely vivid and beautiful colouring, the Kingfisher can be surprisingly easy to miss. It likes to perch in the dappled shade of low, overhanging vegetation, where it can be virtually invisible against a background of yellowing leaves or reeds, and sparkling or dark, rippled water. It is shy, but occasionally lets itself be watched at very close range: a breathtaking experience.

FEEDING

It dives for fish and small aquatic insects, either from a perch or a hover, and eats them at the perch.

DISPLAY AND VOICE

Pairs chase through and over waterside trees in spring. The typical call is a sharp, slightly ringing *keeee* or *ch'keee*, with more of a trill in courtship or territorial displays.

BREEDING

It digs a narrow, round tunnel into an earth bank. It lays 6–7 eggs, which hatch in 19–21 days.

MIGRATION

Some move to the coast in cold weather. Those from eastern Europe move south and west in winter.

Male
Lower mandible black.

Unique green-blue and orange pattern; white on cheeks often conspicuous from side or rear.

Flight very fast, direct, swerving to avoid obstructions or follow course of stream; flies under very low bridges; occasionally flies more slowly and slightly jerkily across a pond.

Vivid blue rump; wings and crown greener in some lights.

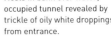

Frequently hovers over water, especially in open sites with few perches; visits small garden ponds; dives with audible splash.

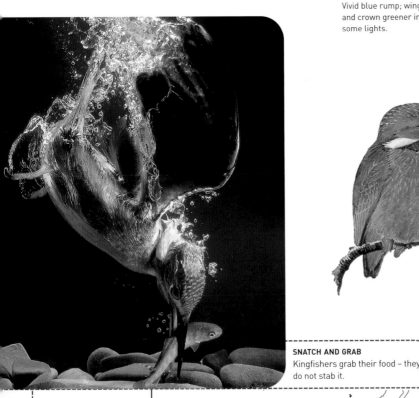

Female
Lower mandible mostly orange-red.

Juvenile is duller, with blackish feet.

Nests in bank over water; occupied tunnel revealed by trickle of oily white droppings from entrance.

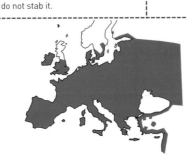

SNATCH AND GRAB
Kingfishers grab their food – they do not stab it.

WHEN SEEN

Oct — March

March to October.

WHERE SEEN
In W Europe, all year; in extreme north of range and east from Germany, mostly March to October.

HABITAT AND INFO

Bee-eater

An elegant, long-tailed, slim-headed bird with stiff, straight, tapered wings, rather like a very elongated Starling. It perches on dead branches and wires, often in groups, and flies in sweeping arcs, wheeling on flat wings with bursts of quick, stiff beats.

LENGTH / 25–27cm (9¾–10½in)
WINGSPAN / 36–40cm (14–15½in)
WEIGHT / 50–70g (1¾–2½oz)

■ **STATUS /** Vulnerable

SCALE v Pigeon

Of the few really exotic-looking European birds, the Bee-eater is perhaps the most glorious-looking of all, both on the page and in real life. Its colours may be muted in early spring and autumn, but its shape and actions are always superb. At its best, its dazzling pattern is rich beyond compare. Bee-eaters are not shy, and with a little patience it is possible to get some wonderful views.

FEEDING
True to its name, it catches insects such as bees and wasps on the wing, in swooping, gliding flights. It takes large ones to a perch to deal with, although it usually eats their stings.

DISPLAY AND VOICE
Males and females behave similarly around the nest, except when males feed females in courtship. The voice is rather liquid, with far-carrying, quite deep, abrupt notes: *quilp*, *prrup*, or *pruuk-pruuk*.

BREEDING
They nest in holes dug in banks or almost flat sandy ground. The 6–7 eggs hatch after 20 days.

MIGRATION
Bee-eaters winter in the African tropics. A few overshoot north of the breeding range in late spring.

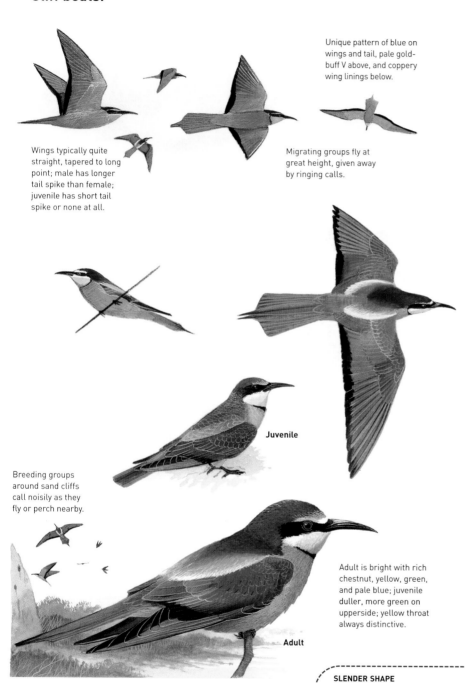

Unique pattern of blue on wings and tail, pale gold-buff V above, and coppery wing linings below.

Wings typically quite straight, tapered to long point; male has longer tail spike than female; juvenile has short tail spike or none at all.

Migrating groups fly at great height, given away by ringing calls.

Breeding groups around sand cliffs call noisily as they fly or perch nearby.

Juvenile

Adult is bright with rich chestnut, yellow, green, and pale blue; juvenile duller, more green on upperside; yellow throat always distinctive.

Adult

SLENDER SHAPE
A slim, upright shape when perched is typical.

WHEN SEEN

Sept — April

April to September.

WHERE SEEN
Breeds S and E Europe, locally north to NE France, E Europe, Russia.

HABITAT AND INFO

SIMILAR SPECIES
Insect-eating Starlings high in sky have similar silhouette, but shorter tail, shorter wings.

Shorter wingtip

Notched tail

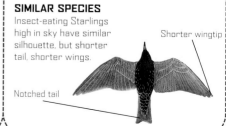

Roller

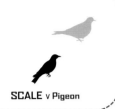

SCALE v Pigeon

LENGTH / 30–32cm (11¾–12½in)
WINGSPAN / 52–57cm (20½–22½in)
WEIGHT / 120–190g (4¼–6¾oz)

■ STATUS / Endangered

This is a Jackdaw-sized, stout-billed, broad-winged bird fond of using exposed perches; nothing else so large has a pale blue head and breast, or such vivid wing colours.

The glorious azure plumage of the Roller is a frequent sight in Africa, where it spends much of the year in the company of other species of rollers, but it comes north to Europe to breed. At times, it can be watched closely as it concentrates on finding food, and is almost oblivious to people in vehicles close by.

FEEDING
Rollers eat large insects and small frogs, caught on the ground after a quick pounce or a short flight from a post, overhead wire, or bush, with an eye-catching flash of blue.

DISPLAY AND VOICE
A displaying male flies over his nesting area with jerky wing beats, gaining height and calling all the time with a harsh *rak rak* note, then drops suddenly with a twisting, tumbling action: a wonder to behold.

BREEDING
Rollers nest in tree holes in parkland or at woodland edges near sunny clearings. The 3–5 eggs hatch in 17–20 days.

MIGRATION
Rollers move to Africa south of the Sahara in autumn. In spring some fly too far north, but they are very rare in north-west Europe.

Adult, summer
Vivid blue, greenish, and rich brown; brightest colour shows on wings in flight.

Upperwing flashes brilliant blue and turquoise.

Flight strong, direct, with slight rowing action of wings.

Juvenile
Rather dull, especially on head and breast, which are browner than adult's.

Typical upright pose on perch, settled on short legs; drops to ground in sudden outburst of blues.

Adult, autumn
Much duller, as fresh feathers have pale buffish fringes.

MUSCULAR SHAPE
The Roller has a broad-shouldered, upright stance.

WHEN SEEN

Sept — April

April to September.

WHERE SEEN
Iberia, S France, rare UK, more widespread E Europe north to Baltic States.

HABITAT AND INFO

Hoopoe

The Hoopoe in flight combines the black-and-white of a spotted woodpecker with unique broad, floppy wings and a thin bill.

LENGTH / 26–28cm (10¼–11in)
WINGSPAN / 44–48cm (17½–19in)
WEIGHT / 60–75g (2–2¾oz)

■ STATUS / Secure

SCALE v Pigeon

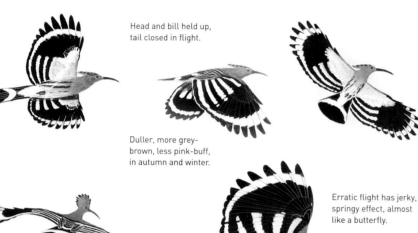

Head and bill held up, tail closed in flight.

Duller, more grey-brown, less pink-buff, in autumn and winter.

Erratic flight has jerky, springy effect, almost like a butterfly.

Crest may be raised in flight.

Crest fans upward and forward when excited, and often immediately after bird settles.

On ground, has shuffling, rolling action on short legs; remarkably easy to overlook.

Bill long, slightly curved.

Surprisingly elusive despite its contrasted plumage, the Hoopoe is easily overlooked as it feeds in the shade of hedges and trees at the woodland edge. It catches the eye only when disturbed, often at close range, and flies off, low and quite quickly.

FEEDING
The Hoopoe feeds mainly on insects such as beetles, various grubs, and caterpillars, as well as frogs and lizards, which it takes from the ground or extracts from bark with its long bill.

DISPLAY AND VOICE
The male calls with his crest raised, from a roof top or bare tree, but displays are not particularly obvious. The call is a far-carrying, soft, quite quick, hollow *poo-poo-poo*.

BREEDING
Nests are found in May and June, in large holes in trees or walls. The sites quickly become fouled by droppings and food remains. The 7–8 eggs hatch in 15–16 days.

MIGRATION
A few remain in southern Europe all year, but most fly south each autumn and return early in spring. Some overshoot to Britain in April and May, and a few appear in autumn.

SPREAD-EAGLED IN SUN
Hoopoes look stranger than ever when sunbathing.

WHEN SEEN

Oct   March

March to October.

WHERE SEEN
Europe north to the Baltic; more sporadic in central Europe; rare in UK and Ireland.

HABITAT AND INFO

Wryneck

LENGTH / 16–17cm (6¼–6¾in)
WINGSPAN / 25–27cm (9¾–10½in)
WEIGHT / 30–45g (1–1½oz)

■ **STATUS /** *Vulnerable*

SCALE v Pigeon

This is a secretive and elusive bird, patterned like a Nightjar, but spending much of its time in trees or hopping on the ground in search of ants. It will turn its head in a slow, curious fashion. It is usually detected by its call in summer.

Its sharp bill, two-forward and two-back toe arrangement, and habit of nesting in holes are clues that the Wryneck is a close relative of the woodpeckers, although it looks quite different. It is difficult to track down, but persistence is worthwhile, since it often allows a close view of its intricate, beautifully coloured feather patterns.

FEEDING
It eats ants, and very little else, digging them from their nests with its bill or extracting them from holes with its long, sticky tongue.

VOICE
The song is a nasal, quite low, complaining *quee-quee-quee-quee-quee*.

BREEDING
The Wryneck nests in holes in trees and walls – but it does not excavate them itself – even if they are already being used by sparrows or tits. Up to 10 eggs hatch after 12–14 days. The young fly when 18–22 days old.

MIGRATION
Wrynecks are scarce but annual migrants in early autumn in much of north-west Europe, including Britain, especially in coastal scrub and dunes, but occasionally well inland.

Resembles sparrow or large warbler in tree; raises tail when hopping on ground.

Tends to look grey with a broad, dark central stripe.

Male

Intricate and beautiful pattern varies: some are more grey, others more rufous.

Male

Male (left) longer-tailed relative to wingtip than female (below).

Once common in Britain, it is now scarce; the use of ant-killing poisons may be to blame.

Female

Pointed bill and long, pointed tongue like a woodpecker's; migrants may visit gardens in search of ants.

COMPLEX PATTERN
A Wryneck often looks peculiar at first glance.

WHEN SEEN

Oct — March

Late March to October.

WHERE SEEN
Breeds over most of Europe but local in west and south-east; migrant in Britain, including northern isles.

HABITAT AND INFO

SIMILAR SPECIES
Nightjar has longer wings; longer, broad-tipped tail; different behaviour.

Aerobatic behaviour

Longer wings

ORDER *Piciformes*

FAMILY *Picidae*

SPECIES *Dryocopus martius*

COMMON NAME Black Woodpecker

Black Woodpecker

A giant woodpecker, it is all-black except for red on its head, its pale bill, and pale eye. It is hard to see despite its size, but its characteristic calls echo far through forests. It has distinctive nest holes.

LENGTH / 45–57cm (17½–22½in)
WINGSPAN / 67–73cm (26½–28½in)
WEIGHT / 250–370g (9–13oz)

■ STATUS / Vulnerable

SCALE v Pigeon

Flight erratic, with Jay-like flaps.

Typical of forest with big pine or beech trees, also suburban parks, gardens where common.

Female
Red only on nape.

Male
Red crown; whitish eye.

Typical slim, gaunt look gives way to puffed-out shape in cold weather.

Broad bill.

Red cap shows prominently in rear view.

In winter, this dramatic bird forages through well-wooded town parks and even gardens, but for nesting it is confined to mature woods with big beech, pine, or larch trees. It is easiest to find in spring and early in the day, when it is most vocal. At other times it can be elusive, despite its size and bright red nape or crown.

FEEDING
It eats mainly ants and both the adult and larval stages of beetles, especially wood-boring grubs. Its sticky tongue is armed with backward-pointing barbs for impaling and extracting grubs.

DISPLAY AND VOICE
It employs a loud, dramatic drumming and an equally loud, melodious *kwih kwih kwih kwih* territorial call, repeated 10–20 times. A plaintive, far-carrying *peee-a* or *ki-ya* is often heard, while in flight it gives a rolled *krrrri-krrrri-krrrri*.

BREEDING
Holes are distinctively oval, 11–12cm (4¼–4¾in) high by 8–11cm (3¼–4¼in) wide. The clutch is usually of 4–6 white eggs.

MIGRATION
A few move quite long distances in winter. Most are resident.

ACORN-SHAPED NEST HOLE
It takes a big tree to accommodate the nest cavity.

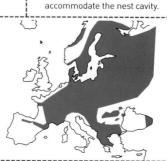

WHEN SEEN

All year.

WHERE SEEN
W Norway, most of Sweden, Finland, Russia; mainland Europe south to Balkans, central France; local N Spain, S Italy; rare outside breeding range.

HABITAT AND INFO

SIMILAR SPECIES
Jackdaw has shorter tail; rounder wingtips; short, dark bill.

Black cap

Jaunty stance

Green Woodpecker

LENGTH / 31–33cm (12–13in)
WINGSPAN / 40–42cm (15½–16½in)
WEIGHT / 180–220g (6½–7¾oz)

■ STATUS / Secure

SCALE v Pigeon

A large, green-and-yellow, long-bodied bird, it is often seen on ground. It flies up into trees with a loud, laughing call.

As common in open heathy places or on rough, grassy pastures as it is in woods, the Green Woodpecker makes itself known by frequent loud calls. If disturbed it flies off low and fast, then sweeps up into a tree, often perching around the back of a thick branch and peering out at the intruder.

FEEDING
Its principal food is ants, both adults and larvae. The bird digs them out of the ground and soft anthills with its relatively weak bill, and licks them up with its extremely long, wide, sticky tongue, which has a flexible, mobile tip.

DISPLAY AND VOICE
It rarely drums against branches, but has loud, ringing calls, evenly pitched but variable in speed: *plue plue plue*, *klee klee klee*, and variants. The Iberian race has a sharper call.

BREEDING
The nest is a 6cm (2½in) wide hole in a branch, often quite low. The 5–7 white eggs hatch after 17–19 days. Chicks fly at 23–27 days.

MIGRATION
Resident.

Undulating flight with 4–5 flaps between swoops.

Striking, bright greenish-yellow rump.

Adult female
All-black moustache.

Dull, worn feathers.

Adult male
Red centre to black moustache; bright green when fresh, wears duller; wings wear to dark brown.

Spanish race
Juvenile with orange-red cap.

Spanish race
Female above, male below.

Juvenile
Spotted and barred below; cheeks and throat streaked; duller than adult.

GROUND FEEDER
Hard frost is a severe test for this insectivorous species.

WHEN SEEN

All year.

WHERE SEEN
Britain (not Ireland or Iceland), S Norway and Sweden, Baltic states and south throughout central and S Europe, except for entirely treeless areas and highest mountains.

HABITAT AND INFO

SIMILAR SPECIES
Grey-headed Woodpecker is slimmer, but has neckless form; paler head with less, or no, red.

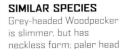

Grey neck

Slender rear

Grey-headed Woodpecker

Like the Green Woodpecker, but it is short-necked, compact, and slim-billed, with a slightly rounder head.

LENGTH / 25–26cm (9¾–10¼in)
WINGSPAN / 45–50cm (17½–19½in)
WEIGHT / 130–180g (4½–6½oz)

■ **STATUS /** Vulnerable

SCALE v Pigeon

Green
Note long head.

Note plain tail without Green's spots.

Grey-headed
Neckless shape.

Juvenile
No red; dull moustache; yellowish on bill; slightly marked below.

Adult male
Red crown; grey nape.

Adult male

Adult female
No red; black moustache.

Plain tail; greenish-yellow on rump.

DELICATE SHAPE
This is a neat, slim, thin-billed woodpecker.

This species is often betrayed by its distinctive call: sufficiently similar to that of the Green Woodpecker to give a good clue, but different enough to sound odd and suggest something else. If the bird can be tracked down, a good view will reveal subtle differences in plumage. It likes small, moist woods, riverside trees, and often small or young trees.

FEEDING
Less specialized than the Green Woodpecker, it eats many ants but varies its diet with more insects and spiders. It also forages more on trees, walls, and rocks.

DISPLAY AND VOICE
Drumming is occasionally heard but the call is most useful: it is slightly sharper, more fluting than a Green Woodpecker's, with the sequence of *ku* or *kee* notes distinctly more melancholy and becoming slower, quieter, and lower in pitch, while fading away.

BREEDING
The 7–9 eggs are laid in a hole excavated in a tree – usually an aspen, beech, oak, or lime.

MIGRATION
Resident, but with some local dispersal.

WHEN SEEN

All year.

WHERE SEEN
S Norway, central Sweden, S Finland, central Europe from middle of France eastward, S to Balkans.

HABITAT AND INFO

SIMILAR SPECIES
Green Woodpecker has large red cap; yellow cheek; different call.

Big red crown

Brighter green

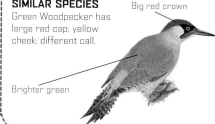

Three-toed Woodpecker

SCALE v Pigeon

LENGTH / 21–22cm (8¼–8¾in)
WINGSPAN / 40cm (15½in)
WEIGHT / 60–75g (2–2¾oz)

■ **STATUS /** Vulnerable

A small, rare, and elusive woodpecker, it is characterized by dark plumage with broken, mottled white markings. It never shows any red.

This is a medium-sized, tame, rather sluggish woodpecker that tends to remain for long periods in one tree. This makes it rather hard to find, but good to watch once located. It lives in northern lowland conifer forests with many damp hollows and dead trees, and in higher Alpine woods of mature spruce.

FEEDING
It digs adult and larval wood-boring beetles from under bark, and takes other insects from the surface. It also eats sap that oozes from holes bored in trees.

DISPLAY AND VOICE
It drums on trees in a long, loud, rapid salvo. Its calls are low and soft compared with a Great Spotted Woodpecker's: *ptuk* or *ptik*.

BREEDING
The nest is a hole excavated in a dead or dying tree, its entrance diameter 4.7cm (1¾in). The 3–5 eggs are usually incubated for just 11 days. The chicks fly after 22–25 days.

MIGRATION
Resident, except for local dispersal. It sometimes moves out from breeding areas, rarely to unlikely places, in small irruptions.

Adult female
Southern race *alpinus*: darker beneath than northern birds; darker tail.

Adult female
Northern race *tridactylus*: blackish above with white back.

Adult female
Race *tridactylus*: some more strongly barred than this; pale tail.

Adult male (right)
Race *tridactylus*: yellow often inconspicuous.

Only one hind toe; most woodpeckers have two.

Adult female
Race *alpinus*: central Europe, Alps, SE Europe; more barred above and below than *tridactylus*.

Both sexes, both races, have striped face unlike any other European woodpeckers; barred back recalls Lesser Spotted (opposite), but it is a blacker bird with smaller white spots.

BLACK-AND-WHITE ZIGZAGS
The broadly striped effect looks unusual on a bird.

WHEN SEEN

All year.

WHERE SEEN
Scandinavia, Baltic states, E Germany, and Poland eastward; locally in Alps, N Balkans, Carpathians.

HABITAT AND INFO

SIMILAR SPECIES
Lesser Spotted Woodpecker has barred back; whiter flanks; some with red on cap.

Red cap

Barred back

ORDER
Piciformes

FAMILY
Picidae

SPECIES
Dendrocopos minor

COMMON NAME
Lesser Spotted
Woodpecker

Lesser Spotted Woodpecker

A very small, elusive woodpecker, often in high twigs (or twiggy undergrowth), it is revealed by its call. It is blurry black-and-white above, with no red beneath.

LENGTH / 14–15cm (5½–6in)
WINGSPAN / 25–27cm (9¾–10½in)
WEIGHT / 18–22g (⅝–¾oz)

■ STATUS / Vulnerable

SCALE v Pigeon

Often up in tree tops in slender twigs.

Male
Bars above may wear into square white patch on back.

Female
Barred underwing often hard to see well against sky in quick, jerky flight.

Chaffinch (top left), Lesser Woodpecker (top right), and Great Spotted (right) to same scale.

Adult male
Red cap (compare juvenile Great Spotted).

Female
No red on head.

Female
Juvenile male has red rear of crown; juvenile female has some red spots.

Barely bigger than a sparrow, this miniature woodpecker tends to stay in the tops of trees or tall, spindly hedges, where it is inconspicuous and hard to find unless it is calling. It occasionally visits gardens, but does not usually feed at peanut baskets (unlike Great Spotted), generally feeding in fruit trees or ornamental cherry trees.

FEEDING
Its diet is almost entirely insectivorous. It hacks out some grubs and beetles from under loose bark, but takes most of its food from the bark surface, often from quite small twigs.

DISPLAY AND VOICE
Its drumming is slightly longer, higher, and more brittle than that of the Great Spotted. The typical call in spring is a peevish, nasal *pee-pee-pee*, with up to 20 notes. It has a rather weak *chik* contact call.

BREEDING
Excavated in a small side branch, the nest hole has a diameter of 3–3.5cm (1¼–1½in). The 4–6 eggs hatch after 11–12 days.

MIGRATION
Resident, with some random dispersal and more extensive movements in the far north of its range.

RED-CAPPED MALE
Dusty plumage is relieved by red on the adult male.

WHEN SEEN

All year.

WHERE SEEN
S Britain; almost all mainland Europe except most of Spain and Portugal and highest, most treeless regions.

HABITAT AND INFO

SIMILAR SPECIES
Great Spotted Woodpecker has big white patch each side of back; big vivid red patch under tail.

Red vent

Bold white patch

Great Spotted Woodpecker

LENGTH / 22–23cm (8¾–9in)
WINGSPAN / 34–39cm (13½–15½in)
WEIGHT / 70–90g (2½–3¼oz)

■ **STATUS /** Secure

SCALE v Pigeon

A handsome, medium-sized woodpecker: black, white, and buff, with splashes of red. It is easily located by its loud drumming from late winter onward, and by its frequent sharp call at all times.

The most common and familiar of the spotted woodpeckers in Europe, this is the yardstick by which to compare others. It is a splendid bird: a wonderful splash of colour in a dreary winter wood, or on a bird table, or in the leafy green of a summer forest. It is equally at home in coniferous or broadleaved woodland, or even in low willow carr.

FEEDING
It eats insects all year and many seeds in winter. It also takes eggs and nestlings. It probes into crevices, digs under bark, and hacks into hard wood, using its strong, stout bill as a chisel, and scoops out food with its long, flexible, sticky, bristled tongue.

DISPLAY AND VOICE
It drums against a branch to produce a sudden, short, fast *brrrrp*. The main call is a loud, sharp *tchik!* A fast rattle is less often heard.

BREEDING
It excavates a nest hole with a diameter of 5–6cm (2–2⅜in). The 4–7 eggs hatch after 10–13 days.

MIGRATION
Resident, but northern populations, especially, sometimes irrupt when food is short.

Typical bounding, undulating flight with steep rise to perch.

Female
Male
Plumage combines large white shoulder patch and extensive red undertail.

Male
Red nape patch obvious.

Female
No red on head.

Black bar across cheek reaches both nape and shoulder.

Juvenile
Red cap of variable extent, edged black.

Juvenile
Underside dusky yellow-buff.

DRAMATIC MALE
This will be a striking visitor to a garden feeder.

WHERE SEEN
All of Europe except Iceland, Ireland, Scottish islands, extreme N Scandinavia, parts of E Spain.

HABITAT AND INFO

SIMILAR SPECIES
Syrian Woodpecker has white band unbroken from cheek to side of neck; paler red undertail.

Paler undertail

ORDER
Piciformes

FAMILY
Picidae

SPECIES
Dendrocopos
syriacus

COMMON NAME
Syrian
Woodpecker

Syrian Woodpecker

A south-eastern woodpecker, resembling the Great Spotted; it is best identified by its head pattern and undertail colour.

LENGTH / 22–23cm (8¾–9in)
WINGSPAN / 38–44cm (15–17½in)
WEIGHT / 60–80g (2–2¾oz)

■ STATUS / Secure

SCALE v Pigeon

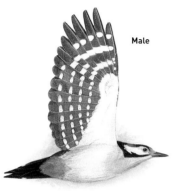

Male

Weak red undertail.

Adult male
Forehead brown; unbroken white cheek bends over shoulder; red nape appears on male only.

Female

Black tail.

Juvenile
Compare with Middle Spotted juvenile.

Great Spotted male
White triangles, outlined with black.

Syrian male

Great Spotted   Syrian

Often shows less white on shoulder than Great Spotted when perched. Red pale and limited in extent.

May lose white line over shoulder in some poses.

Female

In its restricted range in eastern Europe, this is often a quite obvious bird, but you need a good view to be sure that it is a Syrian Woodpecker and not a Great Spotted. These are the most similar of all the black-and-white woodpeckers. It is mostly a bird of lowland woods, orchards, even lines of trees along roads or beside rivers.

FEEDING
It eats mainly insects, but it also eats more seeds, fruit, and nuts all year round than most woodpeckers. It even feeds fruit to its young.

DISPLAY AND VOICE
Bursts of drumming are longer than a Great Spotted's and die away at the end. The typical call is softer than the Great Spotted's familiar *tchik* note: more like a *chuk*, sometimes running into a chatter or rattle.

BREEDING
A hole, 3.5cm (1½in) wide, is dug into a tree branch. Up to seven eggs are incubated for just 9–14 days.

MIGRATION
Resident, but there is some dispersal as it is expanding its breeding range quite quickly in south-east Europe.

TRICKY PROBLEM
Telling this from a Great Spotted is not easy.

WHEN SEEN

All year.

WHERE SEEN
Mostly SE Europe, but has spread north. Still increasing in Poland, Czech Republic, Romania, Ukraine; stable Hungary, Austria, Bulgaria, even declining slightly in Greece, Albania.

HABITAT AND INFO

SIMILAR SPECIES
Great Spotted Woodpecker has black band across lower cheek; bolder red patch under tail.

Red vent

Middle Spotted Woodpecker

LENGTH / 20–22cm (8–8¾in)
WINGSPAN / 35cm (14in)
WEIGHT / 60–75g (2–2¾oz)

STATUS / Vulnerable

SCALE v Pigeon

It is obviously a spotted woodpecker, but rather small, quite dumpy, with a slim bill and a gentle facial expression. It often shuffles and flits around on outer branches.

While its basic pattern is much like that of other spotted woodpeckers, the Middle Spotted's plumage is particularly attractive: flushed buff-and-pink below, and with a particularly bright, almost glowing red cap. It tends to keep high in trees, moving around a lot, making a good, long, close view difficult.

FEEDING

It eats insects all year, mostly picking them from branches and twigs rather than hacking them out of wood or from beneath bark. The bill is a tweezer more than a chisel.

DISPLAY AND VOICE

Drumming is rare. Calls include a throttled *quah quah* or *ahk-ahk-ahk* at varying speed and a rattling *kik kekekekek*.

BREEDING

It excavates a nest hole just 5cm (2in) wide in a decaying tree. It lays 4–7 eggs and incubates them for 11–14 days.

MIGRATION

Resident, except for a few wanderers in the north-east of its range in winter.

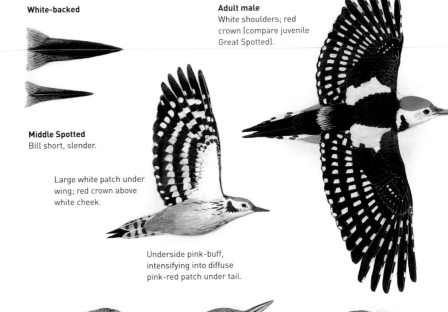

White-backed

Middle Spotted
Bill short, slender.

Large white patch under wing; red crown above white cheek.

Adult male
White shoulders; red crown (compare juvenile Great Spotted).

Underside pink-buff, intensifying into diffuse pink-red patch under tail.

Juvenile
Little red on cap; dull face; round head; weak bill.

Adult female
Like male; wing patch differences are individual variations.

Streaked flanks; underside of tail blends into buff belly.

Adult male
Flame-red crown often raised; white cheek with no dark line joining nape and black side of neck.

FLARED CREST
Males have a flame-coloured crest that can be raised.

WHEN SEEN

All year.

WHERE SEEN
W Russia; Latvia south to Ukraine, Balkans; locally through central Europe north of Alps west to France; rare N Spain, central Italy.

HABITAT AND INFO

SIMILAR SPECIES
Syrian Woodpecker has more black on cap; fewer or no streaks beneath; longer bill.

Bigger bill

Unstreaked body

ORDER
Piciformes

FAMILY
Picidae

SPECIES
Dendrocopos
leucotos

COMMON NAME
White-backed
Woodpecker

White-backed Woodpecker

This is a large spotted woodpecker with bars across the wings and a white lower back, declining and rare in most of its range.

LENGTH / 24–26cm (9½–10¼in)
WINGSPAN / 40–45cm (15½–17½in)
WEIGHT / 105–115g (3¾–4oz)

■ STATUS / Endangered

SCALE v Pigeon

Greyish wingtips.

Adult male
Race *lilfordii*: broader wings and different primary configuration compared with *leucotos* (below); breeds at different altitude; may be separate species.

Greyish wingtips.

Adult male
Central and northern Europe: big white rump; red crown.

Adult male
Race *leucotos*: black hook on cheek; black leading edge to underwing, unlike Middle Spotted Woodpecker's.

Adult female
Races alike.

Red beneath tail, blends into pink-buff belly.

Adult male
Race *leucotos*: central and northern Europe

Adult male
Race *lilfordii*: Balkans, Turkey; very barred on lower back.

The biggest spotted woodpecker, and sometimes more approachable than most, this is generally a rare bird. It must have big, mature woods with a lot of standing and fallen dead wood, and cannot thrive in over-managed woodland or plantations. It has decreased in Scandinavia, and even where conditions are good, pairs are few and far between.

FEEDING
Like other pied woodpeckers, it eats mostly wood-boring beetles, their larvae, and various other insects, but also nuts, seeds, and berries.

DISPLAY AND VOICE
Drumming by males (less often by females) is very loud and accelerates. Calls include a soft *kiuk* and a longer *kweek*, sometimes repeated.

BREEDING
The birds usually dig holes in rotten wood, 25–37cm (9¾–14½in) deep and 6–7cm (2½–2¾in) wide at the entrance. The 3–5 white eggs hatch after just 10–11 days.

MIGRATION
Resident, but a few move quite widely, occasionally beyond the breeding range, in the east of Europe.

DISTINCTIVE RARITY
Good views reveal a highly distinctive character.

WHEN SEEN

All year.

WHERE SEEN
Locally S Norway and Sweden; S Finland, Baltic states eastward and south to Balkans; local Italy, central Pyrenees.

HABITAT AND INFO

SIMILAR SPECIES
Great Spotted Woodpecker has black lower back, white patch either side; stronger red patch under tail.

Red vent

Black back

Skylark

LENGTH / 18–19cm (7–7½in)
WINGSPAN / 30–36cm (11¾–14in)
WEIGHT / 35–45g (1¼–1½oz)

STATUS / Vulnerable

SCALE v Pigeon

This is the classic aerial singer of wide open spaces: a streaky brown bird, bigger than a sparrow but smaller than a thrush, with a short, stubby crest and angular wings that are almost white on the trailing edge.

Despite widespread and even quite catastrophic declines in many areas, largely connected with changes in agricultural practices, the Skylark remains a familiar and generally quite common bird. In spring and summer, the song of the Skylark is still to be heard over large areas of farmland and moorland: one of the most evocative countryside sounds. In winter, Skylarks abandon the upland moors and bleaker heathlands, moving downhill to forage on softer ground, especially on ploughed fields and old pastures. At this time, resident birds are often found in small groups, while migrants to western Europe from farther east tend to be in much bigger flocks.

FEEDING

Skylarks locate food by sight and pick it up with deft, quick movements of their heads and bills. In winter, they eat various seeds, including cereal grains, which they gather from the ground in a low, shuffling walk. They also pick some seeds directly from low stems, and uproot tiny shoots to reach the attached grain in the soil beneath. In spring and summer, they also eat a variety of insects and other invertebrates. Dense, autumn-sown cereal crops tend to make feeding more difficult, and this may partly explain Skylarks' absence from what, at first sight, looks like suitable habitat.

DISPLAY AND VOICE

If both members of a pair survive the winter they are likely to pair again the following spring, so Skylarks are both monogamous and frequently pair for life. The male's song flight lasts 1–5 minutes, and rarely for 10 or even 20 minutes without a break. He flies up silently, at an angle, into the wind, then spirals upward singing. He may reach around 100m (330ft), fluttering on flexed wings, hovering and singing all the time, before a slow descent and a final steep, fast plunge. The song is a wonderful outpouring of fast and varied warbling with a lot of repetition of short phrases. At close range many throaty notes are heard, but at a distance the song has a higher, silvery, whistling quality. Calls include a rippling *chirrrup* and thinner whistles.

BREEDING

Nests are on the ground, neatly lined with leaves and fine stems. The 3–5 eggs hatch after just 11 days. The chicks fly at 18–20 days old.

MIGRATION

Many are seen on the move in autumn or after snowfall, usually in loose, straggly flocks, quite low down. Migration occurs in most areas almost any time between September and March.

Distinctive white outer tail and pale trailing edge to wing above and below.

Plump but long-winged; dusky underwing; sharp breast/belly contrast.

Adult (below right) Darker than bright first winter, as pale feather tips wear off to create colourless grey-buff.

Head rounded with crest depressed; stout pointed bill.

Female, first winter Female's wingtips fall close to tail tip.

Adult male, autumn Male's wingtips fall well short of long tail.

Very long hind claw.

Juvenile Dark, with dark and whitish loops on upperparts giving scaly effect.

First-winter tail.   Adult tail.

WHEN SEEN

All year.

WHERE SEEN
Almost all Europe except Iceland, upland Scandinavia; migrates south and west from Scandinavia and E Europe; resident in west.

HABITAT AND INFO

SIMILAR SPECIES
Corn Bunting has stouter bill; all-dark tail and wings; different action on ground; does not walk.

Thicker bill

Plain tail

Eastern birds wintering in Britain tend to flock more; fractionally larger; paler.

Female
Shorter tail.

Male
Longer tail.

Needs wide open ground, avoiding proximity of hedges or trees, but will sing from a fence post.

Male, first winter
In December.

Variable action and shape; typically bursts of quick wing beats, short swoops; wings angled at front, straight at back, slightly square tips. Compare overhead flocks with Redwing.

Male

Female

Hangs in wind, looking back at intruder.

Always calls when flushed; squats low then dashes away.

FLIGHT PATTERN
Descends with fluttering glide, then drops like a stone before levelling out to hover briefly before landing. In song-flight looks as if suspended on string.

DID YOU KNOW?
Little more than a century ago, Skylarks were almost unbelievably abundant in areas where they are now merely thinly spread: they were caught in vast numbers for food and transferred to the cities for sale. Some English downlands had annual harvests of tens of thousands and some London markets sold 400,000 in a season.

Woodlark

SCALE v Pigeon

LENGTH / 15cm (6in)
WINGSPAN / 27–30cm (10½–11¾in)
WEIGHT / 24–35g (⅞–1¼oz)

STATUS / Vulnerable

This is a neat, streaked lark with prominent head stripes, black-and-white wing markings, and a short tail. It has a slow, bounding flight. Its high circling song flight ends in a plunge to the ground.

A rather small but broad-winged, streaky lark, the Woodlark is best known for its beautiful song. It is quite elusive, often staying well-hidden in short grass or crouching on sandy ground until approached, when it flies off with a peculiarly bounding, almost floppy action.

FEEDING
Woodlarks pick small seeds and insects from the ground in dry places with plenty of bare earth, on heaths or, in winter, on stubble fields.

DISPLAY AND VOICE
During the high, undulating song flight the male covers wide circles over the nesting area. Songs are fluty, liquid, and melodious, in short, usually descending, repetitive phrases without the free-flowing, sparkling sound of the Skylark: *tlu tlu tlu tlu, luee luee luee, teeeoo teeoo tioo tioo tioo*. Ordinary calls include *tit-lee-o*.

BREEDING
The nest is tucked away in long grass near a stump or bush. The 3–5 eggs hatch after 12–15 days.

MIGRATION
Most move south and west in winter.

Looks broad-winged, short-tailed in flight: an almost bat-like outline.

Upperwing plain brown except for leading edge; no pale trailing edge as on Skylark.

Sides of tail duller than Skylark's tail, whiter on corners.

Perches in trees like more slender Tree Pipit, unlike terrestrial Skylark; where common, forms small, quiet, inconspicuous winter flocks.

Well-marked face with rusty- or ochre-brown cheeks; breast striped; belly clean white.

Black-white-black mark on edge of folded wing is very distinctive.

Short, streaked crest; broad cream line over eye almost to back of head, encircling crest.

SQUAT SHAPE
A Woodlark looks short-tailed and rounded, but neat.

WHEN SEEN

All year.

WHERE SEEN
Central Europe, scattered north and west to England, Denmark, S Sweden.

HABITAT AND INFO

SIMILAR SPECIES
Skylark has weaker pale stripe over eye; white trailing edge on wing; white sides to longer tail.

White tail sides

Long tail

Shore Lark

A neat, ground-loving, shuffling lark with prominent head markings, it is likely to get up and fly fast, swerving over a beach or marsh in small groups, before returning to settle again nearby.

LENGTH / 14–17cm (5½–6¾in)
WINGSPAN / 30–35cm (11¾–14in)
WEIGHT / 35–45g (1¼–1½oz)

■ STATUS / Vulnerable

SCALE v Pigeon

Male, Balkans
Broad black band from cheek to chest.

Female, Balkans
Balkan birds have grey backs to match rocky terrain.

Female
No "horns".

Upperwing plain pale brown; tail has narrow white sides, darker outer section and pale centre.

Very thin white outer edge to tail.

Female, spring
Strongest yellow on forehead and throat.

Male, non-breeding
Tiny black "horns"; faded yellow; breast band browner, often with brown smudges beneath.

This is a long-bodied, slim-winged lark, most familiar in winter when it frequents flat, damp areas of salt marsh and wave-washed sand with strandlines and beach debris. In summer, it is a mountain bird of the far north and also, very rarely, in Scotland.

FEEDING
Shore larks eat mostly seeds, supplemented by insects in summer.

DISPLAY AND VOICE
Males display on the ground with bowing actions, showing the colourful head and breast band. The song, sometimes given from the ground but mostly during short, fluttery flights, has short, twittering phrases. Calls include a soft *zeeih* and pure-sounding *tseeep* notes.

BREEDING
The 2–4 eggs are laid in a neat nest of twigs, leaves, and grass in a depression on the ground. They hatch after an incubation of 10–11 days.

MIGRATION
Northerly breeders move south-west to North Sea coasts in winter. In north Africa and south-east Europe, the birds are resident in mountain areas.

UNIQUE FACE PATTERN
Yellow-and-black bands create a highly distinctive effect.

WHEN SEEN

All year.

WHERE SEEN
Central spine of Scandinavia; Balkans; in winter on North Sea coasts, on salt marsh and beaches.

HABITAT AND INFO

SIMILAR SPECIES
Skylark has streaked breast band; paler, more streaked on back; plainer head.

White trailing edge
Streaked breast

Lesser Short-toed Lark

LENGTH / 13–14cm (5–5½in)
WINGSPAN / 24–32cm (9½–12½in)
WEIGHT / 20–25g (¾–1oz)

■ **STATUS** / Vulnerable

SCALE v Pigeon

A small lark, it is like a diminutive Skylark with its streaked breast and slightly crested cap.

A bird of steppe and semi-desert areas, the Lesser Short-toed Lark is most easily seen in Spain along hot, dry river valleys, in bare coastal dunes, and on extensive sun-dried mud, gravel, and rushy places around coastal marshes. It is not very obvious and is easy to confuse with other larks, especially young ones.

FEEDING
In summer, it eats mainly insects, but from autumn to spring its basic food is a variety of small seeds taken from the ground.

DISPLAY AND VOICE
Males have a low, circling song flight, keeping level but sometimes faster, sometimes slower. The song is a continuous flow of metallic, thin, jangly phrases. The call, a useful clue to identity, is a rattled or buzzy *chirr-rit*, *prrt*, or *prrirrik*.

BREEDING
Nests are well-hidden on the ground, typical of the larks. The clutch is of 3–5 eggs.

MIGRATION
There is little coherent migration, but a rather nomadic wandering in winter in Spain.

Female
Narrower wingtip than male.

Wings quite plain; no white trailing edge.

Spanish race
Thin bill.

Crest raised in display.

Turkish race
Asia Minor, north Africa: short, thick bill.

Male
Broader wingtip than male Short-toed Lark.

Longer exposed wingtip than Short-toed's, clearly visible at distance; even longer on male.

Even width of white on tail sides.

Turkish race
Thick-billed, fine-streaked; rare vagrant in west.

Streaked cap; pale around eye; pale throat but whole of breast evenly streaked, unlike Short-toed's.

Adult female

Adult male
Longer wingtip; more attenuated, more Linnet-like shape than female.

LONG AND SLIM
This thin look is typical of hot conditions.

WHEN SEEN

All year.

WHERE SEEN
Locally in N Spain (Ebro Valley), around SE coast, and in SW Spain; rare in extreme S Portugal.

HABITAT AND INFO

SIMILAR SPECIES
Skylark is bigger, not sparrow-sized; white on trailing edge of wing.

Larger size

COMMON NAME
Short-toed Lark
SPECIES
Calandrella
brachydactyla
FAMILY
Alaudidae
ORDER
Passeriformes

Short-toed Lark

This is a small lark with a pale underside, dark cap, and dark spots at the sides of the chest. It is common in southern Europe.

LENGTH / 14–16cm (5½–6¼in)
WINGSPAN / 30cm (11¾in)
WEIGHT / 25g (1oz)

■ **STATUS /** Secure

SCALE v Pigeon

Male
Narrower wings; longer tail than Lesser Short-toed Lark's.

Male

Female

Female
Broader wingtip than male's.

May show dark lower cheek and at side of neck, but no breast streaks.

Eastern race
East European, north African race is pale, rufous-capped, with stocky bill and breast patch; may appear in western Europe, some seen in UK.

Dark band across median coverts; pale midwing band.

Male
Longer tertials than female's; attenuated look.

Fresh

Female

Worn

Long tertials cloak wingtip when fresh; they wear off to reveal more wingtip, but never so much as on Lesser's.

Wingtip detail difficult to see at distance; longer exposed wingtip of Lesser Short-toed Lark easier.

SW European race
Longer bill; chest may be finely marked like Lesser's: check wingtip projection to confirm.

PLAIN CHEST
An unstreaked chest marks out this round-headed lark.

In many areas of the Mediterranean region, this is a common and easily seen little lark. It has its own character, as do many apparently dull, small brown birds. It is lively, frequently in parties or small flocks, and often stays together in tight groups in flight.

FEEDING
It shuffles along the ground picking up seeds, as well as insects in summer. Sometimes it digs for grubs or seeds, or stretches up to pull seeds from dry stems.

DISPLAY AND VOICE
Displaying males flutter upward, circle in undulating flight as they sing, then plummet to earth. The song is quite light, almost spitting in effect, mixed with mimicry of other species, with each phrase descending toward the end. The call is a full, sparrowy *chup* or *chirrup*.

BREEDING
The 3–5 eggs hatch after 13 days. The young fly when 12 days old, but leave the nest earlier.

MIGRATION
Migrating birds cross the Mediterranean throughout its length to winter in northern Africa.

WHEN SEEN

Oct — March

March to October.

WHERE SEEN
Local France, Romania; widespread Iberia, Italy, Balkans; rare but annual vagrant in NW Europe.

HABITAT AND INFO

SIMILAR SPECIES
Lesser Short-toed Lark has full streaked breast band; longer wingtip projection; finely streaked cap.

Longer wingtip

Streaked breast

Crested Lark

LENGTH / 17cm (6¾in)
WINGSPAN / 30–35cm (11¾–14in)
WEIGHT / 30–35g (1–1¼oz)

■ STATUS / Secure

SCALE v Pigeon

This is a common farmland and wasteland lark in south Europe. It flies up with broad, floppy wings and can raise its pointed crest.

In much of southern Europe, Crested Larks are remarkably common and often seen on roadsides and in cereal fields. They can be recognized at a glance by their pale colour, short-tailed, round-winged shape, and floppy flight. They are mostly birds of open, flat, warm lowlands, but often occupy small, sandy patches by railways, docks, airfields, and industrial sites.

FEEDING
They pick seeds, leaves, shoots, beetles, and other insects from the ground, using their strong bills to turn over leaves and stones, and dig or probe into loose earth.

DISPLAY AND VOICE
The song flight is high, fluttering, with some hovering, between spells of level cruising. The birds also sing on the ground. The song is loud and fluty, with short whistles, more complicated notes, and twitters. The call is a pure, liquid, evenly pitched *pee-lee-veee* or *twee-tee-tooo*.

BREEDING
The 3–5 eggs hatch after 11–13 days. The chicks move off at nine days and fly when 15–16 days old.

MIGRATION
Mostly resident.

Pale sandy outer tail.

Puffed out in cold – taut and sleek in heat.

Underwing much more rufous than Thekla Lark's: compare coverts.

Wings are narrower than Thekla Lark's.

Adult
Typical lark pattern with drooping pale feather fringes.

Crest is a spike when flattened.

Pale, blurred, or clearer streaks on chest; belly whitish.

Fresh plumage (above) pale, bright; worn plumage (below) duller, darker.

Bills vary, but typically longer, stronger than Thekla Lark's.

Crest sharp when raised.

Adult
Worn plumage; basic colour can vary with local soil conditions.

First year, late summer

SPIKE HEAD DRESS
The tall spiky crest is typical of a Crested Lark.

WHEN SEEN

All year.

WHERE SEEN
Mainland Europe north to Baltic; absent from large areas in central Europe; very rare vagrant in Britain.

HABITAT AND INFO

SIMILAR SPECIES
Skylark has longer tail; narrower, angular wings with white trailing edge; blunt crest.

White edge to wing and tail

Thekla Lark

A dumpy, shortish-billed lark, it is rather scarce on bushy or bare, stony slopes and rocky plains.

LENGTH / 17cm (6¾in)
WINGSPAN / 30–35cm (11¾–14in)
WEIGHT / 30g (1oz)

■ **STATUS /** Vulnerable

SCALE v Pigeon

Broad, plain wings; orange-sided tail; more contrasted rump than Crested Lark's.

Outer tail contrasty with rich sandy-orange.

Underwing greyer than Crested Lark's, especially on coverts.

Underside of tail dark, obvious in flight; underwing colour hard to see clearly.

Often dives from a height.

Floats high up in sky, with occasional light wing beat; may momentarily close wings in high flight.

Orange on underside of wing can flash to grey at some angles.

Well-marked with dark back when fresh (above); pale when worn (below).

Chest generally firmly, sharply streaked blackish (less on juvenile).

Crest fan-shaped when raised (not a sharp spike).

Adults, late summer
Upperparts worn pale.

While Crested Larks like a range of places that are mostly flat and open – often vast cereal fields – Theklas prefer bushy hillsides with scattered trees, rocks, areas of bare earth, heaths, and woodland edges. They are generally much less easy to find than Crested Larks and less well-known to the average bird-watcher.

FEEDING
They pick insects and seeds from the ground, often discovering them under stones that they flick over – although they do not dig for food like Crested Larks do.

DISPLAY AND VOICE
Song flights are wide circles on weak, fluttery wing beats, but the Thekla often sings from a barn roof, a bush top, or the ground. The song is loud and fluty, with fewer variations than a Crested Lark's. The call is lower, but ends with a long, rising and falling note: *doo-dee-doo-deeeee*.

BREEDING
The nest is a typical lark cup-shape on the ground, lined with grass. A clutch of 3–4 eggs is usual.

MIGRATION
Strictly resident.

CRESTED LOOKALIKE
Crested and Thekla Larks make a difficult pair.

WHEN SEEN

All year.

WHERE SEEN
Portugal, Spain, including Balearics, extreme S France.

HABITAT AND INFO

SIMILAR SPECIES
Crested Lark often has blurry breast streaks; typically sandier; more orange-buff underwing.

Longer bill

Sandier plumage

Calandra Lark

LENGTH / 18–19cm (7–7½in)
WINGSPAN / 35–40cm (14–15½in)
WEIGHT / 45–50g (1½–1¾oz)

■ STATUS / Secure

SCALE v Pigeon

This is a big, heavy, southern lark with a striking wing pattern, heavy bill, and dark chest patches. Its high song flight has slow wing beats.

This big, muscular lark is found in a restricted area of southern Europe in a relatively narrow range of habitats: lowland grasslands and crops, sometimes bushy or with thick, low shrubs, but usually wide open and hot in summer. It is usually easy to see, although even big flocks can disappear from sight when feeding in tall grass.

FEEDING
It eats insects in summer, but seeds and shoots are more important in winter. It digs for food with its large bill, but also picks items from the ground as it runs or walks.

DISPLAY AND VOICE
The male sings from bushes or stones, but mostly in display flight. He circles low before rising to a great height, singing all the time and flying with slow beats of his fully extended wings, quite unlike a Skylark. The song is like a Skylark's in quality, but louder and richer.

BREEDING
The 4–5 eggs, laid in a well-lined hollow on the ground, hatch after 16 days. The chicks leave the nest after 10 days and fly a week or so later.

MIGRATION
Resident in Europe.

Distinctive dark underwing; broad white trailing edge.

Broad, long wings with white rear edge; white sides to tail.

Upperwing has white trailing edge and two pale bars; wings angled down.

Big dark neck patch characteristic, but varies individually and with pose (hunched head hides patch, stretched neck reveals it).

Male sings with tail cocked.

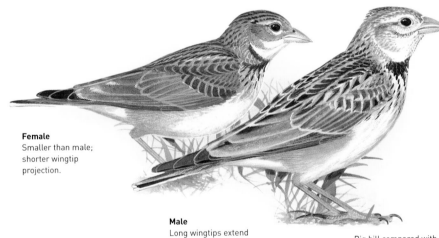

Female
Smaller than male; shorter wingtip projection.

Male
Long wingtips extend well down tail.

Big bill compared with Skylark's; chest streaked at sides, pale in centre.

BOLDLY MARKED LARK
The black neck patch is usually easy to see with patience.

WHEN SEEN

All year.

WHERE SEEN
S Portugal, much of Spain except far north, extreme S France, Sardinia, S Italy; locally in Balkans; rare Britain.

HABITAT AND INFO

SIMILAR SPECIES
Short-toed Lark has smaller patch on side of breast; finer bill; paler underwing and plainer upperwing.

Tiny neck mark

Small size

Dupont's Lark

An upstanding, long-billed lark of dry, sparsely vegetated terrain. It is distinctive, but shy and elusive.

LENGTH / 18cm (7in)
WINGSPAN / 30cm (11¾in)
WEIGHT / 30–45g (1–1½oz)

■ **STATUS /** Endangered

SCALE v Pigeon

This is a strange and elusive lark, found in quite isolated areas of Spain and north Africa, mostly in dry places that are often searingly hot in summer and very cold in winter. Most of these regions have short, often sparse vegetation with areas of bare stony ground, over which the birds run when approached. They are difficult to locate and see well except when singing.

FEEDING
Dupont's Lark takes insects and small seeds from the ground, using its long bill to dig into friable earth, probe tussocks of grass, and split open balls of dung with insects inside.

DISPLAY AND VOICE
Males sing in flight or from the ground, often rising higher in song flight than a Skylark until the bird is almost out of sight. The song is a twittering, Linnet-like affair. The usual call is a nasal *hoo hee*.

BREEDING
Nests are on the ground under a bush, beside a tuft of grass, or against a large stone. The clutch is 3–4 eggs, but other details are unknown.

MIGRATION
Usually resident, with only sporadic dispersal.

Runs if approached, reluctant to fly; often hard to see.

Wings lack pale trailing edge.

Long and rather broad wings give easy, floating flight; long tail with white sides, otherwise quite plain.

Wingtips rather square.

White sides to tail; feather tips spiky.

Slim shape enhanced by upright stance, long bill, slender neck, long legs.

Head alone enough to identify species: pale stripe over eye, complex face pattern, and decurved bill give unique expression.

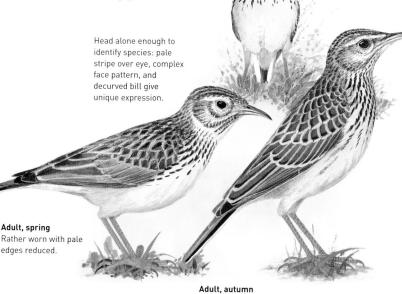

Adult, spring
Rather worn with pale edges reduced.

Adult, autumn
Fresh plumage with neat, pale feather edges.

ELUSIVE PRIZE
Dupont's are rare and difficult larks to find.

WHEN SEEN

All year.

WHERE SEEN
Locally in inland NE Spain and small parts of SE Spain; range has contracted slightly recently.

HABITAT AND INFO

SIMILAR SPECIES
Short-toed Lark has short bill; rustier cap; bold line of dark spots on shoulder.

Short bill

Squat stance

Crag Martin

LENGTH / 14.5cm (5³⁄₄in)
WINGSPAN / 32cm (12¹⁄₂in)
WEIGHT / 20–25g (³⁄₄–1oz)

■ STATUS / Secure

SCALE v Woodpigeon

This is a stocky, broad-winged martin with a shallow tail fork and characteristic white tail spots. It is dull clay-brown in late summer, greyer in fresh plumage. It has a pale underside.

The Crag Martin makes up for a lack of colour by its superb flight. Most elegant of all the swallows and martins, it has a swooping, free-flowing action across the faces of cliffs, or deep into narrow river gorges.

FEEDING

Like other martins, a Crag Martin captures insects in its mouth in the air. In dull, cold weather, it feeds lower over rivers and lakes.

DISPLAY AND VOICE

The call is an occasional short, feeble chirp, easily lost in the dramatic gorges that the birds prefer.

BREEDING

The nest is a mud cup, almost invisible on a similarly coloured cliff face, often just inside a road or rail tunnel. The adults allow a close approach as they sit at the lip of the nest. They rear two broods of 3–5 young between May and July.

MIGRATION

Crag Martins from southern France and the Alps move south each autumn, as far as northern Africa, but in Spain, Italy, and Greece some remain all year.

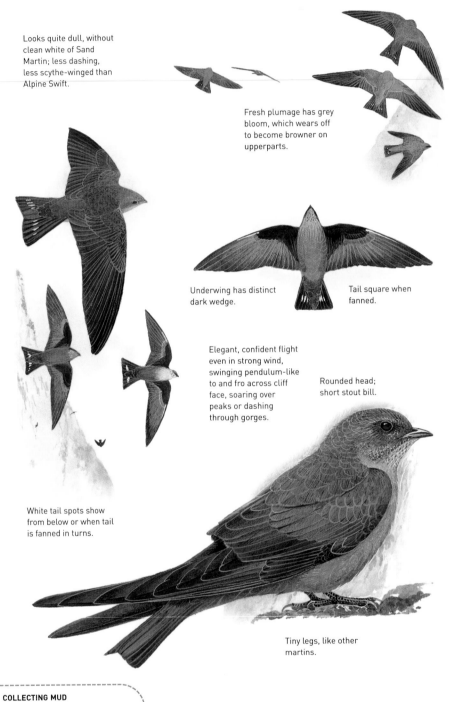

Looks quite dull, without clean white of Sand Martin; less dashing, less scythe-winged than Alpine Swift.

Fresh plumage has grey bloom, which wears off to become browner on upperparts.

Underwing has distinct dark wedge.

Tail square when fanned.

Elegant, confident flight even in strong wind, swinging pendulum-like to and fro across cliff face, soaring over peaks or dashing through gorges.

Rounded head; short stout bill.

White tail spots show from below or when tail is fanned in turns.

Tiny legs, like other martins.

COLLECTING MUD
Crag Martins come to ground frequently when nest building.

WHEN SEEN

Sep / March

Mostly March to September; some all year in the south.

WHERE SEEN
High gorges, cliffs, over rivers; in the Alps, S France, Spain, Italy, Mediterranean islands, Balkans; rare UK.

HABITAT AND INFO

SIMILAR SPECIES
Sand Martin is small; flickery flight; dark band across whiter chest; plain tail.

White throat

Plain tail

Sand Martin

This is a small, fluttery martin with a sharply forked tail and broad-based wings, with narrower tips angled back. Its white underside with a brown breast band is distinctive.

LENGTH / 12cm (4³/₄in)
WINGSPAN / 26–29cm (10¹/₄–11¹/₂in)
WEIGHT / 13–14g (³/₈–¹/₂oz)

■ **STATUS /** Vulnerable

SCALE v Woodpigeon

Underwing and underside of tail contrastingly dark.

All sandy-brown or mud-brown above.

Underside dull white except for breast band.

No tail spots.

Typical wing beat is quick, backward flick.

Often perches on wires, dead trees, or reed stems, sometimes on flat ground or shingle banks.

Flocks roost in reed beds in autumn.

Likes river valleys, flooded gravel pits, sand pits.

Of all the swallows and martins, this is the smallest and weakest in flight, typically feeding low over water with frequent tight twists and turns. Flocks often rise higher, especially if a predator such as a Hobby is nearby.

FEEDING
It hunts small flying insects, often over expanses of freshwater.

DISPLAY AND VOICE
Small groups fly around over the colony, giving short, dry, twittering flight calls.

BREEDING
Sand Martins tunnel into the faces of vertical earth banks, disused or active quarries, and sand pits, where they can occupy scores of holes. Each pair rears two broods of 4–5 chicks each summer.

MIGRATION
Sand Martins are among the earliest of the summer migrants to return in spring. The first may arrive very early in March, often in sleet or snow. They concentrate over lakes and reservoirs seeking insects, but some perish in poor weather. They return in September to Africa, south of the Sahara and almost to the Cape.

TAKING A BREATHER
Sand Martins often rest for some minutes on flat ground.

WHEN SEEN

Oct — March

March to October.

WHERE SEEN
In quarries, gravel, and sand pits, over lakes; most of Europe except interior of Italy, Alps, Balkans.

HABITAT AND INFO

SIMILAR SPECIES
House Martin has darker back, whiter underside; broad white rump band.

Blacker back

Plain white underside

Swallow

LENGTH / 17–19cm (6¾–7½in)
WINGSPAN / 32–35cm (12½–14in)
WEIGHT / 16–25g (½–1oz)

▬ **STATUS /** Vulnerable

SCALE v Woodpigeon

The most attractive, supple, and fluent of the swallows and martins, with a distinctive dark throat and all-dark upperparts. The adult has long tail streamers.

Swallows are among the favourite birds of bird-watchers, although they might be outvoted by fans of the Robin in a public poll. They are symbolic of summer, yet they are in serious decline in many areas where modern buildings offer few nesting opportunities. A nesting pair needs an old barn, or a shed with a broken window – even an open car port will do in a rural village. Unlike House Martins and Swifts, they are not at home in towns: Swallows require open spaces, where they can fly much lower down and swoop close to the ground as they hunt flies. Insecticides are also denying them food. Even the drugs used to worm cattle have had a lasting effect on the populations of insect-eating birds such as Swallows, since they make cow-pats sterile and devoid of flies, beetles, and other insects.

FEEDING
Swallows prefer large flies, such as bluebottles and dung flies, catching them in the air in their open bills. They take fewer aphids and tiny flies than is usual for House Martins and Sand Martins, their average prey size being noticeably bigger.

DISPLAY AND VOICE
Swallows frequently sit on television aerials, dead branches, overhead wires, or other perches close to a nest site, singing with a soft, fast, twittering warble interspersed with a short, wooden trill: a much more sophisticated performance than the martins manage. Other calls tend to be rather liquid and slurred, with a slightly nasal quality.

BREEDING
They build their nests on beams or other small supports against walls inside buildings. The nest is made of mud and straw, and lined with feathers. They lay 4–5 eggs, which hatch after 15 days. In southern Europe, Swallows lay more eggs and rear more broods than in the north. The young fly after 19 days in the nest.

MIGRATION
All Swallows migrate to Africa in the autumn. They gather in flocks first, then move south in about September and October. A very few remain in Europe until December. While many birds skirt around the western or eastern edges of the Sahara, Swallows enter Africa all along the north coast and head off across the desert: a severe test of fitness and stamina. They reach the southernmost parts of Africa and return in spring, reaching Spain in March and Britain by early April.

Colour of underside varies individually, from almost white to deep orange-buff; occasional strongly coloured birds seen in UK, resembling or belonging to Egyptian race.

Compare wing shape with triangular-winged House Martin's and Red-rumped Swallow's.

Breeding adult
Gleaming steel-blue above, browner on wings; deep red forehead and throat and blue breast band unique.

Juvenile
Pale salmon-pink throat; yellow gape.

Adult
Deep rust-red throat.

WHEN SEEN

Oct — March

March to October.

WHERE SEEN
Wide variety of farmland, with open spaces such as pastures with horses, sheep, or cattle, marshes, and over freshwater; almost all Europe except extreme N Scandinavia.

HABITAT AND INFO

SIMILAR SPECIES
Red-rumped Swallow has stiffer action; black undertail; rufous collar; pale rump.

Pale throat

Pale rump

Distinctive row of white
spots across tail easily
seen when tail fanned
in flight.

Wings broad-based but
swept back to a long,
tapered point, more
flexible than House
Martin's or Red-rumped
Swallow's.

Male

Female

Male

Male has longest tail
streamers; female has
mid-length; juvenile
has shorter tail
streamers than both
male and female.

Swallow
Dark rump and throat.

House Martin
White rump, throat,
and body.

Red-rumped Swallow
Buff/orange rump; pale
throat; rusty collar;
black undertail.

FLIGHT PATTERN
Hunting flight typically low,
swerving and swooping
around obstacles in its
path, snapping up large
flies in the air.

DID YOU KNOW?
Swallows have been intensively studied and it is known that females
select mates by a series of assessments, especially involving the
length of tail streamers and the amount of white across the base
of the tail. It is also clear that a longer tail creates extra stress
on the male, and reduces his manoeuvrability when feeding:
successful courtship requires compromises.

?

Red-rumped Swallow

SCALE v Woodpigeon

LENGTH / 16-17cm (6¼-6¾in)
WINGSPAN / 30-35cm (11¾-14in)
WEIGHT / 20g (¾oz)

■ **STATUS /** Secure

This is a swallow with a blue-black back and cap, rusty collar, pale buff-pink rump, and no dark throat. It looks sturdy, straight-winged, and less fluent than the Swallow, flying slower on a straighter course or circling to a height on flat wings.

This distinctive swallow of Iberia and the Balkans combines the blue-black and buff colouring of a Swallow with the pale rump and stiff-winged flight of a House Martin, yet with familiarity it reveals a distinctive character all of its own.

FEEDING
Like the Swallow, it feeds in the air, taking insects on the wing – yet with fewer wing beats, more glides, and higher foraging flights, sometimes in small groups like House Martins.

DISPLAY AND VOICE
A female may perch with her tail raised while a male sidles up to her on the same perch, singing loudly with short, twittering phrases. The typical flight call is a low-pitched, sparrow-like chirp: *tchreet* or *djuit*.

BREEDING
The nest is a cup-like structure of mud under overhanging rocks or eaves, with a characteristic entrance spout. The 2–3 broods of 4–5 young are reared.

MIGRATION
European Red-rumped Swallows winter in Africa, joining others that breed in southern Asia, Japan, and tropical Africa.

Rump two-tone pink or rusty-buff.

Stiff-winged, almost falcon-like soaring.

Black beneath "stuck-on" tail on adult.

Underside pale from chin to vent.

Rusty collar often hard to see in flight, but rules out rare hybrid between Swallow and House Martin.

Juvenile
Lacks tail streamers.

Adult

LEARN THE SHAPE
A stiff-winged, thick-bodied shape is noticeable.

WHEN SEEN

Oct / April

April to October.

WHERE SEEN
In villages and adjacent open, warm countryside in Spain, Portugal, Yugoslavia, Greece.

HABITAT AND INFO

SIMILAR SPECIES
Swallow has dark throat; white tail spots; dark rump.

Dark throat

Dark rump

358

ORDER
Passeriformes

FAMILY
Hirundinidae

SPECIES
Delichon urbicum

COMMON NAME
House Martin

House Martin

A small black-and-white aerial bird, with triangular wings and a forked tail. Its blackish upperparts, marked by a broad white rump, are distinctive. It flies high, with fluttery or flickering wings between short glides.

LENGTH / 12.5cm (5in)
WINGSPAN / 26–29cm (10¼–11½in)
WEIGHT / 15–21g (½–¾oz)

■ **STATUS** / Secure

SCALE v Woodpigeon

Abundant in the clean air over unpolluted towns and villages, House Martins breed throughout Europe. They are especially numerous above old Mediterranean towns.

FEEDING

They tend to feed higher than Swallows, above roof height, often high up with Swifts and frequently in small groups. Swallows tend to be more solitary.

DISPLAY AND VOICE

A pleasant twitter passes for song, in flight near the nest. The call is a dry, simple *chirrup*.

BREEDING

They mostly nest under the eaves of buildings, but in remote parts they still use natural sites on inland or sea cliffs. The nest is the familiar cup of mud, with a mess of droppings below. It may be taken over by House Sparrows in spring.

MIGRATION

On warm autumn days, they gather on roofs to bask in the sunshine or join Swallows on wires before migrating south to Africa, where they live mysterious lives high in the sky, almost out of sight.

Black cap contrasts with white chin, unlike Swallow's.

Forms flocks in autumn.

Underwing dusky; belly white.

Feeds over lakes and reservoirs in spring and autumn, often in large flocks.

Blue-black back; browner wings.

Female

Rump white, duller on young birds in autumn, sometimes stained browner.

Male

Male has longer tail and narrower wings than female.

Unique white-feathered legs.

SEE THE DIFFERENCE
The House Martin's throat is paler than a young Swallow's (bottom).

WHEN SEEN

Oct — March

Late March to October.

WHERE SEEN

In rural and suburban areas throughout Europe, except extreme north and mountain peaks.

HABITAT AND INFO

SIMILAR SPECIES

Swallow has more fluent flight; longer tail with white spots; dark throat; dark rump.

Longer tail

Black rear end

Rock Pipit/Water Pipit

SCALE v Woodpigeon

LENGTH / 16.5–17cm (6½–6¾in)
WINGSPAN / 23–28cm (9–11in)
WEIGHT / 20–30g (¾–1oz)

■ **STATUS /** Secure

| ORDER Passeriformes | FAMILY Motacillidae | SPECIES *Anthus petrosus* | COMMON NAME Rock Pipit |
| ORDER Passeriformes | FAMILY Motacillidae | SPECIES *Anthus spinoletta* | COMMON NAME Water Pipit |

The Rock Pipit and Scandinavian Rock Pipit are usually treated as one species, with the Water Pipit given separate species status. Research for the illustrations on this page shows that the Scandinavian Rock Pipit and Water Pipit are identical in structure, and that the Rock Pipit is the odd one of the trio. Provisionally, therefore, we propose to treat them as three species.

The Rock Pipit is a bird of rocky coasts. It is resident, except for some short-distance movements in winter. Any "Rock" Pipits seen in salt-marsh creeks, on groynes, and around piers in winter, and certainly any inland in spring and autumn, are more likely to be migrant Scandinavian Rock Pipits. This species breeds on coasts, but the whole population migrates in autumn and returns in spring. In Britain migrants appear at inland waters in March–April and September–October. Water Pipits breed on mountains, including high-altitude pastures in the Alps and Pyrenees. They move lower for the winter, often to the north, to muddy freshwater shores, marshes, and brackish pools near the coast.

Rock Pipits hold small feeding territories in winter, and breeding ones (often in a different area) in summer, so songs and aggressive calls towards intruders usually make them easy to locate all year round. Water Pipits are often shy and likely to fly off when approached. A Scandinavian Rock Pipit might go a short distance and double back, while a winter Water Pipit often flies straight to the far side of the lake.

FEEDING
They pick invertebrates from the debris of the strandline and rocks in winter, and insects from grassy areas above the beach in summer. Water Pipits catch insects on the ground, sometimes in flight, or in short leaps or fly-catching sallies.

DISPLAY AND VOICE
Males sing in flight, rising steeply and then parachuting down. The song is a louder version of a Meadow Pipit song, with a stronger trill at the end. Both Rock Pipits call a loud, full *phist* or *feest*. Water Pipit calls are less squeaky than a Meadow Pipit's, less full than those of a Rock Pipit.

BREEDING
Nests are hidden in rocky crevices close to the shore or on grassy slopes. The 4–6 eggs hatch in 14–15 days. Chicks fly at 14–15 days.

MIGRATION
Scandinavian Rock Pipits and Water Pipits migrate. The Rock Pipit is resident.

A complex group of medium-sized pipits, with distinctively dark legs. The Rock Pipit and most Scandinavian Rock Pipits remain dull all year, while the Water Pipit has a brighter, striking breeding plumage.

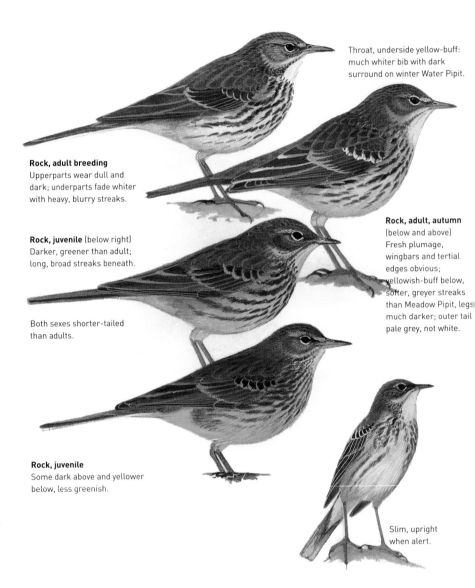

Throat, underside yellow-buff: much whiter bib with dark surround on winter Water Pipit.

Rock, adult breeding
Upperparts wear dull and dark; underparts fade whiter with heavy, blurry streaks.

Rock, juvenile (below right)
Darker, greener than adult; long, broad streaks beneath.

Both sexes shorter-tailed than adults.

Rock, adult, autumn
(below and above) Fresh plumage, wingbars and tertial edges obvious; yellowish-buff below, softer, greyer streaks than Meadow Pipit, legs much darker; outer tail pale grey, not white.

Rock, juvenile
Some dark above and yellower below, less greenish.

Slim, upright when alert.

WHEN SEEN

All year; Scandinavian Rock and Water Pipits in S Britain and W Europe October to March.

WHERE SEEN
Rock strictly coastal in UK and Ireland, NW France. Scandinavian Rock breeds Norway, Sweden, in winter on North Sea coasts and S to Gibraltar.

HABITAT AND INFO

SIMILAR SPECIES
Meadow Pipit is brighter, less grey-olive; paler pink-orange legs; brighter white tail sides.

Plainer head

Paler legs

Rock, adult (right)
Wing breadth equals tail length; narrow-winged.

Scandinavian Rock & Water (right)
Both broad-winged.

Female has shorter tail (sexes alike in Rock).

Scandinavian Rock, male, summer
Typical pattern.

Peachy-pink flush; grey streaks; dusky tail sides.

Rock Pipit is narrow-winged; tail length of male and female the same (right).

Scandinavian Rock and Water Pipits broad-winged; tail of female (left) shorter than male (middle left).

Scandinavian Rock juvenile (right)
Dusky outer tail; like Rock except for broad wings.

White tail side; clear underside; pale stripe over eye; two wingbars; may briefly recall Wheatear when standing upright.

Water, male, summer (above)
No malar stripe; variable spots on chest.

Water Pipit, male, summer
S France/Pyrenees: buff-pink below.

Male Water Pipit, summer
Typical form: pale grey above, pale pink below.

Water, male, winter (above)
Whiter than Rock: dark U surrounds pale bib.

Water, female, early spring
Greyer head than Rock Pipit, browner back, whiter underside.

Rock

Scandinavian Rock

Water

Water Pipit, juvenile
Rufous-brown until November, then greyer like adult.

Water
Leg colour red-brown to dark brown.

CLEANLY STRIPED
Water Pipit's winter pattern is like a cleanly marked Rock Pipit.

WHERE SEEN
Water breeds Alps, Pyrenees, E Europe; winters N to England, Germany, S to Mediterranean.

HABITAT AND INFO

DID YOU KNOW?
A Welsh Rock Pipit has been observed defending a territory all winter, from weeds around the tide line to the rocks well above, but for most of the winter it fed below the high tide line on flies and amphipods. The higher part of the territory became vital later, though, when the flies ran out, and it fed up there on periwinkles.

Richard's Pipit

LENGTH / 18–20cm (7–8in)
WINGSPAN / 29–33cm (11½–13in)
WEIGHT / 30–35g (1–1¼oz)

■ **STATUS** / Rare

SCALE v Pigeon

A large, bold pipit, it strides easily through tall grass, or flies up and away over a long distance, briefly hovering before settling again.

A handful of Richard's Pipits, rarely a few hundred, move west instead of south in autumn and reach western Europe, where they are annual vagrants in favoured places near the coast. Compared with most European pipits they are big, long-tailed, eye-catching birds.

FEEDING
They take insects from the ground, often in tall grass as they walk along. They also catch some in short, leaping flights.

DISPLAY AND VOICE
Their calls are mostly loud, strident, explosive, or sparrowy and sometimes subdued: *shrriw*, *shreep*, *chup*, or *chirp*.

BREEDING
The 2–3 eggs are laid in a bare or scantily lined hollow. They hatch after 23–28 days. The male brings water to the chicks by soaking his belly feathers in a pool. The chicks strip water from the feathers by drawing them through their bills.

MIGRATION
They breed in the steppes of central and eastern Asia. Most move to India and south-east Asia, but a few head west. They cross Siberia to reach Europe and the Baltic and North Sea coasts. In some years they are rare, in others a hundred or more may reach Britain from late September to November.

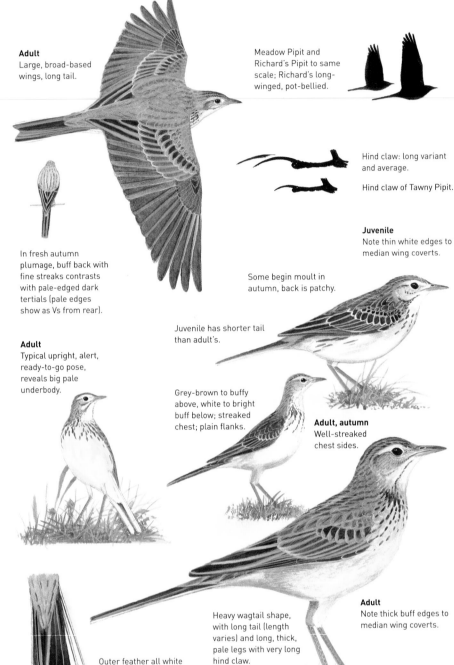

Adult
Large, broad-based wings, long tail.

Meadow Pipit and Richard's Pipit to same scale; Richard's long-winged, pot-bellied.

Hind claw: long variant and average.

Hind claw of Tawny Pipit.

In fresh autumn plumage, buff back with fine streaks contrasts with pale-edged dark tertials (pale edges show as Vs from rear).

Juvenile
Note thin white edges to median wing coverts.

Some begin moult in autumn, back is patchy.

Juvenile has shorter tail than adult's.

Adult
Typical upright, alert, ready-to-go pose, reveals big pale underbody.

Grey-brown to buffy above; white to bright buff below; streaked chest; plain flanks.

Adult, autumn
Well-streaked chest sides.

Outer feather all white except shaft.

Heavy wagtail shape, with long tail (length varies) and long, thick, pale legs with very long hind claw.

Adult
Note thick buff edges to median wing coverts.

FORCEFUL STRIDE
This big pipit can cope with long, thick grass.

WHEN SEEN

Nov

Sept

Late autumn, most end of September to November.

WHERE SEEN
Annual Britain, Belgium, Netherlands, Germany, Sweden; rare or sporadic many other countries.

HABITAT AND INFO

SIMILAR SPECIES
Skylark is stockier; has shorter tail and legs.

Thicker bill

Shorter legs

Tawny Pipit

A big, wagtail-like pipit, obviously pale except in short-lived autumn juvenile plumage.

LENGTH / 16.5cm (6½in)
WINGSPAN / 28–30cm (11–11¾in)
WEIGHT / 35g (1¼oz)

■ **STATUS /** Secure

SCALE v Pigeon

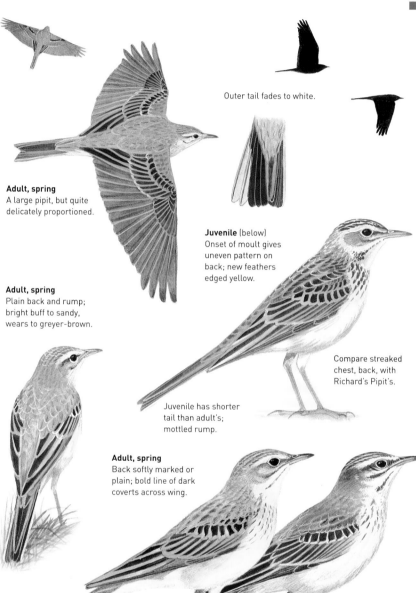

Outer tail fades to white.

Adult, spring
A large pipit, but quite delicately proportioned.

Adult, spring
Plain back and rump; bright buff to sandy, wears to greyer-brown.

Juvenile (below)
Onset of moult gives uneven pattern on back; new feathers edged yellow.

Compare streaked chest, back, with Richard's Pipit's.

Juvenile has shorter tail than adult's; mottled rump.

Adult, spring
Back softly marked or plain; bold line of dark coverts across wing.

Adult, winter
Greyer, slightly more contrasty than in spring.

Wagtail-like shape; slim, pale legs with short hind claw.

This is a big pipit, although only the size of a Yellow Wagtail. It is typical of sunny slopes and dry heaths, sandy fields, and along riversides, but it is generally scarce. It tends to be quite shy, flying up at some distance and going far away if approached.

FEEDING
It picks insects from the ground or short plants in wagtail-like fashion, with short runs, deft lunges, and occasional flutters into the air.

DISPLAY AND VOICE
Males sing from the ground but mostly in a high, long, deeply undulating song flight, with a simple repetition of a ringing *chiree* or *chy-vee*. The call is *tzeep* or *trreep*, a little harsher than the similar call of western Yellow Wagtails; also a sparrowy *chup*.

BREEDING
The nest is of grass stems, on the ground beside a tuft of grass or leaves. The 4–5 eggs hatch after 12–13 days. Chicks fly at 13–14 days.

MIGRATION
This is a scarce, but regular, spring and autumn migrant north of its breeding range, including Britain, usually found on the coast.

SPOTTED WINGS
Dark feather centres make bold markings on the wings.

WHEN SEEN

Oct
April

April to October.

WHERE SEEN
Iberia, locally central and S France; Italy, Balkans, sporadically north to Denmark, extreme S Sweden; rare migrant in Britain.

HABITAT AND INFO

SIMILAR SPECIES
Short-toed Lark is smaller; dumpier; shorter tail; short legs; thicker bill.

Small crest

Short tail

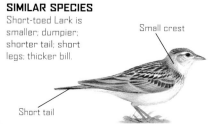

Tree Pipit

LENGTH / 15cm (6in)
WINGSPAN / 25–27cm (9¾–10½in)
WEIGHT / 20–25g (¾–1oz)

■ **STATUS /** Secure

SCALE v Pigeon

A rather bold pipit of trees beside moorland or heath, or at the woodland edge. It is difficult to distinguish from the Meadow Pipit or suspected rarities in autumn, but it is easily identified when singing in spring.

A small pipit, but subtly stronger, more confident than the Meadow Pipit, the Tree Pipit is blessed with a fine song. It is an elegant bird of woodland edges and clearings, felled or newly planted conifers, or scattered trees and bushes both on heaths and high on mountain slopes.

FEEDING
It eats mainly small insects with a few seeds, picking most of its food off the ground, but taking some from leaves or twigs. Now and then it snatches a passing insect from the air.

DISPLAY AND VOICE
Males sing from fence posts, wires, trees, and also in a song flight, typically from a tree top. The Canary-like song rises and falls, stutters, then develops into a series of loud, full double-notes: *chia-chia-wich-wich tsee-a tseee-a tseee-a*. In flight the call is a flat, buzzing *teees* or *tease*.

BREEDING
It nests on the ground. The 2–6 eggs take 12–14 days to hatch.

MIGRATION
Tree Pipits often appear on migration near reservoirs and on the coast. They are detected by their calls.

Song flight descends to tree or bush top.

Subtly different from Meadow Pipit in flight: longer-winged, less hesitant or erratic.

Cleaner below than Meadow Pipit, less obviously darker flanks, whiter belly; flank streaks sharp and fine on pale yellowish ground; whiter median covert tips create more obvious bar.

Adult female

Breeding plumage, worn
Becomes more clearly striped than early spring individual (below).

Heavier bill than Meadow Pipit's.

Adult male, early spring
Diffuse streaked pattern overlaid with cleaner buff-brown hues than Meadow Pipit's.

Breast wears whiter than Meadow Pipit's.

Longer body of male gives it a longer tail than female's.

Juvenile
More buff below than adult.

CLEAN FLANK
The pale side with few streaks is often a useful clue.

WHEN SEEN
Oct
April
April to October.

WHERE SEEN
Breeds in most of Europe except Iceland, Ireland, most of Spain, and Mediterranean coasts.

HABITAT AND INFO

SIMILAR SPECIES
Meadow Pipit is slimmer, more nervous; more streaks on flanks; different call.

Weaker bill

Longer flank streaks

COMMON NAME
Red-throated Pipit
SPECIES
Anthus cervinus
FAMILY
Motacillidae
ORDER
Passeriformes

Red-throated Pipit

A northern pipit in summer that appears elsewhere on migration, often revealed by its penetrating call. Adults are obvious at all times, but autumn juveniles require care.

LENGTH / 15cm (6in)
WINGSPAN / 22–25cm (8¾–9¾in)
WEIGHT / 16–25g (½–1oz)

STATUS / Vulnerable

SCALE v Pigeon

Dark throat patch shows up well when head raised.

Uppertail coverts strongly streaked (detail below).

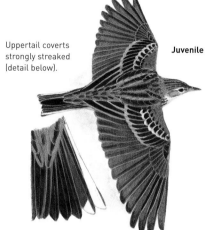

Juvenile

First winter
Many dark breast streaks; obvious dark mark each side of lower throat; two-tone bill.

Quite conspicuous wingbars and pale braces effect.

Most Red-throated Pipits seen on migration in western Europe are in non-breeding or juvenile plumage, but in spring a few – and many in south-eastern Europe – are really colourful. They like clear areas in grassy marshes, damp patches in dunes, and muddy places where livestock comes to water to drink. In summer, they are birds of the Arctic, breeding on the tundra and adjacent fields.

FEEDING
They pick insects, snails, and seeds from the ground and water's edge, or even from seaweed strandlines when on beaches on migration.

DISPLAY AND VOICE
The song flight is high, gliding in wide arcs, with a richer song than a Meadow Pipit. Calls are an abrupt *chup* and more often a high, penetrating note that fades and falls away: *p-seeeeee* or *pee-eeez*.

BREEDING
The nest is on the ground, sometimes a tunnel into a soft mound. They lay 5–6 eggs, which hatch after 11–14 days.

MIGRATION
These Arctic breeders winter in Africa. Migrants are frequent in south-east Europe, rare on coasts of north-west Europe and UK in autumn.

First winter
Bright pale braces above; dark patch of streaks coalescing on side of neck; long, broad, black flank stripes; bright pale wingbar; well-streaked rump.

Female, adult breeding
Very worn plumage, head and breast very pale; many females identical with males.

Adult, autumn

Male or bright female, spring
Distinctive black-and-yellow bill; face and throat, and often whole breast, pale brick-red (some redder or pinker); long black stripes on white flanks; streaked rump. In autumn, red retained, may be yellower at first; pale reddish remains obvious in winter.

RED-FACED ADULT
Adults have more or less red on the face and throat all year.

WHERE SEEN
Breeds N Scandinavia; widespread migrant (most in autumn in Britain, Ireland); some winter Italy, Greece.

HABITAT AND INFO

SIMILAR SPECIES
Meadow Pipit has plainer rump; less boldly striped back; different call.
Plainer back
Unstreaked rump

Meadow Pipit

LENGTH / 14.5cm (5¾in)
WINGSPAN / 22–25cm (8¾–9¾in)
WEIGHT / 16–25g (½–1oz)

■ **STATUS /** Secure

SCALE v Pigeon

A slight, streaked, ground-loving, frenetic bird with a thin bill and spindly legs, white tail sides, and thin, peevish calls. Typically a moorland bird in summer, it is widespread in lowlands in winter.

Almost everywhere this is the most common pipit, the typical little streaky, frenetic bird, always nervous and ready to fly away at the least provocation. On migration in spring, it often appears in little groups by reservoirs, mixed with Pied and Yellow Wagtails, and Reed Buntings, searching the water's edge and nearby grassy areas for early insects. In the hills, it is a summer visitor; on lowland farmland, a winter bird. On lowland heaths and some other rough, grassy places like those surrounding old gravel pits, it can be found all year round. Meadow Pipits are usually approachable and easy to see, but like other pipits and wagtails they may suddenly decide to fly up and away out of sight if disturbed. Pity the poor little pipit: on the moors it is the chief prey of Merlins and Hen Harriers, and its nests are frequently found and parasitized by Cuckoos. However, it remains a common and distinctive bird over vast tracts of open countryside.

FEEDING

It picks insects from the ground and low vegetation in a steady, even walk, with few runs or lunges. It also snatches them from the air as they fly up, but does not follow them in proper aerial fly-catching chases.

DISPLAY AND VOICE

Territorial songs are given in a song flight, a sight-and-sound combination typical of heaths and hillsides in summer. The male flies up from the ground, climbing in a steep, fluttery flight, then sails back down with wings half open and raised and its tail spread, like a miniature parachute or shuttlecock. The song is a long series of thin trills and rattles, accelerating at first, at its best with a more musical trill to finish but without the rich, Canary-like notes of a Tree Pipit. Calls are often given in twos or threes: a short, high, thin *seep seep* or *swip swip swip*, or sometimes more frantic repetitions. Alarm notes at the nest include a shorter *chip*.

BREEDING

The nests are well hidden on the ground: neat little cups lined with grass and hair. The 3–5 eggs are incubated for 11–15 days, and the chicks fly after 10–14 days.

MIGRATION

In Iceland, Scandinavia, and north-east Europe, it is a summer visitor. In Britain and Ireland and much of mainland north-west Europe, it is found all year, but migrates to lower altitudes in winter. In parts of central and southern Europe, it is a winter visitor only.

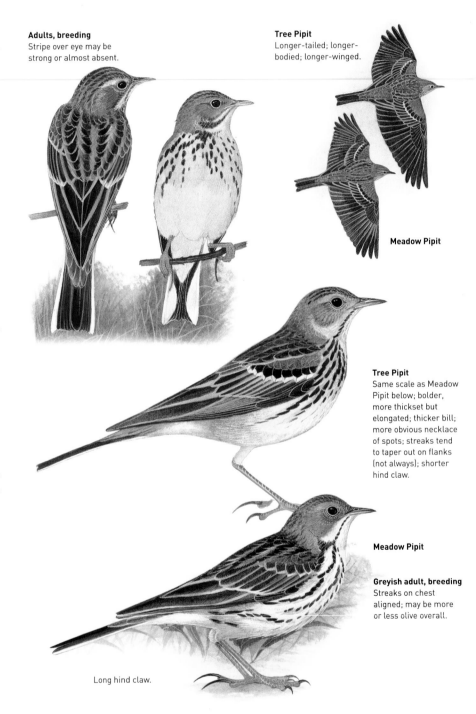

Adults, breeding
Stripe over eye may be strong or almost absent.

Tree Pipit
Longer-tailed; longer-bodied; longer-winged.

Meadow Pipit

Tree Pipit
Same scale as Meadow Pipit below; bolder, more thickset but elongated; thicker bill; more obvious necklace of spots; streaks tend to taper out on flanks (not always); shorter hind claw.

Meadow Pipit

Greyish adult, breeding
Streaks on chest aligned; may be more or less olive overall.

Long hind claw.

WHEN SEEN

All year: Britain and Ireland, N France to Denmark; April to September farther north; September to April farther south.

WHERE SEEN
Breeds Iceland, Ireland, Britain, and mainland Europe south to central France; migrant elsewhere.

HABITAT AND INFO

SIMILAR SPECIES
Tree Pipit has stronger look; plainer flanks; shorter hind claw; different call.

Stronger bill

Plainer flank

CROUCHING STANCE
A nervy, creeping appearance is the norm for this small pipit.

Groups rise in ones and twos, not as a flock.

Parachuting display flight.

Adult, winter
Fluffed out, perched on wire.

Juvenile
Greenish type.

Tail lengths vary slightly.

Juvenile
Yellowish type.

Broad-winged, short-tailed, dumpy look.

Broad white tail side recalls buntings.

FLIGHT PATTERN
Odd wings-down look in flight characteristic of pipits; bounce around the sky, calling, often returning to the same spot.

DID YOU KNOW?
This little brown bird, which is exquisitely beautiful when seen closely, suffers a bombardment from all sides on the moors in spring and summer. It is exploited by parasitical Cuckoos, captured by Sparrowhawks and Hen Harriers, has its eggs and young eaten by foxes and stoats, and forms as much as three-quarters of the diet of the Merlin.

?

Grey Wagtail

LENGTH / 18–19cm (7–7½in)
WINGSPAN / 25–27cm (9¾–10½in)
WEIGHT / 15–23g (½–⅞oz)

■ **STATUS /** Secure

SCALE v Pigeon

Europe's slimmest wagtail, with the longest tail and most exaggerated tail-swinging action, it has a bounding flight with sharp calls.

A bird of rushing rivers, mill races, and upland streams in summer, the Grey Wagtail moves downhill in winter to softer landscapes with calmer, more open waters, as well as visiting the smallest of puddles or the most insignificant garden ponds. It is the most extreme wagtail in shape and actions, but the main clue to its presence is its distinctive flight call.

FEEDING
It flits from rock to rock, walks along gravelly shores, or potters slowly beside pools, picking insects from the ground and the water's edge.

DISPLAY AND VOICE
Males sing and quiver their wings from trees or rocks, or in a pipit-like song flight. The song is a penetrating trill based on the call: a sharp, explosive *tzi* or *tzitzi*, more penetrating than a Pied Wagtail's.

BREEDING
Nests are cups of moss and grass built in crevices in banks, among tree roots or rocks above water. The 4–6 eggs hatch after 11–14 days.

MIGRATION
It moves to lowland areas in winter. Breeders from north and east Europe move south and west as far as Africa.

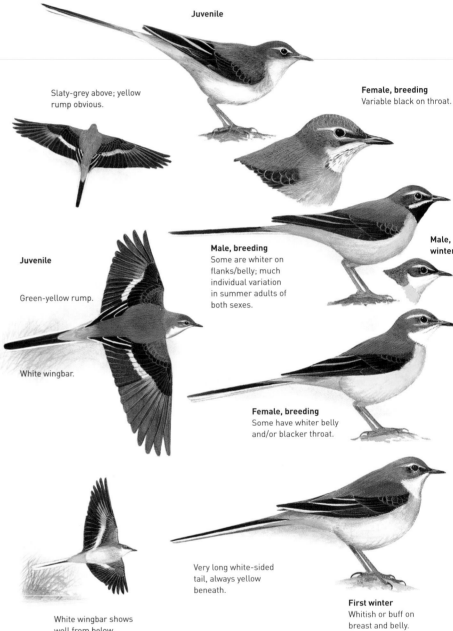

Juvenile
Slaty-grey above; yellow rump obvious.

Female, breeding
Variable black on throat.

Juvenile
Green-yellow rump.
White wingbar.

Male, breeding
Some are whiter on flanks/belly; much individual variation in summer adults of both sexes.

Male, winter

Female, breeding
Some have whiter belly and/or blacker throat.

White wingbar shows well from below.

Very long white-sided tail, always yellow beneath.

First winter
Whitish or buff on breast and belly.

STREAMSIDE DANDY
A spring male looks exceptionally handsome.

WHEN SEEN

All year.

WHERE SEEN
Breeds Ireland, Britain, S Scandinavia south to Mediterranean; in north-east only in summer; central Spain only in winter.

HABITAT AND INFO

SIMILAR SPECIES
Yellow Wagtail has shorter tail; longer dark legs; yellow not so concentrated under tail.

Shorter tail

Dark legs

ORDER	FAMILY	SPECIES	COMMON NAME
Passeriformes	Motacillidae	Motacilla citreola	Citrine Wagtail

Citrine Wagtail

A very variable wagtail. The summer male is obvious, but it resembles Yellow and Pied Wagtails in other plumages.

LENGTH / 17cm (6¾in)
WINGSPAN / 24–27cm (9½–10½in)
WEIGHT / 15–20g (½–¾oz)

■ **STATUS /** Rare

SCALE v Pigeon

Male, spring
Plumage variant in May.

Female, winter
Variant with less yellow on forehead.

Juvenile
Variant with pale forehead.

Juvenile
Wings broader than Yellow Wagtail's.

Male, summer
Yellow head with variable black on neck.

Typical male combines grey back, yellow head, yellow belly, much white on wing.

White undertail (unlike any Yellow or Grey Wagtail).

Female, summer
Back basically grey, rather dark; white wingbars; flanks grey (unlike Yellow Wagtail's).

Dark cap and edge of cheek; yellow over eye curves round behind ear coverts.

Small, variable amount of breast spotting.

Female, winter
White wingbars striking; white undertail.

Juvenile
Pale eye-ring, lores, and cheek spot; pale cheek surround; all-dark bill; greyish back; broad white wingbars; white undertail.

Citrine Wagtails breed in the Arctic tundra, and in mountains and damp clearings farther south. In western Europe, they are vagrants, rare even in the east, although they appear every year and sporadic breeding has been recorded far from the usual range. They are usually found close to water.

FEEDING
They pick insects from the ground and from water, often when wading in the shallows. They also catch flies disturbed by grazing cattle.

DISPLAY AND VOICE
The typical migrant's call is a slightly harsh or buzzed short note, a little more grating but higher, less upswept, than western races of the Yellow Wagtail: *sreep*, *drreep*, or *deesp*.

BREEDING
The cup nest is well hidden in vegetation, in a hollow in a bank, or beside a stone. It lays 4–6 eggs.

MIGRATION
The great majority move south and south-east to the Middle East and India, but a few head west in autumn to reach far-flung coasts and islands of north-west Europe.

CLEAN PATTERN
A spring male is no great identification problem.

WHEN SEEN

Nov
Sept

September to November in W Europe; increasingly in spring.

WHERE SEEN
Breeds locally Belarus, Ukraine, commonly in Russia, rarely and erratically elsewhere; rare migrant/vagrant in most of Europe.

HABITAT AND INFO

SIMILAR SPECIES
Juvenile Pied Wagtail has darker chest band; purer grey back; different call.

Dingy face and throat

Whiter underside

Yellow Wagtail

SCALE v Pigeon

LENGTH / 17cm (6¾in)
WINGSPAN / 23–27cm (9–10½in)
WEIGHT / 16–22g (½–¾oz)

■ STATUS / Vulnerable

A spindly-legged, slim-tailed bird of open, grassy places, often near water or livestock. There are complex races or closely related species.

Recent developments in classifying wagtails suggest that we may eventually separate "yellow" wagtails into several species. The black-headed form of south-east Europe and the mainly yellow type of Britain and northern France are particularly well-marked, and seem to breed alongside other types without hybridizing. Other races are more variable, and the boundaries between them are complex. The variety of racial types has always fascinated bird-watchers, especially in spring, when 2–3 kinds may be seen side by side tripping about in a field of sheep or cattle. Yellow Wagtails like short grass with grazing animals. They favour wet places, especially seasonally flooded meadows, but also breed in fields of cereals close to water. They appear in all kinds of open spaces on migration, from ploughed fields to sand dunes and golf courses. In spring, they often pause in grassy pastures high on mountainsides in southern Europe, waiting for improved conditions before making the final crossing.

FEEDING
Yellow Wagtails eat small insects, picking them from the ground or shallow water while walking steadily, or snatching them in fast runs or lunges (especially insects disturbed by animals). They may chase them into the air, snatching them in their bills or simply knocking them to the ground. They also pick insects and ticks from the backs of animals, especially sheep.

DISPLAY AND VOICE
They pair up from late winter, and form spring flocks soon after migration. Small groups of breeding pairs often gather in suitable areas, with more or less overlapping territories. Males sing from the ground and low perches, or in rather ill-defined undulating song flights. The song is a long, fast, twittering performance of little musical merit. Flight calls vary individually and by race: western birds have a musical, upswept, full *tsweep* or *tsree-ee*; eastern races tend to produce more grating versions of these calls.

BREEDING
Nests are neat cups, built on the ground in grass, lined with fine stems, hair, and wool. The 4–6 eggs hatch after 11–13 days. The chicks leave the nest a few days before they can fly, and fledge at about 16 days old.

MIGRATION
All European Yellow Wagtails move south in autumn, to spend the winter in Africa. A few spend the winter in southern Spain, but most go south of the Sahara. They leave Europe from July and August through to early November, and return in March, April (the majority), and May.

Female
N Scandinavia, "Grey-headed" race *thunbergi*; rare UK.

Male

Female
"Black-headed" race/species *feldegg*.

Female

Whitish wingbars and tertial edges; slim black tail with white sides; flight deeply undulating over long distance.

Female
Italy, race *cinereocapilla*.

Juvenile
Race *flavissima*; compare Pied.

First winter
Race *flavissima*; often seen in autumn.

Female
Race *flavissima*; some greyer, paler, less yellow.

Male, spring
Race *flavissima*; uniquely green and vivid yellow ground bird.

Bottom row of four birds all UK "Yellow" race *flavissima*.

WHEN SEEN

Nov
March

March to November.

WHERE SEEN
Breeds England and Wales, widely over mainland Europe; local in much of S Europe; widespread migrant.

HABITAT AND INFO

SIMILAR SPECIES
Citrine Wagtail has black collar; grey back; white under tail.

Black collar

Grey back

Male, spring
Central Europe, "Blue-headed" race *flava*.

Beware confusion with Grey Wagtail, especially non-breeding; Yellow Wagtail not present in winter in N Europe, unlike Grey.

Male
Italy, race *cinereocapilla*.

Races may be hard to identify: study crown, cheeks, eyebrow, chin, and throat – and note call.

Male
Race *thunbergi*; darkest may look like Black-headed race, but nape duller, back less deep green.

Male
Balkans, "Black-headed" race/species *feldegg*; very rare in W Europe.

Male
Iberian "Spanish" race *iberiae*.

Male
France, "Blue-headed" race *flava*; scarce UK.

Male
Kirghiz steppe, race *bema*.

Male
Romania, SE Russia, races *superciliaris* and *dombrowskii*.

DID YOU KNOW?

The many forms of Yellow Wagtail, combined with common cases of aberrant birds with more grey or less yellow in the plumage than normal, offer an endless source of fascination. The black-headed form of south-east Europe is often separated as a different species. The green-and-yellow headed form that breeds almost exclusively in Britain might be another.

White and Pied Wagtails

ORDER Passeriformes
FAMILY Motacillidae
SPECIES Motacilla alba
COMMON NAME White & Pied Wagtails

LENGTH / 18cm (7in)
WINGSPAN / 25–30cm (9³/₄–11³/₄in)
WEIGHT / 19–27g (⁵/₈–1oz)

■ **STATUS /** Secure

SCALE v Pigeon

A small, long-tailed, fearless, strikingly patterned bird of watersides, housing and industrial estates, car parks, and grassland. It draws attention by frequent, characteristic calls.

The White and Pied Wagtails are usually treated as races of the same species, *Motacilla alba*, but increasingly the Pied is being regarded as a separate species, *Motacilla yarrelli*. Yet whether they are technically races or species, the two are clearly very closely related. The neat, dapper little Pied Wagtail is a British resident: a familiar bird of the suburbs, where it happily feeds on tarmac and concrete, on roofs and beside garden ponds, as well as in many places that are more or less associated with water. It is equally likely to be seen in gravel pits, old quarries, stony rivers, woodyards, railway sidings, and village streets. Over most of the rest of Europe the breeding birds are White Wagtails: common and easy to see in towns and village streets (even deep down in narrow, concrete streets between high walls), along stony river beds, and in more open fields and high, rocky meadows. Both Pied and White Wagtails spend most of their time on the ground, usually away from tall or dense vegetation except when roosting.

FEEDING

Both eat insects washed up at the water's edge throughout the year, and pick others from the ground after short, fast dashes and lunges. They also snatch insects from the air, chasing them in lively, bouncy, tail-flirting runs or in brief, fluttering, fly-catching flights.

VOICE

Male Pied Wagtails do not sing much, but call from roof tops and other raised perches near the nest. Their calls include a cheery, liquid *cheweeoo* or *chiwoo* and a distinctive, harder *chiss-ick*. White Wagtail calls are like those of Pied, but softer, more like *pee-vit*.

BREEDING

They nest in holes in banks, rocks, piles of wood, in old walls, or inside derelict buildings. The 5–6 eggs take 11–16 days to hatch, and the chicks fledge in 13–14 days.

MIGRATION

The Pied Wagtail is more or less resident, with movements to lower ground, urban areas, and the coast in winter. Some birds that breed in northern Scotland move well south within Britain. White Wagtails that breed in Iceland, northern Europe, eastern Europe, and the Alps move south in autumn. They are regular passage migrants in Britain in spring, but less often identified in autumn.

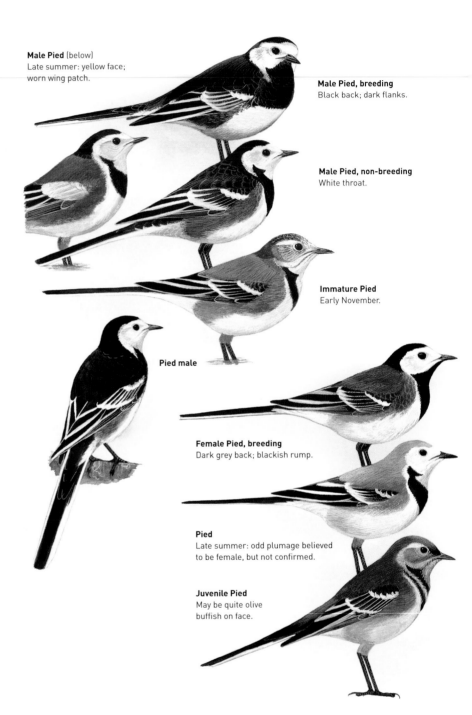

Male Pied (below)
Late summer: yellow face; worn wing patch.

Male Pied, breeding
Black back; dark flanks.

Male Pied, non-breeding
White throat.

Immature Pied
Early November.

Pied male

Female Pied, breeding
Dark grey back; blackish rump.

Pied
Late summer: odd plumage believed to be female, but not confirmed.

Juvenile Pied
May be quite olive buffish on face.

WHEN SEEN

Pied all year in Britain; White all year in C and SW Europe; April–October in north and east; most April–May, September–October in Britain.

WHERE SEEN

Pied throughout Britain and Ireland, rare breeder N France and also irregularly to NW Germany; White throughout Europe.

HABITAT AND INFO

SIMILAR SPECIES

Grey Wagtail has short pale legs; sharper, higher call; yellow undertail.

Yellow undertail

Pale legs

YOUNG WHITE
This pale grey bird with a weak face pattern is a young White Wagtail.

Female Pied
Late summer: black rump merges into tail.

Underwing varies in both races/species; wingbar weak or strong.

Male White
Grey rump contrasts with tail; less dark on uppertail coverts.

Female White, breeding
Most of crown grey; back may be quite dark, dull.

White male
Grey back; pale flanks; pale or browner wing.

Juvenile White

White, first winter
Dull head; grey rump.

Female White, winter

DID YOU KNOW?
Like some of the races of Yellow Wagtail, the Pied and White Wagtails might best be considered as separate species in their own right, with constant differences in colour and small but seemingly consistent differences in call. They are perhaps well down the line between sub-species and species, but not quite there yet.

Waxwing

LENGTH / 18cm (7in)
WINGSPAN / 32–35cm (12½–14in)
WEIGHT / 45–70g (1½–2½oz)

SCALE v Pigeon

■ STATUS / Secure

A soft-plumaged, uniquely crested bird, it is often very tame. The combination of crest, black bib, grey rump, and red undertail are quite unmistakable.

When Waxwing numbers build up after a good breeding season, but the berry crop happens to be poor, large flocks leave northern Europe in search of food elsewhere. These irruptions into countries where Waxwings are usually scarce are among the most exciting events of winter bird-watching.

FEEDING
Groups, rarely large flocks, gather in places with hawthorn or cotoneaster berries, eating greedily and regularly flying off to drink before the next feast. In summer, they eat insects.

DISPLAY AND VOICE
A displaying male shows off his crest and ruffles up his grey rump feathers. He will also pass a berry to a suitably willing female. The song is poorly developed: a version of the typical call which is a rather shrill, silvery trill, with a slight rattling quality at close range.

BREEDING
Pairs build cup nests in belts of tall spruce and pine trees close to open tundra. The 5–6 eggs hatch after an incubation of 14–15 days.

MIGRATION
Erratic movements west and south in winter.

May look plump and rounded, or stretched up into slimmer, erect shape; acrobatic, almost parrot-like, when feeding.

Juvenile duller overall, with streaky belly.

Rusty-red undertail and broad yellow tail tip unlike any other bird.

Female
Short crest.

Flies like Starling, but slightly different body shape: more elongated, with blunter head and broad tail; flocks move in synchrony.

Throat patch shiny and well-defined in male, duller and more blurred in many females (not easy).

Wax-red tip.

Male   **Female**

Immature female

First-winter male

Adult female
Note variation.

Adult male or female
Note white tip.

Sex and age of bird can be determined from a combination of wing pattern, number of waxy tips, length of crest, and width of tailband.

Males have 6–8 large red tips, adult females have 5–8 (usually smaller) tips, immature females have up to 7, or none at all.

Male
Long crest.

Adult and juvenile males have broader tail bar than females.

Front of face foxy-red with white line under eye; black eye stripe.

WINTER SPECTACULAR
In most of Europe, this is a rare winter treat.

WHEN SEEN

All year: November to April in central and W Europe.

WHERE SEEN
N Sweden, N Finland; winters farther south, sometimes to UK.

HABITAT AND INFO

SIMILAR SPECIES
Starling is darker; slimmer body; longer bill; much longer legs.

Longer bill

Longer legs

Dipper

A waterside bird of Wren-like shape, but it is closer to the size of a small thrush. It bobs up and down as if on springs. It has a unique white bib and aquatic behaviour.

LENGTH / 18cm (7in)
WINGSPAN / 25–30cm (9¾–11¾in)
WEIGHT / 55–75g (2–2¾oz)

■ **STATUS /** Vulnerable

SCALE v Pigeon

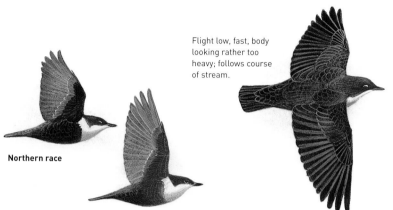

Flight low, fast, body looking rather too heavy; follows course of stream.

Northern race

British race

Typical action is a quick, springy, rhythmic down-up bob of the whole body.

Northern race

North European race has black belly; British race has broad ginger-brown breast band; Irish and Scottish Dippers have darkest heads; central European Dippers are brightest of all below.

Most of body dark grey-black with steely gloss; head browner; white eyelid often seen.

British race

Underwater, Dippers open their wings and lower their heads, using the flow of water over their backs to push them down while they forage for food under stones and weeds.

Large, strong legs and toes give excellent grip on stones even in fast-flowing water.

Juvenile
Paler and greyer; dull whitish below with barred, less crisp bib.

STREAMLINED SHAPE
The smooth shape is made for underwater foraging.

Few birds are quite so restricted to one habitat as the Dipper, which is rarely found away from a stream and then only by water of some sort. In winter, some move to the shore of a large lake or even the sea for a time.

FEEDING
Uniquely among songbirds, the Dipper feeds in and under water, wading, swimming, and diving, to find insects and crustaceans on the water's edge or stream bed. The flow of water against its opened wings helps keep the Dipper submerged.

DISPLAY AND VOICE
Dippers fly along their river territories, calling loudly, and sing from low branches and boulders with loud, rich, warbling notes. The usual call is a short, hard, slightly grating, low-pitched *dzit*.

BREEDING
The nest is always over water, under a bridge or overhanging rock or tree root, sometimes even under the cascade of a waterfall. The 4–5 eggs hatch after 16 days.

MIGRATION
Most are resident, but there is some movement in cold winter weather to lower areas or the coast.

WHEN SEEN

All year.

WHERE SEEN
On clean rivers, less often lake shores, in most of the higher parts of Europe, lowlands in winter.

HABITAT AND INFO

Dunnock

LENGTH / 13–14cm (5–5½in)
WINGSPAN / 19–21cm (7½–8¼in)
WEIGHT / 19–24g (⅝–⅞oz)

SCALE v Pigeon

■ STATUS / Secure

A small, streaky, dark brown and grey bird, found shuffling under shrubberies and through flowerbeds. However, it is also found widely in many habitats from forest to coastal heath.

Best known as little garden birds that sing from the hedge and scuttle into thick cover at the least sign of disturbance, Dunnocks are as likely to be found among the brambles and bracken of coastal clifftops. They are full of surprises when breeding, with extra-pair matings and trios being quite normal.

FEEDING
In summer, they pick insects from the ground and low vegetation. In winter, they eat seeds.

DISPLAY AND VOICE
Dunnocks display in twos and threes by singing and waving their wings, often one at a time, from low perches. The song is a slightly flat, fast warble with less emphasis or melody than that of a Robin. Calls are loud, sharp, simple notes, *tseee* or *tsip*.

BREEDING
A neat nest, lined with hair and feathers, is hidden in a bush or hedge. The 4–5 eggs hatch in 12 days. The chicks fly when 12 days old.

MIGRATION
Birds breeding in northern and eastern Europe move south and west in winter.

Flies with flicking action and gentle undulations, dives into cover.

Adult
Pale belly.

Juvenile
Streaked beneath.

Adult, autumn
Brown cap and ear coverts within blue-grey; pale brown eye; brown wash on flanks.

Pairs and trios wave wings in display.

Rapidly flicks tail open and shut; no white.

Adult, spring
Tiny white spots on wing soon wear off.

Typically feeds in horizontal pose.

Short, thin bill.

Female's tail shorter than male's.

Reddish/orange legs.

Stands more upright when alarmed.

STREAKY GREY
Soft streaks on grey and brown lend a distinctive effect to the Dunnock.

WHEN SEEN

All year in W and central Europe; winter visitor in south, summer visitor in east and north.

WHERE SEEN
Breeds most of Europe except Iceland and Mediterranean.

HABITAT AND INFO

SIMILAR SPECIES
Wren is rounder; short-tailed; much more barred, less streaked, overall.

Short tail

Barred not streaked

Alpine Accentor

Often elusive but sometimes a confiding bird of high-altitude rocks and grassland, it is larger and brighter than the Dunnock, but with much the same character.

LENGTH / 15–17.5cm (6–7in)
WINGSPAN / 22cm (8¾in)
WEIGHT / 25g (1oz)

■ **STATUS** / Vulnerable

SCALE v Pigeon

Adult, spring
Dark streaks above and dark orange on flanks not easy to see at long range; bold streaks under tail.

Yellow bill base obvious, but spotted throat harder to see, often like a pale bar.

Adult, winter
Back wears greyer.

Blackish bar across wing shows well.

Flies low and fast like small thrush.

Adult, autumn
Buff-brown back.

Dull, dark in flight with plain tail but double blackish and thin white wingbars.

In summer, this is a bird of wild, open, windswept mountain regions, usually 1,800–3,000m (6,000–10,000ft) above sea level, with plenty of rocky ground or bare crags. In winter, it may move much lower. It can be located by its song, although distant snatches of song and calls from Black Redstarts or Water Pipits carried on the breeze often confuse the issue.

FEEDING
It eats small insects, spiders, and seeds, picking them from the ground or extricating them from crevices in the rock.

DISPLAY AND VOICE
The song is a creaky trill of uncertain pattern, sometimes more rippling, usually slower than a Dunnock's but more musical. Its calls are rolling *tschirr* or *drru* notes.

BREEDING
Nests are loose grassy cups lined neatly with moss, feathers, and hair, in cavities among rocks. The 3–4 eggs hatch after 14–15 days.

MIGRATION
Mostly resident. Some move lower in winter, but rarely make long-distance movements.

Juvenile
Body like October adult.

Big white tips under tail.

Adult, October
Bright, fresh colours in autumn; dull and worn in summer.

Same scale as Dunnock, opposite.

Male (main bird) has longer tail projection than female (inset).

CRYPTIC PATTERNING
Seemingly bold patterns actually make this a hard bird to see.

WHEN SEEN

All year.

WHERE SEEN
Breeds in highest ranges of central and N Spain, Pyrenees, central France, Alps, Italy, Balkans, and E Europe; rare outside breeding range in winter and only a vagrant farther north.

HABITAT AND INFO

SIMILAR SPECIES
Dunnock is duller; greyer below; much plainer closed wing.

Greyer foreparts

Wren

LENGTH / 9–10cm (3½–4in)
WINGSPAN / 13–17cm (5–6¾in)
WEIGHT / 8–13g (¼–½oz)

SCALE v Pigeon

■ **STATUS /** Secure

A tiny but rounded, deep-bellied bird of dense undergrowth and shady places. It is irascible and inquisitive, with noisy calls and a remarkably loud, very fast song.

Widespread and often very abundant, the Wren can be found anywhere from parks and gardens to rocky islands far offshore. Some isolated island groups have their own races. It is rarely seen in the tree tops, preferring low undergrowth, hedgerows, and shrubs.

FEEDING
It hunts insects and spiders in nooks and crannies in and beneath dense tangles of vegetation.

DISPLAY AND VOICE
Males sing from low perches with a remarkably loud, vibrant, fast warble, more emphatic than the song of a Dunnock and incorporating a distinctive low, rapid trill. Other calls include a harsh *tchurr* and dry *chit-it*.

BREEDING
The male builds several nests, each a ball of grass and leaves with a side entrance, and lines the one chosen by the female. The 5–6 eggs hatch after 14–15 days. Chicks fly at 16–17 days.

MIGRATION
Northern birds move south and west in winter.

Slips through cover or flies to next bush; flight low, fast, and whirring, on tiny round wings.

Tail often cocked.

Pale stripe over eye.

Warm brown; darker bars across wing and flanks.

Loud, very rapid, full-throated song includes distinctive low trill.

Bill slightly curved, tapered.

CONSTANT MOVEMENT
Wrens are energetic foragers, pausing only to call or sing.

WHEN SEEN

All year except much of S Scandinavia and NE Europe, where summer only.

WHERE SEEN
Absent from high mountains, open moors, and N Scandinavia; otherwise almost everywhere.

HABITAT AND INFO

SIMILAR SPECIES
Dunnock is longer; longer-tailed; much greyer on face and underside.

Streaked flanks

Longer tail

ORDER
Passeriformes

FAMILY
Turdidae

SPECIES
Erithacus rubecula

COMMON NAME
Robin

Robin

An unmistakable bird in adult plumage, it is bright when fresh but fades during the summer. Juveniles without red are less distinctive, but have the same alert, intelligent character.

LENGTH / 14cm (5½in)
WINGSPAN / 20–22cm (8–8¾in)
WEIGHT / 16–22g (½–¾oz)

■ STATUS / Secure

SCALE v Pigeon

Robins are bold and confiding in Britain, but much less so elsewhere in Europe, where they tend to be shy. They like deciduous or mixed woods, spruce, parkland with plentiful trees, and, in Britain, gardens, avoiding wide open spaces.

FEEDING
They eat a variety of insects and spiders, taking them mostly from the ground. They also eat small berries in autumn and winter.

DISPLAY AND VOICE
Both males and females are notoriously aggressive, posturing to show off their orange-red breasts in threat displays. The song is a flowing, rich, even warble, clear and rippling. In autumn, it has a rather melancholy quality as each phrase fades away. Calls include a sharp, clicking *tic* or *tic-ikik* and a thin *seei*.

BREEDING
Robins nest in banks, under roots, or in nest boxes with open fronts. The nest is usually a hair-lined cup of grass and leaves. The 4–6 eggs hatch in 13–14 days.

MIGRATION
Many birds from northern and eastern Europe move south and west in winter.

Face and breast clear, unmarked reddish-orange, fading paler.

Both sexes aggressive and territorial; breast patch used in display.

Bluish-grey sides of face, neck, and chest.

Warm brown back; thin pale wingbar.

Juvenile (right)
Pale spots above, dark mottles on gingery chest; tail dull; develops red in irregular spots from centre of chest.

Thin blackish bill; big dark eyes; stands well clear of ground on spindly legs.

VIGOROUS SINGER
Robins sing for much of the year, even at night under streetlights.

WHEN SEEN

All year in south and west; summer visitor in N and E Europe.

WHERE SEEN
Widespread except for Iceland, Norway.

HABITAT AND INFO

SIMILAR SPECIES
Juvenile Nightingale is bigger, with paler eye-ring; more rufous tail.

Rufous colour

Longer tail

Nightingale

LENGTH / 16.5cm (6½in)
WINGSPAN / 23–26cm (9–10¼in)
WEIGHT / 18–27g (⅝–1oz)

■ **STATUS /** Secure

SCALE v Pigeon

A skulking bird with a glorious voice but undistinguished appearance. Its plain face with dark eye and rufous tail are distinctive if seen.

Famous as it is, the Nightingale is not widely known to people in England, where Robins singing at night are likely to be confused with the real thing. Nightingales require dense bushes down to ground level, best provided by coppiced shrubs such as sweet chestnut and hazel, and thickets of blackthorn, bramble, and wild rose. In such places, they are a challenge to see, yet they sometimes sing in full view.

FEEDING

They pick beetles, ants, worms, and berries from the ground, taking them from deep leaf litter and from bare patches in deep shade.

VOICE

The song is superb, but poorly structured. It is recognized by its unique mixture of slow, piping notes, high warbles, and sudden, deep, throbbing and full-throated phrases at great speed, separated by long pauses. Calls include a sweet *hweee* and a peculiar low, croaking, mechanical *kerrrr*.

BREEDING

Nests are cups of leaves and grass built on or near the ground. The 4–5 eggs hatch after 13 days.

MIGRATION

Winters in Africa.

Juvenile (right)
Very dark, wings much darker than adult at first, fade paler by autumn; spotted like young Robin or Redstart.

Rufous tail contrasts with warm olive-brown body.

Undertail and wings rich buff, unlike Thrush Nightingale's.

Very faint malar stripe (dark line from base of bill) at some angles, less marked than on Thrush Nightingale.

Faint breast band on some.

Only slight pale base to large bill.

Bright upperparts and rufous tail separate Nightingale from most Thrush Nightingales (some Russian Thrush Nightingales can be as rich); lower belly whiter.

Sturdier than Robin, hops on ground or through dense vegetation; plain head but pale eye-ring; slight capped effect; greyer side of neck.

Small first primary (dark) shown drooped, equal to or longer than primary coverts.

CHAMPION SONGSTER
Few other birds have the range and vigour of a singing Nightingale.

WHEN SEEN

Sept — April

April to September.

WHERE SEEN

Breeds S and E England, Europe north to S Denmark and Germany, east to Poland, Romania.

HABITAT AND INFO

SIMILAR SPECIES

Garden Warbler is plainer buff-brown, less rufous; shorter, dark bill.

Darker legs

Greyer

Thrush Nightingale

It is very like the Nightingale but more easterly in its range. It is duller, with faint or stronger mottling on breast, duller tail, and more definite dark stripe beside its throat.

LENGTH / 16.5cm (6½in)
WINGSPAN / 24–26cm (9½–10¼in)
WEIGHT / 25–30g (1oz)

■ **STATUS /** Secure

SCALE v Pigeon

Head rounder than Nightingale's; eye-ring less prominent; malar stripe stronger; yellow gape line more marked.

Tail dull rufous; undertail whitish; underparts whitish with faint, fine streaks; fine shaft-streaks on chest.

Stronger pale gape than Nightingale's, darker malar stripe, more mottled breast; plumage variable: some greyer, some more rufous.

Sides of tail, but not uppertail coverts, can be redder in flight; underparts whiter than Nightingale's, but difficult to distinguish.

A real rarity in Britain, this is the eastern counterpart of the Nightingale. It is slightly duller than its relative in appearance, but its equal as a songster. It occupies much the same types of terrain, favouring tall, dense bushes and shrubs in extensive, shady woodland, with soft soil thickly covered in dead and rotting leaves.

FEEDING
It eats mainly insects, varied with a few berries and fruit, obtaining them mostly from the ground. It searches leaf litter and herbs like a small thrush.

VOICE
Males sing from several low perches within their territory. The song is louder, more repetitive, and more staccato than a Nightingale's, with a solemn character. It usually lacks the thin, rising notes, but has many pure, bell-like phrases.

BREEDING
Nests are bulky, made of grass and stems with a fine lining, on the ground in deep shade. The 4–5 eggs hatch after 13 days' incubation.

MIGRATION
Migrates to east Africa in autumn. Rare in western Europe.

First primary very short, hidden beneath primary coverts; usually eight primary tips visible (not seven, like Nightingale); mottled breast may help.

NEAR EQUALS
This is one species that almost matches the Nightingale's song.

WHEN SEEN

Sept — April

April to September.

WHERE SEEN
Breeds extreme S Norway, S Sweden, from Denmark and east side of Baltic eastward, south to Romania.

HABITAT AND INFO

SIMILAR SPECIES
Nightingale has cleaner, paler breast; no or weaker cheek stripe; brighter upperparts.

Brighter back

Plainer throat

Bluethroat

LENGTH / 14cm (5½in)
WINGSPAN / 20–22cm (8–8¾in)
WEIGHT / 15–23g (½–⅞oz)

■ STATUS / Secure

SCALE v Pigeon

A real gem, it is beautiful and tuneful, but secretive in wetlands. Spring males vary and are different from females and young, but all have red tail sides and bold face patterns.

In Britain, the Bluethroat is a scarce migrant, usually in non-breeding plumage and difficult to see, but in spring and summer it is a real joy, combining richness of colour with a fine song. It likes a mixture of open and wooded ground, often frequenting the edges of reedy fens and marshes with willow thickets. It breeds from low plains to high hills.

FEEDING
Bluethroats feed on the ground, scuffling and hopping about in search of insects and seeds.

DISPLAY AND VOICE
Males puff out their throat and breast feathers to exaggerate the central spot as they sing. The song is loud, sweet, and prolonged, varied by a great deal of imitation. It recalls a Nightingale's, but is less richly toned.

BREEDING
It nests on the ground in thick vegetation. The 5–6 eggs take 13–14 days to hatch.

MIGRATION
Winters in Africa (a few in Spain). Migrants appear in varying numbers on western European coasts and islands in late spring and autumn.

Male, breeding
Spain: blue and red bib, no black band.

White line over eye; dark bill with yellow gape patch.

Male, breeding
Netherlands: blue and red separated by black.

Male, breeding
"White-spotted", central and S Europe: central white patch in blue.

Rufous tail sides obvious in flight.

Female, winter
Black and tawny on chest; dark stripe from bill; white over eye and under cheek.

Male, first winter

Female, breeding
Some have blue.

Female, breeding
Bold white and dark stripes; dark breast band.

Male, breeding
"Red-spotted", N Europe: central red patch in blue.

INTENSE GORGET
The metallic blue of the throat is very striking.

WHEN SEEN

April to October.

WHERE SEEN
Breeds locally W and E France, Low Countries, N Scandinavia; erratically across central Europe and east from N Germany into Russia.

HABITAT AND INFO

SIMILAR SPECIES
Nightingale's plain head lacks white over eye; tail more uniform rusty red.

Plainer head

Rufous tail

ORDER
Passeriformes

FAMILY
Turdidae

SPECIES
Cercotrichas
galactotes

COMMON NAME
Rufous Bush-robin

Rufous Bush-robin

Belonging to a family more familiar in Africa, this is a unique bird in Europe. It is lively and jaunty in its actions, with a distinctive long tail, often cocked.

LENGTH / 15cm (6in)
WINGSPAN / 22–27cm (8¾–10½in)
WEIGHT / 20–25g (¾–1oz)

■ STATUS / Vulnerable

SCALE v Pigeon

Flight strong, quick, usually short into nearby cover.

White tail spots larger and obvious underneath.

Western Thin black line.

Eastern Thick black line.

Juvenile, eastern Juveniles more buff; bright feather edges on wings.

The bush-robins are mostly African birds. This is the only species that breeds in Europe, where it likes dry, sunny places such as orange groves, prickly pear thickets, and sandy gorges with bushes. It is lively and almost extravagant in its actions, but it can be extremely elusive. It often flies off into a deep bush if disturbed, but patience may be rewarded when it returns to show itself off on the ground.

FEEDING
It digs large insects and worms from loose soil, catches moths in flight, and snatches flies and wasps while hovering over flowers.

DISPLAY AND VOICE
Males stand upright with drooped wings and fanned tail as a threat to intruders. They sing from high perches with a disjointed but exceedingly rich, varied song, with clear, lark-like notes and throaty phrases like those of a Nightingale.

BREEDING
They build untidy nests of twigs, grass, and roots in bushes. They incubate 4–5 eggs for 13 days.

MIGRATION
It winters in Africa. It is very rare north of breeding range.

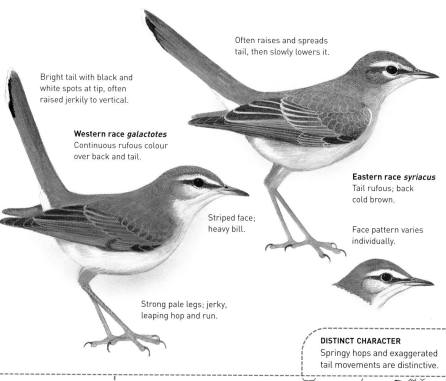

Often raises and spreads tail, then slowly lowers it.

Bright tail with black and white spots at tip, often raised jerkily to vertical.

Western race *galactotes* Continuous rufous colour over back and tail.

Striped face; heavy bill.

Eastern race *syriacus* Tail rufous; back cold brown.

Face pattern varies individually.

Strong pale legs; jerky, leaping hop and run.

DISTINCT CHARACTER Springy hops and exaggerated tail movements are distinctive.

WHERE SEEN
Breeds sparsely in S Spain and Portugal; small numbers in Albania and Greece; very rare UK.

HABITAT AND INFO

SIMILAR SPECIES
Nightingale has plainer head; unspotted tail.

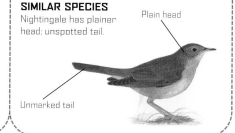

Plain head

Unmarked tail

Redstart

SCALE v Pigeon

LENGTH / 14cm (5½in)
WINGSPAN / 20–24cm (8–9½in)
WEIGHT / 10–20g (¼–¾oz)

■ **STATUS /** Vulnerable

A small, elegant, colourful chat, distinguished by its light rusty-red tail and rump and woodland habitat.

The breeding range of this delightful little chat is curiously erratic: in Britain, it is largely a bird of western woods, but it can be found locally over much of southern and eastern England, too. In the west, it likes old oak woods and scattered oaks on the slopes of rocky hillsides. In other areas, it likes mature oaks with a lot of dead wood in parkland or near lowland heaths.

FEEDING

It picks insects from the surface of leaf litter or from leaves high in trees. It also snatches them from the air in short "fly-catching" flights.

DISPLAY AND VOICE

Males have a rich, full song on arrival at their territories, but soon change to a shorter song close to the nest site as they advertise it to potential mates. This song is sweet, short, and rather unfinished, beginning with several *srree* notes. Calls include a high *hweet* and a harder *tuik*.

BREEDING

It nests in holes in trees, rocks, walls, or, sometimes, nest boxes. Up to seven eggs hatch in 12–14 days.

MIGRATION

Winters in Africa. Regular migrant on W European coasts.

Both sexes have more red on rump than Black Redstart.

Female

Male

Male underwing brighter than that of paler female's.

Male, spring
Slaty-grey above; white forehead; inky black face and bib.

Female

Juvenile

Female and juvenile pale; rump and tail like male's but body mostly buffish; black eye in plain face.

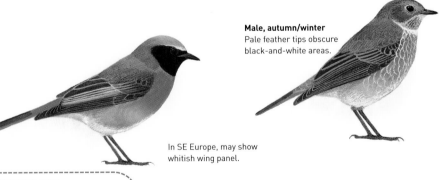

Male, autumn/winter
Pale feather tips obscure black-and-white areas.

In SE Europe, may show whitish wing panel.

HANDSOME MALE
This is one of the brightest of the small chats.

WHEN SEEN

Oct — April

April to October.

WHERE SEEN
Rare in Ireland; local in Iberia; absent from Iceland; otherwise breeds in most of Europe and is a widespread migrant.

HABITAT AND INFO

SIMILAR SPECIES
Black Redstart is very similar in shape, actions, and basic pattern, but more smoky grey.

Darker tail coverts

Paler wing panel

Black Redstart

Typically a bird of old towns and villages, industrial sites, cliffs, and mountain crags. It is also found on coasts and in quarries in winter.

LENGTH / 14.5cm (5¾in)
WINGSPAN / 23-26cm (9-10¼in)
WEIGHT / 14-20g (½-¾oz)

■ STATUS / Secure

SCALE v Pigeon

Male, Iberia
Steely-black with paler cap; bold white wing panel.

Male, first winter
Some first winter males have a little white on inner wing.

Female, first winter

Male

Female

Adult male, summer
Black and slaty-grey with dark reddish tail and vent; immature males much greyer.

Male's tail longer than female's.

Adult female
Sooty brown-grey, darker than Redstart; red more restricted on uppertail.

Note Robin-like shape; dark eye in grey face; dark legs.

Although clearly a close relative of the Redstart, this species breeds in very different habitats. Common in old towns and villages, it is also found on derelict sites and in industrial areas that simulate rocks and cliffs. Many breed on remote cliffs and in mountain gorges far from urban influence.

FEEDING
Hopping and running on the ground, or dropping briefly from a perch before flying back up, the Black Redstart snatches small insects and sometimes picks up small berries.

VOICE
Males sing from roof tops, chimneys, and wires, often on very high buildings, as well as from rocks high above screes and boulder-strewn quarries. The song has short, quick, sweet trills mixed with rattles and a grating, slurred *tch-r-r-rrrrt*.

BREEDING
The nest is on a ledge or in a crevice, in a building, a cave, or on a cliff. The 4-6 eggs take 13-17 days to hatch. The chicks fly in 12-19 days.

MIGRATION
Disperses widely in the autumn to the south and west.

WHITE FLASH
Adult males have well-defined white wing panels.

WHERE SEEN
Breeds locally in Britain; Europe south from S Sweden and Denmark; from N and E Europe moves west and south in winter as far as S Ireland, SW England.

HABITAT AND INFO

SIMILAR SPECIES
Redstart is paler, buffier below; more extensive orange-red on rump and tail.

Brighter tail

Orange underside

Whinchat

LENGTH / 12.5cm (5in)
WINGSPAN / 21–24cm (8¼–9½in)
WEIGHT / 16–24g (½–⅞oz)

SCALE v Pigeon

■ **STATUS /** Vulnerable

Like a slimmer version of the Stonechat, with a white stripe over eye and white in tail. It is typically perched on a tall, thin stem, young conifer, or wire, often in grassier places than the Stonechat.

Sadly declining in many areas where intensive farming has swept away great tracts of ancient, species-rich pasture, the Whinchat needs slender stems rising from rough grassland, heathery slopes, or young, open conifer plantations. Like other chats, it often pauses on open ground near the coast while on migration.

FEEDING
The Whinchat drops from a perch to take insects from the ground, less often taking them in the air.

VOICE
Isolated pairs are often rather quiet, but where several pairs are close together the males sing much more. Their song is Robin-like but with throaty churrs and rattles, and much mimicry. Calls are a scolding *tik-tik* and a rising *huee*, often combined as *huee-tik-tik*, less hard than a Stonechat.

BREEDING
The neat cup nest is extremely well hidden on the ground among thick grass. The 4–7 eggs hatch within 12–13 days.

MIGRATION
All Whinchats leave Europe to spend the winter in Africa.

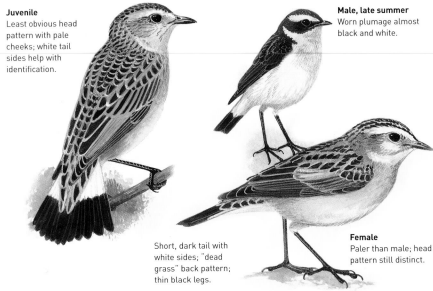

Juvenile
Least obvious head pattern with pale cheeks; white tail sides help with identification.

Male, late summer
Worn plumage almost black and white.

Short, dark tail with white sides; "dead grass" back pattern; thin black legs.

Female
Paler than male; head pattern still distinct.

Much variation in intensity of colour in both sexes, with wear and moult.

Male
Worn and dark; tail pattern conclusive.

Male, September

Female, May

Juvenile, September

Male, spring
Striking white above and below blackish cheeks; apricot breast.

White on tail is very variable: maximum shown on left, minimum shown on right.

TIP-TOP PERCHES
Whinchats like to sit on the very tip of a tall stem.

WHEN SEEN

April to October.

WHERE SEEN
Breeds from N Spain and C Italy north and east through Europe, except for extreme N Scandinavia, Iceland, most of Low Countries, and S Greece.

HABITAT AND INFO

SIMILAR SPECIES
Stonechat is darker; all-dark tail; darker chin; plainer head.

Dark throat

Blacker tail

Stonechat

A stocky little bird, typically seen on exposed perches on bushes or overhead wires, scolding intruders with insistent, tetchy notes.

LENGTH / 12.5cm (5in)
WINGSPAN / 18–21cm (7–8¼in)
WEIGHT / 14–17g (½–⅝oz)

■ **STATUS /** Secure

SCALE v Pigeon

Female
Small white wing marks; all-dark tail.

Male, spring
Short, rounded wings; large white shoulder patches.

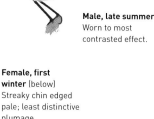

Male, late summer
Worn to most contrasted effect.

Male
Typical posture: black face and throat; white neck patch obvious.

Female
Dark extreme.

Male, September
Spanish race.

Female, first winter (below)
Streaky chin edged pale; least distinctive plumage.

Male, first winter (above)
Dark face and throat, with paler lower edge; all-black tail.

Female
Fades paler below in late summer.

Male, spring
White shoulder patches more exposed in display.

PALE JUVENILE
Young birds are paler and buffier than their parents.

Should you walk close to its nest, the Stonechat will scold you from a bush or wire with endlessly repeated, agitated calls. This is a bird of rough heaths and slopes, moors and hillsides with plenty of gorse, tall bushy heather, and small shrubs. It is fond of the narrow strip between enclosed fields and rocky cliffs on the coast.

FEEDING
Gliding to the ground from an open perch, the Stonechat picks up an insect, sometimes after a short chase, then flies up again – often to a fresh perch nearby.

DISPLAY AND VOICE
Males sing from exposed perches, including wires, and also in bouncy, hovering song flights. They often spread their wing covert feathers to expose large areas of white. The song is a scrappy warble, more uniform than a Whinchat's. Calls are hard, chacking notes and a plaintive *hweet*, often together as *hweet-tsak-tsak*.

BREEDING
The nest is in grass, often with a short entrance tunnel. It holds 4–6 eggs, which hatch in 13–14 days.

MIGRATION
They leave in autumn, often moving to coasts in cold weather.

WHEN SEEN

All year.

WHERE SEEN
Ireland, local Britain, Europe south of Denmark, Germany, Ukraine.

HABITAT AND INFO

SIMILAR SPECIES
Whinchat has paler stripe over eye; pale chin; white each side of tail base.

Pale over eye

White on tail

Black-eared & Pied Wheatear

LENGTH / 14.5cm (5³/₄in)
WINGSPAN / 25–30cm (9³/₄–11³/₄in)
WEIGHT / 15–25g (½–1oz)

■ **STATUS /** Vulnerable

SCALE v Pigeon

Pied Wheatear has the same tail pattern, shape, and behaviour as Black-eared, making it hard to distinguish in some plumages. Black-eared is a neat, bright, handsome wheatear that often perches on bush tops and posts. Its tail pattern is distinctive.

Black-eared and Pied Wheatears form a closely related species pair, not always easy to distinguish. While they are clearly wheatears, both have some characteristics typical of the smaller chats, especially a tendency to perch on bushes. Compared with other wheatears, they are small and slim, and their light weight allows them to perch on quite slender stems. The Black-eared is much the more familiar of the two. It is one of the few birds in Europe with two different plumages: the "pale-throated" and "black-throated" forms. There are also two races, both of which occur in the two plumage forms. Males of the race *melanoleuca*, found east of Italy and Yugoslavia, have more black above the bill than the western race *hispanica*. The eastern black-throated form has more black than the western black-throated form, and in spring eastern birds are greyer, less richly cinnamon-buff, than western ones. The Black-eared Wheatear lives chiefly in the Mediterranean area. It prefers low-lying landscapes with scattered shrubs, rocks, and exposed earth. Stony fields, gullies, heaths, vineyards with rocky walls, and open Mediterranean scrub suit it well. The Pied Wheatear breeds in similar terrain from the western side of the Black Sea eastward, and is a rare vagrant in the UK, typically very late in the autumn.

FEEDING
Both species eat mainly insects, taking them from bare earth and short herbs – typically in short, accurate flights from perches, to which they usually return quite quickly.

DISPLAY AND VOICE
Males sing for long periods from rocks, walls, bush tops, and wires. They have a song flight, expanding their tails to show the large areas of white, then diving in a steep plunge to the ground. The song is a series of short, loud, warbling phrases, with a scratchy effect. Calls are dry clicking notes and short rattles.

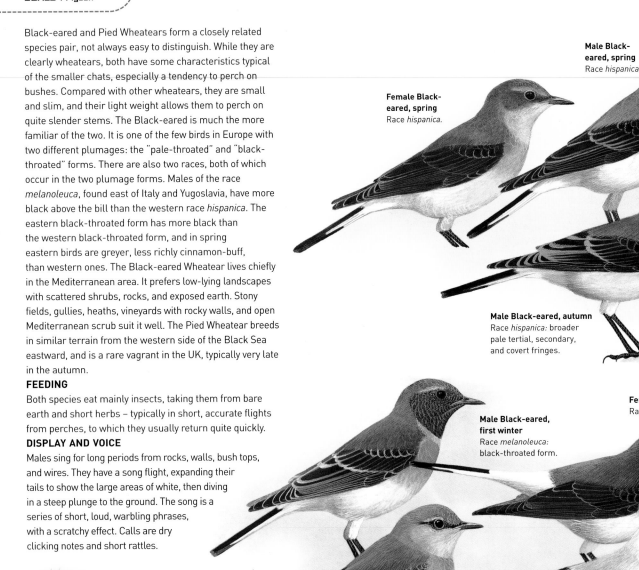

Female Black-eared, spring
Race *hispanica*.

Male Black-eared, spring
Race *hispanica*.

Male Black-eared, autumn
Race *hispanica*: broader pale tertial, secondary, and covert fringes.

Male Black-eared, first winter
Race *melanoleuca*: black-throated form.

Female Black-eared
Race *melanoleuca*.

Male Black-eared, first winter
Race *melanoleuca*: probably pale-throated form.

Male Black-eared, spring
Race *melanoleuca*: orange wears to white.

Compare yellow-brown back, tail pattern, dark wing, and black underwing with Wheatear. Often perches on slender bushes, unlike Wheatear.

WHEN SEEN

Oct — March

March to October.

WHERE SEEN
Black-eared Wheatear: Iberia, S France, S Italy, Balkans; rare migrant elsewhere. Pied Wheatear: extreme E Europe, S Asia; very rare vagrant in W Europe, often very late in autumn.

HABITAT AND INFO

SIMILAR SPECIES
Wheatear has broader black tip to tail; paler underwing.

Greyer

Broader tailband

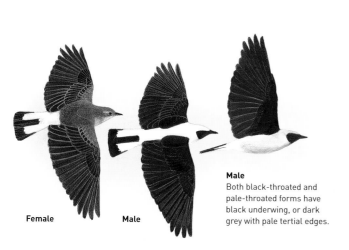

Female **Male**

Male
Both black-throated and pale-throated forms have black underwing, or dark grey with pale tertial edges.

Male Black-eared, spring (below)
Race *melanoleuca*: black throat deeper, black mask wider than *hispanica*.

Male Black-eared, spring
Race *hispanica*.

Variation in tail pattern, all forms: left most like Wheatear, but width of black uneven; right most typical and distinctive, with uneven black tip and thin black line on side.

Female Pied, summer
Tail like Black-eared's; white rump extends higher onto back in all plumages; shorter tail projection than Black-eared's; more rusty- or grey-brown on chest; some are faintly mottled with firmer border against pale belly.

Male Pied
Rare white throat.

Male Pied

Male Pied, spring
Black throat; often grey on crown.

Female Pied, first winter
Typical pale throat; very like eastern Black-eared, but colder back colour, less yellowish below; note scaly back feathers.

Female Pied, first winter
Rare black throat.

STRONG CONTRAST
Spring males have eye-catchingly bright plumage.

BREEDING

Both build a cup nest of grass and moss with a finer lining, on the ground, either in a hollow or beneath a stone or bush, with a heap of fine twigs at the entrance forming a small platform. The 4–5 eggs are incubated for 13–14 days. The chicks fledge after 11–12 days.

MIGRATION

They winter in semi-desert regions in Africa just south of the Sahara. They are rare north of the breeding range, either as "overshoots" in spring or strays in the autumn.

DID YOU KNOW?
These lightweight wheatears can perch on flimsier stems than other wheatears. From these, they take most of their prey from the ground, the rest in short fly-catching flights. During a hatch of insects, fly-catching becomes the most frequent technique. If perches are scarce, they hop on bare ground, or hover if there is dense vegetation, to find food.

Wheatear

SCALE v Pigeon

LENGTH / 14.5–15.5cm (5¾–6in)
WINGSPAN / 26–32cm (10¼–12½in)
WEIGHT / 17–30g (⅝–1oz)

■ **STATUS /** Secure

A small, smart, upright, terrestrial chat with a bold splash of white over a T-shaped black tail. Spring males are beautifully grey above, while other plumages are much more brown and buff.

The first Cuckoo or Swallow may be a more popular symbol of spring, but to many bird-watchers it is the arrival of the Wheatear early in March that lifts the spirits. Usually, it will be a male first, a few days ahead of the females, and he looks unbelievably smart. He may be on a grassy strip near the coast, or on a high chalk down inland, but wherever he is seen, he will probably fly ahead a few dozen yards and then settle again, his vivid white rump catching the eye for a moment before disappearing as quickly. Wheatears behave in the same way in autumn, when migrant birds appear in open spaces with grass, sandy areas, golf courses, ploughed fields, and the shores of lowland reservoirs. In the summer breeding season, by contrast, Wheatears need a combination of short grass on which to forage, and tumbled rocks or stone walls in which to nest.

FEEDING

The birds feed mainly on insects and spiders. They usually take them from the ground, either in short runs with frequent stops to stand upright and look around, or in quick, deft flights from a low perch. A Wheatear tends to fly from a perch to the closest areas of open ground first, then fly farther afield but still return to the same bush or post. Once that area has been exhausted, the bird flies on to a new perch. In this way, it often covers a large area along a linear habitat such as a strip of dunes or shingle behind a beach, or a band of grass along a rough track bulldozed across a moor.

DISPLAY AND VOICE

Wheatear song flights are frequent, quite long and high, with a fast, fluttering action. At the peak of the climb the bird dances in the air before slanting back to the ground. The song is musical and quick, but with many hard notes, creaky calls, and rattles. Calls are typically hard and double or treble: *chak-chak* or *hweet-chak-chak*.

BREEDING

The female builds a rough nest of grass, heather, feathers, and moss in a hole in a wall, a collapsed rabbit hole, a space beneath fallen rocks, or a tunnel into a scree slope. She incubates her 4–7 eggs for 13 days. The chicks move from the nest when about 10 days old and fly after 2–3 weeks.

MIGRATION

Frequently seen on migration outside their breeding areas, Wheatears move south to Africa for the winter. Even breeders from Greenland winter in tropical Africa, passing through Britain in spring.

Female, autumn

Male, first year
Greenland race: crown and ear coverts differ from those of adult.

Adult male, spring
Greenland race: biggest, brightest Greenland birds with longest wings are distinctive, but many are not distinguishable.

Some Greenland birds have shorter tail than European, but not all.

Juvenile female
Primaries browner than young male's.

Male, autumn (left)
Female's wings browner.

Juvenile
Greenland race: longer wingtips than European's, with six visible tips.

Wide, pale primary tips distinguish juvenile from adult.

Autumn birds have boldly contrasted wings, unlike Isabelline Wheatear; more obvious T-shape on tail; wider white rump; grey underwing.

WHEN SEEN

Oct — March

March to October.

WHERE SEEN

Breeds over most of Europe, including Iceland, but sparse and local in France and much of S Spain; a widespread migrant both on coasts and well inland.

HABITAT AND INFO

SIMILAR SPECIES

Black-eared Wheatear has dark underwing; slim tail with narrow black tip curling up sides.

Black underwing

Whiter tail tip

Male, spring
Spanish race: strikingly pale grey and black.

Adult female, spring
Grey bloom wears off to give brown back by June; breast becomes whiter.

Male, first spring
Wings brown; just a thin dark smudge on ear coverts.

Adult male, spring
Black wings; ear coverts have wide black band; back much greyer than Black-eared Wheatear's.

Juvenile

Grey underwing unlike Isabelline or Black-eared Wheatear's.

Simple tailband below.

Immature or adult, autumn to winter

Male, spring
Greenland race: fractionally longer primaries than European race's.

DID YOU KNOW?
Wheatears have spread north-west into North America and also across the Bering Strait from Asia. The North American birds migrate to spend the winter in Africa. Their return journey, almost entirely over the sea in autumn, adds up to more than 24,000km (15,000 miles). These big "Greenland" Wheatears are most often recognized in western Europe in late April and May.

Black Wheatear

ORDER Passeriformes
FAMILY Turdidae
SPECIES Oenanthe leucura
COMMON NAME Black Wheatear

LENGTH / 18cm (7in)
WINGSPAN / 30–35cm (11¾–14in)
WEIGHT / 25–35g (1–1¼oz)

■ **STATUS /** Secure

SCALE v Pigeon

A large, dark wheatear with a striking white rear end, the only all-dark wheatear likely in Europe.

This large wheatear is never common, often occurring just a pair or two at a time in suitable spots with broken rocky slopes, screes, cliffs, and scattered bushes. It is an Iberian speciality, reaching the southern foothills of the Pyrenees, but it also breeds in Morocco and Tunisia, where it must be distinguished from the White-crowned Black Wheatear.

FEEDING
It catches most of its insect prey as it hops about like a thrush or explores cavities under rocks, but it takes some in dives from a perch or in flight. It also eats berries in autumn.

VOICE
The song has a curiously distant, subdued quality even at close range. The call is a thin *pee-pee-pee*, but it also has a hard *chak* in alarm.

BREEDING
The birds nest in cavities in cliffs or walls, laying 3–5 eggs. They hatch after 14–18 days, and the chicks fly within two weeks.

MIGRATION
Higher breeding areas such as the Sierra Nevada are vacated in winter, but little other movement occurs. It is very rare outside its usual range.

Looks big, heavy, broad-winged in flight.

Very striking white tail, rump, and vent.

Paler webs of flight feathers inconspicuous from above.

Typically stocky, but can look very slim in extreme heat.

Male
Black-brown; wings black, but wear browner.

Female/juvenile
Dark sooty-brown; wings black when fresh, but wear to dull brown.

SOBER COLOURS
Black, sooty brown, and white complete this bird's colour scheme.

WHEN SEEN

All year.

WHERE SEEN
Spain, extreme eastern edge of Portugal; almost extinct in extreme S France; perhaps breeds Italy.

HABITAT AND INFO

SIMILAR SPECIES
Spotless Starling has longer shape; no white rump and tail area.

Dark rump and vent

Spiky bill

ORDER
Passeriformes

FAMILY
Turdidae

SPECIES
Oenanthe isabellina

COMMON NAME
Isabelline Wheatear

Isabelline Wheatear

A big, pale wheatear, it is easily confused with some forms of the northern Wheatear: check the structure, face, wing pattern, and tail. It often wags its tail more and runs more than the Wheatear.

LENGTH / 16.5cm (6½in)
WINGSPAN / 27-31cm (10½-12in)
WEIGHT / 25-40g (1-1½oz)

■ STATUS / Vulnerable

SCALE v Pigeon

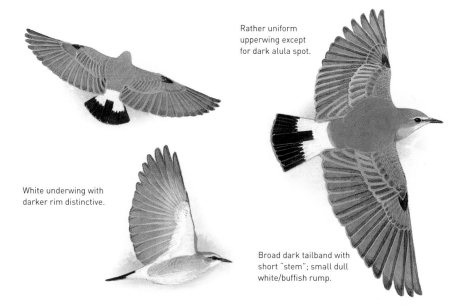

Rather uniform upperwing except for dark alula spot.

White underwing with darker rim distinctive.

Broad dark tailband with short "stem"; small dull white/buffish rump.

Within its usual range, this stocky, pale wheatear can look so striking that its identity is never in doubt. If it turns up as a rare vagrant elsewhere in Europe, however, it is likely to be confused with the northern Wheatear. This makes careful observation essential for a correct identification. It is a lowland bird, found in dry areas from semi-deserts to open fields and scrubland.

FEEDING
It favours ants and beetles, usually catching them on the ground in short, quick dashes. It may also dig them from loose soil, or snatch them in dives from a perch rather like a shrike.

DISPLAY AND VOICE
The song, often given in a low, whirring flight, is rich and musical with much mimicry. Typical calls include a loud *weep* and quieter *cheep* and *wheet-wit* notes.

BREEDING
It usually nests in a burrow made by a Bee-eater or a souslik. The 5–6 eggs are incubated for 12 days. The chicks fledge after 15 days.

MIGRATION
European breeders move to sub-Saharan Africa in winter.

Upright; big-headed; thick bill.

Stripe over eye usually short, well-defined; male has dark line to bill.

Adult, autumn
The darkest extreme: note wing pattern, sharp stripe over eye.

Male, breeding
Note longer tail than female's, but shorter than northern Wheatear's; often more exposed "thigh" above leg joint than on Wheatear.

Juvenile female, autumn
May be sandy or a colder clay colour.

TRICKY CHALLENGE
Identifying this bird requires close concentration.

WHEN SEEN

Oct — Mar

March to October.

WHERE SEEN
Breeds from Greece very locally to Black Sea; very rare elsewhere in Europe.

HABITAT AND INFO

SIMILAR SPECIES
Black-eared Wheatear has dark underwing; narrow tailband.

Black underwing

More white on tail

Rock Thrush

LENGTH / 18.5cm (7¼in)
WINGSPAN / 30–35cm (11¾–14in)
WEIGHT / 50–70g (1¾–2½oz)

■ **STATUS /** Vulnerable

SCALE v Pigeon

A small, sturdy, short-tailed thrush of mountain pastures and rocky slopes. Spring males have bold colouring, other plumages are mostly rusty and barred.

Although its subtlety of colour and pattern make the male Rock Thrush less obvious than might be expected, a close view reveals its true beauty. It is found in grassy Alpine meadows and on high, open slopes with plenty of rocks, dry stone walls, and scattered bushes, often higher up than the Blue Rock Thrush.

FEEDING
It catches beetles and other large insects on the ground, often after a dive from a rock or wire. Sometimes it catches several insects in a shuffling run before returning to the perch.

DISPLAY AND VOICE
The male sings from a perch or in high, fast, fluttering song flights. The song is a soft, flowing warble with much mimicry, especially of the Chaffinch. Calls are a short, hard *tak*, *schak-schak,* and a fluty whistle.

BREEDING
The nest is placed in a crevice in a crag or wall. The 4–5 eggs hatch within 14–15 days.

MIGRATION
A few birds winter in north Africa, but most go south of the Sahara as far as Tanzania.

Male, spring
May have more white on back.

Female, spring
Rich tail and underwing colour aid identification.

Unique tail colour.

Juvenile, autumn
Pale, scaly upperparts; white wingbar; pale orange underside.

Male, autumn
Pale spots wear away in spring.

Back feathers have white tips in spring.

Female, spring
Less white on back than male; grows darker in summer as feather tips wear off.

Younger females more spotted above, paler below.

Male, spring
Unique, beautiful pattern.

Very shy in summer; tame on migration.

ORANGE AND BLUE
A male stands out, unlike any other European bird.

WHEN SEEN

Sept   March

March to September.

WHERE SEEN
Iberia, SE France, Alps, Italy, Balkans, E Europe.

HABITAT AND INFO

SIMILAR SPECIES
Redstart is much smaller, slighter, with narrow dark-centred tail.

Dark throat

Smaller size

ORDER
Passeriformes

FAMILY
Turdidae

SPECIES
Monticola solitarius

COMMON NAME
Blue Rock Thrush

Blue Rock Thrush

Long-bodied, square-tailed, and noticeably long-billed, it is a thrush of rocky crags and gorges. It can be elusive and hard to approach over difficult terrain, but it is not wary around human habitation.

LENGTH / 20cm (8in)
WINGSPAN / 35–40cm (14–15½in)
WEIGHT / 60–80g (2–2¾oz)

■ STATUS / Vulnerable

SCALE v Pigeon

Long wings and tail; strong flight with easy, floating action.

Male

Spends long periods standing still on cliff ledges or boulders.

Juvenile

Female

While the Rock Thrush is a bird of high meadows, the Blue Rock Thrush is more likely to be found in warm, rocky places, including deep, wild gorges and coastal sites with cliffs and buildings. It also lives on large stone buildings that reproduce its natural cliff habitat, such as castles and even the Coliseum in Rome.

FEEDING
Its main foods include insects and small lizards, with a few berries.

DISPLAY AND VOICE
Its song flights are more swooping, less powerful, than those of the Rock Thrush. It often sings from a high perch above a gorge with a far-carrying, rich, throaty warble, recalling a Blackbird or Mistle Thrush but with shorter, simpler phrases. The calls are a hard *tchuk tchuk* and a high *peep*.

BREEDING
It nests in holes in rocks, walls, buildings, or pipes. The 4–5 eggs hatch in 12–15 days.

MIGRATION
The Blue Rock Thrush is a resident or partial migrant, with some winter dispersal to milder areas in the Mediterranean region.

Long bill distinctive.

Female, spring
Combination of blue and barred brown; wings fade browner until moult from July to October.

Wings fade to brown before autumn moult; much duller overall by late summer.

Male
Dark at distance; close-up in good light shows intense blue.

Male, first year

SUBTLE COLOURS
Sunlight reveals an intense, deep, smoky-blue.

WHEN SEEN

All year.

WHERE SEEN
Widespread in Iberia and Mediterranean region, including major islands.

HABITAT AND INFO

SIMILAR SPECIES
Blackbird has shorter bill; longer tail; darker, not barred on body.

Yellow bill

Longer tail

Blackbird

LENGTH / 24cm (9½in)
WINGSPAN / 34–38cm (13½–15in)
WEIGHT / 80–110g (2¾–3¾oz)

■ STATUS / Secure

SCALE v Pigeon

A common garden, woodland, and farmland thrush. The all-black male is unique, the female is darker than any other brown thrush. It raises its tail on landing and gives a loud, hysterical rattle of alarm. It is not found in flocks.

Few birds have such a presence in and around places where people live and spend much of their time: gardens, town parks, woodland edges, tall trees, and farmland with hedges. In all of these habitats, and others, the Blackbird is a familiar neighbour. It draws attention to itself by its loud, persistent, and sometimes irritating alarm notes (especially if there is a cat or a Magpie about), its sudden outburst when scared into flight, and – much more welcome – its beautiful song. Of all the fine songsters of Europe, the Blackbird has the most "musical" song in our terms, with beautifully modulated notes and phrases that seem almost capable of developing into human musical forms.

FEEDING

The Blackbird eats a great many earthworms, and it is most characteristically seen hopping and shuffling across a lawn, stopping periodically to look and listen, lean forward, and then suddenly seize a worm, pulling it from the ground only after a long struggle. It is also a noisy feeder in dry leaf litter, throwing aside piles of leaves as it searches for grubs. It eats various insects, their larvae, berries, and fruit – the berries especially in autumn – as well as occasional newts, fish, and lizards.

DISPLAY AND VOICE

Blackbird displays are overlooked by most people, but they include a variety of postures in which the bird raises, depresses, or fans its tail, and puffs out its rump feathers. Its song, however, is obvious everywhere: a long, flowing sequence of varied phrases, most of which include fluty, throaty, musical notes, which peter out into thin, scratchy, hesitant endings. The song has far less repetition than that of the Song Thrush, and is less wild, more varied, and mellower than a Mistle Thrush song. Typical calls include a staccato *pink pink pink*, especially at dusk; *clink clink* in alarm; a soft, "comfortable" *chook*; a slightly vibrant *seee* in flight; and a loud rattling outburst if suddenly frightened.

BREEDING

The nest is a deep, thick cup of grasses and stems, with a mud inner layer covered by a fine lining. The 3–5 eggs hatch after 12–14 days. The chicks fly after 13 days, leaving the nest a few days earlier.

MIGRATION

A frequent migrant, the Blackbird is often seen at coasts in autumn. Eastern birds move south and west in autumn.

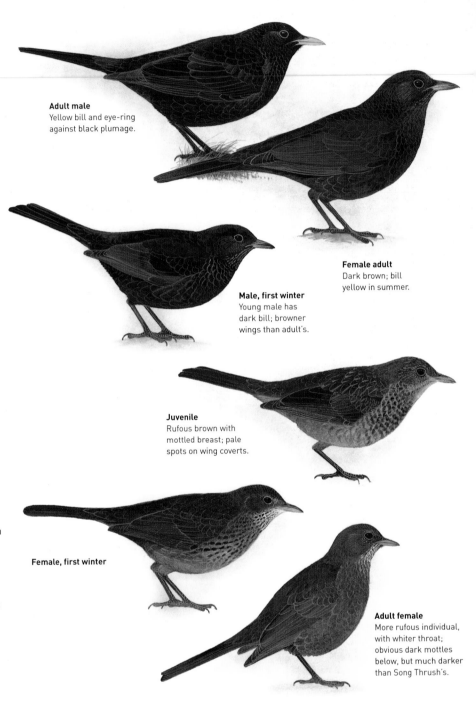

Adult male
Yellow bill and eye-ring against black plumage.

Female adult
Dark brown; bill yellow in summer.

Male, first winter
Young male has dark bill; browner wings than adult's.

Juvenile
Rufous brown with mottled breast; pale spots on wing coverts.

Female, first winter

Adult female
More rufous individual, with whiter throat; obvious dark mottles below, but much darker than Song Thrush's.

WHEN SEEN

All year in most of range; summer only in far north and east.

WHERE SEEN
Breeds Iceland, all but extreme N Scandinavia, and throughout rest of Europe; birds from east of Germany migrate in autumn to W Europe and N Africa.

HABITAT AND INFO

SIMILAR SPECIES
Ring Ouzel has pale upperwing; usually hint of pale, scaly feather edges below.

Paler wing

Sharper wingtip

WINTER STORE
Blackbirds eat many energy-rich berries in winter.

Ring Ouzel
Pale coverts.

Blackbird

Flight direct and strong; wings broad and round; tail long and full.

Pale greyish outer wing of adult male contrasts with black body in flight.

Feeds with series of short, two-footed, bounding hops, runs, and pauses, bending forward to pick up food.

Female
Rounder wings than male's.

Male

Typically raises tail and then lowers it slowly on landing.

DID YOU KNOW?

Many species perform a very quiet, rambling version of their usual song, called a subsong, which is often audible only at very close range. In some, such as the Goldcrest, the subsong is quite unlike the usual song, but the Blackbird's sounds just like a bird giving a quiet, inward, "daydreaming" version of full song. The function has not been satisfactorily explained.

?

Fieldfare

LENGTH / 25.5cm (10in)
WINGSPAN / 39–42cm (15½–16½in)
WEIGHT / 80–130g (2¾–4½oz)

■ STATUS / Secure

SCALE v Pigeon

This is a bold, handsome, gregarious thrush with a distinctively contrasting grey head and rump, a dark back, and flashing white underwings.

A social bird all year round, but it is particularly familiar in its roaming, chattering winter flocks, when it often mixes with Redwings. It likes farmland with tall, old hedges and trees, as well as bushy heaths.

FEEDING
It eats mostly insects and worms taken from the ground, with many berries in autumn and winter.

DISPLAY AND VOICE
Pairs defend their loose nesting colonies against predators, and males sing from a perch or in a song flight. The song is a mixture of weak chuckles, rattles, and squeaks. Calls include a nasal, slightly Lapwing-like *weep* and a chuckling, guttural chatter: *chak-chak-chak*.

BREEDING
The female builds a heavy nest of roots, grasses, and mud in a tree. The 5–6 eggs hatch in 10–13 days.

MIGRATION
Fieldfares migrate south and west in autumn in flocks of 10–100 or more, often moving by day, and return to breed in spring.

Grey rump; black tail.

Bright white underwing coverts obvious (but compare Mistle Thrush's); sharp contrast with dark chest.

White belly striking when perched.

Female (left) longer tailed than male (right); flight strong, quick, often high; flocks have low, throaty, chuckling calls.

Yellow bill with dark tip often conspicuous.

Female (above) has longer tail than male (below).

Handsome grey head, blacker mask, and orange-buff chest with bold black spots; flanks more solidly black in spring.

BOLD APPEARANCE
Fieldfares are striking and confident birds.

Ring Ouzel

A shy, wild, dark thrush of uplands, rocks, and coastal scrub, it has a small head, long square tail, and long wings. It combines the shape of the Blackbird and the Mistle Thrush, but is typically slender.

LENGTH / 23–24cm (9–9½in)
WINGSPAN / 38–42cm (15–16½in)
WEIGHT / 95–130g (3½–4½oz)

■ STATUS / Vulnerable

SCALE v Pigeon

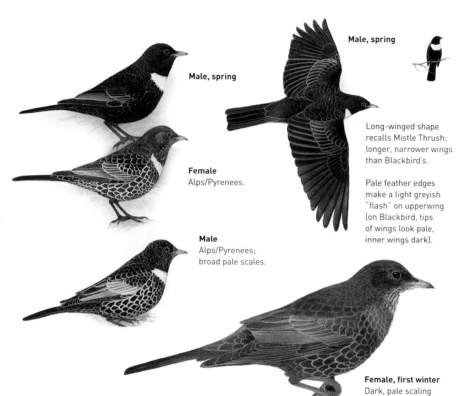

Male, spring

Male, spring

Female
Alps/Pyrenees.

Long-winged shape recalls Mistle Thrush; longer, narrower wings than Blackbird's.

Pale feather edges make a light greyish "flash" on upperwing (on Blackbird, tips of wings look pale, inner wings dark).

Male
Alps/Pyrenees; broad pale scales.

Female, first winter
Dark, pale scaling and chest band often obscured.

Male, winter
Dull breast band; broader pale scales on body.

Female, spring
Brown with pale breast crescent; pale wing panel.

Juvenile
Pale wing panel; black bars on rufous flanks.

In spring and autumn, many people see migrating Ring Ouzels on the coast, or along ranges of quite low hills, but as breeding birds they are restricted to higher ground with rocky tors, cliffs, and crags. The popularity of such places among walkers and climbers puts great pressure on Ring Ouzels in many hilly areas.

FEEDING
They eat grubs, adult insects, and earthworms, supplemented in autumn by the berries of hawthorn, rowan, juniper, and other small trees.

DISPLAY AND VOICE
Males sing from high rocks in early spring, with loud, fluty, melancholy phrases of 2–4 notes, each clearly separated from the next. Calls include a rattle and a loud *tac-tac-tac* in alarm.

BREEDING
Ring Ouzels build their cup nests in vegetation, on steep banks, or in rock crevices. The four eggs hatch after 12–14 days.

MIGRATION
A scarce but regular migrant on coasts and hills away from breeding areas, often early in spring.

WHITE CRESCENT
The white gorget on a summer male is always distinct.

WHEN SEEN

Late February to October or November.

WHERE SEEN
Breeds in N and W Britain, very locally Ireland; N and W Scandinavia, Pyrenees, E France, Alps, Balkans, Carpathians.

HABITAT AND INFO

SIMILAR SPECIES
Occasional piebald Blackbird has darker wing; more irregular white.

Broader shape

Darker wing

Song Thrush

LENGTH / 23cm (9in)
WINGSPAN / 33–36cm (13–14in)
WEIGHT / 70–90g (2½–3¼oz)

■ STATUS / Vulnerable

SCALE v Pigeon

A small, neat, spotted thrush, with a rather plain head pattern and neat, V-shaped spots underneath. It has a loud, bright, repetitive, challenging song.

Song Thrushes that breed in the shrubberies and hedges of parks and gardens do well, but those that live on intensively farmed land find too little food and too few nest sites, and these have been in steep decline for some time. They are justifiably garden favourites, with a most vigorous, energetic song that can include notes of unmatched clarity and purity.

FEEDING
Earthworms and grubs are staple fare, but snails are important, especially in dry periods when worms are hard to find. In autumn and winter, Song Thrushes eat many berries.

DISPLAY AND VOICE
Their displays are rather inconspicuous, but the song is loud and highly distinctive. It includes short phrases, some rich and fluty, others scratchy or strained, each repeated. The typical call is a thin *sit*; also has a hard rattle of alarm.

BREEDING
The nest, lined with hard mud or dung, is built in a tree, shrub, or creeper. The 3–5 eggs hatch after 10–17 days, typically 13.

MIGRATION
Birds from northern and eastern Europe move west and south in autumn, returning in spring.

If flushed, typically flies low into nearest cover (Mistle Thrush flies off far and high).

Longer tail than Redwing's.

Underwing soft orange-buff (white on Mistle Thrush, rusty on Redwing).

Some races look dark.

Often feeds with wings drooped.

Sexes alike.

Juvenile
Streaks above less obvious than on Mistle Thrush.

Neat olive brown; lines of V-shaped spots beneath, on yellow-cream breast.

FAMILIAR THRUSH
This is the most common spotted thrush of parks and gardens.

WHEN SEEN

All year; in north and east mostly April to October.

WHERE SEEN
Throughout Europe.

HABITAT AND INFO

SIMILAR SPECIES
Female Blackbird is much darker; spots below less sharp on darker body.

Much darker

Darker legs

Redwing

This small, sociable thrush is dark above, silvery-white below, with neat lines of dark streaks. Its head pattern is distinctive.

LENGTH / 21cm (8¼in)
WINGSPAN / 33–35cm (13–14in)
WEIGHT / 55–75g (2–2¾oz)

■ STATUS / Secure

SCALE v Pigeon

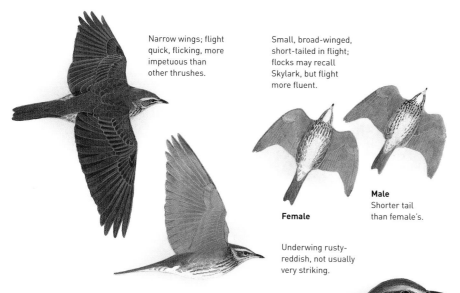

Narrow wings; flight quick, flicking, more impetuous than other thrushes.

Small, broad-winged, short-tailed in flight; flocks may recall Skylark, but flight more fluent.

Male
Shorter tail than female's.

Female

Underwing rusty-reddish, not usually very striking.

Redwings often mix with Song Thrushes and Fieldfares, where they look smaller and darker. In Britain, they are mostly winter visitors, and flocks of autumn migrants can be heard calling at night as they fly west.

FEEDING
They eat insects in summer and many berries in autumn and winter, but earthworms are an important part of their diet throughout the year. They typically forage on the ground, moving a few hops at a time between pauses.

DISPLAY AND VOICE
Males sing from high perches. Most phrases are simple, short, and fluty, with a final light chuckle. Calls include a rattle of alarm and the distinctive high, thin flight call, *seeee*, penetrating and far-carrying.

BREEDING
Pairs may breed in small, loose colonies, each nesting in a bush or shrub. They lay 4–6 eggs in a nest lined thinly with mud.

MIGRATION
Icelandic breeders move to north and west Britain, Ireland, France, and Iberia. Others move south and west.

Bright pale stripes above and below dark cheek patch; yellow bill base.

Juvenile/first winter male (above)
Pale tips to coverts; less organized streaks on underside.

Adult female
Neat lines of streaks bolder in spring; rusty flanks and white vent.

Feathers often fluffed up for warmth in cold winter weather.

FANCY MARKINGS
The head pattern is immediately distinctive.

WHEN SEEN

Oct — April

In north and east mostly April to October; reverse in south and west.

WHERE SEEN
Breeds Iceland, Faeroes, N Scotland, Scandinavia, and N Europe east from N Germany; central, S and W Europe in winter.

HABITAT AND INFO

SIMILAR SPECIES
Song Thrush is more spotted, less streaked; plainer head; buffer underwing.

Plainer head

More discrete spots

Mistle Thrush

LENGTH / 27cm (10½in)
WINGSPAN / 42–48cm (16½–19in)
WEIGHT / 110–150g (3¾–5¼oz)

■ **STATUS /** Secure

SCALE v Pigeon

A large, bold, long-tailed, and long-winged thrush, it is rather wild and aggressive.

This is a big, bold, vigorous thrush, quite capable of attacking an intruding cat near its nest – or, for that matter, anyone who walks too close beneath the nesting tree. In winter, the males defend berry-bearing trees from all-comers. In autumn, however, Mistle Thrushes form flocks, based around family groups, which gather wherever there are abundant berries or a feast of crab apples. These straggling groups, sometimes 30–40 strong, fly from tree top to tree top, staying in contact with their distinctive dry, rattling calls. They are seen far less often in small gardens than Song Thrushes, for they tend to prefer more open places that offer a good view, and plenty of room to escape with a high flight into the distance if disturbed. By contrast, the Song Thrush is content to slip into the nearest shrubbery, or over the garden fence.

FEEDING
The Mistle Thrush finds food on open ground, or in trees and bushes: mostly worms, insects, and various berries. It is less likely to join mixed flocks of other thrushes than the Song Thrush or Blackbird, and it is more vigorous in defence of a fruitful winter feeding territory.

DISPLAY AND VOICE
Mistle Thrushes sing from late autumn through the winter into the breeding season, even on the gloomiest of days. The song is loud and fluty with a strikingly wild and challenging quality. It is far-carrying and probably the loudest song of any European songbird. Each phrase is quite short and simple. It is less varied and developed than a Blackbird's song, but not so high-pitched nor so repetitive as that of a Song Thrush. The usual call is a dry, rasping, almost hissing chatter, with no equivalent among other common thrushes.

BREEDING
These thrushes build their nests early in spring, often on quite exposed branches in tall trees. They line the outer layer of grass and stalks with mud, then add an inner lining of fine grasses. The 3–5 eggs hatch after 12–15 days, and the chicks fledge after a similar period in the nest.

MIGRATION
Birds breeding in the north and east of Europe move south and west in winter, joining the local resident populations. Some from the west of Europe, including Britain, also move south, but most stay in their natal area all year. Migrating birds are generally much less obvious than the more social thrushes.

Paler than other thrushes, with pale edges to wing coverts; greyer when plumage is worn.

Typical stance upright, with small, round head held up, tail angled down.

Breast spots black, round, or broad crescent-shaped; less aligned or V-shaped than on Song Thrush.

Greyer, smaller in Corsica and Sardinia (left) compared with N Europe (below left).

No sexual differences detected.

Powerful on the ground, with long, leaping hops.

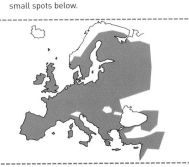

Juvenile
Bold pale spots and dark flecks on back, pale wingbars, and mealy head can be perplexing; dark marks on uppertail coverts; small spots below.

WHEN SEEN

All year in S and W Europe; in N and E mostly in summer.

WHERE SEEN
Breeds in most of Europe except Iceland, N Scandinavia; a summer visitor to the north and east of Denmark and Germany.

HABITAT AND INFO

SIMILAR SPECIES
Song Thrush is smaller, browner, plainer winged; spots more triangular; flanks browner; belly whiter.

Plainer wings

V-shaped spots

Surprisingly large and powerful in flight; almost dove-like shape.

Long, quite pointed wings momentarily close in bounding flight with long undulations, often above tree-top height.

Underwing flashes even more brilliant white than Fieldfare's.

Long wings with row of inconspicuous pale spots; dull white outer tail feathers.

Variable white in tail.

FLIGHT PATTERN
Long, bounding undulations between bursts of wingbeats.

DID YOU KNOW?
In defence of the nest, in this case often remarkably open and easily visible before leaves are on the trees, the Mistle Thrush is famously fearless. It may drive off Magpies and crows, as well as cats, and an attacking pair has been known to kill a Jackdaw. People who walk too close to a nest find the diving attack genuinely intimidating.

Savi's Warbler

LENGTH / 14cm (5½in)
WINGSPAN / 15–20cm (6–8in)
WEIGHT / 12–15g (³⁄₈–½oz)

■ **STATUS /** Secure

SCALE v Pigeon

A long-tailed, slim, small-headed, narrow-necked warbler, it is found in reed beds and is often hard to see. It is similar to the Reed and Grasshopper Warblers.

Being a small, brown warbler of extensive reed beds, this species could be confused with the Reed Warbler, but its relationship with the Grasshopper Warbler becomes apparent with close observation. Its shape and song are both typical of the *Locustella* group of warblers.

FEEDING
It feeds on insects, spiders, and snails that it finds in low growth. It may walk or hop on the ground within deep cover.

DISPLAY AND VOICE
Males sing from reed tops and chase each other across reed beds more visibly than Grasshopper Warblers. The song accelerates into a prolonged trilling buzz lasting half a minute or more: faster, duller, and less ticking than the Grasshopper Warbler's. Calls include a sharp *pit* or *zick*.

BREEDING
A nest of grass stems and leaves is built in tall plants over water. The 3–6 eggs hatch in 10–12 days.

MIGRATION
These warblers move to Africa, probably south of the Sahara, for the winter, but they are rarely seen away from their breeding areas.

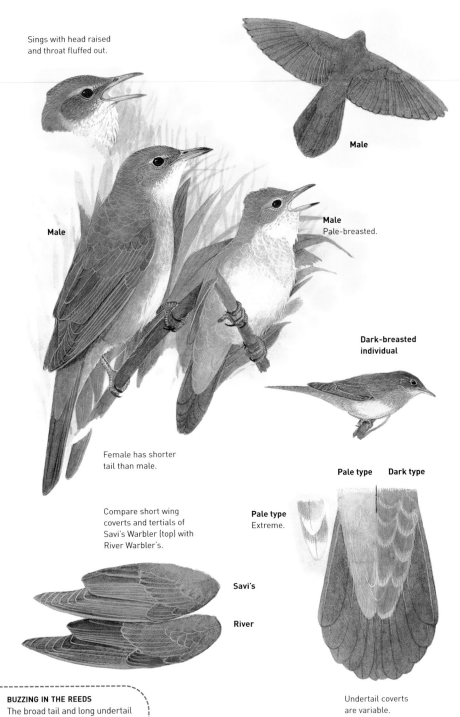

Sings with head raised and throat fluffed out.

Male

Male

Male
Pale-breasted.

Dark-breasted individual

Female has shorter tail than male.

Compare short wing coverts and tertials of Savi's Warbler (top) with River Warbler's.

Savi's

River

Pale type   Dark type

Pale type
Extreme.

Undertail coverts are variable.

BUZZING IN THE REEDS
The broad tail and long undertail coverts are shown well here.

WHEN SEEN
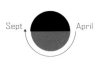
Sept — April

Late April to September.

WHERE SEEN
Very rare SE England; locally scattered through Europe south of Baltic, where extensive reed beds are found.

HABITAT AND INFO

SIMILAR SPECIES
Reed Warbler has shorter under tail coverts; narrower tail; entirely different song.

Longer bill

Squarer tail

River Warbler

This is a dark, slim, round-tailed warbler with a dusky, softly streaked breast. It has typical *Locustella* behaviour, skulking in thickets but singing from one perch for long periods.

LENGTH / 13cm (5in)
WINGSPAN / 15–18cm (6–7in)
WEIGHT / 10–12g (¼–³⁄₈oz)

■ STATUS / Vulnerable

SCALE v Pigeon

While clearly a *Locustella* warbler, resembling the more familiar Grasshopper Warbler in its shape, actions, and song, this is a bird of dense, low thickets, from riverside vegetation to boggy willow, bramble, and birch scrub. It even lives in overgrown orchards and town parks. In recent decades, it has spread westward across north-central Europe.

FEEDING
It finds beetles, spiders, and other small prey items in grass, bushes, nettles, and other low cover.

DISPLAY AND VOICE
Males sing mostly at night from quite high perches. The song has a rhythmic chuffing or fast, pulsing "sewing machine" pattern, with a sharp, metallic, insect-like quality.

BREEDING
Pairs build their nests close to the ground in thick grass or a bush. They lay 5–6 eggs, which hatch after 14–15 days.

MIGRATION
A few appear west of the usual range in late spring or summer. They all migrate to Africa in winter.

Variable but typically darker olive-brown than Savi's Warbler; shorter-tailed shape helpful for identification.

Male
Throat streaks sparse and distinct to broad and blurred; quite unlike Savi's Warbler.

Pale outer primary.

Female's tail (far left) shorter than male's; length may be exaggerated when bird perches with body horizontal and tail angled down.

Female

Round tail; long undertail coverts; average colour left, dark and pale extremes below.

Adult
Pale extreme.

First winter
Dark, no rufous; autumn adult can have rufous wash.

RHYTHMIC SONG
This is a rather plain brown bird with weak patterning.

WHEN SEEN

Aug — May

Mostly mid-May to August.

WHERE SEEN
Local in E Europe from S Finland and N Germany eastward, south to Danube; a rare but increasing summer vagrant in west.

HABITAT AND INFO

SIMILAR SPECIES
Grasshopper Warbler is streaked above, especially on closed wings.

Streaked back and wings

Grasshopper Warbler

LENGTH / 12–13.5cm (4¾–5¼in)
WINGSPAN / 15–19cm (6–7½in)
WEIGHT / 11–15g (³⁄₈–½oz)

■ STATUS / Secure

SCALE v Pigeon

A slim, round-tailed, fine-billed, secretive warbler, found where grass grows up through low bushes. It is usually located by its unique song at dusk or in still, warm, cloudy weather, when it may be seen singing from a more exposed perch.

The Grasshopper Warbler is easier to locate and more familiar than its relatives in the *Locustella* group, and it acts as a yardstick with which the others can be usefully compared. It is a slim bird, with a narrow head and slender bill, a tapered or rounded tail, and long undertail coverts. Most distinctively, the male has a high, fast, ticking or reeling song that may continue without alteration for a minute or more. The vast majority of Grasshopper Warblers seen by bird-watchers are located by this song, but it is so high-pitched that those suffering from high-frequency deafness – common from middle age – cannot hear it at all. Grasshopper Warblers like grassy places with low bushes and small, clumpy thickets. They skulk in these, demonstrating a frustrating ability to avoid being seen. If a Grasshopper Warbler is flushed from cover, it will usually fly off fast and low to the next clump and dive out of sight, often not to be seen again. But if it can be located without alarming it, a quiet and careful watcher may be rewarded with excellent views.

FEEDING

Grasshopper Warblers eat mainly insects, taking them from low vegetation, from the ground beneath clumps of grass or dense brambles, or from the stems of reeds, which they carefully search from top to bottom.

DISPLAY AND VOICE

Little of the display can be seen except for the male singing on his song perch. Typically, this is within a small hawthorn or bramble bush, but he may gradually climb to a clearer perch at the top, or to one side. His song is a remarkable, prolonged performance. At long range it is a light, fast, metallic reel, like a fast freewheeling bicycle, but at close range the individual notes sound harder and more rattling. For a few moments at the beginning of the song the trill is slower and lower, working up to full speed, and it may seem to rise and fall as the bird turns his head. Calls include a quite loud, sharp *tik*.

BREEDING

The nests are thick cups of grass stems and leaves, built on or near the ground in tussocks of grass, sedge, or rushes. Typically 5–6 eggs are laid and incubated for 12–15 days. The chicks fly after just 10–12 days.

MIGRATION

A few are seen away from their breeding areas in spring and autumn, but this is not a commonly seen migrant. All Grasshopper Warblers migrate south in autumn to spend the winter in west Africa.

Male, singing
Head turns from side to side; yellow inside mouth often visible.

Usually olive, some greyer or much yellower; breast unstreaked or with very fine marks, but shows slightly darker breast band.

At long range shows little contrast between upperside and underside, but throat paler.

Long, diffuse streaks beneath tail.

Female has shorter tail than male.

Juvenile female
Very neat with immaculate pale feather edgings and dark streaks; pale eye-ring moderately prominent; typically few flank streaks, but variable.

WHEN SEEN

Sept — April

April to September.

WHERE SEEN

Widespread in Europe but absent from most of Norway and Finland, most of Sweden except for the Baltic fringe, and most of Iberia, Italy, and the Balkans.

HABITAT AND INFO

SIMILAR SPECIES

Sedge Warbler has pale stripe over eye; large plain rump; entirely different song.

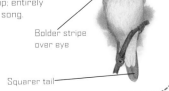

Bolder stripe over eye

Squarer tail

Flight brief and low, diving down or sideways into thick cover.

MOUSELIKE SHUFFLE
Except when singing, this bird skulks in thick vegetation.

Often fans tail in flight as it swerves and dives into cover.

Pale edges to tertials widest on outer webs, slightly diffuse.

Adult, autumn
Dull, yellowish individual.

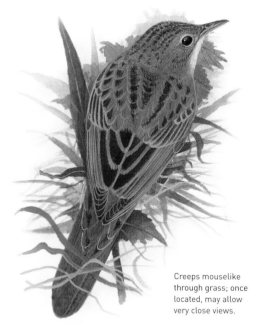

Creeps mouselike through grass; once located, may allow very close views.

DID YOU KNOW?
The high, metallic, reeling song is a severe test for anyone with high-frequency deafness; for many people, it becomes inaudible as they get older. The sound is mostly around 5–7 kHz: this helps give it great penetration, however, and it can be heard in good conditions from as much as 1km (3,300ft), although 500m (1,650ft) is more usual.

Aquatic Warbler

LENGTH / 13cm (5in)
WINGSPAN / 17–19cm (6¾–7½in)
WEIGHT / 10–15g (¼–½oz)

■ **STATUS /** Endangered

SCALE v Pigeon

A striking, small warbler of reed beds and wet scrub. It is often rounder-bodied and less crouched than the Sedge Warbler, and showing more obvious leg.

Never common nor widespread, the Aquatic Warbler has become the object of real concern to conservationists, being one of the rarer and more endangered breeding birds of Europe. It nests in wet marshes with clumps of sedge and iris, and not in the reed-bed habitats used by Reed Warblers. On migration, however, reed beds with plentiful insect food are essential to its survival.

FEEDING
It takes insects from leaves and stems in low vegetation.

DISPLAY AND VOICE
Males move around while singing from perches, or rise in song flights, descending with head raised and tail cocked. The song is a series of short, simple phrases quite unlike that of a Sedge Warbler. Calls include a hard *tak* and a soft *tucc tucc*.

BREEDING
They nest in sedges, laying 4–6 eggs. The eggs hatch in 12–15 days.

MIGRATION
A few reach extreme western parts of Europe, such as south-west England, each autumn. All migrate to west Africa for the winter.

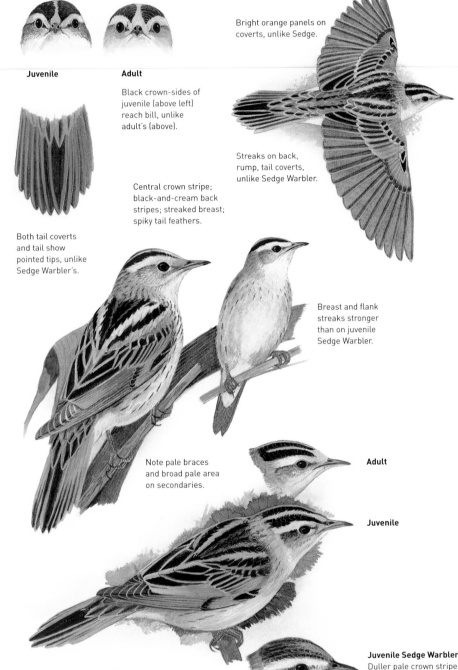

Juvenile | Adult

Black crown-sides of juvenile (above left) reach bill, unlike adult's (above).

Bright orange panels on coverts, unlike Sedge.

Streaks on back, rump, tail coverts, unlike Sedge Warbler.

Central crown stripe; black-and-cream back stripes; streaked breast; spiky tail feathers.

Both tail coverts and tail show pointed tips, unlike Sedge Warbler's.

Breast and flank streaks stronger than on juvenile Sedge Warbler.

Note pale braces and broad pale area on secondaries.

Adult

Juvenile

Juvenile Sedge Warbler
Duller pale crown stripe.

CONTRASTING STRIPES
Black-and-buff lines give a bright appearance.

406

Sedge Warbler

A small, dark, rusty warbler of waterside scrub and thickets, it has a noisy spring song and a striking pale stripe over its eyes.

LENGTH / 13cm (5in)
WINGSPAN / 17–21cm (6³/₄–8¹/₄in)
WEIGHT / 10–13g (¹/₄–¹/₂oz)

STATUS / Vulnerable

SCALE v Pigeon

In spring and summer, waterside sedge and nettle beds, banks of rosebay willowherb, hawthorn clumps, and reed-bed edges are enlivened by Sedge Warblers in full song. They are less restricted to reed beds than Reed Warblers – while often breeding alongside them, they are often found by small ditches or even thickets away from open water.

FEEDING
They take insects from low down in reeds and sedges, from cereals, and from nettles or similar vegetation.

DISPLAY AND VOICE
Males perform a short, rising song flight (unlike Reed Warblers), but also sing from perches. The song is varied and fast. It has a scolding, irritated quality, with buzzing or chattering notes between more musical, rhythmic sequences. It often begins with a few rich, sweet notes. The call is a grating *tucc* or *churr*.

BREEDING
The 5–6 eggs are laid in a deep cup of leaves, stems, moss, and cobwebs, near the ground or over water.

MIGRATION
It winters in tropical Africa, and often stops off in bushy or wet places away from breeding areas.

Rump plain, with blunt tail feathers (slightly pointed on juvenile).

Juvenile
Wings broader than Aquatic Warbler's.

Juvenile
More buff than adult; faint chest streaks sharper.

Song flight.

Wing coverts darker than Aquatic Warbler's.

Note rusty, unmarked rump; black, pale-edged tertials.

Adult
By late summer plumage wears to more uniform, browner appearance.

Adult
Broad white stripe over eye; faint, soft chest streaks; can look silky white against dark bush.

EXCITABLE SONG
Sedge Warblers have a fast, agitated, varied song.

WHEN SEEN

Sept — April

April to September.

WHERE SEEN
Breeds in most of Europe except Iceland, upland Scandinavia, Iberia, S France, and Italy; local in SE Europe.

HABITAT AND INFO

SIMILAR SPECIES
Reed Warbler is plainer above; weaker head pattern; less contrasted rump.

Plainer head

Uniform upperparts

Moustached Warbler

LENGTH / 12–13cm (4¾–5in)
WINGSPAN / 17–21cm (6¾–8¼in)
WEIGHT / 10–15g (¼–½oz)

■ STATUS / Vulnerable

SCALE v Pigeon

A secretive and skulking bird, it is usually low down in dense waterside vegetation. It has rich colours and a striking head pattern.

While the Sedge Warbler is a widespread, successful, and adaptable bird, the similar Moustached Warbler is rather rare, occurring in restricted habitats in south and east Europe. It favours reed and sedge beds with scattered bushes.

FEEDING
It prefers small beetles, but also eats water snails. Both are taken from dense vegetation over water.

DISPLAY AND VOICE
The song is long and rich. It is less scolding than that of the Sedge Warbler's, thinner and softer with fewer jarring notes. It starts with distinctive low, pure notes recalling both the Nightingale's and Woodlark's songs. Calls include a low *trk* and a hard *tac*.

BREEDING
They build an untidy nest of leaves and stems, lined with reed flowers and feathers and attached to plant stems over water. They lay 3–5 eggs in the nest.

MIGRATION
Birds from the north of the breeding range migrate to the south of the range in winter. Otherwise it is sedentary, unlike the Sedge Warbler. Very rare north of usual range.

May sing on exposed perches.

Juvenile
Duller throat.

Cocks tail, unlike Sedge Warbler.

Short tail and broad wings.

Wingtips do not project as far as Sedge Warbler's.

Black streaks on back in fresh plumage wear duller over time; clear, bright rump.

Male
Bold dark cheek patch below white stripe; white throat.

Wingtip projection shorter than Sedge Warbler's.

Moustached

Sedge

Dark crown, bright stripe over eye, and rufous back distinctive; dark, rounded tail, and contrast between white throat and rusty flanks are helpful features.

WHITE EYEBROW
The blackish cap and white stripe over the eye are helpful.

WHEN SEEN

All year.

WHERE SEEN
Very scattered and localized in Spain, S France, Balearics, Italy, and Balkans; also Neusiedler See in Austria, locally Hungary; commoner S Russia.

HABITAT AND INFO

SIMILAR SPECIES
Sedge Warbler has paler crown; less rufous rump; blurry streaks on back; less white throat/rufous flank contrast.

Duller head

Paler body

Paddyfield Warbler

A brownish warbler resembling a Reed Warbler, but paler, rustier, more well-marked on the head, shorter-billed, and longer-tailed.

LENGTH / 13cm (5in)
WINGSPAN / 15–17cm (6–6¾in)
WEIGHT / 10–15g (¼–½oz)

■ **STATUS /** Vulnerable

SCALE v Pigeon

Adult male
Yellowish-rufous rump against dark tail; strong pale stripe over eye.

Male
Long shape when singing; yellow gape.

Adult tail from above (below left), juvenile from below; undertail very dark; juvenile's has narrow, pointed feathers.

Striking head pattern, unlike Reed's, Blyth's Reed's, Booted's, or other difficult warblers'; dark line above wide, whitish stripe over eye; broad, dark eye stripe.

Bill distinctively two-toned.

Warblers are best considered in generic groups, identified by their scientific names: the Paddyfield is an *Acrocephalus*, and so has similarities to Reed and Sedge Warblers. It breeds in reeds beside pools and lakes, sometimes far from a solid shore. It finds such spots in river valleys, or even surrounded by semi-arid steppe.

FEEDING
It picks insects from stems of reeds and other aquatic plants.

DISPLAY AND VOICE
Males tend to sing in full view at the top of a reed stem. The song is quick and varied, more continuous than a Reed Warbler's, and more even than a Marsh Warbler's. Calls are a short *chuk* and a soft, ticking note while feeding: *chek* or *chik-chik*.

BREEDING
A cylindrical nest is suspended from reed stems or in the base of a bush. The 3–6 eggs are incubated for 12 days.

MIGRATION
Paddyfield Warblers go east to winter in India. A very few overshoot in spring to turn up north and west of their usual range.

Male
Both adult and juvenile males have much longer tails than the females.

Juvenile female
Shorter tail than male, very short wingtip; quite dumpy compared to elongated male's.

Quite rusty above, buffy below; throat white; pale base to bill; rump can wear duller.

Bristles beside bill sometimes visible in the field, unlike Booted Warbler's.

SUBTLE DISTINCTIONS
A moderately strong head pattern is distinctive.

WHERE SEEN
Breeds on western shore of Black Sea and eastward through Asia; rare autumn vagrant in NW Europe.

HABITAT AND INFO

SIMILAR SPECIES
Sedge Warbler is softly streaked on back, but less rusty overall.

Stronger stripe over eye

Streaks

Reed Warbler

LENGTH / 13cm (5in)
WINGSPAN / 18–21cm (7–8¼in)
WEIGHT / 11–15g (³⁄₈–½oz)

■ **STATUS /** Secure

SCALE v Pigeon

This is one of the more common *Acrocephalus* warblers, mostly restricted to reeds, but some breed (and many feed) in willows and other dense vegetation. It is the most rufous of the plain brown reed warblers, but individuals with slight variations can sometimes be mistaken for rarities.

Few species are quite so tied to a habitat as the Reed Warbler. It is not, perhaps, as specialized as the Dipper or the Treecreeper, or even the Bearded Tit, but nine times out of ten a Reed Warbler seen in summer will be in a reed bed. They do, however, feed in adjacent willows, even singing and sometimes nesting in bushy thickets, and migrants are often found away from water in unexpected places. These are the ones that can throw even experienced bird-watchers into temporary confusion. In summer, a visit to a reed bed at dawn is well worth the effort, as the chorus of singing Reed Warblers can be unforgettable. Because reed beds themselves are so limited and widely scattered, Reed Warblers may be absent from wide areas but abundant in local pockets of suitable habitat. Reed beds tend to dry out if not managed properly, causing a decline in Reed Warbler numbers. On the other hand, reed growth on the margins of flooded gravel pits can draw them into new areas quite quickly.

FEEDING
They pick insects, spiders, and a few small snails from the leaves and stems of reeds or waterside bushes. The preferred prey depends on its abundance at the time.

DISPLAY AND VOICE
Males sing from a few regular perches; unpaired males sing with the greatest persistence. A singing bird perches on a vertical reed stem in a dense or tall clump, often out of sight, but in calm weather gradually creeps up into full view. Often heard where there are Sedge Warblers, the song of the Reed Warbler is usually quite distinct. It is less angry and scolding. It is more even, rhythmic, and repetitive, with fewer abrupt changes in pitch and speed: typically a low, churring *kerr-kerr-kerr chirruc chirruc chrip chrip chrip chirr chirr chirr* and so on. Calls are mostly soft, low *churrs* and a harder, grating *churrr* of alarm.

BREEDING
Nests are mostly in upright reed stems over water: deep, woven around several stems, and lined with fine grass and hair. The 3–5 eggs are incubated for 9–12 days and the young fly after 10–12 days. Many nests are parasitized by Cuckoos.

MIGRATION
The European population moves to Africa in the autumn. Migrants stop off in thickets near or away from water, inland or at the coast, as well as in reed beds. A few turn up in quite unsuitable habitats on offshore islands, especially in autumn.

Juvenile, first winter
A little more rufous than adult; plumage wears paler, sandier by autumn.

Obvious white throat.

Unstreaked back and plainer face distinguish Reed from Sedge Warbler.

Wingtips tend to be plainer than Marsh Warbler's.

Adult, late summer
Worn plumage sandier brown than spring; rump brighter.

Shorter wingtip projection than Marsh Warbler's.

Compared to Marsh Warbler, tips of greater coverts project farther beyond primary coverts.

Adult, spring
Typically slightly greyer on back than rump, which is more rusty; legs darker, greyer than Marsh Warbler's.

Mouth of both Reed and Marsh Warbler bright orange-yellow, but Marsh sings with bill open wide, Reed less so.

Can adopt dumpy shape when singing.

Sings from reed stem, near top or more often well-hidden; dives out of sight among stems.

WHEN SEEN

Sept — April

April (mostly second half) to September, a few in October.

WHERE SEEN
Breeds from SE Ireland east and south through most of Europe, but missing from Iceland, much of Scandinavia, and upland regions.

HABITAT AND INFO

SIMILAR SPECIES
Sedge Warbler has pale stripe over eye; dusky streaks on back.

Strong stripe over eye

Streaks

IMPORTANT BASELINE
Knowing the Reed Warbler is vital
when identifying its rarer relatives.

Wings rounder than
Marsh Warbler's.

Sometimes shows
whitish over bill,
creating effect of pale
face stripe like Blyth's
Reed Warbler's.

Very slight pale line over
eye, brighter eye-ring;
no broad pale line like
Sedge Warbler's.

Flies off low and fast
over reeds.

Marsh

Reed

Tail shapes vary, but
Reed Warbler's is
generally squarer than
Marsh Warbler's.

Marsh

Reed

Reed

Marsh

Reed Warbler has seven
obvious tips in shorter
wingtip projection,
Marsh Warbler has
eight; paler edges wear
away in summer.

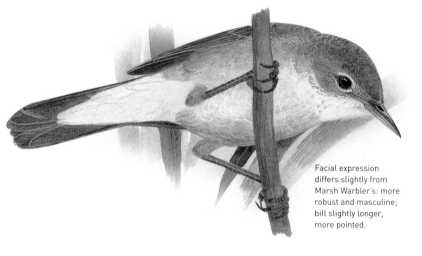

Facial expression
differs slightly from
Marsh Warbler's: more
robust and masculine;
bill slightly longer,
more pointed.

DID YOU KNOW?
Ringing evidence reveals that most Reed Warblers use the same sites
in Africa in winter and return to the same reed bed in which to breed
year after year. In fact, they may even stop at the same sites during
their autumn migrations.

Marsh Warbler

LENGTH / 13cm (5in)
WINGSPAN / 18–21cm (7–8¼in)
WEIGHT / 11–15g (⅜–½oz)

■ STATUS / Vulnerable

SCALE v Pigeon

A dull, pale, brownish warbler of dense vegetation near water, it closely resembles other plain *Acrocephalus* warblers. It looks slim and holds itself horizontally. Its movements are more fluent and graceful than the clumsier Reed Warbler.

It takes more than a casual glance to be certain this bird is not a Reed Warbler, let alone the rarer Blyth's Reed Warbler: the *Acrocephalus* genus is notoriously difficult. Add to that its similarities with some *Hippolais* warblers and the rare possibility of hybridization, and this is clearly not an "easy bird" to identify. Its song helps, but assessing the small differences in shape and pattern takes experience. The habitat can give some useful clues: it is less of a reed-bed bird than the Reed Warbler, with a liking for rank wetland vegetation, including nettle beds, thick growths of tall umbellifers, hawthorns, and many other plants from wild rose to meadowsweet. It does not often occupy vegetation growing from water, preferring the edge of a marsh.

FEEDING
It takes insects, spiders, a few small snails, and similar prey from grass and other stems, or from bushes. Migrants may eat berries in autumn.

DISPLAY AND VOICE
Males sing either openly or from hidden perches in bushes or tall, thick vegetation, often by night (unpaired males sing most persistently, while paired males soon cease). Their song is greatly influenced by the songs and calls of birds heard in winter in Africa: the Marsh Warbler is a superb mimic of both these and European birds. The basic pattern of the song is fluent, flowing, and energetic. It is sometimes gurgling and undistinguished, much like that of a Sedge Warbler, but at its best it is rich and beautiful with Canary-like trills and throbbing, Nightingale-like phrases. At least 99 European and 113 African species have been recognized in its repertoire. Its calls are rather hard and loud, *tacc* or *tchuk*.

BREEDING
The nest is built in tall bushy vegetation, but often close to the ground. It is shallower than a Reed Warbler's nest, and distinguished by more obvious "basket handles" suspending it from upright stems (the Reed Warbler's nest is rounder, with stems growing up through the sides). The female lays 3–5 eggs. They hatch after 12–14 days and the chicks fly within 10–11 days.

MIGRATION
This is a very late arrival in summer in western Europe, in itself a useful clue to identification. A few migrants appear on the coast in early summer and late autumn. The whole European population moves to south and east Africa in winter.

Adult
Subtly narrower wings than Reed Warbler's; tail has hint of paler edge but, as on Reed, may look translucent against the light.

Wing profiles of Marsh Warbler (red) and Reed Warbler (black).

Adult
Taut, tightly feathered shape in summer; flatter head with more delicate forehead/bill profile than Reed Warbler's; angular nape.

Legs paler, browner than Reed Warbler's, but not always conclusive.

WHEN SEEN

Sept   April

From late April in E Europe, May or June in W, until September.

WHERE SEEN
Breeds from extreme SE England locally from France eastward through central Europe, S Sweden, and Finland to most of E Europe and Russia.

HABITAT AND INFO

SIMILAR SPECIES
Reed Warbler is more reddish brown; squarer tail; shorter wingtip.

More rufous

Darker legs

BEST BY VOICE
Identification is easier by song than by visual clues.

Tends to sing more openly than Reed Warbler, from bush or rank herbage, not reeds.

Juvenile, October
Relaxed, fluffed out in cool weather, as often seen on migration; head often rounder than Reed Warbler's.

Juvenile, first autumn
This is the most rufous plumage, very like Reed Warbler's, but legs paler, claws pale (Reed Warbler's dark).

Primary projection (wingtip length) greater than on Reed Warbler.

Tail usually more rounded than Reed Warbler's.

Compare also with Olivaceous Warbler.

Marsh

Reed

Bill fractionally wider than than that of Reed Warbler.

Breeding adults
Tertials and primary tips very dark, often with sharper pale edges than Reed Warbler's; alula usually darker on Marsh.

Acrobatic feeder in dense vegetation; climbs up to pick off insects, drops swiftly out of sight with vertical fall.

Variable colour recalls either wet or dry earth, sometimes faintly tinged greenish above, yellowish below, without rufous flanks of Reed Warbler; duller rump; cold whitish on chin, throat, and belly.

Greater covert and primary covert tips more equal than those of Reed Warbler.

DID YOU KNOW?
The Marsh Warbler's full summer song is a remarkable performance of great richness, with many imitations of other birds joined together in a fluid sequence. Each individual uses several hundreds, if not thousands, of phrases and may mimic more than 100 African birds as well as several of its European neighbours in summer.

Great Reed Warbler

LENGTH / 19–20cm (7½–8in)
WINGSPAN / 25–26cm (9¾–10¼in)
WEIGHT / 30–40g (1–1½oz)

SCALE v Pigeon

■ **STATUS** / Vulnerable

A massive, plain-backed, loud-voiced warbler of reed beds and reedy ditches, with a long bill, dark eye stripe and wide tail in flight.

This is essentially a "giant" Reed Warbler that inhabits dense marshes with tall stands of stout reed, as well as small wet spots with reeds beside rivers or even along deep ditches. It is sometimes very hard to see, but often easy to hear when it sings boldly from an exposed reed top.

FEEDING
It finds a variety of insects in and around the reeds and other marsh vegetation.

DISPLAY AND VOICE
Males sing from reeds, often sporadically by day as if they cannot quite get going. The full song is loud and characterized by a rhythmic repetition of froglike, croaking, grating, and strident notes: *krik krik krik, gurk gurk, eeek-eeek-eeek, kara karra chrruk chrruk* and so on. It also produces a hard *chack* and a *churr*.

BREEDING
A cylindrical nest is attached to thick reed stems. The 3–6 eggs hatch within 14 days.

MIGRATION
It winters in Africa. A few overshoot their normal breeding range on returning in spring.

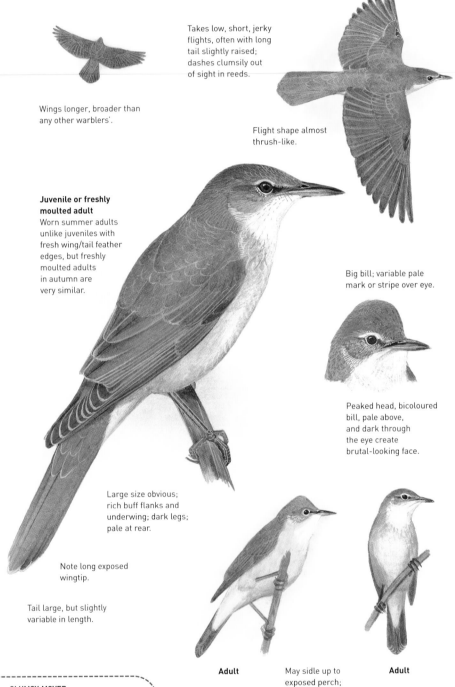

Wings longer, broader than any other warblers'.

Takes low, short, jerky flights, often with long tail slightly raised; dashes clumsily out of sight in reeds.

Flight shape almost thrush-like.

Juvenile or freshly moulted adult
Worn summer adults unlike juveniles with fresh wing/tail feather edges, but freshly moulted adults in autumn are very similar.

Big bill; variable pale mark or stripe over eye.

Peaked head, bicoloured bill, pale above, and dark through the eye create brutal-looking face.

Large size obvious; rich buff flanks and underwing; dark legs; pale at rear.

Note long exposed wingtip.

Tail large, but slightly variable in length.

Adult

May sidle up to exposed perch; head often peaked.

Adult

CLUMSY MOVER
Great Reed Warblers tend to crash through slender reed stems.

WHEN SEEN

March
Sept

March to September.

WHERE SEEN
Breeds much of mainland Europe south of Baltic, but localized; also S Sweden; rare non-breeder in spring in Britain.

HABITAT AND INFO

SIMILAR SPECIES
Reed Warbler is small, not big and clumsy; plainer head.

Weaker face pattern

Much smaller

Blyth's Reed Warbler

One of several plain *Acrocephalus* warblers, but also resembling some *Hippolais* species; elusive and difficult to identify.

LENGTH / 13cm (5in)
WINGSPAN / 17–19cm (6³⁄₄–7¹⁄₂in)
WEIGHT / 10–15g (¹⁄₄–¹⁄₂oz)

■ **STATUS /** Vulnerable

SCALE v Pigeon

Flight feathers edged whitish.

Can look slim and taut on perch.

Broader-winged than Reed Warbler.

A westward spread has made this a more familiar bird in parts of eastern Europe than it used to be. It is a fine songster of willow and alder thickets beside rivers, overgrown ditches, and wet, bushy forests. Unless it sings, it is a serious identification challenge for any bird-watcher.

FEEDING
It finds insects, spiders, and snails both high in trees and in dense bushes, or on the ground beneath.

VOICE
The song is energetic, rich, and full of mimicry, containing many pure, whistling sounds interspersed with harsh or chirping phrases. Its slow pace recalls that of a Song Thrush. Calls are a soft *thik* and *trrk*.

BREEDING
It makes a compact cup-shaped nest in reeds, nettles, or a thick bush. The 3–6 eggs hatch in 12–14 days.

MIGRATION
The entire population moves south-east in autumn, to winter in south Asia. In spring, a very few move farther west than the usual breeding range.

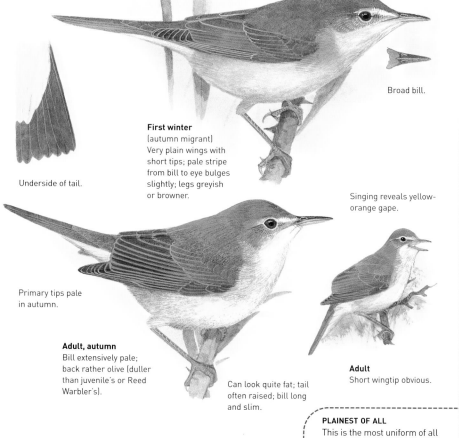

Broad bill.

First winter
(autumn migrant)
Very plain wings with short tips; pale stripe from bill to eye bulges slightly; legs greyish or browner.

Underside of tail.

Singing reveals yellow-orange gape.

Primary tips pale in autumn.

Adult, autumn
Bill extensively pale; back rather olive (duller than juvenile's or Reed Warbler's).

Can look quite fat; tail often raised; bill long and slim.

Adult
Short wingtip obvious.

PLAINEST OF ALL
This is the most uniform of all the reed warblers.

WHEN SEEN

Sept
May

May to September; a late spring arrival in N Europe.

WHERE SEEN
Breeds S Finland, Baltic states, and eastward through Russia.

HABITAT AND INFO

SIMILAR SPECIES
Reed Warbler has more contrast on wing; more rufous rump.

More rufous

Willow Warbler

LENGTH / 10.5–11.5 cm (4–4½in)
WINGSPAN / 17–22cm (6¾–8¾in)
WEIGHT / 6–10g (⅕–¼oz)

■ **STATUS /** Secure

SCALE v Pigeon

This slender warbler is widespread and common in bushes and open woods. Its song instantly identifies it in spring, its call and leg colour help at other times. It slips easily through foliage with occasional forays after insects. It very rarely winters in Europe, unlike the Chiffchaff.

Willow Warblers are, on average, a little longer, a little slimmer, a little "cleaner looking" and fresher than Chiffchaffs, but the differences are subtle at best. Fortunately, their song allows instant identification. While Chiffchaffs arrive very early in north-west Europe – early March onward in Britain, for example – Willow Warblers appear a month or so later. A few Chiffchaffs also remain in winter, while Willow Warblers do not. Habitat differences, however, are not clear cut. Willow Warblers are less likely to be seen within tall, mature, broadleaved woods. They like a variety of bushier places: low willows, mixed thickets of hawthorn, elder, young oak, and various other species growing in abandoned railway cuttings, hedgerows with standard trees, forest clearings, and woodland edges. All these are typical sites. Birch trees are especially favoured as they support thriving populations of insects.

FEEDING
A light, agile, quick feeder, the Willow Warbler slips through foliage while picking insects and spiders from leaves and twigs. It also catches some in the air. A few berries are eaten in autumn.

DISPLAY AND VOICE
In areas where Willow Warblers return in good numbers each year, their sudden chorus of song is one of the great joys of spring. Given from a perch, or while the bird feeds, the song is a particularly pleasing, silvery, lyrical phrase, starting quietly and high in pitch, strengthening in the middle and dying away to a slower, quieter finish. The pattern is Chaffinch-like, but the quality far less rattling. A Treecreeper's song has a similar pattern but is weaker and much less musical, and a Robin's song is stronger and more varied: Willow Warblers repeat their phrase over and over. The call is a more disyllabic *hoo-eet* than that of a Chiffchaff.

BREEDING
The domed nest is built on the ground, well concealed in vegetation. The 4–8 eggs are incubated for 12–14 days. The chicks fly when 11–15 days old.

MIGRATION
Willow Warblers winter in Africa, from Senegal and Ethiopia south right down to South Africa. The silvery song of a Willow Warbler is often heard from a tall African acacia tree. Migrants arrive in mid- or late March around the Mediterranean, and in mid-April in Britain.

Male, spring
May be rather dark olive above, whitish below with clean lemon-yellow wash; pale brown legs (rarely darker); unique song.

Male, summer
Becomes duller with wear.

Female's tail shorter (compare with primary projection) than male's.

Juvenile female
Juveniles commonly seen in autumn; very yellow below and on long stripe over eye, but some much paler; dark-centred tertials.

Adult male
Northern Scandinavia: greyer above, paler below with a hint of yellow, but many indistinguishable from southern birds. Pale birds like this occur on migration in Britain.

WHEN SEEN

Sept — April

April to September.

WHERE SEEN
Breeds widely in Europe north from central France and Alps; also locally in Pyrenees and N Spain; absent from Hungary, Bulgaria, Balkans, Italy, most of Iberia.

HABITAT AND INFO

SIMILAR SPECIES
Chiffchaff is rounder looking; dark legs; pale crescent under eye.

Rounder head

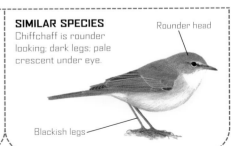

Blackish legs

Male
Flight quick, low, jerky, into nearest thick cover; too small and quick to see detail.

VIGOROUS SONGSTER
Early spring arrivals sing 4–8 times a minute for long periods each day.

Female   **Male**

Female has narrower, rounder wing, and shorter tail.

Juvenile
Yellow beneath wing.

Juvenile

Adult

Compare structure of head (flatter in Willow), also tertial length (pale green) against primary projection (yellow, longer in Willow) and against tail length.

Willow

Chiffchaff
Rounder head, thinner bill; spindly legs always blackish (rarely dark brown on Willow Warbler).

DID YOU KNOW?
Like many other migrants, the Willow Warbler is faithful to particular sites both in summer and in winter. Its presence is often detected in African savannahs by its sweet song, which is used there almost as freely as it is in Europe in spring, presumably as a means of establishing winter feeding territories.

?

Chiffchaff

ORDER	FAMILY	SPECIES	COMMON NAME
Passeriformes	Sylviidae	Phylloscopus collybita	Chiffchaff

SCALE v Pigeon

LENGTH / 10–11cm (4–4¼in)
WINGSPAN / 15–21cm (6–8¼in)
WEIGHT / 6–9g (⅕–¼oz)

■ **STATUS** / Secure

A generally common, widespread, small, slim warbler, it is characterized by rather dull olive-green colours, lack of strong pattern, dark legs, white crescent under the eye, and frequent downward dip of the tail, as well as a characteristic song.

Juvenile
Weak pale line over eye, sometimes stronger, yellower; pale crescent under eye.

Adult, spring
Rounder head than Willow Warbler's.

Adult
May show yellow feathers from underwing poking through.

Sometimes hovers while picking flies from foliage.

Adult, winter
Dull, brownish; legs spindly, very dark (only rarely paler).

Frequent downward bob of tail, unlike Willow Warbler.

Shorter wingtip than Willow Warbler's.

Adult, spring
Western/southern European race collybita: quite bright; dark legs.

Warblers of the genus *Phylloscopus* are mostly small, slender, slim-billed, greenish birds, smaller and narrower-billed than *Hippolais*, and shorter-billed and less brown than *Acrocephalus* and many *Sylvia* species. While these others mostly have simple, hard calls such as *tak* or *churr*, the *Phylloscopus* warblers have variations on a theme of *hoo-eet*. These differences are very useful in identifying and understanding these warblers, and the Chiffchaff and Willow Warbler, being so common and widespread, are the classic *Phylloscopus* benchmark species. They are also a considerable identification challenge in themselves. Chiffchaffs like mature woodland, with a variety of mainly broadleaved trees. The canopy need not be dense and the undergrowth is typically much richer than in woods occupied by Wood Warblers. Migrating Chiffchaffs are often found in much bushier places, including insect-rich willow thickets, especially early in spring.

FEEDING
Insects form almost the whole of their diet, mostly taken from high in trees. They also eat just a few berries in autumn.

DISPLAY AND VOICE
Male Chiffchaffs sing persistently in spring and also on migration, both in spring and autumn. They sing as they wander through the tree tops. The song is an instantly identifiable repetition of simple, short, musical chirps on 2–3 notes. The sequence varies: *chip chap chip chep chep chap chap chip chap*, and may be interspersed with a quiet *churr churr*. The call is more nearly monosyllabic than the notes of the Willow Warbler or Wood Warbler: a simple *hweet*. In autumn, shrill, descending *shlip* or *cheep* notes are heard.

BREEDING
The nest is a spherical ball of grass stems and leaves with a side entrance, on or just above the ground in a bush, thick herbs, or creepers. It lays 4–7 eggs; smaller clutches replace those that are lost, and second broods are also smaller than the first. The eggs are incubated for 13–15 days and the chicks fly at two weeks.

MIGRATION
This is one of the earliest migrants to move north in spring. Wintering areas include the southern fringe of Europe, and north Africa. In spring, migrants often appear first near water where there are insects. In autumn, they are frequent in similar places, such as willow thickets, and also turn up in gardens, often singing briefly. North-eastern races are scarce migrants in north-west Europe.

WHEN SEEN

Oct — March

March to October; all year S Europe; a few winter north to Britain.

WHERE SEEN
All Europe except for Iceland, upland Scandinavia, S Sweden.

HABITAT AND INFO

SIMILAR SPECIES
Willow Warbler has fractionally longer wing and tail; flatter head; pale legs.

Flatter head

Paler legs

Spanish race/species *brehmii/ibericus* (top) has longer wing than European *collybita* (bottom).

Siberian race *tristis* has very yellow or pale yellow underwing.

Western/southern European race *collybita*.

Some birds are intermediate between northern and southern European forms, and not safely identifiable; *tristis* type (right), migrant or wintering in western Europe, merges into *abietinus*.

Adult

Adult
Siberian race *tristis*: cold brownish, buff, and white; may show curved, thin wingbar (compare Greenish Warbler's); rare in western Europe; a few winter in England.

Adult, spring (above)
Spanish race/species *brehmii/ibericus*: bright in spring, wings striped green and oily brown, breast yellow; wingtip longer than most European birds', legs may be paler.

Spanish race/species *brehmii/ibericus* can occur in a duller form (left).

Adult
North European race *abietinus*: colder, greyer than western birds.

DID YOU KNOW?
Chiffchaff songs are well studied: they seem simple and monotonous, with a constant 0.23 second pause between notes, but the phrases, typically lasting around 15 seconds, are of a seemingly infinitely variable sequence. They are so varied that they seem unlikely to help individuals recognize each other.

?

Arctic Warbler

LENGTH / 10.5–11.5cm (4¼–4½in)
WINGSPAN / 16–22cm (6¼–8¾in)
WEIGHT / 8.5–12g (¼–⅜oz)

SCALE v Pigeon

■ STATUS / Vulnerable

This is an obvious *Phylloscopus* warbler but it is stocky, thick-billed, and marked by a thin wingbar (sometimes two) and a long, striking stripe over the eye. Its hard call is a valuable clue.

Often easy to confuse with Greenish Warblers, Arctic Warblers are more northerly breeders but turn up as rare migrants on coasts in western Europe in much the same places. They nest in birch, poplar, or willow stands within conifer forest, usually near water, north to the tree line bordering open tundra.

FEEDING
This is an active warbler, foraging with quick flits and hops through foliage for insects. It flies from bush to bush with a more confident, faster action than most warblers.

VOICE
The song is loud, musical but repetitive, with a few short notes followed by a trill, lower but faster than a Wood Warbler's. The call is distinctive: a hard, Dipper-like *tzik* or *zrik*, or a quieter *zit*.

BREEDING
The domed nest is built on the ground. The 6–7 eggs hatch in 11–13 days.

MIGRATION
All Arctic Warblers winter in south-east Asia, but a handful move south-west in autumn and appear in coastal woods and thickets.

Long whitish stripe over eye stops short of bill; pale half-ring beneath eye only; mottled cheeks.

Plump body gives dumpy look end-on; when relaxed may be quite rounded.

Long and slim when active and alert; very fast-moving through foliage.

Wings longer, more pointed, than on Greenish Warbler.

Greenish
Tiny bill; stripes over eyes meet over bill.

Bill can be long or short in either sex.

Female
Shorter tail than male's; dumpier look.

Typically two wingbars, upper very thin; one or both may wear off, sometimes only from one wing; rear flanks often dusky.

Short-billed individual close to Greenish; long-billed (below) more typical, has aggressive look.

Male
Long tail; long wingtip.

Legs brownish-pink.

Pale-based dagger bill; broad dark band through eye; diffuse streaks on chest.

LONG TIPS
A long-distance migrant, the Arctic Warbler has long, pointed, strong wings.

WHEN SEEN

Sept | June

June to September.

WHERE SEEN
Breeds extreme N Norway and Sweden, NE Finland, N Russia.

HABITAT AND INFO

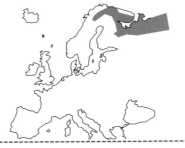

SIMILAR SPECIES
Greenish Warbler has pale stripes over eyes that meet on forehead; weaker bill; different call.

Rounder head

Shorter wingtip

Greenish Warbler

A small, rather bright grey-green and whitish warbler with a thin pale wingbar. It has a rather large, rounded head, but small bill.

LENGTH / 10cm (4in)
WINGSPAN / 15–21cm (6–8¼in)
WEIGHT / 6.5–9g (⅕–¼oz)

■ **STATUS** / Secure

SCALE v Pigeon

Typically active feeder; often raises crown feathers.

Wings shorter, more rounded, than Arctic Warbler's.

Short wingtip compared with Arctic Warbler's.

Single thin wingbar (compare with Chiffchaff's); rarely faint pale tips form hint of second one; some have dark band across tips of primary coverts.

Juvenile, September
Faintly yellow beneath.

Grey-brown legs.

Rear flanks usually cleaner, whiter than Arctic Warbler's.

Adult male

Striking stripe over eye, shorter than Arctic's but narrows over top of bill.

Stripe over eye flares at rear, unlike Chiffchaff's.

Bill small, pale right to tip of lower mandible (Arctic has dark spot).

Adult female, August
Typically rounded, but can look long and slim.

Greenish Warblers like woodland edges and clearings, with birch, aspen, and scattered spruce trees. A slow westward spread has been noted for decades, but although singing birds have been recorded in summer west as far as Britain, they have not bred there.

FEEDING
They take small insects and spiders anywhere from the ground to the high canopy of trees, with agile, quick hops and leaps, fluttering from twig to twig. Wing flicking may help disturb insects, which are then caught.

VOICE
The song is fast, loud and lively, with a Wren-like pattern of chattering and changes in pitch. Calls include a cheery, chirrupy, squeaky note like a call of the Pied Wagtail or House Sparrow: *chi-vee* or *tsi-yip*.

BREEDING
Nests are on the ground. Up to seven eggs hatch in 12–13 days.

MIGRATION
In autumn, Greenish Warblers move to Nepal and India. A few always head west and turn up on north-west European coasts in August and September.

EXCITING FIND
In western Europe, this is a rarity, seen in late summer or autumn.

WHEN SEEN

Oct / April

April to October; a very few in May or June, more in autumn in W Europe.

WHERE SEEN
Breeds west to S Finland, Baltic States, Gotland, very locally along S Baltic.

HABITAT AND INFO

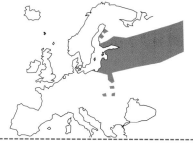

SIMILAR SPECIES
Chiffchaff has dark legs; wingbar absent or weak, but sometimes longer, curved.

Weaker head pattern

Dark legs

Wood Warbler

LENGTH / 12cm (4³/₄in)
WINGSPAN / 19–24cm (7¹/₂–9¹/₂in)
WEIGHT / 7–12g (¹/₄–³/₈oz)

SCALE v Pigeon

■ STATUS / Secure

A long-winged, yellow-faced, white-bellied woodland warbler, it is easily found by following up its distinctive song in its breeding woods. However, it is rarely seen elsewhere on migration.

Of the more widespread leaf warblers this is the largest, most colourful, and also the most exacting in its requirements. It is restricted to tall, leafy woods with open spaces and dead leaf litter beneath the trees: hillside oaks and tall beech woods meet its needs.

FEEDING
It picks insects and spiders from foliage and twigs in trees, usually in less active searching than a Willow Warbler. It also catches flies in the air in fluttering sallies.

VOICE
The song mixes two distinct phrases. Most frequent is a sharp, metallic ticking that accelerates into a short, silvery trill: *ti ti ti tik-tik-tititrrrrrrrrrr*. Interspersed are sweet, sad piping notes: *peuw peuw peuw*.

BREEDING
Nests are in leaf litter on the ground, domed, of grass and leaves. Up to seven eggs hatch in 12–14 days.

MIGRATION
Moves to middle Africa in autumn. Few seen away from their breeding sites in spring or autumn.

Female

Male
Long wings unlike Willow's.

Male
Sings from leafy canopy or open branch beneath.

Juvenile
Tiny sharp white primary tips; broad whitish tertial edges.

Strongly yellow underwing.

Bright yellow stripe over eye and dark green band through eye; variable amount of yellow on cheeks and throat contrasts with silky white belly.

Adult female, spring
Long tail is equal to length of wingtip projection; unusually, female has the longer body.

Male, spring
Short body of male reduces length of tail beyond wingtip.

DOUBLE IDENTITY
Wood Warblers have two kinds of song, given in a mixed series.

WHEN SEEN

Sept — April

April to September.

WHERE SEEN
Widespread Britain, mostly in uplands, rare Ireland; across Europe north to Norway and Sweden and south to Pyrenees, S Italy and N Greece.

HABITAT AND INFO

SIMILAR SPECIES
Willow Warbler is less yellow-and-white below; weaker stripe over eye; different song.

Less green back

Duller underside

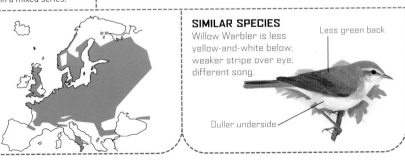

Bonelli's Warblers

Rather like duller Wood Warblers, with no yellow beneath, singing softer, bubbling, trilled songs in southern and eastern Europe, these are both real rarities on migration in north-west Europe.

LENGTH / 11.5cm (4½in)
WINGSPAN / 19–23cm (7½–9in)
WEIGHT / 7–11g (¼–⅜oz)

■ **STATUS /** Secure

SCALE v Pigeon

Yellow underwing contrasts with white belly.

Western, male

Pale over eye but little or no dark mark through it.

Western, male (left)
Greyish about head; greener on wings and rump, but brighter rump not easy to see.

Pale face, greyish cheeks; faint or diffuse pale stripe over eye; complete pale eye-ring.

Western, female
Tertial edges whitish; secondary edges brighter green; greater covert edges and tips bright green; back duller; underparts silky white.

Eastern Bonelli's Warblers, breeding in the Balkans, are now regarded as a separate species from the Western Bonelli's Warblers of the rest of Europe. In the west, they prefer oak woods, birch, beech, or mixed woods with plenty of clearings and bushy undergrowth. Eastern birds occupy similar areas, often in small trees on bushy slopes.

FEEDING
They find insects in the foliage of trees, usually well up in the canopy or out at the edge.

VOICE
Both sing with a loose, bubbly, fast trill, softer than a Cirl Bunting, quicker than Lesser Whitethroat. The Western Bonelli's call is a sharp, finch-like *chweet* or *hoo-eet*. The Eastern's is a hard, dry *tup*, *djip-djip*, or *chip*, but also a wagtail-like *tsioup*.

BREEDING
A ground nest is made under vegetation. The 5–6 eggs hatch in 12 days.

MIGRATION
Western Bonelli's winter in Africa west of Chad; Easterns in north-east Africa. Otherwise, both are rare outside their breeding areas.

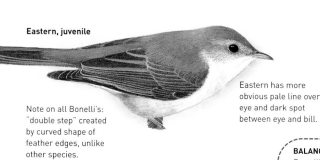

Eastern, juvenile

Note on all Bonelli's: "double step" created by curved shape of feather edges, unlike other species.

Eastern has more obvious pale line over eye and dark spot between eye and bill.

Eastern (above)
Tends to be slightly greyer, rump contrastingly brighter, tertial tips whiter, whitish bar across coverts.

BALANCING ACT
Bonelli's Warblers look for insects high in a tree's canopy or at its edges.

WHEN SEEN

Sept — April

April to September.

WHERE SEEN
Western breeds in Iberia, France, Italy, Alps east to Slovenia. Eastern breeds S Balkans and Turkey.

HABITAT AND INFO

SIMILAR SPECIES
Willow Warbler has stronger stripes through and above eye; plainer wing.

Stronger stripe

Plainer wing

Icterine Warbler

LENGTH / 13.5cm (5¼in)
WINGSPAN / 20–24cm (8–9½in)
WEIGHT / 10–14g (¼–½oz)

■ **STATUS /** Secure

SCALE v Pigeon

A rather large, long-headed, spike-billed warbler with a square tail and short, abrupt undertail coverts. It moves quite heavily through foliage.

Warblers are divided into several groups, each defined by its genus (the first word of the scientific name). *Hippolais* warblers are typified by this one: a medium-large warbler with a rather long, pale, spiky bill. It is stouter, squarer-tailed, longer-winged, and bigger-billed than a Willow Warbler. It is a bird of open woodland and woodland edge, especially with mixed trees, and copses, spinneys, lines of bushes, and overgrown gardens.

FEEDING
Insects are its chief food, with some fruit in late summer.

VOICE
The song is far-carrying and energetic: a striking mix of harsh, strident, and musical sounds, more rapid and powerful than a Marsh Warbler's. Calls include short *tuk* notes.

BREEDING
Its nests are in fruit trees or bushes. The 4–5 eggs hatch within 13–15 days. Chicks fly in two weeks.

MIGRATION
It winters in Africa. A few regularly turn up on the east coasts of Britain in autumn.

Yellow underwing, unlike Olive-tree Warbler.

Cutting edge and base of bill pale orange.

Adult, spring
Green and yellow; long, bright bill; legs typically bluish.

Long wings.

Pale feather edges create pale wing panel.

Typically pale between eye and bill; dark mark from some angles in some lights.

Juvenile

Some juveniles have this stronger head pattern.

Dagger bill, broad from above or below.

Juvenile
Pale edge to tail; strong pale wing panel; no yellow on some individuals. Note long wing projection, long tail.

Wingtips rather long compared with Melodious Warbler's; also compare with Olive-tree Warbler's.

Bold dark eye in quite plain head.

Legs can be brown or bluish.

Adult, spring
Dull, brownish type; white below.

PLAIN FACE
The area between the bill and the eye generally looks pale and weakly marked.

WHEN SEEN

Oct — April

April to October.

WHERE SEEN
Most of Europe east of NE France from central Scandinavia, south to the Alps and Danube region.

HABITAT AND INFO

SIMILAR SPECIES
Melodious Warbler has shorter wingtip; rounder head; plainer wing.

Rounder head

Shorter wing

COMMON NAME
Melodious Warbler
SPECIES
Hippolais polyglotta
FAMILY
Sylviidae
ORDER
Passeriformes

Melodious Warbler

A typical pale green-and-yellow *Hippolais* warbler, it is very like the Icterine. It is rather heavy and thickset, spike-billed, strong-legged, and square-tailed, with a pale facial pattern.

LENGTH / 13cm (5in)
WINGSPAN / 18–20cm (7–8in)
WEIGHT / 11–14g (³/₈–¹/₂oz)

■ STATUS / Secure

SCALE v Pigeon

Broader-winged than Icterine Warbler; quite heavy flight; shows subtle whitish edge to tail.

Juvenile, autumn
Dull, sometimes whitish below with very little yellow, but flushed yellow around throat, neck sides, and on pale wing panel; compare with Marsh Warbler.

Pale eye-ring; pale yellow over and in front of eye; no obvious dark stripe.

Bill quite long, broad, less dagger-like than Icterine's.

This species forms a natural pair with the Icterine Warbler: both are green *Hippolais* warblers, they look very alike, and they replace each other geographically. The Melodious Warbler likes bushy places, tall scruffy hedges, narrow strips of roadside trees, bushy gullies, and waterside woods.

FEEDING
It uses its large bill to seize insects from foliage and in flight, and pulls berries from stalks with a backward jerk. It is clumsy compared with a Willow Warbler.

DISPLAY AND VOICE
Males sing from both deeply hidden and exposed perches. The song begins with quiet, simple notes, followed by a long, fast, chattering of even pitch. Calls include a sparrow-like *tert* and hard chattering.

BREEDING
The nest is a deep, tapered cup of stems and leaves. The 4–5 eggs are incubated for 12–13 days.

MIGRATION
All winter in west Africa. A few appear in spring and autumn on British coasts, mainly in southern and western England. Icterine Warblers are generally east coast birds.

Adult, breeding
Can be very yellow; pale wing patch usually weak.

Legs dull brown or greyish.

Flatter-headed if alarmed, stretching.

Wingtip quite short: it equals tertials on Icterine, but is shorter on Melodious.

Adult, autumn
Worn, dull, can be whiter below; primaries uniform, no pale tips (which show on Icterine).

Typically round-headed; crown feathers sometimes peaked.

Postures vary, but typically pot-bellied.

POT-BELLY
Like other *Hippolais* warblers, it has a stocky body shape.

WHEN SEEN

Oct
April

April to October.

WHERE SEEN
Breeds Iberia, France, Italy, Slovenia; absent from Mediterranean islands.

HABITAT AND INFO

SIMILAR SPECIES
Willow Warbler is slimmer; less green and yellow; finer bill; flatter crown.

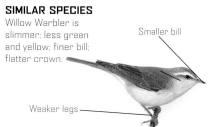

Smaller bill

Weaker legs

Olive-tree Warbler

ORDER Passeriformes
FAMILY Sylviidae
SPECIES Hippolais olivetorum
COMMON NAME Olive-tree Warbler

LENGTH / 15cm (6in)
WINGSPAN / 24–26cm (9½–10¼in)
WEIGHT / 15–25g (½–1oz)

STATUS / Vulnerable

SCALE v Pigeon

This is a really big, long, heavy, spike-billed warbler of olive groves and fruit orchards. It is rather plain and greyish.

Of the *Hippolais* warblers, this is the biggest and most extreme in its long- and broad-billed, stout-bodied, wide-tailed form. It is genuinely a bird of dense olive groves, but it also lives in oakwoods, orchards, and almond plantations. It is typically skulking in its habits and hard to observe, but repays patience and careful watching from a little distance.

FEEDING

It eats insects and other small creatures, as well as figs in late summer. It finds them mostly within the canopy of thick, leafy trees, but also on the ground.

VOICE

A distinctively deep, throaty song is lower, slower, and more uniform than an Icterine Warbler's, combining deep notes with squeaks. Calls are mostly variants on *tuk* or *chuk*.

BREEDING

Nests are made low down in olives, oaks, or smaller bushes. The clutch is 3–4 eggs. Other details are not accurately recorded.

MIGRATION

Its wintering areas are in east and south Africa. In summer, it is almost unknown outside its breeding range in Europe.

Short flights between trees reveal long wings and square tail.

Very pale below; white on belly and underwing; white edge and tip to tail.

Female

A B C

Proportion of "A" (tail projection) to "B" (wingtip projection) to "C" (tertial length) important in identifying *Hippolais* warblers.

Female
"C" dimension shorter on female than on male.

Male (to same scale as female above) "C" dimension long on male.

Bill pale beneath; plain face except pale eye-ring.

Male, spring
"A" dimension long on male: this is a particularly long-tailed warbler.

Very large; very long bill; pale, olive-grey to brownish, with distinct pale wing panel.

MASSIVE WARBLER
This and the Great Reed are comfortably Europe's two biggest warblers.

WHEN SEEN

Sept

May

May to September.

WHERE SEEN

Breeds in SE Europe, mostly Greece and Albania.

HABITAT AND INFO

SIMILAR SPECIES

Icterine Warbler is smaller, often greener; less extreme bill size.

Greener back

Yellow below

Olivaceous Warblers

A small, neat, long-billed, flat-crowned warbler, with short undertail coverts, a deep belly, and a long tail. The latter is often dipped downward as the bird moves through foliage, unlike the similar Reed Warbler's.

LENGTH / 12–13.5cm (4¾–5¼in)
WINGSPAN / 18–21cm (7–8¼in)
WEIGHT / 10–15g (¼–½oz)

■ STATUS / Vulnerable

SCALE v Pigeon

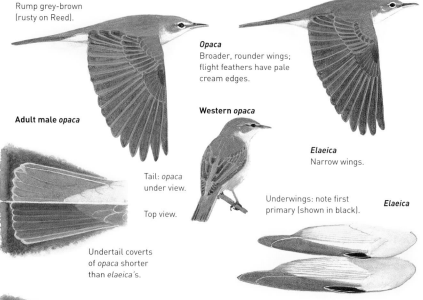

Rump grey-brown (rusty on Reed).

Opaca
Broader, rounder wings; flight feathers have pale cream edges.

Adult male *opaca*

Western *opaca*

Elaeica
Narrow wings.

Tail: *opaca* under view.

Top view.

Underwings: note first primary (shown in black).

Elaeica

Undertail coverts of *opaca* shorter than *elaeica*'s.

Opaca has longer wing.

Opaca

Adult male *elaeica*
Longer undertail coverts than *opaca*'s; tail squarer than Reed Warbler's.

Adult male *elaeica*

A dull *Hippolais* warbler, lacking green or yellow, the Olivaceous is a slender, long-billed bird. It prefers shrubby growth with tamarisk, figs, palms, and various broadleaved trees and bushes, in warm, dry places including dunes. Two closely similar forms are treated here as two species.

FEEDING
It forages for insects in foliage with heavy hops and flits, and takes fruit in summer and autumn.

DISPLAY AND VOICE
The male sings from a hidden perch, but also while moving within a tree and sometimes in flight. The song has a characteristic cyclical pattern, a fast, rising and falling, chattering phrase repeated several times without pause. Calls include a sharp, hard *tack* and *tset-tset*.

BREEDING
Nests are twig cups built in low bushes. The 2–5 eggs hatch in 11–13 days.

MIGRATION
Wintering areas are in Africa from Senegal east to Somalia, just south of the Sahara. It is very rare outside its breeding range.

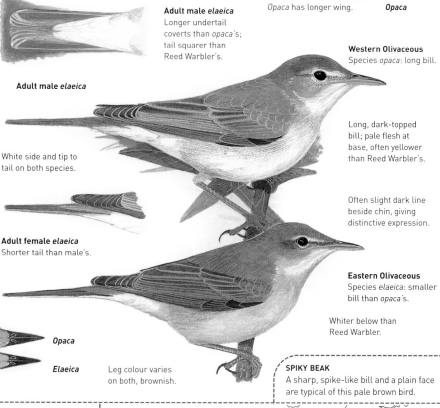

White side and tip to tail on both species.

Adult female *elaeica*
Shorter tail than male's.

Opaca

Elaeica

Leg colour varies on both, brownish.

Western Olivaceous
Species *opaca*: long bill.

Long, dark-topped bill; pale flesh at base, often yellower than Reed Warbler's.

Often slight dark line beside chin, giving distinctive expression.

Eastern Olivaceous
Species *elaeica*: smaller bill than *opaca*'s.

Whiter below than Reed Warbler.

SPIKY BEAK
A sharp, spike-like bill and a plain face are typical of this pale brown bird.

WHEN SEEN

Sept — April

Late April to September.

WHERE SEEN
Western breeds locally in Spain; Eastern in Balkans and E Europe, north to Hungary; rare vagrants elsewhere.

HABITAT AND INFO

SIMILAR SPECIES
Reed Warbler has longer undertail coverts; plainer wings.

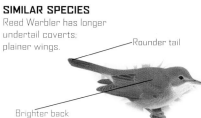
Rounder tail

Brighter back

Booted Warbler
Sykes's Warbler

ORDER Passeriformes
FAMILY Sylviidae
SPECIES Hippolais caligata / Hippolais rama
COMMON NAME Booted Warbler / Sykes's Warbler

LENGTH / 11.5–12cm (4½–4¾in)
WINGSPAN / 18–20cm (7–8in)
WEIGHT / 10g (¼oz)

SCALE v Pigeon

■ STATUS / Rare

Rather Chiffchaff-like *Hippolais* warblers, these are also much like Eastern Olivaceous Warblers, but with a short, usually distinct stripe over the eye and darker lores. Two similar forms are distinguished by structure and song.

The smallest of the *Hippolais* genus, and in some ways the most like a Chiffchaff, the Booted Warbler is also much like a small Olivaceous Warbler. It breeds in varied habitats from dry grassy places and bushes beside fields to green shrubs and riverside thickets. The central Asian form, Sykes's Warbler, is treated here as a separate species rather than a local race.

FEEDING
Perhaps the most restless, quickest feeders of the *Hippolais* group, they find insects anywhere from the ground to tree tops, and catch them in flight. They pluck berries acrobatically.

DISPLAY AND VOICE
Males sing a lot in spring, even at night, but their songs cease when the eggs are laid. The song is a fast, energetic, even phrase, that of Sykes's being harder in quality. Calls are simple *tsik*, *zet*, or *chik* notes.

BREEDING
Up to six eggs are laid in a strong cup of twigs and roots in a bush or herb. They hatch after 12–14 days.

MIGRATION
Most winter in India. A very few stray westward in spring and autumn, rarely to western Europe.

Sykes's Longer, broader wings.

Booted Short, round wings.

Booted

Sykes's

Booted Warbler, female Small, spiky bill; pale-edged tail; pale-edged tertials; pinkish or greyish legs with darker feet.

Male Booted (below) has longer tail than female's (above).

Pale, "milky-tea" colour; whiter throat; pale line over eye subtly edged darker above.

Sykes's, female Larger bill than Booted's; tertials/secondaries often plainer.

Pale-edged tail, pale-based bill with broad base, and paler legs separate both from Chiffchaff; longer tail, short wingtip, pinker legs, upward tail flick separate them from Eastern Olivaceous Warbler.

Male Sykes's (below) has longer tail than female (above).

Greyish legs with darker feet.

Booted Longer undertail coverts.

Sykes's Shorter undertail coverts.

Underwings: note length of first primary (shown in black); underside of flight feathers darker than both Olivaceous Warblers'.

Booted

Sykes's

STRONG HEAD PATTERN Compared with its close relatives, this bird has strong facial markings.

WHEN SEEN

Sept / May
May to September.

WHERE SEEN
Booted breeds in Asia, west to Lake Ladoga, south to Caspian Sea, rare vagrant in western Europe; Sykes's east of Caspian, even rarer in Europe.

HABITAT AND INFO

SIMILAR SPECIES
Olivaceous Warbler has longer bill; flatter head; paler face with less contrasted pattern.

Plainer head

Longer bill

ORDER
Passeriformes

FAMILY
Sylviidae

SPECIES
Cettia cetti

COMMON NAME
Cetti's Warbler

Cetti's Warbler

An extremely skulking warbler, it is hard to see except in short flight across open space – but it has an obvious, loud, explosive song.

LENGTH / 13.5cm (5¼in)
WINGSPAN / 15–19cm (6–7½in)
WEIGHT / 12–18g (³⁄₈–⁵⁄₈oz)

■ **STATUS /** Secure

SCALE v Pigeon

Broad tail of just 10 feathers; may be more rounded; dark rufous undertail coverts.

Tail broad, rounded; may spread and wobble in flight.

Short, rounded wings.

Cocks tail.

Lurks in dense vegetation.

Dark rufous-brown with greyish underside, dull pale stripe of variable strength over eye.

Occasionally appears on open perch to give clear view, when quite tame.

Pale throat and breast against darker flanks.

One of the Asian bush-warblers with a range that extends into Europe, Cetti's Warbler is one of the few warblers resident in Europe all year. It can be approached very closely, but is usually so skulking that it gives scarcely a glimpse as it moves through low, dense, waterside vegetation. It is usually its joyous explosion of song that gives it away – but you may stare in vain at the place from which the song came, until you hear it again from a quite different location.

FEEDING
It finds insects, spiders, and aquatic creatures deep within thick vegetation over or around freshwater.

DISPLAY AND VOICE
Males (and less frequently females) sing from low, hidden perches with sudden, loud outbursts. Two or three separate notes precede a short, fast, rich phrase: *chi-chuwee, chuweewewewewewe!* It has a characteristic loud, staccato *chip* call.

BREEDING
The nest is hidden in reeds or in a bush interlaced with stems. The 4–5 eggs hatch after 16–17 days.

MIGRATION
Resident. Some wander in winter and colonize new sites.

NOISY BUT ELUSIVE
Cetti's Warblers are easily heard, but hard to see.

WHEN SEEN

All year.

WHERE SEEN
S Britain, France, and Iberia east through Italy to Balkans.

HABITAT AND INFO

SIMILAR SPECIES
Reed Warbler is paler; finer head and bill profile; narrower, paler tail.

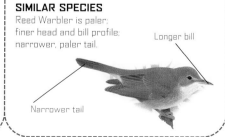

Longer bill

Narrower tail

Whitethroat

LENGTH / 14cm (5½in)
WINGSPAN / 19–23cm (7½–9in)
WEIGHT / 12–18g (³⁄₈–⁵⁄₈oz)

SCALE v Pigeon

■ **STATUS /** Secure

A quite large, long-tailed warbler of low bushy vegetation, with a puffy throat and large head. Its white tail sides, greyer head, white throat, rusty wings, and pale legs are distinctive.

Many of the *Sylvia* warblers are more or less restricted to southern and eastern Europe. The two whitethroats are exceptions, and they in particular (rather than the Blackcap and Garden Warbler) offer a taste of the *Sylvia* character to people living in more northern parts. Both species winter in Africa south of the Sahara, and they suffered enormous declines when the region incurred several successive years of drought. Their consequent rarity in northern areas like Britain helped to draw attention to the fact that protecting migrant birds on their breeding grounds is not enough to ensure their survival if they are at risk elsewhere, at other times of the year. In its breeding range, the Whitethroat likes dry heaths, the edges of woods, and the fringes of fields where there are patches of rough ground. Poorly maintained hedgerows with gaps, and overgrown ditches with nettles and willowherb are ideal. They occupy what is too often described as waste or derelict ground: the kind of habitat that develops around an old gravel pit or along a railway cutting, with a few tall trees but mostly low, bushy thickets scattered over open ground. And most of all, they enjoy a dense, thorny, food-rich bramble patch.

FEEDING
The Whitethroat eats insects, in particular various species of beetles, which it finds by thoroughly searching low bushes and herbs. As the summer progresses it eats more berries, and by autumn berries make up most of its diet.

DISPLAY AND VOICE
Male Whitethroats define their territories by singing from perches such as bush tops and overhead wires. They frequently sing in short, fluttery song flights (which Lesser Whitethroats do not). The song is a short, fast medley of notes, both harsh and sweet, and of variable quality: *cheechiwee-cheechiweechooo-chiwichoo*. The calls are varied, including a churry *wichity wichity wichity*, a croaking *churr*, *wheet*, and a hard *tak tak*.

BREEDING
Whitethroats nest low down in shrubs or in tall herbaceous growth. The 4–5 eggs are incubated for 11–12 days, and the chicks fly at 10–12 days old.

MIGRATION
The Whitethroat spends the winter in Africa along the southern edge of the Sahara, in the semi-arid Sahel zone. Migrant Whitethroats turn up at many places in the autumn, including gardens where they eagerly eat honeysuckle berries.

Male, spring
Head evenly grey, contrasting with white throat.

Bright wing feathers fade to buff during summer.

Female, autumn
Fresh pale tips to primaries.

Juvenile
Bright, buffy, with striking rusty wings, dull tail edges, bright pale tips to primaries; white crescents around eye obvious.

Female, breeding

WHEN SEEN

Sept — April

April to September.

WHERE SEEN
Absent from Iceland, N Scotland, interior of Norway and Sweden, also S Spain; otherwise appears widely across Europe.

HABITAT AND INFO

SIMILAR SPECIES
Reed Warbler has longer, finer bill; less contrasted white throat; plainer wings and tail.

Longer bill

Duller wings

Male, first summer
Adult male fades to similarly dull colours in late summer.

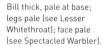

Bill thick, pale at base; legs pale (see Lesser Whitethroat); face pale (see Spectacled Warbler).

Adult (right) has white tail edges and whiter underparts than juvenile (left).

Jerky, erratic, excitable actions; steep climb at beginning of display flight.

Female
Typical pose, diving into low vegetation.

Male
Tail of female and juvenile shorter; note ample wings compared with Lesser Whitethroat.

FLIGHT PATTERN
Song flight from bush, hedge, or wire reveals thin tail.

DID YOU KNOW?
The Whitethroat's food in summer is predominantly insects, but from late summer onward the proportion of energy-rich fruit increases and in autumn and winter berries are the main food. Such food is also essential in spring, to build up energy reserves for the northward migration flight.

Lesser Whitethroat

LENGTH / 13cm (5in)
WINGSPAN / 17–19cm (6¾–7½in)
WEIGHT / 10–16g (¼–½oz)

STATUS / Vulnerable

SCALE v Pigeon

A neat, grey-brown, dark-legged, grey-capped warbler with a bright white throat, it is usually in dense shrubbery, betrayed in spring by its rattling song.

While Whitethroats tend to live in low, bushy vegetation, Lesser Whitethroats go for taller, denser growth. So rather than selecting a straggly hawthorn hedge, for example, a Lesser Whitethroat pair may prefer a tall, dense, widely spreading hedge of hawthorn and blackthorn, punctuated with large trees such as oak or ash. They are also often found in the denser thickets that grow along the edges of broadleaved woodlands. Partly because of this preference for taller, thicker growth, Lesser Whitethroats are less easy to see than Whitethroats – although the frequent singing of a territory-holding male may give away his position. In autumn, they become more conspicuous, visiting elders and honeysuckle to feed on berries along with Blackcaps and Garden Warblers. They sometimes visit gardens, and quietly watching a heavily fruited bush can be rewarding.

FEEDING

Most of their diet consists of insects that they glean from foliage and twigs. They eat a lot of berries in late summer and autumn, and take nectar and pollen from flowers in spring.

DISPLAY AND VOICE

The male sings as it moves around a territory, often from perches hidden in the depths of a bush. Each song is typically given from a different spot within the thicket as it moves, rather than from a single perch. It never sings in flight. The song has a quiet, warbling introduction, often too quiet to be heard at longer range, followed by a hollow, wooden rattle, not nearly so metallic as a Cirl Bunting or Yellowhammer and harder, less bubbling, than a Bonelli's Warbler: a quick *chika-chika-chika-chika-chika*. Calls include a high, thin *seep* and a hard, low *tuk*, not so thick as a Blackcap's *tak* note.

BREEDING

The pair build a nest of grasses and stems in a bush or tree, fixed to creepers close to the trunk or among clusters of suckers, and line it with finer material such as rootlets, moss, some hair, and plant down. The 4–6 eggs are incubated for 11–14 days, and the chicks fly when just 10–13 days old.

MIGRATION

This is an unusual species in that even western populations migrate around the eastern end of the Mediterranean, rather than south through Spain. This means that in Britain migrants arrive and depart via the east coast rather than the south. They winter in Africa south of the Sahara, as far west as Niger.

Male, spring
May be pinker beneath; angle of view and light varies strength of dark patch on ear coverts.

Female, spring
Head paler than that of male, but pattern the same.

Adult, September
Browner; ear coverts slightly darker than cap; note pale primary tips, plain wings, grey legs.

Juvenile, September
Grey cap, dark ear coverts, white eye-ring; wing feathers edged paler (unlike adult's); primaries have neat pale tips.

Eastern race
Paler head and back, but grades into western form so not reliably identifiable in the field.

WHEN SEEN

Sept — April

April to September.

WHERE SEEN

Breeds S Britain, N and E France and east through Europe, north to Norway, Sweden, and Finland; absent from Italy, S Greece, and Mediterranean islands.

HABITAT AND INFO

SIMILAR SPECIES

Whitethroat is paler; longer tail; rufous on wings.

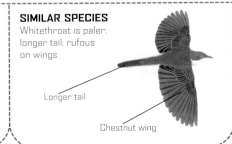

Longer tail

Chestnut wing

Male, singing
Always moves to a new perch before next song.

Easily overlooked when feeding quietly in thick hedge.

Juvenile
Extremely neat; dark edge to cheek and between eye and bill; bright white throat.

Tail of juvenile duller than adult's.

Juvenile   **Adult**

Male, spring

Female, summer

Rounder wings, shorter tail than Whitethroat's.

DID YOU KNOW?

Unlike most migrants, British breeders return from their African wintering areas around the eastern end of the Mediterranean. They travel from there in a single flight in spring, but return in a more leisurely autumn movement, many making a stopover in a small area in northern Italy.

Subalpine Warbler

SCALE v Pigeon

LENGTH / 12cm (4³/₄in)

WINGSPAN / 13–18cm (5–7in)

WEIGHT / 9–12g (¹/₄–³/₈oz)

■ STATUS / Secure

This is a tiny, bright, lively, slim-tailed warbler of Mediterranean scrub.

This is one of the Mediterranean warblers, but it is well distributed through Spain and Portugal as well as on the Mediterranean coastal strip. The Subalpine Warbler is found in bushy, thorny scrub with scattered oaks, as well as open slopes with low heath. It is small, long-tailed, lively, and attractive, but except in spring plumages it can be confusingly difficult to identify.

FEEDING
Insects are its main food, but in autumn it also eats many small fruits and berries. It feeds both low in bushes and higher in oak and olive trees.

DISPLAY AND VOICE
Males sing from perches and in short, fluttery song flights. The song is musical, prolonged, and varied, but rather even-toned. Its calls are a loud *tec*, *tec-ec-ec-ec* and *krrrr*.

BREEDING
The pair build a deep cup of grass stems and cobwebs in a bush or tree. They incubate 3–4 eggs for 11–12 days.

MIGRATION
Subalpine Warblers winter along the southern edge of the Sahara. A few turn up north of the breeding range in spring.

Tail of male.

Tail of juvenile.

Tail of female.

Juvenile
Rather oval wings; longish tail.

Long tail edged white; wings rather plain.

Male, spring
Blue-grey and pink; white moustache; red eye.

South-east European race has darker breast, more abrupt white vent and belly.

Female, spring
Pale ring around brick-red eye-ring; more or less marked white moustache; first year has paler throat.

Female, winter

Juvenile
Brown head; pale eye-ring.

Male, first winter
Grey-brown nape, browner cheeks; dull eye, pale eye-ring; ochre-brown edges on wings.

WHITE STRIPE
The pale line between the cap and throat is obvious on a male.

WHEN SEEN

Sept — March

March to September.

WHERE SEEN
Iberia, S France, Italy, Mediterranean islands, Balkans.

HABITAT AND INFO

SIMILAR SPECIES
Dartford Warbler is darker on back; no white stripe from bill.

Darker back

Longer tail

Spectacled Warbler

Here is a dark-headed, rusty-winged warbler that lives in very short Mediterranean scrub.

LENGTH / 12.5cm (5in)
WINGSPAN / 14–17cm (5½–6¾in)
WEIGHT / 10g (¼oz)

■ **STATUS /** Vulnerable

SCALE v **Pigeon**

Male
Dark cheeks frame white throat; pink chest; white underside of tail.

Adult male has a long, slim, white-edged tail.

Female
Male's tail is longer.

White crescent above and below eye; white throat with blurred grey lower edge.

Wings short and rounded; note rusty patch compared to Subalpine.

Of the various *Sylvia* warblers in southern Europe, this is one of the most restricted in range and habitat. It prefers very low heathy growth on dry, stony slopes, or short vegetation in saline depressions, and it avoids taller bushy growth or trees. Consequently, it is both harder to find and generally less well known than most of its relatives.

FEEDING
Although it eats some fruit in season, insects are by far its most important food. It creeps and hops among low growth, searching for food on the ground and among foliage.

DISPLAY AND VOICE
Males have a typical quick, fluttery song flight. They also sing from a perch. The song is a short, sweet warble. Calls are a high *tseet* and a variety of churring and rasping notes.

BREEDING
The nest is built in very low vegetation. The 3–5 eggs are incubated for 12–13 days. The chicks fly within 12 days.

MIGRATION
A few are resident in the south of France and eastern Spain, but elsewhere it is mostly a summer visitor. It probably winters in north Africa.

Compared with Whitethroat, wingtip projection is short, body small, head large, bill spiky, legs yellower.

Male
Dark head with blackish face; wings show bright rusty panel.

Female
White above and below eye; pale line from eye to bill.

Female, first winter
Bill thin, pointed.

Male, first winter

CHECK CAREFULLY
The blacker face looks obvious, but take care to rule out Whitethroat.

WHERE SEEN
Breeds locally Spain, Balearics, S France, Sardinia, S Italy including Sicily.

HABITAT AND INFO

SIMILAR SPECIES
Whitethroat has longer tail; more streaked wing; paler face; lower edge of throat whiter.

Paler face

Larger size

Sardinian Warbler

LENGTH / 13.5cm (5¼in)
WINGSPAN / 15–18cm (6–7in)
WEIGHT / 10–14g (¼–½oz)

■ STATUS / Secure

SCALE v Pigeon

Always lively but often skulking, drawing attention to itself by its calls, this is a slim, long-tailed, dark-capped warbler of Mediterranean regions.

Warm, bushy slopes and rocky clifftops along Mediterranean shores have many characteristic scents and sounds. They include the machine-gun rattle of this little warbler, which calls over and over again as it skulks and scuttles about in the bushes, or flits across a footpath with its long tail waving, only to disappear from sight. But wait a while and it is bound to poke its head out of the top of a bush to check where you are, since Sardinian Warblers seem to be inquisitive and unable to keep still or entirely out of sight for long. Even so, it might be quite some time before you get a really good, clear view. Sardinian Warblers also move easily through the tops of oaks and pines, as well as varied landscapes of shrubs, herbs, rocks, and very often the shrubberies of gardens and hotel grounds. They are happy to occupy relatively built-up areas so long as some scrubby habitat remains. Their slim shape and long, slender tails make them distinctive, even in a silhouette view or a brief glimpse.

FEEDING
Sardinian Warblers find insects by active foraging, both through low scrub and on the ground. In autumn they also eat a variety of small berries.

DISPLAY AND VOICE
These birds occupy territories throughout the year, but their song is basically restricted to spring and summer. The male sings from an exposed perch on a tree or bush, and also in a short, fluttery song flight. The song is a musical warble with a mixture of harder, rattling notes. The typical call is like a fast, wooden rattle, repeated several times: *tratratratratratra* or *kre-kre-kre-kre-kre*. Males use the call all year. It probably helps them to identify themselves and defend their territories.

BREEDING
The pair build a cup nest in a bush, using grass and plant stalks mixed with cobwebs, roots, and plant down, and lined with finer material. The female lays 3–5 eggs. They are incubated by both parents for 13 days, and the chicks fly when 12–13 days old.

MIGRATION
They are mostly resident birds. In eastern Europe, northerly birds move south in winter, while in western Europe a few move short distances, some to north Africa.

Often cocks and flicks tail.

Male, breeding

Female
Duller than male, but pattern similar; dark head with red eye and white throat.

Leg colour varies, often pinkish-orange.

Male, breeding
Browner-backed individual.

Often crouches with head low, flitting through low vegetation or on ground beneath, with tail raised; also in taller trees.

Juvenile
Duller and browner; wing feathers edged paler; flanks dark.

WHEN SEEN

All year.

WHERE SEEN
Widely in Iberia, locally S France, Italy, Balkans, and Mediterranean islands; occasional vagrant outside breeding range.

HABITAT AND INFO

SIMILAR SPECIES
Orphean Warbler is bigger, heavier; less extensive black head; less grey below.

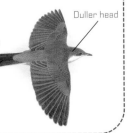

Duller head

Shorter tail

Female, first winter

Male, breeding
White throat shines brightly against grey chest and black cap.

Broad white band across underside of tail.

White spots on tail.

Juvenile
Long thin tail and narrow-based, broad wings.

Tail of juvenile.   Tail of adult.

Male, breeding
Always looks grey.

DID YOU KNOW?
Although a warbler of Mediterranean scrub, this bird is common in a relatively wide range of habitats, from almost bare ground to holm oak woodlands. It is more frequent than most around buildings and in gardens. In favoured areas, densities reach 40 pairs or more (even as many as 93) per square kilometre (²/₃ square mile).

Dartford Warbler

LENGTH / 12.5–14cm (5–5½in)
WINGSPAN / 13–18cm (5–7in)
WEIGHT / 9–12g (¼–⅜oz)

■ STATUS / Vulnerable

SCALE v Pigeon

A tiny, long-tailed warbler, it is small-billed but peaky-headed. It is usually elusive and skulking. It may perch on bush tops or fly low with its long, slightly flicking tail trailed behind. Its short, soft, buzzing churr is distinctive.

In southern Europe, the Dartford Warbler is found on warm slopes with short, aromatic herbs and dense, thorny scrub. In southern Britain, it is confined to heaths with gorse and heather, mixed with a few pines. Being resident in Britain, it suffers severely in hard winters, and this causes marked fluctuations in numbers.

FEEDING
It takes various small caterpillars and other invertebrates from foliage and vegetation close to the ground.

VOICE
Males in spring briefly abandon their skulking habits to sing from bush tops. The song is an even, rapid, churring warble. Calls are distinctively slurred, buzzy *jrrrr* notes.

BREEDING
The birds build their nests of moss, wool, and grass, deep within gorse or heather. Up to five eggs are incubated for 12–13 days.

MIGRATION
Although basically resident, Dartford Warblers make sporadic movements when high numbers put too much pressure on their food supply.

Adult male, spring
Britain, May: Blue-grey head, browner-grey back, looks dark and slaty; equally dark brown-red underparts.

Adult male
Long, slim tail; broad wings.

Pale throat spots may align in slight moustache.

Tiny spiky bill.

Juvenile male
Northern France, August.

Adult female
Slightly browner than male; may look dull and greyer.

Bright orange legs.

Adult male
North-west Spain, May.

Pale outer tail feather.

Female, first winter
Eastern Spain, January: dull brown, dark eye.

Male, first winter
Wears duller in summer, often lacks white throat spots; female paler below.

PUFFED UP IMPORTANCE
When singing or aggressive, the Dartford Warbler raises its head and neck feathers.

WHEN SEEN

All year.

WHERE SEEN
On Mediterranean scrub and heaths: S Britain, NW France, Iberia, Italy, Mediterranean islands.

HABITAT AND INFO

SIMILAR SPECIES
Whitethroat is paler; obvious white throat; rufous on wing.

Paler head

Rusty wings

Marmora's Warbler
Balearic Warbler

Two southern species, very like the Dartford Warbler, but the adults are a more uniform pale grey, with longer tails. The male Balearic Warbler has a white throat and paler underparts than the male Marmora. The bill, leg colour, and call are also different.

LENGTH / 13–14cm (5–5½in)
WINGSPAN / 25–30cm (9¾–11¾in)
WEIGHT / 10–15g (¼–½oz)

■ **STATUS /** Vulnerable

SCALE v Pigeon

Male Marmora's

Male Balearic
Longer tail, slighter build, and paler underparts than Marmora's. Note bill orange, not pinkish, and legs pale orange-brown.

White throat patch characteristic of male Balearic, and often conspicuous.

Juvenile Marmora's
Sardinia, May.

Skulking habits; often invisible in a tiny bush even at close range.

Legs darker brown on average than those of Balearic Warbler.

Adult male, Marmora's
Corsica, December: looks plain, pale grey with pale belly, but a close view reveals browner feather edges on darker wings; bright red eye and eye-ring.

Female Marmora's
Corsica, February: females and immatures can be difficult to separate from Dartford and Balearic Warblers.

Male Marmora's, first winter
Corsica, December: adults paler when freshly moulted in autumn, with slight pale spotting on throat; plumage wears darker, and pale spots are lost.

Marmora's has white spot at base of bill (not on Balearic's); bill pinkish, throat grey.

GREY TWIN
This species looks like a grey Dartford Warbler.

These two warblers are even more restricted in numbers and range than the very local Dartford Warbler, which has now replaced the Balearic in Menorca. They are birds of exposed coastal scrub and higher heathy places, often found among rocks with sparse herbaceous growth.

FEEDING
They pick small insects, spiders, cocoons, and similar minute creatures and their young from foliage near the ground.

VOICE
The song of the Marmora's is a short, sweet, twittering warble; that of the Balearic is more grating. The call of the Marmora's is a hard, throaty *tak*, while that of the Balearic is a nasal *tsrek* or *trt*.

BREEDING
The nest is a neat, deep structure of moss and grass, sited deep inside a small bush. Up to five eggs are incubated for about 12 days.

MIGRATION
Balearic Warblers are resident, but some Marmora's Warblers move to the coastal areas of north-west Africa. There are rare vagrants in Britain.

WHEN SEEN

All year.

WHERE SEEN
Marmora's: Sardinia, Corsica, small islands in area, and Pantelleria. Balearic: Balearic Islands, but not Menorca.

HABITAT AND INFO

SIMILAR SPECIES
Dartford Warbler has browner back; reddish underside; juveniles more alike.

Darker back

Rusty below

Rüppell's Warbler

LENGTH / 14cm (5½in)
WINGSPAN / 18–21cm (7–8¼in)
WEIGHT / 10–15g (¼–½oz)

■ **STATUS /** Secure

SCALE v Pigeon

A quite large, thick-necked, grey warbler, recalling the Sardinian Warbler but much more restricted in range. The pale edges on its wing feathers are always distinctive.

Restricted to the extreme south-east of Europe and Turkey, this warbler is normally found only on dry, sunny slopes with thorny bushes, aromatic herbs, and scattered trees. It is less active than most smaller warblers, skulking but not especially shy, so it is usually quite easy to watch once located. It is often attracted to rocky places, especially where scrub grows up from deep clefts.

FEEDING
It forages for insects within the cover of trees and bushes. It also eats berries in autumn.

DISPLAY AND VOICE
Males sing from a perch or in a "parachuting" song flight. The song is a mixture of short, dry chattering phrases and clear whistles. Calls are a hard *tak* and a ticking, "clock-winding" *tictictictictic*.

BREEDING
The nests are solid structures of grass and stems, sited in thick, thorny bushes. The 4–5 eggs are incubated for 13 days.

MIGRATION
The wintering area is in Chad and Sudan. In Europe, very few turn up outside the breeding range.

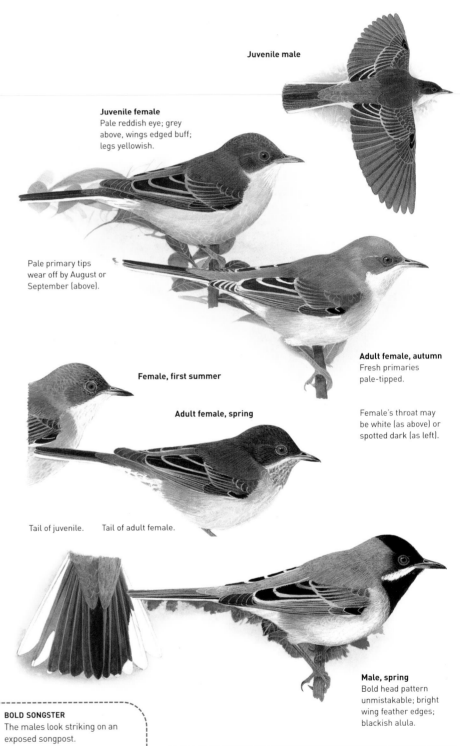

Juvenile male

Juvenile female
Pale reddish eye; grey above, wings edged buff; legs yellowish.

Pale primary tips wear off by August or September (above).

Female, first summer

Adult female, spring

Adult female, autumn
Fresh primaries pale-tipped.

Female's throat may be white (as above) or spotted dark (as left).

Tail of juvenile. Tail of adult female.

Male, spring
Bold head pattern unmistakable; bright wing feather edges; blackish alula.

BOLD SONGSTER
The males look striking on an exposed songpost.

WHEN SEEN

Sept — March

March to September.

WHERE SEEN
Breeds S Greece, Crete, a few Greek islands, Turkey.

HABITAT AND INFO

SIMILAR SPECIES
Orphean Warbler is browner; plainer wing; dark legs.

Browner back

Plain wing

COMMON NAME
Orphean Warbler

SPECIES
Sylvia hortensis

FAMILY
Sylviidae

ORDER
Passeriformes

Orphean Warbler

This is a big Mediterranean warbler with a dark head and obvious white throat. It has a heavy bill and thick legs.

LENGTH / 15cm (6in)
WINGSPAN / 20–25cm (8–9¾in)
WEIGHT / 15–30g (½–1oz)

■ **STATUS /** Secure

SCALE v Pigeon

This large warbler is a bird of the Mediterranean and Iberia, found in open woodland and tall bushes on shrubby slopes, in olive groves, and in orchards. It is easy to overlook, but it often attracts attention with its song.

FEEDING
The Orphean Warbler eats mainly insects in summer and berries in autumn. It feeds in larger bushes or trees rather than scrubby undergrowth, picking food from the foliage.

DISPLAY AND VOICE
Males sing loudly, but usually from a hidden perch inside the canopy of a tree or bush. In western Europe, the song is a loud, repetitive warble in short, distinct phrases. In the east, it is flowing and varied, almost Nightingale-like at its best. Calls are simple hard *tak* or *tek-tek* notes.

BREEDING
The nest is a well-built cup of grasses and stems lined with cobwebs and moss. The 3–5 eggs hatch after 12–13 days.

MIGRATION
Orphean Warblers winter in Africa. They are rare vagrants outside their breeding range.

Upperside of adult tail contrasted with underside.

Broad, round wing; wide tail.

Male, first winter
Dark; dull on head, but dark cheeks contrast with throat; bright flanks.

Male (above) has longer body, giving longer tail projection, than female (below).

Female, breeding
Pale eye.

Bill long and heavy.

First summer
Both male (left) and female (right) first summer have dark eyes.

Male, breeding
Blackish crown and cheeks blend into dark nape.

DUSKY HOOD
This bird has a deep, dark hood rather than a narrow cap.

WHEN SEEN

Sept — April

April to September.

WHERE SEEN
Breeds patchily Iberia, S France, Italy, Balkans, including Crete, but absent from other Mediterranean islands.

HABITAT AND INFO

SIMILAR SPECIES
Sardinian Warbler has longer, narrower tail; greyer; more extensive blackish head on male.

Greyer underside

Long tail

Barred Warbler

LENGTH / 15.5cm (6in)
WINGSPAN / 15–20cm (6–8in)
WEIGHT / 12–15g (³/₈–¹/₂oz)

SCALE v Pigeon

■ **STATUS /** Secure

This is a bulky, broad-tailed, pale-eyed warbler with stout legs and bill that often moves heavily through low bushes. Its thin, pale wingbars, dark bars under its tail, and pale tail sides/corners are distinctive.

Big, heavy, almost clumsy for a warbler, and in summer almost resembling a Wryneck in some ways, the Barred Warbler is usually easy to identify, but not to see. It skulks in low bushes and undergrowth, particularly in banks of brambles, thorn bushes, and overgrown woodland edges.

FEEDING
It eats insects in summer and takes berries in autumn, using its large bill to pluck them from twigs with a firm grip.

DISPLAY AND VOICE
Males skulk even in spring, but they sing from trees (not while moving around as other *Sylvia* warblers do) or in a song flight. The song is a vigorous warble with much mimicry, especially of Red-backed Shrikes. The typical call is a hard or rattling *trrrt* or *tsak* like a Blackcap.

BREEDING
The nest is often close to that of a Red-backed Shrike. The 4–5 eggs hatch within 12–13 days.

MIGRATION
Barred Warblers winter in east Africa, but a few move west in autumn to reach north-west Europe, including the east coast of Britain.

Grey arrows beneath tail are characteristic.

Wing long, pointed.

Upperside of adult tail contrasted with underside.

Male (above) larger-bodied than female (below), giving longer tail projection.

Male, first autumn
Dark eye and bill tip.

Female, breeding
Yellow eye; weak barring.

Male, first spring
Retains dark eye.

Male, spring
Weak barring in first year, more in second, strongest in third.

Grey legs.

WASTE REMOVAL
The chick's droppings, in a faecal sac, are easily removed.

WHEN SEEN

Aug — May

May to August; migrants in west August to September.

WHERE SEEN
Breeds very locally S Sweden and Finland, widely south of Baltic east from E Germany and N Italy.

HABITAT AND INFO

SIMILAR SPECIES
Garden Warbler is plainer overall, especially tail and head; no wingbars; shorter tail.

Plain tail

Browner wings

Garden Warbler

A relatively large warbler with a round head and stubby bill, otherwise it has few distinctive characters. It is soft and subtle in colouring, with a rich, flowing song.

LENGTH / 14cm (5½in)
WINGSPAN / 20–24cm (8–9½in)
WEIGHT / 16–23g (½–⅞oz)

■ **STATUS /** Secure

SCALE v Pigeon

Fast, flitting, rather Robin-like flight.

Female
Gentle face with large eye a distinctive feature of the species.

Male
Round head, thickish bill; notice the plain face with pale eye-ring and subtle grey patch on side of neck.

Tail coverts of male extend beyond wingtips.

Fresh plumage neatly edged paler buff on wing feathers; generally unmarked, soft olive-brown; paler beneath, with just a hint of a paler line over the eye and paler throat.

Wingtips of female equal in length to uppertail coverts; male has longer tail/body extension beyond wings.

Juvenile female

Fresh juveniles can look warm yellow-buff below, but become paler in time.

An inhabitant of mixed woods and shrubberies with dense undergrowth, the Garden Warbler shows little in the way of colour, but has a beautiful song. Even experienced bird-watchers have to see the singers to be certain some Garden Warblers are not Blackcaps, despite the slight differences in their songs. Despite its name, the Garden Warbler is not common in gardens, although it will come to feed on honeysuckle and other berries.

FEEDING
It eats mostly insects, with a variety of berries in autumn.

DISPLAY AND VOICE
The song is typically long, fluent, and rather less exuberant than a Blackcap's, without the slightly higher, fluty acceleration in the middle, but many are practically indistinguishable. Calls are a slightly softer *tsak* and a chuffing *ch ch ch*.

BREEDING
The 4–5 eggs hatch after 10–12 days. The chicks fly just 9–12 days later.

MIGRATION
They leave for Africa in August–October and return in April.

SUBTLE COLOURS
Garden Warblers have little pattern and no bright colours, but are appealing birds.

WHEN SEEN

Sept / April

April to September, a few in October.

WHERE SEEN
Open woodland; most of Europe except S Spain, N Scandinavia, most of Ireland.

HABITAT AND INFO

SIMILAR SPECIES
Female Blackcap has pale rufous-brown cap.

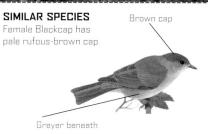

Brown cap

Greyer beneath

Blackcap

LENGTH / 13cm (5in)
WINGSPAN / 20–23cm (8–9in)
WEIGHT / 14–20g (½–¾oz)

■ STATUS / Secure

SCALE v Pigeon

A large, thickset but sprightly warbler, it can be sluggish in movements, especially if feeding on berry clusters on honeysuckle or elder. It is sometimes aggressive, noisy, with hard, abrupt calls and a brilliant song.

From a woodland thicket in early spring comes a rich warbling song: a rapid, throaty performance, initially subdued but quickly becoming a faster, louder outburst. The Blackcap is back. Yet, while traditionally a summer visitor in Britain, the Blackcap has changed its habits and is now often seen in winter as birds from central Europe move west to replace UK breeders that fly south in autumn. These winter birds frequently appear in gardens, dominating smaller birds at the bird table.

FEEDING
It eats insects and berries, plus food from bird tables in winter.

DISPLAY AND VOICE
Few displays are seen but the song is frequently heard. It has shorter phrases than the prolonged song of a Nightingale or thrush, and is more rushed. Calls are the hard, short *tak* notes typical of *Sylvia* warblers.

BREEDING
The small, rounded cup of thin stems in a low bush holds 4–5 eggs. They hatch after 10–12 days.

MIGRATION
Most winter in the Mediterranean area and north Africa.

Rear body looks silky white from below.

Female

Male

Juvenile male
Duller and darker above and below than adult female, with darker cap.

Pointed outer tail feathers show this is a male.

Spring male
Fresh grey, becoming browner later in the season; striking black cap; grey above bill base unlike Marsh Tit or Willow Tit.

Spring female
Bright red-brown cap; grey collar; olive-brown back.

Wingtips of female equal tail coverts; male has longer body, tail extends farther beyond wings.

BRILLIANT SINGER
This is one of the best songsters among Europe's warblers.

WHEN SEEN

All year, but most April to September; increasingly winter in W Europe.

WHERE SEEN
Open woodland, parks with plentiful undergrowth and shrubberies: all but extreme N Europe.

HABITAT AND INFO

SIMILAR SPECIES
Sardinian Warbler has longer, narrower, dark tail; more black on head.

Darker cheeks

Longer tail

Fan-tailed Warbler

A tiny warbler that is sandy, round-bodied, and thin-tailed in side view, but broad- and short-tailed from rear. It is most easily seen in frequent song flights over grassland.

LENGTH / 10cm (4in)
WINGSPAN / 12–15cm (4¾–6in)
WEIGHT / 10g (¼oz)

■ **STATUS /** Vulnerable

SCALE v Pigeon

Tiny, very active, strikes perky poses on grass and bush tops.

Song flight rises steeply, then with wide ranging undulations; *tzip* call at each bound.

Adult, late autumn

Flight quick, weak, flitting, wings short and round, tail fanned; clear orange-buff rump.

In Africa, there are many species of *Cisticola* warblers, but this is the only one found in Europe. It requires large areas of grassland, damp or dry, with sparse bushy growth at most, and more or less bare earth beneath. Cereal fields make a fair substitute in places. It is typically seen beside coastal marshes or around the fringes of salt pans or shallow lagoons.

FEEDING
It picks small insects from soft, level ground beneath grass or cereal stems.

DISPLAY AND VOICE
The best way to detect Fan-tailed Warblers is to listen for their distinctive song. Males have a high, undulating song flight, calling at each bound with a sharp, metallic, vibrant *tzip, tzip, tzip*. They also sing from a perch.

BREEDING
The nest is a pear-shaped, bottle-like mass of grass and cobwebs with a high side entrance, fixed to tall stems. The 4–6 eggs are incubated for 13 days. The chicks fly at 14 days.

MIGRATION
Resident. Hard winters cause severe declines, but periodic dispersals help populations recover.

Adult, late autumn
Fresh plumage in November: tail plain from side; black streaks on wings; fine streaks on crown, which wears more solidly dark.

Long toes grasp slender stems.

Juvenile
Richer buff than whiter-bellied adult.

Underside of tail has black-and-white spots; left side shows wider white spots, right side shows duller or worn variation.

Adult, breeding
Whole plumage wears dull and dark.

DEAD GRASS PATTERN
Contrasted streaks create excellent camouflage in dried grass.

WHEN SEEN

All year.

WHERE SEEN
Iberia, local W and S France, Italy and Mediterranean islands, S Balkans.

HABITAT AND INFO

SIMILAR SPECIES
Sedge Warbler is bigger; less cute face with bold stripe over eye; more blurred streaks on back.

Bold stripe over eye

Longer tail

Goldcrest

LENGTH / 9cm (3½in)
WINGSPAN / 13–15.5cm (5–6in)
WEIGHT / 5–7g (⅕–¼oz)

■ **STATUS /** Secure

SCALE v Pigeon

A minute woodland bird that combines some features of warblers and tits. It is oblivious to human presence, especially in autumn and winter when foraging low down in bushes and undergrowth.

Tiny, fearless, often indeed simply ignoring people, the Goldcrest is a familiar bird of coniferous trees and thickets. It likes parks and gardens with yews and ornamental firs, and woods with spruce and silver fir (it is less attracted to Scots pine and larch). In winter, it roams widely through low thickets of willow and alder.

FEEDING
It picks tiny insects and spiders from twigs high up in dense trees.

DISPLAY AND VOICE
The crest is fanned in display. The song is thin, rhythmic, fast, with a flourish at the end: *tidl-de-ee tidl-de-ee tidl-de-ee tidl-de-ee-didl*, or *cedar cedar cedar* at a distance. Calls are needle-sharp, both less shapeless and more emphasized than those of a Long-tailed Tit: *seee seee*. Both song and calls are a test for high-frequency hearing loss. Many people cannot hear them.

BREEDING
A tiny nest of moss and lichen suspended from a twig holds up to 11 eggs. They hatch in 15–17 days.

MIGRATION
Many northern breeders move south in winter. Others are resident or wander short distances.

Forages high in trees; often hovers, catching insects in foliage.

Yellow crown stripe often very thin in narrow black cap.

Tiny, dumpy, or quite slim; pale area around eye; faint dark moustache; two pale bars on blackish wing.

Adult female
Yellow crown stripe.

Male
Bright orange centre to crest, fanned broad and flat in aggression or display.

Thin dark legs with paler feet.

Constant wing flicking reveals white underwing.

Juvenile
Plain crown; pale around eye.

Broad pale wingbar often has V-shape.

MINUTE ACROBAT
Goldcrests are so lightweight that they can explore the tiniest of twigs and stems.

WHEN SEEN

All year.

WHERE SEEN
Widespread breeder, absent from Iceland, N Scandinavia, S Spain, and Portugal; winter visitor to much of S Europe.

HABITAT AND INFO

SIMILAR SPECIES
Chiffchaff has dark legs; plainer cap, but pale line over eye; plain wings.

Plain wings

Dark legs

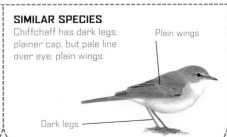

Firecrest

A tiny woodland gem, revealing bright colours in close views, but often a dull silhouette high in trees. Its song is typically unlike Goldcrest's, and its calls are subtly different.

LENGTH / 9cm (3½in)
WINGSPAN / 13–16cm (5–6¼in)
WEIGHT / 5–7g (⅕–¼oz)

■ STATUS / Secure

SCALE v Pigeon

Through much of Europe the Firecrest is quite common, but in Britain it is much rarer: a treat in winter or at the coast on migration, and a rare find in summer. It likes mixed woodland with holly and oak, maples within conifer forest, and pure conifer stands, especially spruce.

FEEDING
It eats similar food to the Goldcrest, but often feeds in more open places. It is less restricted to conifers.

DISPLAY AND VOICE
Males display with their crown feathers widely spread. The distinctive song lacks the rhythmic repetition and flourish of a Goldcrest: an accelerating *zi zi zizizizizii*. Calls are slightly lower and firmer: *zit* or *zizi*.

BREEDING
The nest is an elastic cup of moss, lichens, and cobwebs similar to the Goldcrest's. Up to 12 eggs are incubated for 15 days, and the chicks fly when they are about 22 days old.

MIGRATION
Mostly resident, but some move south and west. A few winter in southern Britain.

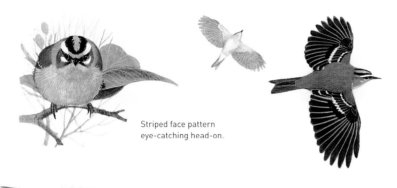

Striped face pattern eye-catching head-on.

Female, winter

Male fans crown in display.

Adult female
Crown stripe rich orange-yellow; broad black band each side of crown; yellowish forehead, broad white stripe over eye may look wedge-shaped; grey cheek.

Juvenile
Lacks crown pattern; dull pale stripe over eye.

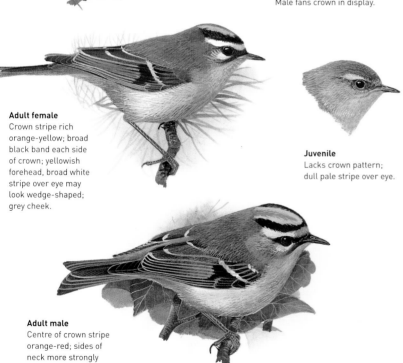

Adult male
Centre of crown stripe orange-red; sides of neck more strongly bronzy-orange; whiter below than Goldcrest.

AGGRESSIVE DISPLAY
The crest is fanned out sideways in excitement.

WHEN SEEN

All year.

WHERE SEEN
Breeds very locally S Britain; widespread in Europe north to the Baltic and east to Baltic states, Bulgaria, and Greece.

HABITAT AND INFO

SIMILAR SPECIES
Goldcrest has plainer face with pale eye-ring, not stripes.

Pale face

Buff beneath

Spotted Flycatcher

LENGTH / 14cm (5½in)
WINGSPAN / 23–25cm (9–9¾in)
WEIGHT / 14–19g (½–⅝oz)

■ **STATUS /** Vulnerable

SCALE v Pigeon

A Spotted Flycatcher perches on open twigs or fences, high or low, and snatches insects on the wing with sudden, fluttering sallies. Tiny legs, upright stance, long wings, and a longish tail combined with a relatively flat head and thicker bill prevent confusion with brownish warblers.

Not every bird with character has obvious plumage patterns or bright colours. The Spotted Flycatcher is a clear case of a species with basically dull, brown plumage yet a really distinctive and individual appeal. It is bright-eyed, ever on the lookout for insects, lively, and active. It is always a joy to watch and welcome back in spring. It often draws attention to itself by its acrobatic fly-catching behaviour, despite its lack of conspicuous colours. Spotted Flycatchers are among the last of the summer visitors to Europe to arrive in spring: indeed, some of their traditional territories may not be occupied until the very end of May, or even early June – to the relief of those people who wait for "their" flycatcher to return to a familiar garden or park perch. This is a bird of tennis courts, churchyards, and park benches; also of creepers on walls, the ivy around an old apple tree, or an open-fronted nest box fixed on a stump among the climbing roses and clematis flowers.

FEEDING
A Spotted Flycatcher catches flies and other insects on the wing with a quick sally from its perch and a loud snap of its bill. It needs clear air and open space to see and hunt its prey. It may use perches as low as gravestones or as high as bare branches at the tops of trees. Unlike a Pied Flycatcher, it often flies out from a perch, catches its fly, and returns to the same place.

DISPLAY AND VOICE
An undemonstrative bird, the Spotted Flycatcher has an insignificant song that most people would not recognize: a brief, thin, squeaky repetition of a few short notes. The calls are similarly short, scratchy, and slightly creaky or squeaky in character: *tseet*, *sirr*, or *tsee-chup-chup*.

BREEDING
The nests are often built among creepers, sometimes on old thrushes' or wagtails' nests. Some sites are used year after year. They may use nest boxes or even half coconut shells placed out for them, but they need a shallow dish or open-fronted box, with a clear view for the incubating bird. The 3–5 eggs hatch after 12–14 days. The pale-spotted chicks fly when 12–16 days old.

MIGRATION
European breeding birds move into central and southern Africa, where Spotted Flycatchers are common in parkland and savannah regions. Most migrate in September, but a few stragglers remain into October, mainly at coastal sites. They return in May.

Sits upright with alert, intelligent air, often flirting its long wingtips, watching intently for flying insects.

Bill looks slim from side, but more substantial than most warblers'; viewed from above, has typically broad fly-catcher form, with fine bristles at base.

Juvenile male
Silver-grey and buff feather centres on crown, ear coverts, back, and scapulars produce pale-spotted effect above; wing feathers broadly edged yellow-buff.

Underside pale, silvery-white on belly: typically gives very pale-fronted look to upright bird.

Adult female
Soft, fine streaks on crown; broader, gentle streaking on chest; upperparts mostly plain, pale olive-brown to grey-brown, but wing feathers have obvious pale edges.

Male is longer-tailed then female.

Short legs set well back; long tail and long head profile create upright, alert look on perched bird.

WHEN SEEN

Sept · May

Mostly late May to September.

WHERE SEEN
In gardens, parks, open woodland clearings; in coastal bushes or shelter belts on migration; almost throughout Europe except Iceland and exposed moorland or mountain areas.

HABITAT AND INFO

SIMILAR SPECIES
Garden Warbler has much plainer wing; less upright, on longer legs; unstreaked crown.

Plain wing

Longer legs

May drop to the ground to snatch an insect, but most prey caught in the air from a perch.

Long-winged and narrow-tailed in flight, with angular, straight-winged shape.

Juvenile

Pied Flycatcher
Note pale wingbar, white edges to tertials and short, white-edged tail.

Adult male

DID YOU KNOW?

Flying insects form the great majority of the diet of this bird, but it can only catch and swallow single insects, being unable to store and carry them in its bill. Adults, therefore, concentrate on larger insects to feed to their young than they eat themselves, making visits to the nest more efficient.

Pied Flycatcher

SCALE v Pigeon

LENGTH / 13cm (5in)
WINGSPAN / 21–24cm (8¼–9½in)
WEIGHT / 12–15g (³/₈–½oz)

■ **STATUS /** Vulnerable

A neat, quiet, round-headed bird with a bold eye in a plain face and some white in the wing. It breeds in open woodland, but migrants often appear in low scrub or more unexpected places.

Male Pied Flycatchers are splendid little birds with a beautifully contrasted pattern. In autumn, the males have a duller brown-and-white version of the same pattern, like summer females and juveniles, yet they remain striking, if unobtrusive in behaviour. They can be surprisingly elusive in the woods where they breed, and once the nesting season is over it is a virtual mystery where they spend the few weeks before they migrate: they simply melt away into the woods. Like Redstarts and Wood Warblers, which are often linked in the minds of bird-watchers – in Britain at least – as birds of the western oakwoods, they like leafy canopies above open, tree-shaded spaces. Overgrazed slopes under oak, with no undergrowth, are ideal. The clear space allows them room to manoeuvre when feeding.

FEEDING
The Pied Flycatcher catches small insects, both in the air and on the ground after fluttering dives from a perch. It is more of a ground feeder than the Spotted Flycatcher. Protein-rich caterpillars are vital food for chicks in early summer.

DISPLAY AND VOICE
Males find territories around suitable nest holes or (especially in Britain) nest boxes. They sing frequently at first, with a simple, hesitant phrase, changing in pitch: *tri tri tri, trip trip, chichi-chwee*. Calls include a loud *hweet* or *whit* and a sharp *tic*, often combined as *whee-tic*.

BREEDING
The nest is in a hole in a tree such as might be used by a Blue or Great Tit. Such holes are often in short supply, and many woods with thriving Pied Flycatcher populations had few or none at all until nest boxes were put up for them. This bird responds to their provision more positively than any other, occupying suitable woods in high densities once the shortage of nesting holes is no longer a problem. The nest is made of leaves, roots, and bark, lined with feathers, fine roots, and strips of soft bark. The 6–7 eggs are incubated for 13–15 days. The chicks fly when they are 14–17 days old.

MIGRATION
Pied Flycatchers spend the winter in west Africa, between the Sahara and the Gulf of Guinea. In spring, they return quite swiftly, with relatively few stopping off on coasts or at other places where they do not breed. In autumn, however, they are more widespread and northern birds are regularly seen on coasts in August and September. They are also seen in smaller numbers inland.

Adult female
Small, narrow white primary patch may show or be hidden.

Female resembles a small female Chaffinch with only one wingbar and white edges to tertials; not streaked like Spotted Flycatcher.

Adult male typically has two white spots on forehead, but sometimes just one.

Female, first winter
Thin white streaks in wing; pale brown wings; white side to tail.

First winter female shows more or less marked dark malar stripe below bill.

Some have more white in wing, including white primary bar.

Short black legs.

Adult female
Whiter below than immature bird.

Male, first winter
Blacker wings than young female; some show pale edges to smaller coverts.

WHEN SEEN

Oct — April

April to October.

WHERE SEEN
Breeds N and W Britain; locally Iberia and France; more widely across N and central Europe, but absent from Italy, SE Europe, and Mediterranean islands except Mallorca.

HABITAT AND INFO

SIMILAR SPECIES
Spotted Flycatcher has streaked crown; lines on wing thin, buff, not white.

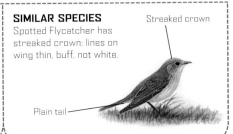

Streaked crown

Plain tail

Juvenile, August
Typically smaller white wingbar than adult female.

Male, breeding, Spanish race
Large single forehead patch; extensive white in wing; pale grey patch on back; no white in tail.

Male, first summer
Browner wings than full adult; fly-catches from a perch, but does not return to it; often forages on ground.

Male, breeding
Tiny white spot at base of primaries, beyond primary coverts, varies.

Male, breeding

Female, breeding
First winter may have similar white pattern, but slight individual variation.

DID YOU KNOW?
Unlike the Spotted Flycatcher, which winters widely through Africa south of the Sahara, European Pied Flycatchers mostly move west then south in autumn, to feed up in Iberia, before moving on to a small area of West Africa close to the Gulf of Guinea coast. In spring, they may briefly hold territories in Spain to feed up again before moving on north.

Collared & Semi-collared Flycatcher

LENGTH / 13cm (5in)
WINGSPAN / 12-13cm (4¾-5in)
WEIGHT / 10-15g (¼-½oz)

SCALE v Pigeon

■ STATUS / Vulnerable

This is a pair of strikingly contrasted species that forage high in the trees in east and south-east Europe.

The eastern counterpart of the Pied Flycatcher, with even more contrasted plumage, the Collared Flycatcher lives in warmer regions with tall broadleaved woodland. It hunts more in the tree tops, and less often on the ground than the Pied Flycatcher. The closely related Semi-collared Flycatcher, once considered a local race of the Collared, is mostly found in mountain woods of oak and hornbeam.

FEEDING
They catch airborne insects in fly-catching sallies, and take insects and larvae directly from foliage.

VOICE
The song has a Robin-like quality, but is slower, more broken, with a mixture of harsh whistles. It is longer, but less loud, than a Pied Flycatcher's. Calls include a thin *eeep*.

BREEDING
They nest in tree holes. They lay 4–7 eggs, which hatch in 12–14 days.

MIGRATION
Wintering in Africa south of the Sahara, they move south through the Mediterranean in autumn, only rarely west of their breeding ranges. A very few overshoot in spring.

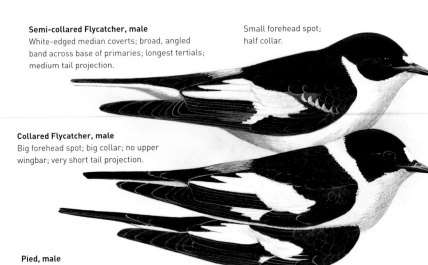

Semi-collared Flycatcher, male
White-edged median coverts; broad, angled band across base of primaries; longest tertials; medium tail projection.

Small forehead spot; half collar.

Collared Flycatcher, male
Big forehead spot; big collar; no upper wingbar; very short tail projection.

Pied, male
No upper wingbar; very small primary patch; longest tail.

Semi-collared
Tail shorter, wings longer than Pied's; pale lower back; white across primary bases.

Semi-collared, female
Thin half collar; thin primary patch.

Collared, female
Wide half collar; thickest primary patch.

First winter bird (far left and below) has incomplete white tertial tips compared to adult's (near left).

Collared
Body of tail is short; pale lower back; broad white on primaries; white collar complete.

EXCITING SIGHT
A spring male is an extravagantly patterned flycatcher.

WHEN SEEN

Sept — April

April to September.

WHERE SEEN
Collared: east from W Germany and Italy through central Europe, north to Baltic islands. Semi-collared: much more local, breeds Greece, Bulgaria, Turkey, Azerbaijan.

HABITAT AND INFO

SIMILAR SPECIES
Male Pied Flycatcher has no collar on the neck and a narrower wing patch.

Less white in wing

Dark neck

ORDER
Passeriformes

FAMILY
Muscicapidae

SPECIES
Ficedula parva

COMMON NAME
Red-breasted
Flycatcher

Red-breasted Flycatcher

One of Europe's most delightful small birds: tame and confiding, it flits about in the tree tops, occasionally flying out to snap up a tiny insect in the air, when it reveals its distinctive white tail patches.

LENGTH / 11.5cm (4½in)
WINGSPAN / 18–21cm (7–8¼in)
WEIGHT / 10g (¼oz)

■ STATUS / Vulnerable

SCALE v Pigeon

Often cocks tail.

Bold white side patches on black tail distinctive in all plumages.

Autumn juvenile
Peachy-yellow or dull orange-buff below; pale wingbar; pale eye-ring.

All the flycatchers are delicate, engaging birds, but in many ways this is the most charming of all. It is tiny, tame, active, and characterized by a boldly marked tail. It prefers tall trees with thick undergrowth, near water, orchards, and vineyards.

FEEDING
It hovers to glean insects and spiders from tree foliage, mostly within the middle canopy. It also catches a few in the air or on the ground.

DISPLAY AND VOICE
Its song is loud and far more attractive than that of other flycatchers. It has a silvery, melodious character as if combining Wood and Willow Warbler songs. Calls include a Robin-like, but distinctive, *zit* or *zirrt*.

BREEDING
The nest is in a hole in a tree or wall. Five or six eggs are incubated for 12–13 days.

MIGRATION
In winter, Red-breasted Flycatchers move to southern Asia rather than Africa. They take an easterly route in autumn, but a handful go west instead and turn up as rare, but regular, migrants in western Europe.

Male, first summer
Reduced red.

Male, summer
Dark brown; greyish on cheeks and neck, white beneath; orange-red gorget.

Adult female
No grey or red on head; whitish throat above soft brown breast band.

TINY SPRITE
This is a wonderfully cute, perky little flycatcher.

WHEN SEEN

Oct
April

April to October.

WHERE SEEN
Breeds S Sweden, Germany and east across NE Europe; also locally south to Balkans.

HABITAT AND INFO

SIMILAR SPECIES
Spotted Flycatcher has plain tail; streaked crown; pale lines on wings.

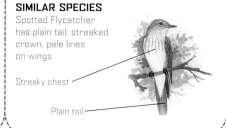

Streaky chest

Plain tail

Bearded Tit

LENGTH / 16cm (6¼in)
WINGSPAN / 16-18cm (6¼-7in)
WEIGHT / 12-18g (³/₈-⁵/₈oz)

■ STATUS / Vulnerable

SCALE v Pigeon

A uniquely long-tailed, small songbird of reed beds and marshes. Its bright, tawny plumage, striped wings, and ringing calls make identification straightforward, but it can be difficult to see.

Unless forced to leave its native reed bed and roam more widely by lack of food, or because there are too many individuals in one small marsh after a good breeding season, the Bearded Tit is a strict resident in freshwater (or slightly brackish) marshes with dense reeds. Consequently, it has a very localized distribution, and it is easily wiped out from large areas if its fragile wetland habitat is destroyed.

FEEDING
It eats small insects and seeds, taken from reed heads and the leaf litter at the base of the reed bed.

DISPLAY AND VOICE
Their displays are relatively inconspicuous in the dense reeds, but Bearded Tits are easily heard, giving a variety of abrupt, ringing, or twangy notes, especially *tying* and *ping*.

BREEDING
Nests are well hidden in reeds, over water, or in dense leaf litter, lined with reed heads. The 5–7 or more eggs hatch after 12–13 days.

MIGRATION
Usually resident, it sometimes makes wide-ranging winter movements over Europe.

Male, first winter   Female, first winter

Young male in winter has dusky marks from the bill to the eye; young female has pale grey mark there.

Flight low, fast, quite whirring over reeds; birds may fly high in autumn before leaving reed bed, but often decide to stay and dive back again.

Adult female
Plain face; bright tawny-buff crown and back.

Adult male
Blue-headed with unique black moustache.

Juvenile male has black back until autumn; juvenile female has dusky streaks; by winter they are both plainer tawny-brown.

Male   Female

FLAMBOYANT MOUSTACHE
The drooped, pointed moustache is unique.

WHEN SEEN

All year.

WHERE SEEN
In reed beds (in winter, less often in reed mace and sedge); breeding range very erratic over Europe from Sweden, Britain, and Spain eastward.

HABITAT AND INFO

SIMILAR SPECIES
Long-tailed Tit has rounder, more neckless shape; stubbier bill; lacks tawny-brown.

Less brown

Blacker tail

ORDER
Passeriformes

FAMILY
Remizidae

SPECIES
Remiz pendulinus

COMMON NAME
Penduline Tit

Penduline Tit

A tiny, tit-like bird of waterside habitats. Adults have a unique black mask from the forehead across the cheeks (beware confusion with much larger Red-backed Shrike).

LENGTH / 11 cm (4¼in)
WINGSPAN / 20cm (8in)
WEIGHT / 8–10g (¼oz)

■ **STATUS /** Vulnerable

SCALE v Pigeon

Adult male
Most boldly marked with black and rufous on pale grey head.

Adult female
Duller mask, not reaching forehead, and paler breast; note round head, sharp, triangular bill.

Flight quick, flitting, usually low or from tree top to tree top.

Blackish tertials with pale fringes and well-marked wings at all ages.

Nest begins as narrow horseshoe, develops into broad pouch, finally has spout added high on one side.

Immature
Dusky, incomplete face mask; white chin; buff underside.

Wing coverts form broad bar of rich rusty-brown.

Juvenile
Lacks mask, face being pale buff with diffuse white stripe over eye.

Unrelated to the typical tits, the Penduline Tit is a marsh bird that likes a mixture of reeds and reed mace, tall poplars, and willows. It is easily overlooked, but its characteristic call draws attention to it once learned.

FEEDING
It forages for insects and a few small seeds, usually in reed beds in winter, but more widely in summer.

VOICE
Its song is a rather quiet development of its high, thin call – a quite long, simple *tseeeh* or *tseeuh*, rather stronger and longer than the similar call sometimes heard from a Reed Bunting.

BREEDING
The nest is extremely distinctive, made of reed mace down and poplar or willow catkins, fashioned into a deep pouch with a short entrance spout near the top and hanging from the end of a thin twig. The clutch of 6–8 eggs hatch in 13–14 days.

MIGRATION
Birds from eastern Europe move south in winter, but southern birds are resident.

ENTRANCE SPOUT
The remarkable nest has a protruding side entrance near the top.

WHEN SEEN

All year.

WHERE SEEN
Mostly in poplars and willows, in damp farmland mixed with reed-fringed streams and ditches, in Europe and the Mediterranean fringe; spreading west; in reed beds in winter.

HABITAT AND INFO

SIMILAR SPECIES
Bearded Tit is much browner; longer tail; striped wings.

Paler back

Long tail

Long-tailed Tit

LENGTH / 14cm (5½in)
WINGSPAN / 16–19cm (6¼–7½in)
WEIGHT / 7–9g (¼oz)

■ **STATUS /** Secure

SCALE v Woodpigeon

No other bird of bushes, trees, and woodland edges has such a combination of tiny bill, round body, and long, stick-like tail. The black, pink, and dusky white colouring is equally distinctive. Small parties usually move from bush to bush in a thin stream, calling as they go.

Despite marked variation from place to place across Europe, all Long-tailed Tits are immediately identifiable: tiny, round-bodied birds with minute bills and long, slim, straight tails giving a distinctive "ball and stick" shape. They are sociable birds, showing more of an affinity with the babblers than with the true tits. Whole families may roost together in their elastic nest to keep warm. Not many European species exhibit such regular close body contact. In winter, they huddle together in parties to conserve energy, for they suffer badly in hard weather, especially when heavy snow or spells of hoar frost and glazed ice lock away their food. Fortunately, they have the ability to rear large broods of young, so they are able to bounce back given a few years when the winters are milder.

FEEDING
Most of their food is animal matter: tiny insects, including larvae of all kinds, and spiders and their eggs. They usually forage high in the tree canopy or in the top of the shrub layer, and rarely on the ground.

DISPLAY AND VOICE
Winter flocks are based around family parties. These break up in spring, so avoiding inbreeding, although previous adult pairs may remain together. Pair formation is a subdued affair. The two birds perch side by side and shiver their wings, the female slightly opening her wings a little away from her body. Voice plays little part: both sexes have a quiet, twittering song of no fixed pattern. They call all the time, however, to keep contact as they move through the trees: high, colourless, single or repeated *seee* notes, a soft but slightly metallic *pit*, and a trilled *purrrp*.

BREEDING
Despite their social nature, Long-tailed Tits nest in solitary pairs, but additional helpers may assist a pair to feed their large brood of hungry young. The nest is an extraordinary flask-shaped construction of moss, lichen, and spider silk, with a side entrance and a thick feather lining, usually in a low, thorny bush. Up to 12 eggs (highest numbers in the north) are laid and incubated for 13–17 days. The chicks fly at 14–18 days old.

MIGRATION
Long-tailed Tits are mainly resident and do not usually travel far. In some years, however, the populations in north and central Europe build up to high levels. If there is then a shortage of food they are sometimes forced to move to other regions in spectacular irruptions.

Adult, British Isles
Dark race *rosaceus*, with black head bands.

Juvenile (below)
Typically white crown but blackish upperside lacks pink on scapulars.

Adult, northern Europe
Pale race *caudatus*, with all-white head.

Adult
Intergrades between dark and pale races occur.

Juvenile

Adult, breeding
British type (left) grades into grey-backed type found in Italy (opposite page).

Adult, breeding
Black/pink/white plumage; bright white edges to wing feathers; white-sided tail.

WHEN SEEN

All year.

WHERE SEEN
In mixed woods, farmland with tall hedges and bramble brakes, thickets, gardens, and parks; almost all Europe except Iceland.

HABITAT AND INFO

SIMILAR SPECIES
Pied Wagtail has much longer legs; longer bill; less rounded shape; black bib.

Longer bill
Longer legs

Adult
Dark-headed.

Adult
White-headed.

Nests in bush (far left) or fork of tree (left); nest is faced with lichen, hair, and feathers; note yellow gapes of young calling to be fed.

Adult, breeding (right)
Grey-backed type found in Italy.

Adult   **Juvenile**

Adult has long central tail feathers, while juvenile has short ones.

Increasingly visits garden peanut baskets; may feed on ground, holding tail slightly above horizontal.

Adults, breeding
Central Iberian/Corsican form (left); Sicilian form (right).

FLIGHT PATTERN
Typical party flying in line astern from tree to tree, at roughly 30-second intervals.

DID YOU KNOW?
Few European birds perch so close together as to touch, but this, one of a small group of related species scattered through Asia, Europe, and the Americas, will do so when roosting or simply resting. It forms small, tight-knit social groups all year, easily observed as they move through woods and hedgerows, but pairs separate out to nest in distinct territories.

Sombre Tit

LENGTH / 14cm (5½in)
WINGSPAN / 21–23cm (8¼–9in)
WEIGHT / 17–19g (⅝oz)

■ **STATUS /** Secure

SCALE v Pigeon

Its Great Tit proportions and black-white-brown-buff pattern with no bright colours make this bulky, bold bird unique within its range.

Even compared with a Great Tit this is a bulky little bird, and much bigger than the similarly patterned Marsh and Willow Tits. It is also less acrobatic in its behaviour. It occupies warm forests of oak, willow, poplar, or conifers, as well as orchards, and favours slopes with a mixture of trees and big rocks.

FEEDING
It picks caterpillars, grubs, and adult insects from trees and shrubs, or takes them from the ground beneath to be eaten on a nearby perch. It rips seedheads to pieces with its bill, acting more like a finch than other tits.

VOICE
The song is a loud, repeated phrase, which is variable but with a buzzy effect: *chriv-chriv-chriv*. Calls include a deep, chattering, un-tit-like *chrrrt* or *chaerrrrr*, and a high *si-si-si*.

BREEDING
A hole in a tree or among rocks is lined with feathers and wool. The 5–7 eggs are incubated for 13 days. The chicks fly when 22 days old.

MIGRATION
Resident, except for short-distance wandering in winter.

Underside plain, pale buff.

Very wide bib and cap striking in most views, especially from front; white cheeks create narrow wedge.

Tail plain, greyish, with only faintest pale edge.

Wing feathers edged pale.

Sometimes works its way up tree trunks, like a Nuthatch, in search of food.

Large black cap and broad black bib outline white cheeks.

TRIANGULAR BIB
The black-and-white head pattern is strikingly bold.

WHEN SEEN

All year.

WHERE SEEN
Breeds south from Slovenia to Greece, and east to Romania and Turkey.

HABITAT AND INFO

SIMILAR SPECIES
Willow Tit has black crown; smaller bib.

Small bib

Dumpier shape

Siberian Tit
Azure Tit

The Siberian Tit is a big brown, grey, and white tit, with a large bib and cap outlining broad white cheeks. The Azure Tit is uniquely blue and white, with no yellow. A faint yellow flush indicates a hybrid with the Blue Tit. Most such hybrids lack yellow, but have a short tail and blue cap.

LENGTH / 13cm (5in)
WINGSPAN / 19–21cm (7½–8¼in)
WEIGHT / 10–15g (¼–½oz)

■ **STATUS /** Secure

SCALE v Pigeon

The Siberian Tit is a bird of old, undamaged and undisturbed northern conifer forests with plentiful, streaming lichens, although it also breeds in birch forest. The largely central Asian Azure Tit prefers riverside willows and damp scrub.

FEEDING
Both birds eat small insects, spiders, and seeds. In winter, the Siberian Tit visits rubbish tips and sometimes bird tables to find food. It hides food among twigs and pine needles, to be rediscovered later during normal foraging.

VOICE
The calls of the Siberian Tit are like a Willow Tit's, but less emphatic and not so drawn out at the end: *zi-zi tah tah tah* or *tchay*. The song is rasping and unmusical: *cheeurr cheeurr cheeurr* or *prrree prrree prrree*. The Azure Tit's call is more like that of a Blue Tit.

BREEDING
Nests are in tree holes or rotten stumps lined with soft wood chips, moss, and hair. Up to 10 eggs hatch in 15–18 days.

MIGRATION
Both are resident.

Siberian Tit
Back has grey bloom when fresh, wears off to brown.

Wings and tail edged pale grey, wearing to dull brown (below).

Siberian

Siberian Tit
Cap is dark brown; back warm ochre-brown.

Bib is rough, fluffy, and loose-looking.

Azure Tit
Pure Azure Tit has white uppertail covert spots and pure white on tail.

Azure Tit
Long slim tail; broad white band across blue wing; head pattern recalls Blue Tit, but crown white.

DENSE FEATHERS
The rounded shape is typical of a bird in cold conditions.

WHEN SEEN

All year.

WHERE SEEN
Siberian breeds mid-Norway, N Norway, and Sweden, N Finland, N Russia. Azure breeds in Russia; only a very rare vagrant farther west.

HABITAT AND INFO

Marsh Tit

LENGTH / 11.5cm (4½in)
WINGSPAN / 18–19cm (7–7½in)
WEIGHT / 10–12g (¼–³⁄₈oz)

■ **STATUS /** Secure

SCALE v Pigeon

It is difficult to distinguish from Willow Tit on sight, but the Marsh Tit's loud, bright *pi-chew* call is distinctive. It looks grey, neat, smooth, and glossy-capped.

Bright, lively, and acrobatic in its behaviour, the Marsh Tit lacks bright colours, but its subtlety is itself attractive. It poses a real identification problem, since it so closely resembles the Willow Tit: even experienced observers may confuse them unless they call. The Marsh Tit likes woods – often drier, with more mature trees, than the places favoured by Willow Tits. A beech wood is ideal, but it also lives in wooded parks or mixed woods.

FEEDING
It eats insects and spiders in summer, and seeds, berries, and nuts in winter, including beechmast.

VOICE
The song is rather infrequent: a rattling or bubbling *schip-schip-schip-schip*. The most distinctive call is a loud, explosive, bright *pi-chew*, quite unlike the Willow Tit. It also has a buzzy *chicka-dee-dee-dee*.

BREEDING
A hole in a stump or branch is used for nesting. The 6–9 eggs hatch after 13–15 days and the chicks fly when 17–20 days old.

MIGRATION
Resident.

Marsh

Willow

Juvenile

Hammers food and feeds on ground more than Willow Tit does.

Male
Long tail.

No white nape or wingbars as on Coal Tit; black chin and more black in front of eye than Blackcap.

Neat shape, with head in proportion (compare with Willow Tit on opposite page).

Flanks may look whiter in spring and summer, and on juvenile.

Female
Shorter tail projection than male's.

Black cap and small black chin; plain brown upperparts, but variable pale wing panel can be quite marked; flanks typically less rich than on Willow Tit.

Adult

Adult
Scandinavia, central Europe: larger, greyer, with pinkish wash on flanks.

NEAT AND PALE
The smart, pale grey-and-black effect is distinctive.

WHEN SEEN

All year.

WHERE SEEN
S Britain, N Spain, and France eastward, north to S Sweden and Norway; absent from most of Spain, Mediterranean coastal areas and islands.

HABITAT AND INFO

SIMILAR SPECIES
Blackcap has fine bill; narrower cap; grey in front of eye; no black bib.

Narrower cap

No bib

Willow Tit

A chunky, thick-necked, bull-headed bird with a big, dull black cap, large black chin, typically warm-coloured flanks, and pale wing panel. Its deep buzzing call is a helpful clue.

LENGTH / 12–13cm (4³/₄–5in)
WINGSPAN / 17–18cm (6³/₄–7in)
WEIGHT / 9–11g (¹/₄–³/₈oz)

■ **STATUS /** Vulnerable

SCALE v Pigeon

Central Europe
Intermediate form, less buff than British birds.

Wide head, broad white cheeks unique to Willow Tit.

Large cap of Willow Tit duller black than that of Marsh Tit, but often not easy to judge; bib frequently more diffuse.

Willow Tit

Marsh Tit

Longer black cap and broader head than Marsh Tit's; long head; short back.

Marsh Tit
Shorter head; longer back; usually less obvious wing panel.

Willow Tit
Pale edges to flight feathers most distinct in rear view.

Flanks more strongly washed rusty-buff than Marsh Tit's.

Scandinavian race
Larger, paler, greyer, with whiter cheeks; whiter beneath.

Looking like a stocky, slightly more richly coloured, less neat and tidy version of the Marsh Tit, the Willow Tit can be hard to distinguish. It is more often seen in willow and alder thickets and marshy places, in dense, tall hedgerows or bushy places beside heaths, and in upland birch woods. Both visit gardens and peanut baskets.

FEEDING
It seeks out insects, spiders, seeds, and berries, mostly rather low down in bushes.

VOICE
Males sing a simple, repeated, liquid, and sad *tsew tsew tsew tsew* and more rarely a short warble. Calls include a harsh, buzzing, thickly nasal *zi taah taah taah taah* or *eez eez eez*, which is rougher and deeper than Marsh Tit calls, and thin *zi zi* sounds. It never gives the *pi-chew* that is characteristic of the Marsh Tit.

BREEDING
Holes are chipped out of rotten stumps. The 6–9 eggs are incubated for 17–20 days.

MIGRATION
Mostly resident, but some wander short distances in winter.

PALE CHEEKS
The broad pale cheek is especially obvious on northern birds.

WHEN SEEN

All year.

WHERE SEEN
From Britain and NE France east through central Europe, north through Scandinavia, locally south to Italy and Balkans; absent from Iberia and Iceland.

HABITAT AND INFO

SIMILAR SPECIES
Marsh Tit has shiny cap; plainer wing; neater bib; different call.

Glossy cap

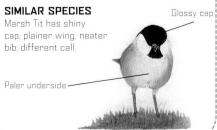

Paler underside

Crested Tit

LENGTH / 11.5cm (4½in)
WINGSPAN / 17–20cm (6¾–8in)
WEIGHT / 10–13g (¼–½oz)

■ **STATUS /** Secure

SCALE v Pigeon

A tiny, lively, acrobatic tit of coniferous woods, it can be located by its trilled, purring call and is identified by its unique crest.

In Britain, where Crested Tits are confined to Scotland, they are strictly pine forest birds. Elsewhere in Europe, they like mixed woods, even beech forest or cork oak in places. They are not quite so easy to watch as other tits. They seem a little shyer and are less likely to make a close approach.

FEEDING
Their chief foods are insects, spiders, and conifer seeds. In a few places, they come to peanut baskets in winter. They store food, rediscovering it later during normal foraging in the winter and spring.

VOICE
Crested Tits' songs differ little from their calls, which are distinctive and very useful in locating them. They have a quick, purring, stuttering character: *chr-r-r-r-rrrup* or *pt-rrr-r-p.*

BREEDING
The female excavates a hole or enlarges a smaller one, and lines it with moss, hair, and wool. The 6–7 eggs are incubated for 13–16 days. Chicks fledge after 18–22 days.

MIGRATION
Resident.

Often difficult to see as it forages in tall trees.

Basically warm brown above, buffy below, with black-and-white head.

Juvenile
Crest short, dull; face pattern weaker.

Crest varies in length; black feathers edged white in streaky pattern.

At nest site: a hole excavated in a pine trunk.

Adult
Black cheek crescent; black bib.

Very active as it climbs trunks and branches looking for food.

PINE SPECIALIST
The Crested Tit prefers coniferous forest or pines in mixed woods.

WHEN SEEN

All year.

WHERE SEEN
Local in N Scotland; widespread Europe except extreme north and Italy; local in Hungary, Romania, Bulgaria.

HABITAT AND INFO

SIMILAR SPECIES
Marsh Tit has neat, smooth black cap; small bib; and plainer cheeks.

Smooth cap

Plain cheek

Coal Tit

A miniature, acrobatic bird of conifers, often visiting garden feeders. The bold white patch on the back of its head is characteristic.

LENGTH / 11.5cm (4½in)
WINGSPAN / 17–21cm (6¾–8¼in)
WEIGHT / 8–10g (¼oz)

■ **STATUS /** Secure

SCALE v Pigeon

Fast, bounding in flight, with large head, short tail.

Coal Tit (above) barely bigger than Goldcrest (below).

White wingbars prominent.

Glossy black head with oblong nape patch, bold white cheeks, large triangular bib.

Adult
Europe: continental birds are greyest on back.

Adult
Britain, Iberia: back plumage more olive.

Irish   **British**

Irish bird (far left): yellowish on cheeks and nape.

Lacks blue, green, and yellow of Blue Tit; no central stripe on underparts.

Tiny, almost Goldcrest-like, lacking bright colours but with boldly patterned plumage, the Coal Tit is a charming little bird. It prefers conifer trees, principally spruce, and is far less common in deciduous woods.

FEEDING
Its feet and slim bill are adapted to searching the tightly bunched, long needles of conifers for insects and spiders, their eggs and young. They also hide a lot of food in such places. They probably forget where, but find it again in the course of normal foraging.

VOICE
Their songs recall a Great Tit's but are less strident: a rhythmic *teechu teechu teechu* or *tchuwee tchuwee*. Their calls also have a sweet, full quality: *chiwee* and *syew*, and also a high, thin *seeee* and a sharp *spit*.

BREEDING
They nest in holes in trees and in the ground. The 8–9 (rarely more) eggs are incubated for 14–16 days. The chicks fly when 19 days old.

MIGRATION
Parts of northern populations move south in autumn, sometimes in very large numbers.

DOUBLE BAR
Two wingbars on the greyish upperparts are always obvious.

WHEN SEEN

All year.

WHERE SEEN
Absent Iceland, N Scandinavia, otherwise widespread in Europe; largely a winter visitor in Mediterranean areas.

HABITAT AND INFO

SIMILAR SPECIES
Great Tit has black nape with no white patch; broad stripe down chest; extensive yellow and green.

Black belly stripe   Yellow

Blue Tit

LENGTH / 11.5cm (4½in)
WINGSPAN / 17–20cm (6¾–8in)
WEIGHT / 9–12g (¼–⅜oz)

■ **STATUS /** Secure

SCALE v Pigeon

A bright, tiny garden favourite, looking blue, pale green, or light yellow according to the angle of view and light. It usually looks plainer at a distance, and brighter and more contrasted at close range.

Deciduous woods with abundant caterpillars in spring provide the best breeding habitats for the Blue Tit. It also nests in gardens, often in nest boxes, but most suburban plots do not provide enough insect food for really successful breeding and brood sizes are consequently rather small.

FEEDING

It eats insects, especially caterpillars, spiders, buds, and seeds. Peanuts are garden-feeder favourites. It takes food from the tips of thin twigs that cannot support heavier Great Tits.

DISPLAY AND VOICE

In spring the male's fluttering display flight involves frequent inspection of suitable nest holes. The song is a quick, stuttering trill, *tsee tsee tsee trrrr*, and most calls have a similar quality: *tseee-tseee-tseee tsit* and *churr-rr-rr*.

BREEDING

Nests are made in tree holes and other cavities. Females lay 7–16 eggs, which take 12–15 days to hatch. The chicks leave the nest quietly after 16–22 days.

MIGRATION

Resident, but some continental birds winter in Britain.

Flight is quick, direct; lands on perch with sudden "stop dead" effect.

Short display flights are fluttering "butterfly" glides from tree to tree.

Highly acrobatic when feeding.

Juvenile
The pattern is familiar, but the colours are dull; yellow face and greenish cap most obvious differences from adult.

Blue cap, white ring around top of head; white cheeks and blue-black chin unique.

Spring male
At his brightest the male looks vivid blue on cap, wings, and tail; these areas become dull with wear.

In winter roams woods, gardens, and hedges in mixed flocks with other tits and finches.

LIGHTWEIGHT
Small size and strong feet combine to give great agility.

WHEN SEEN

All year.

WHERE SEEN
Mixed and deciduous woods, hedges, parks, and gardens; in winter also reed beds; all Europe except Iceland, N Scandinavia.

HABITAT AND INFO

SIMILAR SPECIES
Great Tit has big black cap; bold white cheek patch; wide white bars across wing; broader stripe on chest.

Black crown

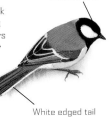

White edged tail

Great Tit

Compared with the Blue Tit, it is a bigger, heavier, bolder bird, marked by vivid white cheeks on a blue-black head and a long, dark stripe down the centre of the yellow chest. Its spring song is a strident, simple repetition of two notes.

LENGTH / 14cm (5½in)
WINGSPAN / 22–25cm (8¾–9¾in)
WEIGHT / 16–21g (½–¾oz)

■ STATUS / Secure

SCALE v Pigeon

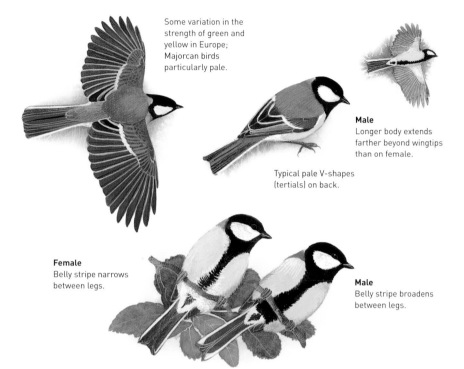

Some variation in the strength of green and yellow in Europe; Majorcan birds particularly pale.

Male
Longer body extends farther beyond wingtips than on female.

Typical pale V-shapes (tertials) on back.

Female
Belly stripe narrows between legs.

Male
Belly stripe broadens between legs.

Some English birds now pale yellow below, perhaps caused by a break in the food chain.

Female has matt black on head; male deep blue.

The largest and boldest of the tits, the Great Tit is not so common as the Blue Tit in most gardens, nor in the mixed bands of birds that wander in search of food in winter.

FEEDING
Its greater weight makes the Great Tit less acrobatic than the Blue and Coal Tits, and less able to gather food from fine twigs, so it tends to feed more on larger tree trunks. It also feeds on the ground, often under beech trees where it eats fallen beechmast.

VOICE
The spring song is a loud, strident, but joyful repetition of simple notes, with many variations: *tee-cher tee-cher* or *suee-suee-suee*. Calls include a loud *chink!* and many churrs and thin *seee* notes.

BREEDING
It nests in holes in trees, walls, or preferably nest boxes. The 5–11 eggs hatch after 12–15 days. Like the Blue Tit, it rears just one brood each year.

MIGRATION
Some continental birds move south and west. British Great Tits are resident.

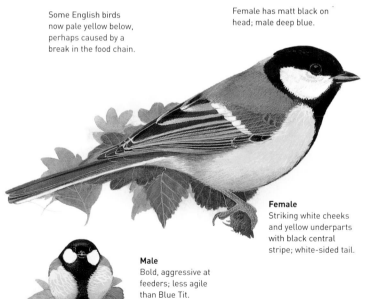

Female
Striking white cheeks and yellow underparts with black central stripe; white-sided tail.

Juvenile
Dull cap; yellow cheeks; short central stripe underneath.

Male
Bold, aggressive at feeders; less agile than Blue Tit.

EYE-CATCHING FACE
The big, white cheeks create a striking pattern.

WHEN SEEN
All year.

WHERE SEEN
Mixed woods, parks, and gardens; all of Europe except Iceland and highest mountains.

HABITAT AND INFO

SIMILAR SPECIES
Blue Tit has white ring around blue cap; dumpier shape; plainer blue wings and tail.

Blue cap

Blue wings

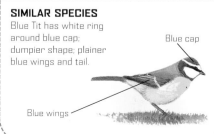

Treecreeper

LENGTH / 12.5cm (5in)
WINGSPAN / 18–21cm (7–8¼in)
WEIGHT / 8–12g (¼–³⁄₈oz)

■ **STATUS /** Secure

SCALE v Pigeon

A mouse-like, shuffling bird that creeps up trees, often spiralling around trunks and out onto smaller branches, hanging underneath, and probing with a fine, curved bill.

Now and then a Treecreeper is seen on a wall or even a cliff, but these are exceptions to the rule: it is a bird that normally spends its life wholly on the trunks and branches of trees. It likes parkland, mixed and deciduous woods, hedges with tall trees, and pine forest, especially where its range overlaps with Short-toed Treecreepers.

FEEDING
It finds insects, spiders, and some seeds by diligently searching the rough bark of trees, typically climbing spirally up one trunk before flying down to the base of the next.

VOICE
Its song is frequent and a little like a Goldcrest or Willow Warbler: thin, musical, and quick, with a terminal flourish. Confusingly, it often mimics the Short-toed Treecreeper. The call is a high, thin *tsreee*.

BREEDING
Nests are in cavities under loose bark. The 5–6 eggs hatch in 13–15 days. Chicks fly in 13–18 days.

MIGRATION
Resident, but some northern birds wander in winter, sometimes in large numbers.

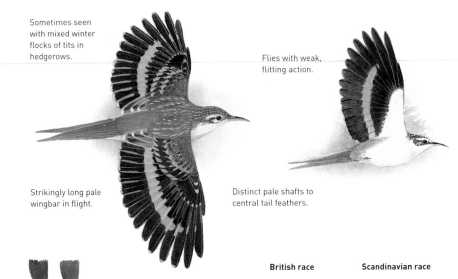

Sometimes seen with mixed winter flocks of tits in hedgerows.

Flies with weak, flitting action.

Strikingly long pale wingbar in flight.

Distinct pale shafts to central tail feathers.

Pale primary tips of Treecreeper (above left) more even than V-shaped tips of Short-toed Treecreeper (above right).

British race

Scandinavian race

Note short, open V-shape of pale band across primaries (longer, more acute shape on Short-toed Treecreeper's).

Each bird excavates a body-shaped recess in soft bark and sinks into this to roost with fluffed-out feathers.

Long, often forked, brown tail pressed against tree.

Mottled brown upperparts, but some more spotted, looking like mottled lichen; more orange on rump; white underside.

Scandinavian birds have brighter stripe over eye and whitest underparts; faintly washed buff and palest grey on British race.

A TIGHT GRIP ON LIFE
Treecreepers cling to tree bark throughout their lives.

WHEN SEEN

All year.

WHERE SEEN
Breeds Ireland, Britain, very local central and N Spain, N and E France, Italy; more widely through E Europe, Norway, Sweden, Finland, south to Balkans.

HABITAT AND INFO

SIMILAR SPECIES
Short-toed Treecreeper has a different call and song; duller underside contrasts more with white throat.

Different song

Duller flanks

Short-toed Treecreeper

It is almost identical to Treecreeper. The safest way to identify is by the song, since checking plumage features requires exceptional views and close attention to the finest detail.

LENGTH / 12cm (4¾in)
WINGSPAN / 18–21cm (7–8¼in)
WEIGHT / 8–12g (¼–³/₈oz)

■ STATUS / Secure

SCALE v Pigeon

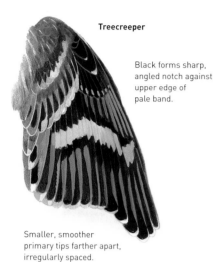

Treecreeper

Black forms sharp, angled notch against upper edge of pale band.

Smaller, smoother primary tips farther apart, irregularly spaced.

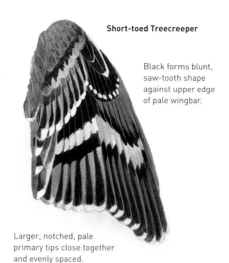

Short-toed Treecreeper

Black forms blunt, saw-tooth shape against upper edge of pale wingbar.

Larger, notched, pale primary tips close together and evenly spaced.

Typically pale edge of longest alula feather is complete and of even width.

The treecreeper pair present as great an identification challenge as any in Europe: the best bet is to listen for the song or to go by distribution and habitat. Short-toed Treecreepers are more lowland birds than Treecreepers, occupying a variety of broadleaved and conifer woods, often with dense undergrowth.

FEEDING
Like the Treecreeper, it creeps about like a mouse on trees, searching for insects and spiders, insect eggs, and pupae. It is perhaps slower in its movements, with more hops and tight spirals.

VOICE
The song is distinctively different from the Treecreeper's: less flowing, less thin, a series of distinctly separate notes, *teet, teet, teet-er-oi-tit*. The call is more piping, less drawn out or thin, and sometimes almost explosive, sounding like *sreeet* or *zeet*.

BREEDING
It nests in bark cavities. The 6–7 eggs will hatch in 13–14 days, and the chicks fly in 16–18 days.

MIGRATION
Resident in Europe. A rare vagrant in south-east England.

Some birds have darker, more rufous-cinnamon rump than Treecreeper's.

Typically duller beneath than Treecreeper; greyish or browner on flanks, with contrasted white throat.

Plain tail without pale shafts.

Compared with Treecreeper, has longer, more acute pale V across primaries.

Sometimes looks rounder-bodied than Treecreeper, with tail more sharply angled into tree.

COMPLEX PATTERN
Streaks, spots, and bars create excellent camouflage.

WHEN SEEN

All year.

WHERE SEEN
Iberia, France, north and east through Europe to S Denmark, Poland, Hungary; south as far as Italy, Balkans, Crete.

HABITAT AND INFO

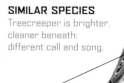

SIMILAR SPECIES
Treecreeper is brighter, cleaner beneath; different call and song.

Brighter colours

White underside

Nuthatch

LENGTH / 14cm (5½in)
WINGSPAN / 16–18cm (6¼–7in)
WEIGHT / 12–18g (³⁄₈–⁵⁄₈oz)

■ STATUS / Secure

SCALE v Pigeon

A dumpy, large-headed bird with a square tail, grey above with black mask, unique in most of Europe. Its noisy calls echo around woodlands.

As the Dipper is forever tied to the river, so the Nuthatch must live on the larger branches and boles of big trees, with only an occasional excursion to feed on open ground, old walls, or rocks, or even from a basket of peanuts.

FEEDING
It eats a wide variety of insects, nuts, and berries, and often stores them in autumn. It wedges large insects and tough seeds in crevices in bark or walls so it can break into them more easily with its sharp, stout bill.

DISPLAY AND VOICE
It displays with strange head-waving movements in spring. Songs are loud, ringing, and far-carrying: a fast trill or a slower series of rounded, almost human whistles. The calls include a sharp *twit* like a pebble striking ice, and a loud, tit-like *sit*.

BREEDING
The nests are in holes, usually in trees, with mud plastered at the entrance. Up to 11 eggs are laid on a layer of bark and chippings.

MIGRATION
Resident, but in northern Europe many may move south in autumn when numbers are high.

Weak flight with looping undulations.

Black-and-white tail, unlike Rock Nuthatch's.

Exceptionally agile, does not use tail as prop.

British race
Soft blue-grey and pale orange-buff with richer flanks.

Much whiter underparts in far north and eastern Europe (below right).

Italy and Balkans
Bill narrow, pointed.

Sweden

Spain

BIG APPETITE
Large nuts and acorns are wedged in bark for easy feeding.

WHEN SEEN

All year.

WHERE SEEN
Breeds from Wales and England east through S Norway and Sweden, sporadically Finland, east through Russia, and south to Mediterranean.

HABITAT AND INFO

SIMILAR SPECIES
Rock Nuthatch is bigger; paler; whiter beneath; plain tail.

Plain tail

Whiter underside

Rock Nuthatch
Corsican Nuthatch

The Corsican is a small, neat nuthatch of mountain pine forests. The adult male has black-and-white head stripes. The Rock Nuthatch of south-east Europe is a bold, eye-catching bird that flits jauntily between rocks and ruins, giving strident, far-carrying calls.

LENGTH / Rock 15cm (6in); Corsican 12cm (4¾in)
WINGSPAN / 23–25cm (9–9¾in)
WEIGHT / Rock 25–35g (1–1¼oz) Corsican 10–15g (¼–½oz)
■ **STATUS /** Secure

SCALE v Pigeon

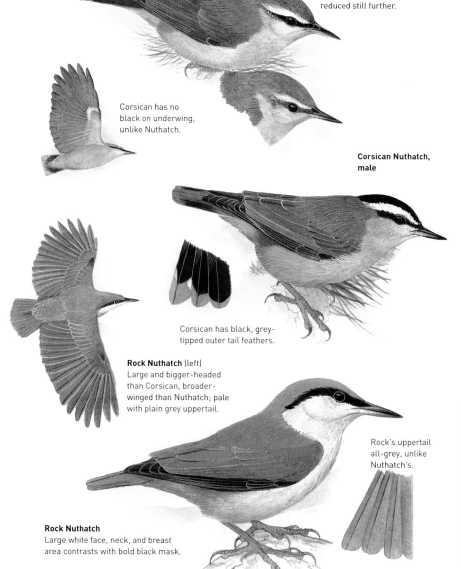

Corsican Nuthatch, female
Duller grey and whitish head; juvenile has pattern reduced still further.

Corsican has no black on underwing, unlike Nuthatch.

Corsican Nuthatch, male

Corsican has black, grey-tipped outer tail feathers.

Rock Nuthatch (left)
Large and bigger-headed than Corsican, broader-winged than Nuthatch; pale with plain grey uppertail.

Rock Nuthatch
Large white face, neck, and breast area contrasts with bold black mask.

Rock's uppertail all-grey, unlike Nuthatch's.

The Rock Nuthatch is a Balkan equivalent of the Nuthatch that lives on limestone crags and scattered hillside rocks. It is often conspicuous at Ancient Greek sites. The Corsican Nuthatch lives in mountain forests of Corsican pine, with 2,000–3,000 pairs confined entirely to Corsica.

FEEDING
Rock Nuthatches eat mainly insects, with seeds and snails in winter. Corsican Nuthatches feed on pine seeds, except from May to August, when they eat insects and spiders.

VOICE
Rock Nuthatches are noisy birds. Their loud trills, repeated at varying speeds, echo among the rocks and ancient columns and are audible at great range. Corsican Nuthatches have quieter trilling songs and a variety of short, whistled calls.

BREEDING
Rock Nuthatches make flask-shaped nests of mud against rocks or on buildings. Corsicans nest in holes in pines. The holes are left unplastered.

MIGRATION
Both species are resident.

BOLD ROCKHOPPER
Rock Nuthatches are noisy, easy to see and distinctive.

WHEN SEEN

All year

WHERE SEEN
Rock Nuthatch: along Balkan coasts, widespread in Greece, Turkey. Corsican Nuthatch: confined to forests of central Corsica

HABITAT AND INFO

SIMILAR SPECIES
Nuthatch is darker below; black-and-white patches on tail; simple black line through eye; bright rufous flanks.

Black line

Black-and-white patches

Wallcreeper

LENGTH / 16cm (6¼in)
WINGSPAN / 30–35cm (11¾–14in)
WEIGHT / 25g (1oz)

■ STATUS / Secure

SCALE v Pigeon

An extraordinary, elusive, beautiful bird of gorges, mountains, and crags, it is quite unmistakable. It flies with a jerky, skipping action. Its short flights while feeding include spins, dives, and flutters.

No European bird is more beautiful than this unreal-looking creature. It may require a long search in difficult terrain, but when it appears the Wallcreeper is stunning, making all the trouble worthwhile. It may fly high onto a barren cliff or drop into a gorge, but if you can reach the spot you may get very close views. In winter, Wallcreepers often move lower in gorges or appear on large buildings in the mountains. The bird bobs like a Dipper and constantly flicks its wings. It may remain in one spot for a long time, restlessly leap from rock to rock, or spiral away out of sight on rising currents of air.

FEEDING
It captures insects and spiders under overhangs, beside rivulets, or from the walls of buildings. Shady, moist spots are often preferred.

VOICE
The elusive song is a repetitive, high whistle: *ti-tiu-treee*. The call note is a piping *tuee*.

BREEDING
It nests in a hole in a cliff face, usually above the tree line, but lower in eastern Europe.

MIGRATION
Moves lower in winter.

Male, winter
Flicks wingtips as it feeds.

Male, summer
Variable black throat against grey.

Spots on midwing more orange-red; from distance, white spots more obvious than red.

Female, summer
Variable black throat with white surround.

Female, winter
Bill slimmer than male's.

Juvenile
Outer tail has smaller white tips.

Outer tail of adult male.

BOLD WHITE SPOTS
Round white spots are usually revealed on the spread wing.

WHEN SEEN

All year.

WHERE SEEN
Breeds in N Spain, S France, Alps, N Italy, Balkans; rare vagrant outside breeding range.

HABITAT AND INFO

SIMILAR SPECIES
Nuthatch has larger head and dagger bill; does not flick wings.

Dark eye stripe

Grey wing

Lesser Grey Shrike

This is an eastern shrike with long wings, a relatively short tail, and a stout bill. Its large white patches on narrow, pointed wings are obvious, especially in flight.

LENGTH / 20cm (8in)
WINGSPAN / 30cm (11¾in)
WEIGHT / 30g (1oz)

■ **STATUS /** Vulnerable

SCALE v Pigeon

The Lesser Grey Shrike is an open country bird of dry southern grasslands with scattered shrubs and trees. More contrasted and pinker beneath than the more northerly Great Grey Shrike, it looks more compact and less rangy.

FEEDING
Like other shrikes, it takes large insects, small reptiles, and small birds, but grasshoppers and beetles form the bulk of its diet. It requires drier, sunnier habitats than other shrikes mainly for this reason.

VOICE
It is generally quiet, but in spring a varied, chattering, thrush-like song includes mimicry of other species. Unmated males sing loudly, while paired birds have a quieter song.

BREEDING
The nests are neatly made cups of twigs and rootlets. The 5–6 eggs hatch after 15–16 days.

MIGRATION
Most arrive from Africa in May and leave again in August to September, when many are seen in the eastern Mediterranean region.

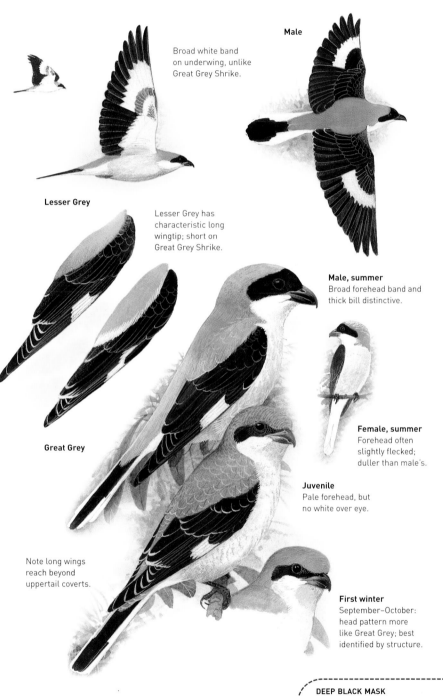

Male

Broad white band on underwing, unlike Great Grey Shrike.

Lesser Grey

Lesser Grey has characteristic long wingtip; short on Great Grey Shrike.

Great Grey

Note long wings reach beyond uppertail coverts.

Male, summer
Broad forehead band and thick bill distinctive.

Female, summer
Forehead often slightly flecked; duller than male's.

Juvenile
Pale forehead, but no white over eye.

First winter
September–October: head pattern more like Great Grey; best identified by structure.

DEEP BLACK MASK
Males have extra deep black forehead patches.

WHEN SEEN

Sept
May

Mostly May to September.

WHERE SEEN
Breeds in extreme S France/NE Spain, but mostly Italy and SE Europe; rare vagrant north and west of this range, mostly in late spring.

HABITAT AND INFO

SIMILAR SPECIES
Great Grey Shrike has longer tail and relatively shorter wingtips; pale forehead; less stout bill.

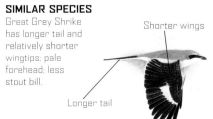

Shorter wings

Longer tail

Great Grey Shrike

LENGTH / 24–25cm (9½–9¾in)
WINGSPAN / 30–35cm (11¾–14in)
WEIGHT / 50–80g (1¾–2¾oz)

■ **STATUS** / Secure

SCALE v Pigeon

A large, long-tailed, short-winged shrike, it is often perched boldly on top of a bush or tree, or on a wire, flirting its tail or balancing by twisting it to one side.

Shrikes are exciting and charismatic birds, yet although they often perch on the exposed tops of bushes or even on overhead wires, they can be notoriously hard to find. Great Grey Shrikes like heathland with scattered trees and bushes, forest clearings, and rough ground with scrub, from marshes to farmland. The similar Southern Grey Shrike *Lanius meridionalis* is a recent split from the Great Grey Shrike, having previously been considered the same species. It occupies dry, warm, bushy places with scattered trees, olive groves, and orchards. The eastern forms of these shrikes are rather complex, and the inclusion of some within the Great Grey or Southern Grey remains contentious. One of these forms, the Steppe Grey Shrike, is best considered as a full species: *Lanius pallidirostris*. This is a rare migrant to the UK and Western Europe and has been confused with the Great Grey.

FEEDING

The Great Grey Shrike takes large insects from the ground after gliding down from a perch. It also kills various mice, voles, and small birds. These shrikes often impale large prey on thorns or wedge it in twigs to make it easier to tear apart. The Southern Grey eats more lizards because of its southerly distribution, but otherwise the variety of food and feeding techniques are the same.

DISPLAY AND VOICE

Pairs may remain together all year, but in some areas males stay in the territory in winter, vigorously defending it against intruders, while females move away. Both sexes sing, the males to attract mates. The song of both species is a rough mixture of warbles and coarse, chattering notes. Surprisingly, very few calls are heard in winter.

BREEDING

The nest of the Great Grey Shrike is a mixture of stems, roots, and moss, woven around twigs in a tree. The 4–7 eggs hatch after 15–17 days. Southern Greys select the fork of a tree, or twigs in the canopy well out from the trunk, as the base for a bulky nest of twigs, and incubate 5–7 eggs for 18–19 days.

MIGRATION

Northern populations move south and west in winter. Other populations include both resident and migrant groups. A few Southern Greys cross the Strait of Gibraltar in spring and autumn, but most remain in or close to their breeding areas in winter.

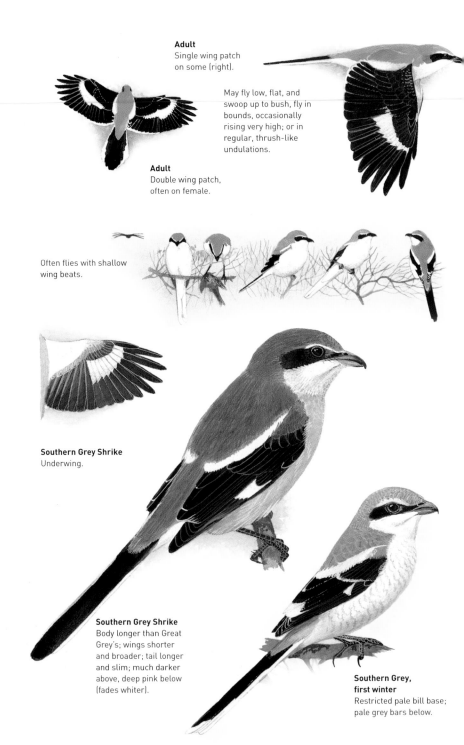

Adult
Single wing patch on some (right).

May fly low, flat, and swoop up to bush, fly in bounds, occasionally rising very high; or in regular, thrush-like undulations.

Adult
Double wing patch, often on female.

Often flies with shallow wing beats.

Southern Grey Shrike
Underwing.

Southern Grey Shrike
Body longer than Great Grey's; wings shorter and broader; tail longer and slim; much darker above, deep pink below (fades whiter).

Southern Grey, first winter
Restricted pale bill base; pale grey bars below.

WHEN SEEN

All year; migrant Great Greys in NW Europe September to April.

WHERE SEEN
Great Grey breeds through N and central Europe; migrates west to Britain and south to the Mediterranean. Southern Grey breeds S France, widespread through Iberia; also Middle East; rare vagrant outside range.

HABITAT AND INFO

SIMILAR SPECIES
Lesser Grey Shrike is darker above, pinker below.

Longer wing

Black forehead

472

Steppe Grey Shrike
Long narrow wings with huge white primary patch.

Southern Grey
Contrasting white throat and pink breast; bold white patch on outer wing only.

Race *homeyeri* in Ukraine has structure of Great Grey but paler, more white on wing, tail, and rump.

Eight primary tips show on drooped wingtip: long tip is critical identification point.

First winter
Pale in front of eye; pale bill.

Adult
Female may have faint chest bars.

Some populations have paler bill base.

Steppe Grey Shrike
Paler, with shorter body than Great Grey's, longer wingtip; narrower wings with big white primary patch.

Wingtip partly hidden under tertials when tightly tucked up.

Unmistakable grey/black/white, with black mask, grey back, black-and-white wings.

Juvenile
Faint pale bars above, browner bars below; pale base to bill; wingbar wears off; primary patch small.

Wingtip shows seven primary tips, four in a close group (compare with Steppe).

Adult
Single (top) or double wing patch variations.

DID YOU KNOW?

Perhaps because it lives farther north and needs to store more prey, but mainly because it catches larger prey that is more difficult to manipulate unless fixed, this shrike impales and wedges more food than the other European species. Young birds seem instinctively more inclined to wedge their prey between twigs than to impale it on thorns or barbed wire.

?

Woodchat Shrike

SCALE v Pigeon

LENGTH / 18cm (7in)
WINGSPAN / 25–30cm (9¾–11¾in)
WEIGHT / 25–35g (1–1¼oz)

■ **STATUS /** Vulnerable

A typical shrike, at times obvious, at times elusive, it is patterned with rusty cap and white shoulders.

Shrikes have a distinctive habit of dashing across open spaces and swooping to new vantage points. The Woodchat Shrike is typical, but its flight is less undulating than others and it tends to choose higher perches. It prefers farmland with scattered trees, tall hedges, bushy slopes, or the aromatic heath, spiny bushes, and trees found in Mediterranean areas.

FEEDING
It eats insects, especially big beetles, catching them on the ground after dropping from a perch. It also occasionally catches small birds.

DISPLAY AND VOICE
Pairs stand face to face, very upright, bobbing their heads and calling. The song is a prolonged mixture of warbles and harsh chatters. Calls are infrequent, but varied, with a creaky *kiwik* and a hard *grack kjak kak*.

BREEDING
The nest is lined with hair and wool. The 5–6 eggs hatch in 14–15 days. Chicks fly in 15–18 days.

MIGRATION
Woodchat Shrikes winter in Africa south of the Sahara.

W Mediterranean islands: no white wing patch.

Juvenile Mainland birds have pale primary patch.

Adult female Fresh, pale edges; peachy wash.

Often perches on wire or high twig.

Adult female

Underside of adult tail.

Mark in front of eye looks whiter in some lights; buff/peach wash wears away.

Adult male Pale edges worn off; bold primary patch.

Female's head paler than male's; black reduced.

Adult female Worn plumage; white rump.

Underside of juvenile tail (compare with Masked Shrike's).

Juvenile has pale rump/uppertail coverts; black tertials with rufous-buff edges (compare with Masked Shrike).

Juvenile Pale scapulars; buff greater coverts.

Distinct bars on flanks.

First winter

BOLD PATTERN Even this female is strongly contrasted and distinctive.

WHEN SEEN

Oct   March

March to October; most vagrants May–June, August–September.

WHERE SEEN
Widespread in Iberia, S and E France; locally S Germany and south through Italy, Balkans, Greece, Turkey.

HABITAT AND INFO

SIMILAR SPECIES
Southern Grey Shrike is grey above, pinker below; no rufous on head.

Grey back

Longer tail

ORDER
Passeriformes

FAMILY
Laniidae

SPECIES
Lanius nubicus

COMMON NAME
Masked Shrike

Masked Shrike

An unusual shrike, it is the only European one with a white forehead. Its white shoulders and buff flanks are distinctive.

LENGTH / 17–18cm (6¾–7in)
WINGSPAN / 24–26cm (9½–10¼in)
WEIGHT / 15–25g (½–1oz)

■ **STATUS /** Vulnerable

SCALE v Pigeon

Female
Pied effect; very long, dark tail.

Male
Strikingly pied in flight.

Juvenile undertail more pied than Woodchat Shrike's.

Juvenile
Dull, but broad white wing patch.

Juvenile male
Bolder underwing than the Woodchat Shrike; female has smaller white outer panel.

Male
Fresh spring plumage: chest wears white by September.

Female
Duller, greyer than male, but white forehead, neck sides, shoulders equally distinct.

Dark parts of both sexes wear solidly brown-black by autumn.

Juvenile
Centres of back feathers, scapulars, greater coverts all greyer, paler than Woodchat Shrike's; tertials pale-centred; rump darker; tail blacker.

This species is restricted to hot, sunny parts of south-east Europe in summer. It breeds in areas of cultivation with olives, almonds, or other orchards mixed with stone pines and thorn bushes. It is frequently hard to see, perching inside or low down on the edges of bushes. A small, slender shrike, it is easily identified when adult, but in juvenile plumage it looks similar to a Woodchat Shrike.

FEEDING
Like other shrikes, it takes mostly large insects, with the occasional small lizard, often flying out from hidden, shady perches.

DISPLAY AND VOICE
The song is a fairly long, repetitive performance with a rhythmic, cyclical effect. Its calls include a short, dry rattle and a short, hoarse *chair*.

BREEDING
The nests are well hidden in small trees or bushes, built of leaves and twigs and lined with a variety of softer material such as feathers or hair. The 5–6 eggs are incubated for about two weeks, and the chicks fly at 18–20 days.

MIGRATION
A scarce migrant through the Middle East, to and from Africa.

ON THE ALERT
This bird gives the typical bright, wide-eyed shrike impression.

WHEN SEEN

Oct — March

March to October.

WHERE SEEN
NE Greece, Turkey.

HABITAT AND INFO

SIMILAR SPECIES
Juvenile Woodchat shrike is browner, especially on wing; paler tail; darker back.

Darker back

Browner wing

Red-backed Shrike

SCALE v Pigeon

LENGTH / 17cm (6¾in)
WINGSPAN / 24–27cm (9½–10½in)
WEIGHT / 25–30g (1oz)

■ STATUS / Vulnerable

A small, upright, colourful shrike, the male is distinguished by a bold combination of black, grey, pink, and chestnut. Females and the young are more puzzling, but they share the same hook-billed, strong-clawed, square-tailed character.

Despite substantial declines and reductions in range, this remains the most typical shrike throughout much of western and central Europe. In Britain, its status has declined from that of a common breeding bird to complete absence, other than as a scarce spring and autumn migrant, mostly on the coasts. It is hard to say why, but the reduction in large insect prey is probably to blame, more so than habitat change. Although it often occurs in warm, sunny areas with a good deal of bare ground, and is capable of breeding in quite dry, hot areas, the Red-backed Shrike can also survive in lush, green, damp places such as the small meadows and bushy hedgerows on the slopes of the Pyrenees and Alps.

FEEDING

Beetles form the bulk of its prey, together with other insects. It also captures small birds and lizards. It chases insects in the air in rapid, twisting pursuits, but spots most of its victims on the ground and catches them after a long, descending swoop from a perch. It carries even small insects back to a perch to be swallowed, and impales large prey items on thorns or barbed wire. This has two functions: it creates a larder of food for future use, but it also helps the shrike dismember large or tough meals.

DISPLAY AND VOICE

The male establishes a territory by moving around from perch to perch and singing. Any neighbouring males call and sing in retaliation. The songs, often given from tree-top perches or high wires, are prolonged but subdued warbles intermixed with a variety of harsh notes and much mimicry. If a female is nearby the song becomes a more excited, rapid twittering. Calls include loud, hard chirps, *cha* or *chee-uk*, and a short, hard alarm note, *tak* or *tek*.

BREEDING

The nests are often built in thick thorny bushes, sometimes in taller trees or even woodpiles. Various kinds of rubbish, from paper or cloth to string, are included in the structure, which is neatly lined with grass, hair, moss, or reed mace down. The 3–7 eggs are incubated for 14 days. The chicks fly after a further two weeks.

MIGRATION

European Red-backed Shrikes spend the winter in Africa, some in Kenya but mostly farther south. In Europe, small numbers appear on coastal strips outside the breeding areas, especially in autumn.

Juvenile
Rufous, but barred on back, uppertail coverts, flanks.

Juvenile

Female
Grey-headed type.

Male
Blue-grey cap and broad black mask, contrasting with bright, pale, pink-washed underside.

Thin white edge to tail.

Black tail broadly edged white.

WHEN SEEN

Oct — April

Mostly April to October; most breeding areas vacated by August or September.

WHERE SEEN

Breeds in S Norway, S and E Sweden, Finland and most of Europe south to N Spain, Italy, Balkans; absent from Iceland, Britain, Ireland, and most of the Low Countries.

HABITAT AND INFO

SIMILAR SPECIES

Juvenile Woodchat Shrike is greyer; line of whitish feathers along shoulder; darker tail.

Paler shoulder

Blacker tail

IMPRESSIVE MALE
This is perhaps the most colourful and
attractive of the shrikes.

Male
A few (especially in
eastern Europe) have a
thin white line at base
of primaries.

Female variably bright,
plain rusty-brown
above; tail narrowly
edged white.

Female
Brown-headed type.

DID YOU KNOW?
Red-backed Shrikes impale prey on thorns throughout their
territories, but almost never wedge it. The impaling habit is instinctive
in young birds and does not need to be learned. Great Greys fix
their prey by wedging or impaling mainly to help dismember it,
while Red-backed Shrikes do so to store food.

Rose-coloured Starling

LENGTH / 21.5cm (8½in)
WINGSPAN / 37–40cm (14½–15½in)
WEIGHT / 70–90g (2½–3¼oz)

■ **STATUS /** Secure

SCALE v Pigeon

A blunt-billed, dumpy starling of open ground. It is social, but as a vagrant is usually solitary. It is often seen in dull immature or non-breeding plumages.

Essentially Asiatic, with variable numbers reaching Europe from year to year, Rose-coloured Starlings live in semi-desert and dry grassland areas – although they must have access to water. They roost socially, often in reed beds and bushes far from their favoured feeding areas.

FEEDING
They feed on the ground, where they eagerly capture swarming grasshoppers and locusts. They also eat grapes, other fruit, and seeds in autumn and winter.

VOICE
Their song is like a Starling's, but even less musical. Their calls are harsh, rasping notes.

BREEDING
Colonies, often large, nest in holes in rocks and buildings. The 3–6 eggs hatch after 15 days.

MIGRATION
In autumn, most Rose-coloured Starlings move south-east, to India. Small numbers move north-west in spring and autumn. Occasionally, large flocks invade south-east Europe in spring (but fewer and smaller flocks recently owing to declining numbers).

Flight like Starling's, but wings more tapered at base, less triangular.

Juvenile
Contrasting pale rump.

Female
Newly moulted: buff tips wear off to reveal pink.

Breeding adult
Unmistakable pink and glossy black.

Some very pale juvenile Starlings mistaken for this species; check shape and colours of bill.

OBVIOUS STARLING
Despite the colour, its mannerisms reveal this to be a typical starling.

Juvenile
Dark eye in plain face; round head; blunt, thick yellow bill.

Remains pale brown into winter, unlike Starling; note darker wings, pale rump.

WHEN SEEN

Oct

May

May to October.

WHERE SEEN
Sporadic breeder in Balkans, especially N Greece, Turkey; rare but regular in Italy and west as far as Britain and Ireland; rarely Iceland.

HABITAT AND INFO

SIMILAR SPECIES
Juvenile Starling is darker, browner, more uniform, without contrasted pale rump; dark bill.

Dark bill

More uniform colour

Spotless Starling

A thickset, dark starling that is unspotted in summer. It has a restricted range around the western Mediterranean, often near towns.

LENGTH / 21–23cm (8¼–9in)
WINGSPAN / 38–42cm (15–16½in)
WEIGHT / 75–90g (2¾–3¼oz)

■ STATUS / Secure

SCALE v Pigeon

Usually seen in towns and villages and on nearby farmland and pasture, this is a bird of Iberia, the extreme south of France, Corsica, Sardinia, and Sicily, as well as adjacent parts of north Africa. Common Starlings move into its range in winter and the two species may then flock together, but mostly they separate for the breeding season.

FEEDING
Like Starlings, they forage on the ground, walking and running, often in small groups, to find insects in summer and seeds in winter.

DISPLAY AND VOICE
Males sing from roofs, aerials, and overhead wires, with a prolonged, Starling-like song that includes longer, louder whistles and purer, fluty notes. Alarm notes are similar to a Starling's: *fit* or *chip*.

BREEDING
The 4–5 eggs are laid in a hole in rocks or under a roof tile. They hatch after 11 days' incubation.

MIGRATION
Resident.

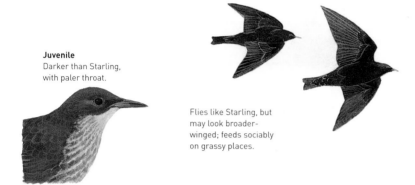

Juvenile
Darker than Starling, with paler throat.

Flies like Starling, but may look broader-winged; feeds sociably on grassy places.

Long throat feathers.

Pointed back feathers.

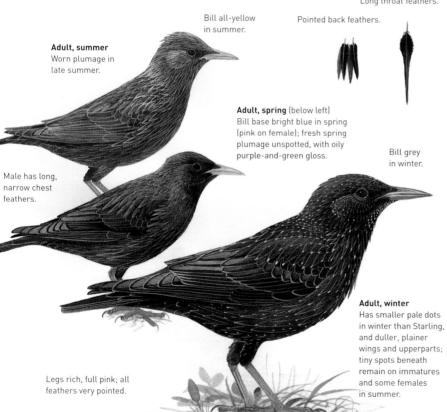

Bill all-yellow in summer.

Adult, summer
Worn plumage in late summer.

Adult, spring (below left)
Bill base bright blue in spring (pink on female); fresh spring plumage unspotted, with oily purple-and-green gloss.

Bill grey in winter.

Male has long, narrow chest feathers.

Adult, winter
Has smaller pale dots in winter than Starling, and duller, plainer wings and upperparts; tiny spots beneath remain on immatures and some females in summer.

Legs rich, full pink; all feathers very pointed.

IMMACULATE BLACK
Summer males are entirely unmarked glossy black.

WHEN SEEN

All year.

WHERE SEEN
Extreme S France, Spain, Portugal, Corsica, Sardinia, Sicily.

HABITAT AND INFO

SIMILAR SPECIES
Starling has larger spots on body and especially under tail in winter; pale-edged wing feathers.

Spotted body

Spots under tail

Starling

LENGTH / 21.5cm (8½in)
WINGSPAN / 37–42cm (14½–16½in)
WEIGHT / 75–90g (2¾–3¾oz)

■ STATUS / Secure

SCALE v Pigeon

This is a sharp-faced, square-tailed, fast-walking, boisterous bird. It is common, familiar, sociable, and quarrelsome. Its pointed head and triangular wings are distinctive in flight.

Before their recent widespread decline, Starlings could often be seen in winter in huge flocks, drifting like smoke across the sky, sometimes numbering tens or hundreds of thousands. The flocks gathered to roost in reed beds and woods, sometimes millions together. Such concentrations are rarer now because changes in agricultural practice have reduced Starling numbers in most areas. Yet in some town centres, tens of thousands can still be seen gathering in the winter dusk to roost on giant bridges and other man-made structures. They attract Sparrowhawks, and sometimes Peregrines, which swoop through the flocks trying to catch a late meal. Starlings remain familiar in gardens all year, squabbling over food in winter, singing from roofs and aerials in spring, and nesting in roof spaces and eaves where cavities still exist. Most, however, nest in woodland or in old trees on farmland. They feed on more open ground, especially grassland.

FEEDING

A foraging Starling typically probes in the grass, opening its bill to make a small but distinct hole, hoping to grasp some large grub such as a leatherjacket. It will eat insects of many kinds, seeds, grain, and food put out on bird tables. In winter, especially, flocks gather around animal feed troughs, on refuse tips, and in other places where food is unnaturally concentrated. They also search seaweed on beaches for small invertebrates.

DISPLAY AND VOICE

Males sing with their bills open and held upward, and their wings loosely flicked open at each side. The song is a mixture of wheezy notes, rattling trills, and clicks, with more musical whistles and a variety of mimicry. Calls include a buzzy *churrr* on takeoff, a loud, whistled *teeuw*, a grating *tschee-eer*, squawking notes, and a sharp *klik* in alarm – a cue to look for a Sparrowhawk overhead.

BREEDING

Starlings build their nests in holes, such as woodpecker holes in trees, large nest boxes, and under the eaves of a variety of buildings. The nest is made of straw, grasses, roots, and other material, lined with feathers and moss. The 4–7 eggs are incubated for 12–13 days, and the chicks fly when they are 20–22 days old.

MIGRATION

Northern and eastern breeding birds move west and south in autumn. Many of these migrants reach Britain in late autumn, to join the resident Starlings.

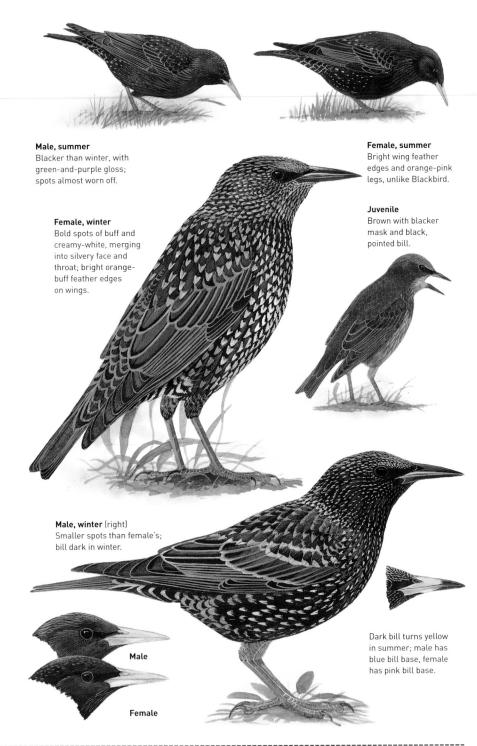

Male, summer
Blacker than winter, with green-and-purple gloss; spots almost worn off.

Female, winter
Bold spots of buff and creamy-white, merging into silvery face and throat; bright orange-buff feather edges on wings.

Female, summer
Bright wing feather edges and orange-pink legs, unlike Blackbird.

Juvenile
Brown with blacker mask and black, pointed bill.

Male, winter (right)
Smaller spots than female's; bill dark in winter.

Male

Female

Dark bill turns yellow in summer; male has blue bill base, female has pink bill base.

WHEN SEEN

All year.

WHERE SEEN

Breeds widely south to Pyrenees; absent S Italy, S Balkans; in winter, range extends south to Mediterranean area.

HABITAT AND INFO

SIMILAR SPECIES

Blackbird has rounder head, less sharp-faced; longer tail; rounder wings.

Rounder shape

Long tail

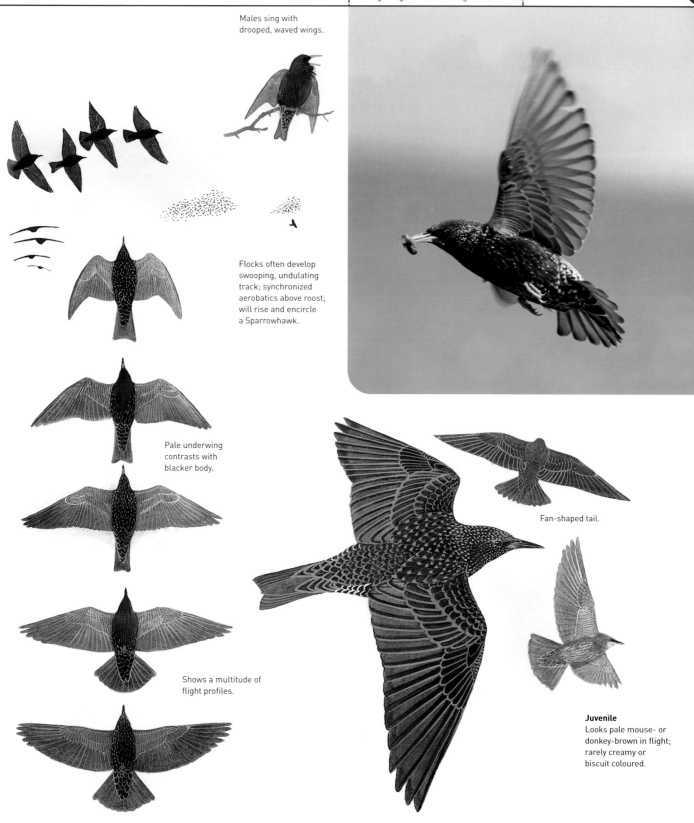

Males sing with drooped, waved wings.

Flocks often develop swooping, undulating track; synchronized aerobatics above roost; will rise and encircle a Sparrowhawk.

Pale underwing contrasts with blacker body.

Shows a multitude of flight profiles.

Fan-shaped tail.

Juvenile
Looks pale mouse- or donkey-brown in flight; rarely creamy or biscuit coloured.

FLIGHT PATTERN
Flight typically fast and direct; singly, often making long, straight bee-line to nest or feeding place.

DID YOU KNOW?
The muscles that open the Starling's bill are especially well-developed, so that it can probe and open its bill forcefully to make a hole in the soil. Its skull is narrow and its eyes can swivel forward so that it can see into the hole, aided by unusually good low-light vision. It can also swivel its eyes back to look for approaching predators.

Golden Oriole

SCALE v Pigeon

LENGTH / 24cm (9½in)
WINGSPAN / 35cm (14in)
WEIGHT / 55g (2oz)

■ **STATUS /** Secure

A thrush-sized, long-winged, secretive bird of leafy tree tops. Despite the male's vivid plumage, it is extremely hard to see unless it flies to another clump of trees. The buttercup-yellow and black of the male is unique in Europe, but the female resembles Green Woodpecker.

In a picture a male Golden Oriole looks stunning: in reality it is sensational. Few birds are quite so vivid, yet few are so difficult to see well. An oriole's presence is usually betrayed by its song, from the depths of a poplar plantation or a streamside copse, but it may take hours of patient watching to get more than a glimpse. Now and then, though, it allows a clear, close, and truly memorable view.

FEEDING
It takes caterpillars, beetles, and berries in leafy tree canopies, more rarely from lower vegetation.

DISPLAY AND VOICE
Males advertise their territories with frequent songs, especially at dawn and dusk. Females sing less often. The song is full-throated and fluty, but short: a yodelled *eee-oo*, or *weedle-eeoo*, *doo-dl-iu*, or similar. Both sexes make a cat-like squawl.

BREEDING
The nest is slung within a horizontal fork high in a tree. The 3–4 eggs hatch after 16–17 days.

MIGRATION
Iberian birds move south, probably into west Africa. Birds from farther east take a more south-easterly course to east Africa.

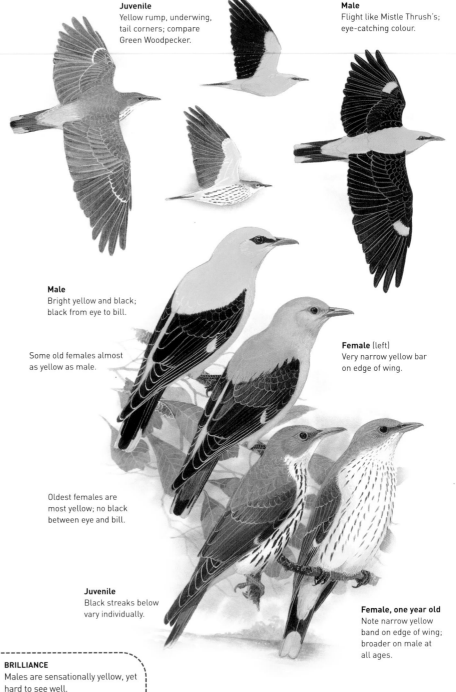

Juvenile
Yellow rump, underwing, tail corners; compare Green Woodpecker.

Male
Flight like Mistle Thrush's; eye-catching colour.

Male
Bright yellow and black; black from eye to bill.

Some old females almost as yellow as male.

Female (left)
Very narrow yellow bar on edge of wing.

Oldest females are most yellow; no black between eye and bill.

Juvenile
Black streaks below vary individually.

Female, one year old
Note narrow yellow band on edge of wing; broader on male at all ages.

BRILLIANCE
Males are sensationally yellow, yet hard to see well.

WHEN SEEN

Sept — April

April to September.

WHERE SEEN
Europe south of Baltic; rare breeder in E England, S Sweden.

HABITAT AND INFO

SIMILAR SPECIES
Green Woodpecker is less likely to perch across branch; larger bill; red cap; plainer beneath.

Red cap

Spiky tail

Nutcracker

A uniquely white-spotted, chocolate-brown bird with dark cap and wings, it has a vivid white undertail and tail tip. It is closely associated with pines, but turns up in unlikely places during irruptions. It is much bigger than the Starling.

LENGTH / 32–33cm (12½–13in)
WINGSPAN / 52–58cm (20½–23in)
WEIGHT / 125–190g (4½–6¾oz)

■ **STATUS /** Secure

SCALE v Pigeon

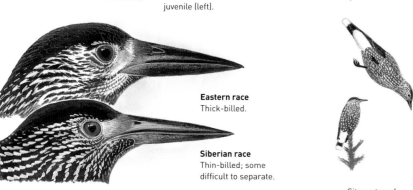

White tail tip obvious from rear.

Broad wingtips; white bars under wing; white streaks on middle primaries; unique white-black-white undertail.

Thin pale tips to primaries on adult (far left); wider on juvenile (left).

Drops like a stone from perch.

Eastern race
Thick-billed.

Siberian race
Thin-billed; some difficult to separate.

Sits on top of pine trees.

Bold white spots on body, black cap and wings, and white splash under tail produce unique pattern.

The Nutcracker is a remarkably handsome and fascinating bird of northern or high-altitude coniferous forests. Given a good view it is unmistakable, yet wishful thinking accounts for many reports based on misjudged Starlings or young thrushes!

FEEDING
Nutcrackers do eat nuts (chiefly hazel), plus conifer seeds (especially Arolla pine), berries, and various insects. They bury large stores of food under leaf litter or moss, and these are essential for seeing the birds through each winter.

VOICE
In summer, they use harsh calls. In winter, they are silent.

BREEDING
Although they often live in flocks, pairs separate out even in winter, and they nest independently of their fellows. The nest is made against the trunk of a conifer. The 3–4 eggs are incubated for 18 days and the young fly within a month.

MIGRATION
Mostly resident, especially in the west of their range, Nutcrackers sometimes move west and south in autumn in search of food. Few survive these irruptions to return in spring.

COALESCING SPOTS
The background brown is almost obscured by white spots in fresh plumage.

WHEN SEEN

All year; in west vagrants usually September to spring.

WHERE SEEN
S Scandinavia, Germany, and Alps eastward; mostly in mountains.

HABITAT AND INFO

SIMILAR SPECIES
Juvenile Mistle Thrush has smaller bill; much longer tail; no contrasted white patch under tail.

Small pale bill

Pale legs

Jay

LENGTH / 35cm (14in)
WINGSPAN / 52–58cm (20½–23in)
WEIGHT / 140–190g (5–6¾oz)

■ **STATUS /** Secure

SCALE v Pigeon

A colourful, elusive, sometimes noisy bird, it is most obvious when collecting and transporting acorns in autumn.

Bold, noisy, beautiful, and, in the main, unfairly persecuted, the Jay is an intriguing species. In most forests, it is wild and shy, justly so as the gamekeeper is against it. In gardens and parks, however, it may become more approachable if it is left alone.

FEEDING

The Jay eats nuts, seeds, berries, insects, and occasional small mammals or birds and their eggs. In autumn, it collects huge numbers of acorns and buries them for future use, memorizing their location so it can retrieve them in late winter and spring.

DISPLAY AND VOICE

Males raise their crest and rump feathers in aggressive displays. Calls include a nasal *miaow* and, most typical, a loud, rasping, tearing screech, like *skairk!*

BREEDING

The 5–7 eggs are incubated for 16–17 days. They are laid in a coarse twig nest in the fork of a tree.

MIGRATION

Jays are resident in the west and south, but some birds from the north and east move south in search of food each winter, sometimes in sizeable flocks.

Blue wing patch more or less conspicuous depending on view.

Typical flight around tree-top height except when moving long distances; wing beat mostly below horizontal.

White rump often raised in flight.

Glides down to feed or collect acorn.

Broad black tail.

Big white rump obvious on ground and especially in flight.

Crown raised in anger, alarm, or curiosity.

Bold black moustache and white chin obvious.

Darker in west, greyer in north, pinker in south of Europe; juveniles have less intense colours on the body.

Moves on ground with leaping hops and sideways shuffles.

MULTICOLOURED CROW
Large areas of white and black dominate the blue in most views.

WHEN SEEN

All year.

WHERE SEEN

All Europe except for Iceland, extreme N Britain, N Norway, Sweden, parts of interior Spain.

HABITAT AND INFO

SIMILAR SPECIES

Hoopoe has boldly barred wings; barred tail; longer bill.

Narrow bands on wings

White bar on tail

Siberian Jay

An orange-and-grey bird of the northern taiga forest, the Siberian Jay is unlike any other European species. It is shy in summer but tame around forest camps in winter.

LENGTH / 30cm (11¾in)
WINGSPAN / 40–46cm (15½–18in)
WEIGHT / 80–100g (2¾–3½oz)

■ **STATUS /** Secure

SCALE v Pigeon

Deep orange on wings and on tail sides.

Very orange below; may moult central tail feathers together, so tail looks all orange for short time.

Short, broad wings; adept, agile flight.

Extent of orange varies individually; some buff, others grey below.

Juvenile
Darker, browner, duller than adult.

Adult
Dark cap; pale bristles over bill; pink patch under bill shows when throat pouch extended by food.

The Siberian Jay likes dense tracts of unvarying, undisturbed forest, untouched by people. Yet in contrast with the Jay, it is unafraid of humans when they appear in its remote forest home. It is a camp follower, appearing beside tents and camp fires. It prefers areas of Norway spruce and Scots pine, but may also be found in larch and birch. Logging and forest disturbance have caused widespread declines in recent years.

FEEDING
Much more of a hunter than the Jay, it captures small mammals and birds, and eats nestlings and eggs. It also scavenges from dead animals. Nevertheless, much of its food is seeds, berries, and insects, and it caches seed stores for use in winter.

DISPLAY AND VOICE
There is much aggression and calling when Siberian Jays are feeding, but the flocks move silently. The song is a low, varied chattering. Typical calls are harsh repetitions of *eee* or *eeer*.

BREEDING
The 3–4 eggs are laid in a loose nest of twigs in a conifer, and hatch in 16–20 days.

MIGRATION
Resident.

SMALL-BILLED JAY
The distinctive jay character is evident on this grey-brown bird.

WHEN SEEN

All year.

WHERE SEEN
Norway, Sweden, Finland, N Russia.

HABITAT AND INFO

SIMILAR SPECIES
Jay has white rump; white patch in wing; black moustache.

White rump

White wing patch

Magpie

SCALE v Pigeon

LENGTH / 44–46cm (17½–18in)
WINGSPAN / 52–60cm (20½–23½in)
WEIGHT / 200–250g (7–9oz)

■ **STATUS /** Secure

Despite its long-tailed elegance, the Magpie has a jaunty, jerky air. It is bold and inquisitive on the ground, but rather weak and uncertain in the air.

Many people detest the Magpie because of its reputation for killing songbirds, yet it is a bold, intelligent, highly attractive bird with a talent for thriving in modern suburban conditions. In Britain, it is now returning to the countryside after centuries of persecution.

FEEDING
Insects, especially beetles, as well as berries, seeds, and all kinds of scraps form the bulk of a Magpie's diet. In spring, it eats eggs and nestlings, and rarely small adult birds, but it prefers to eat insects whenever they are available.

DISPLAY AND VOICE
Groups of Magpies sometimes gather in mysterious communal displays or in pre-roost flocks. They communicate with their bold plumage and long tails and various loud, harsh calls, especially a staccato *cha-cha-cha-cha*.

BREEDING
A roofed, mud-lined fortress nest of thick twigs is built in a tree or tall hedge. The 5–7 eggs are incubated for three weeks.

MIGRATION
Resident.

Adults
Sexes alike; juvenile has short tail at first.

Spanish birds may have blue spot behind eye.

Nests high in trees or tall hedges.

Wings largely glossed blue; tail green with purple toward tip.

Adult
A good view reveals "black-and-white" plumage is a more complex mixture of iridescent colours.

Bouncy, leaping, sidling hop and quick walk; often waves and flicks tail; mature birds have longer tails.

GLOSSED ON BLACK
Iridescent colours overlay the basic black.

WHEN SEEN

All year.

WHERE SEEN
Throughout Europe except N Scandinavia, Iceland, extreme N Britain, high Alps, and some Mediterranean island groups.

HABITAT AND INFO

SIMILAR SPECIES
Jay has short black tail; bold white rump.

Paler body

Shorter tail

Azure-winged Magpie

Long-tailed, elegant shape, soft colours, and complex social behaviour make this species unmistakable.

LENGTH / 34–35cm (13½–14in)
WINGSPAN / 38–40cm (15–15½in)
WEIGHT / 70–75g (2½–2¾oz)

■ STATUS / Vulnerable

SCALE v Pigeon

Pale patch on wing.

Soft blue wears paler, more purplish.

Adult

Flight smoother than Magpie's, with more constant wing beats and direct track.

Adult
Soft blue and pinkish-buff, with black cap; blue wings and tail look rather dull and slaty, not vivid.

White leading edges to outer primaries.

Juvenile
Scaly cap.

Juvenile

Agile, bouncy gait and almost parrot-like exploration of tree trunks and vegetation.

Adult

EXCEPTIONALLY NEAT
This is a smooth, velvety-looking bird with subtle colours.

This dramatic species lives in Spain and Portugal. A similar-looking species occurs in eastern Asia and Japan. It roams through the open forests, cork oak groves, and stone pine-covered sand dunes in small flocks, looking and behaving like something between a Magpie and a Jay. Where it occupies plantations it seems to exclude otherwise locally abundant Magpies.

FEEDING
It eats beetles, seeds, and fruits, mostly found on the ground. It stores acorns, olives, and pine seeds.

DISPLAY AND VOICE
After each breeding season, family parties from the small breeding colonies form flocks. These defend large communal territories from other flocks. Calls are many and varied, typically a husky *schrie*.

BREEDING
The nest is a bowl of twigs mixed with dung, mud, and roots, built in the top of a tree far out from the central crown. The 5–7 eggs hatch after 15–16 days. The chicks fly after a further two weeks.

MIGRATION
Resident.

WHEN SEEN

All year.

WHERE SEEN
European range W, central and SW Spain, SW Portugal.

HABITAT AND INFO

SIMILAR SPECIES
Jay has short black tail; bold white rump.

White rump

Black on wings

Chough

SCALE v Pigeon

LENGTH / 39–40cm (15½in)
WINGSPAN / 68–80cm (27–31½in)
WEIGHT / 280–360g (10–12½oz)

■ **STATUS /** Secure

A glossy crow, it is lively and entertaining as it flirts its wings and tail, calls loudly, and flies with graceful but bounding, energetic swoops and undulations. Its red bill is distinctive.

Of all the crows this is the most ebullient, lively, energetic, and graceful in all its actions. In Britain and Ireland, it is mostly coastal, but elsewhere it inhabits inland cliffs and gorges, and mountain peaks. It needs areas of old, unfertilized turf, preferably grazed by cattle or sheep all year.

FEEDING
Ants are important, as are various other insects found in or under animal dung or locally in mats of seaweed, especially in winter.

DISPLAY AND VOICE
Choughs display great agility in flight, revelling in their mastery of the air with exaggerated swoops and dives over or alongside cliffs. They call loudly: typically a yelping, explosive *pchi-oow!* or *keyaaa*.

BREEDING
They build their nests in deep caves, quarries, mine shafts, under dark overhangs in cliffs, or in derelict buildings. The 3–5 eggs are incubated for 17–18 days.

MIGRATION
Resident. It is almost unknown outside breeding areas.

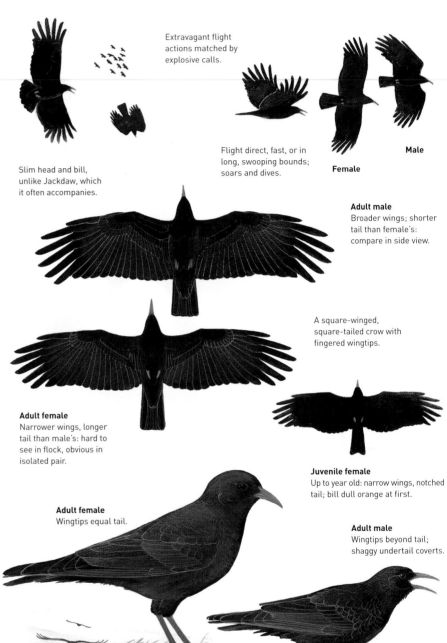

Extravagant flight actions matched by explosive calls.

Slim head and bill, unlike Jackdaw, which it often accompanies.

Flight direct, fast, or in long, swooping bounds; soars and dives.

Female

Male

Adult male
Broader wings; shorter tail than female's: compare in side view.

A square-winged, square-tailed crow with fingered wingtips.

Adult female
Narrower wings, longer tail than male's: hard to see in flock, obvious in isolated pair.

Juvenile female
Up to year old: narrow wings, notched tail; bill dull orange at first.

Adult female
Wingtips equal tail.

Adult male
Wingtips beyond tail; shaggy undertail coverts.

Red legs, red bill distinctive.

FINGERED WINGS
The broad-winged shape is distinctive once learned.

WHEN SEEN

All year.

WHERE SEEN
SW Scotland, Wales, W Ireland, extreme NW France, S France, Iberia, Sardinia, central Italy, Sicily, Balkans, and Greece.

HABITAT AND INFO

SIMILAR SPECIES
Jackdaw has rounder wing; longer tail; grey on nape.

Grey nape

Rounder wings

Alpine Chough

Smooth, glossy, and highly gregarious, this is a crow of high-altitude pastures and snowy peaks, distinguished by its rounded tail and yellow bill.

LENGTH / 38cm (15in)
WINGSPAN / 65–74cm (25½–29in)
WEIGHT / 250–350g (9–12½oz)

■ STATUS / Secure

SCALE v Pigeon

Its name betrays the restricted habitat of this bird: it lives in or around mountains, crags, and nearby montane grassland, descending to meadows in high valleys mainly in winter. It is also frequent around ski-lifts and high-altitude resorts. In the Alps, it reaches 3,000m (9,800ft) above sea level.

FEEDING
It forages for grasshoppers, leatherjackets, and other insect food in rough grass. It also eats refuse and scraps around ski resorts.

DISPLAY AND VOICE
The Alpine Chough is quite as acrobatic in its social displays as the Chough. Its calls are highly distinctive: a high, penetrating, far-carrying *chree* or *tree* and a more rippling, softer, *chirrish* or *zirrrr*.

BREEDING
The nest is on a ledge in a cave, tunnel, or mine shaft, often in darkness inside a deep cave, reached through a small entrance. The 3–5 eggs are incubated for three weeks.

MIGRATION
Resident, but moves up and down mountains with changing weather conditions.

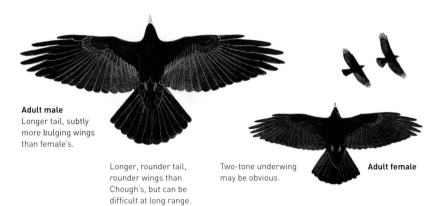

Adult male
Longer tail, subtly more bulging wings than female's.

Longer, rounder tail, rounder wings than Chough's, but can be difficult at long range.

Two-tone underwing may be obvious.

Adult female

Huge, swirling, fast-moving flocks sweep across valleys.

Males

Often covers vast areas in huge mountain landscapes, but also tame around buildings, ski-lifts.

Easily overlooked with Choughs and Jackdaws; rounded wing and tail more Jackdaw-like.

Long, slim, tapered, and small-headed.

Adult

Juvenile

Adult
Stubby yellow bill like big Blackbird, but legs red; very smooth, glossy, immaculate plumage.

TAPERED SHAPE
The deep body tapers narrowly front and back.

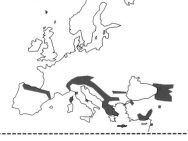

WHEN SEEN

All year.

WHERE SEEN
N Spain, Pyrenees, Alps, Corsica, Italy, Balkans, Greece.

HABITAT AND INFO

SIMILAR SPECIES
Chough has squarer wings; shorter, squarer tail; red bill.

Red bill

Shorter tail

Jackdaw

SCALE v Pigeon

LENGTH / 33–34cm (13–13½in)
WINGSPAN / 67–74cm (26½–29in)
WEIGHT / 220–270g (7¾–9½oz)

■ **STATUS /** Secure

A bold, noisy, agile crow, it is rather pigeon-like in outline and flight actions, with a distinctive black cap and pale nape. Flocks are full of nervous energy, flying off at great speed, soaring over cliffs or buildings or circling above woods. They frequently mix with Rooks.

All crows are credited with more intelligence than most other birds, and the Jackdaw, in particular, is a real character, even among the crows. It is difficult to believe that it is not genuinely clever. It is a bird of temperate regions, avoiding excessive heat or cold, yet it occupies a broad range of habitats from coastal cliffs to inland crags, from quiet cathedral closes to busy, noisy supermarket car parks, from old woods and parks to warm Mediterranean slopes. It is a social bird that roosts and nests in groups, and to thrive it needs plenty of holes in trees or buildings, or sheltered, overhung ledges. This requirement gives it a localized and patchy distribution.

FEEDING
Jackdaws feed in pairs or small groups, often mixed with larger numbers of Rooks and Stock Doves. They take almost all their food from the ground, except for caterpillars when they are abundant in foliage. They eat acorns, but not from beneath oak trees in a wood. They prefer to forage on open fields, lawns, and derelict ground, finding insects, seeds, berries, and scraps. At the coast they often feed on the beach. Some Jackdaws develop a taste for eggs, including those of cliff-breeding seabirds. They do not store food for the winter as much as other crows.

DISPLAY AND VOICE
Flocks are often to be seen flying around crags or over trees, revelling in the wind, sometimes more or less synchronized in their movements. They call loudly. Pairs seem to come together through such behaviour, with little obvious display. Calls include a sharp, squeaky *kya*, or *kee-yak* ("Jack"); also a great variety of grating *kaarr* notes, *yapping ya!* or *yip* sounds, and clucks and hisses.

BREEDING
They build their nests in a great variety of places, ranging from old chimneys (sometimes in use) and cavities in church towers or other buildings to holes in trees and rock faces. Rabbit holes are sometimes used, as are Black Woodpecker holes. Jackdaws may restrict hole-nesting species such as the Stock Dove by monopolizing suitable nesting sites. The 4–6 eggs hatch after 17–18 days' incubation. The chicks fly when 28–36 days old.

MIGRATION
Northern birds move west to south-west in autumn. They migrate by day, often with Rooks. Continental Jackdaws reach Britain in October and November.

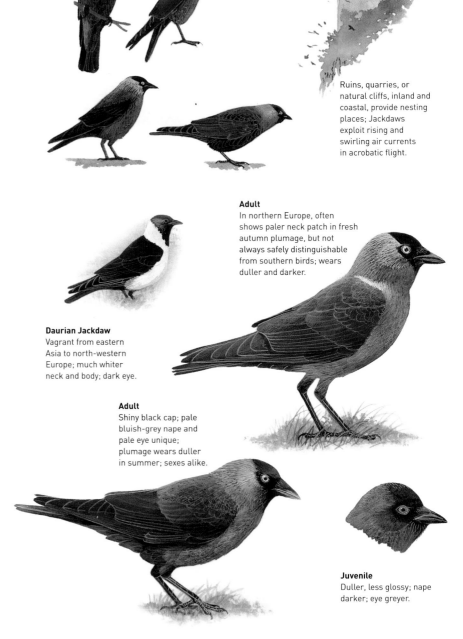

Ruins, quarries, or natural cliffs, inland and coastal, provide nesting places; Jackdaws exploit rising and swirling air currents in acrobatic flight.

Adult
In northern Europe, often shows paler neck patch in fresh autumn plumage, but not always safely distinguishable from southern birds; wears duller and darker.

Daurian Jackdaw
Vagrant from eastern Asia to north-western Europe; much whiter neck and body; dark eye.

Adult
Shiny black cap; pale bluish-grey nape and pale eye unique; plumage wears duller in summer; sexes alike.

Juvenile
Duller, less glossy; nape darker; eye greyer.

WHEN SEEN

All year.

WHERE SEEN
Breeds in most of Europe, except for Iceland, NW Scotland, most of N and inland Norway and Sweden, and parts of N and W Iberia.

HABITAT AND INFO

SIMILAR SPECIES
Rook is larger; longer, narrower wing; more rounded tail.

Longer bill

Heavy body

Lively, quick to drop down to investigate potential food; upright or forward-leaning on ground, with quick walk, jerky hops; flirts wings and tail.

Flocks often found in urban or suburban situations, around ruins, cathedrals, old houses with big chimneys, civic buildings.

Rook (above)
Long wings, rounder tail.

Jackdaw

Rook
Larger, longer-winged, longer-headed than Jackdaw.

Jackdaw

Glides with wings angled; sometimes dashes off in fast flight with wings bent well back; soars on spread wings and tail.

Dark grey-black wings and tail contrast with paler body.

Not so square as Chough.

FLIGHT PATTERN
Typical flight shapes, with slightly rounded wings swept back, protruding head but small bill, short, slim tail. Wing beats much quicker than Rook's, with snappy, jerky action.

DID YOU KNOW?
Jackdaws show considerable signs of intelligence, yet can seem stupid when building a nest. Sticks dropped into a narrow cavity soon create a stable structure, but some pairs will drop sticks through a small hole into a large opening, even through a wall to the other side, and then add hundreds or thousands more, building up vast piles.

Raven

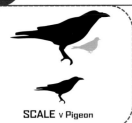

LENGTH / 64cm (25in)
WINGSPAN / 1.2–1.5m (4–5ft)
WEIGHT / 0.8–1.5kg (1¾–3¼lb)

SCALE v Pigeon

■ **STATUS /** Secure

A Buzzard-sized, all-black crow distinguished by a long, arched bill, long head and neck, and a wedge- or diamond-shaped tail. In flight, its long head/neck and tail give it a more obvious cross-shape than other crows, while it wings are long, fingered at the tips, and often angled at the wrist.

This is the world's biggest and most impressive crow. Seen on the ground at long range it is not always easy to separate from the Carrion Crow, but in flight its shape and actions are always distinctive, as are its calls. It is usually associated with wild and remote landscapes: mountains, crags, coastal cliffs, even deserts. Yet in many areas it lives quite happily on the fringes of towns and cities, flying over built-up areas quite regularly. It is also at home in softer, farmed areas with mixed landscapes of rolling fields and patchy or extensive woodlands.

FEEDING

Compared to other crows, the Raven is more capable of killing small animals such as rabbits, mountain hares, and medium-sized birds. It eats a great deal of dead meat, too, such as sheep or deer found dead on the open hill, rabbits killed by road traffic, or carcasses washed up on a beach. It also eats insects such as big beetles and fat caterpillars, as well as shellfish on coasts. In fact, it eagerly devours almost anything edible.

DISPLAY AND VOICE

Non-breeders form flocks, but breeding pairs defend territories, mainly through aerial advertisement. Ravens regularly roll over in flight (a sideways roll with half-closed wings, then back again). Other aerobatic and soaring flights help them communicate with each other. Calls are important, too: even when far apart pairs stay in contact with loud calls that can be individually recognized. Typical calls are hoarse, full-throated and far-carrying, such as *prruk-prruk* or *cronk cronk*, with a barking quality. Others are more metallic, ringing notes: *tonk tonk*. A quiet song includes variations on these notes, together with a variety of clicks, rattles, and softer, more musical sounds.

BREEDING

Raven nests are built up year after year in traditional sites, on ledges under overhangs on cliffs, in quarries, or in tall pines or oak trees. In undisturbed regions, the birds may nest in lower situations. The nest is made of thick, gnarled sticks, lined with earth, dung, and roots, a layer of moss and grass, and a final lining of wool, hair, and lichens. The 4–6 eggs are laid in late winter or early in spring, and incubated for 20–21 days. The chicks fly after 45 days.

MIGRATION

Resident, but few northern birds wander in winter, and immatures disperse from their native areas.

Wing shape of juvenile or full-feathered adult smooth and graceful; moulting adults often show notch on trailing edge, emphasizing angle.

Feathers of crown and throat often raised, giving exaggerated large-headed effect.

Spread primaries create loud rasping sound in display flights.

Carrion Crow
To same scale as Raven, below.

Throat feathers pointed, may be raised to create "beard", especially when calling.

WHEN SEEN

All year.

WHERE SEEN
Breeds in most of Europe, but absent from large lowland regions including much of England, France, the Low Countries, and parts of central Europe.

HABITAT AND INFO

SIMILAR SPECIES
Carrion Crow has shorter wings; shorter, squarer tail; less accomplished flight.

Smaller bill

Shorter tail

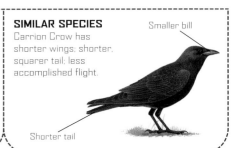

CARRION FEEDER
Dead animals attract Ravens in undisturbed areas.

Long head/bill projection.

Raven
With Carrion Crow (below right) to same scale.

Tail rounded or wedge-tipped (compare Rook).

Carrion Crow
Rather square with short, square tail.

Raven

Raven has longer, more shapely wings than Carrion Crow's; longer head and neck; longer tail with rounded tip when closed.

Heavy arched bill most powerful of any crow's.

Adult
Neat, all-black plumage; long wingtips and tail; tail may extend beyond wings (above) or not.

FLIGHT PATTERN
Flight powerful, with deep, regular wing beats, but also much soaring, gliding, and aerobatics.

DID YOU KNOW?
Breeding pairs maintain territories, but adolescents, unpaired adults, and all Ravens in winter are remarkably social. Large gatherings, of 50–100, or sometimes more, give the impression of pure enjoyment in the way they interact and exploit their powers of flight. Occasionally, flocks of 1,000 or more have been recorded, drawing birds from tens, perhaps hundreds, of miles.

Carrion Crow

LENGTH / 45–47cm (17½–18½in)
WINGSPAN / 93–104cm (37–41in)
WEIGHT / 540–600g (19–21oz)

■ **STATUS /** Secure

SCALE v Pigeon

This is a big, black, broad-headed, and thick-billed crow, tightly feathered and smooth. In flight, it is square, short-headed, with fingered wings, quite heavy and deliberate, not so acrobatic as the Rook or Raven.

Its taste for dead meat has given the Carrion Crow a bad reputation, yet it is an undeniably impressive, even handsome bird. Its intense blackness, solid build, thick bill, and bright, intelligent eyes give it great character. Despite persecution, it survives on farmland, at the edges of woods, and on coasts, often feeding on beaches.

FEEDING
It takes mostly large insects and grain, supplemented by whatever small rodents, birds, and nestlings it can catch. It also eats eggs, dead fish, molluscs and scraps. Hundreds may feed together on recently manured fields and refuse tips.

DISPLAY AND VOICE
Both sexes, but mostly the male, call while bowing with wings raised above the fanned tail. Calls are harsh, deep, *kraaa* notes, falling in pitch, often repeated without variation. The songs are rarely heard mixtures of soft calls and mimicry.

BREEDING
Big stick nests in trees, or bushes in open areas, contain up to six eggs. They hatch after 18–19 days.

MIGRATION
Resident.

Squarer wings and tail than Rook or Raven.

Deep wing beats; glides with wings slightly drooped.

Typical flight shapes: compare with Rook's; not easy to separate at long range.

Calls loudly with forward bowing action, from high perch.

Adult
Heavy and powerfully built; stout bill more arched than Rook's.

Thigh feathers tighter than Rook's.

COAL BLACK
Everything about the Carrion Crow is shiny black.

WHEN SEEN

All year.

WHERE SEEN
Most of Britain, throughout Iberia, France and east to Germany, Austria, north to S Denmark.

HABITAT AND INFO

SIMILAR SPECIES
Rook has longer, rounder, more tapered wings; rounded tail; angled forehead.

Peaked crown

Deeper body shape

Hooded Crow

SCALE v Pigeon

A striking, handsomely patterned crow, it is identical to the Carrion Crow in its shape and behaviour.

LENGTH / 45–47cm (17½–18½in)
WINGSPAN / 93–104cm (37–41in)
WEIGHT / 540–800g (19–28oz)

■ **STATUS /** Secure

Black head, wings, and tail contrast with grey body; unmistakable.

Flight shape and actions like Carrion Crow's; much bigger, paler than Jackdaw.

Often in pairs or small groups, sometimes larger gatherings at rubbish tips or along coasts in winter.

Hybrid Carrion x Hooded
Hybrids occur along borders of range; variable between pure extremes.

Adult
Body grey, but variably tinged fawn, beige, or pinkish, partly depending on light and surrounding colours; wings glossed green-blue.

The Hooded Crow is now treated as a separate species, but it was previously considered a race of the Carrion Crow. Where the two meet they may hybridize, but the bulk of both populations breed only among themselves and remain pure.

FEEDING
To a great extent, Hooded Crows rely on refuse and offal in winter and insects in summer. They eat fewer eggs and kill far fewer small animals than is commonly believed. They forage on beaches, around animal feed, and on pastures with animal dung.

DISPLAY AND VOICE
Their behaviour and calls are much the same as those of the Carrion Crow. Some calls are perhaps slightly less harsh in character.

BREEDING
The nest is like a Carrion Crow's, built of thick sticks lined with soil, moss, roots, wool, and feathers.

MIGRATION
In winter, many northern birds move south to the coasts of the Low Countries, fewer to Britain. Western birds are resident.

HANDSOME PATTERN
Pale grey and black make an appealing combination.

WHEN SEEN

All year; migrants on coasts October to April.

WHERE SEEN
Breeds N Scotland, Isle of Man, Ireland; N Denmark, north and east through whole of Scandinavia, Russia; E Europe south to Italy, Corsica, Sardinia, east to Balkans and Turkey.

HABITAT AND INFO

SIMILAR SPECIES
Jackdaw is smaller; grey only on neck; body dull slaty-black.

Darker body

Smaller size

Rook

LENGTH / 44–46cm (17½–18in)
WINGSPAN / 81–99cm (32–39in)
WEIGHT / 460–520g (16–18oz)

■ **STATUS /** Secure

SCALE v Pigeon

A big, black crow with a strong, purplish-blue gloss. Its steep forehead, pointed bill, and hanging underpart feathers give it a distinctive shape. More waddling, narrow-shouldered, and broad-bodied than the Carrion Crow on the ground; rounder-tailed and more pointed-winged in flight. It is noisy and sociable, feeding in fields and at rookeries.

Rooks are not everyone's favourite birds, but they are undervalued. They are surely inseparable from the typically British countryside of open parks with clumps of trees, spinneys, and copses surrounded by farmland, ploughed fields, and stubbles among old, dense hedgerows and churchyard limes. There will always be Rooks in such places, calling with their lovely, rich voices, often in sharp counterpoint to the bright, squeaky calls of Jackdaws mixed with them. Yet Rooks are now equally likely to be seen feeding beside motorways, looking for insects dashed to the side by passing traffic, or even scrounging scraps of bread and biscuit in motorway service car parks, surprisingly tame and bold.

FEEDING
Their staple diet for much of the year is earthworms and various large insects, especially beetles. Rooks forage on pasture, ploughed fields, and cropland. Freshly turned earth is ideal for snapping up worms and grubs, while newly sprouted cereal fields and land fertilized with farmyard manure provide opportunities for Rooks to search for insects and seeds with their steady, rolling walk. They usually feed in flocks, almost always on the ground, only rarely taking caterpillars from foliage. At times, they eat newly drilled grain and ripening cereals.

DISPLAY AND VOICE
Rooks often display on and around their tree-top nests, with much bowing, lowering, or raising of half-opened wings and fanning of their raised tails. Their calls are varied, with frequent strangled, almost ringing, trumpeting calls mixed with rattles and churrs in a kind of song. Their usual call is rougher, flatter, and more open-ended than the Carrion Crow's: a more even *kaah kaah kaah*.

BREEDING
The nests are mostly built high in tree tops, rarely on an open side branch or near the trunk. They are substantial structures of sticks, lined with roots, moss, clay, feathers, and various rags or bits of paper. Pairs often steal material from neighbouring nests. The 2–6 eggs hatch after 16–18 days. The young fly when 30–36 days old.

MIGRATION
Breeding birds from Asia and north-east Europe move south and west in winter, more obviously in cold winters. British and Irish Rooks are resident, and joined by many from the Baltic in winter, especially in the east.

Noisy social behaviour around tree-top nests is distinctive, with familiar croaks and far-carrying, strangled metallic notes.

Juvenile
Bill and face black; head and neck dull, rest of body more glossy.

Good views reveal bright purple-blue gloss on adults.

Adult male
Bare parchment buff/white face with flexible pouch beneath chin; steep forehead; long, pointed bill.

Adult female
Wingtip reaches tail tip, unlike male's, in which tail protrudes.

Juvenile Rook   **Carrion Crow**   **Adult**

WHEN SEEN

All year in Britain and Ireland; winter only in S Europe.

WHERE SEEN
All of Britain and Ireland except N Scotland; absent from most of Scandinavia, S France (except in winter), Iberia, and Italy; mostly only in winter in much of central and SE Europe.

HABITAT AND INFO

SIMILAR SPECIES
Carrion Crow has flatter crown; blunter bill; squarer wings and tail; tighter underside feathering.

Blunter bill

Squarer tail

Carrion Crow
Wingtip slightly broader, squarer; head and bill slightly heavier.

Rook
Wingtip rather tapered when angled backward.

Wingtip fingered when fully spread; tail slightly wedge-shaped or rounded at tip, inviting confusion with Raven at long range.

Rook

Tail closed in direct flight; wingtips outstretched, tail fanned out and rounded in soar.

Compare wingtip shape (more pointed) with squarer shape of Carrion Crow (below).

Carrion Crow

Small groups often soar in tight circles; capable of rising to considerable height in warm air or in wind against hillside.

Rook

FLIGHT PATTERN
Typically direct, flat flight with regular wingbeats. Also soars.

DID YOU KNOW?
Rooks are nothing if not gregarious: there are records of rookeries containing more than a thousand nests, with one in Scotland reaching 6,700 and an Irish rookery perhaps 10,000 pairs strong. Nevertheless, the average rookery has fewer than 50 nests. Rooks are usually widely spread in relatively small groups. Night-time roosts, however, often exceed 1,000 birds.

House Sparrow

LENGTH / 14–15cm (5½–6in)
WINGSPAN / 20–22cm (8–8¾in)
WEIGHT / 19–25g (⅝–1oz)

■ **STATUS** / Secure

SCALE v Pigeon

A busy, bustling, noisy bird with bright, chirrupy calls, streaky above but plain beneath. The female has a broad pale band above the eye; the male, a grey cap and black bib. Their tails are plain, without the white sides or coloured patches of many buntings and finches.

House Sparrows hop and chirrup their way through life in all kinds of places inhabited by people: from town parks and railway stations to suburban gardens and farmsteads. In Britain, there is some evidence that House Sparrow numbers in gardens are declining, although in most places this remains a common bird.

FEEDING
Adults eat seeds, and to a lesser extent shoots, buds, and berries. They feed their chicks on insects.

DISPLAY AND VOICE
A male will hop around females on the ground or on a roof, his head and tail raised, his wings slightly open and lowered. His song is a jumble of chirruping notes. Calls include a bright *chirp*, *chweep*, *chrrup*, and *chirrup*.

BREEDING
The nests are large, oval balls of grass, lined with feathers, and usually well-hidden. The 3–5 eggs are incubated for 11–14 days.

MIGRATION
Virtually sedentary.

Male, winter
Note plain tail, white wingbar.

Female
Mid-brown; thin wingbar; broad buff line over eye.

Sparrows often chase pigeons in flight.

Adult, winter
Undersides entirely unstreaked on both sexes.

Female

Male

Slim when alert, often dumpy when feeding.

Adult male, winter
Adult male's bib is at its smallest, least well-defined in winter.

Female, summer

Male, summer

Male (right) has longer body than female.

Male has longer bib and cleaner head pattern in summer.

ROUGH CUSTOMER
A winter sparrow loses its smart appearance and jet black bib.

WHEN SEEN

All year.

WHERE SEEN
Farmland with cereal fields and weedy stubbles, gardens, town parks, shrubberies, and hedgerows; all Europe except Iceland and high northern mountains.

HABITAT AND INFO

SIMILAR SPECIES
Tree Sparrow has brown cap; white collar; white cheek with square black spot; buffer rump.

Brown cap

Black spot

Tree Sparrow

Both sexes are much like the male House Sparrow, but slightly smaller, rounder, often with a cocked tail. The face pattern and brown cap are the best clues.

LENGTH / 14cm (5½in)
WINGSPAN / 20–22cm (8–8¾in)
WEIGHT / 19–25g (⅝–1oz)

■ **STATUS /** Vulnerable

SCALE v Pigeon

House Sparrow

Two white wingbars; brighter, buffier rump than House Sparrow's.

Underwing warm orange-buff: cold grey on House Sparrow.

House Sparrow

Tree Sparrow

May look slim, but feathers fluff up in cold weather, when it looks very round; tail often cocked.

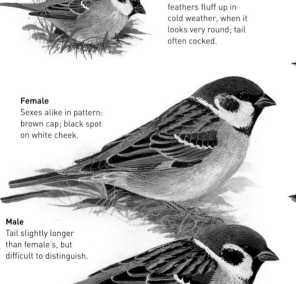

Female
Sexes alike in pattern: brown cap; black spot on white cheek.

Male
Tail slightly longer than female's, but difficult to distinguish.

Tree Sparrow, winter
Bill has pale base.

Tree Sparrow, summer
All-black bill; white neckring distinctive in both summer and winter.

Tree Sparrows seem to have always undergone marked fluctuations in numbers and distribution, but recent declines in western Europe, including Britain and Ireland, seem especially severe. In some areas, they have become rarities where once they were frequent.

FEEDING
They take plant and animal foods according to their abundance, supplementing seeds – picked from both plant stems and the ground – buds, and a few berries with insects of all kinds, from tiny springtails and thrips to grasshoppers and beetles.

DISPLAY AND VOICE
Like other sparrows, the male shows off his dark bib in stretching and bowing postures, raising and quivering his tail and drooping his wings. The song is an excitable series of chirrups. Calls include chirps and a particularly distinctive, deep *tek*.

BREEDING
Tree Sparrows nest in holes in trees or walls. The 2–7 eggs hatch in 11–14 days.

MIGRATION
North-eastern breeders move south in winter. Birds breeding in the British Isles are resident.

DISTINCTIVE HEAD
A brown cap and black cheek spot make this bird easy to identify.

WHEN SEEN

All year.

WHERE SEEN
Deciduous woods, farmland; absent from N Scandinavia, Iceland, parts of Scotland and Ireland.

HABITAT AND INFO

SIMILAR SPECIES
House Sparrow is grey on crown; plain cheek; greyer rump; larger bib in summer.

Grey crown

Greyer rump

Spanish Sparrow

LENGTH / 15cm (6in)
WINGSPAN / 20-22cm (8-8¾in)
WEIGHT / 20-25g (¾-1oz)

■ STATUS / Secure

SCALE v Pigeon

A highly gregarious, lively sparrow that congregates in noisy flocks before roosting. The contrasty summer males are obvious, but the dull winter males and other plumages less so. Note the colour of its cap and streaked underparts.

A male Spanish Sparrow in spring is a superbly handsome bird, although its other plumages are less distinguished. It is associated with people, but far less so than House Sparrows in most areas, preferring trees and shrubs, often willow thickets, typically near lakes and marshes. It is more of a town bird where House Sparrows are absent.

FEEDING
Groups eat insects and buds in bushes. Large, dense flocks may gather to feed on grain and insects in fields.

DISPLAY AND VOICE
More gregarious than House Sparrows, Spanish Sparrows live in flocks throughout the year and breed in colonies. Males sing at the nest to attract mates. Its song is like a House Sparrow's, but more strident: *cheeli-cheeli-cheeli*. Calls are varied chirps.

BREEDING
Breeding colonies may consist of thousands of nests in trees or bushes, on pylons, in the "basements" of White Stork nests, or in holes.

MIGRATION
Mostly resident, but some eastern European populations migrate in dense flocks to the Middle East and Africa. A rare vagrant north of its range.

Male, summer
Rusty-brown cap, white marks near eye, black bib, and bold white cheeks; extreme wear produces almost black back.

Summer male

Female
Back sometimes more heavily marked; underparts softly marked with subtle streaks, but these often obscure and match those of House Sparrow.

Bill heavier than that of House Sparrow.

Male, winter
Pale feather edges create a hoary, greyish or cold buff look with obscure black marks; grey mottles below.

Male, summer
Gradual wear of pale tips from winter to spring gives vivid breeding plumage with much intense black, including flank streaks.

SPLENDID MALE
For a sparrow, this is a striking and boldly patterned bird.

WHEN SEEN

All year.

WHERE SEEN
Scarce S and central Spain, E Portugal, Sardinia; commoner Balkans, especially Greece, Turkey.

HABITAT AND INFO

SIMILAR SPECIES
House Sparrow has grey crown; greyer cheek; unstreaked underparts.

Grey crown

Plain underside

Italian Sparrow

A stable hybrid form of sparrow, it is most like the House Sparrow but with some features resembling its other ancestor, the Spanish Sparrow.

LENGTH / 15cm (6in)
WINGSPAN / 20–22cm (8–8³⁄₄in)
WEIGHT / 19–25g (⁵⁄₈–1oz)

■ **STATUS /** Secure

SCALE v Pigeon

This is something of an enigma: the Italian is apparently a long-established, self-perpetuating, stable hybrid between the Spanish Sparrow and the House Sparrow. It is more like the Spanish Sparrow in the south – almost purely Spanish in Western Sicily and Malta – but less so in the north. This is an unusual situation, as hybrids tend to be at a disadvantage and typically soon disappear unless interbreeding between the parent species takes place again.

FEEDING
In much of Italy, Italian Sparrows feed in towns, more like the House Sparrow than the Spanish.

DISPLAY AND VOICE
In courtship, they behave more like the House Sparrow than the Spanish Sparrow, and have similar chirping calls.

BREEDING
In many areas, they nest in buildings, much like House Sparrows. Their nests are rough, domed structures of grass and straw. The 4–6 eggs hatch after 11–13 days.

MIGRATION
Italian Sparrows are mostly resident, but there is some evidence of movements to the Middle East and north Africa in winter.

Male, summer
Crown and nape rich chocolate brown; cheeks white; large black bib, but flanks obscurely marked at most; upperparts lightly marked.

Male, summer

Female, winter
Dull, pale head; pale-based bill larger than that of House Sparrow.

Male
Winter plumage (above) has pale tips obscuring crown colour and bib; summer pattern (right) revealed as tips wear away.

INTERMEDIATE FEATURES
The brown cap recalls a Spanish Sparrow, the plain underside a House Sparrow.

WHEN SEEN

All year.

WHERE SEEN
Italy, Corsica, Crete, Rhodes.

HABITAT AND INFO

SIMILAR SPECIES
Spanish Sparrow has bolder white cheek; blacker streaks above; streaked underside.

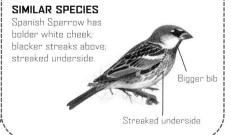

Bigger bib

Streaked underside

Rock Sparrow

LENGTH / 14cm (5½in)
WINGSPAN / 21–23cm (8¼–9in)
WEIGHT / 20–28g (¾–1oz)

■ **STATUS /** Secure

SCALE v Pigeon

A chunky, pale, sparrow-like bird of semi-arid, stony or rocky places, it is often heard before it is seen. It is undistinguished unless its head stripes or tail spots are visible.

In southern Europe, nasal, twangy, cheery calls from rocky gullies, roadside cuttings, even the roofs of old, decrepit stone buildings, will often lead to a group of neat, streaky, pale birds: Rock Sparrows. They like sunny places, often exposed and barren, as well as sheer cliffs in sun-warmed gorges. However, they also enjoy greener, cultivated places with fig trees, olives, and thickets. Ancient walls around towns and villages are often ideal.

FEEDING
They eat seeds and berries all year, but feed protein-rich insects to their chicks.

DISPLAY AND VOICE
Males sing to attract 2–3 mates. The song is very simple: one, two, or three syllables based on the call, which is a nasal, piercing, far-carrying *pey-ee* or *peeyuee*. Calls are repeated for long periods.

BREEDING
Nests are in rock crevices, or holes in buildings or earth banks. The 4–7 eggs hatch in 11–14 days. The chicks fly at 16–21 days.

MIGRATION
Resident, apart from some local dispersal in autumn.

Tail from above (left) and below (right): size and shape of spots vary between individuals.

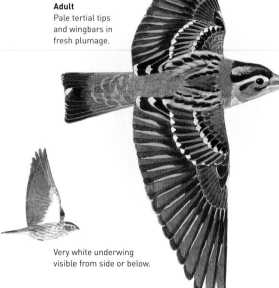

Adult
Pale tertial tips and wingbars in fresh plumage.

Very white underwing visible from side or below.

Striped flanks, mottled undertail coverts often show well, unlike House Sparrow; compare female Spanish Sparrow.

Adult (left)
Pale crown stripe and line behind eye distinctive; yellow breast spot often hard to see.

White tail tip obvious from below; spots show from above when tail is spread.

Juvenile
Duller head; no yellow on chest; more buff than adult.

Adult
Tertial tips and wingbars wear away on old feathers.

SUBTLY DIFFERENT
The streaky pattern is easily overlooked in a hot, dry environment.

WHEN SEEN

All year.

WHERE SEEN
Widespread in Iberia, S France, Corsica, Sardinia, S Italy, S Balkans; very rare vagrant outside breeding range.

HABITAT AND INFO

SIMILAR SPECIES
House Sparrow has weaker head pattern; unstreaked underside; no white tail spots.

Plain crown

Plain tail

Trumpeter Finch

A small, thickset, stub-billed finch that lives in arid and often stony places, it is usually inconspicuous, but is betrayed by its call.

LENGTH / 12.5cm (5in)
WINGSPAN / 25–28cm (9³/₄–11in)
WEIGHT / 17–20g (⁵/₈–³/₄oz)

■ **STATUS** / Vulnerable

SCALE v Pigeon

Adult male
Bright pink rump.

Pale underwing; black tail.

Juvenile

Immature male
October plumage shown: drab, brownish rump dull against blacker tail; bill already pink-orange.

Adult female
Fresh plumage dull and brown; bill variable but dull; rump pale sandy-pink.

Juvenile

Adult male
Bright bill; plain greyish head with dark eye; pink/brown with black wingtips; pink rump; wears paler overall.

Juvenile
Nondescript; dark eye in plain face; dark wing and tail tips.

This is essentially a bird of Middle Eastern and African desert fringes, even penetrating far into real, barren desert, especially where there are rocky outcrops or crags. A few Trumpeter Finches occur in Europe, where they have found a suitable niche in the "desert" of south-east Spain.

FEEDING
They pick seeds from the ground, occasionally directly from short herbs. They are inconspicuous when feeding, shuffling around or flitting short distances.

DISPLAY AND VOICE
Males sing in wide, circling, fast song flights, with short glides. They also sing from the ground. The song is a nasal, long-drawn-out, peculiar note, often compared with a tiny toy trumpet. Other calls are more abrupt, such as *chik*, *kek*, or *tset*.

BREEDING
The 4–6 eggs are laid in a nest in the shade of a rock or tussock. They are incubated for 13–14 days.

MIGRATION
Although basically resident they make some nomadic movements, usually associated with their need for freshwater.

DESERT SPECIAL
This stubby billed finch is a bird of stony, arid places.

WHEN SEEN

All year.

WHERE SEEN
Extreme SE Spain; N Africa and Middle East; extremely rare vagrant elsewhere.

HABITAT AND INFO

SIMILAR SPECIES
Linnet has white streaks in wing and tail; red forehead in summer; white belly.

Small bill

Streaks on wing

Hawfinch

SCALE v Pigeon

LENGTH / 18cm (7in)
WINGSPAN / 29–33cm (11½–13in)
WEIGHT / 50–60g (1¾–2oz)

■ **STATUS /** Vulnerable

One of the larger, heavier finches, it is large-headed, big-billed, and short-tailed. It perches upright in tree tops, looking bull-necked and crossbill-like. It also remains more secretively within foliage, or on the woodland floor. Small groups fly up into trees when disturbed.

Hawfinches are usually found in open woodland, woodland clearings, and mature avenues with shrubby understorey, especially of cherry and hornbeam. In southern Europe, they can be found in olives and almond orchards. These are enigmatic birds: they seem to be genuinely scarce in most places, even when woodland areas seem suitable for them to colonize. In other areas, they are seen year after year in traditional spots, along particular avenues, or beneath the same clumps of beech and hornbeam trees. Here they can be approached with great care and watched while they feed, but the least disturbance sees them off and away, high into the trees or even far across the tree tops out of sight. Their chunky shapes and rather long, tapered wings with bold white or semi-translucent bands, combined with their fast, bounding flight, make them easy to identify – if only you can see them.

FEEDING

Its muscular cheeks and broad, deep bill allow the Hawfinch to break larger seeds and nut kernels than other finches. It is famously fond of cherry stones (and capable of dealing with them), but is also associated with hornbeam, beech, elm, crab apple, and maple. It eats buds, too, and in summer, caterpillars and other grubs. In late summer, it turns to raspberries, rose hips, and other fruits.

DISPLAY AND VOICE

Males approach females with drooped wings dragged along the ground, swivelling from side to side to display their white shoulders. More rarely, they perform butterfly-like courtship flights. Their song is quiet: a broken series of sharp notes in no particular pattern. Their calls are sharp, Robin-like ticking notes: *tik* or *tzik*, becoming a more explosive *tzick!* in flight or a louder version in alarm.

BREEDING

The nests are sited in old, gnarled oaks or fruit trees, well-hidden among tangled foliage or in the cover of ivy or honeysuckle. Often made of thin birch twigs strengthened by stiffer twigs of oak or bits of bark, they are lined with grass or lichen, never feathers. The 3–5 eggs are incubated for 11–13 days by the female only. The chicks fly after 12–13 days.

MIGRATION

Most Hawfinches remain in the same area all year round, but northern populations are more migratory. Juveniles move farther than adults, and females more than males. British Hawfinches are apparently resident, but occasional ones and twos appear in unexpected places.

Frequently in spindly twigs at top of trees; feeds inconspicuously on ground despite large size, flying up vertically when disturbed to perch half-hidden behind branch.

Juvenile
Underside barred brown; chin pale; face dull.

Female, summer
Richly coloured, with orange-brown crown against pale grey neck; grey secondaries behind white wing patch (black on male).

Male, summer
Blue-black on wings; broad, heavy head with deep, sharp-pointed bill give distinctive silhouette.

WHEN SEEN

All year.

WHERE SEEN
Absent from Ireland, most of Scandinavia; sporadic and local in most of Britain and rest of Europe, but in S Europe more widespread in winter.

HABITAT AND INFO

SIMILAR SPECIES
Chaffinch has smaller head; longer dark tail with white sides; pinker beneath.

Small bill

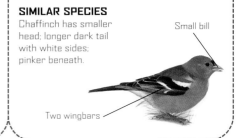

Two wingbars

Male, summer
Bold underwing pattern against dark body; bill marked with black in summer.

Adult, winter
Wings have strong white bars, easily seen in brief flight views; white tail tip can be obvious.

Bill is all-pale in winter.

Juvenile/first-winter
Wing pattern dull; white parts streaked dark; bill yellowish.

Female
One year old.

Female

Primaries have unique billhook shape.

DID YOU KNOW?
Many European Hawfinches are migratory and southern France and northern Italy are particularly important wintering regions. As with many other species, juveniles tend to migrate farther than adults, but there is also a sexual difference, as females move farther than males. In Spain, for example, the majority of incoming birds in winter are female.

Brambling

LENGTH / 14–16cm (5½–6¼in)
WINGSPAN / 25–28cm (9¾–11in)
WEIGHT / 19–23g (⅝–⅞oz)

■ **STATUS /** Secure

SCALE v Pigeon

A richly coloured, long-winged, short-legged finch, it has narrower wings and a shorter tail than the Chaffinch, but with obvious resemblance. Often found with Chaffinches, its white rump and orange wing panels are useful identification clues, but females are difficult to pick out in a mixed flock.

In summer, Bramblings are birds of northern birch forests with open heathy clearings, or mixed birch and conifers with plenty of light, airy woodland edge. A few can be found in late spring singing in similar habitats much farther south, including heaths in Britain, but they very rarely stay to nest. In winter, Brambling numbers are very variable in most areas, depending on the success of the breeding season and the availability of food. In some winters, Chaffinch flocks feeding beneath beeches or in weedy fields may attract similar numbers of Bramblings, while in other winters they are few and far between. Some immense flocks have been recorded in central Europe. Bramblings are often attracted to Chaffinches, and feeding Chaffinch flocks are often the best places to look for these more boldly patterned relatives. Males can be easy to spot, but females and immature birds are much duller and surprisingly hard to find. Their mixture of black, white, and orange, rather than brown and pink with bold white wingbars, separates them from the Chaffinches.

FEEDING
Bramblings feed mainly on insects in summer, but seeds are critically important to their survival in winter. They take most of their food from the ground, and may join Chaffinches gleaning seeds scattered on the ground beneath bird tables.

DISPLAY AND VOICE
Males in spring sing from high tree-top perches. The song is a simple rattle between deep, nasal, monotonous *dzweee* notes, recalling a Greenfinch. Their flight calls have a harder tone than a Chaffinch's, easily distinguished with practice: a *tchek* or *tch'k* rather than the Chaffinch's soft *tsup*. Another distinctive call, based on a typically finch theme, is a twangy, nasal *tsweek* or *tswairk*.

BREEDING
Built in a tree or bush, the nest is a neatly constructed cup woven from grass and stems, with various fibrous plant materials, lichens, and feathers. Typically 5–7 eggs are laid and incubated for 13–14 days by the hen. The chicks fly when two weeks old.

MIGRATION
They make irregular, large-scale, long-distance movements when food supplies fail in the north. Some remain in southern Scandinavia in mild winters, but normally many move south into central Europe. Smaller numbers head west to Britain and Ireland, and further south to Iberia.

Male, spring
Black head develops before pale feather edges wear off to reveal black back.

Orange breast contrasts with white belly, even in head-on view, unlike any Chaffinch.

Spotted rear flanks.

Intensity of orange varies.

Male, winter
Mostly yellow bill obvious, unlike any Chaffinch.

Female, breeding
Spotted flanks; back may wear to plain brown.

Female, winter
Pale nape and dark cheek surround; only small orange patch above bend of wing.

WHEN SEEN

Oct — April

In N Europe mostly April to October; elsewhere September to April or May.

WHERE SEEN
Breeds throughout Scandinavia and east into Russia; winters widely throughout Europe, but absent from Iceland.

HABITAT AND INFO

SIMILAR SPECIES
Chaffinch has white shoulder band; dark rump; less white on belly.

White wingbars

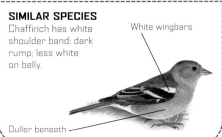

Duller beneath

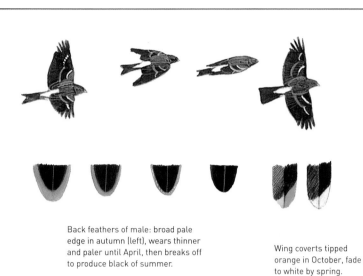

Back feathers of male: broad pale edge in autumn (left), wears thinner and paler until April, then breaks off to produce black of summer.

Wing coverts tipped orange in October, fade to white by spring.

Juvenile
Narrow rump has snaky look as bird rises.

Female, winter
Yellowish underwing, black undertail, and white belly, unlike Chaffinch.

Long, narrow white rump patch.

Male, breeding
Solidly black head and back distinctive; steely bill.

Male, breeding
Contrasted black, white, and buffy orange.

Male, autumn

Orange-buff and white shoulder patch; buff wingbar.

Female, autumn
Broader wingtip than male's.

FLIGHT PATTERN
Typical finch bounding flight with open-shut wing action.

DID YOU KNOW?
In winter, Bramblings occasionally form vast flocks where beech seeds are temporarily abundant. In central Europe, some large roosts have been estimated to contain over 10 million birds. In Britain, numbers vary from year to year, but about 9,000 is typical.

Chaffinch

LENGTH / 14.5cm (5¾in)
WINGSPAN / 25–28cm (9¾–11in)
WEIGHT / 19–23g (⅝–⅞oz)

■ **STATUS /** Secure

SCALE v Pigeon

A common finch showing much white when it flies, but this may be hidden when it's standing. Large flocks are rather loose and less synchronized than those of smaller finches. It frequently feeds on the ground under trees or in open fields.

Chaffinches are common and familiar birds in many areas, yet unaccountably scarce in some others. In many rural regions, they are remarkably tame and bold around car parks and picnic sites, often hopping about looking for crumbs and even taking food from people's outstretched hands. They are also frequent visitors to gardens. Yet winter flocks in open fields are wary of any disturbance, and all too ready to fly up and move off to the nearest hedge or tall tree. These flocks generally lack the sudden movements and tight, coordinated flights of Greenfinches and Linnets. A male Chaffinch is a seemingly discordant mixture of colours – pink, blue, black, white, green, and reddish brown – yet the bird is not nearly so gaudy as such a list implies; the overall effect is soft and subdued. A bright male in spring is, nevertheless, a real treat. The song is a bonus: one of the most welcome sounds of late winter, and continuing into summer, it is a lively, energetic performance – if not the most musical.

FEEDING
In summer, Chaffinches take huge numbers of caterpillars and other insects from tree foliage. In winter, seeds are much more important, mostly taken from the ground. Chaffinches hop about in fields, gathering a variety of grass and herb seeds, and they also search for tree seeds, especially beechmast, on the ground in woods and parkland.

DISPLAY AND VOICE
A courting male displays his bold white wing markings, drooping one wing and tilting over toward a female. He also sings from prominent perches, using a simple, lively, rattling, and cheery phrase with a faster flourish at the end: *chip-ip-ip, cherry erry erry, chipip-tchewee-oo*. The length and complexity of the song varies individually. Calls include a far-carrying, sharp *fink* or *pink* much like the call of a Great Tit; a simple, slightly vibrant whistle; a rising *wheeet*; and a sharp, fine *zee*. In flight, a Chaffinch makes an abrupt but soft *tsup* or *yup*, repeated but not running into a trill: a frequently heard and easy clue.

BREEDING
The nest is an immaculate little cup covered with moss and lichen, in a tree or tall bush. The 4–5 eggs hatch after 12–13 days, and the chicks fly at two weeks old.

MIGRATION
Large numbers of Chaffinches move south and west from northern and eastern Europe in autumn. They are common migrants along North Sea coasts.

White wingbars exposed in threat or display; may be hidden by overlapping feathers when feeding.

Wing feather fringes worn narrow and whitish.

Male, spring
Clear blue cap; blue bill; rich pink underparts.

Female, spring
Olive-brown, becoming greyer during summer.

Female, autumn
Dark sides, pale centre to nape more subtle than on Brambling.

Juvenile
Buff rump.

Male, winter
Spring colours obscured by buff feather tips.

Female, winter

WHEN SEEN

All year except in N and NE Europe, where mostly April to October.

WHERE SEEN
Throughout Europe except for Iceland and extreme N Scandinavia.

HABITAT AND INFO

SIMILAR SPECIES
Brambling has orange-buff shoulder; yellow bill in winter; white rump.

Orange shoulder

Whiter belly

Upright stance, peaked head distinctive.

Male

Female

Wingbars striking; rump green, no white.

Male, summer
Belly darker and underwing whiter than Brambling's.

Female, summer
Dull olive and greenish, but white bars obvious.

Male, first summer

Male, summer
Broad white band on forewing, narrow second bar, white tail sides; wings broader at tip than female's.

DID YOU KNOW?
Chaffinches tend to form single-sex flocks in winter, when females migrate farther south than males. The Swedish naturalist Linnaeus, who devised the system of Latin names for flora and fauna, saw only male Chaffinches in his country in winter, and named the Chaffinch *coelebs*, from the Latin for bachelor.

?

Greenfinch

LENGTH / 15cm (6in)
WINGSPAN / 25–27cm (9³⁄₄–10¹⁄₂in)
WEIGHT / 25–30g (1oz)

■ **STATUS /** Secure

SCALE v Pigeon

A sturdy, sociable finch, marked by yellow streaks along (but not across) its wings and tail, and with a distinctive, large, pale orange-pink bill. Feeding flocks fly up in dense, synchronized groups when disturbed.

There are smaller finches that are equally green and yellow, but none are so large and sturdy, or so plain and unstreaked as the Greenfinch. It is a bird of tall, overgrown, thorny hedgerows, orchards, old gardens, and parks, with plenty of trees and belts of tall, leafy trees such as limes and poplars. In winter, Greenfinches move to open fields, the edges of salt marshes, and even lake shores where seeds are heaped up in the waterside drift by the wind. They often mix with Sparrows, Chaffinches, and other seed-eaters such as Reed and Corn Buntings.

FEEDING

A seed-eater, the Greenfinch likes large seeds such as cereal grains and the bunches of seeds inside rose hips, which are too tough and leathery for smaller-billed species. Rarely, it feeds in small herbage, more usually in bushes and trees, or on the ground. It may jump up to seize the stem of a plant such as a dandelion in its bill, then hold it down under one foot. Greenfinches are also fond of peanuts and sunflower seeds taken from bird tables and hanging feeders.

DISPLAY AND VOICE

Males sing from a perch and in flight, using a strange, fluttery, bat-like flight action on widely spread wings, looking as if they must fall from the sky at any moment, but continuing in wide spirals at tree-top height. Their song is a loud, staccato, trilling rattle, varied with more musical notes and a droning, wheezy *dzweee*. The usual flight call is a chatter or trill, less hard than a redpoll's, but firmer than a Linnet's: *chichichichichichit*. Their many other calls include a looser trill: *chil il il il*, a loud, Crossbill-like *chup*, and a twangy *diuwee*.

BREEDING

The nest is a large one, made of twigs, roots, grass, and moss, and lined with fine hair and plant down. It is usually built against the trunk of a hedgerow bush or tree, or in a strong fork. Conifers are preferred, especially early in the season when cover is otherwise sparse. The 4–6 eggs hatch after 11–15 days. The chicks fly after 14–18 days.

MIGRATION

Many Greenfinches from north-east Europe move south and south-west in autumn, and others from the south and west of the range disperse to a greater or lesser extent. They spend the winter entirely within their breeding range, but numbers increase in Mediterranean countries.

Crossbill may look equally green, but has dark wings with no yellow.

Adult male
Song flight on outstretched wings, bat-like fluttery beats.

Siskin has yellow (and black) bar across wing instead of along its edge.

Male

Female

Adult female, winter

Adult male, winter
Duller than summer bird.

WHEN SEEN

All year.

WHERE SEEN

Throughout Europe except for central upland Scandinavia, N Finland, and N Russia.

HABITAT AND INFO

SIMILAR SPECIES

Chaffinch has white band on wing; white sides to tail; plain face.

Narrower bill

White across wing

Flight shape chunky with long, pointed wings; short but deeply forked tail.

Yellow stripe on wing breaks into series of streaks in flight; yellow tail sides then more obvious.

Adult male, breeding
Brightest, with most yellow.

Adult female
Duller than male; less yellow, but unstreaked.

Adult male, spring
Wings largely grey with yellow patches.

Dark face gives angry frown.

In Spain, yellow on belly.

Juvenile female
Brownest plumage; least yellow, most streaked.

Adult female, spring

DID YOU KNOW?
Unlike other finches, Greenfinches will crack open unripe seedpods to reach soft seeds. They bite through the soft stones of unripe *Daphne mezereum* seeds in gardens to get at the kernels. With other fruits, such as yew berries and blackberries, Greenfinches also eat only the seeds and discard the fleshy parts of the fruit.

Siskin

LENGTH / 12cm (4³/₄in)
WINGSPAN / 20–23cm (8–9in)
WEIGHT / 12–18g (³/₈–⁵/₈oz)

■ **STATUS /** Secure

SCALE v Pigeon

This is a tiny, neat, contrasty finch of pine forest and mixed woodland that visits gardens in late winter and spring. Outside the breeding season, it feeds in tight-knit, coordinated flocks.

In winter, Siskins dash in and out of the tops of spruce, alder, and larch trees in tight, coordinated, busy-looking flocks. They are often mixed with redpolls, sometimes with Goldfinches: all of them tiny, delicate birds. Siskins visit gardens, especially in March and April, and a close view of one on a peanut basket reveals just how minute it really is: barely as big as a Blue Tit. Size alone is a good clue to its identity, especially combined with the green, yellow, and black patterns of a male, but against a grey sky in winter Siskins often appear as little more than silhouettes. Then, their calls provide the best means of separating them from redpolls.

FEEDING
Siskins feed mainly on the seeds of pine, spruce, alder, and birch, as well as some shorter herbaceous plants. In summer spruce or pine seeds are essential. Siskins are less likely to feed on the ground than redpolls, although they do take seeds washed up alongside rivers and pools beneath alders in late winter. A Siskin uses its slim bill to tease out seeds from cones, although its bill cannot penetrate so deeply as the larger Goldfinch's.

DISPLAY AND VOICE
Pairs are formed in winter flocks and occupy territories together when they return to breeding areas in spring. Males often sing close together and in wintering areas, suggesting that song is more important in pairing than territorial defence. The song is a lively, prolonged twittering, interspersed with chattering and nasal notes, and with a wheezy note toward the end. Calls are distinctive, typically with a ringing, twanging, metallic quality, such as a descending *teeyu* and a rising *tsooee*. Flocks make a fast, rattling twitter and short, hard *tet* or *tut* notes.

BREEDING
The nest is usually high in a conifer, fixed to a hanging, outer twig. It is made of twigs, heather, grass, moss, and bark, lined with hair and plant down. The 3–5 eggs hatch after 12–13 days, and the young leave the nest when 13–15 days old.

MIGRATION
In northern Europe, the Siskin is mainly a summer visitor. Elsewhere some individuals return year after year to the same wintering site. Others visit various sites and may even change from country to country in different years. In the south and west, many Siskins are resident.

Adult male, breeding
Distinctive black cap and chin; lime-green to yellow neck and chest; banded wings.

Male, first winter
Black cap obscured by pale tips; breast pale, streaked.

Adult female, breeding
Heavy streaks on white underside; broad black and narrow yellow wingbars.

Small, active, agile, with deeply forked tail and long wings; sharp, slim bill for probing into cones.

Juvenile

WHEN SEEN

All year; in the north, mostly April to September.

WHERE SEEN
Almost the whole of Europe except for extreme N Norway and Sweden; leaves most of Scandinavia and Russia in winter.

HABITAT AND INFO

SIMILAR SPECIES
Greenfinch is bigger; darker; no crossbars on wing; darker rump; large, pale bill.

Plain head

No wingbars

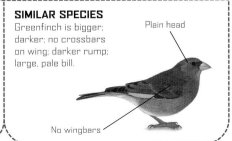

PEANUT SPECIALIST
Bird feeders are invaluable in spring when natural food is scarce.

Adult male
Yellowest on rump; adult female (far right) more streaked; narrow yellow bar on wing.

Adult female

Juvenile
Brownest plumage, but wings already distinctive with black and yellow.

Adult male
Yellow wingbar broader, black narrower, than on female at all ages.

Adult female
More streaked than male.

Distinctive black-and-yellow bands on wings and bright rump, yellowest on males.

Juvenile lacks yellow in tail.

Male
Black cap in spring and summer; white below with fine streaks.

Juvenile male
Yellow across base of primaries broader than female's of any age.

DID YOU KNOW?
Feeding on peanuts in gardens began in the 1960s, associated with late winter and early spring when natural foods have been exhausted. In recent years, the availability of niger seed for garden feeding has seen a further boom in numbers. Northern European Siskins will stay in mainland Europe in some winters, but visit the UK in others, even returning to the same gardens.

?

Serin

LENGTH / 11.5cm (4½in)
WINGSPAN / 18–20cm (7–8in)
WEIGHT / 12–15g (³⁄₈–½oz)

■ **STATUS /** Secure

SCALE v Pigeon

A tiny, fast-flying finch with oval, leaf-shaped wings, a tiny bill, and, in males, a bright yellow forehead and rump. It often makes constant jingling calls.

There are many serins in Africa and Asia, including the canaries, but the two on this page and the opposite page are the only ones that breed in Europe. The Serin is a tiny, lively bundle of colour and song, widespread in Europe but especially common in Mediterranean areas.

FEEDING
Serins feed mainly on the ground and in low herbs, eating seeds and a small number of insects.

DISPLAY AND VOICE
Males sing from high perches, and in song flights over and beyond the boundaries of their territories. The song is a fast, jingling, or sizzling (glass-splintering) trill, higher, faster, and more prolonged than a Corn Bunting's. Their calls include a rippling trill in flight, as well as a rising *tsooet*.

BREEDING
The nests, tiny cups of stems and lichen lined with feathers, are usually in dense conifers. The 3–4 eggs hatch within 12–13 days.

MIGRATION
Northern breeders move south in autumn. Southern ones are mostly resident.

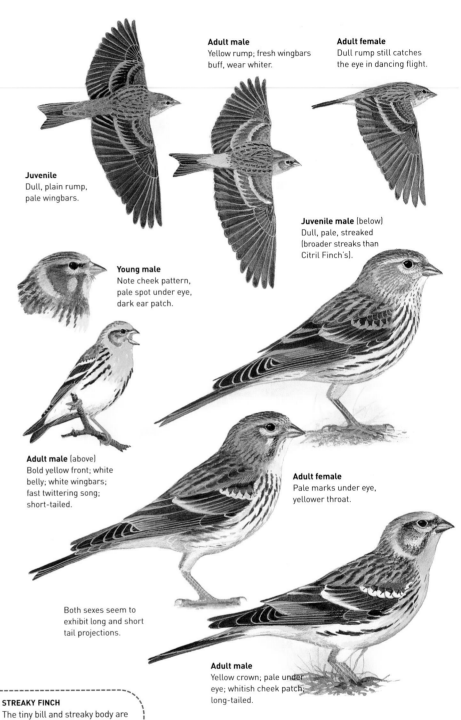

Adult male
Yellow rump; fresh wingbars buff, wear whiter.

Adult female
Dull rump still catches the eye in dancing flight.

Juvenile
Dull, plain rump, pale wingbars.

Juvenile male (below)
Dull, pale, streaked (broader streaks than Citril Finch's).

Young male
Note cheek pattern, pale spot under eye, dark ear patch.

Adult male (above)
Bold yellow front; white belly; white wingbars; fast twittering song; short-tailed.

Adult female
Pale marks under eye, yellower throat.

Both sexes seem to exhibit long and short tail projections.

Adult male
Yellow crown; pale under eye; whitish cheek patch; long-tailed.

STREAKY FINCH
The tiny bill and streaky body are always obvious.

WHEN SEEN

All year in S Europe; in central Europe mostly March to October.

WHERE SEEN
Breeds widely across Europe south of Baltic; rare and sporadic in Britain.

HABITAT AND INFO

SIMILAR SPECIES
Greenfinch is bigger; darker; no crossbars on wing; darker rump; large, pale bill.

Plain body

Streak on wing

Citril Finch

This is a small, neat finch of high-altitude forest edge, with unique green, grey, and yellow plumage.

LENGTH / 12cm (4¾in)
WINGSPAN / 18–20cm (7–8in)
WEIGHT / 12–15g (³/₈–¹/₂oz)

■ **STATUS /** Vulnerable

SCALE v Pigeon

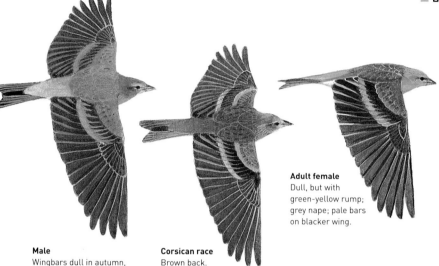

Adult female
Dull, but with green-yellow rump; grey nape; pale bars on blacker wing.

Male
Wingbars dull in autumn, wear brighter by spring.

Corsican race
Brown back.

This is one of the few species essentially restricted to Alpine environments, preferring high woodlands with a good deal of spruce and clearings such as Alpine meadows, right up to the tree line. It can be elusive, but it may be tame enough to allow excellent views once discovered.

FEEDING
It eats seeds, especially grass seeds, but often those of spruce and pine, plus insects in summer. It feeds mainly on the ground. It sometimes forages in trees, but is less agile than the redpolls or Siskin.

DISPLAY AND VOICE
In spring, males sing close together in small territories. The song begins with a few distinct notes followed by short, variable phrases with a buzzy or tinkling quality.

BREEDING
A neat nest of grass, roots, and spiders' webs, lined with hair and feathers, is made in a conifer. The 4–5 eggs are incubated for 13–14 days.

MIGRATION
Resident, except for movements downhill in winter to avoid heavy snowfall.

Male
Some have pale yellow face.

Female
Usual deeper yellow face; grey beneath variable.

Juvenile
Streaky, but fine lines below; two pale wingbars.

Male
Yellow bars on black wing, green wing panel; grey hood distinctive.

Corsican/Sardinian race
Brown back.

MOUNTAIN FINCH
Citril Finches like woodland edges in mountainous areas.

WHEN SEEN

All year.

WHERE SEEN
Breeds in E France, Alps, Pyrenees, and mountains of N Spain, Corsica, Sardinia.

HABITAT AND INFO

SIMILAR SPECIES
Serin has streaked back and breast.

Paler wing

Streaks beneath

Goldfinch

SCALE v Pigeon

LENGTH / 12cm (4³/₄in)
WINGSPAN / 21–25cm (8¹/₄–9³/₄in)
WEIGHT / 14–17g (¹/₂–⁵/₈oz)

■ **STATUS /** Secure

A small, delicate, boldly patterned finch, it is gregarious and easily seen, except when nesting secretively in the foliage of leafy trees.

Despite becoming a garden bird in places, and even learning to feed from hanging feeders, the Goldfinch is essentially restricted to places with plentiful seeds on tall herbs. It does not like clean farmland with no weeds. It revels in untidiness and rough, overgrown places.

FEEDING
Seeds of thistles and similar tall plants are essential, especially when soft, milky, and half ripe. In winter, it also takes alder and pine seeds. It feeds acrobatically in small groups, directly from the seed heads, using its feet to manipulate stems.

DISPLAY AND VOICE
Gregarious, but separating into pairs in spring, Goldfinches defend small territories but feed elsewhere. The song is a long, rambling, twittering version of the call, which is distinctively liquid and slurred, and varies between pairs: *chwee*, *chlui*, *tutitee*, or *tuleep*.

BREEDING
They nest in the outer twigs of tall leafy trees. The 4–6 eggs hatch within 11–14 days.

MIGRATION
Northern birds move south in winter to the Mediterranean.

Juvenile
Wings and tail as adult's, but broader, buffer feather tips; plain head with no red or black.

Quick, springy, bounding flight, with constant slurred, liquid calls.

Adult (right)
Unique bold red, white, black head pattern and black wings with broad yellow band above.

Female has less intense black face patch, less extensive red than male.

Adult, spring
Cinnamon to buff-brown breast patches; may join in bar across chest on female.

Adult male, autumn
Flight and tail feathers have buff tips, which soon fade to white.

Adult male, spring
Wing and tail feathers lose pale tips with wear; during the spring the back becomes paler, less rich brown; cheeks get whiter, nape patch bigger, face glossier red, and underside slightly greyer.

Adult, winter
Pale tips make head duller, more buff; broad pale tips to flight feathers; rich buff flanks most extensive on female.

TEAZEL TEASER
Goldfinches tweak seeds from spiky seed heads.

WHEN SEEN

All year.

WHERE SEEN
From Britain and S Scandinavia south throughout Europe.

HABITAT AND INFO

SIMILAR SPECIES
Greenfinch has yellow on wing more restricted; no black on wing or tail.

Plain head

Streak along wing

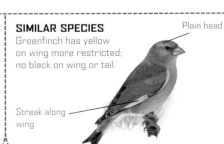

Bullfinch

This is a thickset, rather slow-moving, heavy-looking, but quite acrobatic finch with a striking, broad white rump. It is often evident as it dives out of sight through a hedge or into a thicket.

LENGTH / 14.5–16.5cm (5¾–6½in)
WINGSPAN / 22–26cm (8¾–10¼in)
WEIGHT / 21–27g (¾–1oz)

■ **STATUS /** Vulnerable

SCALE v Pigeon

Male

Female

Female
Black cap as male's; pale grey hind neck and wingbars; big white rump; black tail.

Juvenile
Like female except no black on head, browner wingbar; black wings, white rump, and black tail distinctive, separate it from bigger-billed Hawfinch, Brambling, and Chaffinch.

You might expect such a subtly but beautifully coloured bird to be easy to see, but it is often rather elusive, drawing attention to itself only by its low, fluted calls. It often feeds in pairs at the edges of woods or hedges, quietly slipping out of sight if approached.

FEEDING
Bullfinches specialize in eating soft buds and green shoots, and nibbling small seeds from fruits on the twig. With their blunt, rounded bills, they are unable to pick small seeds from the ground. Insects are vital in summer for feeding their young.

DISPLAY AND VOICE
The song is rarely noticed: a long-sustained, varied mixture of calls and whistles with a vibrant, reedy quality. The calls are simple, clear, pure whistled notes, typically *piew* or *phew*, but with hoarser variations.

BREEDING
A loose nest of twigs in a thick bush or tree contains 4–5 eggs. These are incubated for 12–14 days.

MIGRATION
Mostly resident, but northern birds move south in winter.

Male, NW and W Europe
Smaller than northern race; less extensive white rump; duller breast (palest Britain, redder NW Europe, reddest Spain).

White wrap-around rump and vent, and square, blue-black tail distinctive at all times.

Male, N Europe
Large, heavy, with very wide white rump; deep, vivid pink underside; some washed pink above.

SOFT COLOURS
Bullfinches have subtle, smooth colours, but strong patterns.

WHEN SEEN

All year.

WHERE SEEN
Breeds throughout Europe except for high areas of N Scandinavia.

HABITAT AND INFO

SIMILAR SPECIES
Chaffinch has pale crown; white shoulder patch; dark rump; white-sided tail.

Pale cap

Two white wingbars

Mealy Redpoll

LENGTH / 13–15cm (5–6in)
WINGSPAN / 20–25cm (8–9¾in)
WEIGHT / 10–15g (¼–½oz)

SCALE v Pigeon

■ **STATUS /** Secure

A large redpoll, broader- and squarer-winged than the Lesser Redpoll. Its red cap, black chin, slim form, deeply forked tail, and dark flank streaks beside a white belly are typical of the redpolls.

Individual variations in redpolls have bedevilled their identification and classification. Here we accord full species status to the Mealy and Lesser Redpolls and split the "Arctic" birds into the Arctic and Hoary Redpolls, on the basis of a suite of characteristics that include structure and plumage. We also treat a fifth group, breeding in Greenland, as a separate species. They remain an identification challenge. Icelandic birds require further research.

FEEDING
Mealy Redpolls eat small seeds, including those of birch, alder, willow, and grasses.

VOICE
The call is like the Lesser Redpoll's metallic, chattering, far-carrying *chut-chut-chut* that blurs into song with sharp, fast rattles between calls.

BREEDING
Nests are usually in small willows, poplars, birches, or alders. The 4–5 eggs hatch in 10–12 days.

MIGRATION
Most Scandinavian birds move south-east in autumn, but in some years large numbers wander south-west and reach Britain.

Juvenile, October
Browner than adult; narrow white rump at most.

Juvenile male, Hoary
Clear white on rump.

Juvenile male, Mealy
Female has narrower, less square wings, very like Hoary's.

Adult female, January
Streaked whitish rump.

Juvenile, August
Most like Lesser.

Juvenile male (left)
Some have whiter rump like adult's.

Male, first winter (below centre)
Typical small bill; streaked white rump and undertail distinctive.

Female, winter (above)
Showing the large-billed northern form *holboellii*, which forms a small minority in western Europe in winter; streaks beneath tail separate Mealy Redpoll from Hoary and Arctic.

Male, January (right)
Broad pale wingbar obvious; pink-red breast more like Lesser Redpoll's; Arctic and Hoary paler pink, not so red.

Arctic, Hoary
Legs densely feathered, with fluffy "shorts", unlike Mealy's.

Mealy

FROSTY LOOK
The Mealy Redpoll has a white background with browner streaks.

WHEN SEEN

All year; in N Europe mostly April to September.

WHERE SEEN
Breeds in N Sweden, Norway, Finland, N Russia; range fluctuates.

HABITAT AND INFO

SIMILAR SPECIES
Lesser Redpoll is darker; wingbar deep buff; dark rump.

Browner body

Buff wingbar

COMMON NAME
"Arctic" Redpolls

SPECIES
Carduelis hornemanni,
C. exilipes & C. rostrata

FAMILY
Fringillidae

ORDER
Passeriformes

'Arctic' Redpolls

Here are two thick-feathered, round-headed, small-billed, white-rumped "Arctic" redpolls and a large, dark, heavily marked, rather Twite-like form from Greenland, all with typical redpoll red caps and black chins.

LENGTH / 13–15cm (5–6in)
WINGSPAN / 21–27cm (8¼–10½in)
WEIGHT / 10–16g (¼–½oz)

■ STATUS / Secure

SCALE v Pigeon

Hoary, male (above)
Whitest of all redpolls, like a snowball when white rump is fluffed out.

Hoary, juvenile female
Smallest, but still substantial; unmarked white rump.

Greenland, juvenile male
Broad-winged, long-bodied; dark, with three broad flank stripes; buff wingbar and throat recall Twite.

Arctic, male (above)

Arctic, winter male

Hoary, juvenile male
Bold white rump; small red cap.

Hoary and Arctic both plain white beneath tail.

Arctic male
Bright buff head; dark wings; white belly; broad, square wings (Hoary's narrower at tip).

Arctic (above)
White bars on black wings; very long wingtips; very white below; big white rump; feathery "shorts"; tiny bill.

Bill rather deep; mostly tawny-brown; rump brownish.

Greenland juvenile male

Tiny bill; wide head; bull neck.

Greenland
Thickly streaked beneath tail.

Adults are whiter on flanks, but boldly striped.

SNOWY MALE
Some Arctic Redpolls look like tiny snowballs.

Redpolls from Arctic regions are treated here as three species: a dark Greenland one, *rostrata*, a north Canadian group, *hornemanni* (Arctic Redpoll), and a north Siberian group, *exilipes* (Hoary Redpoll). All three are rare visitors to north-west Europe, including the UK.

FEEDING
They eat small seeds, such as those of birch, alder, willow, and grasses, along with insects in summer.

VOICE
Their calls are very like those of Mealy and Lesser Redpolls, with a basic, hard *chut-chut-chut* pattern, the notes perhaps a little slower or more well-spaced. They are quiet birds in winter.

BREEDING
All three species nest low down in small trees or shrubs. The 4–5 eggs hatch in 11–12 days.

MIGRATION
Usually there are just short-distance movements, by part of the breeding population, but in some years larger numbers move south in Scandinavia and may reach Britain. Greenland breeders winter in Iceland, along with the resident Icelandic population.

WHEN SEEN

All year; in NW Europe November to March.

WHERE SEEN
Breed Finland and extreme N Norway, Greenland, Canadian Arctic; rare vagrants elsewhere.

HABITAT AND INFO

SIMILAR SPECIES
Mealy Redpoll has streaked rump and undertail coverts.

Bigger bill

Streaky rump

Lesser Redpoll

LENGTH / 11.5–14.5cm (4½–5¾in)
WINGSPAN / 20–25cm (8–9¾in)
WEIGHT / 11–16g (³/₈–½oz)

SCALE v Pigeon

■ **STATUS /** Vulnerable

This is a tiny, quick-moving, acrobatic redpoll, rather dark brown and well streaked, with a black chin. It flies in tight, coordinated flocks, often mixed with Siskins.

Lesser Redpolls have enjoyed decades of expansion followed by sudden declines. The increases were related to increased planting of conifers in Britain, and of birch and alder on dunes in the Low Countries, but the declines are puzzling. They became suburban birds for a time, but they are essentially birds of the northern woods.

FEEDING
The staple food is tiny seeds, especially of birch, which they take from the trees or the ground below.

DISPLAY AND VOICE
The song, given in looping, undulating flights, is a fast, metallic, reeling trill interspersed with staccato flight calls: *tchuch-uch-uch-uch*, harder, less jingling than a Greenfinch's. A nasal, twanging *tsoo-eee* is often used.

BREEDING
A small, neat cup of twigs, bark, flower heads, and leaves, in a shrub or tree, contains 4–6 eggs. They hatch after 10–12 days.

MIGRATION
Western birds move short distances. Northern and eastern birds much farther, sometimes in widespread irruptions in search of food.

The smallest redpoll, lighter in bulk and narrower winged than the Mealy.

Flocks feed acrobatically in trees.

First winter
Red cap, unlike autumn/winter Linnet.

Dark bill in late spring.

Male, spring (above)
Deep red crown; extent of pink-red on breast and rump varies; some very eye-catching.

Male

Female, autumn
Always duller than male, usually more buff; in summer, wears dark brown above and whitish below.

Juvenile female
Narrower wing than adult's.

Juvenile
Black bib; no red cap; typical long, slender rear body and wingtips; long tail.

Wingbars, buff flanks, white belly recall Twite.

Female, winter
Fresh feathers edged whitish; some white on rump.

Deeply forked tail.

Female, spring
Lacks pink-red breast of male.

ROSY GLOW
Spring brings a strong pink flush to the male Lesser Redpoll.

WHEN SEEN

All year; in N Europe mostly in summer.

WHERE SEEN
Breeds N and central Europe south to France, Alps, Danube.

HABITAT AND INFO

SIMILAR SPECIES
Mealy Redpoll has pale areas all whiter; more white on rump; white wingbar.

Paler body
Whiter wingbar

COMMON NAME
Scarlet Rosefinch

SPECIES
Carpodacus
erythrinus

FAMILY
Fringillidae

ORDER
Passeriformes

Scarlet Rosefinch

This is a slim-tailed but heavy-bodied, large-headed, fat-billed finch with a bold dark eye. It is dull in most plumages except for two wingbars.

LENGTH / 15cm (6in)
WINGSPAN / 22–26cm (8¾–10¼in)
WEIGHT / 21–27g (¾–1oz)

■ **STATUS /** Secure

SCALE v Pigeon

A western representative of a chiefly Asiatic family, the Rosefinch is a colourful bird in male breeding colours. The other plumages are dull and undistinguished. There has been a general westward spread and increase in its numbers in central Europe, with the beginnings of colonization in several western European countries.

FEEDING
It uses its thick bill to open buds and soft or unripe seeds. It also eats soft fruit, shoots, and other vegetable matter, as well as insects.

VOICE
The song consists of a variety of bright, whistling or piping phrases, with a marked rising and falling pattern. Calls include a short *zik* or *zit*.

BREEDING
The nests are well hidden in thick scrub or herbage. The 4–6 eggs hatch after 11–12 days.

MIGRATION
In autumn, Rosefinches migrate to Pakistan, India, and east to China. Small numbers of immatures move west and may appear in western Europe, especially in coastal areas.

Adult male
Red rump; pinkish wingbars; deeply notched tail.

Juvenile, September
Two wingbars; dark tail (no white).

Juvenile (left)
Rounded bill; black eye in plain face; streaked chest.

Juvenile

Adult male
Strawberry-red head, chest and rump of variable extent.

Dull head, but dark eye and stubby, dark bill obvious.

Immature male, spring
Two thin wingbars; greenish above, pale beneath; nondescript.

Compare with buntings: most have white in tail; Corn Bunting is much bigger, more striped on head.

Juvenile, autumn
Beady eye; two wingbars; streaked chest.

Adult female
Soft breast streaks; only one strong wingbar.

RED FOREPARTS
This is a plain bird in summer with red on the head and breast.

WHERE SEEN
Breeds S Norway, much of Sweden and east from Germany; more locally through central Europe and along North Sea coasts.

HABITAT AND INFO

SIMILAR SPECIES
Linnet has white streaks on outer wing and tail; chestnut back.

Streaked wingtips

White on tail

Linnet

LENGTH / 13.5cm (5¼in)
WINGSPAN / 21–25cm (8¼–9¾in)
WEIGHT / 15–20g (½–¾oz)

■ STATUS / Secure

SCALE v Pigeon

This is a slender, petite, gregarious finch with a light, dancing flight. It feeds on the ground beneath vegetation rather than on the stems and foliage. Its warm colours with darker wings and tail, each marked with streaks of white, are distinctive.

One of several relatively featureless, small, brown finches, the Linnet is distinguished by the plumage of the spring male, which develops a beautiful flush of crimson. It is a bird of dry, open ground with abundant bushes and herbs. It breeds on open heaths, at the edges of higher moors, on farmland with uneven hedgerows, and high in the foothills of the Alps and Pyrenees where low hedges cross flowery green meadows. In winter, Linnets are often found in flocks on open farmland, on salt marshes, and weed-grown shingle, and around freshwater marshes where seeds collect along the edges of pools and ditches.

FEEDING
Linnets are essentially seed-eaters, taking fewer insects than other finches, so they require waste ground and are unable to survive in areas of weed-free agriculture. Less agile than the redpolls and Twite, which gather seeds while clinging to plants, they feed mostly by standing on the ground and picking seeds from overhanging stems, or from the soil beneath.

DISPLAY AND VOICE
Males frequently sing from bush tops, even in late winter flocks. Their small territories are defined by singing: a rather quiet, musical, fast, repetitive medley of fluty whistles, warbles, chirrups, and trills. Calls include a typical small finch twitter, which is metallic, quick, dry, and lighter than the hard notes of a redpoll: *chichichichit* or *tet-tet-terret*. Like other finches, it also produces a plaintive *tsooeet*.

BREEDING
Linnets are sociable even in summer, gathering where seeds are abundant. Several pairs can exploit small areas of plentiful food (unlike the Chaffinch, for example, which feeds its young on caterpillars and must defend a larger territory to ensure a sufficient supply). The nests are neat, tiny cups of twigs and roots, lined with hair and wool. The 4–6 eggs hatch after 12–14 days' incubation, and the chicks fly when 10–17 days old.

MIGRATION
In autumn, most Linnets move south-west to winter in the south of the breeding range, mainly around the Mediterranean. Many coastal areas, particularly, see straggling groups and sometimes larger flocks of Linnets on the move in autumn and spring. In countries such as Britain and France, Linnets are residents, summer visitors, winter visitors, and passage migrants!

Male, breeding
Variable amount of red on crown and chest; back unstreaked rusty-brown.

Female, breeding (above)
Warm brown with only fine streaks; pale marks above and below eye and on cheeks.

White sides to tail and streaks on wings a good clue, but compare Twite.

Male, autumn
In fresh autumn plumage, dull feather tips obscure red beneath; they gradually wear off to reveal brighter colours.

Female, winter
Compared with Twite and redpolls, Linnet is a plainer, redder brown above, brighter buff below, with greyer head and whiter throat.

Constant face pattern: pale around eye and on cheeks.

Juvenile
Dullest and streakiest plumage with hint of wingbar; compare with Twite.

WHEN SEEN

All year; mostly summer in north and east of range.

WHERE SEEN
Breeds through most of Europe, except for Iceland, most of Norway and N Sweden; in winter mostly south from Britain, Denmark, and Germany to Mediterranean coast.

HABITAT AND INFO

SIMILAR SPECIES
Twite has plain buff throat; stronger white streak on side of closed tail; yellow bill in winter.

Tawny throat

Buff wingbar

BUSH-TOP WATCHER
Linnets keep an eye on their
surroundings from a prominent perch.

Males

Female

White on wing and tail
breaks into separate
streaks when spread;
obvious in flight.

Female

Juvenile

Male
Rump wears paler
and greyer.

DID YOU KNOW?
Because they eat seeds, which can be locally abundant, Linnets often
nest in loose colonies and socialize all year round. Although males
hold small territories around the nest and have strong, melodious
songs, flocks frequently sit together in bush tops and produce
a cheerful chorus of twittering calls before moving off to
roost for the night.

?

Twite

LENGTH / 14cm (5½in)
WINGSPAN / 21–25cm (8¼–9¾in)
WEIGHT / 15–20g (½–¾oz)

■ **STATUS /** Vulnerable

SCALE v Pigeon

Although clearly closely related to the Linnet, the Twite often looks more like a redpoll with its warm buffy-brown colour and pale wingbar.

In some ways, the Twite seems to lie half-way between the Linnet and the redpolls, but it is most closely allied to the Linnet. A bird of low vegetation or the ground, it is even more terrestrial than the Linnet. It breeds in more northerly or higher regions, where it is associated with upland farms and coastal crofts. It frequents salt marshes in winter.

FEEDING
Twites pick small seeds from the ground or herbs, and from the vegetation washed up along tide lines.

DISPLAY AND VOICE
Males circle with flapping wings and glide while singing. They also sing from perches. The song is Linnet-like, but more twittering and metallic, less musical, with a nasal jangle or twang. Calls include a redpoll-like *tup-up-up*, which is harder than a Linnet's, and a nasal, twangy, almost rasping *twaa-eet*.

BREEDING
The 4–6 eggs, are laid in a nest on the ground in heather or herbs. They hatch after 12–13 days.

MIGRATION
Upland breeders move to the coast in winter. Northern birds head south to central Europe.

Male, October
Pink rump begins to show in September/October, brighter by spring.

Juvenile
A "ginger" bird in the field, with tawny throat.

Winter flocks sweep round in tight, calling groups before dropping silently out of sight.

Female
Shorter tail.

Pink rump of male becomes brighter as brown tips wear off.

Scandinavian bird, winter
Particularly buff.

Bill grey in summer, yellow in winter.

Compare tail pattern with Linnet's.

Female, breeding (above)
Worn plumage dark, white on tail reduced, wingbar narrow; face more buff; overall less rust/ginger than Linnet.

Juvenile male (above)
Bright and buffy; wingbar broad buff; white streak along wing and obvious white tail side.

Female, autumn
Yellow bill; broad orange-buff throat; wingbar like redpoll's, white streak like Linnet's.

TAKE A CLOSE LOOK
Twites are beautiful on close acquaintance.

WHEN SEEN

All year; April to September in N Europe.

WHERE SEEN
Breeds Norway, Ireland, N Britain; winters Sweden, Denmark, E England, Low Countries, central Europe.

HABITAT AND INFO

SIMILAR SPECIES
Lesser Redpoll has no white streak on edge of wing or tail; dark chin.

Plain tail

Black chin

ORDER
Passeriformes

FAMILY
Fringillidae

SPECIES
Pinicola enucleator

COMMON NAME
Pine Grosbeak

Pine Grosbeak

A very large thrush-sized finch of the far north, it is shy in summer, but remarkably tame in winter. Flocks may feed in suburban areas, but rarely stray far south. Its size, deep bill, and black wings with white feather edges are distinctive.

LENGTH / 18.5cm (7¼in)
WINGSPAN / 30cm (11¾in)
WEIGHT / 50–65g (1¾–2¼oz)

■ **STATUS /** Secure

SCALE v Pigeon

This remarkable bird lives in the forests of the far north, to the edge of the tundra, both in conifers and in birch woods. In winter, some move into towns to find food.

FEEDING
It takes buds, shoots, seeds, and fleshy berries both from trees and from the low shrubs beneath them, or at the forest edge. It is acrobatic when feeding, often hanging upside down almost like a small parrot or a Waxwing, but using its bill to cling on or to grasp berries like a Crossbill.

DISPLAY AND VOICE
Both sexes sing, males most loudly, with a short phrase of yodelling, fluty, rich whistles. Calls include a Bullfinch-like flute and soft, silky sounds, and also a loud *tui-tui-tui*.

BREEDING
The female builds a large nest of ragged twigs, lined with moss, lichen, and roots, against the trunk of a tree. The 3–4 eggs hatch after an incubation of 14 days.

MIGRATION
Mostly resident, but some migrate short distances. All are likely to move when food is short, with Russian birds moving into north-east Europe.

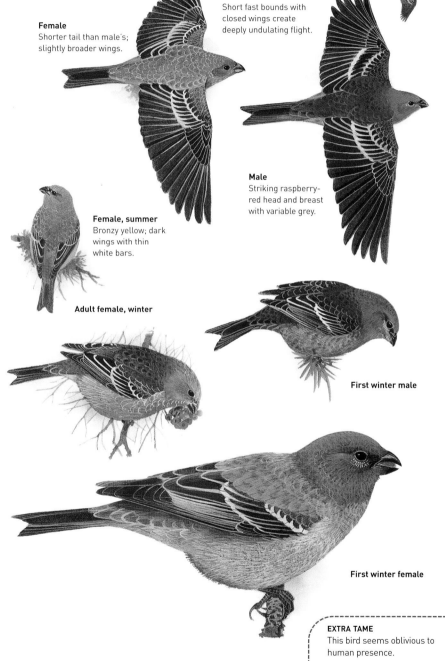

Female
Shorter tail than male's; slightly broader wings.

Short fast bounds with closed wings create deeply undulating flight.

Male
Striking raspberry-red head and breast with variable grey.

Female, summer
Bronzy yellow; dark wings with thin white bars.

Adult female, winter

First winter male

First winter female

EXTRA TAME
This bird seems oblivious to human presence.

WHEN SEEN

All year; around fringe of breeding range mostly August to April.

WHERE SEEN
Breeds locally Norway, Sweden, Finland, Russia; rare vagrant to south and south-west of breeding range.

HABITAT AND INFO

SIMILAR SPECIES
Crossbill usually has plainer wing; bigger, more hooked bill on bigger head.

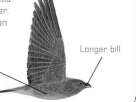

Longer bill

Slimmer body

Parrot Crossbill

ORDER Passeriformes
FAMILY Fringillidae
SPECIES Loxia pytyopsittacus
COMMON NAME Parrot Crossbill

LENGTH / 17.5cm (7in)
WINGSPAN / 30–33cm (11¾–13in)
WEIGHT / 50–70g (1¾–2½oz)

■ **STATUS /** Secure

SCALE v Pigeon

A thickset, heavy-billed finch, it is remarkably similar to the Crossbill and Scottish Crossbill and often difficult to identify, although typical, large-billed males are distinctive.

Crossbills worldwide have adapted to local conditions and appear in a range of forms, with different bill sizes, plumage intensities, and calls. In Europe, this is the biggest, and feeds on the toughest seeds. It lives in tall, open pines in northern forests, less often in mixed coniferous woods.

FEEDING
Parrot Crossbills feed in the canopy, extracting seeds from the cones of Scots pine, less often spruce. They use their feet and bills to manipulate the cones. Falling scales and empty cones give a clue to the presence of birds feeding silently above. They also eat some insects in summer.

VOICE
Calls may be deeper and louder than a Crossbill's, but some are indistinguishable: *kop kop*, *choop choop*, and a very hard, deep *cherk cherk*.

BREEDING
They nest high in conifers at the forest edge. Females lay 3–4 eggs very early in spring.

MIGRATION
Normally resident, they sometimes wander in search of food, periodically irrupting in large numbers that may penetrate south of the Baltic.

Adult male
May have very thin, pale wingbar.

Adult female
Colours as Crossbill's, but bill deeper, with blunter tip.

Juvenile male
Pale buff with dark streaks, dark wings; young male already big-billed.

Crossbill **Parrot Crossbill**
Bill and head wider than those of common Crossbill.

Adult male
Massive bill; tiny eye; often a thick ruff on hind neck; some males pale grey.

Female's bill is smaller than male's (shown in outline).

Both sexes particularly long-tailed at all ages.

Typically feeds quietly in pines or flies off with deep, loud calls; often drops to puddle to drink.

HEFTY BUILD
Head, bill, and body are all heavily built on this bird.

WHEN SEEN

All year.

WHERE SEEN
Breeds Scandinavia, Baltic states, eastwards through Russia.

HABITAT AND INFO

SIMILAR SPECIES
Crossbill's bill is less heavy, not running so evenly into forehead.

Lighter build

Smaller bill

Two-barred Crossbill

A slim, neat, small-billed crossbill with a distinct
wing pattern, it is often seen with other crossbills.

LENGTH / 15cm (6in)
WINGSPAN / 26–29cm (10¼–11½in)
WEIGHT / 30–40g (1–1½oz)

■ **STATUS /** Secure

SCALE v Pigeon

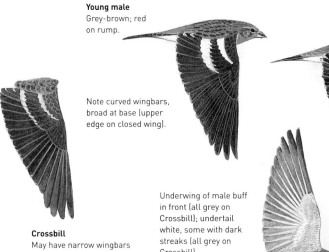

Young male
Grey-brown; red
on rump.

Note curved wingbars,
broad at base (upper
edge on closed wing).

Crossbill
May have narrow wingbars
of different shape.

Underwing of male buff
in front (all grey on
Crossbill); undertail
white, some with dark
streaks (all grey on
Crossbill).

Adult male

Juvenile
Greenish, streaked, wingbars
already distinct.

Some have heavier bills
(lower mandible still slim).

Tertial tips V-shaped
or stepped, not
smoothly curved
as on Crossbill.

Adult female
Worn plumage, October.

Adult female

White tertial tips large
and obvious.

Adult male
Cherry-red to pink-
red unlike Crossbill;
blacker wings.

BRIGHT WINGBARS
The pure white bands are
conspicuous on this species.

A small, distinctive and bright crossbill, this is a bird of larch
and spruce forest with a mixture of other trees. It prefers
woodland edges in some areas, dense forest in others.

FEEDING
It feeds mainly on larch and spruce seeds, taken from
cones on the trees, but it may eat alder, birch, and other
seeds. It also takes insects from pine needles in summer.

DISPLAY AND VOICE
The male sings within a small territory. The song is
distinctively fast, with rattles, buzzy notes, trills, and
musical whistles. It is more like redpolls or a Canary
than other crossbills. Calls are high, dry, and less metallic
than the calls of other crossbills: *kip kip* or *tyip tyip*.

BREEDING
Nests are made of dead twigs and stems in spruce trees.
The 3–5 eggs are incubated for 14–15 days, and the chicks
fly at 22 days old.

MIGRATION
Usually resident, but like other crossbills it has to make
local movements in some years to find food. Every few
years, larger numbers move much farther afield. Some
then reach Scandinavia and, rarely, Britain.

WHEN SEEN

March
July

July to March.

WHERE SEEN
Mostly visits Finland, Norway,
and Sweden from N Russia.

HABITAT AND INFO

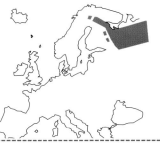

SIMILAR SPECIES
Crossbill has no white
tertial spots, even if
there are thin white
wingbars; thicker bill.

Plainer wings

Heavier body

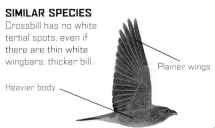

Crossbill

Scottish Crossbill

ORDER	FAMILY	SPECIES	COMMON NAME
Passeriformes	Fringillidae	Loxia curvirostra	Crossbill
Passeriformes	Fringillidae	Loxia scotica	Scottish Crossbill

SCALE v Pigeon

LENGTH / 16.5cm (6½in)
WINGSPAN / 27–30cm (10½–11¾in)
WEIGHT / Crossbill 30–50g (1–1¾oz)
Scottish 35–50g (1¼–1¾oz)
■ **STATUS /** Crossbill Secure
■ **STATUS /** Scottish Endangered

Wonderfully entertaining to watch, Crossbills feed quietly and inconspicuously in trees, now and then calling loudly before flying off. While common Crossbills are widespread in spruce, larch, and often Scots pine, and Parrot Crossbills are more northern birds of pine forest, the Scottish Crossbill is a more or less intermediate form found in the ancient Scots pine forests of northern Scotland. It is Britain's only unique species. Identification is a challenge, for bill size and calls are of limited use in the field.

FEEDING
Crossbills prise the seeds of pine, spruce, and larch from cones, using their curved bills and tongues to extract the seeds while they manipulate the cones with both bill and feet in almost parrot-like fashion. They visit water to drink several times a day. Scottish Crossbills eat mostly Scots pine seeds, using the typical crossbill technique.

DISPLAY AND VOICE
Male Crossbills sing from exposed, high perches or in a slow display flight. It is a hesitant, varied warble mixed with buzzy notes, calls, and trills. Calls are distinctive, staccato, loud, and explosive: *chip chip* or *jip jip* but vary between populations. Like other crossbills, male Scottish Crossbills sing from perches in the nesting territory, but whole flocks may sing on cold, sunny days in winter or spring. Calls include a deep *chup* – distinguishable with experience, but difficult for most people to recognize given the variation of Crossbill and Parrot Crossbill calls.

BREEDING
Crossbills nest in the tops of trees, laying their eggs very early in the year, but also in late summer, depending on the cone crop. The 3–4 eggs hatch in 14–15 days. Scottish Crossbills' nests are typically high in a pine, in the centre or out on a wide branch, near a clearing. The 3–4 eggs are incubated for 12–14 days.

MIGRATION
Resident to dispersive, Crossbills sometimes move long distances to find food, turning up in conifers in some unexpected places. Scottish Crossbills are resident, except for local movements when food is short.

Scottish Crossbill
Underwing paler than Crossbill; some very heavy-billed, big-cheeked, but not so square-billed as Parrot Crossbill; very difficult to identify in the field.

Crossbill
Four primary tips visible beyond tertials; short tail; undertail covert (shown) dark-centred, grey at sides.

Adult male
May be rich strawberry-red, brighter on rump.

Crossbill
Five primary tips exceed tertials on some; long tail; undertail coverts of some individuals (perhaps populations?) have much white, as shown.

Acrobatic feeding on cones; cracking sounds and falling cones often heard.

Groups with recognizably different calls appear to maintain discrete identities.

WHEN SEEN

All year; Crossbill often late summer in areas outside breeding range.

WHERE SEEN
Crossbill: local in Britain, Iberia, France, central and SE Europe; widespread N and E Europe.

HABITAT AND INFO

SIMILAR SPECIES
Parrot Crossbill has heavier head; bull neck; thicker bill; small-eyed look.

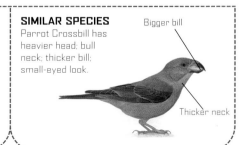

Bigger bill

Thicker neck

All crossbills are very similar and difficult to identify: all males are red with dark wings, all females grey-green, and all have remarkable bills with crossed tips. They feed quietly in conifers, fly off noisily, and frequently come to water to drink. Some populations are long-bodied, others short-bodied, giving a short- or long-tailed effect. Bill size and calls also vary, but these variations do not seem to be related. They are highly irruptive and populations may temporarily breed in areas not normally occupied.

Parrot
Deep angle.

Scottish
Heavy bill.

Crossbill
Majorca.

Crossbill
Sweden.

Crossbill
Moscow.

Crossbill
Britain (may be visitor or resident).

Crossbill
Portugal.

Scottish
Some Speyside birds.

Crossbill, adult male
Short-tailed.

Crossbill
Darker underwing than Scottish (but paler than shown in some populations).

Short-tailed type.

Long-tailed type.

Adult female
Variably green or grey, rump bright yellow-green or bronzy-yellow; rarely shows pale wingbars.

Adult male
Some are large and heavy; some have marked white wingbars as shown; tertial tips tiny, unlike those of Two-barred Crossbill.

Adult male
Grey and orange colours depend on timing of moult; typically slimmer-necked, rounder-headed than Parrot Crossbill.

Juvenile
Pale buff with strong dark streaks; bill not crossed (or only weakly) at first.

WHERE SEEN
Scottish: N Scotland only.

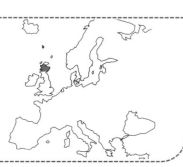

HABITAT AND INFO

DID YOU KNOW?
Crossbill taxonomy is complex, still being studied intensively around the Northern Hemisphere. Various forms, more or less nomadic and hardly distinguishable visually, have different calls and songs, and these differences seem to be permanently retained. There is potential for recognizing several distinct species in Europe and several more in North America.

?

Corn Bunting

SCALE v Pigeon

LENGTH / 18cm (7in)
WINGSPAN / 26–32cm (10¼–12½in)
WEIGHT / 40–55g (1½–2oz)

■ **STATUS /** Secure

A large, heavy-billed, fat-bodied bunting with no white in the tail. It recalls the Skylark, but it typically perches on overhead wires, bush tops, hedgerows, and raised clumps of earth and does not walk for long periods over open ground.

The Corn Bunting has become scarce in intensively farmed landscapes in recent years, after a period of increase and spread. Such population fluctuations are normal for many species, but birds such as the Corn Bunting have been hard hit by the increasing use of insecticides and herbicides, which make it very difficult for them to find sufficient insects to eat in summer and seeds in winter. In southern Europe, however, the Corn Bunting is still a common bird. It is often seen from roadsides as it perches on wires, or on top of straggly bushes beside fields. While the brighter Crested Lark flies up from the roadside verge or runs about on bare places, the more sluggish Corn Bunting hops quietly on the ground and tends to be far less conspicuous when feeding. In winter, at dusk, Corn Buntings can sometimes be seen flying overhead in small groups toward their communal roosts – which may involve scores or hundreds of birds where they are still common – drawing attention with their distinctive flight calls.

FEEDING
A ground feeder, the Corn Bunting finds seeds, shoots, and – especially in summer – insects on arable fields or grassy, bushy slopes. In autumn, it gleans waste grain from the stubble of harvested cornfields. It is far less likely to visit farmyards and similar places than the Yellowhammer, except in the most severe weather.

DISPLAY AND VOICE
Males often pair with several females. They arrive on the nesting grounds earlier than females and sing, but after mating they have little to do with them. A male usually sings from an obvious perch, but sometimes from a low clod of earth or stone. The song is a brief, fast, jangling phrase, beginning with separate ticking notes and ending in a tuneless, metallic jingle (often likened to a quick shake of a bunch of keys, or breaking glass). The songs may be heard all day long, throughout the summer. Calls include a loud, slightly liquid, abrupt note: *quit*, *quick*, or *plip* with an emphasis on the final "click".

BREEDING
The female builds a loose structure of grass, green stems, and roots on the ground in grass or herbage. She lays 4–6 eggs and incubates them for 12–14 days.

MIGRATION
In some areas, Corn Buntings are resident, in others they move short distances. Smaller numbers migrate south into Mediterranean countries and north Africa.

Streaks on chest often make dark central V-shape.

Sings with head raised, held back, and bill wide open.

Drooping tail and humped back may give untidy look on perch; often flicks tail.

Large bill with S-shaped cutting edges; deep, broad shape unique among buntings; compare Skylark.

Bill from front.

Female
Short tail.

Juvenile
Warmer buff.

Adult
Worn plumage, June/July.

May be confusing when feeding quietly on ground; note large, pale yellow-brown bill, trace of pale moustache, dark-streaked chest.

Male
Longer tail.

WHERE SEEN
From England and Scotland, Denmark and Germany, south and east into Middle East and north Africa.

HABITAT AND INFO

SIMILAR SPECIES
Skylark walks on ground; more even breast band; white on trailing edge of wing and tail sides.

Trailing edge

White tail sides

JINGLING SONG
A singing bird reveals the typical bunting bill-shape.

May briefly dangle legs as it leaves a song perch.

Longer flights are undulating and powerful, with bursts of beats between brief closures of wings.

All pale tawny-brown with darker streaks; paler rump and plain tail with no white sides.

Male (left) has broader, rounder outer wing than female (right).

Female
Shorter body than male's produces shorter tail.

Male, autumn
Fresh plumage in October/November.

Plain tail with no white sides, unlike Yellowhammer's and other buntings' or Skylark's.

DID YOU KNOW?
The Corn Bunting remains in a small area all its life. There is so little mixing that males living only 30km (18 miles) apart may sing in different dialects, their distinctiveness maintained by a lack of contact with others. Once a local population is lost – through habitat changes, for example – it may take years for the species to return even if the habitat is restored.

Ortolan Bunting

LENGTH / 16–17cm (6¼–6¾in)
WINGSPAN / 22–26cm (8¾–10¼in)
WEIGHT / 20–25g (¾–1oz)

■ **STATUS /** Secure

SCALE v Pigeon

A slim, sharp-faced bunting with a pinkish bill, yellowish line beneath the cheek, and fine pale eye-ring. It is typical of upland meadows and hot stony slopes with low bushes.

The Ortolan is a round-headed, longish-billed, plump, long-tailed bunting of open slopes and pastures with scattered bushes and trees or forest edge. In southern Europe, it is perhaps most familiar on hillsides with a mixture of a few tall trees and many more low bushes and aromatic herbs, but it ascends to greener, softer regions with grassy fields and clumps of trees. Farther north, it likes plantations and forests of pine and birch with clearings. There are a number of other small, neat European buntings with a similar pattern to the Ortolan, especially Cretzschmar's Bunting, with which it is easily confused. Changing farming methods have caused a widespread and serious decline in Ortolan Buntings, especially in the west but increasingly elsewhere as agriculture is intensified in eastern Europe. It seems that the removal of hedges, elimination of field weeds, and reduction in crop variety is to blame, with a consequent loss of nesting sites and food.

FEEDING
The Ortolan feeds mainly on insects, with some seeds in autumn and winter. It picks caterpillars from trees and can even catch flying insects, but its long bill is best adapted to seizing insects and seeds on the ground and manipulating them between the sharp cutting edge and the tongue. This splits and peels seeds, and removes the legs or antennae of insects so the bird can swallow them more easily.

DISPLAY AND VOICE
Males sing to advertise their territories and to attract mates. They use the same perches repeatedly, mainly in bushes (often not quite at the top, so the singers can be hard to spot), in trees or on wires, but they also sing from the ground. The song is characteristic, tuneful, but short, with a clear, ringing quality. A simple phrase, descending at the end, is repeated several times, then again at a different pitch: *tsee-tsee-tsee-tsu-tsu-tsu*. Calls are rather abrupt, fuller than a Yellowhammer's: *tsip* or *twik* in flight, and a thinner *tsee-up* or *tseeu* in summer.

BREEDING
The female builds a nest on the ground – often in cereals or potatoes, among thick grass or on a rough slope – using stalks and stems lined with finer grasses, roots, and hair. She incubates her 4–5 eggs for 11–12 days, and the chicks fly when 12–13 days old.

MIGRATION
All European Ortolans migrate south in autumn. They spend the winter in Africa well south of the Sahara, mostly in the east.

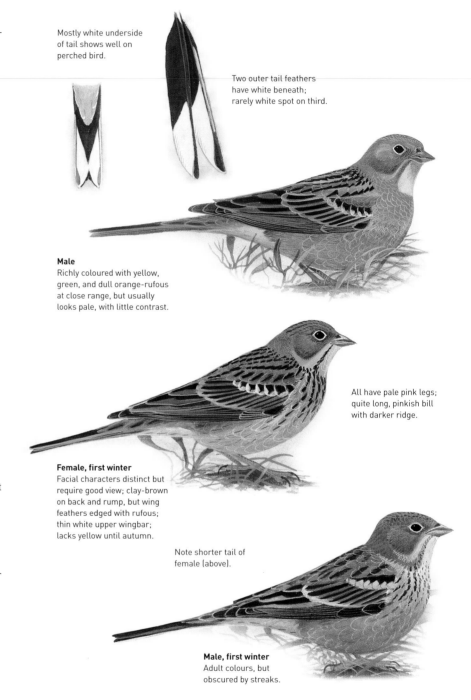

Mostly white underside of tail shows well on perched bird.

Two outer tail feathers have white beneath; rarely white spot on third.

Male
Richly coloured with yellow, green, and dull orange-rufous at close range, but usually looks pale, with little contrast.

All have pale pink legs; quite long, pinkish bill with darker ridge.

Female, first winter
Facial characters distinct but require good view; clay-brown on back and rump, but wing feathers edged with rufous; thin white upper wingbar; lacks yellow until autumn.

Note shorter tail of female (above).

Male, first winter
Adult colours, but obscured by streaks.

WHEN SEEN

Oct — April

April to October.

WHERE SEEN
Breeds from Sweden and S Norway east through Finland to Russia, and south to Germany and Poland; also from Iberia through S France and Italy to E Europe and the Balkans.

HABITAT AND INFO

SIMILAR SPECIES
Female Yellowhammer has no pale eye-ring; less pink bill; more obvious rusty rump.

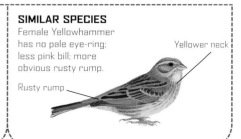

Yellower neck

Rusty rump

CURIOUS EXPRESSION
The light eye-ring gives a
characteristic facial appearance.

Male, breeding
Green chest looks pale,
but whole bird darkens
with wear.

Female, breeding
Distinctive facial
expression with sharp
bill, flattish forehead,
yellowish stripe under
cheeks, but compare to
Cretzschmar's Bunting.

Female, first winter
Female has shorter
tail, blunter wings
than male's; note
pale eye-ring.

Male
Longer tail and
more pointed wings
than female's; pale
eye-ring; pink bill;
green chest.

Male

DID YOU KNOW?
Males are often easily located by their frequently repeated song. Yet,
despite these apparently territorial songs, they often have very weak
territories, with unpaired males tolerated and other paired males
often singing close by, even nesting within 50m (165ft).

Yellowhammer

LENGTH / 16-17cm (6¼-6¾in)
WINGSPAN / 23-29cm (9-11½in)
WEIGHT / 24-30g (⅞-1oz)

■ STATUS / Secure

SCALE v Pigeon

More elongated and sharper-faced than finches, the Yellowhammer is a slim, long-tailed bunting, often found in small groups and mixed with finches and sparrows outside the breeding season. In summer, males typically perch on bush tops or posts, repeating their simple, metallic songs.

Few birds call in the heat of the afternoon on a summer's day, but the Yellowhammer sings his cheerful, repetitive song all day long, all summer through. A typical bunting, its long body, slender white-edged tail, and flat-topped head – with a thin upper mandible and more bulbous lower one – distinguish it from all the finches and sparrows. Yellowhammers are characteristic birds of heathland with bushes and open grassy spaces, farmland with hedgerows between pastures, and grassy strips with mixed gorse bushes and bracken above coastal cliffs. In farmland areas, they have declined with the loss of hedgerows, and especially the loss of winter food: stubble fields and stackyards are now rare, and seed-eating birds like the Yellowhammer are suffering as a result.

FEEDING
In winter, Yellowhammers eat seeds, shoots, spilled cattle food, and other scraps foraged from fields and under hedges. In summer, they eat more insects. They feed on the ground, often in scattered flocks, and frequently with Chaffinches, Reed Buntings, and House and Tree Sparrows. If disturbed, they move to the nearest hedge or tall tree with a quick, jerky flight action, showing the extensive white sides of their flicked tails.

DISPLAY AND VOICE
The male usually sings from an exposed perch: a bush top or open branch, or a fence post or wire on more open ground. The song is somewhat variable, but typically a short series of sharp, metallic notes, often repeated, with the penultimate or final one higher or lower than the rest: *tit-it-it-it-it-it-teeee-tip*. Call notes are also sharp and metallic, and distinctive once learned: *tswik or twitik* and a more rasping *dzu*.

BREEDING
The nest is a rather bulky structure of grasses and straw, lined with finer grass and hair to form a soft, smooth cup. It is usually at the base of a hedge or close beside the roots of a bush, or in a low bank. The 3–5 eggs hatch after 12–14 days, and the chicks fly when 11–13 days old.

MIGRATION
Some northern European Yellowhammers reach Britain in winter, but most of the birds in Britain and Ireland are resident. Birds that breed in northern and eastern Europe move south to wintering areas in Spain, Italy, and Greece.

Male, spring
Striped head wears to all-yellow by August; cheek stripes variable.

Male, spring
More rufous variation; duskier below.

Dull breast of winter male becomes bright yellow and rufous in spring.

Yellow undertail coverts, but underside of tail mostly white.

Male, first winter
Male long-bodied, with rump and tail extending farther beyond wingtips than female's (below).

Female, breeding

Juvenile female
Wingtip/tail position indicates female; less white in tail than male's, but still conspicuous; juvenile's slightly less white than adult female's.

Adult male
Some males more streaked beneath than others.

WHEN SEEN

All year; only winter in much of Spain.

WHERE SEEN
Farmland and grassy uplands with hedges, woodland edge; all Europe except N Scandinavia, Iberia, and extreme SE in summer; general southward movement in winter.

HABITAT AND INFO

SIMILAR SPECIES
Corn Bunting is bigger; bulky; large pale bill; dull rump and plain tail.

Big bill

Plain tail

Female, breeding

Adult female, winter
Note fine streaks on crown and lower face; streaked chest; clear greenish-yellow belly.

Female (left) has shorter tail and narrower wings than male (right).

Tail pattern.

Male
Rich rusty-red rump characteristic of all ages, both sexes.

Distinctive mixture of greenish-yellow and chestnut-brown with blacker streaks, yellower belly, and streaked flanks; orange-rusty rump rules out Cirl Bunting.

Adult female
Duller and less yellow than male; rump similar.

DID YOU KNOW?
The typical summer song is often written "a little bit of bread and no cheese": a simple repetition of a short, metallic note, slightly intensifying in volume but otherwise remarkably uniform, usually followed by one or two longer notes. Sometimes the emphasis is on a longer "no" followed by a shorter, lower-pitched "cheese", sometimes on a higher, longer, stronger "cheese".

Cirl Bunting

LENGTH / 16cm (6¼in)
WINGSPAN / 22–26cm (8¾–10¼in)
WEIGHT / 21–27g (¾–1oz)

■ **STATUS /** Secure

SCALE v Pigeon

A neat, slim bunting, with a distinctive olive rump against rusty back, and yellowish below. The males are strongly patterned. It has a frequent song and short, high, thin, elusive call note.

Cirl Buntings are typical of warm, lazy summer days in southern Europe, where sunshine bathes the bushy slopes or fills the orchards and vineyards with light. At the northern edge of their range, they rely more on old meadows and bushy hedgerows in summer, and weedy stubbles with plentiful seeds in winter.

FEEDING
They feed mainly on various seeds taken from the ground, but grasshoppers are important in summer.

DISPLAY AND VOICE
The song is the best clue to a Cirl Bunting's presence in summer: a simple, short, metallic trill, fast and dribbling or slower, more of a rattle, on one note. It is harder than the trill of Bonelli's Warbler, and lacks the usual longer note at or near the end of a Yellowhammer's song. The call is frustratingly difficult to pinpoint: a short, high, soft *sip*, often repeated.

BREEDING
The 3–4 eggs are laid in a well-hidden nest low in a bush or creeper. They hatch after 12–13 days.

MIGRATION
Almost entirely resident.

Juvenile
Like pale brown Yellowhammer, but rump dull, not rusty; sharp streaks on buff below.

Adult female
Dull rump; long tail with white on sides.

Adult male
Rusty on wings and tertials, framing olive rump.

Outer tail has limited white.

Adult male
Head pattern obscured by pale feather edges in winter.

Adult female, spring
Looks like a pale-throated male in spring.

Adult female
Sharp-faced, with flat crown; slightly more striped face than Yellowhammer's; dull crown with no central stripe; rufous scapulars against duller wings.

Adult male (below)
Black, yellow, and green head and breast unique.

HANDSOME PATTERN
Male Cirls are among the most attractive of the buntings.

WHEN SEEN

All year.

WHERE SEEN
Breeds extreme SW England, most of France, Spain, Portugal, Italy, Mediterranean islands, Balkans, Turkey, and locally in NW Africa.

HABITAT AND INFO

SIMILAR SPECIES
Yellowhammer has rusty rump; more orange-rufous on back and wings; less red-brown.

Pale throat

Yellow breast

Cretzschmar's Bunting

Very like an Ortolan Bunting except for the orange and grey on the head of the male, instead of yellow and greenish. It is generally more rusty-buff overall with dark streaks. The eye-ring is white, not yellowish.

LENGTH / 16cm (6¼in)
WINGSPAN / 23–26cm (9–10¼in)
WEIGHT / 20–25g (¾–1oz)

■ **STATUS /** Vulnerable

SCALE v Pigeon

A south-eastern equivalent of the Ortolan Bunting, this is a colourful bunting of low, rocky places with scattered bushes, often near the coast or on islands. It seems to be intermediate between species such as the Ortolan and Cirl Buntings, which require more vegetation, and buntings of barren rock or desert farther south.

FEEDING
Of all the buntings, this is perhaps the most terrestrial, foraging entirely on the ground for small seeds and sluggish insects.

VOICE
Males have a simple song, less ringing or musical than an Ortolan's. There are usually 3–4 notes, the last one longer. The usual call is a sharp *tchipp*.

BREEDING
The nest is sheltered by tussocky vegetation and rocks, usually on a slope. The 4–5 eggs hatch in 12–14 days.

MIGRATION
In autumn, Cretzschmar's Buntings move south via the Middle East to winter in Sudan and Eritrea.

Adult male
Longer, more pointed wings than female's.

Adult male
Warm brown rump; sharp black streaks on rusty back.

Tail pattern.

Adult female, autumn
Whitish eye-ring; buffy face; short pinkish bill; pinkish-beige underside; rusty rump.

Adult male, spring
Dark streaks, pale fringes to body feathers in spring before they wear off; rather greenish effect on wings and chest, but throat orange, unlike yellow of Ortolan Bunting's.

Adult male, summer
Immaculate by midsummer; blue-grey head with pale orange marks; white eye-ring; solidly orange to rusty brown underneath, darker than throat (Ortolan more uniform in tone).

ROCKHOPPER
Stony slopes and deep rocky valleys are typical habitats.

WHEN SEEN

Oct — March

March to October.

WHERE SEEN
Breeds in most of Greece and some Aegean islands (but not Crete), Turkey, Cyprus, and Middle East; extremely rare vagrant farther north or west of this range.

HABITAT AND INFO

SIMILAR SPECIES
Ortolan Bunting is greener on head; yellower on throat and stripe below cheek.

Green head

Yellow chin

Black-headed Bunting

LENGTH / 16–17cm (6¼–6¾in)
WINGSPAN / 26–30cm (10¼–11¾in)
WEIGHT / 25–35g (1–1¼oz)

SCALE v Pigeon

■ **STATUS /** Secure

A big, solid bunting, it is big-billed and long-bodied. Males are obvious, but females and juveniles require care in identification.

A large, bright bunting of high summer in south-east Europe, this is a rare early-summer visitor to the north. It likes open, airy places with warm sunshine penetrating open olive groves and vineyards, and orchards and fields with surrounding hedges, overgrown walls, and small copses.

FEEDING
It eats insects in summer and seeds at other times, picked from the ground and from among leafy vegetation.

DISPLAY AND VOICE
Males sing from prominent perches at any height, all day long, and also sometimes while in flight. The song is short, but develops into a full, throaty warble. Calls are short and hard, like *cheuh* or *chup*.

BREEDING
It nests in a thorny bush or vine, laying 4–5 eggs. The eggs hatch after 14 days.

MIGRATION
They migrate to India in early autumn, returning in late spring. A few overshoot to north-western Europe in June.

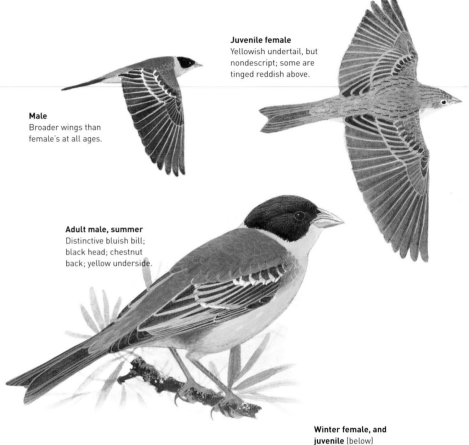

Juvenile female
Yellowish undertail, but nondescript; some are tinged reddish above.

Male
Broader wings than female's at all ages.

Adult male, summer
Distinctive bluish bill; black head; chestnut back; yellow underside.

Adult male, winter
Colours dulled by pale feather edges.

Thickset, but active and agile; pale edges to wing feathers create paler panel; no white in tail.

Winter female, and juvenile (below)
Yellowish undertail; faint streaks only on chest.

Weak, pale eye-ring.

Female, summer
Strong yellow below; large greyish bill.

Dusky chest patches may be obvious.

LATE SPRING SINGER
Males are easy to identify in summer plumage.

WHEN SEEN

Aug — May

Mostly late May to August.

WHERE SEEN
Breeds locally in Italy; more continuously along Balkan coasts of Adriatic and through Greece, Turkey, and Cyprus; rare vagrant elsewhere.

HABITAT AND INFO

SIMILAR SPECIES
Yellowhammer is streaked on head and underside; rufous rump.

Streaked back

Yellow-breasted Bunting

A slender, sharp-billed, streaky bunting with a flush of yellow on the face and underside. Spring males are unmistakable.

LENGTH / 14–15cm (5½–6in)
WINGSPAN / 8–9cm (3¼–3½in)
WEIGHT / 17–28g (⅝–1oz)

■ **STATUS /** Secure

SCALE v Pigeon

Male, summer
Broader-winged than female.

White underwing on young male (buff on female).

Juvenile female
Female narrow-winged.

Male, year old
Winter adult has all-yellow throat.

Male, summer
Unique black face, yellow and chestnut breast bands, white wing patch.

Some juveniles much paler, almost unstreaked below; a few intensely streaked.

Pink on bill.

Tail pattern of female; some have white only on outer tail feather.

Yellow over eye; dark border to cheek; pale eye-ring on juvenile and female; two wingbars.

Juvenile female
Pale yellow over eye, on throat; thin pale centre line on crown; rump grey-brown, striped, unlike Yellowhammer.

Female, summer
Very worn wing and scapular feathers; streaks on back recall House Sparrow.

Pale centre line on crown.

UNIQUE PATTERN
The breast band and wingbar create an unusual effect on the male.

Like the larger Black-headed Bunting, this is a bird that moves to Asia, rather than Africa, in winter. It is a much more northerly breeding species, however, that is unfamiliar throughout most of Europe, but occasionally encountered as a vagrant. In some places, such as Shetland, it is seen every year.

FEEDING
It eats insects in summer, but otherwise this is a seed-eater, feeding mostly in or beneath long grasses.

DISPLAY AND VOICE
Pairs breed in small, loose groups, with nests sometimes very close together. Males sing from low bushes, with a melodious, jingling phrase. Calls include short, sharp notes sounding like *tik, zip,* or *tzip.*

BREEDING
The nests are built in grass tussocks or tree roots in wet areas, or on the ground where it is dry. The 4–5 eggs hatch after 13–14 days.

MIGRATION
In autumn, an eastward, then southward, path takes them to south-east Asia. A few go the wrong way to end up in north-west Europe.

WHEN SEEN

Aug ← → May

Mostly late May to August.

WHERE SEEN
Breeds eastward from Finland; vagrant in Britain, Scandinavia, Italy.

HABITAT AND INFO

SIMILAR SPECIES
Yellowhammer is less crisply streaked above; weak wingbars.

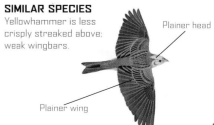

Plainer head

Plainer wing

Little Bunting

LENGTH / 13–14cm (5–5½in)
WINGSPAN / 18–20cm (7–8in)
WEIGHT / 15–18g (½–⅝oz)

■ STATUS / Secure

SCALE v Pigeon

A smart bunting, closely resembling the Reed Bunting when not in breeding plumage. Its most reliable identification features are centred on the head and bill.

Rare in western Europe, this small, neat bunting is a breeding bird of the far north. It likes moist, shrubby tundra in summer, rather than the more open spaces occupied by Lapland Buntings and the thicker woods preferred by Rustic Buntings.

FEEDING
Although they take insects in summer, Little Buntings are usually seen feeding on seeds in crops, on ploughed earth, or on footpaths.

DISPLAY AND VOICE
Males sing from tree tops, with a variety of buzzy phrases and unmusical clicks. Calls are short, sharp, quiet clicks, unlike those of a Reed Bunting: *tik, zik, stip,* or *twit.*

BREEDING
A small, neat nest is made under the shelter of a grassy or mossy tussock, often in a thicket of willow, birch, or alder. The clutch is of 4–6 eggs.

MIGRATION
North European breeders migrate to south-east Russia and China. A few move westward instead, reaching western Europe as vagrants.

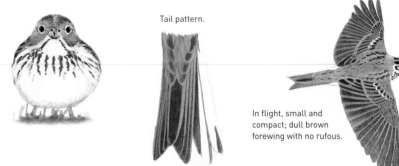

Tail pattern.

In flight, small and compact; dull brown forewing with no rufous.

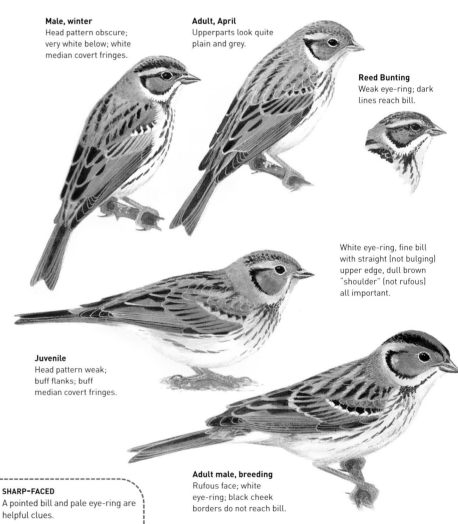

Male, winter
Head pattern obscure; very white below; white median covert fringes.

Adult, April
Upperparts look quite plain and grey.

Reed Bunting
Weak eye-ring; dark lines reach bill.

White eye-ring, fine bill with straight (not bulging) upper edge, dull brown "shoulder" (not rufous) all important.

Juvenile
Head pattern weak; buff flanks; buff median covert fringes.

Adult male, breeding
Rufous face; white eye-ring; black cheek borders do not reach bill.

SHARP-FACED
A pointed bill and pale eye-ring are helpful clues.

WHERE SEEN
Breeds eastwards from N Finland; vagrant Britain, Scandinavia, France, and the Low Countries.

HABITAT AND INFO

SIMILAR SPECIES
Reed Bunting female has more convex bill; weak eye-ring; different call.

Thicker bill

Longer tail

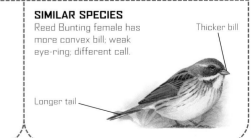

Rustic Bunting

A distinctive bunting in summer, but autumn migrants are easily mistaken for Reed Bunting despite their rusty rump and pale, peaked crown.

LENGTH / 15cm (6in)
WINGSPAN / 14–17cm (5½–6¾in)
WEIGHT / 15–25g (½–1oz)

■ STATUS / Secure

SCALE v Pigeon

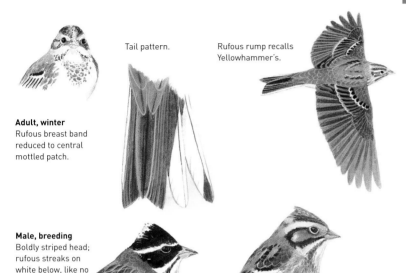

Tail pattern.

Rufous rump recalls Yellowhammer's.

Adult, winter
Rufous breast band reduced to central mottled patch.

A breeding bird of northern woods, the Rustic Bunting prefers wet places with willow, birch, or conifers growing from riversides or swampy ground. With a slightly less northerly range than Little or Yellow-breasted Buntings, it is more familiar in much of Sweden and Finland.

FEEDING
It typically forages on the ground like other buntings, looking for seeds, but also takes many insects and spiders in summer.

DISPLAY AND VOICE
Males sing from high perches with a short but melodious, even mournful, phrase. Calls are short, sharp and high: *zit* or *tik t'k*.

BREEDING
Nests are on or near the ground, in tussocks or root tangles beneath bushes. The 4–5 eggs hatch within 11 days. The chicks leave the nest well before they can fly.

MIGRATION
In autumn, western breeders move east, then south, to spend the winter in China or Japan. A few move west instead, reaching western Europe in autumn.

Male, breeding
Boldly striped head; rufous streaks on white below, like no other bunting.

Female, winter
Peaky crown; rufous flank streaks.

Adult male, winter
Dull black stripes on rich buff face; pale cheek spot; flanks heavily marked rufous.

Juvenile female, September
Weakest head pattern; note peaked crown, black corners to cheeks with white spot; rufous flank streaks; pinkish legs.

CONTRASTED COLOURS
The bright white underside is often obvious clue.

WHEN SEEN

Aug — May
Mostly late May to August; vagrants September to November in west.

WHERE SEEN
Breeds Sweden, Finland, Russia; vagrant Britain, the Low Countries, France.

HABITAT AND INFO

SIMILAR SPECIES
Yellowhammer female has dark streaks on yellower underside; weaker wingbars and head pattern.
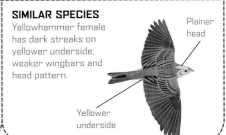
Plainer head
Yellower underside

Reed Bunting

SCALE v Pigeon

LENGTH / 15–16.5cm (6–6½in)
WINGSPAN / 21–26cm (8¼–10¼in)
WEIGHT / 15–22g (½–¾oz)

STATUS / Vulnerable

This is a richly coloured bunting with much rufous-brown, cream, and black and a broadly white-sided tail. A breeding male is unmistakable, but other plumages need care.

Male Reed Buntings in spring are unmistakable, but juveniles and females are sufficiently like several scarcer species to raise hopes of a more exciting find. Consequently, like other common buntings and finches, they are sometimes treated as the haystacks in which rarer needles might be discovered. Not that Reed Buntings are not interesting birds to watch in their own right. They like mixed fen, with sedges, irises, reed mace, and purple loosestrife mixed with reeds. Lines of willows beside rivers, or alongside flooded gravel pits, also make very acceptable habitats. In some areas, they may breed in damp places on upland hillsides, with rushes and long grassy tussocks. In winter, Reed Buntings remain close to wet places for the most part, but often feed in what stubbles they can find. They also regularly visit gardens. They are frequently to be seen mixed with Yellowhammers, Corn Buntings, Chaffinches, and sparrows.

FEEDING

They pick most of their food from the ground, often from among the stems of bushes and tall marsh plants. They eat mainly seeds and buds, but in summer they also take many insects and spiders.

DISPLAY AND VOICE

Males sing their short, jingly songs repeatedly from low perches in spring and summer. The typical Reed Bunting song is a short series of discrete notes followed by a trill. Unpaired males have a faster song, while paired males have a slower, less interesting version with longer spaces between the notes. The usual call is a soft, quite full *seeoo* or *tseup*, very distinctive once it is learned. In spring, they give a very thin, high *seee*. They do not give any of the ticking calls typical of other buntings.

BREEDING

The nest is well hidden in a dense tussock of sedges or grass, or in the base of a bush growing from a damp marsh. The 4–5 eggs are incubated for 13 days, and the chicks fly when about 10–12 days old. They leave the nest 3–5 days earlier, to clamber about in nearby vegetation.

MIGRATION

In spring, small migrating parties often appear on grassy places beside freshwater pools or lakes on their way to higher or more northerly breeding areas, usually accompanying Meadow Pipits and Pied Wagtails. Scandinavia and eastern Europe are almost entirely vacated in autumn as the birds move south and west.

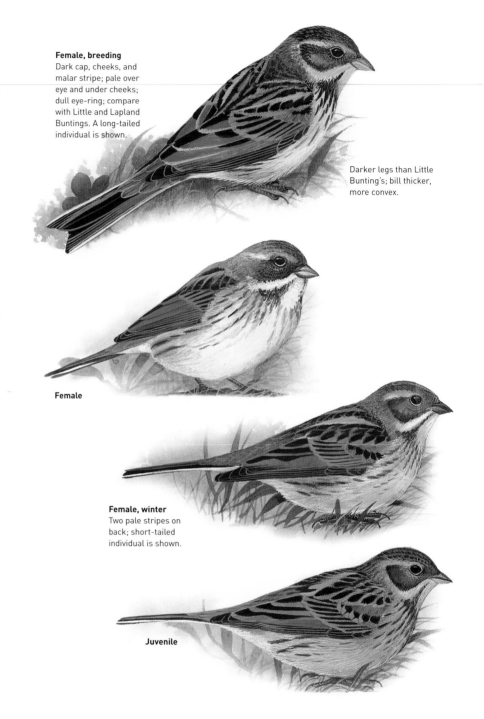

Female, breeding
Dark cap, cheeks, and malar stripe; pale over eye and under cheeks; dull eye-ring; compare with Little and Lapland Buntings. A long-tailed individual is shown.

Darker legs than Little Bunting's; bill thicker, more convex.

Female

Female, winter
Two pale stripes on back; short-tailed individual is shown.

Juvenile

WHEN SEEN

All year in W and central Europe; March to October in N Europe; October to April in most of S Europe.

WHERE SEEN
Breeds Britain and Ireland, mainland Europe south to central France, locally S France and Iberia; in winter, from Baltic south to Mediterranean coasts.

HABITAT AND INFO

SIMILAR SPECIES
Little Bunting has neat, straight-edged bill; white eye-ring; ticking call.

Bright eye-ring

Shorter tail

Male, breeding
Long-tailed bird; all pale tips worn off head.

Male, late summer
Very worn; dark above.

Tail often flicked to reveal broad white sides.

Female, summer
Narrower wings than male's.

The difference in body size of males is a puzzle that has yet to be resolved.

Male, autumn
Long-tailed individual.

Male, winter
Tail has white sides; note much broader wings than female's.

Rufous shoulder patches.

Male, spring
Short-tailed individual.

Black-and-cream on back; more rufous on wings, becoming darker with wear.

DID YOU KNOW?
The song has been described as "boring", even "irritatingly repeated", but is pleasant enough. It is certainly simpler, more disjointed, and more monotonous than that of most other buntings or finches, but it is typical of a warm summer's day at the edge of a lake or marsh. Shorter songs can be given at the rate of 20 per minute for many minutes on end.

?

Lapland Bunting

LENGTH / 15–16cm (6–6¼in)
WINGSPAN / 25–28cm (9¾–11in)
WEIGHT / 20–30g (¾–1oz)

SCALE v Pigeon

■ STATUS / Vulnerable

This is an inconspicuous bunting in most plumages, with spring males obvious, but others more difficult. Blackish ear-covert corners, dark mottled stripes beside throat, mottled breast sides, and rufous midwing panel are all helpful features. It is more terrestrial than the Reed Bunting.

Superficially like a Reed Bunting, the Lapland Bunting also has a lot of the Snow Bunting's character about it. It is a similarly low-slung, short-legged, feathery-thighed bird of the far north, which visits low-lying coastal marshes and muddy tide lines in winter. It can be remarkably elusive in long, tussocky grass, but a close view is rewarding, especially of a well-marked male. A hint of the summer pattern often remains even in winter, and the colouring always has a pleasing richness and complexity. Wintering birds in eastern Europe are often far from the sea, but in western Europe they remain more or less coastal. In summer, they avoid the rocky terrain favoured by Snow Buntings and breed in shrubby tundra with dwarf birch and willow, or mossy places with scattered stones and shallow pools.

FEEDING
In midsummer, an abundance of flies provides their main food. At other times they feed mainly on seeds. Lapland Buntings run on the ground, stopping to pick up seeds or shuffling up to tussocks of vegetation to search the stems for insects. They occasionally feed in low bushes, but rarely on really bare, open ground.

DISPLAY AND VOICE
The song flight is a pipit-like performance, with a steep, silent ascent followed by a wide, spiralling descent with full song. This is lark-like, full-throated, but short: *teeTOOree-tooree-treeoo*. The calls are worth learning, as they frequently draw attention to migrants and wintering birds: a bright, metallic *teeu* and a tuneless and flat, hard drumming or stuttering rattle, *t'k-r t'k-r t'k* or *tikitikitik-teu*.

BREEDING
Nesting is timed so the birds can feed their young on the brief midsummer abundance of flies in the far north. They build their nest on the ground, in a hollow or sheltered by a tussock, frequently near water and often sheltered by an overhanging spray of birch or willow. The 5–6 eggs hatch after an incubation of 11–13 days. The chicks leave the nest before they can fly, which they do after just 9–10 days.

MIGRATION
All European breeding birds move south in autumn, becoming rather scarce migrants and local winter visitors in eastern Europe and around the North Sea.

Juvenile female
Dull; dark rufous wing panel edged white; heavy black striping below.

Juvenile male
Two pale back stripes join pale, curved wingbar; bright nape.

Juvenile
Pale, buffy type most like Reed Bunting; note rufous wing panel.

Male, spring
Pale crescent behind black face; black breast; black streaks on white flanks; bright rufous nape.

Female, winter
Paler central crown; plain cheeks with black corners; mottled chest around white V.

Note long wingtip projection compared with stubby tip of Reed Bunting.

WHEN SEEN

May to September where breeding; on W European coasts, September/ October; wintering areas, October to April.

WHERE SEEN
Breeds Arctic Russia, N Finland, N Sweden, Norway; winters Denmark, S Baltic coasts, Netherlands, E Britain; also Hungary and Ukraine.

HABITAT AND INFO

SIMILAR SPECIES
Reed Bunting has weaker head pattern with duller nape; plainer wing without rusty central panel.

Plainer head

Duller wings

RICH COLOURS
Lapland Buntings have strong, bright, earthy colours.

Female, summer
Bright nape; broad buff stripe over eye curves under dark-edged ear coverts; yellow bill unlike Reed Bunting.

Pale underwing coverts; lark-like shape, with long, straight outer primary.

Tail dark with little white on edges.

Female, first winter
Tail of female looks longer than male's.

Long wings; forked tail; bounding flight.

Male, winter
Mottled black/grey forewing; rusty midwing panel; fine white wingbars.

Wings long and narrow compared to Reed Bunting's.

Female (left) has broader wingtip than male's (right).

Adult's tail has bright white; juvenile's tail is dull white/grey on outer feathers.

Adult   **Juvenile**

DID YOU KNOW?
This species breeds around the edge of the Arctic, with the only gap in its circumpolar range being Iceland. It faces an uncertain future as climate change warms the Arctic fringe and its habitat is simply shrinking northward, finally to disappear, or to be left in only the most extreme northerly islands and peninsulas.

Rock Bunting

LENGTH / 16cm (6¼in)
WINGSPAN / 22–26cm (8¾–10¼in)
WEIGHT / 21–27g (¾–1oz)

■ **STATUS /** Secure

SCALE v Pigeon

A richly coloured bunting with a unique head pattern, it is usually on or close to the ground and rather unobtrusive.

Often inconspicuous and detected only by its call, this sober little bunting reveals a neat pattern and rich colouring if seen clearly. It likes a mixture of bushes and rocks, where scrub meets open spaces such as alpine meadows and grassy slopes at the upper edges of forests. It is not, however, restricted to really high ground and often descends to the lowlands in winter.

FEEDING
It eats seeds and buds all year, insects in summer. It feeds on the ground, standing on stems to bend them over to reach seeds, or in bushes.

VOICE
The song is similar to that of a Dunnock or a short, weak Wren. The usual calls are a short, thin, elusive, yet penetrating *seee* and a harder *zit*.

BREEDING
The nest is built in a crevice or below a bush growing from between boulders. The clutch of 4–5 eggs hatches after an incubation of 12–14 days.

MIGRATION
Resident except for short downhill movements in winter.

Female, spring

Broad wings; long tail; rufous rump; grey-and-black bill in all plumages.

Male, winter
Whitish breast streaks.

Sinister face.

White coverts below; grey forewing above.

Grey, whitish, and black head stripes always distinctive.

Male, first winter
Broad white outer tail feathers.

Male, summer
Unique pale grey/rusty orange contrast.

Juvenile
Greyish throat and chest; dull bill.

Both male and female wear to duller colours when breeding.

Rufous rump, white wing lining, grey forewing characteristic of species.

ELUSIVE VOICE
Rock Buntings are often heard, but hard to locate.

WHEN SEEN

All year.

WHERE SEEN
Breeds SW Germany, S France, the Alps and Apennines, higher parts of the Balkans and E Europe, and most of Iberia; in winter, more widely in lowland Italy, Greece.

HABITAT AND INFO

SIMILAR SPECIES
Yellowhammer is paler, yellower beneath; different call.

Paler head

More orange rump

Snow Finch

This is a large, sparrow-like, thickset bird of high altitudes, with a lot of white in the wing.

LENGTH / 17cm (6³⁄₄in)
WINGSPAN / 34–38cm (13½–15in)
WEIGHT / 30–40g (1–1½oz)

■ STATUS / Secure

SCALE v Pigeon

Adult, summer
Back duller than in spring; white across primary coverts.

Adult, winter
Pale face; yellow bill.

Juvenile
Streaks on hindwing; all-black primary coverts.

Male, spring
Black bill; dull black face and throat; reddish-brown back.

Male, spring
Dusky black throat.

Juvenile

Often droops black inner coverts so white partially obscured.

Adult, winter
Yellow bill; white throat; paler back; grey head always distinctive.

More sparrow than finch, this is a bird of alpine habitats, moving only a little lower in winter. It spends most of its time on the ground, on rocks, or on roofs. It breeds in exposed, often partly snow-covered areas, near grassy slopes above the tree line and on screes. In winter, it hangs around high ski villages, the back yards of hotels and border stores, and farm buildings.

FEEDING
Insects and spiders are most important in summer, seeds in winter.

DISPLAY AND VOICE
Winter flocks disperse in spring, breaking up into solitary breeding pairs. The males sing to defend their territories, both while perched and in flight. The song is a varied, sparrow-like, sometimes prolonged chirruping. A hoarse *szi* or *tseeh*, often repeated, is a frequent call.

BREEDING
Nests are in cavities in rocks or banks. The usual clutch is 4–5 eggs, hatching after 13–14 days.

MIGRATION
Snow Finches make small movements to lower, milder altitudes in winter.

MOUNTAIN-TOP BREEDER
Snow Finches must be sought on high peaks and plateaux.

WHEN SEEN

All year.

WHERE SEEN
Breeds Pyrenees and NW Spain, Alps; locally central Italy; very locally on highest areas through the Balkans.

HABITAT AND INFO

SIMILAR SPECIES
Snow Bunting head lacks plain grey; much more tawny-brown in winter.

Browner head
Different tail

Snow Bunting

SCALE v Pigeon

LENGTH / 16-17cm (6¼-6¾in)
WINGSPAN / 32-38cm (12½-15in)
WEIGHT / 30-40g (1-1½oz)

■ **STATUS /** Vulnerable

A long-bodied, short-legged, heavy bunting, it is starkly pied in summer and richly coloured in winter, when it often shows little white until it flies.

Long, low-slung, and short-legged, the Snow Bunting is quite different from the typical farmland buntings of the lowlands. In summer, it is a mountain bird, but while some remain on the hills throughout the year others move to the coast. There, lively, engaging flocks live on sand and shingle beaches and the salt marshes just inland from the shore. These winter flocks feed inconspicuously, but may suddenly fly up and dash along the beach, flashing their white wing patches as they go. They then either double back or just dive back to the ground. They may seem to stop dead and disappear but, with care, it is possible to approach them and get a close view. Their rich colours and varied patterns are always fascinating. In summer, Snow Buntings are different birds: they must be sought on the highest cliffs and screes in Scotland, where they are rare, in Scandinavia, or on bleak, rocky places beyond the tree line in Iceland and the remote Arctic islands.

FEEDING
Snow Buntings search the ground intently for seeds, shuffling forward on their short legs. They avoid grassy fields, but in much of Europe they visit arable land with stubbles and ploughed fields. In north-west Europe, seed-rich muddy and shingly patches beside salt marshes and, less often, stony ploughed fields are typical feeding habitats. In summer, they also eat insects. These and spiders form the sole diet of the chicks.

DISPLAY AND VOICE
Males attract mates and defend territories by singing. They sing from high boulders and in short, rising song-flights. Their song is loud and musical, with fluty two- or three-syllable notes like *turee-turee-turee* and *sweeto-swevee-seeetuta*. In winter, two calls are distinctive: a loud, clear, full *too* or *tuu* and a silvery, rippling, twittering trill, *p-trrr-iririp*.

BREEDING
The nest is located in a deep crevice between boulders, or on a scree slope. In Arctic areas, nests are often built in buildings or other stone structures, or even in discarded tins or boxes. The 4–6 eggs are incubated for 12–13 days. The young are fed in the nest for a further 12–14 days.

MIGRATION
In winter, Snow Buntings vacate the northern parts of their breeding range, but elsewhere many birds remain in the breeding areas. Large numbers move south and west to lowlands and coasts.

Female/juvenile (far left) Much paler under wingtip than adult male (left).

Male, breeding Brown of winter plumage wears off to reveal smart black and white.

Female, breeding Plain white beneath; Norwegian birds may wear much browner.

Long black wingtips tight over tail, long body, tiny feet characteristic of species.

Juvenile female Back may be more rufous or much greyer; note cheek patch, yellow bill, small black feet almost hidden, white on wing.

Female, winter May lack breast band.

Female This plumage believed to be adult.

Great variation in winter appearance may reflect area of origin.

Male, winter (right) White forewing means male; complex rusty-orange head and breast pattern wears off in spring.

WHEN SEEN

All year; in wintering areas, mostly October to March.

WHERE SEEN
Breeds Spitsbergen, Iceland, Norway, highest and northerly parts of Sweden, N Finland, N Scotland; in winter, hills and coasts of Britain, North Sea coasts, east through N and E Europe.

HABITAT AND INFO

SIMILAR SPECIES
Lapland Bunting has dark cornered ear coverts; far less white in wing, which has white-edged rufous central panel.

Pale crown stripe

Dark wings

COPIOUS WHITE
Much of the snow-white is hidden on
a perched bird.

Juvenile male
Median coverts
all-white, creating
white wingbar.

Dark wing with broad
white band (above)
may indicate second-
year female or a
different race.

Female, winter

Juvenile male

Male, winter
Maximum amount
of white on wing.

**Juvenile female,
midwinter**
More rufous in autumn,
but wears to duller
colour in winter.

Male
Some have dark rim
to primary coverts.

Back of male bright
in autumn; duller
from November
until spring.

Females at all ages
have dark-centred
median coverts.

Flocks fly fast and low,
wings swept back, with
flickering jerky action.

Wings long and
pointed; tail
short, forked.

DID YOU KNOW?
This is an active bird, more so than most buntings, living on open
ground over which it can run quickly and easily. When disturbed it
often prefers to run before taking flight. Flocks fly around quickly,
with a variety of swift bursts using quick wing beats, undulations
on closed wings, short glides, and long, low skims across
the ground before finally settling again.

GLOSSARY

Abrasion The effect of wear, chiefly on feathers. It is especially marked on the pale parts that lack the dark pigment melanin, because this strengthens the feather. White tips or pale spots at feather edges may wear off, changing a plumage pattern quite markedly. Abrasion can make bright colours duller, but dull tips may also wear away to reveal brighter colours beneath.

Adult A mature bird whose plumage no longer changes with age.

Alula The small feathers on the "thumb" or bastard wing, often prominent on birds of prey, which use it to control the airflow over the wing, but visible on the folded wings of most species.

Axillaries A small group of feathers underneath the base of the wing, in the bird's "wingpit".

Bar A "bar", or a barred pattern, refers to lines across a feather or plumage tract (as opposed to streaks or stripes, which are lengthwise). A Chaffinch, for example, has wingbars, and a Kestrel has a barred tail.

Bill The beak, made up of two parts, the upper and lower mandibles, each covered with a bony sheath.

Bleaching The fading of feathers in sunlight. Combined with abrasion, this can radically alter the appearance of a bird without any change of feathers. For example, the blackish wing feathers of many immature gulls in autumn fade to brown by the following spring. More subtly, the grey feathers of an adult gull become tinged with beige when faded and worn. Some large birds of prey grow glossy black-brown feathers that fade to dull brown or even pale buff as they are bleached. "Old" and "new" feathers can often be detected from this, indicating the state of moult, but parts of feathers usually covered when the wing is folded remain darker than those constantly exposed.

Breeding Pairing, laying, and incubating eggs, and rearing young.

Breeding plumage The bright plumage in which birds display at rivals and court potential mates, typically in spring and summer but in some cases in winter prior to the breeding season. Male ducks, for example, are at their brightest in winter but become dull when the females are on eggs or tending young.

Brood The young birds hatched from one set of eggs. A "second brood" results from another set of eggs laid later during the same breeding season.

Call Call notes are distinct from songs and are used in many situations: most calls are "contact calls" used by social species to keep in touch or alarm calls used to alert others to potential danger.

Clutch A set of eggs laid within a few days and incubated together.

Coverts The short feathers that cover the leading edge of a bird's wing.

Diving duck A type of duck that dives underwater to feed, unlike a "surface feeder", which feeds either by filtering food from the shallows or by up-ending to reach more deeply without submerging. Diving ducks always submerge from the surface while swimming, not by plunging from the air.

Duck A general term for an individual of any of the species of ducks, the smaller species of the *Anatidae;* more specifically, a female of such a species, as opposed to a drake (male).

Eclipse The plumage acquired in early summer by male ducks (drakes), in which bright colours and patterns are lost so the birds resemble dark females. By this time drakes do not need to display, so they adopt better camouflage while they moult their wing feathers: a process that may make them flightless for a time.

Emargination A marked narrowing of the web on the outer side of a feather. On many birds of prey emargination of each

outer primary, together with a deep notch on the inner side of the adjacent feather, produces "fingered" wingtips. On small birds such as warblers, emargination can usually be examined only on a bird in the hand (or on a close-up photograph) but it may be important in identification.

Family A taxonomic category in the hierarchical system of classification of living things. Families bring together genera (the singular is "genus") and are grouped into orders. Genera group species with obvious close relationships; families group genera that are related. Groupings within a family reveal distinct similarities, but between families there will be obvious differences. Families tend to have simple equivalent English names (such as "grebes" or "owls") and are more useful to birdwatchers than orders.

Feral Wild birds derived from domestic or captive stock that has either escaped into the wild to form breeding populations, such as town pigeons, or been introduced, such as Greylag Geese in lowland Britain.

First year A bird in its first year of life: a term applied to plumages after "juvenile". In species with very distinct plumage sequences, such as larger gulls, the autumn and spring moults produce a sequence from juvenile to first winter, then first summer, second winter, second summer, and so on.

Flushed Startled from cover, usually by the close approach of a potential enemy.

Form A variant or "morph" within a "polymorphic" species that occurs in two or more plumages, such as the Arctic Skua, which has "pale", "intermediate", and "dark" forms (sometimes called "phases", which is misleading because each individual retains one plumage that does not change with time). Such forms occur together and interbreed freely; they are not races or subspecies.

Genus See *Scientific name.*

Gliding Flying without active wingbeats, either using momentum to maintain height and speed or losing height to gain forward movement.

Gonys The fusion of the two sides of the lower jaw near the tip of the bill; on gulls, for example, it may create a marked angle.

Gorget A band of colour or pattern around the chest.

Hybrid A cross between two species. Hybrids are usually infertile but wildfowl, in particular, may produce fertile hybrids that may be very difficult to identify, some looking confusingly like other species.

Immature Not yet fully adult and sexually mature: implies that plumage will change (becoming closer to adult pattern) with increasing age, but not always so. Different species progress to adulthood over different lengths of time: for example, a Herring Gull may be visually distinguishable in its first, second, third, and sometimes even fourth years before becoming adult, after which its age cannot be judged by plumage pattern, but smaller gulls may become adult within a year.

Irruption An irregular mass movement, usually caused by a food shortage, that results in birds occurring outside their usual range. Not to be confused with regular migration.

Juvenile A young bird in its first set of feathers, in which it makes its first flight. Juvenile plumage may be short-lived before being replaced at the first moult.

Lore The area on a bird's head between its eye and bill.

Migration Regular movement between geographical areas from season to season, for example between summer breeding areas in Europe and wintering areas in Africa. Some migrations are much shorter and may involve, for example, movement from inland hills to lowland areas on the coast. Species

that migrate may be described as "migrant" and individual birds seen during migration as "migrants".

Moult The replacement of feathers. Birds moult in a strictly ordered fashion at specific times of the year, which in some cases vary between sexes and age categories. A moult may be partial (typically replacing head and body feathers, but not those of the wings and tail) or complete; complete moult may take place in a continual sequence or may be suspended for a period, such as during migration.

Order A taxonomic category used in classifying living organisms into a hierarchical system; a subdivision of a class (birds form the class Aves) grouping together families; all order names end in "-iformes". The groupings put together families with a supposed relationship but this is often speculative.

Pair A male and a female that breed together. In many species, however, a single polygamous male may mate with several females; in fewer species the reverse occurs. In some polygamous species, such as harriers, a male may help rear the young of more than one mate, but usually a male that mates with several females takes no part in caring for the eggs or young.

Passage migrant A bird that appears in a certain area only while on passage during migration, in spring and/or in autumn, neither nesting nor spending the winter in the area. Some individuals of a species may be passage migrants while others of the same species may breed or winter in the area. Green Sandpipers, for example, appear in Britain as passage migrants in spring, very rarely as summer visitors, commonly as passage migrants in autumn, and regularly in smaller numbers as winter visitors – but none are strictly resident.

Plumage The whole set of feathers on a bird; also used when describing birds that change according to age, season, or sex – for example, juvenile plumage or summer plumage.

Primary feathers The long wingtip feathers; together with the secondaries, they form the flight feathers or remiges.

Race A local variant of a species, also known as a subspecies, that breeds within a defined geographical area and has evolved a slightly different form, colouring, or pattern from birds of the same species elsewhere. Most races are difficult to identify in the field, but some are well marked. Particularly distinctive "races" are often elevated to the status of separate species.

Resident A bird or species found in the same area all year round.

Roost To "sleep"; also a gathering of birds that may come together at night, or for example at high tide when wading birds are displaced from mudflats or beaches.

Sailing Used to describe a bird of prey flying in a wind or updraft without wingbeats, with a rather different appearance from a similar bird gliding or soaring – but these three intergrade.

Scientific name The name, typically based on Latin or Greek, printed in italics and labelled "species" at the top of each page in this book. There are normally two words, but the full name may consist of three. The first (always with a capital initial) is the generic name, or "genus", and the second is the specific name; the two form a unique combination that defines a species. The third name, if any, identifies a subspecies or race. The scientific name is useful because the genus is applied to a group of species that share similar characteristics and are closely related. For example, the Reed and Marsh Warblers of the genus *Acrocephalus* have much in common, but Savi's Warbler and the Garden Warbler (*Locustella* and *Sylvia* respectively) are quite different, both from *Acrocephalus* warblers and from each other.

Secondary feathers The shorter flight feathers on the trailing edge of the wing, between the primaries and the tertials.

Soaring Flying with wings fully spread and not flapping, often on warm, rising air currents, typically circling and gaining height (unlike gliding, which is moving directly forward without wingbeats).

Song A particular vocal performance used to attract mates and/or announce an individual's presence and claim to a territory. The songs of different species are mostly very distinctive and help in identification (for example, the simple repetition of a Chiffchaff compared with the flowing cadence of a Willow Warbler) but some species display marked variation between individual birds.

Species A particular type of bird (or other organism) that interbreeds with others of the same type to produce fertile young. For example, the Song Thrush *Turdus philomelos* is a species, while the Mistle Thrush *Turdus viscivorus* is another species in the same genus. The precise definition of a species is, however, debatable and the status of several "species" in this book is still unclear (see the smaller shearwaters, gulls, and crossbills). Hybrids between species are exceptional, and typically produce infertile young, but they are more frequent in some bird families, especially wildfowl.

Streak A lengthwise mark along a feather or plumage tract, such as a dark streak along the back or flank (as opposed to the crosswise "bar").

Sub-adult An immature bird in a plumage that is neither juvenile nor adult (but, by implication, closer to an adult in appearance).

Subspecies See *Race.*

Summer visitor A bird (or species) that visits an area in summer to breed (such as the Swallow, which moves to Europe in spring, breeds, then departs in autumn to spend the winter in Africa); also, therefore, a migrant.

Tarsus The lower part of the exposed leg, above the foot. It is actually the tarso-metatarsus, roughly equivalent to the human foot; the "foot" of a bird is equivalent to human toes. The tarsus is usually the most obvious part of a bird's leg, below the exposed joint.

Tertial feathers The innermost set of trailing feathers on each wing, between the secondaries and the body.

Vagrant An individual bird that has turned up well outside its usual range by accident – for example, a North American warbler blown across the Atlantic in the autumn; popularly, a "rarity".

Wader A typically coastal or marsh bird that often feeds by wading in shallow water, known in North America as a "shorebird". Neither term is satisfactory because the families of "waders" include some species that do not wade much or at all (such as the Dotterel) nor live by the shore for much of the year (Lapwings breed on fields, Curlews on moors). On the other hand, some birds that do habitually wade (such as the Grey Heron and Spoonbill) are not referred to as "waders" in the sense used as a handy shorthand reference to plovers, sandpipers, and their allies.

Wear See *Abrasion.*

Wildfowl The group of birds that includes all the swans, geese, and ducks.

Wing formula The structure of the wing described according to the relative lengths of the primary feathers on the spread wing (rather like the relative lengths of fingers on a human hand) together with any emargination of those feathers. With some difficult warblers, for example, the wing formula, which is practically constant within species, can help with identification (see, for example, the Willow Warbler and the Chiffchaff).

Winter visitor A migrant that appears in the non-breeding part of its range – for example, the Fieldfare winters in England but breeds in Scandinavia and northern Russia.

INDEX

Page numbers in *italics* refer
to treatments in detail.
Many species are known by
several names. The most common
alternative names are indexed with
cross-references to the name by
which that bird is known in this book

ACKNOWLEDGMENTS

Front endpapers: l © David Tipling; r © Roger Tidman
Back endpapers: l © David Tipling; r © Arco/Alamy

The following photographs are © David Tipling:
Pages 2–3, 8, 22, 23, 24, 28, 29, 30, 31, 33, 34, 37, 39, 41, 43, 45, 47, 49, 50, 51, 52, 53, 54, 55, 57, 58, 59, 60, 61, 65, 67, 69, 71, 73, 74, 75, 77, 80, 82, 84, 85, 87, 88, 89, 90, 91, 92, 93, 95, 98, 99, 101, 103, 104, 105, 106, 107, 109, 110, 111, 115, 120, 121, 122, 123, 124, 126, 133, 136, 139, 141, 145, 146, 151, 153, 155, 157, 159, 160, 163, 165, 167, 171, 173, 182, 185, 186, 187, 189, 190, 191, 193, 195, 196, 197, 198, 199, 200, 201, 203, 204, 205, 206, 207, 209, 210, 211, 213, 215, 217, 218, 220, 221, 222, 223, 224, 225, 226, 227, 228, 229, 230, 231, 233, 235, 237, 239, 241, 242, 244, 245, 246, 247, 249, 253, 255, 257, 259, 260, 261, 263, 267, 269, 271, 273, 275, 277, 281, 289, 290, 291, 292, 293, 296, 301, 303, 305, 307, 308, 309, 310, 311, 313, 315, 316, 317, 319, 320, 321, 324, 331, 332, 333, 334, 335, 336, 337, 338, 339, 340, 343, 344, 345, 347, 348, 352, 355, 359, 363, 365, 366, 367, 371, 372, 373, 374, 375, 376, 377, 378, 380, 382, 385, 387, 389, 395, 396, 398, 399, 405, 407, 409, 411, 417, 422, 438, 444, 445, 446, 451, 457, 458, 459, 460, 461, 462, 463, 464, 465, 466, 468, 473, 479, 481, 483, 485, 486, 491, 493, 494, 497, 498, 499, 500, 505, 507, 509, 511, 513, 516, 517, 519, 524, 528, 531, 535, 537, 539, 541, 543, 549

The other photographs are as follows:
Page 4 © Roger Tidman; 6 © blickwinkel/Alamy; 25 © Les Wagstaff/Alamy; 26 © Roger Tidman; 27 © Yari Peltomaki; 35, 48 © Roger Tidman; 62, 63 © Markus Varesvuo; 64 © TOM VEZO/Minden Pictures/FLPA; 76 © Yari Peltomaki; 78 © Aquila/M C Wilkes; 79 © Aquila/D Robinson; 81 © Roger Tidman; 83 © Aquila/Juan Simon; 86 © Jari Peltomaki; 94 © Roger Tidman; 96 © F Dhermain; 97 © Yvon Toupin; 108, 112, 113 © blickwinkel/Alamy; 117 © blickwinkel/Alamy; 118 © Elvele Images/Alamy; 125 © Roger Tidman; 127 © Aquila/Juan Simon; 128, 129, 130, 131 © Roger Tidman; 135, 137 © Yari Peltomaki; 143 © Roger Tidman; 147 © blickwinkel/Alamy; 149 © Yari Peltomaki; 161, 169 © Markus Varesvuo; 175 © blickwinkel/Alamy; 177 © Markus Varesvuo; 179 © FLPA/Alamy; 181 © Markus Varesvuo; 183 © Aquila/C Greaves; 184 © Arco Images/Alamy; 188 © Yari Peltomaki; 194 © Aquila/Alan Wilson; 208 © Markus Varesvuo; 219 © Yari Peltomaki; 243, 248 © Roger Tidman; 250 © Yari Peltomaki; 251, 264, 265 © Roger Tidman; 278 © David Hosking/FLPA; 279 © Roger Tidman; 283 © Aquila/Hans Gebuis; 284, 285, 286, 287, 288, 294, 295 © Roger Tidman; 297 © Aquila/MikeWilkes; 299 © Roger Tidman; 312 © Yari Peltomaki; 314 © Roger Tidman; 318 © Aquila/Mike Lane; 322 © Roger Tidman; 323 © Peter steyn/FLPA; 325 © H & J Eriksen; 326 © Markus Varesvuo; 327 © NHPA/Jordi Bas Casas; 328 © blickwinkel/Alamy; 329, 330 © Roger Tidman; 341 © Markus Varesvuo; 346 © Aquila/D Robinson; 349, 350, 351, 353, 356, 357 © Roger Tidman; 360 © Aquila/Conrad Greaves; 361 © Roger Tidman; 362 © Yari Peltomaki; 369 © Roger Tidman; 379 © Markus Varesvuo; 381, 383, 384 © Roger Tidman; 390 © Aquila/Mike Wilkes; 391 © Roger Tidman; 392 © Aquila/K Carlson; 393 © Aquila/R T Mills; 397 © Yari Peltomaki; 401 © Roger Tidman; 402 © Aquila/Mike Lane; 403 © Markus Varesvuo; 406 © Aquila/Denzil Grieg; 408 © FLPA/Silvestris Fotoservice; 413 © Aquila/Hans Gebuis; 414 © Roger Tidman; 415 © Markus Varesvuo; 419 © Roger Tidman; 420, 421 © Markus Varesvuo; 423 © Roger Tidman; 424 © Aquila/Hans Gebuis; 425 © Roger Tidman; 426 © Jan Van Der Knokke/Foto Natura/FLPA; 427 © Roger Tidman; 428 © Yari Peltomaki; 429 © Roger Tidman; 431 © Roger Tidman; 433 © Aquila/P Smith; 434 © Aquila/Kevin Carlson; 435 © Aquila/J Simon; 437 © Aquila/Kevin Carlson; 439 © Aquila/Mike Wilkes; 439 © Aquila/J Wagstaff; 440, 441 © Roger Tidman; 442 © Aquila/Kevin Carlson; 443 © Roger Tidman; 447 © Yari Peltomaki; 449 © Roger Tidman; 452 © Aquila/Ulf Antonsson; 453 © Markus Varesvuo; 454 © Roger Tidman; 455 © Aquila/Mike Lane; 467, 469, 470 © Roger Tidman; 471 © Aquila/Conrad Greaves; 474 © Roger Tidman; 475 © Aquila/Kevin Carlson; 477 © Roger Tidman; 478 © Markus Varesvuo; 482, 487, 488, 489 © Roger Tidman; 501 © Panda Photo/FLPA; 502, 503, 514 © Roger Tidman; 515 © Martin Woike/Foto Natura/FLPA; 518 © Aquila/Mike Wilkes; 520 © Brian Bevan/Ardea; 521 © Aquila/Denzil Grieg; 523 © Roger Tidman; 525 © Yari Peltomaki; 526, 527 © Markus Varesvuo; 533 © Roger Tidman; 536, 538 © Roger Tidman; 540 © Hannu Hautala/FLPA; 545 © Yuri Artukhin/FLPA; 546 © John Hawkins/FLPA; 547 © Robin Chittenden/FLPA

The publisher would like to thank Philippa Bell, Fiona Kellagher, Anatole Beams, Dave Farrow, and Amber Dowell for their assistance.